IT STARTED IN NEBRASKA

MY LIFE IN BIO BITS

6-19-12

Dear Willard...

These stories are in the order
that I remembered them ... not in
the chronological sequence in which
they occurred. Keep me up-dated
from your place and I'll try to
do the same. Pleasant reading!!!

Fraternally

Phil

IT STARTED IN NEBRASKA

MY LIFE IN BIO BITS

BY

PHILIP N. RAYNARD

www.bookstandpublishing.com

Published by
Bookstand Publishing
Morgan Hill, CA 95037
3134_7

ISBN 978-1-58909-729-2

Printed in the United States of America

ACKNOWLEDGEMENTS

To my wife, Ann, who encouraged me to write these Bio Bits. She was a private person who was never interested in recording her own stories, but she did enjoy sharing her memories with her family and friends. To our daughters, Coral and Holly, whose frequent questions about my life on the farm and in the Navy made me realize these stories' worth, and to our grandchildren, Ryan and Mackenna, who inspired the publication of this collection.

Phil and Ann Raynard, 2007

INTRODUCTION

I was born and reared on a ranch in the Nebraska Sandhills near Stapleton. My studies at the University of Nebraska were interrupted by World War II. I returned from service as a Naval Aviator to become an Animal Science major with a Journalism certificate. I was the first person hired in an agribusiness company's newly created executive training program and held several positions with that firm including advertising manager. I later became a field editor for *Western Livestock Journal* and then published the *California Cattleman* for 16 years. During this time I became a ranch real estate broker and still operate my own ranch sales firm, based in Auburn, California, but involving ranches throughout Northern California.

These sketches, written at the urging of my daughters and the impulse of the moment, hopscotch through the years, beginning with the events that took place during the drought and depression of the 1930s and including my current life (but not necessarily in that order), so family members could know something of my experiences. These incidents are the kind of thing I wish my parents and grandparents had recorded. They could have given me and members of my family items of historical interest, which were lost forever with the passing of those who were involved and who could have written about them, but didn't. These stories are roughly chronological, but in something like "popcorn" order, like watching corn in a popper and guessing which kernel will pop next. You should feel free to enjoy, criticize, edit, or especially, to write your own.

This is written for people who wish parents or grandparents had left a written record—no matter how fanciful—knowing that memories may fade in the time between the event and the writing. And it is for people who wish they had the courage to write about themselves, their family and friends. Reading this should convince you that you can do it and that it is, for the most part, interesting to read.

It is in this reference that I offer my Bio Bits. They cover many experiences and give at least one person's perspective of his place in the world and a skinny slice of history's pie not previously seen in print.

Table of Contents

Phil's Bio Bits

Navy Bio Bits

The Day I Killed the Boar

Pigs are normally curious and friendly or oblivious to people in their area. This pen had a good mix of mature sows with their fall litters of piglets. And to be sure there would be new pigs next spring, this pen also had a large red Duroc Jersey boar. Boars are generally the passive herd sires of pigdom but they guard their turf, which is pretty much all the area within a short charge toward any intruder. Boars have an advantage in this enforcement by being large—frequently 500 to 600 pounds or more—and having serious tusks that extend well beyond their lips if more than a year old, which this one was. He also had an attitude of protecting turf well beyond the imagination of most boars elsewhere in the world of pigs.

I was 9. Jack, my younger brother, was 6. We rode a horse to the one-room country school just over 2 miles away by cutting across the pastures, which was easy this time of year with the cattle in the winter feeding pens near ranch headquarters. This meant we could leave the gates open from home to school so we got home before dark after the 9-to-4 school day. This was a good arrangement for a ranch family who needed to get all the work possible from the kids. In early fall, after the corn was mature but not dry enough for storing in the crib, we "snapped" the corn (ears were handpicked or snapped from the stalks without removing the shucks) and the wagon full of corn was parked in the pig pen. We then fed the hogs by scooping the twice-daily feedings of corn from the wagon onto the ground where the pigs enjoyed corn on the cob, so to speak, leaving the cobs, with shucks attached, all over the pig pen.

The old Copper Clad cook stove in the kitchen would burn wood, coal, chips or corn cobs, among other possible fuels. The fire created heat for cooking meals, heating water in the reservoir attached to the firebox and heating the home during cold winter days and nights. It was the duty of farm-bred kids to do ranch chores. In our case this included picking up the cobs from the pigpen, removing the shucks and filling about six bushel-sized peach baskets with cobs every evening before dark to keep the kitchen stove fired for the next 24 hours.

Along with the responsibility of picking up six baskets of cobs and trying to get a decent amount of help from 6-year-old Jack, I had the on-the-scene duty to keep Jack safe from the red boar. As October slipped into November with not even one half-serious attack from the potential menace it got progressively harder to convince Jack to keep his distance from Big Red. There was a gradual tendency for us to feel comfortable with the shrinking radius for our "safe distance" from the boar.

On this particular evening, I set another basket full of cobs over the fence outside the pigpen and turned back just in time to see Jack thrown high in the air, then hit the ground screaming like a wounded banshee. Immediately I

1

was concerned with my little brother's safety but I also knew I'd get a razor strop massage on my backside and the lecture of the season for not protecting Jack from the red boar. Fortunately for me, for that instant at least, our dad had recently finished disassembling some aging A-frame individual hog farrowing houses, leaving piles of 1-by-8 and 2-by-4 lumber in storage and waiting to be re-assembled into other hog houses.

There was what appeared to be a boar-sized club, a 2-by-4 about 3 feet long, between me and the boar, which I picked up, swung as hard as I could and smashed full blast between the eyes of the red boar. He dropped dead as if he'd been shot and I picked up my screaming, dirt-laden but un-bloodied brother and headed for the house. I told our frantic mother that I had watched him every minute for weeks—trying to save my backside—but while I was putting a basket over the fence, Jack had just gone too close and the boar had charged Jack and thrown him in the air.

Jack had a loud cry, especially when it served his purpose. By now his noise had attracted our dad—on the run, straight to the house—from his evening chores of feeding livestock near the barn. When the story was re-told and Jack gave up his crying, I had to drop the other shoe. "I killed the red boar," I confessed. "I just picked up a 2-by-4 and hit him so I could get Jack away from him," I pleaded. Next move—straight to the pigpen as a family unit, including 2-year-old brother Dick—to see the dead boar.

When we got to the pigpen, that red boar had totally disappeared. He had not only died, he had apparently gone to hog heaven. It was getting late in the evening and nearly dark but that pig was absolutely not in the herd. Finally we found him in a "sitting" position a good distance from the herd and feeding area. As our dad walked toward him, the boar began squealing and shaking his head. We left the pen and the boar to himself and his headache. He had fully recovered by the next day, except that he forever kept his distance from boys picking corncobs in peach baskets. My parents were so relieved that Jack hadn't been torn to shreds—and the boar was still alive—that they entirely forgot the razor strop.

Red, the Irish Setter, enrolls in Cat 101

We always had dogs on the ranch. And most of our dogs were useful, like greyhounds, the triple threat dogs. Good playmates for growing boys, they bark at everyone who rides into the yard and besides, they catch coyotes. But that's another story. We never knew whether it was the good pheasant hunting and frequent invasions by out-of-state hunters with their retrievers or whether he had just been made an offer he couldn't refuse by a neighbor with a litter of Irish setter pups. Anyway, Dad showed up with a pup.

Irish Setters give new meaning to the word energy. Our home ranch was a mile wide, a mile-and-a-half long with a long 40 on the side. Much of it was visible from the headquarters. As "Red," the setter pup, reached near full size for skeletal structure he far surpassed full size for energy. Look up in early morning and you might see him near the northeast corner of the ranch running south at a full gallop and a few minutes later you'd see him near the west boundary going north at the same gait. Next he'd jump up on you near the barn with tongue and tail both wagging.

Every ranch also needs a few cats. For damage control, if nothing else. We had a dandy calico mama cat that had at least one litter of worthless kittens every year. Worthless for what they contributed, but valuable in their motivation to make the calico mother cat the best hunter in that part of Nebraska. She kept the population of pocket gophers at almost zero on 40 acres of alfalfa, just feeding those litters of kittens.

When the spring litters of kittens were big enough to travel, Calico Mama had a place under the Siberian pea hedge near the ranch house that she used as a summer place, and where they could learn about the world but be relatively hidden from whatever ranch dog was the current menace. Red found the haven and would stand with his nose at the entrance, tail wagging like a flag in the breeze, waiting for a kitten. He made a sport of picking up the half-grown kittens by the head and "retrieving" them to various locations.

One morning, returning from his usual survey romp around the ranch, Red stuck his nose in the nest to get another mouthful of kitten. Instead, he got a nose full of Calico Mama. Red began yelping and running at his bounding gait toward the barn some 50 yards away, with Mama hanging from his nose, claws firmly planted. At the barn, Red lay down and began rolling in pain on the ground, dislodging Mama.

She made straight for the nest full of kittens. Red saw me and came running and whimpering, big drops of blood on his nose artfully dispersed in a double cat's-paw pattern. He got no sympathy from me, nor ointment. Throughout his life, his wagging tail gave away his excitement whenever he was near a cat and especially the cat's den, but his memory never let him get close enough for another meeting with Calico Mama.

Frostbite on the Plains

I rode a horse to the one-room Nesbit Elementary School for eight years. The school was located some 3 miles from our house by county road but just over 2 miles to the north, cross country, if you rode through pastures and opened three gates. School board members had thoughtfully provided, in addition to a coal house and outhouses for boys and girls, a barn for stabling students' horses during the day. My grandparents' house was about a half mile east of the school but about the same distance from our house as from the school.

Bad weather was probably not invented in Nebraska but you didn't have to spend many winters on the plains to get well acquainted with blizzards.

Weather fronts generally come to the Sandhills area on a northwest wind. Temperatures in the range of 20 degrees below zero are commonplace. Tie that with winds of 20-to-35 miles per hour and heavy snow and you have an ugly day. The one thing worse was the above formula with a northeast wind. Northeast winds had high moisture, making them more chilling and penetrating to both man and livestock.

It was just such a February morning when I was 9 or 10 years old that both my parents decided it was too cold to let brother Jack go to school but I was on my second or third year of perfect attendance so no thought was given to my staying home. I was bundled up in almost all the clothes I owned: some winter underwear, two pairs of overalls, heavy shirt, sweater, winter coat, dad's socks pulled on over my overshoes, heavy mittens, winter cap

Raynard family ranch house in Stapleton, Nebraska, after gentle snowfall. Cement blocks, made from native sand in homemade forms, and construction by my Grandpa (W.C.) Raynard.

with ear tabs and a heavy scarf wrapped around my face and tied with barely a crack for vision. Getting on a horse wearing that uniform is more than a simple test of athleticism. Fortunately we threw the three gates open at this time of year when we took the cattle out of the pastures between home and the school so I didn't have to dismount—and re-mount—to open and close gates on the way to school. When I finally got to the last range of hills and almost in sight of the school, I could see no smoke, which meant the teacher, having decided it was too cold to have school, had not gone to the schoolhouse and had not built a fire. At this point it was about an equal distance to school or my grandparents' house. I knew Grandma had a fire. The school didn't. I was cold but I still figured that one out.

When I got there I tied the horse in Grandpa's barn and waddled to the house. Grandma started unwrapping me, layer by layer, checking for frostbite on ears, nose, fingers, toes, etc. I don't know whether I was tough or just lucky but Grandma didn't find any frostbite. A few minutes later, at 9 a.m., just as school should have been starting, Grandpa came in from doing chores. He always kept a sort of country weather bureau with official thermometer, etc. At 9 a.m., it was minus 32 degrees with a wind from the northeast.

But Grandma goofed—she didn't take my pants off. Some days later—and continuing for months—skin began flaking off from the outside of my right thigh where it had taken the full blast of a northeast wind while riding north toward school. To this day I have no feeling in an area of skin about 2 inches by 8 inches on the outside of my right thigh. I never learned if I got credit for a "bonus" day on my continuing perfect school attendance record.

The Road Builder

Things were not easy for a young family trying to make a living on a small farm/ranch in the Nebraska Sandhills during the '30s. In what might be called nepotism, since Grandpa was a County Supervisor, my dad had been given the "contract" to continue a longstanding highway project of making a cut in the hill, putting the dirt in the valley below. This attempt to flatten the hill or at least make the slope more gentle, had been going on intermittently for years but, with very little county budget for such niceties, progress had been slow at best.

When the field work was caught up in summer, we spent a few days with a four-horse team on the county road along the east side of our property. A Fresno scraper is a dirt-moving machine from the horse-drawn era similar to a cross between a giant snow shovel and a big tin can with both ends still attached and about half of the side removed, making a hollowed-out scoop. The one we used was about 4 feet wide. The edge that cut into the ground was razor sharp. The only control was an iron handle extending 4 or 5 feet from the rear center of the scoop which the walk-behind operator used to control the depth of cut (when loading) or dump the load when at the deposit area . . . reins in one hand; depth-control lever in the other.

Most of the dirt in this area was blow sand with about 1 to 2 inches of topsoil and rare or occasional layers of clay. Handling the depth gauge when loading sand was easy. Like fishing for bluegills. But if you hit clay, the sudden jerk on the blade created a leverage that threw the handle up in the air like having a 20-pound lunker take your bait. The operator must let go in a hurry if there was a serious pull on the handle; the power of a four-horse team ensured that the handle was going up, with or without the operator.

When the scraper was empty, the handle was high in the air. A rope was tied to the end of the handle so you could pull the rope to bring the handle down and get the scraper in a position to take on its next load. Nine-year-olds like to tag along on jobs like this. And the rope was such an attraction that what father in his right mind could deny his kid the thrill of holding onto the rope? And after so many loads of pure sand it was easy for the most responsible father to yield to days of begging to let the kid hold the handle to control the depth of the cut—just this one time. "But be sure that you let it go—fast—if it really pulls like hitting clay."

Who could guess that just a couple of loads later the scraper would hit clay, or that the kid who would absolutely remember to let go. . .forgot. Four horses pulling a Fresno scraper can create serious leverage compared with the gentle pressure it takes to load the scraper by raising or lowering that handle an inch.

By the time it occurred to me that I should let go of the handle, I was on my way to outer space. Only then did I let go of the handle, and replacing it by grabbing two hands full of air, found instead that my hands were full of hame knobs—the most available part of the harness on the gentle team in the middle of the four-horse hitch. My dad died in 1970. I'm sure he took the secret of his indiscreet supervision to his grave. I guess I never realized it until now, but that was always my favorite team of horses after that.

Quiet Road Rage in the Sandhills

Summers in the Nebraska Sandhills are long and hot. Frequently they are also dry. Before irrigation wells were discovered, dry land alfalfa generally made a good first cutting. Sometimes the second, third or fourth cuttings were good, sometimes not or even non-existent, depending on how often and how much it rained. Little wonder a lot of residents are regular churchgoers.

One dry summer day we were moving a fair-sized drove of cattle a few miles up the county road to a neighbor's range we had leased. County roads in this part of the country were made with a four-, six- or eight-horse team on a road grader that left a reasonably planed sand surface wide enough for two cars to meet and pass. It was often months or years between gradings on all but the most-travelled roads. The day after a rain, the sand-surfaced roads, like the beach at Daytona, are firm as concrete. After some weeks without rain, the surface was like a flat sand dune. Our road had not been serviced in ages except for our cattle tracks, leaving a layer of loose blow sand several inches deep.

A neighbor living a few miles up this sand-surfaced road was more into farming than cattle and had purchased more machinery than most of the neighbors, especially during the depression of the 1930s. Despite limited credit available to agricultural buyers, he often owed money to machinery manufacturers. As we drove the cattle toward our leased pasture, a new Chrysler came upon us from the rear, driven by a man wearing a suit, snap brim hat and wrist watch. When he slowed, then stopped, he became stuck in the sand. After a few demonstrations of how not to drive in sand, he was really stuck and asked if we could pull him out.

My 10-year-old brother Jack wanted to be a cowboy in the worst way, but always had a deep interest in cars. He slid off his horse and was giving the new car a keen eye as the driver got out to explain to our dad he was going to see our machinery-buying neighbor, and we got the idea he was a collector from the home office. Jack climbed into the driver's seat and asked the company rep how to use the steering column gear shift. Apparently pleased with the kid's enthusiasm, he explained in detail all the car's features.

Jack started the car, gently rocked it forward, then backward, a few inches at a time, then a few feet. Finally, with no signal from anyone, he backed the car up to a fairly firm, wide spot in the road, turned the car around heading back toward town and backed it near our conference site, then turned off the ignition and climbed out. Without even finishing his next question or explanation to us, the company rep slid into the seat and disappeared back down the road. I have since wondered if our neighbor ever appreciated the extra time he got between payments on his machinery because of a sandy road and a 10-year-old driver with understanding beyond his years.

Phil Meets Angus

In most of Logan County, Nebraska, there is a scarcity of certain items well known to much of the world. This was especially true in the 1930s. For example, Ben Fledderman had a small farm at the edge of town—and the only flock of sheep in the county. Jess Kesslar was the only Democrat in our precinct if not the whole county. Hadley Ranch really only half qualified. Their home ranch was in the next county but their summer range bordered ours for about a half mile. The Hadleys raised Angus.

For the uninformed, Angus cattle are black (some have a red gene that spawned what is now the Red Angus breed), originally imported to America from Scotland. As a breed, they have maternal females and produce excellent carcass animals selling today at a premium as "Certified Angus Beef." Some years ago, a few Angus families had antisocial tendencies. They were wild, even combative, especially mother cows with young calves at side.

We rode the summer range several times a week, checking cattle health, water, fence and strays. We shared a windmill and stock water tank with a neighbor who raised purebred Herefords. Not only were they Herefords, they were Certified Anxiety 4th (a special strain) Herefords. Two of his weanlings gave me my start in the cattle business. But my problem was not with them.

As I rode the perimeter fence, I noticed one of Hadley's black cows, on their side of the fence, had a tin can on her toe. She appeared to be a 2-year-old heifer with her first calf at side. And she was limping badly. Like all ranch-bred kids, my next job was to take the can off her toe. There was a "let down" on a nearby knoll so I jumped off my horse, let the wires down and led my horse across the fence into their pasture. The heifer didn't seem to be tame so I took down my rope, tossed a loop over her head and snubbed the rope to my saddle horn.

I went down the rope toward the heifer to remove the can, as I would have done with any of our Hereford-Shorthorn cattle; the black heifer met me

7

halfway with a loud bawl and a continued charge until she hit the end of the rope. Then she bolted away from the horse and backed into the rope until it began to cut off her air supply. Fortunately, my horse had been trained to face the heifer and keep the rope tight.

When I decided it was safe—the heifer had choked herself near collapse—I approached her again to remove the can. (Ranch boys can be slow learners.) The heifer discovered new life, charging me again. I again ran outside the limit of the rope. When she couldn't hit me, the heifer charged the horse, hitting the horse several times and then sticking her head under the horse's belly, trying to flip the horse in the air. But soon the horse backed into the rope, tightening it around the heifer's neck and she was choking again.

When I decided she was occupied with her own problems, I walked back to the horse, climbed into the saddle and began to wonder how I was going to get my rope back. She was choking badly, her front feet wide apart. I started taking up slack, dallying up the rope until I could get close enough to the heifer to get the rope off. Inch by inch I made it, reached down and grabbed the rope at the loop and let go of all the slack. I don't know how long the heifer limped with that can but several years passed before I had an objective attitude about Angus cattle.

Alien Visits Nebraska Bedroom in the 1930s

The ranch house was built by my grandfather shortly after he homesteaded in about 1908. He made the cement blocks out of native sand, one block at a time. The house was square, with four rooms downstairs and two bedrooms upstairs. When a kitchen was added a few years later, it had a basement with 32-volt Delco electric generator and shelves full of storage batteries that furnished power for a retro-wired home and ranch out-buildings.

The upstairs bedrooms were lighted by a bare bulb in the ceiling with a pull-chain on/off switch. A cord was tied to the pull chain and anchored to the head of the bed I shared in the south bedroom upstairs with brother Jack. We had shared a bed ever since Jack got pushed out of the crib when he was 2 ½ years old by the birth of brother Dick.

Jack was a quirky bed partner. When any kind of flu or childhood illness hit the country, other kids caught it and ran a little fever for a day or two. So did Jack, except that a couple of degrees of fever pushed Jack over the edge. He went totally out of his mind, talking gibberish like, "Just wait a minute, Phil, I got to get this thing fixed," when he had nothing at hand to get fixed. Next morning he had no memory of the event and I was the only one who knew what happened. Jack also might start a conversation that continued an idea from days ago with no introduction. It was sometimes hard to know if Jack was fully conscious or fully asleep.

I believe I was 13 and Jack was 10 when I was awakened in the middle of the night by the light coming on. Jack was beating the floor with his boot. "What is going on?" I asked him. I knew he wasn't making sense but I didn't even know he was sick. Jack kept saying "the dirty sonofabitch, killin's too good for the dirty sonofabitch," as he banged his boot on the floor.

I had learned to ignore his insane night-time outbursts as long as possible but this time I just had to get his attention, even though I knew the answer would not be coherent. Jack obviously had another fever. "What are you doing?" I finally asked him. "You'll wake up the folks downstairs," I reasoned aloud, with the hope that the possibility of their wrath at such goings-on might return him to his senses. Without missing a beat, Jack continued, "A wasp just got in bed with me. Killin's too good for the dirty sonofabitch!" This time, Jack was awake.

Good Fences

We have all heard that good fences make good neighbors. While I had not yet appeared on the scene at the time this took place, I can repeat a "family" story my mother told me about the time when bad fences also made good neighbors. Incidentally, almost all the farm families in the early 1920s milked cows, separated the milk, sold the cream and fed the milk to the pigs.

My mother was a member of the Brothers family. The fence between the Brothers ranch and the Johnson ranch was probably a good enough three-barbed-wires-on-split-cedar-posts kind of fence. It might not keep all the stock on the right side of the fence all the time but at least it kept the tame ones at home. Time had done the fence no favors and there had been plenty of that since the fence was built or last repaired. Simply, when the Johnson pasture got a bit overgrazed just across the fence from a fine field of Brothers corn waving in the August breeze, the herd of Johnson milk cows marched, almost in military formation, through the fence and into the corn.

While Uncle Hank (my mother's older brother) had chased the cows back into their pasture several times and touched up the fence repairs, the cows were too attracted to the lush cornfield to be contained by the fence, no matter how freshly repaired. Efforts to get the Johnsons to keep their cows at home were not paying off either. When the score got to be Cows 7-Corn 0, the secret weapon arrived. Edna, my mother's younger sister, came home from her summer term at college. Edna was an activist, a tough farm girl, a tiger. She was a candidate for the "don't get mad; get even" award.

When the Johnson milk-cow herd made their now regular afternoon safari into the Brothers cornfield, Hank asked Edna to help him chase them home. She had a better plan. Normal milking time was about 5 p.m. Edna got Hank to help her bring the herd to the Brothers barn where she milked every cow, then turned them back in the cornfield, just in time for the Johnson afternoon roundup. We do not know how much milk those freshly milked cows gave to the Johnsons at the evening milking a few minutes later. We do not know how long it took for the Johnsons to figure out what had happened but, mysteriously, those milk cows had eaten their last stalk of Brothers corn and contributed for the last time to their "bad neighbor" reputation.

Don't Steal Gas from Grandpa's Tank

We lived so far from the school bus route that there seemed no way for me to go to high school. But my grandparents only lived a mile from the bus and they had once boarded a cousin who did chores for her keep during the school year. I asked Grandma if I could stay with them, acting as if it was my parents' idea. She tentatively agreed. Then I asked my parents, acting like it was her idea.

My dad, who had gone to only one year of high school, had visions of a free hired man after I finished the eighth grade. My mother had gone to high school and "Normal School," becoming a teacher. She thought I should go on but she wondered if they could afford to lose a worker, right now when times were so hard—maybe later. School finally won and I started getting acquainted with Grandpa's chores.

He took pains to show me the gasoline storage tank that was just a few feet inside a 10-foot door on an overhead track in the south end of the shop. It was about a 200-gallon tank on a stand several feet in the air, with home-built steps so the tank wagon man could carry the big 5-gallon buckets of gas from the truck to the tank on delivery day (tank wagons didn't have pumps in those days). Grandpa was sure someone was stealing gas from this tank. But he didn't call the sheriff; in those days, you just did what you had to do.

Grandpa was a master carpenter and blacksmith with a mechanical mind and a Rube Goldberg flair. He was thinking of a plan that would stop this thief. He had put a lock on the faucet but he was sure the thief was siphoning out of the refill opening on the top. He wanted me to watch for clues, tracks or anything that could help. A bumper crop of weeds covered the ground outside the big shop door. Who leaves a track in weeds? Eager to get involved, I cleared out all the weeds by hoeing down to bare dirt, all along that side of the shop.

The shop was about 50 or 60 yards west from the ranch entry road and 10 yards north of the hog pen fence. This area, the full length of that distance, from the buildings out to the fence, was also a block of weeds. It seemed that this would be an inviting path to the gas barrel if all the weeds were gone. In later years I wondered if it was really such a good idea or if my own Grandfather would con me into getting rid of that weed patch for him. Anyway, such sleuthing was a real adventure for me and those weeds didn't have a chance.

Two or three weeks passed and not a hint of the gas thief. And good thing. Grandpa was working on his plan but it wasn't ready. He didn't want to do real bodily harm to anyone, just show the thief that we know who he was so he wouldn't do it again. The job of checking every morning began to get boring. Then one crisp fall morning it happened. Even though it was on the side of the shop away from the house, we could see the floodlight the minute we went out before dawn to do the morning chores.

Grandpa had set up multiple booby traps—each independent of the other, in case one or more of his ideas failed to work as planned. When the big door was opened a few inches, a string of tin cans would fall from the gable roof to clang on the floor below. A rifle mounted above the door fired a bullet into a tempered steel disc that went ZING! A bucket mounted above the door dumped 5 gallons of icy cold water on anyone in the area of the opening door. Then a floodlight up under the peak of the roof (100 watts was the biggest bulb available for the old 32-volt system), newly installed for the occasion, flooded the whole south side of the shop.

Since it had been a couple of weeks between the time Grandpa set the trap and when the varmint finally came to spring it in the middle of the night, we were all dead asleep. We never did learn what time of night it happened, but it appeared that everything had worked as planned. And after all that preparation, there was a harvest.

A 10-foot piece of hose, no doubt intended to be used to siphon the gas, was the first item, just outside the slightly open garage door, then a pair of gloves, followed by a heavy-duty funnel a few feet away and finally, a 5-gallon gas can—the kind used by tank wagon operators—near the wood gate leading into the hog pasture about 30 feet from the shop door.

Did the scorched earth clearing of the area outside the shop door by the boy with the hoe contribute or did Grandpa just get some weeds cut for free? At least we could see from the marks in the sand that the 5 gallons of water had hit its mark. And the footprints across the freshly plowed hog pasture went in the direction of a wide spot in the road (parking place) behind that field on a line in the direction of the suspected neighbor's house. The steps were so far apart, the runner had to be much taller than the suspected neighbor . . . unless he was scared and running very fast.

Raking Rattlers

Few ranchers ever had too much feed for the cattle they owned, especially during the 1930s in the Nebraska Sandhills where it seems yields rarely came up to "average" and near crop failures were commonplace. Under such conditions any rancher that had the cheap labor of a few growing boys, was always on the lookout for more hay ground. We leased the Catterson Place for several years. It wasn't a big producer but the east half had apparently never been fenced so it was used for hay ground instead of pasture.

We made hay out of native prairie grass on this ranch for several years. We had acquired a tractor with a mounted sickle bar mower that really went round 'n round the field—in a hurry—when it came to cutting hay. My brother Jack loved the tractor but the folks felt he was too young to drive anything as dangerous as a mower. I refused to use the tractor for anything that could be done with horses. That put our dad on the tractor mower while I raked the hay into windrows with a team on a sulky or dump rake.

Raking hay with a totally dependable team on a summer day starts out dull and reaches a high level of boredom after a couple of hours. The only excitement is counting the number of windrows, comparing how fast the tractor moves vs. the team, trying to stay alert enough to dump the rake at every windrow and deciding how many more laps before I can stop at the camp wagon for a drink of water without getting chewed out for wasting time. The team gets to know the routine so well that they follow the edge of the raked area with a rare nudge from the driver.

Then why would Tim, the dependable horse on the right side of the rake tongue suddenly charge to the left as if he wanted to jump over both the rake tongue and Tony, the equally dependable horse on the left? It happened so fast I was almost dumped off the rake

Mowing hay with team, which I did plenty of until we got a tractor mower. I hated the tractor, its noise and exhaust fumes; my dad liked it so I "advanced" to driving a team on the rake. Photo: J.C. Allen & Sons.

seat. Gathering my composure and the reins, I pulled back hard to the right but this always-responsive team now seemed to have jaws of steel.

They turned sharply to the left but I was totally unable to get them back on track. I then guided them in a large circle with the idea of returning to the spot where the team had balked, then continue raking. My sales pitch was not working. The team absolutely would not go past the spot where they had stopped. They stuck their noses as near to the ground as the check reins allowed, then veered aside.

When I looked at the ground where the rake should have gone, the grass seemed to be crawling. Apparently the tractor mower on its last round had made chopped snake out of a den of prairie rattlers. One snake had been

12

chopped into several pieces. Two others became both hostile and mobile when the mower cut off their rattles plus a few inches of body. But if they wanted to strike a horse, they'd have to hurry. My team was giving them a wide berth.

I eased them back to the camp wagon, calmed them nearly to their gentle and dependable state, then walked back to put the wounded rattlers out of their misery. Then I carefully moved every piece of snake I could find to a previously raked area but the team would not go near the battle zone area, approximately 40 feet in diameter, even several days later. This was not the break from boredom I might have ordered or ever imagined but it surely put some excitement in a dull afternoon on the ranch. And as long as we made hay with horses, I never worried about finding a snake on the hay stack.

The French Belgian in Nebraska

Until tractors came on the scene in the 1930s or 1940s, the horsepower for farm work was all delivered by horses. Almost all ranches had a band of horses that included both draft horses and saddle horses. A horse weighing more than 1,600 pounds would be rare in our area, while draft horses in the Corn Belt frequently hit 2,000 to 2,400 pounds. Corn Belt horses were frequently purebreds of the leading draft breeds, Percheron, Belgian, Clydesdale or Shire. Draft horses in our area were pretty much horses of mixed breeds.

McPherrins had the biggest ranch in our neighborhood. Their home was a sway-backed soddy (walls made by piling blocks of prairie sod) on a gentle hill near their meadow, about a mile from our house. They had several hundred cows and made hay on hundreds of acres of sub-irrigated hay meadow at the head of the South Loup River. They ran a band of nearly 100 draft horses including the brood mares and growing stock and a few dozen saddle horses.

In the belief that more horsepower per horse was a good thing, they imported a Belgian stallion from France to use in "upgrading" their breeding and produce bigger horses when mated to their mares. He was a giant strawberry roan with the longest head I had ever seen on a horse. We could hardly wait to see his first offspring. They began coming about a year later and, even though the foals were large, most of the mares foaled without serious trouble.

It seemed to take forever, but finally the first foals were 3 years old and it was time to begin training them to pull their weight in the ranch operation. This was done by handling the colt until it was familiar with people, doing cosmetic things like mane, tail and hoof trimming, and getting the youngster comfortable with people. But these half-Belgians were big. There was no chance for a mere man to overpower any one of these horses. They had better be gentle.

The first one to get the "gentling" treatment hated every minute, every move and every person who came near. He bucked, kicked with rear feet, struck with front feet, bit everything within reach and squealed like an echo chamber full of giant snared rabbits. McPherrin fences were so tight we jokingly said you could play them with a violin bow. Their corrals were heavy duty, always made of over-size lumber with bolts instead of nails. They were "animal proof," so to speak.

The young gelding couldn't get away but he gave them no cooperation. They then tried gelding No. 2 . . . and No. 3 . . . and not one was corrigible. They now had three crops of these half-brothers and sisters on the ranch and the mares were carrying another crop. What would they do for horsepower if four crops of these colts wouldn't work? In time, a few worked in four-horse-abreast hitches with three gentle horses. The next year some worked in two-horse hitches with one cross-bred and one gentle horse. Then they tried two half-Belgians in a team.

We often exchanged work with McPherrins. When their hay was ready for cutting and ours wasn't, we helped them and vice versa, with a team or two on the mower or rake or sweep. One day we were cutting alfalfa and they brought a team on a horse-drawn mower—the first time I had seen two of these strawberry roans in the same hitch. We had made a few rounds of the field when Ed McPherrin drove his team-drawn mower over a pheasant nest. When the pheasant hen took off, so did the team pulling the mower—at full gallop with heads high in the air.

Ed pulled on one rein in an attempt to turn them in a circle to the right. On the second time around, the circle got lop-sided and they approached a fence from an angle just before an open gate. The horse on the left side went through the gate, the one on the right didn't, and the mower began knocking over posts and rolling up a giant ball of the wire that had previously been a fence. When the load got too heavy for them to pull, the team just stood frozen but trembling. We brought our biggest and most dependable team, tied one of the roans to each of our horses and began "undressing" the runaways one strap at a time. Ed was so glad to be out of the mess, his embarrassment hardly showed.

And what did happen to the progeny of the imported stallion? The first few went to Beutler Bros., rodeo contractors, and became the first of the "big" rodeo broncs. Cowboys were experienced at riding the lightweight, saddle-bred horses but these gave an entirely different ride. They weighed hundreds of pounds more than any rodeo horse anyone had ever ridden and when these horses hit the ground, riders lost their "seat" and were bucked off on the next jump. No bronc rider stayed aboard for a qualifying ride through

14

the first rodeo season and dozens stayed in bucking strings for years. Welcome to America!

Breathless on the Barn Floor

Ranch kids handle a lot of responsibility. I had ridden long enough and well enough for my parents to send me off to kindergarten 2 miles away on a horse. My mount stood in a stall at school all day, and then we returned home in the evening. Three years later brother Jack and I rode double to school. When Dick started two years later, we graduated to two horses but the routine continued through eighth grade. Field work with four-horse teams on cultivators began when I was 10 years old.

All the ranch work was done with horses until we got the first tractor when I was about 12 years old. My dad liked the tractor as did brother Jack. I was not sold on anything that had to be driven every minute. I admitted that horses might only have a one-digit IQ, but that tractor didn't have a brain in its head. We stood draft horse stallions to breed neighbors' mares for several years. We used ours in two-, four- and six-horse hitches. I drove them but never liked stallions much better than tractors. But we had one stud that I really did like.

In the late 1930s, we got an Army remount stallion from the Fort Robinson Cavalry station to use ourselves and to "improve the quality of horses in the area." In the '30s and '40s, army buyers bought potential mounts throughout our area according to strict qualifications. No rancher wanted to breed his saddle mares to a Thoroughbred, the breed of race horse that ran in the Kentucky Derby, etc., because we knew that race horses had a bad temperament and couldn't handle cattle. Army Cavalry remount horses, on the contrary, were the best you could get. Years later I was shocked to learn they were one and the same. The "Jockey Club" on the registration papers was another name for horses of the Thoroughbred breed registry.

"Red" was a handsome, well-muscled, bright sorrel horse standing 15 hands 2 inches with a small star on his forehead and a white ankle on one rear foot. When I saw Three Bars, the famous Thoroughbred sire of Quarter Horses, many years later, I felt that I was seeing Red all over again. I never learned much about his history but he was great under the saddle and handled as gentle as a gelding. He was the only stud I ever really liked. The only time he ever acted up was when he was near another stallion.

We kept him in a box stall that had an outside exercise run. Even though he never acted like a stallion, the box stall was for the stud at our ranch, period. I could open the door and he'd come to be haltered or bridled. I had a routine of leaving the box stall door open and riding him bareback to get the mail at our box about a quarter mile from the house. When we got back I'd rein him over to the gate in front of the house, wedge the mail in the gate, remove the bridle or halter, then grab the barn door track as we got to the barn and let him slide out from under me at a fast trot or gallop and return to his stall. One summer day we made the mail run and I grabbed the track as usual . . . except . . .

As I was stretched out, firmly gripping the track and hanging in space, body parallel to the barn floor nearly 8 feet below, I was reminded of what I forgot until then. Red was wearing a saddle . . . not as slick as bareback when it comes to sliding off. Finally, after hanging horizontally in space for what seemed a very long time, I could hold on to the track no longer. I fell to the barn floor, flat on my back. I just had to lie on the floor until, gasp after gasp, breath returned. Red did his part. He went back in the box stall and was waiting for me to shut the door as soon as I was able.

Banker Pete's Wild Horses

Before, during and after the bank holiday in 1933, there were hard times on the farm. F.E. Peterson was president of the Bank of Stapleton. As such, he held the fate and future of most people in our community in his grasp. He was understanding, if not generous, in dealing with borrowers, but perhaps nobody could have envisioned so many years of both bad economy and bad weather as hit our area.

Despite his ability to "divine" which farmers would be able to repay in time and which had no chance, he presided over some foreclosures. Farm foreclosures today result in selling tractors at auction but tractors in those years had four feet and they didn't bring enough money to bother with an auction. Pete simply took the horses to one of the ranches where he had foreclosed the land, and turned them out to pasture.

In a few years, he had many acres of essentially wild horses. When a borrower in Pete's good graces, including my dad, needed more horsepower for the season, you went to his horse ranch, picked out as many as you felt you needed for the year, took them home, broke them to work, and used them for the year, FREE for the feed. Pete gained too. Wild horses were worthless. Well-broke teams had some value. I don't know how many horses we broke over three or four years but it was six or eight a year; some made good teams.

We raised some row crops and used six-horse hitches on machinery. If you had solid horses in the center and outside of a six-abreast team, you could hitch anything that would wear a harness in slots 2 and 5 in the hitch by tying them securely to the reliable horses on both sides of the trainee(s). One of the problems with success in anything, though, is its tendency to breed overconfidence in the participants.

In our case, this resulted in Whitey and Dynamite. They were both "senior citizens." Gray horses get whiter with age, from steel gray as 2-year-olds to nearly white at 8 to 10. When a horse is nearly white before he is broke to

16

work, a trainer had better pick any other horse from a band of 50 to 100. But Dad "liked" him so Whitey was ours for the year. Dynamite was a good looking black gelding that had bluffed at least two previous attempts by "farmer-trainers" to show him the error of his ways and make him "useful." We gave him one more chance.

Whitey acted like he had been handled before. We had a stout narrow stall so we could bring two or three horses (including the unbroken one) in the back, then slide one side over, narrowing to single file. A broke horse was first in line and we led it out the front gate. The wild horse came next. We fed him oats and began grooming to make him comfortable (in sight of other horses). After a positive response from the horse, we tried a halter. Whitey did not kick or rear like some wild horses. He endured hitching in six-horse teams but would pull back, kick, bang his head and abuse himself when tied in a stall.

Dynamite was a real bully. He chased cattle in the pasture, charged other horses with teeth bared when running loose in the corral. He gave us the slip the first few times we tried to get him in our restraint stall. But we did get him in the stall, haltered him and snubbed him to a big, gentle horse. We got a harness on him and hitched him several times in a six-horse team. He never pulled a lick.

Another bank borrower had taken four horses but he got sick and Pete wanted us to go pick up the horses. We agreed if he would take back Whitey and Dynamite so he said the veterinarian would come to pick them up. We were convinced that these two horses were useless and beyond hope. But little did we know. Our dumb vet entered them in amateur night at a rodeo try-out. They both found new careers where they thrived by working eight seconds once or twice a week for years.

The Best Christmas Ever

We had a brockle-faced cow. She had blotches of red on her face that would have been solid white if she had been pure Hereford. Most of our cows calved in the February-to-April period. She was one of few that calved in fall. And she was prolific. She had twins the week after Armistice Day (November 11) and a single calf just a year later. Then I was cleaning the barn the next year when she had twin heifers—on Armistice Day. How my brother Jack and I wished those calves could be ours.

Nebraska had been through several years of drought. This was a decent rain year but after so many dry years, people were afraid to be optimistic. The "cousins" had come from Canada to visit but our parents were not in a generous mood. We knew at an early age there wasn't any Santa Claus. I was beginning my sophomore year in high school and trying to make the football team. I wasn't a regular but I got to play. I wanted a "letter sweater" in the worst way but we couldn't spare enough money for that.

Our mother had her priorities straight. She saw to it that the family went to church and put money in the collection plate several times a week but we never had money for anything we wanted. She would rather have a family of broke, unhappy Christians than whatever the alternative might have been. We knew from years of experience that Christmas in our family was a church holiday. We never had a tree. Our traditional Christmas disappointment was softened to an extent because we had no electricity, no radio except for a splurge once a year or so when they bought a battery that ran down after a few months, only a couple of trips per year to the city and no paper except the weekly *Stapleton Enterprise*. We were not teased by slick advertising to buy, buy, buy. But Jack and I would speculate—hoping against fate—about what we might get.

Then came Christmas morning. We each got an orange, some nuts, a little candy . . . and a Bible. We never knew whether our long faces changed their plans or whether they planned it as a lesson in character building. It's even possible that our dad did it on his own. But when he told us we were each getting one of the month-old twin heifers as a Christmas present, we yelled *Merry Christmas* as we ran . . . all the way to the barn.

Home Brew in the Milk House

It wouldn't do justice to either Hank or the term to call him my "Drinking Uncle," because he was a pretty sober guy. He was, however, my uncle. And he did like a cool, tall one on a warm summer evening. Hank made a batch of home brew about every summer—a few cases per batch. I don't know if you need a cool place to make beer or if it was just a little unused space, but Hank made his beer in the milk house.

If you didn't live on the plains in the 1930s, before refrigerators, you have no way of knowing that the coolest place around was in a concrete-walled building under large trees with freshly pumped cool water flowing through a concrete chamber or tank about 2 feet wide and in three depths. The shallow end was for small containers such as gallon jars of milk, crockery containers of butter, salad and other foodstuffs.

The deepest level came up to the neck of 10-gallon cream cans, stored until filled and taken to the railroad depot in town for shipment to the creamery company that made butter from it and mailed a check to the farmer. The mid-level part of the tank was for middle-sized containers. The old windmill just outside the milk house seemed to always be pumping and the cool water came out of the ground and directly into the shallow end of the tank. The milk house provided space for the cream separator, a rack for empty, clean cream cans, milk pails and whatever it was inconvenient to

18

store someplace else. At certain times this included some containers for the brewing process and/or a few cases of freshly bottled beer. This was after the repeal of prohibition so it was not illegal but my teetotalling parents refused to admit that they knew of Hank's activity, much less condone it.

It was late summer, about the first weekend after we had finished the threshing run in the neighborhood. We went to Grandma's house for Sunday dinner (Hank was my mother's older bachelor brother who ran the place after my grandfather died). Some of my cousins, including Albert, who was a year older than I, also came to dinner. I think I was 10, he was 11. After dinner we climbed up the windmill tower, did a tour of the barn—upstairs haymow and all—and eventually the milk house, which was only 15 or 20 yards from the house. Then we left the milk house, slamming the door, which had a tendency to stick open or shut.

Home brew, as bottled by Uncle Hank, tended to be about as unstable as nitroglycerine. The slamming door was an adequate shock to cause some of the bottles to blow their tops—and thus began a chain reaction a bit like a string of Fourth-of-July firecrackers. By now it was about time to leave Grandma's milk house and go home for any of several reasons.

We did not get asked to take inventory or even clean up the mess in the milk house. I suppose Hank was upset but my parents had mixed emotions. Should they be harsh with me for the thoughtless horseplay or thrilled that we had exploded a fair percentage of Hank's embarrassing vice? The incident was never mentioned by my parents and is probably long forgotten by everybody but me. I wanted to taste the stuff.

The Country Preacher

They may have deserved each other. The rag-tag, broke-but-not-foreclosed band of near-Dustbowl farmers of the '30s and the country preacher. With the double desperation of the bad economy and the record drought, about the only ray of hope was going to heaven someday. But some quirk of human nature forced them to keep on praying for better times in this life.

A few of the neighbors drove to church in town. There were three churches there. Most of the inhabitants of our little community, for reasons known only to them, didn't endorse any of these beliefs, though. But they were determined to go to church and to have their own preacher, even if it meant sharing him with another band of believers. He preached early at one location, then drove about 15 miles to preach a late sermon at the next gathering. Each group met at its own neighborhood one-room schoolhouse.

The turnover of these itinerant preachers was high. We had one that was really a pretty good guy. He had a wife and two kids, lived in a vacant house at the back of a neighbor's ranch and drove a team of loaned horses—one from our band and one from a neighbor's—on a wagon loaned by another.

19

These were desperate times. After a year or so, he finally got hired by a real church somewhere and we went back to new-convert types who "threw down the bottle and picked up the Bible" in their first solo outing from the "preacher-nursery-and-save-factory."

They were good at visiting the parishioners "in their homes" and were good at hitting these homes at mealtime. This occasion might also be followed with the observation that "if this gauge is working, my gas tank seems to be nearly empty," followed, if the farmer didn't volunteer to fill up at the gas tank, by "I wonder if you could be so good as to loan me a couple of gallons."

One such evening, after a good family supper, we picked up the milk pails and began our trip to the barn for the evening milking where we hand-milked 20 to 30 cows. Uncle Bill, my dad's younger brother, was working for us as a hired hand. Someone volunteered that the reverend would be welcome to help us milk, to which he answered, "I'd surely be glad to help you but I've milked about three-fourths of a cow in my life." And in a split second, Bill responded to my dad, "Hey, Harvey, you don't have a three-teater, do you?"

Where's Edward?

E.J. "Old Mac" McPherrin was our neighbor. He was also the strong paternal influence in the McPherrin family. Their home was on a nice rise at the edge of a large sub-irrigated hay meadow. There was one big cottonwood tree at the northwest corner of the house. Otherwise, E.J. could sit in the house and look over much of the ranch with binoculars, which he frequently did. Their house was about a mile from ours. I know well because we had a phone. They didn't.

If anybody wanted to talk to McPherrins on the phone, they called us. You guessed it: I got to ride to their house. Sometimes I had a brief message to carry, if there was nothing of a personal or financial nature. Otherwise the message was for them to come to our house and pick up their end of the call. In bad weather, I sometimes wished they would get a phone. But it wasn't all bad. Mrs. McPherrin served me homemade Grape Nuts ice cream, made in their gas-powered Electrolux refrigerator, one time when I took them a phone message. It was good stuff.

Mac had a Model T Ford coupe. He drove it to town a few times a year and he drove it to church almost as often. Otherwise, McPherrins did it with teams—they had good horses and lots of them. They also had three sons and a daughter. John, the first son, was a thoughtful, mechanical, quiet type. Edward was second in line, the extrovert and the horseman. Margaret was the daughter and Old Mac's prize. Robert was the youngest, about three years ahead of me in school.

Calling Mac a dominant personality was being generous. None of the children ever married while he was alive. As much as he hated surprises, one afternoon in the fall of 1934, he was driving past the "mailboxes on the wheel" (a landmark where McPherrins owned land on three corners of the crossroads) and noticed Edward's horse in a small pasture on the corner. The saddle cinch was loosened and the reins were dragging on the ground. But Ed was not there.

Mac had just come from his house. When he found Ed missing, he went straight to our house, about a mile away. He started calling neighbors to see if anyone had seen an accident or knew what had happened to his mysteriously absent No. 2 son, who was probably 25 years old. No Ed. He had vanished and nobody would have noticed, for the moment, if the horse had been in a less obvious pasture, but this was at a corner of the highway.

If Mac, the man who loved to be in control, had any cool in reserve, it didn't show. He was red-faced and rubbing his thinning white hair frantically. He sat near our telephone, praying to hear anything from anyone. Then a car drove into our yard—a brand new 1935 Ford sedan. And Ed, the missing son, was driving. He had come to show us, his neighbors, what he had done.

His distressed father was so glad to see him return from apparent death, all he wanted to know was "What happened?" Ed had heard the local Ford dealer had a new car in the show room, decided to buy it, and had caught a ride to town with the tank wagon man. He had to park his horse somewhere so he just opened the gate and put him in the field. Mac may have forgiven his son, but he never drove that car.

The Spunky Nesbit Schoolteacher

It's no wonder kids got a good education in the one-room school. Students in the lower grades got the benefit of overhearing next year's lesson as the more advanced classes recited on the stage area in the front of the room. And the kids learned more than textbook material from the other students, who could be several years older or younger.

The job was a textbook example of time and people management to keep 24 to 30 boys and girls in eight grades under control while following or exceeding the assigned course of study. At Nesbit School, where I spent eight years, the teacher was also the janitor, fire-builder, school nurse, producer and choreographer for seasonal school performances, and campus cop. She probably also would have been the psychiatrist if that specialty had made it to the plains by that time. And we had to pump drinking water with a hand pump at recess time. Two of the teachers I had at Nesbit were among the best in my life. My first and second years were under Caryl Johnson, a teacher who started us on phonics so we really learned word sounds, spelling and usage.

Grace Clark taught when I was in the fourth, fifth and sixth grades. She was small in stature and fresh out of school. And her first year was the year that Mick, Ray and Bob were all physically mature, over-age (15 or 16 years old) eighth graders from families in our district with the most casual attitude about school, especially regarding the importance of school decorum.

The three had not been discipline problems the previous year. That teacher was from a local family and had several years' experience. But boys can mature a lot in a year and the new teacher was unknown to the kids in the district until the first day of school. From day one, the three had tried to match their newly found macho with the new teacher's discipline. Then one day during the morning recess, Bob made a remark out in the schoolyard that upset the teacher. She sent him back inside the schoolhouse as discipline.

When he refused to go, she grabbed his pants in the middle of his back with her right hand and began to march him toward the school. He whirled around expecting her to go flying across the schoolyard. No deal. When her feet touched the ground again, she grabbed on with both hands and, while he was about 6 feet tall and she was barely more than 5 feet and only a few years older, she lifted him up until his feet barely touched the ground and they went straight to the schoolhouse door.

"Robert," she said, "You'd just as well get it straight right now. You are the student here; I am the teacher. And it's going to be that way from now on. Now make yourself useful and ring the bell. Recess is over." Everyone on the school grounds gasped. Bob was not only one of the "big kids," he was the leader. But, exactly as he had been asked . . . or ordered . . . he rang the bell. And so, in another sense, did the teacher. She rang his bell and every potential bully in the school heard it loud and clear.

This may not have been traditional "visual education" but it was visual and, boy, was it educational. Years later, after she had married and moved to a nearby community, I asked if she had anticipated the showdown. She said she felt, from the first day, it might happen with any one of the three big boys but she decided she would win or lose during the first showdown. Is it any wonder kids learned a lot in the little old one-room school?

Runaway Well Digger

You don't need to be a hydrologist, geologist, or even a water witch to find underground water in the Nebraska Sandhills. It's right there. All the water you want. Wherever you want a well. And it's not very deep. Badgers frequently dig a little hole when they want a drink unless it's a really dry season. But even though the area is figuratively awash in water, people still need wells, fortunately for Alvie, the well man of the 1930s.

They don't drill wells in this area; they "wash" them. A well man needs a power source, a portable tower to stabilize and direct the joints of pipe as they wash down and are lowered into the ground, a water storage tank and a pump with hose. Alvie used a 1929 Buick as his power source. His home-made derrick of spiked-together 4-by-4s that hinged on a two-wheel trailer was towed behind the Buick. He had a belt pulley on the right rear hub of the Buick. He blocked the left wheel, jacked up the right one and a belt from the hub ran the pump that forced the water down the pipe.

If you wanted a 3-inch well, the well man set the first joint of 3-inch pipe on the ground inside the portable tower, stuck a 2-inch pipe inside, and hitched it up to a hose, pump and water supply. As the pressure of the water going through the 2-inch pipe washed the sand from inside the 3-inch casing, it was lowered into the hole in the ground. When the first joint of casing pipe was mostly into the ground, another joint of pipe was screwed onto the first joint and the washing continued. A perforated sand point, screwed to the bottom, finished the well.

The Buick had either a blown muffler or a cut-out. It was not necessary for Alvie to honk the horn to announce his arrival. Maybe that gave the Buick more power, I never asked. And Alvie may have needed extra power on occasion, but it didn't help one sleepy summer afternoon. I was cultivating corn with a four-horse team in a field along the road between our place and the Barner farm. That road had been graded and had ditches on both sides of an elevated grade.

Alvie rarely drove faster than 20 miles per hour. I heard him coming past Barners' house and about a quarter mile to the T in the road. At the T, Alvie made a left turn onto the road along the edge of the field where I was working. He got about halfway around the corner, and then seemed to drive straight into the ditch, where he was stuck, Buick, trailer, derrick and all.

Even though he had few teeth left, Alvie chewed tobacco. He tipped his head back as he chewed, with tobacco juice trickling down the corners of his mouth until it was spitting time. When he was on the derrick, it was a good idea to give him room. And, with the absence of teeth and presence of tobacco juice, his enunciation left a good bit to be desired.

I thought my team might be able to pull the car and trailer out so I drove them the 30 yards to Alvie's disaster and asked him if I could help. And I had to know, "What happened?"

"Well, I was comin' down the road and turned the corner. I guess I missed the brake and hit the gas and . . . that . . . Buick . . . just . . . went . . . like . . . that," slapping his face-up left palm with his open right hand. It seemed that his Buick just outran Alvie's reflexes.

Depression Cash Crop

Herding turkeys challenged your patience but not your intelligence. After a year of this, my parents decided I was ready to graduate to new assignments. Or maybe I just went from age 11 to 12. I liked driving a team much better and since I had little brothers to take over, who could deny them such a character-building opportunity in ranch employment.

Turkeys are curious about everything that moves, shines or shouldn't be there. At other times they can be panicked by almost all the same things that they normally like. They eat grain, gravel, many green, growing things, jewelry, worms, bugs and jillions of grasshoppers. They may peck at a grasshopper only to have it fly 10 to 20 feet, with the turkey in hot pursuit, often making the catch on the second or third hop.

When they were only a few weeks old, we began driving them in one big herd around the edge of our alfalfa fields. In an hour or so, their crops were bulging with free feed and we gave another chance at life to many new alfalfa leaves, adding so much value to the price of a ton of hay. As both they and the crop of grasshoppers got bigger, the tours got longer and went to twice a day. A bamboo stick worked as a "shepherd's crook" but it did more for the herder than the herd.

Turkeys flock around a snake or small animal. They go berserk in thunderstorms. I never knew what lightning did because the clap of thunder that followed often made them collect in huge piles, suffocating any that you didn't get unpiled quickly. Crossing the path of a coyote with a herd of turkeys was unpredictable. A coyote would normally love to find a single turkey but herds were baffling. The turkeys were curious and often chased the coyote.

Turkeys were a "niche" crop in several ways. In spring, we bought 300 to 400 day-old poults and about a pound of starter feed for each. Not a big cash outlay. After that feed was gone, they got a little farm-grown cracked grain and the rest of their growth came from grasshoppers, which they harvested by the ton, one at a time. This not only fed the growing turkeys, but it dramatically thinned the perennial bumper crop of the alfalfa-loving hoppers giving new life to acres of alfalfa hay.

It also gave a return from another farm resource, kids too young for other productive work. When the new corn crop was mature enough to begin picking, it gave a calorie boost to the nearly mature birds for the few weeks before market near Thanksgiving. And since there was very little cash outlay, the sale price was almost pure profit, something every family needed during the depression.

We wore old shoes and overalls at the start of the new school year until we sold the turkeys. Then we went shopping—like the first rain after a long drought. On the trip home, we got bologna sandwiches on sliced baker's bread. What a treat! The rest of the year we ate home-cured dried beef, corned beef and ham—on homemade bread. Yuck. Our practical parents saved a few turkeys at least for Thanksgiving and Christmas dinner, although the homegrown herders would have gladly seen the last one go to market. Ben Franklin allegedly campaigned for the turkey instead of the bald eagle as our national bird. If true, I can guarantee that Ben never herded turkeys.

Stranger in the Road

If you happened to be in Tryon, Nebraska, in the late 1930s or early 1940s, you must have been on a rare mission or else you were badly lost. The road ran from Stapleton through Ringgold to Tryon and, if you were really determined, you could go all the way to Flats and Arthur. The road maps called it Nebraska "Highway" 92. In fact, it was a graded dirt road from Stapleton to Tryon. But then it soon became two tracks (one for each wheel) across the pasture.

Not far out of Tryon, in midsummer, you might find strange objects in the middle of your "highway." Rancher George Snyder had heard that he could make more money with crossbred cattle—that their calves gained more and brought a bigger paycheck. Anyway, George bought some Brahman bulls to use on the predominantly white-faced Hereford cows. No, the bulls were not in the middle of the road. They were far away in a bull pasture.

But those cross-bred, half-Brahman calves, while hating to be alone, had minds of their own. Their mothers dutifully stayed in the pastures. The fences on either side of the road had only three strands of wire and posts that were further apart than normal in some areas. They were no challenge for these floppy-eared, brockle-faced babies. When only a few weeks old, they got through the fences and stared at oncoming traffic from their position in the middle of the sort of "imaginary" road.

Some of the cows had been bred to Hereford bulls. These calves, with the solid white faces, never seemed to be in the road. Traditional Sandhills ranchers were quick to condemn the "goofy-acting mongrels." When we saw the first of the Brahman bulls we understood, partly. They were gray, nearly white, tall with slim bodies and a hump at their shoulders and huge, droopy ears. And you could not separate these bulls. They did not like to be alone and had the athletic ability to get across the fence for a party.

Brahman bulls were being used in the bull-riding competition at rodeos but few ranchers had ever been close to one unless they sat near the arena at the county fair and rodeo. That's where I got my first close-up. Cousin Raymond and I were a year and a day apart in birthdays and about 3 feet apart at the rodeo. In our sparsely-populated county, the fairgrounds grandstand held about 200 people. The rest watched from cars parked outside the V-mesh fence around the arena. Our cars were parked directly across the arena from the chutes, about 3 feet apart with front bumpers 2 or 3 feet from touching the fence. We were sitting on the front fenders during the bull riding when the riders were bucked off and the hazers rode near the bull to return him to the corral. I have since learned that if there is one thing Brahmans like less than being alone, it is being crowded.

In a show of displeasure over being alone, while trying to elude the hazers, one bull jumped the 6-foot arena fence, landing between our cars and missing us by inches. Bug-eyed and speechless, we learned great respect for the athletic ability of Bos Indicus, the Brahman bull. Those cross-bred calves didn't escape George Snyder's pastures and play in the road because they were mean, but rather, just because being half-Brahman, they could.

The Best "No Hunting" Sign

Growing up with cattle in Nebraska, you learn how to ride to check the cattle, the fence and drinking water almost in your sleep. When school started in the fall we still had chores to do and limited daylight so thorough checking of cattle was pretty well limited to Saturdays. This continued as long as there was a field with grass standing. When the grass was gone, cattle were brought in to nearby fields where they were fed hay until spring.

South Dakota and Iowa both fought for the reputation as the best places for pheasant hunting. We didn't have a fraction of the hunters that hit the fields in either of those areas but we probably had as many pheasants. And a big bonus for pheasants in our area was the protection of the shelter belts of trees planted as windbreaks during the Dust Bowl days of the 1930s.

Like many of our neighbors, we planted a few rows of grain sorghum, corn or millet between the rows of trees to develop habitat and winter feed for pheasants and other birds. Hunters could walk down the rows of trees in one of these plantings—see and possibly get decent shots at several pheasants—but most of the birds ran ahead and never flew. If you posted two or three hunters at the end of the rows, the whole party could frequently "limit out" in one pass as the birds flew when they ran out of tree and brush cover. Hunting was good and we had been discovered by hunters so we always posted "No Hunting" signs near the trees.

On the Saturday morning that opened the pheasant season, hunters would park at the end of a tree planting, waiting with dogs and guns for the opening minute. One such morning I was on the first leg of fence riding when I noticed a bunch of hunters and two parked cars. I knew that we had not given anyone permission to hunt so I rode to the corner to see if they were friend or foe. Strangers with Missouri license plates.

I was only 14 but I felt possessive about our rights and asked who gave them permission to hunt and they said "the owner." I asked what his name was. They mumbled a name I couldn't understand or did not know. I asked where "the owner" lived. They pointed to Barners' house (it was visible, ours wasn't). I was having trouble with the fidgety half-broke horse I was riding. He kept turning to left and right as we talked.

I told them they pointed to the wrong house so I knew they didn't have permission and they had better move on. They started talking among themselves and I thought I might have gone too far. There were six of them and only one of me. And I almost had my hands full with my horse that was young and tired of standing still and began turning around again. Suddenly they jumped in their cars, dogs, guns and all, and left.

When I got home and talked about the hunters and the mystery of their sudden leaving, it occurred to our hired man that they had probably noticed the gun, a 30-30 carbine, we always carried in a scabbard under the stirrup fender on the horse's right side. A few days later we heard from one of the neighbors that hunters had driven into his place to ask permission to hunt and told him they had been threatened and run off by a boy on a horse with a rifle a few miles up the road.

Spraying Out a Prairie Fire

My parents took a trip to visit relatives in Canada in August of 1947. The other kids went along but Jack and I stayed at home to look after the ranch. We were both back from service in the Navy. I had taken a break from college and Jack was working at the ranch and running cattle in exchange for part of his work. Summer work was pretty well behind us except for putting up a little "last cutting" hay.

We had finished raking alfalfa about mid-afternoon and were returning to headquarters when I happened to look toward the northwest and saw a big puff of smoke. Immediately we knew—prairie fire! We had a nearly new spraying machine with a 300-gallon redwood tank, PTO-driven pump and platform for the operator to stand on, mounted behind the tank on the rear of a two-wheel trailer. We always cleaned it after use, then filled it with water in case of fire and parked it in the shop to be ready for any emergency.

I went to the house and got on the phone while Jack hooked the spray rig to the John Deere tractor. At this time of year the grass was fairly mature but rarely over 18 inches to 2 feet tall. Fire will run but is not really dangerous to buildings unless it hits a structure squarely. It can eat up a lot of feed in short order, however. We still had crank phones mounted on the wall. I cranked out a "general ring" for everybody on the line to hear and answer. When I told the neighbors about the fire, all the neighbor men on our phone line were away from the house.

Mrs. Gibbs came on the line first, went to look, then came back and said "it's straight north of our house." Mrs. Kjar looked next and said "it's southwest of us." I told them to call town and neighbors for volunteer fire fighters, and that Jack and I were on our way, at 15-plus miles per hour, 4 miles away with the sprayer. When we arrived at the fire, it had burned about 100 to 150 acres. The Sandhills in our area were mostly gentle terrain with little or no growth of trees or shrubs—just grass.

I stood on the rear platform with a 10-foot wand that had a spray nozzle at the end. The fire was burning with a flame not more than 2 or 3 feet high. Jack geared down to about 5 miles per hour and drove with a tractor wheel on the edge of the flame. I laid a spray pattern of water on the flame and we almost totally wiped out the fire as the tractor drove along the fire line.

We had disposed of about 2 miles of flame and had only a few hundred yards of fire left when the first neighbors arrived with barrels of water, wet sacks, shovels and traditional fire-fighting equipment. All that was left to do was hit a few flare-ups and burning cow chips. This was the first use of a portable spray rig to fight prairie fire in the area. One of the neighbors told us, jokingly, to get rid of that thing. "This fire didn't even get big enough, nor last long enough to justify a party after it was out. That rig takes all the fun out of fighting a prairie fire."

Ernie Brown's Roan Team

Several county and state fairs still hold pulling contests. Most have gone to tractor pulls. A few still get teams to enter and there are several horse fanciers who spend many dollars to keep stables, breeding programs and moving vans to get their teams from one "pull" to the next. I never cared much for the show biz side of horses but a good team doing their job well always got my respect. Furthermore, no tractor ever did.

I really enjoyed working with horses and so my dad let me pick the horses I was to use for whatever job. We had one team of blacks that drove my dad crazy but I could get them to do almost anything. We didn't drive many mare-gelding teams but this was my team. I knew their foibles and they endured me. Named for distant neighbors, Maude was a shy breeder so except for being in heat a few times a year, she worked like a gelding. Charlie could do more than most teams. He would ease gently into a pull— and just keep pulling; Maude hit a little harder but might not pull quite as long if the load didn't begin moving.

Getting a heavy load started is a problem for most teams. They "lean into" the load, tightening the tugs but when the load doesn't budge, they quit pulling, period. Charlie would tighten up the tugs and the load would almost always begin to move when Maude leaned into the hitch. If it was especially heavy, I walked around in front and took their bits—one horse in each hand—and smoothed their release of power.

I knew Ernie Brown, his wife and their kids. But we did not live close enough to the Browns to exchange work, although a couple of neighbors

28

lived between us and exchanged work both ways. They often bragged that Ernie Brown's roan team could pull whatever was the load of the moment. I never saw horses walk on water but the neighbors would have me believe that Ernie's roan team could do that too.

In our area, all the fields were sandy and, except for a few days after a good rain, country roads can be even worse than the fields. One day we were filling silos with fresh-chopped green corn stalks. This was before field choppers; two men rode a horse-drawn "sled" with knives that cut the stalks, while they gathered corn. Then they stopped the horse and piled the green corn on a wagon.

My favorite team could pull "almost any load." Sorry the photographer cut off their feet and lower legs.

When the wagon had a good load, the driver pulled it away and drove to the silo where the cutter chopped the green corn stalks into silage. Another wagon replaced it in the field. One neighbor, this day, filled his wagon a bit too full and, when he pulled it toward the silo, the sand in the road got deep and his team quit. He could not make them pull again. Since it was evening quitting time, he unhitched. He said that Ernie Brown's roan team could pull the load up to the silo but that first we would have to off-load some of the corn in the morning.

The other wagons were full when we quit that night so we had no empty to use in the morning to get rid of his overload. I was sick of his talk and said that if Ernie Brown's roan team could pull that load, my team could pull it. Then it hit me—I'd hitch Charlie to the end of the tongue and pull the load with one horse. I had nothing to lose. Everybody knew that no one horse could budge that wagon. I took him by the bit, eased him into the load and when it moved, I stayed with him and he pulled it 20 to 30 yards to the silage chopper. I don't know if the roan team fell into a hole that day or if Ernie sold them but our neighbor never mentioned them again. It seems a shame but I never did see Ernie Brown's roan team pull a load.

To Make it Shine

The one-room school was a great place to learn. We learned the curriculum from course of study. We learned from the higher grades' recitation. We learned from the interaction of students in all the grades, far more than a room filled with children of only one age group. We saw imagination at its best and sometimes the weird things others did that we would never do.

When I was in the seventh grade, our teacher was a home-grown product with a handicap: her students included two of her nephews. The older brother was a decent student who handled the relationship well, not asking, giving, nor expecting special treatment. The younger brother, a first or second grader, might have acted the same with another teacher, except that he simply could not remember to use her last name. Instead of Miss Bakewell or even Aunt Pearl, to Howard she was Pearlie. It did not lessen her authority. We all understood.

Howard was not stupid. He just did things so differently from "normal" that some people mistook him for stupid. His desk was by the window. When he saw a daddy long-legs spider crawling up the outside of his window, he began talking to the spider aloud, giving it directions. He was not embarrassed when everybody was at his side, watching him do or say something most inappropriate for school.

When we came back into the schoolhouse after the noon-hour recess on a nice spring day, the teacher sat in the chair at her desk in the front of the room. A minute later she acted as if something was wrong with her desk. She touched a spot on the desk with a finger, then another spot, and then she smelled her finger. It was not the normal way to start an afternoon. In a rural, one-room school, though, you were well-served to expect the unexpected.

She stood up and got a serious look as she asked, "does anybody know what is on my desk?" Howard held up his hand.

"I do, Pearlie," he said in his usual slow, thoughtful manner.

"What is it?" she continued.

"Mucilage," Howard answered promptly, but slowly.

"Well, it's all over my desk," she said in exasperation. "Who did it?"

"I did, Pearlie," Howard said in open, unflinching innocence.

"Whatever for?" she questioned.

"To make it shine," Howard said with expression—and in total innocence. He really was not stupid. But he did do things differently.

A Tractor in His Coat Pocket

One day when I was about 10 or 11, I went to town with my dad to do some shopping and get some parts for a machine. It seemed to be a busy Saturday. We had to wait for service at the dealership. And looking back, it was little wonder that we had to take our place in line. The man at the front of the line, I was to learn, was Zell Russell, who, I was able to tell, must have been a rich farmer. He wore a suit jacket over his bib overalls, the well-off farmer's business uniform in the 1930s. And he wore a snap brim felt hat, which was not typical farmer attire. He had apparently bought a new tractor, either from stock or order, and was ready to take delivery.

The mechanic at the dealership started the engine right there in the shop. I had never been that close to a tractor with its engine running, especially a brand new tractor. But it wasn't the pop, pop, pop of the John Deere that made my eyes almost glaze over from staring. The buyer was standing only a few feet away from me and was paying for the tractor.

When the dealer showed him the price of the tractor on the order form—I didn't see how much it was—Zell Russell reached into the side pocket of his suit coat and took out a roll of bills. It looked like he had wrapped a bill around a half-inch dowel or spool or maybe a large pencil. Then another bill and another until the roll was about 3 inches in diameter. He had a rubber band stretched around the roll to keep all the bills in order.

He removed the rubber band, took a couple of ones off the outside of the roll and then began peeling off $100 bills. I didn't even know they made $100 bills. I don't remember for sure but I believe the tractor cost $1,400 or $1,500. He paid the full amount with $100 bills and got back some change, but the roll didn't even get smaller by taking off that many $100 bills. I don't remember if I asked my dad where he got the money or not—rumors were about that he was into bootlegging since this was around 1933 or 1934, just after the repeal of the prohibition amendment. I never saw proof but I never forgot that roll of bills.

Sunday Glue Makers

My family went to church every Sunday morning at our one-room country schoolhouse when I was growing up. And there was a second service Sunday evening. A few times a year my parents would let me go home with Victor Gibbs (or vice versa) after the morning service, then return to the proper parents at the evening service. This was a treat since it gave us new scenery and new bread. My mom always made white bread; his made whole wheat. We didn't have many exciting moments for 10-year-old boys in the 1930s in the Sandhills.

One Sunday I went home with Vic and we found a good afternoon project that needed some glue to complete. We knew that flour and water made paste but we needed real glue. We found some old pieces trimmed from horse hooves and the leftovers from dehorning calves; everybody knows they make glue out of horns and hooves. In the orchard we found some nice balls of dried tree sap that just had to be good in glue. We decided to use some wheat flour since that went into paste.

We put them in a gallon syrup can with a lid that you could really press on good, then we added some water and put the mixture on the back part of the kitchen stove to cook. But the fire had been allowed to go out after

Sunday dinner was prepared so our project would just have to wait until they had a fire in the stove again. We got distracted and found other projects for the rest of the afternoon.

Farm families followed a pretty rigid schedule that included washing on Monday, ironing on Tuesday, etc. The laundry water was heated in a reservoir that was attached to the end of the Copper Clad kitchen range, fired by cobs, wood, coal or other fuel. Farm wives fried and boiled in pans and pots that sat on top of the stove and baked in an oven that was surrounded by flame in the firebox.

The reservoir had only one side exposed to the fire. Water did not boil, but it got hot enough for laundry with a good fire in the firebox, which was a good time to bake in the oven or cook on top of the range. Mrs. Gibbs built that kind of fire on Monday morning but I didn't get the news until Vic came to school on Tuesday.

It seems that the roaring fire designed to heat the laundry water also heated the top of the cook stove, including the area on top of the stove well away from the normal cooking area. Our Sunday glue-manufacturing process became activated with the presence of heat. We had firmly pounded the lid on the gallon can, but the water inside began producing steam. Without warning, the lid headed for outer space with a noise like popping a giant paper bag. Our glue embossed the Gibbs' kitchen ceiling and the laundry got interrupted as Mrs. Gibbs tried to collect her wits. And did we have a good formula for glue? It was some time before I went home with Vic again but according to his mother, that lid and the glue really stuck.

For Good Measure

It was never clear to me how it happened that there was one each of several exotic but frequently needed pieces of hardware within our Nebraska Sandhills community but rarely was there more than one of a kind anywhere in that area. Maybe it came down to the fact that if a neighbor had one that I could borrow, why buy one? We had a Fresno scraper (dirt mover) and a chain drill that were handy but rarely used pieces of equipment. When we needed to use either one, we had to remember who had borrowed it last, and what we might have that we had borrowed from that neighbor that we'd better return when we went to retrieve our tool.

A chain drill attaches to a brace and bit with a bicycle-type chain that goes around the post or item being drilled. The chain puts pressure on the drill as it bores its way through the wood. We needed it to help hang some corral gates. Barners had borrowed the drill last, as we remembered, so I rode along as my dad drove to their place to borrow it back. When we drove into the yard, only 8-year-old Lamoyne, nicknamed Dinky, was at home. The family had all gone someplace for an hour or so, leaving Dinky. He was sitting on the ground with an old dishpan nearly full of dirt, counting.

My dad went to the shop to see if he could find the chain drill. I watched the counting event. In this pan of dirt, he had many small worms—grubs about half an inch long. He picked them up, one at a time, and put them in the pan of dirt. Then when they were all in the pan, he dumped the contents, dirt and grubs, on the ground and began picking them up and counting again.

I watched as he counted the grubs from the ground to the pan: one hundred five, one hundred six, one hundred seven and finally, at one hundred thirteen, I went to the shop to see if I could help my dad find the drill. When I came back, Dinky took a deep breath, got to his feet and acted like the event was concluded. I asked how many grubs were in the pan. "A hundred twenty-three," he said.

Then I noticed a couple of grubs still on the ground that he hadn't put into the pan. I said, "There are two that you missed; now you have a hundred twenty-five." Without any hesitation he said, "No, I still have a hundred twenty-three. I have several extras for good measure." Sandhills thinking at its best. And Lamoyne Barner grew up to become a banker.

The Family Provider

Probably the most desperate year in rural Nebraska when I was young was 1934. It was the peak of the drought and depression. We had a short crop of first-cutting alfalfa but between drought and the grasshoppers, we had no other crop to harvest. We stacked weeds as a substitute for hay, hoping it would keep the thin and nearly starving livestock alive until next year.

When 1935 came, we had excessive, cold spring rains that killed some of the weakest cattle but we did raise better yields of most crops. Prices for farm-grown produce of every kind stayed at low levels but it was a much-improved living over the previous year. I had an old hand-me-down BB gun from my Uncle Bill that wouldn't shoot and I wanted a real gun for Christmas. We almost literally "lived off the land" by hunting rabbits and birds for food. I was 11 and I just knew I could help.

Christmas morning brought the answer to my prayers. There was a rifle— a .22 caliber, single-shot, bolt action—that I later found in the Sears catalog for $5.10 plus shipping—and a box of ammo. I could hardly wait to go hunting but was told I had to wait until afternoon—after Christmas dinner. Christmas was a cloudy, threatening day. Without waiting for dessert, I put on coat, cap and boots, and headed out to the fields.

The ground was almost fully covered with snow from a recent storm with a few melted spots near corn stalks, posts or anything that was capable of absorbing a little heat from recent sunny days. I was sure the best hunting place for pheasant or rabbits (regular family fare) would be the cornfield, so I put a shell in the gun and headed for the nearest cornfield.

The first sight of game was a pheasant that jumped and flew far out of range. After plodding several hundred yards through shallow drifted snow I froze. I thought I saw a pheasant's head about 10 yards away, sitting in a protected spot under a couple of bent-over corn stalks. Yes, it was a head. I saw an eye blink. I was near pay dirt for a hunter.

As I raised the rifle it occurred to me: I hadn't sighted in the gun. Would it shoot high or low, left or right? I couldn't waste this shot—a family dinner hung in the balance—so I aimed carefully behind and below the head, hoping to hit the greatest body mass, although as "meat hunters" we usually tried to save the meatiest parts. I squeezed the trigger.

Crack! That was the only shot I had in my single-shot rifle. The pheasant flew straight up in the air as if blown out of a vertical pipe. My spirits sank as the bird went up. Then, almost like delayed action, the bird collapsed and fell to earth, and hit the ground just inches from the exact spot from where it had flown. Christmas prayer No. 2 had been answered. Guess who set a record in the quarter-mile sprint with pheasant in one hand, rifle in the other? And after taking the game to show the family, I went straight out behind the barn for a practice shot—to find that the rifle's sights were dead on target. Santa had already sighted-in the rifle for me.

Livestock Wisdom Gone Sour

His name was Jake. I don't know where my dad found him but he worked for us as a hired hand for a couple of years. To me, he may have seemed bigger than he really was. I was 12 or 13 years old. To me he seemed tall as a windmill. My mother, who washed his clothes along with the family laundry, said he wore a 20x38 shirt (the largest size carried in most stores) and the sleeves didn't come anywhere near to his wrists. He bought a new hat when he found one big enough to fit because stores rarely stocked one that large.

Today he would have had a cleft palate. In those days it was a hare lip. He probably got too big to go through the schoolhouse door by about the third or fourth grade so he just stuck with livestock, observing. And boy, did he observe! He told me that livestock knew a lot but people were still smarter. In the early 1930s, he took me to a tiny field on our ranch to show me that a big herd grazed every bite but in big fields they left tufts of grass to get overripe and unpalatable.

He said that if we would fence off enough small fields so cattle would graze all the grass in that field flat to the ground, then move cattle to the next field that a ranch would run more cattle because they didn't waste those tough clumps and all the grass grew back evenly. Jake had invented what would later be called "cell grazing" but had no idea it would later be re-invented and promoted by people with multiple college degrees.

He knew that each animal had a "comfort zone" that applied to handling livestock whether gathering a herd or doctoring a single calf. He could convince cattle and horses—even spooky ones—to go through narrow gates. He listened to horses years before Monte Roberts, the "horse whisperer," but never put it in writing. He listened to all livestock. He remembered what they told him. He told me but I was too young to remember much of it. Years later I would find myself thinking, "What would Jake have said or done?" when handling stock in difficult situations.

Jake was sure that heifers reached sexual maturity younger and came into heat earlier if they were penned with bulls than with only females. He showed me how to tell if a cow was a fertile and regular breeder. Jake knew from experience, that lean, clean-necked females were more fertile than the ones that had thickness of fat, muscle or skin in the neck and jaw area.

One day I noticed a halter lying on the floor of the stallion's box stall. I knew that it would be trampled into the stall floor and ruined if not retrieved so I went in the stall and picked up the halter. When I came out, Jake said, "Phil, you did something I don't want you to ever do again." I was shocked. I really respected Jake and his advice but I thought I had done the right thing by saving the halter.

I asked him what was wrong with getting the halter. "You think you picked up a halter," he said, "but you really trusted a stud." My explanation that I rode the stud with a halter to get the mail and rode him all over the country, even to breed mares, didn't make any difference to Jake. He said, "Phil, there are temporary exceptions but studs are just good for two things: breedin' and fightin'. If you trust one long enough, no matter how good a friend you think he is, he'll do one of 'em to you and they ain't either one good." I don't know how he spelled his last name, S-O-U-R or S-A-U-E-R. It was years before I learned that we had an option on the spelling. To me, he was always Jake Sour, our livestock magician.

Red Beam R.F.D.

There are mail carriers and then there are mail carriers. During all of my growing-up years, our mail carrier did more than carry the mail. During my life on the ranch, C.W. "Red" Beam was our carrier. Our mailbox was a half-mile from the house. And in those drought and depression years, nobody wasted 19-cents-per-gallon gasoline driving to get the mail.

We either walked or rode a horse and, while the mailman delivered six days a week, we generally picked it up a couple of times per week unless we expected an order from Sears or Wards. Our carrier was an extension of our shopping mall. He delivered large packages to the house if we didn't have a closed gate but left a note if we did. If we sent a letter to someone on the route, it cost 1 cent less (2 cents instead of 3) and he cancelled it with an indelible pencil.

We lived by the alarm clock. If my parents forgot to wind it at night, we didn't know what time it was. We had a radio but its battery never lasted many months and then we had to wait until we sold turkeys the next fall to get money for a new battery. We had a telephone but my mom was embarrassed to ask somebody what time it was. More than once I walked to the mailbox early, with alarm clock in hand. Red always had a watch so I could set the clock.

Once, when a neighbor's wife died, people on the mail route prepared food for the family every day for weeks. People on the route put food in their mailboxes and Red delivered the care packages. People on the part of the route Red visited before he reached the victim's family prepared foods to eat today and those later on the route prepared bread and items that could store. Red took those and delivered them the next day. Do you suppose your delivery person would or could do that today?

His wife was a standout teacher at the one-room country school when my younger brother and sister attended. They had four children, one in my class in high school and another, my protégé in ag journalism in college and at the Alpha Gamma Rho (AGR) fraternity house, who later went to law school and became a federal judge. Red never took himself too seriously and maintained that he was just glad to be able to do his job.

Our small-town newspaper publisher once wrote that Red Beam always entered your office voice first. And when faced with the comment that he surely had bright kids, Red commented that his kids should be bright—they had such a brilliant woman for a mother and a smart aleck for a dad. But pure chance gave him a problem not faced by most carriers. My dad's name was Harvey Raynard (frequently misspelled as Raymond) and further down the route was Raymond Harvey, Red's brother-in-law. Who had a better excuse if he delivered to the wrong box?

A Little Mechanical

When I was growing up, every boy had a jack knife. You just wouldn't go outside without that knife in your pocket. You could always whittle yourself through boring times if you had your knife. And most boys would whittle on a stick until it had a point on one or both ends. All boys ended up with a pile of shavings. But when Russell Gibbs whittled he always made something. It might have been the head of a horse, ready for mounting on a chessman, a bird, a coiled snake, a cube or a ball. He had a knack—maybe a compulsion—and a load of talent.

36

He began doing taxidermy, mounting birds and rabbits when he was in first or second grade; repairing old clocks the next year. One of the "big boys" when I started to country school, he was five or six years ahead of me. He drove a one-horse buggy with his younger sister and brother. The "dash" board was decorated with a hand-carved horse head mounted on each end.

Our school had wide, side-by-side desks made for two students. They had a seat on the front for the kids in the next desk ahead. They had the typical sloping hardwood writing surface, iron ends and a book compartment below. Russell did not want people looking in his desk so he made a hinged front door that locked at the top, but there was no visible lock. I later learned that he had drilled a hole all the way—nearly 3 feet—from end to end. He pushed a wire into a tiny hole at one end to lock the door and into the other end to unlock it.

He went to a trade school after high school and I didn't see him much until one summer after I was home for a few days. This was a few years after the first U.S. moon shots. I heard that he was also at home so we got together to visit about what we had been doing. He had been working for a precision parts firm that did work primarily for U.S. government space projects including moon exploration.

The Pentagon would order a unit that controlled rockets, jets, cameras, etc. The order would describe the functions, the length, width, shape and weight and tell them to make it. He was making patent models for inventors in his spare time and told me he had been working on a little motor. He said, "I just happen to have it with me," and took a lip vial out of his watch pocket for me to examine.

This motor was little larger than a lead pencil eraser. It was powered by a flashlight battery. His boss saw it one day and asked to borrow it. He put it in one of the magnifying desk weights to show off the business to some military brass on their next visit. They were impressed and the boss asked to keep it. Russell said he wanted to keep this one since it was his first; that he was making another for the boss. It was a lot smaller so it was more impressive— and you just plugged it into a wall electrical outlet to make it run.

I was not surprised at what he was doing. It took me back to a day at Nesbit School when I was in the second or third grade and he was in the eighth. I was one of the "little kids" in a lower grade so I sat in a desk near the front of the room while the big boys sat in the bigger desks at the back. At the front of the room was an elevated stage where the teacher's desk was located and where there were seats for the students to recite.

I confess to having a wandering eye and to knowing other people's business at least as well as my own. But it was quite a surprise one dull afternoon when, without notice, I saw a large mouse or small rat run right up the aisle past my desk, from the back of the room to the front, then turn 180 degrees just before it got to the elevated stage and return to the back of the room. Russell had combined watch-making with taxidermy. Not your run-of-the-mill eighth grader, but one with a rare talent at an early age that continued to grow.

Desperation in a Haystack

The harvest was far from being up to normal in Nebraska in 1933. I was a boy of 9, not ready for field work nor for much responsibility, but I knew we were having hard times. If my parents knew how bad it would get in the next couple of years they would probably have left the area, except for two things: they didn't know any place else to go and they didn't have enough money to get out of town.

If it didn't rain much in 1933, it was not a hint of how dry 1934 would be. The deep-rooted and always reliable Cossack alfalfa produced about half a crop for the first cutting and nothing for the rest of the year. The corn never got above knee-high. It did not tassel nor set an ear. Rye, which was planted in the fall and harvested the next summer, produced a little pasture when it became obvious that it would not mature into any grain.

We planted some acreage of sorghum crops such as milo, for grain, and Sudan grass, for hay, as drought insurance. They had been recommended by the county ag agent since they survived under drought conditions. This turned out to be a curse. Under any conditions, sorghum crops can kill cattle with prussic acid poisoning if eaten green. Drought makes it instantly lethal. Several cows that broke out of the pasture to sneak a bite of the only green feed on the ranch died with the Sudan grass leaves in their mouths.

The native pasture grasses barely grew enough stems for cattle to graze. There was no hope of cutting hay on the fields normally harvested. What would we have to feed the cattle? We had to carry them over the winter and into the next year when it might rain. Even 1934 was not so dry that we didn't have weeds. We had a fair crop of Russian thistles and Kochia (fire weed) in the fields that should have been growing crops of corn, rye, milo and Sudan grass.

Nobody that we knew had ever harvested crops of weeds. Weeds were weeds, or were they? If we cut them, we left the ground without any cover to protect the soil from blowing away in the wind but these weeds seemed to be our only hope, so we mowed, raked and stacked numerous tons. I was 10 years old but we had no money to hire help so I tramped the loads of "hay" down to pack the stack.

If you ever have to handle these crops, take the Russian thistles. Kochia has dust on it that makes your skin itch, turn red and burn like fire. Taking a bath may give temporary relief but there's a reason they call it "fire weed." It does not burn your legs quite as bad when you handle it some months later, at feeding time. We never learned whether cattle really liked this weed-patch in a stack or not. They had nothing else to eat and it kept most of them alive.

The spring of 1935 was almost the answer to 1934. It rained and rained in the spring. Our cows were desperately weak from malnutrition. Some fetuses were aborted, some calves were premature. Veterinarians came in to test for brucellosis. Looking back on it, when I was working in the livestock feed business, I became convinced that we had nutritional abortion, not brucellosis. It was an example of a rare ill wind that blows nobody good. My dad got paid in real money—enough to help in our desperate time—for guiding the state vets from ranch to ranch. We did not have a good crop in 1935 but we had something—and that year the drought finally broke.

Wedding in Tryon

A vacation to most of the struggling ranchers in the Nebraska Sandhills in the 1930s was when it rained in the daytime and we got under cover to be sure we wouldn't get struck by lightning or absorb a few raindrops that might better have fallen on the ground. Otherwise we worked all the time but had no money to take a trip or even buy vacation clothes. So it was a welcome, if curious, notice in the weekly *Stapleton Enterprise* and *Tryon Graphic,* inviting all people in the area to attend the wedding of Mike David's daughter to Sammy Ellis.

I have no idea when Mike David came to Tryon or where he came from. He had owned and operated the Tryon Store for as long as I could remember. And he had four beautiful daughters. The first had married Taft Haddy and they ran the Flats store at a crossroads about 20 miles west of Tryon, population 4, counting the two Haddy children. The population of Tryon, the first town west of our ranch, was about 150 at that time but smaller today.

One daughter was married to Tom Solomon, who became the high-profile sheriff of Sarpy County, the next county south of Omaha, and Offutt Air Force Base, home of the Strategic Air Command. This was the third of Mike David's daughters to be married. I don't remember if the other "public" weddings were held in our area but this was a memorable event in the eyes of a very countrified early teenager.

My parents didn't want to go because the David family belonged to some religion that we had never heard of and went to the "Orthodox" church, whatever that meant, in North Platte. They may have been "foreigners" with slightly olive skin and black hair but everyone knew that Mike's word was always good and he ran a first-rate general store. Finally, many of the people in our community decided to go, even if they weren't family friends. "I guess that's just the way they celebrate a wedding," my mother concluded.

It was a fairly hot summer day in the mid 1930s. Tryon had two wide streets. One was the "highway" running east and west. It was a graded dirt road, actually part of the officially marked "Highway 92" that became a two-track trail as you left Tryon going west. The other was the north-south main street, also dirt. Mike David's store was on the northeast corner of the intersection. The wedding was in the community auditorium, big enough for the family and close friends. The rest of the guests, possibly 200 people, were standing in the street out front. When the ceremony ended, they served "Neapolitan" ice cream bricks, cake and punch. It was the event of the year. And it was the first time I ever saw or tasted Neapolitan ice cream.

Supply and Demand

Looking back, it hardly seems fair. And maybe it wasn't fair at the time but, when you have what they want, you are in the catbird seat, so to speak, and if you don't accept the best offer, you have nobody but yourself to blame. We had dogs at the ranch as long as I can remember. For many years our dogs were greyhounds and they were used to catch coyotes.

A good coyote pelt would bring $8 to $10 and some years we could get $15 for a good one. That was equal to two or three days' pay at a decent farm job. You could do the job best in mid-winter when pelts had good fur, you had spare time and couldn't make a dollar anywhere else in the area. Coyotes thrived in our area so our only expense was raising the dogs and having a horse (sometimes we hunted from an auto) to get to brush patches or good coyote hiding areas.

Coyotes are in some ways the smartest and most enduring wild animal but we often found them doing really dumb things. Some days we rode for hours to find and catch one coyote. One day we rode through a patch of brush and weeds not larger than 10 to 20 acres in a grassy plain of several hundred acres. We jumped five coyotes and were lucky enough to have all of the hounds in our pack decide to chase just one of the coyotes.

The hounds caught him in about 100 yards. We tied him on the saddle and went back through the brush, jumped two—apparently from the original five—and the hounds caught them both. When we went through the brush again we jumped the fourth and then the fifth coyote. That's about $50 income in only a couple of hours. Good greyhounds had value.

One of our neighbors liked to hunt. He had good luck raising horses but bad luck with greyhounds. When he heard about our five-in-one hunt, he just had to own three of those dogs. We normally carried four or five in a pack but we left the rest (frequently two to four dogs) at home. He rode over to our place almost as soon as he got the news.

Nobody had ever put a dollar value on a dog in our area, but we knew how to barter. We started when Ed offered a good grey gelding that my dad felt would be a good mate for a black horse we had and needed to match. But three dogs—it would take a lot more than the grey. Ed had a green-broke team of 4-year-old sorrels that were not as big as most good ranch teams but what they lacked in size, they made up for in other traits.

Ed switched and offered the sorrel team for three hounds—but the trade had to include Pete, the big, brindle-colored dog. Then my dad made his final offer—he would include Pete and his littermate, Eppie, (she was the fast one, Pete was the killer) and another hound, but it would take both the sorrel team and the grey. Ed McPherrin had a ruddy complexion but he turned a blushing red when he said OK to the deal. He knew he had paid too much but he couldn't let this deal get away if he wanted to be a real coyote hunter.

Ed did his share of hunting for a few trips through their ranch, which was a real coyote nursery. But he finally told us that we could hunt anywhere on their ranch except in the cattail area between their ranch house and the hay meadow. He just didn't have enough time to hunt far away from home. The dogs retired early and I saw Pete, the big brindle-colored one with the crushing jaws, several years later enjoying his twilight years lounging in the shade of the house.

The grey turned out to be a good horse and a mate for our black. It took a year or two before we finally found how good the sorrel team would become. Paddy, the horse that hitched on the left, was high strung. Mick, his mate on the right, was more than high strung; he was nearly crazy. They moved under rein and hitched as if they were almost steroids covered with horsehide. But did they make a team for a Champion hay sweep! They could be sweated into a lather but they went out on a fast trot for every last load of hay on the longest day.

Dumb Crooks: See Everett

The town of Stapleton, Nebraska, was established while my mother was a girl and the new high school was opened just in time for her last year at the school. The first graduating class had two students who had transferred from Gandy High School. Her only classmate was Everett Bakewell. This didn't make Everett a member of our family but he shared a lot of years in our little community with my mom.

When I returned to the 50th anniversary of my high school graduation, mom also returned for her 75th. If you guessed that she was the lone survivor, you're right, but not by much. Mom was 92 at the time. Everett had died at age 88. What graduating class from any school can top that for average longevity?

Like almost everyone in Logan County in those days, Everett grew up on the farm and, while he may or may not have begun farming immediately, he was well established when I first knew him. Everett believed in scale. He fed more cattle than any of his near neighbors and raised more hogs and planted more acres of corn, most of which normally got harvested and generally

41

needed more hired farm hands than any of his neighbors. He may have been the original example of the expression "a day late and a dollar short."

He never knew within a truckload of his inventory of almost anything. But he had a good heart. He would always help a neighbor in need. It was no surprise that Everett frequently helped his neighbor on the north. A hard-working and honest farmer had died at a relatively young age, leaving a widow with three or four school-age children. They continued on the farm and did their best to make a living even though the oldest son was hardly ready to take over. They kept a large flock of hens, raised turkeys and a few pigs. Otherwise, they sold the grain they raised to increase their meager income from livestock.

One day the family returned from a trip to town and noticed that a large sow was missing. They had just weaned her litter and had her confined to a small pen near the farmhouse to separate her from her litter while her udder dried up and the pigs forgot about nursing. A quick search of the farm found no sow, but it did turn up distinctive truck tracks in front of the loading chute near the hog pen.

The mother called the sheriff, who came immediately to the farm, got a good description of the sow, including her color, size and earmarks. It was sale day at the North Platte livestock auction. The sheriff called the Lincoln County sheriff in North Platte, who sent a deputy to the auction yard where the thieves were just backing up to the loading dock with the sow aboard.

The thieves were taken to jail while the sheriff continued the investigation. Authorities held the sow, which matched the owners' description and which they claimed when they went to North Platte. The tire tread marks checked out and the stupid thieves were quickly sentenced for theft. Had they only known, they could probably have filled their truck with stolen pigs only a few hundred yards across the fence, at Everett's pigpen, without the theft ever being detected or even suspected. Dumb crooks.

Christmas at Grandma's

Living in the Nebraska Sandhills in the 1930s made you a candidate for a little excitement. That is because little excitement was available. Very little. It was a long way to town and we didn't go often. It was even further to the city—in our case, North Platte, with a population of about 10,000, where we went about twice a year. Otherwise we went to school, country church and sometimes we went to borrow something from a neighbor, or vice versa.

My brother, Jack, was three years younger than I. He didn't understand that we couldn't have everything in the Sears catalog. Being the big brother, I had the job of helping Jack learn the facts of life. I had been a member of the family long enough to know that Christmas was a church holiday but Jack still believed in Santa Claus, literally and figuratively. And Jack was a positive thinker—a true believer to the end.

I must have been about 10 years old, so Jack was 7. We slept in the basement. The entry to the basement was outside. The house was on a knoll with three steps up to the entry on the south side of the house. The basement stairs were just to the west of the house steps with about seven or eight steps down to the level of the basement floor. The weather could be pretty foul and, during a blizzard, snow drifted up on the south side of any house, barn or fence post.

The basement had a regular door but there was a poured cement stairwell on each side with a sloping top and a pair of doors hinged from both sides that met in the middle. When Jack and I went to bed in the winter, we let the doors down as storm protection. Our basement bedroom was not heated, but it was all underground except for a small sill window. It may not have been warm, but it never froze—or almost never.

It was Christmas Eve and we were going to Grandma Raynard's house for Christmas dinner. We never had a Christmas tree but Grandma had one that she used every year. I don't know if they had plastic in the 1930s but this synthetic tree was about 18 inches tall and had built-in colored Christmas lights with bulbs that lit when plugged into the 32-volt current from batteries backed up by a Delco generator. She used that tree year after year. It might not have been fancy to most people but it was really special for me. I would just sit and stare at it whether it stood watch over any presents or not. For me, a Christmas tree, any Christmas tree, not only beheld magic—it was magic. We never had one.

It was beginning to snow when we went to bed so I checked to see that the storm doors were shut tight. Jack and I went to bed but visions of Grandma's house kept us from sound sleep. In time we woke up; I don't know which of us woke first. We did not have a clock nor any light but a kerosene lantern which we could light—but only for emergencies. We decided it must be Christmas so we put on our heavy winter coats (winter bath robes) and felt our way to the door. I could hardly push the storm doors open with so much snow on them.

We finally got up the stairs all the way to the steps to the house and banged on the door before deciding it was OK to just go in. The door was never locked—there may not have even been a key. Our parents came out of the bedroom in shock. "Do you know what time it is?" they asked in horror. When they told us it was 3 a.m., I knew we should have stayed in bed but it was hard for me, and impossible for Jack, to accept. They let each of us open a small present, then back to bed. Despite the snow, a few hours later we got to Grandma's to see her Christmas tree.

Brock Has the Kitchen Sink

Before it fell down, I saw the small house on the rented farm where my parents lived after they were married and where they still lived when I was born. I do not remember our living there nor do I have any recall of our first years in the house built on the school section where we lived until I was in high school. Nebraska gave sections 16 and 36 in every township not privately owned at the time to the schools. School sections were leased, not sold, and the rent was paid to support the schools. Lessees frequently built improvements as they would have done on deeded land since the lessee had perpetual right of renewal and the right to sell the leasehold.

My parents built a two-room home with basement and outhouse, a 300-hen house, a one-car garage/shop, a shed row barn with six two-horse stalls and milking stalls for about 20 cows. I don't know which was built first or how long it took to build them all. The house did not have indoor plumbing. I remember that we had a Model T coupe. We had a hired man named Floyd "Brock" Kelly. He had a Dodge touring sedan with a rear seat and a black, convertible top.

When the kitchen sink arrived, it was a day to remember—and it is my most vivid early memory. They took Brock's car to the railroad depot to get it since a big sink with attached drain board in a wooden crate would be much too big to fit in a coupe. I have a fuzzy memory of watching the men digging a trench for the water line from the wooden barrel on the mound near the windmill that stored the family water to the kitchen side of the house.

I don't know how old I was and I don't remember whether brother Jack was born yet or not. But I do remember when the long car drove up in front of the house. My mother yelled, as I remember it, "Brock has the kitchen sink." It must have been a great day for her. I don't know how long it took to attach the water pipe. Cold water, that is. We never had a hot water faucet in that house. After all, who needed hot water? There was a reservoir attached to the kitchen range that heated all the water you could use, except maybe for Saturday night baths.

"Pay-Per-View" in the 1930s

It is difficult if not impossible to relate the experiences of any era to people who did not live through them. How do you know what poor means if you have never known a rich person? We didn't know that we were poor. We knew that we didn't have any money to spend but nobody had money to spend. We would have been hungry if we had not raised a giant garden, picked and canned hundreds of jars of vegetables and fruit to feed the family until the next summer.

We got the weekly *Stapleton Enterprise* newspaper whether we paid or not. We got the *Nebraska Farmer* because the subscription salesman would take a few dozen eggs or other farm produce to pay for the next year's paper. But neither of these had much news of the world. Grandma Brothers somewhere found the money to take the daily *Omaha World Herald*. Our trips to her house gave me occasional and welcome windows to the outside world. I really wished we could afford to get a newspaper every day like she did. What a luxury!

Grandpa and Grandma Raynard had a 32-volt electric generator with a row of storage batteries in the basement for electric lights and Grandpa had a radio that always seemed to be in working condition. Grandpa liked news. But it seemed that radios of that era were often inoperative because "a tube was out." Thankfully, diodes and their electronic kin replaced the undependable vacuum tubes of the 1930s and '40s. We had a radio but it operated on batteries and a new battery only lasted for a few weeks or months, then we were without a radio until the next fall when we sold the turkeys or some other surprise financial windfall brought a little cash.

But just because we had no money and few contacts with the outside world, don't think we didn't have occasional excitement and/or culture. Joe Louis was the world champion heavyweight prizefighter. His fights were always broadcast on the radio, as were frequent fights of challengers for his or other titles. Fowlers were great fight fans. They always seemed to have a radio and we went to their place on numerous summer evenings to listen to the fights—not unlike ordering pay-per-view on cable or going to the neighbor's to watch a special event on TV.

Once when I was about 10 or 11 years old, one of the Fowler boys was our hired man and I got to go with him to a Fowler near-family reunion. They had a bunch of big boys who worked for several neighbors. They had a homecoming for the fight and I think they all brought a guest or two. My mother was aghast when she learned that Mrs. Fowler and her daughters had made some fruit punch (it may have been Kool-Aid if it was made at that time) for the whole crowd. There must have been two dozen people. I think my mother was shocked to learn that they had enough glasses to serve all of us and at how much it must have cost.

But listening to the fights on radio was not as simple as we might imagine today. There were very few radio stations in Nebraska or surrounding states and most were not very powerful. On a good night, a lucky radio operator might "run the dial" and bring in a station from Lincoln, Omaha, Shenandoah, Yankton, Denver, Salt Lake City, Chicago, St. Louis, Kansas City, Nashville, New Orleans or even Calgary. It was not uncommon to have the fight carried on more than one station but there was so much squealing and static that the operator of the Fowler radio switched from one station to another, trying to keep a signal for us to hear.

Then there was the summer that the Stapleton Commercial Club showed free Saturday night movies on the side of the courthouse. There was a vacant lot beside the courthouse with a nice, white-painted side, just made to be a movie screen. Our hired man went to town on a Saturday night and my parents once agreed that I could go to town with him. When we got home a little late and they learned that he had innocently taken me to the movie, he was fired on the spot (everybody knows movies are sinful). But by morning they decided they needed a good hired man, there was no replacement, and he "had learned his lesson."

Bud Wouldn't Lie

I was not present for this occurrence but I'm sure it happened. Bud Danker wouldn't lie. As far as I knew, Bud had always lived in Ringgold, the next town west of our ranch. In the 1930s, Ringgold had a general store, a little church and a total population in the range of 12 to 20, depending on what month of what year. Bud had a small farm with a big barn across the road from the store.

With his four-horse team, he bladed the highway from Ringgold, about 10 miles west to Tryon, the county seat of McPherson County, and about 12 miles east, past our ranch, to the beginning of the graveled road that ran through Stapleton, county seat of Logan County. This was Highway 92 and, even though it was a dirt road, it had the signs to prove that it really was Highway 92. Bud carried lunch and feed bags with oats for his team for the noon-time rest stop.

One day Bud was repairing a culvert at the edge of Ringgold with the help of a neighbor when Sebe (pronounced Seeb) Smith, a local rancher, rode up with his horse at a gallop. He was carrying a shovel. Sebe had something of a reputation as a liar. Sometimes he'd manufacture a whopper right on the spot. At other times he would just bend the truth enough to leave his audience guessing at whether what he'd said was really true or not. He relished his reputation, which was surely earned, and he enjoyed getting full credit for his accomplishments.

He reined in his horse, they exchanged greetings and the neighbor who was helping Bud with the road work said, "Sebe, stop and tell us a lie."

"I would, but I don't have time," Sebe answered, without changing expression. "You know Mrs. Miller has been sick in the hospital in North Platte. She died last night and I'm on my way with this shovel to help dig the grave. The funeral is tomorrow afternoon at 2 o'clock at the church in Tryon," and he spurred his horse back to a gallop. The neighbor showed up at the church the next day to attend the funeral and waited a good while before he decided that Sebe had given him exactly what he had asked for.

Morning Roundup

We worked a lot of horses in the 1930s and early '40s. We farmed about 400 acres of alfalfa, corn, rye and a few other crops on the home ranch and frequently leased some additional hay or crop land and some summer pasture. We got a used John Deere tractor and mounted sickle mower in about 1940 but it was used mainly for mowing hay and plowing. I hated the tractor. It made too much noise, you could not trust it to go anywhere on a loose rein like a good team and besides . . . it made terrible, ear-ringing noises . . . and it had bad breath.

We had two or three four-horse teams or two six-horse teams under harness a lot of the days from early spring through harvest time. We turned the horses out on summer nights to roll in the dirt and graze in the pasture. It saved on hay and cleaning stalls and they seemed to refresh and relax better. This meant early morning roundup every working day. And I was generally the roundup rider.

Our main saddle horse during several of these years was a tall, brown gelding named Tony with a rare pedigree. He was out of Floss, a Hambletonian-Thoroughbred cross that could fly, either loose or under saddle, and a chance breeding to a French Draft akin to a small Percheron (draft horse breed) stallion. Tony was quite a blend of size and power along with good top speed and he could trot for miles.

My grandfather had a fine driving team, reputedly Hambletonians. I never saw Floss and Tony but they allegedly were the best driving team in the area. I barely remember her last foal, also named Floss, sired by one of Frank Stanley's Thoroughbred stallions. Frank Stanley was a neighbor who owned a large band of horses of various breeding. He contracted with county fairs in the area to put on the whole arena show except for the rodeo.

He had enough Thoroughbreds to stage several races. He also hired jockeys to ride the various races, had some pinto mares that jumped hurdles going around the track with foals that took the hurdles right beside their mothers. And he had a Shetland pony race, with monkeys wearing denim overalls and red bandanas riding as jockeys. I had seen a Stanley show a couple of times so I often thought about them when I rode our Tony, the leggy brown gelding.

Tony was good under the saddle both as a rope horse or cutting and driving herds. I often rode him bareback to round up the workhorses. He sometimes forgot his good training when bareback. He didn't really buck, but he would crow hop a little, especially when chasing horses. One morning a few horses decided to leave the band and I made a run to bring them back.

The Sandhills are called Sandhills because they are. Under the thin cover of grass, only a couple of inches down, is plain old blow sand. And with the drought of the '30s, or in little swales after a rain created some runoff, sand came to the surface. This morning roundup, Tony tried to buck as we started down a slightly eroded sandy area. He lost his footing and did a complete somersault. I flew off his bare back to one side, fortunately. When he got on his feet there was sand all over the area where I had been sitting. We were both unnerved but I never let go of the reins. I climbed on his back again and brought the horses home. I don't think Tony ever bucked again—at least not with me.

Early Maturity or Child Labor?

You grew up fast on a Nebraska Sandhills ranch in the 1930s. When I see kids today that are in such a rush to do "grown up" things, I recall my growing up. We did different things. I learned to ride young enough that my parents sent me 2 miles to kindergarten in a one-room schoolhouse on horseback. I can't remember when I first drove a team with no adult present but looking back, I must have been stupid to ask permission. Little did I know what was ahead.

I had reached my mature height—nearly 5'6" inches—at 12 or 13, a big enough frame to have nearly 2 inches to spare over the 5'4" needed to be accepted for Naval aviation cadet training some years later. At 14 or 15, I was muscular enough to do a man's work at doctoring cattle, digging post holes or loading and unloading a bundle rack as we exchanged work with the neighbors in the community grain threshing crew. My coordination was miles ahead of those string-bean types in high school football and it was fun to block and tackle the less-coordinated big guys. But it surely changed the definition of "leisure time" when it came to describing a teenager.

In the drought of 1934, our fields of corn didn't mature beyond the tassel stage so we put all our effort into cutting and stacking every stem of grass, crop or weed that grew, hoping to have something to feed the cattle. I was only 10 but I could push hay around, helping build the haystack with a pitchfork. On my days off from stacking, I walked behind a weighted harrow with four-horse team to level the ridges between the rows of shriveled corn. I learned that "bag balm" is a lot better than talcum or Vaseline when the chafing between your legs begins to bleed. I hated walking behind the harrow so much that I welcomed the opportunity to stack whatever kind of hay we were making—from weeds such as Russian thistles, fire weed mixed with our scanty crop of alfalfa.

With that work history, I cultivated the corn with a four-horse team during the summer of 1935 when I wasn't helping stack hay. It rained in 1935, especially in the spring, so the alfalfa made a pretty good first cutting with lots of hay to stack. Mid-summer dry days reduced the later cuttings, but it was a bonanza compared with 1934. I graduated to being the main stack builder, with little help, when the hay was ready to bring in from the field and put in haystacks.

In 1936 and '37, when I was in the seventh and eighth grades, we couldn't afford the wages for a hired man so I got the job, but for no pay. I did field work with a team for six days a week from the day school was out until it began again in the fall. I found several arrowheads and other Indian relics

Making hay "the old way" in the "old days" (courtesy of Duane Gray, O'Neill, Nebraska) where the Gray family made hay in the northeast end of the Sandhills with almost the same equipment that we used near Stapleton, in the southwest end of the Sandhills about 100 miles away. Gray had the foresight and resources to assemble the crew for this photo, including mowers, rakes, sweeps, "overshot" stacker, the man on the stack and the man who drove the stacker team. Invention and development of the modern baler made this obsolete.

that had been uncovered in the drought and wind of the "dust bowl" years. I got loaned to a neighbor during hay-making time. I didn't like their horses so I told them I could build stack—and they let me—until somebody noticed that I wasn't on top of the stack, which was up to about 12 to 15 feet high.

Someone found me on a pile of loose hay beside the stack. I had apparently passed out with heat stroke and walked off the stack. The summer temperature was nearly 100 humid degrees in the shade, which did not exist on top of a haystack. Luckily, someone doused me with cold water but the event ended my career as a stacker, at least for the rest of that day. I still can't take much hot sun on my head.

You Need a Banker

Grandpa Raynard died during my first year in high school. I was staying with my grandparents, doing chores for my room and board to be near enough to the bus route to go to high school. My dad and grandma formed a partnership to operate the ranch. Then about a year later, grandma died. During the

1930s, the drought and depression made it almost impossible for anybody in agriculture to keep operating, much less make a profit.

Couple those hard times with medical bills and it was little surprise that the family attorney said the estate probably did not have enough assets to pay the costs of probate. He suggested that if any member of the family had the desire—and could get a banker to agree—that the other heirs simply sign off and keep the land in the family.

The family members included four girls and two boys. The birth order was two girls, then my dad, then two more girls and brother Bill. Bill was the first to opt out of consideration. My dad said he would consider it if nobody else wanted to take it—if he could get bankrolled. He got an OK from the bank. Then one of the sons-in-law decided he wanted to take over and it was agreed that he could try. The banker had kept my dad operating for years and they were comfortable with each other. But he wouldn't sign on with the son-in-law so the heirs signed over their interests to my dad and wished him well. It was good for family relations that the banker made the decision.

While he couldn't have had a clue about the future, it was a good time for my dad to get started on a new ranch. He was lucky that Grandpa had picked what turned out to be a good ranch. We had a decent crop in 1939 and we took the first trip in years and the last vacation I was ever to take with the family. We saw bears and my Uncle Lee in Yellowstone, where he was a saddle-horse guide, then visited his family (dad's sister Lyndall) in Montana and mom's sister Edna and her family in Portland and made a trip to the agate beach on Oregon's Pacific coast.

The drought was over and stable markets through the World War II years gave a new lease on life to anybody who began ranching from ground zero in 1939. Being a decent stockman and farmer who had learned to get by on little spending during the drought and depression of the 1930s, the good times began to roll and my dad paid off everything before retiring and building a new home in Stapleton in 1965. The county's first irrigation well, put down after the war, assured a crop every year. It all happened because he had a banker who said OK when it counted.

Matches and the Twin

I never learned to ride a bicycle. When I was at the age when most people learn to ride a bike, we had neither the money to buy a bike nor a place with something solid, like pavement or hard dirt, to ride on. I helped hold the bike in a vertical position for the first attempts when our daughters learned to ride but they didn't get any first-hand instructions from me on how to do it. Their mother, on the other hand, loved riding her bike and she was a skilled biker.

Nebraska's Sandhills area is not known for its good soil and it had few paved roads until recent years. The farm-to-market roads that bordered our

50

ranch along the full north and east sides were dirt. The road on the north got bladed with some regularity when Bud Danker patrolled it, driving his four-horse-powered road grader up the road and back. When I graduated from high school, the only pavement in Logan County, including the high school town of Stapleton, was the sidewalk that crossed Main Street as it ran from the drug store to the post office. The rest of Stapleton's main streets had once been gravel surfaced and were graded a few times per year. I don't know if the secondary or residential streets were ever graded.

During the drought years we had a hired man named Lloyd Masterson. My little brother, Dick, was just getting started on his vocabulary and had difficulty in pronouncing Masterson, so he invented an abbreviation. Dick called him "Matches." Lloyd had a couple of other identifying features. He wore shirts with zippers instead of buttons. He said he was too sleepy in the morning to button a shirt straight but they always zipped straight. He also had a motorcycle, an Indian Twin, he called it. I think that "twin" meant two cylinders. I do not know whether other bike engines at the time had more, or fewer, cylinders. I am not and never was a "biker."

On a particular school day our parents wanted to pick Jack and me up from school en route to an evening event. Problem: We rode horses to school each morning, stalled them in the school barn during the day and rode them home in the evening. How would we get them home to ride to school tomorrow without the trip back to school to bring them home at night? Lloyd volunteered to take us to school on his 'cycle so we could leave the horses at home. This was in about 1933. I don't know the age of the bike. It normally ran well but it was far from new.

This was the first and last time I ever rode on a motorcycle. School was nearly 3 miles from home by road. Our roads were not fancy. They had once been graded, but that was some years earlier. Meantime our dad sometimes bladed them with a four-horse team, hopefully a day or two after a rain, so the sand could be managed a little and rearranged to resemble a road. Long strips of roadway would otherwise be wind-blown, eroded down to a layer of clay, which made a rough roadbed. The layer of sand that had once covered the clay would be drifted into dunes. These were sometimes a challenge to an automobile and it took a near-miracle to ride over them with a bike. It didn't help to have two school kids hanging on to the rider.

Looking back, I give Lloyd credit for completing the job. Jack rode up front on the gas tank; I rode on a poorly padded bracket over the rear wheel—and held onto Lloyd for dear life. We had to get off and walk a few times to get the cycle across miniature sand dunes in the road but I don't remember that he ever killed the engine. That would have really chilled the experience. I trusted my horse but not this bike. We got to school before the bell and were the envy of all our schoolmates. But it was a once-in-a lifetime event, thankfully. I don't think any of our biking trio was ready to try another trip over those sand-drifted roads.

Stapleton Lotto

Every small-town merchant faces the problem of customers running off to the nearest city to buy because they get greater selection, lower prices or perhaps just for adventure. Stapleton is about 30 miles from North Platte. North Platte is not a big city (about 10,000 at that time) but Stapleton is tiny (under 400 at that time; smaller now). The last time I was there it was down to a bank, a hardware store and a meat locker where you could order groceries from another town.

In the 1930s we had a doctor, a dentist, a drug store, an attorney, two car dealerships, two lumber yards, three grocery stores, and the Campau family even had a movie theater that had shows on weekend nights plus matinees. But even with all this service, people went to North Platte for many purchases, so the merchants started a Saturday afternoon drawing for cash. Customers registered at the merchants and for several years, at 2 p.m., Ryan Stalnaker pulled his team and dray wagon, the town's long-time freight delivery service, onto the vacant lot near the post office, at one corner of the town square, to serve as a stage for the drawing.

The head of the merchants' club brought out the drum with the names inside. I remember that during the drawing one summer day, when a name was drawn, Dr. Hyland, the dentist, from the open window in his upstairs office across the street, yelled, "I've got him up here."

"In your chair?" questioned one of the officials.

"No," Doc answered, "On my books." It seemed to me and most of the other kids that the officials waited much too long for an answer.

There was a $5 and a $10 ticket each week that absentees could win. But you had to be present to win the big prize, the $20 drawing. And it rolled over to $40 the next week if unclaimed. When it got up to $60, the crowd at drawing time spilled into the street. Once, when it got to $80, even my parents went to the drawing. Jake Linderman, a recent high school graduate, won the prize. Merchants were sure that the Saturday drawing attracted shoppers, but when Jake took his money and spent it out of town, it was more than the businessmen could take and the drawing was soon abandoned.

Forget About the Parking Lot

I can understand why our kids today can hardly wait until they get a license to drive a car. I was plenty anxious to get mine—sort of a rite of passage— and we weren't really going any place when I was 16 years old compared with the possibilities that exist today, but it was really a big thrill anyway. In

52

our low-population county, there was no DMV office. A highway patrolman came to our county clerk's office once a month and gave new license candidates a once-over and a test drive for the kids that had passed the magical 16th birthday.

I'll never know what I did right, or wrong, but when it was my turn (I think there were three eligible candidates that day) he asked me how long I had been driving. I reluctantly but honestly—I shrunk a bit—answered "four or five years." Then I quickly added that it was just on the ranch, not on the highway except with my dad. I don't know why but I got a pass from him, without a ride, and the county clerk issued my license that day. Both the other applicants had to take driving tests with the patrolman. They may have felt cheated or did I just have an honest face?

A good many years, probably two million miles behind various steering wheels and many ideas have passed since that time and frequently when I am trying to find a parking place I am reminded of a trip to Europe a few years ago. Not every place has the traffic situation quite as well managed as we found in Stockholm but we stayed at a hotel in the middle of the city. We could take an elevator down from our room to the street level. If we rode the elevator one level lower, we could board the train to the airport and two levels lower was Eurail, which went everywhere in Europe. The train to the airport stopped inside the terminal, where you could buy your ticket, check your luggage and board your plane. I never learned if they have parking lots or taxicabs in Sweden. We never needed one. And I don't know how many labor unions were bent out of shape over such an arrangement but I believe the citizens were well served. I know we were.

I don't know if they have labor unions in Sweden but I think of the many years that the Bay Area Rapid Transit train track ended a couple of miles from San Francisco Airport so the ungrateful cabbies could "harvest" a few dollars from all air travelers to take them from the end of the BART line to the airport terminal where the train should have gone. Imagine which politicians got how much from the cab companies for making that original arrangement and who lost their jobs when reason finally prevailed and the track was extended so cabs were no longer needed for those last few miles. I'm the first to admit that there are plenty of places that trains won't go. It takes a lot of traffic to pay for trains but once done, riding the rails surely simplifies travel. For somebody who did his earliest traveling either by foot, horse or Model T Ford, almost any change is an improvement in travel time and comfort.

Guess What We're Doing Saturday?

Almost all of the original homesteaders on the plains in the early 1900s built sod houses. Sod was free for the plowing. The soddies were not fancy but they were stable and protection from almost everything except tornadoes. The tornado threat, coupled with the need for a cool storage room in the years before refrigeration gave good reasons to have a cave. Most of our neighbors in the Nebraska Sandhills in the 1930s had either a cave dug into a hillside, a poured cement cellar or a basement "safe room" if a home had been recently built.

Most of the original sod houses had been abandoned by the time I appeared on the scene. The only people that I remember living in sod houses were my Aunt Pearl (my mother's oldest sister) and Uncle Clarence, Chet and Edith Barner (oldest son Earl Dean went through 12 grades of school with me), the McPherrins (they had no telephone so I rode a horse to their house with phone messages for years—their soddy was in use until the late 1940s) and one in the west part of the county whose owners' names I can't recall. Sod houses tempered outside temperatures. They picked up earth cooling in summer and earth warmth in winter, responding like above-ground caves. But they were not "tornado-proof," as a tornado would tear off the unprotected roof almost as easily as if it were frame construction.

Our house (only two rooms and a path to the outhouse) was frame construction built when I was about a year old. It had a full basement with cement floor and clay tile walls. It was built into a slope with the north end of the basement underground and a short staircase entry on the south. The southeast corner was used for a hired man's bedroom (later for brother Jack and me) with a small window facing south. The balance of the basement housed the cream separator and storage shelves for the many jars of garden produce canned every year to feed the family.

The north wall was lined with crockery containers (3, 5 and 10 gallons), our "deep freeze" counterpart of the 1930s during a lot of the year. Some were filled with hams, bacon and pork shoulders being cured in salt brine, later to be hung to dry until used. One would have cuts of beef being cured for dried or corned beef. One was filled with shredded cabbage on its way to becoming sauerkraut and others were filled with cucumbers en route to becoming pickles. There must still be gallons of pickles in that basement. I know I filled a lot more crocks than we ever used.

Other crocks held pork chops fried and "put down" in enough melted lard to cover the layers of meat. Lard solidifies when chilled, preserving the meat. The meat was later retrieved from the crock, heated to melt off the lard and served for dinner. Beefsteaks and roasts were also "put down" in fat for storage and taken out prior to re-heating for family meals like we retrieve cuts from the freezer today. If not for salt cure and fat storage, farm families would have had little meat except in freezing weather. We also canned some cooked meat in glass jars.

Elsewhere in the basement we had a bin for potatoes, a barrel for apples, kegs for onions and a 5-gallon can with a sealed top for dry beans. Beans were my favorite—no sorting. A dirt-filled "planter" held root crops—parsnips, turnips, carrots. It seemed that every Saturday we had to work on the apples, sorting them carefully and removing any with soft spots—to be eaten before they spoiled, both the soft apple and its neighbor—and the same for potatoes and onions.

We stored squash and pumpkins for weeks in the fall. Tomatoes could be "ripened" hanging on the vine in the basement. Picking and storing everything we grew could quickly get boring. But potatoes were the worst. They could be stored for months but grew sprouts in storage and we had to handle every potato every few weeks to rub the sprouts off and take out the ones beginning to get soft and eat them before they began to rot. Did we feel abused? Doesn't every kid who has to work Saturdays? It wasn't so bad. At least we were not on the streets. How can you get into trouble sorting produce in the basement?

Hunting season was really the welcome Saturday break, both after I was old enough to handle a gun and earlier, when I was just allowed to tag along and be the retriever. We had greyhounds. They are great on coyotes but they didn't understand bird hunting very well. Sometimes we got enough game that we had to cook and can the extras; nothing went to waste. But like our neighbors who had to "live off the land" in the depression of the 1930s, we let mother nature store them live, out in the fields, until we needed a meal.

Farm kids worked long hours every day in summer with the exception of some Saturdays and all Sundays. We generally took the week's eggs to town and every grocery store bought eggs. We actually traded eggs for groceries. It was possible to get money back if you had enough eggs or bought few enough groceries on that trip. It generally worked out that we owed the grocer. And there would be a tiny paper sack with a few pieces of hard candy in the corner of the grocery-filled egg crate for the kids—at no charge.

The kids' No. 1 Saturday summer job in our family was hoeing weeds in the garden and around young trees. We had to work fast to get the job done in time to go to town in the afternoon—not every Saturday, but maybe one or two Saturdays per month. And we had a serious garden. We raised enough vegetables to preserve for family meals for the entire upcoming year. That took two to three jars of something for each of two meals per day plus tomato juice or some kind of fruit juice for breakfast for the next year.

Grandpa Raynard had planted a large orchard soon after he homesteaded and it always had cherries and apples for the picking. Grandpa told me once that the nursery where he had purchased his trees guaranteed to buy the produce if shipped to them in Nebraska City when the trees matured. He thought it was simply a sales gimmick—yes, they had sales "incentives" in 1908, too. All Grandpa wanted was a good "family" orchard. He didn't plan to sell fruit. But when the trees really came into production he shipped barrels and barrels of apples for several years, returning far more than the trees had cost. There were also the apple picking and cider making days in the fall and storing barrels of apple cider, some turning into vinegar. Yes, the cider and vinegar barrels were stored in the cellar, cave or basement, as were the cream cans until the Saturday trip to town.

We picked vegetables from the garden by the bushel, then shelled peas, cut beans and peeled tomatoes for canning. Our farm was pretty sandy and dry. We could barely keep cottonwood trees alive but then somebody introduced Chinese Elms. They grew big in spite of the poor soil and drought. Oh yes, the kids carried several pails of water on Saturdays to irrigate each of the newly planted Chinese Elm trees for their first few years. We did not have the good soil with a shallow water table like Grandpa's orchard area so we had no fruit trees.

We picked our fill in Grandpa's orchard and we went to the Dismal River to pick choke cherries, currants and wild grapes so we had jelly and jam for our home-made bread. Wild plum bushes in a thicket northwest of Grandpa's house, near the bee hives, were on the thorny side and I don't think anybody else was motivated enough to invade the brush for the fruit. The plums were too sour to eat but my mom's plum butter was the best thing that ever happened to a waffle.

The plum bushes had died or never grew in the center of this wild plum thicket—a secret world where brother Jack and I had our own little farm when our family moved there after Grandpa died—a miniature built-to-scale barn, fence and all. Grandpa had made a poured cement storm cellar with an air vent in its dome-shaped roof near the main ranch house. It was totally tornado proof and a better temperature-controlled storage place for produce than the basement of our previous house.

Butter! I forgot the butter. Our churn was a 3-gallon crockery churn. Its crockery lid had a hole in the center equipped with a dasher made from a stick with boards in a cross attached to the end of the stick. Enough ups and downs with that dasher in a couple of gallons of cream made butter. I don't know if that magic worked every day, but it made butter on Saturday when I churned it. My high school ag class (called farm management) assignment was planning work for operating a farm. Classmate Vic Gibbs said his dad planned his work. He planned all week what he was going to have Vic do on Saturday. We needed something to do; after all, we didn't have radio, TV, daily papers or near neighbors to help us kill time.

The Great Financial Equalizer

Banks and parents in years gone by, cooperated—or perhaps colluded, I was never sure which—to encourage the saving ethic in kids. Relatives and traveling salesmen seemed prone to giving pennies to young kids, which we were encouraged to save. When you opened a bank savings account for a dollar or more, the bank gave you a piggy bank to take home and use to deposit the coins occasionally given to preschool-age kids.

My piggy bank was in the form of a small barrel about 3 inches in diameter and 4 inches tall. One end came out when unlocked with a key. The bank kept the key. When you collected enough pennies to shake well, you took your barrel bank to town where the banker pulled out his key, emptied the barrel, recorded the addition to your savings account, added the accumulated interest and sent you home pennies richer for the experience.

My savings account had grown to $5.61, as I remember it, when the bank holiday of 1933 was approved by Congress. My dad banked at the Bank of Stapleton, which we knew was the best bank to have. Earl Dean Barner went through 12 years of school in my class. His family farm headquarters was about two miles from ours. His relatives were richer or more generous than mine. He often bragged that he had more than $12 in his savings account and, while the experience of feeling poor was probably educational, it annoyed me that he had more money; the fact that he bragged about it was, to me, unforgivable.

Then came the bank holiday after Roosevelt took office in 1933 when all banks closed for a day or two and counted their money. Our Bank of Stapleton opened the next morning and I still had $5.61 in my account. Earl Dean's account was at the Farmers Bank, across the street from Bank of Stapleton. Before the bank holiday, we argued about which bank was best like we argued about whether Fords or Chevys were best. Oh yes, his family had a Chevy. We had a Ford. I guess we had a lot of differences, now that I look back on the experience.

Anyway, the Farmers Bank did not re-open after the bank people counted their money. In fact, the Farmers Bank never re-opened. While they did give back a small percentage of deposits many months later, Earl Dean was greatly sobered and I do not remember that he ever bragged about his comparative wealth again.

Snow Banks in the Dust Bowl

The financial crash of 1929 didn't hit Nebraska farm families—or at least our family—as hard as the drought and dust bowl years that followed. In the Nebraska Sandhills, a south wind in the 1930s found dust to blow around almost the day after a rain and if the ground had been plowed in recent years, it was serious dust. We and our neighbors had plowed many too many acres for the kind of weather we got. I didn't check rain gauges in 1932 or '33 and I wasn't old enough to have vivid memories of whether we had a trend toward lower rainfall but I was told that harvests were below average.

I do remember 1934. I was 10 years old and began driving a team in the fields. Winter moisture allowed seed corn to sprout and plants got a few inches tall in some fields before the drought gave their tender green stalks a sun tan. In a few well-protected, fertile valleys some stalks survived long enough to tassel but I don't believe our farm produced a single ear of corn. And the wind seemed to blow almost every day, drifting sand into sandbanks behind fence posts, buildings or anything permanent.

Sand blew into our house leaving dusty layers on window sills, furniture, floors and everywhere it could settle. The wind generally blew its hardest during the daylight hours, easing off at sundown. Then we could take the top layer of bedding off and shake the dust onto the floor before going to bed. Our house had a south door. It wasn't our front door or our back door or side door. It was the only door. We only had two rooms plus the basement, which only had an outside entry.

The door lock had a keyhole that you could look through—and sand could blow through—but if we had a key, I never knew about it. Nobody ever threatened to break into any home in our community so nothing was ever locked. That didn't make it totally safe, however. Ten-year-olds go barefoot in summer. The wind blew so hard on one of our windy days that it blew the door open. I was standing near the door when it came open with such force that it totally peeled back and tore off the big toenail on my right foot. That was a windstorm to remember.

By early summer, the crop failure was obvious. We had only a short first cutting of alfalfa. Then we cut and stacked weeds—Russian thistles—in hope the cows would survive the winter. Most of the depleted herd made it to spring but we lost calf after calf to nutritional abortion. Rain began in the spring of 1935 and the mood of the depressed farm families improved. But the relief was short-lived and we had another very short crop, although we did have some corn to pick and most of our alfalfa fields produced at least half a crop. The south winds continued but we carried on. We were too poor to leave and we had no place to go.

One of my regular summer jobs was rounding up the cows for the evening milking in the late afternoon when I wasn't working in the fields and sometimes I left the field early to make the evening roundup. Jack was three years younger than I and an eager 7- or 8-year-old can tag along with the best, but his contribution was getting off the horse and scattering the herd while trying to pick a thistle head in the middle of a cattle drive, then crying when he got stickers in his fingers. He ignored all my attempts at discipline because he knew that I couldn't carry out any threat. My parents were just as unreasonable as Jack was.

I had to bring him home in one piece and our parents always defended the younger one. Jack was a good playmate when we were playing but I hated being responsible for him. He always wanted to go where I went, which was a problem, sometimes a serious problem. Many afternoons the sky was filled with dust. You could hardly breathe and sometimes we couldn't see the cows

58

until we were only a few hundred feet away. Jack was eager to go, but was often crying, with muddy streaks down from his teary eyes, by the time we got home with the cows.

I still remember the worst storm. The sky was so full of dust when chore time arrived that we could hardly see the gate at the far end of the corral. The pasture and the cows were lost in the blowing dust. Jack was always at his worst on days like this and I begged to leave him at the house but Mom insisted that if he wanted to go, he was my charge for the moment.

If you grow up on a ranch you learn a few rules of nature. Cattle always put their tails to the wind and drift so they would be at the most downwind point of the pasture. We went down the fence from the gate, followed it around the corner, and soon found the herd, milling in a compact group, having given up trying to graze on any grass or weeds still living in the pasture. But breaking up the cow party and heading them home was just about as challenging as handling Jack. He and the cows were bawling. Fortunately, the cows stayed in a tight herd and we had a fence to follow back to the barn because we couldn't see enough of the countryside to even get our bearings.

This was not the first milking when we had to strain every drop of milk through a towel to remove dust before running it through the cream separator. Sanitation standards have changed since those years. Everything exposed for even minutes was dust-covered and there was no escape. Few dust-proof storage containers had been invented by 1934 and if any existed, we didn't have them. And the winds continued into 1935 after a spring with near-normal rain.

Sand had drifted into dunes at locations on every farm and every county in the Midwest. The wind would blow away everything loose beside a barn, a tree or a post, then settle a mountain of sand into a dune a few feet away. Dunes drifted over the pasture fences. We plowed the sand away from fences to keep livestock in the pasture. The V-mesh fence around the house yard had a drifted sand pile 3 feet high along the fence at the northwest corner of the house and blown out trenches resembling gullies made by rivers overflowing their banks.

We had finally plowed enough sand away from fences or dug out the posts and wire, re-building where necessary to keep the stock in the pastures when the winter of 1935-36 arrived. Early in 1936, we were hit by the heaviest snow that had hit the area in years, and the continuing winds made The Blizzard of '36 a most memorable one. The harder the wind, the firmer the snow bank. What fun to walk over the yard fence around the house!

No sooner had we plowed years of accumulated sand away from pasture fences than we were plowing snow away. The wind had drifted snow banks so hard that grown cattle and horses walked over the fences on top of the snow at many locations on the ranch and didn't break through the crust. The drifts were solid from the ground up. In fact, the snow was badly mixed with sand and the dirty frozen mess lingered well into spring.

The Family Trip

The Sandhills community was working itself out of the 1929 financial crash and the Dust Bowl days of the early or mid-'30s. Happy days might not have totally returned by the summer of 1939, but our parents felt they could afford a family trip. I don't remember that the word *vacation* was used to describe it and for good reason. It was a trip to visit relatives and we had two adults and five kids in a two-door sedan, spending nights at tourist courts (predecessor of low-price motels) and campgrounds; hardly a vacation for anyone. But we went anyway.

Aunt Lyndall (my dad's oldest sister) and Uncle Lee lived in Belgrade, Montana. This was to be our first stop, except that our route took us through the Black Hills in South Dakota at the time the Mount Rushmore sculpture was half-finished. It was interesting to see the men, hanging in baskets on the mountain face, chiseling away the rock. At the Rushmore tourist facility we saw a ceiling-high model of what the finished mountain would become.

All this was fine, but I had never seen a big pine tree up close and we drove through forests of them. There was one at a campground with cones that actually sparkled in the sun. I just had to climb up to see what made pine cones sparkle. I collected plenty of tree sap as I climbed up to the cones but then I got to the mother lode of sticky. All those sparkles turned out to be beads of sap oozing from green cones and, oh, did it cling!

We went to visit Aunt Edna (my mother's baby sister) and Uncle George near Portland. They had just built a new home but, as modern and accommodating as it was, it was not as big a deal for me as Aunt Edna's high-speed driving over the snaky roads to the agate beach or my first look at the Pacific Ocean. I was not ready for the Oregon roads that curved around small mountains and large trees with total disregard for north and south.

En route, we stopped to see my Uncle Lee, who had a summer job as a saddle-horse guide and dude wrangler in Yellowstone Park, and then we went to visit his family. They were living on a ranch in the Gallatin Valley near Belgrade, north of Yellowstone. Not only was this the first time I had had a chipmunk eat a nut from my hand or watched wild bears being fed by park rangers, it was the first time I had seen either a bear or a chipmunk. Our weather had been wonderful so I was surprised that Aunt Lyndall covered her tomato plants in late August to keep them from freezing. A lesson in weather geography for me.

My cousin, Raynardine, was a few months younger than I. Brother Jack was nearly a match, age-wise, for her sister, Bonnie. I don't remember if we were trying to hide from our younger sibs or just exploring but we were in the loft, half-filled with loose (not baled) hay. The hay gave way and I slipped over the edge, sliding feet first down some 10 to 12 feet, through the open door in the hayloft floor and another 10 feet to the ground floor below. It happened in a flash but, on taking inventory, I found one shoe sole was entirely torn off and the skin on my ribs and under my arms was scraped raw on both my right and left sides. I later realized how lucky I was that the carpenter who built the barn had placed the spaces in the hayloft floor directly over the mangers without a board to straddle. I was shaken but received no broken bones or even heavy bruises.

"Number Please"

As your fingers punch out a number on the buttons of a phone, remember, if you will, that this is at least the third generation of phones during my conscious lifetime. As a boy on the farm, we had the old wall phone in a wood box. It had a crank on the right side and a cut-off switch on the left that resembled a large spring-loaded fork with two tines. The phone connection was made when you picked up the receiver and broken when you hung up the receiver as its weight grounded the connection.

To make a call, you lifted the receiver and turned the crank. If you wanted to call someone on your line, you cranked out their number. Our number was 88F14—one long and four shorts—when we lived on the old school section. To ring this number you turned the crank two to three revolutions for each long and half a turn for each short with a pause of a second or two between each signal.

Sometimes you needed to make a "general ring" on your line, like the time when the rest of the family went to Canada. Jack and I were babysitting the ranch when we spotted serious smoke to the northwest. I made a general ring and everyone within hearing distance answered the phone and identified themselves. That fire didn't have a chance.

When we moved to take over my grandparents' ranch, our number was 82F22—two longs and two shorts. If you wanted to call someone not on your line, you made one long, continuous ring and you were greeted with a "Number please" response from the operator somewhere called "Central."

Small town operators got to know their customers, their phone numbers and many of their voices. They also got to know many of their quirks and habits. I was living in Ogden, Iowa, in 1952. An old high school and college friend, George Campau, was a traveling salesman. He happened to be in the area and called Ogden information to get my phone number.

Lois Van Meter, one of the operators, sometimes stopped at our feed dealership to visit as she walked home from work. George's call happened to come on her line. She told him that she thought he could catch me having dinner at Rudy's Cafe. Did he want her to call me there? Under other conditions he would probably been satisfied with simply getting my number but he couldn't resist. He had her call me there and warned me I was a marked man in that town. Des Moines had dial phones; one day I took two of the employees from our dealership to the factory in Des Moines and Orville Sparks, who was nearing retirement age, wanted to call his daughter who lived in Des Moines. He asked me to dial the call for him. He had never used a dial phone and wasn't sure how to do it.

"Zeppie" was Central at Stapleton for the last of many years' operation before the phone system went in one step from crank wall phones to state-of-the-art service with underground lines and all the goodies. I never knew whether she was a real snoop and rumor monger—it seems a shame to have such a great job and not be one—but she knew both the community business and the personal lives of those hardy phone subscribers.

I don't know how many people have ever known a real person whose first name was "Zeppelin." Hers was. But then her dad was our neighbor, George Andre. He named his youngest son James Commercy France Andre after the port he left or entered as a doughboy in World War I. Since blimps (also called zeppelins) were used in coastal defense, he may also have been frightened by a blimp. And in her later years, his daughter slightly resembled one. I don't know if Zeppie ever left home beyond the telephone office, but she was a clearinghouse for community news whenever the need arose.

Several years after I left town, a severe storm hit during an evening school event, closing several of the traffic arterials and most side roads. My sister was caught at the school and, when she tried to call home, Zeppie recognized her voice and said, "Barbara, your mother is at your Aunt Pearl's, Rollie is at the Delfs', your mother has already called your dad and I guess you are staying with Maureen McCants." The telephone company may someday sponsor a blimp to convey its messages . . . but it won't have the local impact that our Zeppelin had during the years she spent as Central.

Underground Refrigeration

Grandma Brothers' milk house had cool, freshly pumped water constantly running into and through a cement tank to keep milk, cream, salads and all sorts of perishables from spoiling. We had a wooden barrel on a mound near our well. Our windmill pumped cool water into the barrel. The overflow pipe stood near the top of the barrel so we always had a barrel full of fresh, cool water before the stock tanks below got water for the livestock. Jars of milk and cream hung on strings in the barrel to keep cool with our refrigeration system for the 1920s and '30s.

Then we happened upon a new invention—the icebox. It was an insulated cabinet akin to the modern refrigerator except that the insulation was probably not so efficient and the coolant came in the form of blocks—blocks of ice. In cities, the ice man made his route once or twice a week, delivering large blocks of ice to all the homes with ice boxes—and got money to pay for the convenience. But this convenience had not come to the country. We had to find our own ice.

Ambler's lake, a nice body of water during summer, was about 3 or 4 miles away—halfway between our ranch and town. It was the nearest reliable source of clean, thick ice during the winter. We dug a pit for ice storage, then went to the lake when the ice was about a foot thick and, using a special large saw, cut blocks of ice. I think the expression, "heavy lifting," came from those who had loaded blocks of ice by hand, with ice tongs, onto a wagon, for the trip home. With the ground frozen underneath, it was quite a ride behind a team of horses.

We put an insulating layer of straw on the bottom of the pit or cave, then a layer of ice blocks and another layer of straw, etc., until we had stored the amount of ice we felt it would take to get through the summer. It was sort of an underground solid-ice igloo. We built a roof over the top of the ice pit to minimize melting from the heat of the sun when summer came. Still, the blocks would shrink to a fraction of their original size by late summer.

"Making ice" was a winter job, akin to "making hay" in summer and, being a youngster, I mainly watched. Historic as the event may seem today, the nostalgia evaporated as fast as one of the blocks of ice when the Servel company introduced the Electrolux refrigerator that ran on liquid propane gas (some ran on kerosene), several years before electric power came to rural Nebraska. But there was another real benefit from having those blocks of ice in a pit outside the house; we didn't have to go to town to get the ice to make homemade ice cream.

I Never Could Eat Potatoes

Jack was a good brother but he may not have been a "normal" one. He was three years younger and I should have had all the advantages. At least I had him on size and maturity, but Jack used his wits. He used me as a training ground for his head-on encounters with our parents. I never knew whether he invented a scheme or whether, in developing strategies, he would shamelessly try any angle and when one worked, he'd polish his technique and use it again later.

Smallpox was about the only disease with a vaccine in the 1920s and '30s. We got all the others—chicken pox, measles, etc., even bad colds—as kids. Jack ran a fever with every disease and just a couple of degrees pushed him over the edge of coherence. We shared a bed after baby brother Dick moved him out of the crib when Jack was 3 and I was 6. I had to listen to his midnight madness every time he was sick. My mother was sure that he was incoherent because he had a fever. I began to think he was just gaining credibility for the next time he wanted to get his way in a family argument. He blended imagination with madness.

Jack's imagination could suck you into his games. He would pull a large weed out of the ground and then, holding it at his backside below his belt line and letting the leaves hang as a tail, Jack was mounted on a fine horse. We had rodeos on these weed horses when neighbor kids came to visit.

A thicket of wild plum grew at the north end of the cherry orchard and a few hundred yards from the garden. We found a bare area in the middle of the brush patch known only to Jack and me. We had to crawl on our bellies to get in to this, our imaginary farm. Lumber for our built-to-scale barn came from the packing box for the new cream separator. Corn cobs were the livestock; those with no shucks attached were cows. If a few shucks were still attached, enough for Jack to imagine a tail, that corn cob became a horse.

Crafty as he was at merging his conscious with not-so-conscious moments, he was quick to seize any opportunity. At 10 or 11, I was on the short side while Jack, at 7 or 8, was the string bean type. When our mother commented one day that "at the rate he's growing, I believe Jack is going to be taller than Phil," Jack quickly pleaded, "Then will you put me older?"

If Jack had one totally predictable trait in his early years, it had to be that he was unpredictable. He would sometimes listen and respond reasonably to instruction or threat but at other times swing a shovel or broom in circles, to keep me from forcing a response. I remember his running until he collapsed, dead tired, when chased by sweat bees. Trying to reason with him at such a time was futile.

Jack spent more time with me than with our parents. I never knew a sure way to make Jack make sense but I learned to live with him as he was. Our dad never did. Dad was impatient with everybody and everything. They often held each other at a standoff but Jack did not hold grudges. I think he really believed what he was saying and he would be his good old mellow self only moments after a major altercation. Imagine the frustration when a 4-year-old son leaves food on his dinner plate. The father orders him to clean up his plate, and hears a totally straight-faced son say, "I never *could* eat potatoes."

The Mirage

Ten-year-old kids know a lot today. Maybe they know things that they don't need to know, but that wasn't the case in 1934, '35 and '36. If 10-year-olds, or their parents, were listening to the news of the day on March 6, 2000, they would have heard that MGM Grand, a Nevada gaming company that owns a few casinos by that name, had agreed to buy The Mirage, another Nevada casino, for something over $4 billion. That landmark has been built since my last visit to Las Vegas, but I have seen a few mirages elsewhere.

64

My dictionary describes a mirage as "an optical phenomenon in the desert or at sea by which an object appears displaced above, below or to one side of its true position as a result of spatial variations of something illusory." I imagine that is what Steve Wynn, the builder and owner of The Mirage, had in mind when he named it. An optical phenomenon.

I was 10 years old in 1934. That was the driest of the terrible drought years in our area of Nebraska. I had a fair vocabulary for a country kid but I don't know whether I had known the meaning of the word "mirage" until one hot, dry day in a middle of a summer filled with hot, dry days. We were living on the school section where my parents had built a farmstead when I was a year old. Farming there was barely more than an existence in normal years but it became desperate during the drought.

One day I looked east down our driveway and saw what first appeared to be strangely shaped clouds just above the horizon. My dad was returning to the barnyard from one of the fields and I ran, excited, to ask if he had noticed the strange show in the sky. He yelled at my mother and she called Grandma on the phone to see if we were crazy and "seeing things" or if it was real. Grandma went outside and looked to the east. Above the large, mature apple orchard east of her house, Grandma could see it too. Nebraska wasn't near a sea, maybe we really were in a desert. During the 1930s, it was a desert in fact, if not in the newspapers.

It began at the east horizon line and was about as high as the width of your hand at arm's length. It stretched from northeast to southeast several "hands" in width. I remember the sun as being high in the sky, which was a dark summer blue without a cloud in sight. The color was gray similar to a cloud, but in silhouette with sharp definition and the scene was obviously a town. There was the city water tank on its tower that looked to be at least two stories tall.

My dad said it looked like it was the town of Arnold. It was in almost the right place for Arnold, which was actually 25 to 30 miles east of our ranch, except that he didn't think the position of the water tank and the elevator were right for Arnold. If that mirage was an illusion, it was very real to a 10-year-old. We saw several more in the next couple of years—I don't remember whether it was three, four or more—but none with such memorably sharp definition.

With the return to more nearly normal weather pattern and a diminishing numbers of day-after-day searing heat after 1936, we saw no more mirages. Dustbowl survivors were a hardy lot, but the drought years gave cause to question almost everything, including your own mental health. Believe me when I tell you that you never want to see a real mirage from the place where you live and especially if you're trying to make a living by farming there.

Grandpa Wasn't a Big Talker

My grandfather, William C. Raynard, kept his family together during the drought and depression years but he didn't leave much of a record, public or private. In fact, if I hadn't lived with my grandparents to be near to the bus route so I could ride the school bus to high school, doing chores for my room and board, my recollection of his life might be limited to little more than a marker in the Loup Valley cemetery and a few old records of land ownership. Even his official signatures were burned in the county courthouse fire in the 1960s.

He was born in Ontario, Canada, and moved with his family to Manitoba, in the Pilot Mound area southwest of Winnipeg, at an early age. He married my grandmother, Ethel Elizabeth Evelyn Kerfoot, and after their first daughter was born in Canada, moved to Keya Paha County in northern Nebraska in 1897, where they homesteaded a property near Carns, taking out naturalization papers to become citizens. But after their second daughter and my dad were born, they took the family to Idaho in 1900 where he got work with the Potlatch Lumber Co. as a mechanic and repair man for its lumbering operations.

Returning to Nebraska in 1907, he homesteaded in Logan County in what was to be the family home base for another generation. The next year he built a cement-block house with blocks he made from native sand. It had four rooms downstairs and two bedrooms upstairs. A new kitchen (with basement) was added later. He built a landmark horse barn with gambrel roof over its upstairs hayloft, a granary, shop, a milk-cow barn and hen house. He finally built a two-bedroom hired man's home by the orchard. He had a married hired man as long as I can remember. The hen house was replaced by one made from straw bales—the first I ever saw or heard of—neatly plastered inside and out, when the old house blew down in the early 1930s.

Grandpa was not a gregarious person but he met people well. I remember him as a member of the county board of supervisors for many years. This was an elected office and I remember his name on the ballot but I can't imagine him on the campaign trail. I don't know my age at the time, but Grandpa's politics prompted me to ask one of the hardest questions my parents ever had to answer. Nebraska law allowed a candidate to file on both party tickets if unopposed for election so voters would have someone to vote for, regardless of party affiliation.

I was proud to find his name in the sample ballot printed in the *Stapleton Enterprise*. He was listed as a Republican. But horror of horrors, I noticed that he was also listed as a Democrat. "How come Grandpa is a Democrat?" I asked my parents. There were few Democrats in our county and almost none in our precinct. I don't remember their answer but at that time they wished

Grandpa hadn't been so eager for votes. At any rate, he was re-elected as long as he lived.

Grandpa had the best farm shop I ever saw. He had a large forge, anvil, long bench with leg vise and a wall full of tools, mostly handmade, but you couldn't tell from looking at them. He also had a large tool chest he had made while in Idaho that looked like the finest factory-made one in the world. He bought the hinges and metal corners but he hand-sawed and hand-planed every board and had hand-fitted every mortise-and-tenon joint in every bin and drawer.

He also had a set of about a dozen special wood planes with blades to make moldings from quarter-round to exotic shapes that he had made, blade and all, from select lumber and steel, which he tempered. My Uncle Bill, the youngest of the family, got the tools in Grandpa's estate settlement. I went to the auction of Bill's personal property after his death. My sister, Barbara, wanted the chest so I bid and bought it for her. An antique tool collector outbid us for the planes, which he described as "the best I ever saw," and was shocked to learn they were handmade.

In March, 2000, I returned to Lincoln for an anniversary meeting of my college fraternity and visited with Willard Waldo. He took the job as Stapleton ag teacher upon his graduation from the University of Nebraska and was my Uncle Bill's ag teacher and football coach. He recalled holding farm welding classes in 1933 or '34 in my grandfather's shop, described as the best he had ever seen.

Grandpa almost never started a conversation but he sometimes volunteered a little to a discussion. I saw a photo with cattle and sheep in the same photo and asked why he didn't raise sheep now. He didn't answer that, but he recalled once when he and his sister were playing in a field in Canada. A ram made butting motions at them. When they ran away, the ram chased them. His sister got them behind a large rock and spread her skirt over it. The ram charged the skirt, butting the skirt-camouflaged rock so hard he killed himself. I still don't know if that's the reason he didn't raise sheep. Grandpa wasn't much of a talker.

We had a tall, brown gelding named Tony that I liked to ride. Grandpa said Tony should be a good horse to drive, if not to ride. Grandpa had a driving team named Floss and Tony. While he had no registration papers, he said they were full-blooded Hambletonians and could trot, pulling a top buggy without breaking gait, almost all the way to town, 8 miles away. "There aren't many teams like them," he almost boasted. Floss had a daughter (also named Floss) sired by a Thoroughbred stud owned by Frank Stanley, a racehorse breeding neighbor. Our tall, brown Tony was her son.

Grandpa had a large orchard—in fact, two orchards. There was a large apple orchard east of the house, probably two acres, and a cherry orchard about half as large, west of the house. When I asked about the trees he explained that he wanted to raise their own food including cider in the fall, some for vinegar. The nursery in Nebraska City promised to buy the fruit in future years. He thought it was just "sales talk," but when the trees matured he shipped barrels of apples by rail for several years, returning far more money to him than the trees had cost.

When I was helping do chores, we had a baby calf that was unthrifty and I was concerned about its health. Grandpa reassured me by telling me it was not nearly as sick as calves he had saved in Canada when their mothers died or quit giving milk because of illness. He said they made "hay tea" by steeping timothy hay in hot water and feeding it to calves, keeping them alive, if not in the peak of health, until they could survive, and later thrive, on dry feed.

Grandpa milked a fairly large herd of dairy-cross cows. He once showed me the official registration certificate for a Holstein bull. I was so impressed with the fancy border, gothic type and gold seal on the pedigree that I memorized the bull's name: Lord Pontiac Segis Dekol Butterboy. I was later to learn that those were all famous bloodlines in the Holstein breed of dairy cattle. Maybe his genes helped to make Grandpa's herd give more milk.

I remember our Canadian relatives' comments about Will and Ethel (Grandpa and Grandma) living "down in the States" where they "don't have a King or anything." I never felt that Grandpa had such loyalty to the crown. I remember a Sunday in the 1930s when my grandparents came to our house for Sunday dinner. We didn't get a daily paper and rarely had a battery for our radio. Grandpa seemed to always have a radio and was bringing us up on the news of the world. He said the King had been riding on his white horse and returned with a bad cold. In the days that followed, King George died, leaving the throne to Prince Edward, not my grandfather's favorite royal, who later abdicated his throne.

Grandpa introduced me to "bag balm," a long-sold salve to heal cracks in cows' teats and udders or almost any other sore on man or beast. I stayed with Grandpa and Grandma when my brother Dick was born. I was too close to the action for a 5-year-old when the cows came into the barn. As I climbed a partition, a board came loose, puncturing my lower lip with a nail. He wiped off the blood and a generous coating of bag balm assured a quick return to good health, but I still have a scar on the inside of my lower lip to remind me of that incident so many years ago.

Grandpa always had a twinkle in his eye and I remember that he had a small gold inlay in an upper left molar that showed when he smiled. He liked to have a young grandchild on his lap in the wingback leather rocker, listening to the tick of his watch. My memory isn't good enough to put me in that place of honor but I know I must have had my turn. He would somehow always find a piece of horehound candy for a deserving kid. I never had a "sweet tooth" but candy from Grandpa was a welcome treat.

We have a copy of a family photo taken in 1918 or '19 when Uncle Bill was a baby. In that photo, Grandpa had a generous, if not a full, handlebar moustache. I don't remember him wearing a moustache but he was stone bald as early as I can remember. My dad apparently got some of those genes. He had thinning hair from my earliest memory but he did retain enough hair on top to justify an occasional combing throughout his life.

Grandpa never practiced "one-upmanship," at least in public. I once saw him at the top of his game, satisfied enough to almost act proud. Gasoline had been disappearing from the tank inside the shop. Locking the spigot didn't help so he guessed the thief was siphoning out of the bung at the top of the tank, mounted high on a stand. His "Rube Goldberg" gotchas did the job, with the thief leaving his hose, funnel, 5-gallon pail, and tracks, never to return. Grandpa's homemade noisemakers, waterfall and flood light, triggered into action as the thief began to open the shop door, had spooked our late-night gasoline customer, never to return.

Grandmothers are for Quilts and Cookies

Kids need grandmothers. They fill a niche unique in family relationships. They were my universal, God-given source for quilts and cookies. When I was very young I didn't know much about either grandma, but I was always glad to visit either one. They lived about a mile apart and within 3 miles of our house. We saw Grandma Raynard at church every Sunday and, in later years, the Bakewells took Grandma Brothers to church, but that didn't count as a visit to me.

We didn't visit their houses very often. Grandma Brothers was my "quilt" grandma. She always had a quilt in progress. She had one of the big, square, two-story farm houses from the 1920s. It had a big parlor that was rarely used by people but it had heavy-duty eye-screws in the ceiling that suspended a quilting frame. A rope from each corner of the frame was threaded through pulleys attached to the eye-screws and the rope ends were secured to the wall. The frame could be pulled up to the ceiling to accommodate company, then let down to lap height when Grandma had time to stitch.

Grandma Raynard was my "cookie" grandma. She had the Canadian way of pronouncing *south* as *sowth* and her grandson Harold was *Harrold*. I never knew if this was an extension of her Canadian pronunciation but no matter what recipe she used, she pronounced them *coookies*, to sound like *kook-ease*. I was never big on sweets. I was the kid who cut off the frosting, leaving it on the edge of the plate as I ate the cake. Everyone waited to watch me eat the frosting later. But I didn't eat it. Frosting was too sweet—almost made me gag. It still does. But not Grandma's *coookies*.

I ate everything Grandma made. She almost invented sugar cookies, but she also made uncooked oatmeal, nut and marshmallow cookies, chocolate coconut cookies and raisin-filled cookies that had Fig Newtons beat hollow. She never entered a recipe in the county fair, which was fine by her grandkids. We had one of the country's great natural resources to ourselves.

As we got older, the relationships got more complicated. One day Grandma Raynard had a quilt frame suspended in her parlor with a quilt in progress. That didn't destroy her image as she still had the well-filled cookie jar but it gave her a new dimension. I was shocked to find that she also raised a great garden and later learned that she had furnished a grouse for the dinner table with a single-shot rifle more than once when the family lived in Idaho.

Grandma Brothers also confused the picture about once a year when she would have some cookies for the grandkids, but never enough to "spoil" us or to earn a reputation that might become difficult to maintain. She didn't have much formal schooling but amazed me while confounding my dad by routinely adding a bunch of numbers in her head as they were read to her. She also frustrated my dad over her political convictions. My dad never saw a bad Republican or a good Democrat and Grandma was a Democrat to her dying day.

It never occurred to me that she had a previous life but I was to learn that as a girl of 16 or 17, she worked as a cook and housekeeper for Buffalo Bill Cody at his Scout's Rest Ranch in North Platte. Actually, she worked mainly for Buffalo Bill's daughter, who lived at the ranch regularly while Cody, himself, mainly used the ranch as a base for a rest-stop when he returned to the area from his world-wide tours.

Grandma Raynard was generally happy and showed it by singing as she worked. If she was aware of, or affected by, what her neighbors were doing, she didn't let on. Grandma Brothers was a little more high strung and might raise her voice in disapproval of a neighbor's new car or idea. She boarded schoolteachers for our country school for years and was pretty much an unflappable character. But she couldn't contain her normally cool demeanor when I came driving home, unannounced, from overseas duty in the Navy during WWII, with both her youngest daughter, Edna, and my brother Jack as surprise passengers. That was the only time I ever saw her cry.

The Feed Team

I know that agriculture is a noble profession because the professor in one of my college classes said it was. It is also more likely a way of life than any other profession. A shopkeeper or lawyer rarely lives and sleeps at the shop. Most of the farmers and ranchers I know live, eat and sleep where they work. Farming in the old days meant raising a little of everything. You always had something to sell and, if one crop earned low prices, another might do better.

70

Down on the farm these days, stock is fed in feed bunks or troughs filled with semi-automatic augers from central storage units or with large feed trucks driven down alleys, with the feed mixture weighed by automatic scales as it is deposited in cement feed troughs. There was a time when that was all done by hand with a manually operated system—that means by a human with a scoop shovel, from a wagon pulled by a team of horses. I know this is true because I did it.

It took a sizeable band of horses to operate a farm. We often took out two or more six-horse hitches or three four-horse teams, day after day, for field work. We needed teams to plant and cultivate, to cut and stack hay all through the summer but things eased up for a few weeks until corn harvest when we needed several two-horse teams to pull wagons. When corn was picked by hand, ear-by-ear, we always tried to have it out by Thanksgiving. Then we settled down to winter feeding of whatever livestock we wintered on the farm.

We "sledded" hay from the stacks with a four-horse team to feed the cowherd but it was a two-horse team that pulled the feed wagon, feeding grain to pigs and cattle in the feedlots. Every farmer learned by trial and error which two horses from his band were the most reliable to pull the feed wagon, whether loaded or empty, in stormy or fair weather. They always moved when the driver clucked to them and stopped, just as dutifully, when he yelled "whoa."

We had a crop of foals every year that would grow up and become the feed teams of tomorrow. Every farmer had extra horses in the fall and winter that did nothing but eat until field work began the next spring. Many of these were taken to horse sales, bringing welcome income and cutting off the feed bill. Next spring we would break some of those 3-year-olds to replace the horses that were sold.

There have always been opportunists who make a good living in a "niche" market. Such is the case with horse traders. During the winter and spring days we were frequented by horse traders of two types. One was the guy who drove into the yard with a team on a wagon, often with a horse or two snubbed to the team he was driving, and sometimes leading several horses behind. He would try to buy . . . or sell . . . horses or, if he had a horse that appealed to the farmer, he would look over the farmer's band and pick one or more to swap.

The other type was the "carload" trader. He drove a car and always knew what kind of horse he wanted to make a train carload to ship to buyers "back east" or "in the south." He bought during winter in the cold country and shipped his horses to farmers in milder climates for their use in spring field work months before we needed them in Nebraska. This was a nice source of income for almost-always money-starved farmers.

To a horse trader, there were horses—and then there were horses. He knew he had hit pay dirt if he could trade a farmer-feeder out of his "feed" team. He could make lavish promises to a potential buyer, with confidence, if he was selling the "feed team" from almost any farmer. It was even better if he saw the farmer's kids—the younger the better—driving the team.

My dad was pretty much a run-of-the-mill Nebraska farmer who would not have impressed many people as being astute. But he had spent enough years in the unforgiving Sandhills trying to make a living that he had learned a few lessons. And when it came to trading horses, he didn't go out traveling the roads but sat at home, a bit like the trapdoor spider, patiently waiting for an unsuspecting victim, ready to pounce.

When it came to horse trading, he made use of all the family's assets. Early in the fall, he decided which two horses needed selling and looked good enough together to be a team. We fitted the best harness on them and stood them in the first stall. If there was a good place to get a high price for two less-than-great horses, this was it. I was small for my age but able to handle almost any horse and get good response from whatever team we used.

From early fall, whenever a horse trader showed up, no matter what time of day, our dad would say, "Boys, I think it's time to feed." Jack and I would dutifully go to the barn, harness the team, hitch them to the feed wagon and pull into one of the feedlots. One year we sold three "feed teams" before spring work began. That was asking a lot from two unsuspecting farm kids but we delivered. And we were too naive to the ways of the world to even ask for a commission.

Hallelujah, Brother!

The United States' Midwest has often been referred to as the "Bible Belt," because of the concentration of fundamentalist churchgoers and churches, along with so-called "fire and brimstone" preachers. This combination was regularly enhanced by traveling evangelists or revivalist preachers who would attract large groups to tent meetings, rented halls or traditional churches. These types made up a large group that spawned Billy Graham, Oral Roberts and a few others who became famous, along with hundreds or thousands of preachers who never became known outside a small area for a few years, especially the 1930s and '40s.

While the larger cities have many activities to absorb the energy and dedication of the citizens, small towns and rural enclaves have a limited list of possible social, intellectual or religious groups to join and, if you live there, you have your choice to be a member of some of the local clubs or a loner with few friends or even neighbors who will openly accept you and your family. The hardy group of farmers in the Nesbit community met at the Nesbit School with whatever itinerant preacher they could find, rather than worship at any of the more established churches. We were on some Bible school's "sucker" list.

Stapleton had Presbyterian, Catholic and sometime Free Methodist churches. Gandy had a Methodist church that had a Sunday school for years, even if they couldn't keep a regular preacher and there was a community church in Tryon. The Nesbit worshipers found something wrong with every one of these groups and continued to worship alone, but they did join the area churches in holding "Sunday School Convention" meetings once a year at one of the Protestant churches. Keeping a preacher was always a problem. There were five or six of the families that were there every Sunday no matter what happened. A handful of others showed up on some Sundays. Sometimes they shared a preacher with one or more of the other area churches who came early to our service, then drove to his regular church service. Other times they had an itinerant evangelist type or a practice preacher from North Platte.

My parents were not as emotional as some of the neighbors but they didn't miss a chance to expose their kids to this brand of religion. We went to church and Sunday school every Sunday morning, then again Sunday night for an evening service. Prayer meeting was Wednesday night, summer or winter, since there was no appropriate time or place otherwise for the "saved" members to "testify" to their neighbors about the wonders of being a Christian. Revival meetings were held at least once a year. Some years there were even more. The star at these events would be some evangelist who came from somewhere and it seemed that the further away, the better. These might run every weekday night for a week or 10 days or even longer. I always felt they lasted as long as there was money in the collection plate.

My mother knew that her duty as a mother required that all her children be "saved" and become good Christians. I remember the worst of the sessions beginning when I was about 9 years old and Jack was 6. Our parents did not apparently think that Jack was old enough to understand going to Hell at age 6, but as I reached 10 or 11, they were sure that I should be saved and, if I wasn't, they were failures as Christian parents. The pressure to get their boys saved continued for years. My mother explained that it would surely make her happy. She never asked if it would make me happy.

I remember one particular session at the Nesbit schoolhouse. The school was a good-sized one-room schoolhouse with a stage across the front, elevated about 6 inches for the full width of the room. The teacher's desk sat in the front center of the stage, facing north, with chairs or benches at the east side where the members of the grades reciting lessons sat. The piano sat at the west side of the stage.

There were about six two-student desks in a row on the east side and six in the center of the schoolhouse facing the teacher's desk and the stage, and another four desks in the west row, which was shortened by the stove in the northwest corner of the room. The schoolhouse was built with no windows on the south end nor on the east and west sides of the stage but a full row of five or six windows on the east side and one on the west. The entry door was at the north end joining a vestibule or outer entry where we hung our winter coats, across most of the north end with front steps on both the north and east sides of the covered entry.

When revival time rolled around, the evangelist worked from a bob-tailed pulpit that sat on the teacher's desk and the 6-inch-high stage became an altar. The "saved" volunteers knelt at the makeshift altar. After the preacher warmed up the crowd with a sermonette, he pleaded with both the congregation and God for a "bountiful harvest" of new Christians. He began his "altar call" asking for both the saved and sinners to come forward. A couple of the middle-aged women who always seemed to need saving were first to the altar.

As the preacher continued his call, his volume increased and so did his urgency. People trickled one by one to the altar. After the preacher warmed up the crowd a little more, the hard cases began going forward. The music, even as delivered by a couple of local, self-proclaimed Gospel singers, backed by the school piano, voiced appropriate lyrics to move sinners to see the light. "Come, brother, come sister," the preacher chanted. Then, when one of the holdouts went to the altar, the preacher shouted, "Hallelujah, Brother, Praise the Lord." It was too unbelievable for a Hollywood movie.

Our neighbor, "Old Mac" McPherrin, went to church a couple of times a year. His daughter, Margaret, came to Sunday church fairly often but none of the other McPherrins, except that Old Mac would come to the revivals for a night or two almost every time they came around to get saved again. Oswald McNeill was another revival regular, even though he only came to church a couple of times a year otherwise. Even Chet and Edith Barner, whose farm bordered ours and whose oldest son, Earl Dean went through 12 years of school in my class, never went to church, but sometimes came to a revival meeting. I never asked them why.

The desks and seats in the schoolhouse were arranged with the bigger ones at the back of the room, then the size reduced with the kindergarten and first graders in the front row. It was hard for the adults to get into the small seats in the front so the kids had to sit near the front with grownups in the back. Jack and I sat together. Our agreement with each other was never spoken but we both needed the security of having somebody as a fellow holdout when the pressure built to its peak and the sinners were wall to wall, two rows deep, at the altar.

Jack was not a great student during his first few years in school. He lived a miserable life when under the nose of our mother, who would accept nothing short of perfection from her kids. Jack couldn't read well in the early grades and seemed indifferent to school. Then the teacher discovered that Jack was nearly blind in one eye from amblyopia or "wandering eye" ailment. His eyes didn't focus properly and our country eye doctor may not have diagnosed his problem nor fitted glasses properly. At any rate, Jack wore glasses all his life from early age, but he didn't need to see or read well to know a phony faith peddler when he saw one. Jack had great instincts. He was also direct. I always knew what Jack liked or didn't like. If Jack didn't get what he wanted, it was because those in power just didn't listen to his pleas . . . or disagreed with him.

I tried to reason with my mother. Why, I asked, should I want to be a Christian if their preachers were so stupid they didn't even know good grammar and couldn't get a decent job? Most of the revivalists that came our way bragged to us that they had "found God." They didn't endear themselves to me by boasting of their former evil lives and how they had "picked up the Bible and thrown down the bottle" when I didn't know what kind of bottle they were talking about. I knew they had nothing to say that I wanted to hear. I thought they should either use good English and good grammar or shut up. I was embarrassed to be in the same room with them. But my mother wouldn't listen. I told her I couldn't see what they meant when they yelled, "Hallelujah, brother, praise the Lord." And it offended me when they yelled in church. I told her these preachers couldn't get a decent job and I didn't even want to be near such low-grade people. My mother never seemed to give my ideas any consideration. They were CHRISTIANS!

I remember one particularly challenging night revival meeting when most of the assembled crowd was repenting at the altar but the preacher railed on. We were sitting in the third row from the front in the far west row of seats and there wasn't a soul left in any of the seats near us. When it seemed to me that we had to be the last targets in the room, Jack leaned toward me and spoke directly in my ear. "You ain't goin' up, are you, Phil?" he begged. "Not unless they drag me," I assured him. It never occurred to me to ask if he was going, nor to thank him for sticking with me. That was just assumed, in our desperation to survive.

I was not thoughtful or analytical enough to understand why I hated to get up, do chores and ride the horse off to school early the next morning after being kept up half the night doing something that I hated. Jack and I recalled those awful nights and days a few times in adult life. We never asked our parents why they subjected us to the most awful abuse we could have imagined short of being beaten to a bloody pulp but I'm sure neither of us ever forgave them.

We decided, without asking, that our mother felt it was her duty as a parent to make us Christians. I don't think she ever realized that her duty might have been balanced with some responsibility as a parent to consider the obligation to the welfare of the kids. Jack and I bore the brunt of our parents' early bad parenting. They seemed to soften their heavy-handed approach to rearing Christian children after their early failures with us and softened with each succeeding child, finally becoming nearly normal if over-protective parents by the time baby Barbara came along. They let her and brother Rolland have dates, participate in school events and even go to school dances. As Jack once said of our younger siblings about the training we did on our parents, "They owe us plenty." And neither of us ever felt a great need to go to church again for any reason. What we got as youngsters would last anybody at least one lifetime.

A Corncob in the Radiator

I have been in many severe rainstorms. Sometimes it seemed as if I would be washed off my horse, or if driving, that my car would be washed or blown off the road. I have been near the ominous, twisting tail that sometimes develops on the bottom of a dark-colored cumulonimbus storm cloud on several occasions. If you grew up in "tornado country," as I did, these are scary times. You cannot fight a tornado and win. The best you can do is try to protect yourself.

Nebraska, I have been told, is not in the middle of "Tornado Alley," the most common area for tornados running through Oklahoma, Kansas, Missouri and a few southern states, but there were numerous killer storms in the Nebraska Sandhills during my time there. Nearly every home had an underground storm cellar or at least a "safe" corner, normally the southwest corner of the basement with a cement wall on two or more sides. A tornado whirls in a counter-clockwise direction and normally moves from the southwest to the northeast.

Some of the "old timers" had a fairly good ability to predict weather based on experience from observing weather in that area. Official reporting was primitive, with a limited number of weather stations that reported temperature, wind speed and direction, barometric pressure, cloud cover and precipitation as of a given hour. Newspapers sometimes had weather maps—if you got a newspaper—but these were primitive and our area got daily papers least a day late. We were to wait years for weather satellites, color television and Doppler radar.

We always kept an eye on the sky but during tornado season we were doubly alert. Storms could sneak up on you but normally you watched for extremely dark clouds that were sometimes nearly black with a greenish cast at the bottom. A tornado seemed to come with a roar, like the giant turbine it would frequently become. Our tornado watches were in daylight because we couldn't see them coming at night. The heat of the afternoon or early evening air made a storm more severe so there were more storms during daylight.

I remember one that hit our ranch headquarters at night when I was in high school. The steel fan blades of the windmill were neatly wrapped around the hub at the center of the wheel but the mill "engine" was still atop

76

the tower of the windmill. The tail, made of sheet metal, was broken off and carried several hundred yards away to the edge of the apple orchard. The two pieces were attached to a steel pipe with steel reinforcing rods from the base to the ends of the tail at the top and bottom of the tin blades. These rods were wrapped around the center pipe.

Near the windmill tail, a giant 40-year-old apple tree was uprooted from a solid stand of similar trees, and left standing on its top with its roots pointed toward the sky. A hay wagon had been moved nearly 100 feet from its normal parking place and while the rack stayed with the wagon gears, the small pile of loose hay that had been in the wagon was spread over the orchard area about a football field away. We did not lose a shingle off any roof as proof that our storm was really a tornado but we were convinced that this wind had some strange habits if it was not, in fact, a "twister."

The most memorable tornado in our area came before I could remember in detail but I'll never forget the "magic" of the Lambert Tornado. Burke Lambert had a highly improved farm at "Lambert's corner" on the highway between our ranch and Stapleton. The improvements were on the south side of the highway and included two giant gambrel-roofed barns and the square, two-story ranch house that were about 100 feet apart in a saw tooth configuration with the south end of the house even with the north end of the middle barn and its south end lined with the north end of the west barn. A few other buildings also sat nearby.

Burke had great mule teams. All the field work and hay making on the farm was done with mules. The southwest barn had space for milk cow stanchions, grain and hay storage. The middle barn had a giant haymow upstairs with a long north-south passage way through the center of the barn with large doors rolling on tracks at the north and south ends of the barn. Wide, two-horse (or two-mule) stalls were side-by-side along the full length of the barn. A hay manger was located at the front of each stall, along the outside barn wall with openings in the upstairs floor over every manger so hay could be pitch down from the loft into the mangers. Feed boxes for grain were built next to the stall partitions for each animal. The top board of the manger was a full-measure 2-by-12 with holes drilled for the halter ropes that tied the animals in the stalls.

The tornado struck in the evening just after the teams were in from the hay fields, harnesses removed and grain fed for the night meal. The barns were located about 80 to 100 feet south of the highway. Across the road was a hay meadow that stretched north from the road to the South Loup River for a quarter-mile or more. It had been a cloudy but dry late summer day and the crew had been mowing and raking hay, preparatory for stacking.

As the Lambert family began eating the evening meal, skies darkened and rain began to fall, typical for a summer thunderstorm in Nebraska. But without notice, a strong wind began and rain came down with a vengeance for several minutes. Then the wind and rain nearly stopped, replaced by a deafening roar that was interrupted by banging noises. It was too early in the evening for full darkness, but the large farmhouse, where the family and farmhands had felt safe, shook as the storm progressed. In only minutes it was over. Burke climbed the basement steps and looked outside to see if there had been wind damage.

The middle barn where the mules were tied was gone as if it had never been on the farm. The mules were found in the hay meadow, having been transported several hundred yards across the highway to the north. And some were still tied by their halter ropes, one by one, to pieces of the mangers from the barn—shaking as they stood, frozen with fear. The hay meadow around the mules was filled with splintered boards, sharp, pointed ends driven into the ground at wry angles, including some of the split manger boards with trembling mules still attached.

The grand, square two-story farmhouse now had only one story. All of the upstairs was gone, and almost as neatly as if it had been sawed, certainly not blown away by a tornado. The first person to use the bathroom found a 3-foot-diameter cast iron wheel from a horse-drawn hay mower sitting in the bathtub. The porcelain was not chipped but one of the tub's legs was broken off. The pane in the bathroom window was broken but the hole was not large enough for the wheel to pass through. They removed the wheel by rolling it down the hall. Carpenters later converted the two-story home into a bungalow. Straws, by the thousands, from harvested grain and newly mowed hay, had been driven into the southwest side of tree trunks, sticking out like hair on a dog's back, among other "impossible" events.

The Lambert family car, a four-door Chevrolet touring car with canvas top, had been parked in the center driveway near the south end of the middle barn that had blown away. Darkness came before they could find the automobile but the next day after the storm, they began to count the losses. The first barn, the most southwest of the improvements, did not have even a shingle blown off, yet the barn between it and the farm house had been picked up, the ground under it seemingly swept clean, with the harness, saddles, hay and other contents found in the meadow across the highway, and the top story was removed from the house. But where was the automobile?

Two haystacks had been built about 40 yards south of the middle barn. The stacks were still in place, although some of the hay had been blown down between them. In a few days the loose hay between the stacks began to settle into a strange shape. Under the storm-blown hay they found the car—without a scratch—almost. Some automobiles of the 1920s had the radiator cores fully exposed and that particular model, instead of having straight coolant tubes, had cores in an unusual zigzag-shaped honeycomb pattern.

When the hay was removed from the top of the car, they found a corn cob pushed far into the honeycomb core but the radiator was not leaking. Without thinking, someone removed the cob, and in hindsight, expected the coolant to pour from the radiator. It didn't leak even a drop. Myron Lambert was a year behind me in school. I remember that he drove that car to high school on occasion in the late 1930s and the radiator, with the hole where the corn cob had been, was still on the car. It had never been repaired and it still didn't leak. That's a tornado to remember.

The School Picnic at Bay's Grove

It seems that our American society likes to see its events conclude in an orderly way. We like an identifiable closure to clear the air or clear our heads and give us permission to move on to the next project. I never knew when it began, but we had a tradition at the rural Nesbit School that brought closure to the school year. I was never one for ritual or formality but I did look forward to the last day of school. Several parents drove to the school, picked up all the kids, which varied in my memory from about 20 to nearly 30, and went to Bay's grove.

I never knew if George Bay had been one of the original homesteaders or not but he was about the vintage of my grandfathers and E.J. McPherrin, "Old Mac," whose ranch was a couple of miles wide and lay between ours and the Bay place. Both our ranch and the Bay place had large cottonwood groves planted at the headquarters. There was a "tree claim" advantage to the homestead contract for planting trees. If this is true, it was a credit to the government policies of the time as there were not many native trees when the settlers arrived.

The school term ended around the 20th of May. The Bay grove was about a quarter of a mile south of the highway. Most of the area from the highway to the grove was sub-irrigated meadow with the South Loup River wandering through the meadow. The trees were many years old and must have been 60 to 100 feet tall. They were just getting into full leaf and the cottonwood seeds, along with the cotton that let the wind blow the seeds around, seemed to carpet our picnic area. The meadow also supported a heavy crop of dandelions that were always in bloom for our picnic. Cows with baby calves were generally on the meadow. And George Bay was one of our few neighbors who raised sheep. Ewes with baby lambs were always a hit with the school kids as most did not have lambs at home. It was almost a storybook setting but we didn't know it. We had done it every year and it was fun but we had nothing for comparison. What do kids know?

I don't know who brought the tables but there were two rows. One was the food table. To me it seemed long, and with enough homemade potato salad and beans and Jell-O and wieners and hamburgers and cold fried chicken and lemonade and iced tea for a threshing crew—or a couple of dozen kids from kindergarten through eighth grade and a handful of parents.

79

The other table was even longer and it had benches of large, split logs along both sides. About the time we were ready to start through the cafeteria line, George Bay always showed up to share our picnic dinner with the current crop from Nesbit School.

As I remember, he always looked the same. He was a tiny man with ruddy cheeks, a flowing white mustache, sweat-stained cowboy hat and his jeans stuffed inside his boots. Year after year he arrived leading a Shetland pony that had survived several Bay youngsters who were now all grown and married. Who knows how old the pony was; it didn't matter. But I remember his color; he was a bay pony. He was ready to give rides to especially the youngest of our group. Most of the older kids had horses at home and shunned the pony ride.

The South Loup River started at a series of springs in a large swampy hay meadow area on the McPherrin ranch but it was in a normal stream bed by the time it got through the fence to the Bay place. It was only about a foot deep, 8 or 10 feet wide and too cold in May for serious wading, but we all had to try. By the time we got back to the old one-room schoolhouse in late afternoon, we were all ready for summer vacation.

More Than a Hired Man

He wasn't officially a member of the family but he was a fact of life in many of the farming/ranching operations in our area of the Nebraska Sandhills when I was growing up. This unique employment category was probably the result of the economy of the time during the depression and drought of the 1930s and continuing until World War II. Most male high school graduates or dropouts had little chance for employment in a high-paying job in their home communities or by going to the big city. There were not many jobs for skilled labor, even fewer for unskilled laborers. And there were no government agencies with unemployment checks for anybody. A desperate family might get a "relief" check from the county for $21 per month if they lived in our area.

A few of the ranches in our area had a house for a married hired man. My Grandpa Raynard's ranch had a nice two-bedroom house sitting at the edge of the cottonwood grove and he normally hired a married man. We barely had a home on our small ranch for the family so our hired man had to be single, slept in the basement "bedroom," and was, for many purposes, another member of the family. It wasn't part of the deal but the farm kids learned plenty from the hired man—much of it never known to the parents— and while most of our hired men were very careful about telling any stories unfit for young boys, our parents never knew for sure what we did learn from our hired men.

80

My dad always leased enough land from neighboring property owners to be sure he had work for his hired man. And he could get as many horses as needed, free for breaking them, from our banker, who had a ranch full of horses that he had repossessed during the hard depression years. The first hired man that I can remember was Brock Kelly. His real name was Floyd but the Kelly kids gave each other the names of neighbors as nicknames. Brock was the only one that stuck. He was a gentleman, was always a bachelor and became a lasting friend to my brother, Jack. He was the youngest of the neighboring Kelly family that went to school with my parents. He knew stories about all our neighbors, nothing sinister, but he taught me most of the lore of our neighborhood in the couple of years he worked for us.

Ralph Klee wandered into town from Colorado, looking for work, and our banker sent him to our place, knowing that Brock was leaving to work on a larger ranch for more pay than we could afford. I had mainly tagged along with Brock and rarely contributed more than standing in an open gate to keep the cattle from going through or being a gofer for ropes, straps, buckets, etc. I had been riding as long as I could remember but I was old enough to start driving teams when Ralph came along. He was patient with horses and was patient when teaching me about handling teams and horses in general.

Ralph bragged about our good harness, commenting that he once worked for a Colorado farmer who had big, good horses but the harness did not have any breeching or cruppers to hold back the wagons when going downhill. The owner said he thought it was a "poor team that couldn't outrun a wagon when they had a head start." Ralph always wore wide-brimmed hats to protect his red, freckled skin and red hair and hated to shave his tender face. I never knew if there was an employment agency or who served in that position in our community to find a hired man, nor why they left. Did they get tired of living on a starvation wage and decide there was something better in the next town or state, or did my dad tell them to part company and get on down the road?

I did know in one case when Ralph took me to town on a Saturday night. There was no movie theater in the county but during the depression years the city fathers arranged to set up rows of plank seats on the empty lot between Jenkins barber shop and the county court house. Then they showed a free movie on Saturday night on the north wall of the court house. The wall was already painted white so it made a decent movie screen. When Ralph told my parents why we got home late, he was fired on the spot. "He had to know that all movies were evil," was their reasoning for the complaint.

However, he was a good hired man and it was the middle of summer when it was a tough time to get a replacement so my parents decided by Sunday morning that he had "learned his lesson" and re-hired him, apparently without prejudice. I was fascinated by Ralph's Valet brand safety razor. It had a slot for a razor strop and the blade flipped over to strop the blade on one side when you pulled the razor toward you and the other side when you pushed the razor away. I never saw another Valet before or since.

Jake Sauer was the next hired man to have a real influence on my growing up. He blew in from Texas and I have no idea how or why he wound up working at our place but in the long view, I'm glad he did. I have no idea how big he really was; I know that my mother said he wore a 20-38 shirt, the biggest size stocked at almost any store, and the sleeve cuffs were well above his wrists. He bought a hat or cap whenever he found one that fit him, which was not often. He knew it might be a long time before he found another to fit. He did not have much schooling as I remember his once saying he got too big to go through a schoolhouse door for the fourth grade.

Today he would have had a cleft palate. In the 1930s, the time of Jake's era, he had a harelip and was a little difficult to understand when he spoke. But Jake knew more about cattle and horses and ranching and grass and the outdoors than anyone I ever knew, possibly in my entire life. He could look at a heifer or cow and tell whether she would be an easy breeder and good mother. He invented the idea of holistic resource management before Allan Savory did in South Africa, but not by that name, and showed me in the 1930s why grass needs cattle as much as cattle need grass. He taught me a good bit of understanding and respect for working with potentially dangerous male breeding animals: bulls, stallions, boars, etc.

Ervon "Fat" Fowler was not fat. He was not as big as Jake, but a big man by most standards, and must have earned his nickname as a baby because he was a raw-boned and muscular guy. His heavy black beard and contrasting gentle demeanor reminded me of the Steel Vent Piston Rings ads of the time with the heavy-bearded giant in a flower patch plucking petals one at a time from a large daisy. The action line proclaimed, "Tough, but oh so gentle." He became engaged and later got married while he worked for us. I remember the indicator of those hard years and limited money was the fact that he and his girlfriend wrote "penny" postcards instead of letters in sealed envelopes. But they saved enough money in a few years to rent a farm and begin farming on their own. He was a good influence for me at the time since he leaked a little of the off-the-farm world to me as I neared high school age, which my parents would never have done, nor approved of if they had known. I was not aware that I had learned from each man what I was ready to learn . . . and what my parents would never have told me.

The routine on a livestock and crop operation was disturbed for two specific events every year: small grain harvest in summer and corn harvest in the fall. We generally had a field of oats. Sometimes oats would be planted as a nurse crop for new alfalfa seeding since it germinated quickly and gave wind and sun protection for tender new alfalfa plants. Then as both grew, the oats ripened and we generally harvested that crop. When we threshed the

82

oats, we got both grain to feed horses and calves and oat straw, which was a more nutritious hay crop than most other kinds of forage that we grew.

This harvest time usually came shortly after the Fourth of July holiday. If we had a wet spring and summer the alfalfa crop sometimes grew fast and we might cut the alfalfa and oats together before the oats ripened. We used a mower that cut the stems much closer to the ground than the grain binder. The mixed alfalfa-and-oat hay was great feed for calves and horses and brought a high price if we had a few extra tons to sell. We often exchanged work with neighbors at haying and grain harvest time but we might also hire day laborers, if any were available, for a few weeks.

The heavy time for extra labor came at corn picking time. In the 1930s, no mechanical corn picker had been invented, or if there was one, it never made it to our area. This meant that corn was picked by hand, one ear at a time. This was a job that lasted weeks or months. The equipment required was a gentle team of horses, a wagon with "back" or "bang" board on one side of the wagon that was a temporary extended side of the wagon that stuck up 3 or 4 feet above the normal wagon box. The man picking the corn could concentrate on walking between two rows of corn, picking every ear of corn from both rows, then without looking, throw the ears in the wagon by throwing against the back board in a single motion instead of having to carefully drop the ears in the wagon box.

A top corn picker with experience in a field with a good crop could pick up to 150 bushels per day. The entire Corn Belt held harvest festivals featuring corn-picking contests where the best hand pickers worked for a given period of time. Then judges went through the field to gather ears that the picker had missed—for a deduction—and he got another deduction for every ounce of cornhusks left on the ears harvested. President Truman outlined his new farm policy at the Iowa State Corn Picking contest. That was probably the all-time largest crowd and all-time news coverage for a corn-picking contest. When mechanical pickers replaced the hand pickers, contests continued, but lost the drama of man against the elements. A man is not a fair match against a machine and a tractor does not pull with the drama of a team of draft horses.

When corn picking time came, the regular hired man was put on piece rate pay, along with an extra corn picker or two or three, all of whom were paid on the basis of cents per bushel. They were normally paid from a half-cent to a cent to 2 cents per bushel, depending on the year and the price of corn. Migrant workers came to town for corn picking. We generally had three corn pickers. The ritual began when corn was mature and dry enough to put in wire mesh corn cribs to continue drying without spoiling. It continued until the last ear of corn was picked.

Then the corn would be shelled off the cob and sold or stored at some later date when the corn had dried enough to keep in a bin without spoiling.

Corn shelling machines were a little like threshing machines for small grain, wheat, rye, oats and grain sorghum, except that the corn on the cob was already in the crib so there was no need for the many teams, bundle racks and the large threshing crews.

Thanksgiving was the target date. If the corn was picked by then, the family and corn pickers celebrated with a giant oyster stew feed with ice cream for dessert. It was homemade ice cream since the only ice cream available other than homemade was a nickel a dip at the drugstore and none was packaged to take home. Just as well; we didn't have a refrigerator. All the extra corn pickers were out of a job and went down the road after the corn was picked except for the regular hired man. In some of the hardest depression years when there was no work anywhere and nobody had any money to pay for help that was not absolutely needed, the corn pickers would stay on through the winter and do whatever ranch work could be done for room and board plus "wages" varying from around a dollar to possibly 2 dollars per month. I was not quite mature enough to pick corn and I didn't understand the economics but I enjoyed the fall activity.

Our Welcome Traveling Salesmen

You may have heard, or on rare occasion even used the expression, "As exciting as watching grass grow." After school was out in May and continuing to the beginning of the new school year in September, life on the farm was lonely and boring. We kids weeded the garden, hoed the weeds along the driveway and fence rows, herded turkeys and, after I got to be 10 or 11 years of age, I began driving a team in the field on harrows, cultivators, hay mowers or rakes. It was not a thrill to drive a team but it beat the other jobs and at least it was a signal of maturity. It was probably just as boring in the winter except that we were in school during most of the daylight hours. It was an exciting day when anyone disturbed the calm by coming to our place, especially in summer when the days were long.

I don't know how our parents felt, but we kids were surely thankful for traveling salesmen and horse traders. We were almost glad to see the dreaded (by us kids) traveling country preachers. The unexpected visitor always made it an occasion and it was an occasion for the whole family. During the 1930s (and probably the '40s; I was not at home after I went to college and the war began in 1941), when a salesman stopped to do business, he was invited in for dinner (dinner was served at noon) or supper, the evening meal. After the meal, he was welcome to present his proposition. It was just the unspoken rule, if he won't eat with you, you don't buy from him. Some of the meals were plain and often short on variety but it was hearty, high-energy food and there was almost always plenty of it.

The Stapleton Enterprise sent us a bill once a year, which we never paid, but the paper kept coming. They could not afford a salesman. But the *Nebraska Farmer* and the *Capper's Weekly* did have subscription men. We took the *Nebraska Farmer* in good years and bad. He would take barter like chickens, eggs, fresh vegetables or anything that he could eat or convert to cash in town. We only got the *Capper's* in years when we had just sold something or were flush with cash. After all, it cost $1 per year or 5 years for $3. I don't think we ever took the 5-year deal.

Two horse traders were regulars every year. Clarence Greb always wore stylish (to us) clothes, drove a good, new car to make his rounds and bought horses "to fill a carload for the southern market." Feagins (I guess I never knew his first name) drove a team on a wagon with a bunch of horses trailing, being led behind the wagon or snubbed to the team he was driving. It was a shock one day to see one of our neighbor's teams being trailed behind his wagon when he drove in to our place. I don't remember if I ever knew what they got in return.

My mother especially looked forward to a visit from the Raleigh man. She felt that she couldn't bake without Raleigh vanilla. And our poor farm family was never too broke to afford a few boxes of spice. She bought from the Watkins man only if her supply was low and the Raleigh man was overdue. I remember that one time somebody came by selling cleaners but all he got was a free meal—no sale. She got a set of dishes, one dish at a time, in her dishwasher detergent and, until I was in high school, we made laundry soap in the big cast iron tub using animal fat when we had butchered an animal. A farmer from nearby Ringgold or Tryon, with relatives in the Ozarks, stopped every fall with a load of genuine cane sorghum in his sputtering Model T Ford truck. He always arrived just before dark and my dad always bought a gallon. I wish he would call again. I'm still searching for sorghum that tastes that good on a waffle.

Barners' Horses Turn to Iron

It was the spring of 1935, as I remember, that we had a rainy springtime. It was our first sign of a break in the drought that compounded the national depression to bring financial ruin to many hard-working farmers in the Midwest. Aside from the wet spring, the thing I remember most was that our neighbor on the west, Chet Barner, traded his whole band of workhorses for a Farmall tractor as his power unit for the future. I was not really surprised that Chet would be the first in our community to get a tractor. He was not a bad horseman but he liked engines and I didn't think he really felt loyalty to horses like I did.

We got the *Nebraska Farmer* magazine, where I saw the tractor ads, and I had seen new tractors in town. My uncle Hank had an old Fordson tractor that he used to run his feed grinder but I don't think he ever pulled a machine with it. Frank Wooters was the John Deere dealer across the street from Baskin & Salisbury, the International dealer. I had been inside both dealers when we bought parts for our old machinery but it just hadn't occurred to me that anybody in our community would actually own a tractor. We had always farmed with horses and I never thought that it would ever change so I was shocked to see Chet riding that red tractor to plant corn. He had used a team to disc weeds under for seedbed preparation just a few days earlier. And Earl Dean, the oldest Barner son, who went through 12 years of school with me, hadn't said a word—maybe he didn't even know the deal was hatching.

It was nearly a quarter of a mile from the school house to Barners' field and all the kids in Nesbit School strained to watch that tractor rush across the field to plant corn. It was much faster than a team, we all agreed. And in the spring mornings, as we rode our horses along the edge of the field on our way to school, and again in the evening on our way home, we got to see the miracle of the tractor at work. Don't say there was no excitement in the Sandhills. And then we noticed the crooked rows where the corn had been planted. A disaster. We were ashamed for our neighbor.

Farmers tended to judge their neighbors' proficiency as much by their rows as by the yield. You could never be a great farmer in the eyes of your neighbors if you couldn't plow a straight row. Chet Barner was never the master of the straight row when he drove a team on the planter but you should have seen his first field that was planted with that tractor. He barely kept it inside the fence. He got the hang of it a little better with practice but he said there was the same number of plants in 40 acres whether the rows were crooked or straight. That was probably true but we were embarrassed by our now "sloppy" but formerly neat neighbor.

A few weeks later I began to philosophize, wondering why it was Chet and not Irving Gibbs who bought the first tractor. The Gibbs boys were all mechanical and only Russell showed real interest in livestock. Ralph had gone to college and was some kind of an engineer for the State of Nebraska. Roland had a motorcycle. Wouldn't it follow that their dad would have the first tractor, I reasoned.

Where did Chet Barner earn the right to be the first? Barners had a Chevy and we had a Ford. Earl Dean and I already argued about which car was best. Now, since we did not have a tractor, I had to be the defender of horses vs. tractors and neither of us knew anything about tractors. But this was just the first of the inevitable. Even my dad bought a John Deere tractor (used) a few years later that did much of the heavy work around our place. Brother Jack liked the tractor so I never tried to make friends with that noisy monster at our place. I did the horse work and enjoyed it, despite its slower pace. As it turned out, a few years later, Chet bought a threshing machine to go with his tractor and threshed the grain for our neighborhood and beyond for years to come. The tractor was here to stay.

Jada, Jada

I learned to ride at a very early age on a bay mare. Her name was Jada. She was one of the possessions my dad brought to the marriage in 1923, named from the lyrics of a popular song of the era, "Jada, Jada, Jada Jada, jing, jing, jing," recorded by young Tommy Dorsey's band, among others. I don't know how songs became popular at the time since there were none of the music outlets we know today. Traveling troupes played at the Chautauqua houses—even Stapleton had a Chautauqua house—and dance bands played music. I don't know where they learned what was "popular," or how it got that way.

THE SALE OF THIS SONG WILL BE FOR THE BENEFIT OF THE NAVY RELIEF SOCIETY. THE SOCIETY THAT GUARDS THE HOME OF THE MEN WHO GUARD THE SEAS.

My parents didn't go to dances. My mother, who played the piano, had sheet music for dozens of songs but no records. Many families had pianos but few had Victrolas, the trade name for record players. I never went to a movie in the "silent" days but I have been told by knowing, authoritative people that a pianist or small musical groups played background music for the movie but it was mostly classical music. Later, songs were made popular from being played or sung in the "talkie" movies when they came along.

The few radio stations of the day were barely more than an experimental way to advertise. Most call letters came from the initials of the business' name. The earliest station that I can remember was KMMJ, Clay Center, (later moved to Grand Island) Nebraska. Its reason for being on the air was to sell baby chicks for the Martin M. Johnson hatchery. WOW in Omaha was owned by the Woodmen of the World fraternity. WHO in Des Moines was named for the "With Hands Only" creed of its founder, Col. Palmer, who was also a founder of Chiropractic medicine. KMA, Shenandoah, Iowa (later Omaha) advertised farm seeds for the Earl May seed company. Our few radio stations broadcast a few hours daily on some days, no printed schedules, no networks, no disc jockeys, no TV. My mother had a piano, as did the school, but there was no record player at the school, which had neither a telephone nor electricity.

Jada was broke to ride as a 3-year-old in the year I was born. She was bred to a spotted pony two years later to get a pony for me to ride. When "Midget" was born, she wasn't spotted, she was just plain brown, but became a great "kid pony" as she outgrew her genes and her name to become every bit as large as her mother. Jada was not a reliable "kid pony." She panicked upon hearing gunfire. She shied every time a pheasant was flushed from cover within 20 to 30 yards and she did not "rein tie," (stay put when the reins were dropped so a dismounted rider would always have a horse to ride). But she was what we had. Midget did become that reliable horse, but she was just a baby when I began riding to attend the Nesbit one-room, eight-grade, country school at age 5. I rode Jada.

It was 3 miles by road from home to school and just over 2 miles through the pastures to school when gates were opened after cattle came home in late fall when the grass quit growing and we began feeding hay. How many parents would send kids off to begin their school careers today on a sub-zero winter morning riding a horse that snorted at the odor of a dead animal and shied when a pheasant flew out of cover or even a moving tumble-weed? Three years later Jack started to school and Midget was getting broke to ride. We started the year riding double on Jada but by spring and each year thereafter we took both horses and stalled them together in the school barn. Times and values have changed.

Phil (approximately 2 years) on Jada with greyhounds, our "family pets" on the ranch, which also kept the coyote population under control.

When brother Dick started school two years later, Jack rode Jada and Dick rode double with me on Midget. Normally surefooted, Midget stumbled one day and both horse and riders were spread over the roadside. A fast learner, she liked getting rid of her load and stumbled again the next day with the same results. Stumbling became a homebound ritual. I told my dad, who gave me spurs to wear and dig her sides the next time she stumbled. Still smart—and smarting, she never stumbled again. Midget was first bred the year I started college and foaled a good saddle horse with the spots we expected from her but which she never had. Two years later, when I was in the Navy, she shattered a leg bone while pushing cattle up a loading chute and had to be destroyed. Each of the three foals Jada raised after being "retired" at age 20 became a first-rate saddle horse.

Jada had the run of the ranch in her declining years, free to eat from the stack of the best fourth-cutting alfalfa, spend the night there if she chose, in the barn if the weather justified it, exercise in the yard, on our entry road or even on the graded dirt highway. While I cannot testify to the veracity of this report, our neighbors along the way told us that old Jada was seen walking alone one day, in sight of their ranch house, on the road where she had carried our family, one by one, to the one-room school. This route was nearly 6 miles round trip—to the ranch where we lived when I started school and back by the short way past the school house and another half mile to our yard—a mare on a mission of fulfillment, so to speak, completing the circuit. The next morning, apparently satisfied by retracing the route traveled daily for much of her useful career, she was found near her favorite haystack, dead at the remarkable age of 29 years.

Music for "Ja-Da," the 1920s hit for which our bay saddle mare was named.

A Cow Named Tidy

I did most of my growing up when we lived on a "school section" (Section 16, Dorp Precinct) during the 1920s and '30s. Nebraska operated under an act of the legislature which gave Section 16 and 36 in every township (in areas where the named sections were not already owned by citizens) to the schools. The tenant on a school section never got title to the land. The "rent" was paid to the state and the amount was based on some magic number closely akin to taxes on a comparable property in the area. To encourage development and building on these sections, a tenant (owner) was given perpetual right to re-lease the property.

Having a school section was similar to ownership. The owner/tenant could sell the right of "ownership" to a new buyer but transferred a "right" instead of a deed. My parents' first real home was the two-rooms-with-path model on a school section they purchased after spending their first two years of married life on a farm they rented from Freed Wilcox. They built the house, garage, barn with hay yard inside a windbreak and a chicken house. It was the barn and chicken house—with their occupants—that allowed the family to eke out a living. We raised the "dual purpose" Durham (Shorthorn) cattle that were reputedly good for both milk and beef. The barn had four two-horse stalls on the east end, then a row of wooden stanchions for milk cows in the west end. I don't remember the exact number but we could house more than 20 milk cows.

The cows that gave the most milk got to spend the cold winter nights inside the protection of the barn. We often milked more cows than that but the extras had to bed down outside, then were brought in for milking after some of the better producers were milked and turned out to drink. We brought several new heifers into the milking herd every year to replace older cows that were culled because of age, health, low production or failure to breed back promptly. The ones giving the most milk got to stay in the herd but they got another bonus. They got names.

Each year's crop of heifers was named in a different sequence. One year we used flowers. I remember a roan heifer named Pansy. There were Violet, Tulip, Rose, Marigold and Cosmos. Fuchsia was a dark red heifer with white spots shaped much like stripes. We used up several flower names, but Pansy and Fuchsia were the best producers and stayed in the herd for years. I don't remember when we named new heifers after neighbors but most of them had been culled and gone to market by the time I began milking. Nearby towns didn't do well in our dairy. A roan heifer did stay for a couple of years but what cow would want to be called Arnold?

One year we had Beet, Carrot, Onion, Pepper, Spinach and Tomato but it upset my mother since it confused the cows and garden vegetables so we had to rename them. I don't remember any of them in the herd. I do remember a

90

mostly white cow with red spots that was the daughter of a cow they got from a neighbor in a trade for hay. The neighbor's last name was Tidy. That was our best family. Tidy and her daughters were good milk producers, with good disposition and always had a calf on schedule. She produced several daughters that were named Tidy I, Tidy II and Tidy III. And she was the favorite of our barn cats.

Every barn needs a few cats to control the mouse and rat population that goes with hay storage. And those cats gathered around at milking time for their treat of fresh milk in a pie tin. Our "sometime" dairy barn recreation (we milked the string of 20-plus to well-over 30 cows by hand) was squirting milk directly from the cow, hitting the cat squarely in its waiting open mouth. Those Tidy heifers were the best for feeding cats too. Some cows would kick when you bent their teats sideways. I think this was when Dad began breeding the herd out of the dairy business by crossbreeding to Hereford beef bulls; this was about the time when I left home to go to college. It was a busy time that would now be called a hard life and I don't need to do it again. It probably is not experience that will help anybody get a job today, but it's fun to recall such an "earthy" time as long as I'm reasonably sure, if not positive, that it won't return.

Storm Coming

"Storm coming" is an expression that gets your attention in any location where I have lived or visited. But it has a different meaning where any of several severe weather words are used. Hurricanes, tornados, blizzards or sandstorms have the inclusion of wind along with whatever other factor describes the storm. And almost all, except sand storm, involves rain or snow being driven by the wind. The most notable sandstorm I ever experienced was when I was growing up in Nebraska in the 1930s during Dust Bowl days when we endured years of drought and windstorms with the relocation of topsoil from thousands of acres in several Midwest and Southwest states. We had drifted sand dunes several feet deep and hundreds of yards long where there had formerly been fields and fences.

I recall many days when brother Jack and I went to bring the milk cows in from the pasture when we were unable to see very far, but one day especially when we couldn't see fences or other landmarks for more than 30 to 50 yards. There was also a trip from Palm Springs to Los Angeles when I got acquainted with California desert sandstorms for about 30 or 40 miles. The sand was hard on the paint job and the ruined windshield couldn't have been more completely etched with acid.

I flew a few hurricane patrols when I was stationed at NAS Banana River in Florida to locate Atlantic storms and we were ordered to fly through the eye of one storm. This was an operational training base and the first assignment for me and other new pilots after getting our wings. It was a scary trip for the student pilots but our instructor was a veteran of numerous storms who assured us that our plane would hold together. We flew through miles of heavy rain as we neared the storm. Rain and turbulence became severe at the wall of water at the edge of the cone. When we got into the eye of the storm, it was dead calm and the water surface was flat and glassy with no wind and it looked as if the surface was a few feet higher than in the turbulent water nearby. The eye of that particular storm was several miles across. We had new respect for the people who designed and built that patrol bomber we were flying. We were in the fringes of a few typhoons (the far-east Pacific name for hurricane) when I was in the Philippines and saw the destruction these storms bring but the difference I saw was the location and name, not the effect. (I understand this storm is called a Williwaw near Australia.)

The "Armistice Day Freeze" was one of the weather events I will remember forever and it had neither severe wind nor precipitation. This shocker happened on the night of November 10 and morning of November 11, 1940. My dad maintained that the average "killing" frost in our area of Nebraska was September 27. We never knew what was killed in a killing frost. I felt that was when the green left the corn stalks and the last cutting of alfalfa was not going to get any taller. A killing frost meant the growing season was over but we did not expect to see the onset of blizzards, snowdrifts and serious winter weather for perhaps several weeks.

We usually had a good stretch of Indian summer with a little morning frost on the pumpkins, cornstalks, etc., but the sap did not disappear from the trees. I wore a jacket when I ran to catch the school bus but not a winter coat. We had no weather channel to forecast tomorrow's weather and the newspapers (which we did not get), never had a reliable weather forecast or predicted temperatures. So it was a shock to the Sandhills on the morning of November 11 when the morning temperature was down below zero. It shocked many trees to death. We had three groves planted as shelter belts in the 1930s that were getting nicely established. Thousands of these trees did not survive the shock.

The "Blizzard of '49" was another landmark weather event. I had returned home from college for Christmas in 1948. As we approached the end of the year the weather bureau forecast a severe storm on its way. I was working to earn my way through college and needed to be back in Lincoln so I left home on one of the last days of December to be ahead of the storm. No reason to wait and drive in a snowstorm when we had good weather right now. I was one of the few in our fraternity from western Nebraska who came back early.

The storm hit its peak the next day in western Nebraska and took a full day or more to reach across the state. It was the storm of the century in all but the few eastern counties. In Lincoln, we had a heavy snow but no disaster. Back home in Stapleton, everything drifted shut. Our ranch tractor had a front-end loader, so they were able to move enough snow to pass through some gates and get hay to the cattle. They cleared the ranch road out to the highway but the drifts were too deep to get anywhere near town. Wayne Salisbury lived at the old Ed Salisbury ranch just southeast of Stapleton but most of his cattle were at the ranch west of town, about halfway out to our ranch.

When the storm was over, Wayne got Homer Empfield to drive his bulldozer to the ranch by road, over fences or wherever they had to go to get through. They cut snowdrifts so the cattle could get out of the protection of the old "tree claim" grove, spread out a haystack for feed and opened another passage so the cattle could get to open water. All the neighbors did what they could to help themselves but it was several days before most could leave home. A strip of the new Highway 83 just north of Stapleton was graded high enough above the nearby land that it blew clear of snow. A few of the neighboring rancher pilots shoveled their planes out, flew to town and landed on the snow-free highway, ready to help their neighbors.

The storm covered a lot of the Midwest but the heaviest snowfall and drifts seemed to be in the northwestern two-thirds of Nebraska and especially the Sandhills. In Lincoln, classes began on schedule after the Christmas-New Year vacation. But it was not business as usual at the Alpha Gamma Rho (AGR) fraternity house. A lot of our members were from the heart of the Snow Belt—the western half of the state. One by one they began to show up for classes. Jim Monahan hired a pilot to pick him up, along with a couple of other students from the Hyannis area of the Sandhills, and fly them to Lincoln as soon as the weather cleared.

As the severity of the storm became known nationwide, *Life* magazine photographers headed for blizzard headquarters looking for damage, dead cattle or whatever they could find to make gripping pictures. Our county was one of the hardest hit, with drifted snow but only two head of cattle were confirmed dead from the storm. It was ironic that Wayne Salisbury had purchased two new bulls and put them in the barn for protection when he heard the storm was coming. This was the new barn, the best in the county. After the storm he went to the barn to check on his new high-priced bulls. The barn was almost airtight, but enough snow blew in through the tiny cracks to drift absolutely full of snow to the peak. They dug out the new bulls and found them dead—the only cattle killed in our county as a direct result of the storm. They had suffocated inside the barn, filled to the rafters with fine flakes of drifted snow.

Hurricanes, drought, sandstorms, blizzards and extreme cold snaps are not high on your list of fun things but they have one thing in common. They do not often include thunder-and-lightning storms. There is little thunder and lightning in California. Tornados are most at home in the Midwest and develop in severe thunderstorms. I have never been caught within a few hundred yards of "ground zero" of a tornado but I have been too close for comfort to several and I never saw a dry one. They all followed or were closely co-mingled with heavy rain and thunderstorms loaded with active lightning strikes and deafening thunder claps.

There's an old saying that "lightning never strikes twice in the same place." Don't you believe it. All our buildings in Nebraska had lightning rods with cables to ground any strikes. We had a "lightning hill" of 4 or 5 acres in our south pasture fenced to keep cattle out during thunderstorm months after three cattle were killed on that knoll over several years. Many other ranches had done the same. Lightning does strike in the same place twice, or even more, in many cases. If you noticed that I have not included earthquakes in this comment on natural phenomena, it is because storm clouds do not gather in advance of an earthquake. Some people believe that animals change behavior just before a quake but predicting is not taught in college, the weather bureau has not learned to predict a quake and the art is still less accepted than water witching. Some day we may learn to predict when an earthquake will strike, but not yet. People who study earthquakes, animal behavior and tea leaves still have open-ended job opportunities.

A Pile of Bulls

The Union Pacific branch line ended in Stapleton. The train turned around in Bob Baskin's pasture. Bob discovered credit and bought every ranch near him that he could finance, just before WWII. Prices rose and he became the biggest rancher in the area along with having a nice financial statement and credit for being very smart. The note was coming due on a small ranch he had purchased and for the moment he was strapped for cash. Since breeding season was over, he decided he could sell his bulls and get enough money to make the payment.

He ordered some cattle cars and herded the bulls to the railroad stockyards. In a small town—and ours was really small—this was a big event. By the time they got all the bulls in the stockyards, a fair crowd of idlers and local experts had assembled to see the excitement. In spite of the help, they got one car loaded and started on the second car when the bulls began to get unhappy with being crowded. They finally got the second car loaded and shut the door. The engineer pulled the train up to where the third door was abeam of the loading chute. Just as they began loading the third car, the bulls in the first two cars really got unruly.

Everybody in town knew John Collier, the long-time depot agent. They were amazed that he, a man of average size, could pick up a 10-gallon can of cream in each hand, deftly swinging and lifting each, one at a time, from the ground to the platform of the freight wagons at the depot. He handled the telegrams and delivered messages along with freight tickets as routine items. This day he had to improvise.

Nothing would quiet the bulls on the two cars and their bellowing upset the ones yet to be loaded. John had an idea and ran up to the engine for a visit with the engineer, who then built up a head of steam and hit the throttle. The cars jerked and clanged, then began to roll forward, shaking the footing under the two carloads of bulls, and hopefully shaking their confidence.

He ran forward a few car lengths, then locked all the brakes on the train, piling the bulls against and on top each other at the front of the cars. Then he built the steam up and put the train in reverse, restacking the pile of bulls in the other end of the cars. When he finally stopped the train with the door of the next empty cattle car in front of the loading chute, those bulls stood frozen and shaking as the rest of the bulls went aboard, and out of town with the evening train.

Visitors From the North

I was curious about my Canadian relatives at an early age but I had little ability to imagine what, if any difference, there might be between "us" and "them." I knew that we had bad winters in Nebraska but things were worse in Canada, unless our relatives exaggerated. I remember a letter that Grandma got from one of her sisters in January saying the weather had been fine. It was cold at night but it got up to zero nearly every afternoon and, if you looked up in the sky at noon, you could almost see the sun above the blowing, shifting snow.

Travel, communications and expectations changed a lot from 1938 to the 21st century. Long distance phone calls were all made manually with live, flesh-and-blood people pushing a "jack" to connect your local line into one of the long distance lines. You turned the crank on your wall-mounted telephone to reach the "central" operator in your town. Then another operator connected your call to a "central" operator in a major city and another operator connected that to the next major city, etc. It could easily take 10 to 15 minutes to reach a person who lived a few states away.

Calls to, or from, Canada were only made in case of dire emergency. A sick person would generally be either dead or recovered before a letter arrived. Travel was by train or auto until the 1940s, when the Greyhound bus began to offer connections not on the railroad track. Road-building on a big scale would have to wait until after World War II. Road maps of the era showed Highway 92 reaching from Omaha, at Nebraska's eastern border on the Missouri River, westward nearly 250 miles to Broken Bow. That part had been paved. But the signs continued along a dirt road with graveled surface for about 55 more miles to Stapleton and along a graded dirt road for 27 more to Tryon. It continued another 40 miles to Arthur except that it was a two-lane trail from Tryon to Arthur. No, the Greyhound did not come to Arnold, Stapleton, Tryon or Arthur. We were "frontier." Incidentally, Highway 92 was paved all the way to Arthur by the turn of the century.

Except for the brief visit by a few relatives for my Grandpa's funeral, I met the first of my Canadian relatives during the summer of 1938. It was the

Canadian relatives pay a visit to us in Stapleton (1937). Back row, l-r: Great-Aunt Lou Kerfoot, my Grandma Raynard, Clarence Windsor, Great-Aunt Mina Windsor, Mabel Windsor holding my baby sister Barbara, my mom holding my brother Rowdy, my Grandpa Raynard, my dad, and me. Front row, l-r: my brothers Dick and Jack, Great-Aunt Edie Masson, Keith Windsor, with my Uncle Bill Raynard seated in front.

summer after my freshman year in high school. I had lived with Grandma and Grandpa Raynard, doing chores for my room and keep, to be near enough to the school bus route that I could go to high school. Grandpa had been ailing with heart trouble and died before the year was out. This brought a new agenda for our family. We became partners with Grandma in the farming operation; Grandma and Uncle Bill moved to the little red house in the cottonwood grove and our family moved into the big house.

I do not remember how many Canadian relatives came for Grandpa's funeral. They arrived and left while I was busy at school or doing chores so I barely saw them. I was just a 13-year-old school kid. But the next summer we had a truck-full of family visiting Grandma. Headed by Aunt Edie and Aunt Lu, Grandma's sisters, we had a load of Manitobans. Aunt Edie had been widowed for several years but her four children, Harold, Beth, Marjorie and Hugh, (in birth order) made the trip. Harold was farming and he had a nearly new Ford truck that they converted into a 1930s substitute for a van for the trip, alternated drivers and drove straight through from Pilot Mound, Manitoba to Stapleton, Nebraska. The group included Mel Andrews, whose sister had lived with Grandma and gone to high school in Stapleton some years earlier after her mother died. I do not remember her very well but she was about Aunt Lil's age and I was fascinated that she owned and played the musical instrument of the day, a mandolin.

We were harvesting rye with a horse-drawn grain binder, which cut the stalks of grain, tied them into bundles, then toted several bundles on a carrier until the operator tripped it, dumping the bundles in a windrow. The grain was cut before the kernels were fully dried so we stood the bundles on end in

Four horses on the grain binder harvesting rye. The binder automatically cut the stalks, sized the bundle, tied it with "binder twine" and kicked the new bundle into a carrier to be dropped into windrows by operator. No more need for scythe harvesting. Photo courtesy of J.C. Allen & Sons, "rural life" photographers of W. Lafayette, Indiana.

teepee-shaped "shocks" in the field so the grain would dry. It might be a few days or several weeks until the shocked bundles were hauled to the thresher, which flailed, shook and fanned the grain out of the heads, separating the grain from the straw, then blew the straw into a pile while elevating the newly threshed grain into a bin. Harvesting small grains, such as rye and wheat, generally began around the first of July in our area, just at the peak of the summer heat. Harvesting and shocking the grain meant walking through the fields from windrow to windrow. It also meant handling the bundles with bare or gloved hands since nobody had figured how to stand the bundles on end in the fields with pitch forks. Nobody, that is, except our Canadian cousins. Once we got the hang of shocking bundles with a fork from them, our efficiency went up and stoop labor gave way to the more modern method meaning the laborer could shock more grain and was less tired by evening.

Uncle Bill, our hired man that summer, worked with the Canadian cousins to finish shocking our fields in record time, then hired out earning vacation money from our neighbors. A difference in terminology entered the scene, however. When we arranged the bundles in shocks by hand, we called it "shocking" grain. When they did it using pitch forks, they called it "stooking." Neither we nor they knew why. And before the community changed to using forks as a common way to harvest, combines came along. Combines are machines that cut the grain, then threshed it in the same operation, putting the grain in an onboard grain bin while blowing the straw on the ground. It was more efficient for harvesting grain but it was the end of the straw pile that was such a nostalgic asset, especially on ranches with livestock operations.

Brother Jack and Beamy Christiansen

My brother Jack was born with a "Beamy Christiansen" complex, or if not born, it was acquired early in life. Beamy was everybody's friend. This sometimes meant not straining for high goals or expectations. He made few demands and was accepting of his lot in life. This was a wonderful character trait for this imaginary person from our play world—my brother Jack, three years my junior, and me. Beamy was, I think, Jack's alter ego. I have no idea where Jack got the name—he was only 7 or 8 years old at the time—but it was fitting. In his life, Jack was a friend to almost anybody who needed or wanted a friend. He was never judgmental. On rare occasions he might not make himself available to certain people but he was generally accepting of any friend, rich or poor, warts and all.

And who was Beamy Christiansen and why did we need him? Brother Jack and I had a real, if imaginary ranch, in a clearing in the middle of a wild plum thicket at the end of the cherry orchard that we entered by crawling some 15 to 20 feet on our bellies under the brush. This tended to make it our exclusive domain. We each had our imaginary owners of this hidden Shangri-La. Mine was Lloyd Lowell (don't ask me where I got the name; it just happened, but Mr. Lowell was nearly Mister Perfect, who I later saw as the person my mother wanted her first born to be). Lloyd had gone to the best schools, owned acres and acres of the best soil in Nebraska, was knowledgeable on many subjects. The livestock on his imaginary ranch were the best. He had a new truck to haul whatever needed to be bought or sold. But not Beamy! He was Mister Everyman. He had a used pickup truck with several dents and many miles, a copy of most of our neighbors. Fortunately, we never had to explain how these totally different people happened to be partners on this ranch within the plum thicket.

And was it, you may ask, a real ranch? You bet your life! We even had a sizeable barn, made from the lumber that came disguised as a packing crate for the new cream separator—fully planed one-half inch by 4- or 6-inch white pine boards. We carefully disassembled the crate and sneaked every board into our ranch in the middle of the plum thicket like we got everything else in to the ranch, by crawling in on our bellies with the prized possession, where we reassembled the shipping crate into a large barn (by our measurements) with haymow above the stalls and stanchions in the "L" shaped dairy barn at one side of the main structure. Jack was three years younger but he was all I had.

Imagination? We had no source for real model horses and cattle so Jack's imagination settled it: Corn cobs! A few shucks still attached to make a tail meant it was a horse. No shucks meant it was a cow. Our dad allegedly raised the best red-cob white corn in the area, which made for red cows and sorrel horses with white manes and tails. When colors

Phil (standing) with brother Jack (seated) for Christmastime photo when Jack was nearly 2 years old, Phil nearly 5 years old.

faded with time and weather we could trade for fresh ones that hadn't been exposed to weather. And what happened to Beamy and Lloyd? They were probably casualties of World War II. I don't remember that either went to war nor that either came home after the war. As per the song made famous in its regeneration by General MacArthur upon his retirement, "Old soldiers never die, they just fade away." Only their memory remains.

Maybe My Grandpa Lived in the "Dark Ages"!

Both of my grandfathers were horsemen. That is a loose description that nearly compares with the statement of today that they both drove cars. My Grandpa Brothers was born in Iowa in 1856. His given name was Dennis, but he was known to everyone as Den. His reputation as a horseman followed him when he left the family settlement near Marshalltown, Iowa, in 1890 to travel west and homestead in Logan County in the Sandhills area of central Nebraska. He was known as a horse trainer and horseman with a magic touch, not unlike a gifted auto mechanic of today who could make the machine in question perform beyond the imagination of its maker. And his ability at both horse training and horse trading was allegedly the best. I remember a possibly jealous neighbor commenting, when I was a teenager, that "Den Brothers might have done better to spend more time farming and less time training horses." But he apparently made the best of his ability and, in those years, a man's ability as a horseman would compare with mechanical abilities of today's young men, their reputation and social success. Nobody ever told me if his accomplishments with horses helped him meet and marry my grandmother, whose family already lived in the area.

I never knew Grandpa Brothers. He was seriously ill when I was born in 1924 and nearly bedfast with what they called TB of the bone, allegedly from having had so many bones broken by horse training mishaps. But as the story goes, and possibly was improved with re-telling, he always wanted Baby Philip put in bed beside him when we visited. He died when I was only a few months old so my knowledge of him and his abilities is only hearsay. I remember having seen a snapshot many years ago of me lying on the bed with my bedridden Grandpa. I hope that some family member can furnish a copy for my memory bank. If, as claimed by his doctor, his ailment was not contagious, it might explain why none of my younger siblings, born after Grandpa died, caught "horse fever," like I did, preferring horses to tractors.

Grandpa Raynard was born 13 years later, in 1869, in Ontario, Canada but the family moved to a farming area in southwest Manitoba, just across the U.S./Canadian border from North Dakota. They later left Canada to homestead in Keya Paha County in northern Nebraska in 1898, where my dad was born, then moved to Idaho, where Grandpa worked as a sawmill mechanic, craftsman and maintenance man with the Potlatch Lumber Co. at the lumber town of Bovill, in big timber country east of Moscow. After a few years (in 1906) the family moved back to Nebraska. This time they took up another homestead on a property that touched the Brothers claim. He broke virgin sod and raised corn and rye and later, alfalfa, like the neighbors who were settling the area. He eventually grew his homestead to a thousand contiguous acres that included several hundred acres of excellent nearly level soil that produced good yields of alfalfa.

Grandpa Raynard was also a horseman but he made no claim to matching his neighbor, Den Brothers, for horse magic. However, I remember his telling me one day of a driving team he had—a pair of matched Hambletonians named Floss and Tony—that regularly trotted the 8 miles from the farm to town rarely breaking gait. Then he added, almost embarrassed that I could think he was bragging, that "they might have been

100

the best driving team in the area" (imagine the substitution of an expensive convertible to put it in today's terms).

But Grandpa Raynard's genius was in the shop. He could work with his hands and he could see possibilities unimagined by many people. He once told me that he could always "fix things." This was the talent that got him the job with Potlatch Lumber Co. and, while examples were all over the ranch, you might have to be told that the tongs in his blacksmith shop were "homemade," as was the wooden tool chest and a full set of shaping planes with bits in the shape of many moldings used for trim in home construction. They all appeared to be fresh from the factory. He had built (or supervised the building of) all the barns, granary, shop and other farm outbuildings and even made the forms, then the blocks, from native sand, to build the cement-block ranch house. He imagined, then built, a culvert with bridge planks, in a cut of earth near the crest of a hill (and under a county road through the ranch) that was wide enough and high enough to drive cattle and horses, including a horse and rider, from a pasture south of the road, through the culvert, and into the large corral at the headquarters. Almost anyone else would have had gates on both sides of the road to open and close with every trip, forever. Often-used corral gates hung by large hinges from railroad tie posts with a wheel holding up the outer end that allowed for easily rolling the gate open and shut.

I was not old enough or mature enough during the lifetime of either grandfather to even think of the question, much less ask it, regarding their choice of livestock breeds. My earliest memory of the Brothers cowherd was of red and roan cattle, indicating that Shorthorns were the breed of choice. They were the popular dual-purpose cattle of that era, meaning that even if they produced a good carcass at the butcher shop, the females gave a pretty good pail full of high-butterfat milk—good for the farmer who marketed cream. But the Raynard cowherd had some black-and-white, blue roan and other exotic exceptions to the red and roan color pattern. I once saw the breed registration papers of a purebred Holstein bull he had owned, and Grandpa Raynard, as I recall, even had a few sheep. But above all his selection of livestock, I remember that he always had someone living in the two-bedroom hired man's house. I don't remember ever seeing my Grandpa harness or drive a team of draft horses. The hired man—and he had good ones—always did the field work while Grandpa was planning, building or fixing things.

Both of my grandfathers saw automation begin with the steam engine replacing teams that turned a shaft in a circle to furnish the power needed to grind grain, bale hay and perform the processing needed for farm operations. The first mechanical threshers and corn shellers were run with large steam engines. Miniaturization of the "steamers" made them suitable for field work, followed a few years later by gasoline- and diesel-powered tractors. Grandpa Brothers never owned a tractor but his son, my Uncle Hank, made the switch to tractors. He had a Fordson that permanently sat at the granary to furnish belt power in grinding grain for livestock feed and he was among our first neighbors to have a John Deere tractor for field work.

Hank liked horsepower but he just didn't share his father's attraction to horses. Grandpa Raynard was a holdout, never owning a tractor. He died in 1938. My dad finally bought a used John Deere that we used for field work, especially plowing, and it had a detachable power mower that was a real speed demon when it came to cutting hay in the alfalfa fields and on the native pasture hills, compared with horse-drawn mowers. I know because I rode a horse-drawn dump rake for many miles, making windrows of the newly mowed grass that the tractor-mounted mower had cut and laid down. I appreciated what the tractor could do but I never liked it and always did the horse work while I was at home. Brother Jack, even though he wanted to be a cowboy in his early years, adopted the tractor and, to my eternal joy, was always first in line for it and all motorized equipment, making it easy for me to use and enjoy our good teams of horses.

My grandfathers both lived to see the invention of the airplane, but neither ever rode in one. I didn't really ever know my Grandpa Brothers and I never thought to ask anyone what he would have thought about the new inventions and the way they changed our lives but I got the idea that both my grandfathers would have accepted them as inevitable and mostly as desirable. It would probably not have enticed either to try it. But I am sure neither would have been surprised that I was the first in either family to have a pilot's license or even to fly, not because I was a daredevil or future-seeking youngster, but simply because I was born at an appropriate time for such activity. Grandpa Brothers never lived to talk on a telephone.

Both families (Grandpa Raynard had a big console radio from my earliest memory) learned to take the telephone and phonograph in stride. Both were among the first in the neighborhood with electric power, when, in the 1920s, they each bought 32-volt Delco power plants with the long row of storage batteries and wired the barns, outbuildings and the houses. Grandpa Raynard was a beekeeper with several hives at the end of the cherry and plum orchard near the alfalfa fields. He also had a cider press and every fall the extended family would gather to pick apples and squeeze out the juice, storing the barrels of cider in the cool of the cement storm cellar. Neither ever saw television nor a cell phone. I don't know if either grandfather was a hunter but neither, to my knowledge, even owned a gun. Not true of my grandmother Raynard. She was reputed to be a keen shot, at least in her early life, using a single-shot rifle to bring in an occasional grouse or pheasant for the dinner table.

I never heard my Grandpa Raynard, nor Grandma either for that matter, make a negative remark about any of the neighbors or relatives. If they had a disagreement with anybody it was kept to themselves as far as I ever knew and I had some opportunity to overhear their comments since I lived with them during my first year of high school. Small wonder that Grandpa, both discreet and thrifty, was re-elected county commissioner (supervisor) by his neighbors, year after year, to spend the county's tax money. He might make a diplomatic comment about a possible difference of opinion with someone but never a direct challenge or attack.

This was not true for my Grandma Brothers. She had her personal rating service for all the neighbors and most family members, including her own children and grandchildren. Your standing could be worse or better by the week, depending on her latest report. She was often vocally critical of neighbors, friends and family, including my dad, which often embarrassed other family members, but I do not recall hearing or knowing of her ever being critical of my Raynard grandparents. Maybe, as longtime neighbors, they were immune from the perils of Grandma Brothers' scorn. And the old adage about "voting with your feet" was obvious when I asked to do chores for room and board with Grandma Raynard so I could ride the bus to high school, but I never asked to stay with Grandma Brothers, even though the farms were side-by-side on the school bus route.

A Lesson in Multiplication

Our summer pasture joined Edgar Fowler's. We shared a well and the large stock water tank sat with half on each side of the fence. The Fowler family had come from Texas a few years earlier and brought a herd of cattle with them. Not only were they Herefords, the red beef cattle with white faces and other body markings, they were Anxiety 4th Hereford cattle. Airtight Anxiety 4th. This meant that these cattle were closely line bred descendants of the sire that helped found the Hereford breed, never introducing any blood that did not trace to the old bull. Cult followers are not new.

How is a kid in the isolated Nebraska Sandhills going to know whether Anxiety 4th cattle were better than any others? I barely knew what a "purebred" was. My high school ag teacher said a herd could be improved by using purebred bulls, which seemed a fair recommendation. And I knew that I had just been given an opportunity to get in the purebred cattle business by our neighbor and I didn't want to let it get away.

Fowlers had purchased a new bull, test-bred him to a few cows but didn't think the offspring (two heifers and a few bulls) fit the "pattern" of their cattle. I thought they were his best two heifers. Through the summer of my second year in high school, we visited often about how I could buy the two heifers. I had a heifer that had been given me as a Christmas present the previous year. I had a sow and her eight pigs as an FFA project. I might get a little more than $100 for the whole outfit so I finally got Edgar to agree to sell me the heifers for $50 apiece at weaning time, if I could raise the money.

We made the deal. At that time, the mother must be at least 26 or 27 months of age for the Hereford Association to register her calf. To keep the heifers away from bulls until they were 18 months old, we kept two fences between them (with other heifers) and any bull and I checked them every day. It had to be a virgin birth because there was never a bull in the heifer field and never a heifer got out. But one of my heifers gave birth to a nice heifer calf (ineligible for registry) just before she was 24 months old. That year we bred both heifers. They both had heifer calves in the spring of my first year in college. But the plot thickens.

The Japanese bombed Pearl Harbor on December 7, 1941, during my first year in college. I had to register for the draft after my birthday in February, 1942 and at college we began discussing our preferences and possibilities in the military. I decided that Naval Aviation was the hardest to get into, so I'd try that. If I couldn't make it, the Army Air Corps was next hardest, etc. I was accepted by the Navy and my dad agreed to keep my cattle while I was in the service—for half the bull calves. I knew it was a sucker deal. They had not produced a bull calf at this time and this was sure to change, but it was the best offer I had.

Those original heifers plus the one born to the 2-year-old mother gave me three more calves in the spring of 1943, five produced heifers in the spring of 1944 so I had 13 females by the time I got my Navy wings in September 1944 and went to Operational training. The spring of 1945 brought eight more calves, all females, for a total of 21 head by the time the war was over. The Navy kept me on duty in the Philippines and Hawaii until the summer of 1946. This was a contribution my dad made to the war effort with little return. But payday came in 1946.

My Hereford females had 13 calves in the spring of 1946 but eight were bulls. He finally had four bulls for payment after feeding that whole outfit for four years. And my herd had grown to 26 females. But almost stranger than the all-female production for five years is the fact that the original cow that calved as a 2-year-old without ever being seen with a bull, produced nine females in nine years that all looked just like her and nobody ever saw her breed or even be in heat. I'll never try to convince you that she "selfed" or reproduced without a male contact but you didn't check those heifers at least once every day during the summer of 1940 like I did. I still wonder about that, but I know for sure that Anxiety 4ths can multiply.

Real Money

I didn't know that I was through growing when I was a sophomore in high school. Some people explained it by saying I "matured young." I was able to do a man's work at 14 or 15 and in our family I had full opportunity to prove it. We had a sandy soil that was allegedly good for growing rye. I never knew if such was the case—or perhaps it just wasn't much good for wheat. With either, if you had any kind of a crop, you had to harvest it.

Harvesting grain in our area was done in a three-stage operation. First it was cut with a "binder" that cut the stalks and gathered them in bundles, the machine automatically tied them with "binder twine" and kicked the bundles

Threshing grain from "bundle racks." Running a "rack" was hard work, as the operator loaded dozens of bundles from shocks in the field to fill the rack, then the team pulled the load to the threshing machine (grain separator) where the operator pitched the bundles, one at a time, into a hopper. The machine then sorted the grain from the straw, sending the grain into a wagon and blowing the straw into a pile, a favored material for bedding livestock stalls in winter. We raised rye, which did better than wheat in our sandy soil. Straw is also good "low nutrient" livestock feed. Several neighbors exchanged work to get the 8 or 10 hay racks on the job so there would always be two loaded, ready to unload (one bundle from each rack at a time) into the threshing machine's "hopper." The expression "They eat like threshers," came from watching the threshing crewmen dig into high-energy farm food at noon and evening meals plus mid-morning and mid-afternoon lunches. Photo courtesy of J.C. Allen & Sons.

onto a carrier, and the operator dropped them in rows. Then workers arranged the bundles into shocks, where the grain dried. Later, the grain would be threshed or separated from the straw by large threshing machines.

Threshing was a community event. The neighbors exchanged work, helping each other on what was called a "threshing run" that sometimes ran several weeks and included eight or 12 farms. It took from eight to 12 racks (depending on distance from field to thresher), each pulled by a team of horses. The team and wagon with bundle rack went from shock to shock with the operator alongside on foot, loading the shocks onto the rack until it was filled. Then the teams pulled the loads to the thresher where the drivers unloaded, two racks at a time. The grain separator or threshing machine was placed where the farmer wanted a giant straw pile to be located. The thresher had a feeder where two hayrack loads, one on each side, could unload at once with the driver unloading the bundles, one at a time with a pitch fork, into the feeder. The threshed grain was augured to a waiting wagon and hauled to a storage bin. The straw was blown by a giant fan out a blower into a straw pile to be used later for feed or bedding. This was man's work. We worked long days. The expression "they ate like threshers" came from watching the threshing crew consume food, prepared by a kitchen full of neighborhood women, at mealtime.

It was the summer after my high school sophomore year. Our obligation on the run was ending Thursday. Dewey Fattig asked me if I could work for him as our run ended and it moved to the next neighbor. He wanted to go fishing on Friday and Saturday. I told him I'd ask my dad. Dad asked how much I would get paid. "Dewey said $5 a day with my team, $3 with his team. He wanted to give his team a rest." Dad said, "Well, I guess it's OK if you want to, but that sounds like an awful lot of money." He was right. Dewey gave me a $10 bill. It was the first one I ever earned.

Melons Are Ripe

Lewis Mitchell was a good farmer in our area—a pillar of the community in the eyes of most—when I was growing up. Mitchells had no children but raised three boys as their sons. After the boys were grown and gone, Lewis apparently had a case of "empty nest" syndrome. He had always planted watermelons in the cornfield on the south side of the highway, just beyond the corral east of his house. The melons were always several rows away from the road so nobody knew they were there unless they had inside information. I don't know how the word got around from generation to generation, but high school boys knew "where." Lewis told us "when." He ran a six-word ad in the Stapleton Enterprise: "Boys, melons are ripe. L.C. Mitchell."

We never knew if the girls also knew and played dumb about the whole affair, but it could be one of the more exciting Saturday night events in our normally boring community. I have heard that young folks in the New England states steal "roasting ears," ears of corn at the right stage for roasting over an open fire, then consuming same with assorted beverages.

Corn was no big deal in Stapleton. We stole watermelons . . . two or three couples, or sometimes there would be two or three carloads of kids in the party. We told the girls how risky it was and what a mean old farmer this Mitchell guy was, but the melons were worth it. We drove the last few

106

hundred yards with the headlights off—so we wouldn't alert the farmer. Then we parked at the edge of the road and slipped through the fence and into the cornfield.

The first male to reach the melons always *sshished* in a loud whisper, "Over here." After sorting and thumping to detect the proper ripeness, we'd pick a melon for each couple. The leader of the raid would have an uncontrolled cough and immediately the lights went on in the Mitchell house. The door opened and the raiding party heard clearly in the otherwise still night, "Who's there?"

Of course, there was never an answer. The door closed and the lights went off. It made a good show and it was an effective, if countrified way, to impress the girls. If you wanted to make a really deep impression, you "inadvertently" ticked the car horn while you were getting out of the car. You apologized to the girls while reassuring them that you were too far from the house for the farmer to hear.

If you followed this ritual (with the car horn), the group got the melons picked and ready to return to the car and the leader coughed as usual. Then, after the lights came on, instead of asking "Who's there," a deafening BANG! as Lewis fired his shotgun in the air. I don't know the medical or politically correct term for it but even when you know it's coming, the noise from a shotgun blast makes your pulse quicken on a dark night.

One fall I was home from college for a weekend. A friend had arranged a double date for us with two teachers new in town. After mollifying their misgivings about "stealing," the date proceeded until the shotgun fired. The girls ran through the corn in panic. It took us at least a half hour to find the girls and get them out of the field and back in the car. After we got them "quieted down" and reassured that our "aggressive" farmer was safely back in bed, the girls would not let us go back in the field to retrieve the melons without several minutes of reassurance. You can be sure we never told them the rest of the story.

The Right Place at the Right Time

I had made a deal with my grandparents to do chores for my room and board while going to high school. We lived several miles from the bus route which made the idea of going to high school impossible. The bus went a quarter of a mile from Grandma's house on the outbound route and a mile from the house an hour later when it returned on the road to town. Since you can do a lot of chores—or get a little sleep—in that time, I ran the mile and caught the in-bound bus except on the days with the worst weather.

New frontiers bring new problems. At home, I had never needed money since I had no opportunity to spend any. We went to town most Saturdays to ship the 10-gallon cans of cream on the train to the creamery in Minnesota.

We also took the case of eggs we had gathered during the week which we "traded" to the grocery store for groceries. The grocer put a small paper bag of hard candy in the corner of the egg case along with the groceries.

I was the oldest child so I often got to take the trip, but did not like sweets so I always took the candy home and hid it behind the desk, until my little brother found my cache and made himself sick, but that's another story. The whole family also went to North Platte once a year in the fall to collect the money when we sold the turkeys and did the family fall shopping. We knew we didn't have money to spend in either trip off the farm, so we didn't need money, as kids, because we had no chance to spend it.

But now I was going to high school. I was in town every day. A town with a population of more than 300 people and several stores was just full of opportunities to spend money. And high school kids need the kind of stuff those stores sold. But my parents told me when I left home to go to school that they would buy my clothes but I was on my own otherwise. That meant no money. As my good fortune, a few weeks after school started, the preacher notified the parishioners who attended the Sunday Church services at our country schoolhouse that he could no longer arrive early to build fires in the schoolhouse. I needed to earn money so I told them I would build the fires on Sundays if they would pay me.

They volunteered to pay 25 cents per Sunday and since I hadn't yet learned to "bargain" I had my first job for money. I had to get up at 4 a.m. and hike nearly a mile to the school in winter cold, but I had the first real spending money in my life. And in 1936 you could actually buy things for 25 cents. A Hershey bar cost a nickel. A bag of mints or a pack of gum was a nickel. A pair of athletic socks for football practice cost 60 cents. What more could a new high school student want from a job?

Salisbury Steak

Ed Salisbury was not really a cattle baron but he was a pretty influential guy in our town. He had two fairly large ranches, owned half of the International Harvester machinery dealership and a chunk of stock in the Bank of Stapleton. But I think he made a big part of his income doing the job he did best—as an order buyer of cattle. And like most successful people, Ed had good connections and willing accomplices.

I don't know how many landmark clients he had around the area but my dad was Exhibit A in the area west of Stapleton. Our ranch was that awkward size. We were either the biggest of the little ranchers or the smallest of the big ones. Our management probably had much to be desired but at least we grouped our calving dates so most of our weanlings were about the same size—important if you expect to get top price.

108

At market time, Ed came to our place first. He would make almost any deal to buy our calves. We had livestock scales and checked weights on our stock several times during the year, especially before weaning time, and went to the sale barn a few times to see what similar stock was bringing. We tried to be ready for him. But one way or another, he bought our calves, at a good price. Then my dad bragged about the price to everyone—just what Ed wanted. He verified both the fact that Ed had made the deal and the price ceiling for the season.

Then he went up and down the road buying neighbors' calves. He'd tell them, "you have a few calves just as good as Harvey's (my dad). He'd offer them the same price he'd paid for ours—for maybe a fourth of their string. Then he'd dock the price a few cents a pound for some that were too big and a few cents for the ones that were too small, etc. Then they would brag to the neighbors that Ed had paid them "the same price as Harvey's."

He would be right on the market price for the select few, but make an extra $5 or $10 per head on the others. When he matched them with others the same size and color, they sold just fine with no penalty. Ed cultivated his friendship with cattle raisers, remembered their names and often reminded them of the shrewd deals they had made with him, true or not.

I haven't seen it used so much recently but for many years, hamburger steak on restaurant menus all over the country was called "Salisbury steak." As one who grew up and saw our cattle sell to Logan County's No. 1 Cattle Buyer, I automatically assumed that it was named after Ed. Now I wonder how many other things I knew that weren't true. After all, if you can't believe in a Salisbury steak, what can you really depend on?

All in Good Time

Not long after I graduated from high school, my Aunt Lil (dad's youngest sister) wrote to me from her fairly new job as a County Home Demonstration Agent in Hawaii and said that she and her sister, Marge, wanted to get a watch for me as a graduation present. Did I want a pocket watch or a wrist watch? And she had good reason to ask.

This was 1941, when real men mostly still used pocket watches. A lot of men with town jobs like jewelers, pharmacists, store clerks and schoolteachers were getting wrist watches but it was mostly men in the cities. Stapleton store owners, mailmen, auctioneers, cattle traders, bankers and, of course, farmers, were not ready to do anything so un-masculine as to be the first in their town to wear a wrist watch.

I remember a representative for a farm machinery company who got his car stuck in the sand when he came upon our cattle drive. He was wearing a wrist watch—one of the first people working in a rural or agriculture-based job that I remember as wearing a wrist watch. Since I haven't ridden on a train for many years, I don't know if conductors still carry pocket "railroad" watches but they certainly had to be the last to change if, in fact, they have.

The offer of a graduation present was a pleasant surprise. I had no quick decision for Aunt Lil because I sensed this was an important moment. I didn't want to be too avant-garde and be laughed at by my neighbors for picking a wrist watch, nor too conventional in asking for a pocket watch if wrist watches were indeed to be the watch of the future.

I considered the decision from as many angles as I could, with my limited ability to anticipate the future. I knew I was going to college. I knew I would be working to earn the money to stay in school but I didn't know what kind of work I would be doing. Would I be better off with a wrist or pocket watch? Then, almost out of the blue, the decision was obvious. There would always be somebody around with a watch. I could ask what time it was.

What if my job had an early morning schedule? Who would see that I was awake to get to work on time? I may have been the only graduate in the world to request one, but the watch I needed for a graduation present was an alarm clock. They bought the best Baby Ben they could find and it kept me on time for more than a year before I went in the Navy—and for a good many more after the war . . . when I got home to reclaim it from the closet.

Talk about a "practical" gift; what more could a graduate want from a timepiece? Maybe it wasn't sexy but it was an "enabler." It enabled me to show up for work on time whether that meant 4 a.m. to run an early morning milk route or a job that fell into a more conventional time frame. And it solved another problem—the "watch" decision. By the time the Baby Ben had quit being dependably 'alarming' every morning, the wrist watch had caught on and sent most pocket watches to retirement but people still get up to the r-r-r-ring of a Baby Ben.

Not Ready for Prime Time

My Grandma Brothers, as a teenager, had been a housekeeper at Buffalo Bill Cody's Scout's Rest Ranch near North Platte, where he frequently visited, but it was his daughter's residence. Grandpa came to Logan County from Iowa. He was a horseman and horse trainer. My mother was the third of four daughters in her family. Her only brother and the family's first-born, my Uncle Hank, became the family's "hired man" after his father died when I was a few months old. Pearl was the oldest girl and was apparently the "hired girl" while Helen, the next born, paired with my mother, Eunice, in work and play. Edna was the baby of the family and the most spirited of the lot. My mother finished high school and attended a year at "Normal" school in teacher preparation. Edna, who took Home Economics at the University of Nebraska, was the first and only one to graduate from a full four-year college. I believe that was in 1927. Pearl and Helen generally went to church

110

but their parents were not dedicated churchgoers. My mother was the only go-to-church-three-times-a-week member of the family—a quiet but dedicated religious zealot.

My Grandpa Raynard came to the United States from Canada to homestead as the head of a young family. Lyndall had been born in Canada and Hazel shortly after they immigrated. My dad was next and the first son. I don't know what had influenced him but Grandpa was an Orangeman, an anti-Catholic group in action to this day in Northern Ireland. I seem to remember a comment from my dad at some early date that he was sorry he couldn't be an Orangeman. I don't know why, maybe there was no local club. He was, however, a Catholic hater and member of the Ku Klux Klan. I never asked why and he never told me. I remember finding his white robe while probing in a dresser drawer when I was in the early grades. I was known in the late 1920s and early '30s when I was 6 to 9 years old as "Spook Raynard's Bright Son."

I never knew whether my dad was really as religious as my mother was, or as she wanted him to be, but he went along with the game. They seemed to have a negative attitude about most of our neighbors on many issues but they joined with the ones they most often criticized and the most religious of the lot, in keeping the renegade non-denominational country church service going. In retrospect I can see they were an austere, puritanical group. Nobody in this little group would attend a dance or a movie, which were both "evil," as were smoking, drinking and associating with people who did. The women generally wore dark and plain clothing with no style when I was young . . . and no makeup. My mother had naturally wavy hair. I have no idea how she convinced the neighbors that she didn't go to a beauty parlor, also evil.

The totally rural area where my parents' families lived was just over 8 miles to Stapleton. The families gathered around the one-room Nesbit School with little in common except that they were all poor, all trying to raise families on what they could produce on sandy farms and none of the religious "rebels" wanting to join the Presbyterian church or worse yet, the Catholic church, in Stapleton. Most felt from tradition that they "should" have some religious influence in their lives so they rallied around the schoolhouse, giving a meager income from the Sunday collection to whatever otherwise unemployed preacher they could find.

I never knew whether it was part of the religious ritual or whether they were just charter subscribers to the "spare the rod and spoil the child" policy but I guess I was quite a disappointment to my mother, being her firstborn and unable to live up to her expectations. Since my dad shaved with a straight razor, I suppose it was natural that the razor strop became the weapon of choice for teaching their number one son what it took to be perfect. I have no idea when I got whipped for the first time, nor how many times it occurred. It was almost always more than once a week and sometimes almost every day. I got all A's on my report card but that wasn't good enough after I made the "mistake" of getting an A+. That treatment can jangle your nerves. Jack frequently got a few licks but I was often accused of not setting a good example for him and I got whipped for his less-than-desired behavior.

My mother was generally the one who carried out the punishment and she was the worst—often in a rage—but sometimes she would explain my offense to my dad and make him spank me. Finally, at age 11 or 12, I jerked the strop out of my mother's hand and told her that beating me didn't make me better and if she ever hit me with it again I would kill her. I don't know if I would or could have done it but I was at the end of my world and it was impossible for me to reason with her to neutralize her frustration that mostly did not include me except for punishment.

We didn't have much to talk about for a long time after that but I think she realized that I had good reason to do it and having physical maturity at an early age, I was probably big enough and strong enough to do it. In any case, the beatings stopped. I don't know if she ever regretted her conduct or if she gave a second thought to it. Neither of us ever mentioned it. None of the other kids in our family, to my knowledge, got much corporal punishment except a few times when Rolland got caught responding to baby sister Barbara's unseen teasing after I left home for college.

We were taught to say "thank you" but aside from that, neither of our parents gave any advice to any of the children, to my knowledge, about growing up or how to conduct ourselves with our neighbors or in the world around us or what to expect from others. Our parents rarely if ever told us how to act in public and if we were to learn anything about personal conduct it was when we were punished for doing wrong. Unfortunately we didn't know it was wrong until they handed out the punishment. We did ask questions a few times about various subjects but if it was a topic that our parents were sensitive about, instead of answering, they generally said "that's a stupid question" and I was smart enough to know I shouldn't ask it again.

We were pretty much alone in the world, left to learn from our observations but we rarely went any place outside our little protected community to see how other people lived, to get an objective view of things. I was aghast the first several times I saw grown people hug or kiss in public. I do not recall ever seeing any member of our family either hug or kiss anybody more than 2 years of age at any time, family member or friend, privately or in public, under any condition. We said "hello" and sometimes shook hands. Our little church group functioned a lot like Quakers or Amish—free from any outward sign of emotion. It takes a lot of discipline to respond normally after years of such inhibited conduct.

I had heard a good bit about high school from classmates and others in our country school by the time I got to the eighth grade but I hadn't been prepared for what to expect. Then shortly after the end of my eighth grade year my parents began telling me that I might have to delay going to high school. We lived more than 3 miles from the bus route and times were financially so hard that we couldn't afford to pay a hired man. They had decided that I would be the hired man until something changed to make more money for our family. I knew that my two classmates at Nesbit School were going and it seemed to me that almost everybody that I knew had gone to high school and, while I didn't know what to expect, I knew that I wanted to go. I had to find a way, by whatever means I could use.

It occurred to me that one of my cousins had done housework and stayed with Grandma to go to high school one year. She and Grandpa were getting older and might like to have someone do part of the chores and housework. Their house was only a mile to the bus route so if they agreed to my imaginary plan, I could go to high school. I felt that Grandma would be the easiest to sell so I approached her first. I didn't claim outright that it was my parents' idea but did explain that we had a problem, living so far from the bus, and sort of suggested that I was asking her, with their approval. She said that they had an empty bedroom and she could use some help. Maybe it would work out if Grandpa also needed help with his chores.

With this as leverage, I suggested to my parents that Grandma said they might want me to do chores for room and board so I could ride the school bus. As it turned out, neither my parents nor grandparents were great communicators and both took my word for it and I had made a deal that assured my going to high school. To my surprise, this turned out to be my first sales job. My parents never officially told me that I could stay with my grandparents, they just told me that they would buy my clothes, two new shirts and overalls, but could not give me any other money to spend. I knew they would keep their word about the money . . . and they did.

I was not told anything about what I could expect or how to conduct myself when I started to high school. Earl Dean Barner had been a neighbor and classmate for all my eight years at Nesbit School. Freida Fowler joined our class later so I knew at least two members of my high school freshman class when I got there and I had some cousins in the upper grades so I wasn't a total lostling, but our family had as little contact as possible with families outside our community. I was totally without guidance and generally without friends. I observed . . . and tried to follow the lead of my new classmates.

The worst crisis of my freshman year came about a month into the school year. The class voted for 10 cents class dues from every student. I had no dime and I didn't know where to get one. I knew I couldn't ask my parents for money. My grandparents sometimes left a few coins lying on top of the dresser in their bedroom but I wouldn't take money from them. They let me stay with them to go to school. I knew my parents wouldn't give me 10 cents and I couldn't face either asking my grandparents or stealing it. I considered dropping out of school but that would be shameful. I didn't know how I could face them if I dropped out and went home. I considered suicide, and as the deadline to pay our dues approached, I pondered the various ways and how long I could stall paying dues before I carried it out. Deadline was Friday. Running home from the bus on Thursday evening I saw something shiny on the graded dirt highway. I stopped to check it out. There was my dime, and just in time. I had flashbacks of this crisis for years.

The school bus route went a quarter of a mile from Grandma's house on its way out early in the morning and its late evening route back to town but it also got to a mile from the house later in the morning and earlier in the evening. I took the longer distance and practiced my mile run technique which gave me an extra half hour to sleep or do chores except on a few of the worst blizzardy winter days. I learned to get up in the morning and make my lunch. I already knew how to gather eggs, milk cows and feed livestock, which were part of my chores. I also got my first job a few months into the year, earning 25 cents a week for lighting a fire in the schoolhouse stove at 4 a.m. Sunday morning so it would be warm for church services later in the morning. I had a double win going for me. I was in high school and I now had 25 cents a week to spend.

I got good grades—all A's—except algebra. The first-year math teacher and I just couldn't get tuned to the same frequency. I was lucky to get a C-plus, the lowest grade I ever got in high school. But I wasn't having much fun. I did not know how to handle social situations. I had few people to observe except my dad, who was always negative in his comments about other people. Every person with German origin was a "kraut," Italians were "wops," everyone with religious affiliation other than his little country congregation were suspect and Catholics were evil. He was merciless in teasing anybody and everybody, especially the young couples of dating age who showed an interest in each other.

I silently admired a few neighborhood teens but everyone, at some time, fell victim to my father's slurs, which made me wonder just who and what could get his approval. I couldn't face the idea of my being the target of his spears but I couldn't imagine how to avoid them. Neither parent volunteered advice or even a suggestion of how I should conduct myself in public. They refused to give serious answers to my questions on what to expect and how to conduct myself in school. It was easy to learn what I shouldn't do but I couldn't get any positive input. I sometimes asked Grandma what I should do but she said she didn't know, she hadn't gone to high school.

I reached my physical maturity fairly young. My voice began to change in 7th grade; I reached my full height before I started to high school and had muscular development to do a man's work in most jobs. A few facial hairs became whiskers during that first year in high school but my dad had never talked about such a possibility, anything personal was taboo so I would never bring up the subject. I found an old straight razor of his that I honed until it was sharp enough to cut off my early crop of whiskers. Lucky because I had no money. I was a real ugly duckling, socially. And just as well. There were few possible social occasions and I had no money or ability to attend.

One day in late fall my dad told me that he heard I had walked downtown during the noon hour from the high school with some of the Catholic boys. He said he would prefer that I didn't associate with Catholics. I didn't know whether my classmates were Catholics, Protestants, Christians or heathens. It had never occurred to me to ask and it didn't make any difference to me. I may have been pressing my luck but that really upset me. He had dozens of chances to give me important advice but never did. I told him I had no idea which kids were Catholic and which were not. If it made any difference to him, I wished I was a Catholic. At least they don't tell their kids who to walk downtown with. I think that was the last religious lecture I got from my dad.

My hormones were not working enough to make girls interesting. I had no training in social conduct and surely no preparation for meeting girls. My parents had such negative comments about every girl outside our little church group that I couldn't have considered a date with any of them and no girl in our church group interested me in the slightest so it was easy to sit on the sidelines. Besides, there was no place to go and I wouldn't have considered being seen by my parents with any girl. During the summer after my freshman year my parents hired my cousin, Mildred, to help my mother with canning and cooking for our extra summer farm workers. She was 2 years and one school grade my senior. One evening, her boyfriend drove out to see her and brought Vera Mae Ambler, one of the most desirable high school juniors. I went for a ride with them but I panicked when they parked and began to cuddle in the front seat. I was in the back seat with one of the most popular girls in the high school but I couldn't get home fast enough. My immaturity really wrecked their plans for the evening.

The next year I was assigned a school locker beside the one assigned to Norma Jean Merritt, a really cute freshman. She got friendlier as the school year progressed and one day she asked me to help her get a big book down from the top shelf in her locker. When I retrieved the item, she thanked me and put her hand on mine in a manner I'd never experienced. I guess it felt good but I was so self-conscious and uncomfortable about the contact that I looked in every direction to see if anyone saw it. I finally got a little more comfortable with my classmates and considered asking one for a date during my senior year but when I asked my dad if I could use the car to attend some event he killed the idea so, having no transportation, I gave up and I had never had a date nor kissed a girl before I graduated from high school.

I did know a little about the human body since my mother had given me half of a University of Nebraska Extension Service or USDA bulletin on the body and sexually acquired diseases during my sophomore year. She gave me only the male half. The bulletin had been torn in two and she had disposed of the female section. It's good that I had classmates or I might never have known about boys and girls except that I already imagined they functioned like farm animals. I had been present during the breeding of farm animals and had assisted in births of cattle, horses, pigs, dogs and cats before anyone ever told me—officially—about people. I will never know what my parents were thinking about. Maybe they were uncomfortable with knowing I needed their help and hoped they'd find an easy way to tell me, or that someone else would.

We did not live in a socially active community but there were a few school functions where parents were invited. I brought home numerous invitations for my parents to high school events but they never attended a single one except for the baccalaureate ceremony before my high school graduation. I guess that was OK because a minister came and preached to us. I believe they really did plan to attend my graduation because they bought a new suit for me to wear. They were saved from actually having to take me to school and from attending my last high school function by the violent cloudburst that struck just before we were ready to leave for town. Only a few from my class who lived in the south end of town near the school actually attended the graduation ceremony.

I learned to stay out of almost all extracurricular activities because some required meetings after school hours and if I couldn't do it in time to catch the school bus, my parents did not allow it. I never went to a high school party in four years nor any event, in or out of school, that might turn into a dance because my parents knew that dancing, in and of itself, was evil. Students in high school ag class participated in livestock judging as part of the classwork. I made the school judging team and my parents let me go to the state judging contest, where we had to stay overnight in North Platte, 30 miles away. I guess they trusted our ag teacher.

As the winner of the state contest, I automatically qualified to represent Nebraska in the national contest with expenses paid for me and my chaperone. But it was in Kansas City. That was too far away, so I was not allowed to go and see how I could perform against the best in the country, even though my ag teacher would again be my chaperone. He was really upset. It's a big honor for a teacher to produce the best in the state with a chance to compete with the best in the country. I was terribly disappointed, but not surprised.

They reluctantly let me go out for football because we were such a rural school that practice was over in time for all team members to shower and catch the bus. It was not a big deal to them as long as I was home in time to do my work. The bus waited until after the game when we had home games. I was a team regular for two years but my parents never attended a single game. I had to beg and agree to do extra work at home to get permission to go with the team to every out-of-town game, which meant I would miss doing my normal evening chores. I had to ask for a ride home with our neighbors, the Barners, the same neighbors my parents criticized for not going to church but who understood my parents and my problem. I felt so guilty. We never took their kids anywhere. I will always be grateful to them for helping me to live at least a little of what was a normal high school life for everyone else.

Big Ears and Idle Moments

I was in Stapleton in late August 1941, a few days before I would leave home for the first time. In a few days I would go to Lincoln to begin my college career. I knew little about what to expect when I got to the University. I didn't even know any good questions to ask. My parents had kept me on such a short leash—protecting me from all the bad influences in the world—that I had not been able to make even casual friendships with anybody beyond our immediate family and my high school classmates.

I had not been much of a customer for our bank but I had trusted the Bank of Stapleton with all my money up to that time. I don't think my balance was over more than $20 so the bank personnel had little chance to know me except for the fact that "Pete," the president and major stockholder had nursed my dad's farming operations through the depression and the drought and hadn't foreclosed. As the firstborn, I had accompanied my father on some trips to the bank. Bank personnel included Mr. Peterson, the bank president, and John Link, the only other employee, who also happened to be the cashier and son-in-law of Ed Salisbury, the largest, if not the only stockholder, other than Mr. Peterson.

The impact of my leaving wouldn't be noticed by anyone but me and a few of my family members so it didn't take long to say my goodbyes. But I was in town and I felt the urge to tell Pete, the banker, goodbye, so I walked into the bank. Pete was busy in his office so I sat down on the bench to wait my turn. He was talking to George Mudd, one of the county's most successful ranchers and the owner of what was almost surely the best herd of commercial Hereford cattle in the area. It was quiet. The conversation from the open door to Pete's office was a lot louder and a lot more interesting than the ticking of the bank clock, the only other noise in the bank at the moment.

I knew it wasn't good manners to listen to private conversations but I had no choice. I overheard Mr. Mudd tell Pete that he was getting on in years, that it was hard to hire good help and he had no family. He had decided to sell his herd in the fall and retire. Our cowherd, like many of our neighbors who milked cows and sold cream, was primarily Shorthorn breeding but we still wanted steers to qualify for beef buyers. We had crossbred to Hereford bulls for a few years but much of the herd still did not yet have the Hereford white face. My dad had commented that the family might milk fewer cows after I was gone to college. When I heard about the Mudd cattle going to market, I saw opportunity. I could see instant beef herd improvement by selling the poorest of our herd and replacing our "culls" with the best heifers from the Mudd herd.

I rushed in to Pete's office, excusing myself for hearing the conversation for intruding. Once there, I said, "Mr. Mudd, if you're going to sell your cattle, what would you think if somebody bought the top 40 or 50?" Heifers could upgrade our herd in one move, I explained. It wouldn't cost us much to exchange for your best, you'd get paid the same as if you sold them to someone else and you could keep some of your cattle in the county. "I haven't told my dad about the idea," I warned them, "but I plan to." I'll never know whether my dad thought that I had a good idea or that Pete had a good idea but he made the deal. Except for the pair of purebred Hereford heifers I bought from Edgar Fowler and their offspring, the Mudd heifers gave our herd its first transition to take a milking herd into the beef business.

Betcha a Beer

A semester or so after I returned to college following my hitch in the Navy, I had decided I wanted a journalism major but I wasn't sure I wanted to transfer from Ag College to Arts and Science. This was before Nebraska opened a full-fledged "College of Journalism." A Journalism major was possible from either college. I needed a course in soils if I stayed in Ag but it wasn't an accepted course if I went to Arts and Science. Then I learned that a geology course could fulfill an Arts and Sciences science requirement and that Ag College would substitute it for soils. This geology course gave me another semester, at least, to have it both ways.

The lecture was as dry as you would expect (I could never convince myself to fall in love with rocks) but the lab, which met for three hours once a week, became unexpectedly exciting. We made a couple of field trips in the first few weeks but back on campus, the lab teacher held up a rock, asked us what kind of rock it was. It looked to me as if it might have had a volcanic birth, I looked around and seeing no volunteers, I said, "igneous." From the table behind me I heard, "metamorphic."

In the first or second lab I had noticed two girls who came to class together and sat together at a lab table. I turned to see where this "metamorphic" had come from and it was the cuter (in my opinion) of the pair. I looked at her and again said, "igneous." She responded, "metamorphic"—and after a brief pause she added, "betcha a beer." I told her she had better be right about the rock because I doubted that she was old enough to buy if she lost. Minutes later it was break time and I suggested we walk a block off campus to the theatre to get popcorn before lab resumed.

118

In 1947, I did not know of a boy who had been asked for a date by a girl and maybe this didn't qualify, but it was close enough to get my attention. My wits may not have been as sharp as Kay's but before the bag of popcorn was gone and lab resumed, I had made a coffee date to schedule the beer date. Our weekly trip to the theater for popcorn during break time continued through the semester. We dated frequently during the next two years, inhibited mainly by her constant urge to "go steady," something I wasn't ready to do, even with her. She always called after a break-up to see if I was still dating—and I always was. But I can't recall whether that rock was really igneous or metamorphic.

If I Can't Publish, I'll Study Journalism

It was the summer of my junior year in college. I was visiting at home in Stapleton and was talking with Mentor Brown, the publisher of my hometown newspaper, the *Stapleton Enterprise*. He knew I was a journalism student and asked if I knew of anyone, including myself, who would be interested in taking over his paper. It just happened that a row of newspaper dominos was ready to be toppled. Even Mentor didn't know about the last possible one.

Jack Beisner had been a professor in the U of N Journalism Department specializing in country newspapers, typography, etc. I knew him but had not taken a course from him. He had left school the previous year to buy the *Custer County Chief* in Broken Bow, one of the better county newspapers in Nebraska. The Grand Island *Daily Independent* had been offered to Beisner, who talked to Mentor Brown about moving from Stapleton to Broken Bow.

I had recently visited with Hugh Priest, owner/publisher of the *Tryon Graphic*, the newspaper in the county west of home. When he learned that I was taking journalism, he immediately offered me his paper for free. It turned out that he was a local rancher who had sold his ranch a few years earlier and wanted to retire to town. The only house for sale in Tryon, the county seat of McPherson County, was owned by the newspaper publisher.

Hugh wanted the house but the printing plant was in the basement so the buyer had to take the newspaper. He was a logical publisher, he explained to me in Sandhills logic, since he had finished a year of college. Hugh had previously tried to sell the paper. He had tried to give it away but nobody in the county knew, nor wanted to learn, newspaper publishing. The previous owner had made a living from legal advertising. Neither owner had tried to sell outside the house. Advertisers simply came in or called in their ads.

The *Tryon Graphic* had a nearly new press. The *Stapleton Enterprise* had a nearly new linotype machine. Immediately I could see putting the two papers together in these side-by-side, low-population counties. Folding the paper one way put the *Tryon Graphic* on the front page with the *Stapleton*

Enterprise inside; folding the other way reversed the papers. I always had mixed emotions about spending my life in rural Nebraska but I was beginning to like the idea of taking over these two papers. Attorneys were drawing up the contract when the deal for the Grand Island paper came unglued. After I went back to college in September I never again seriously considered becoming a country newspaper publisher.

Collegiate Press at Work

I didn't eat at the YMCA cafeteria often. Most of the time I ran back across the street from the Ag College campus to the Alpha Gamma Rho (AGR) fraternity house for lunch. One day I made a lunch appointment with Harold Cleal, a fellow Ag Journalism student. As editor of the *Cornhusker Countryman*, the ag college magazine, I was meeting to discuss an article that Harold wanted to write. He had complained to me about the stingy servings and I told him he was just looking for trouble.

He said that he frequently ate at the YMCA cafeteria near the downtown campus and got a lot better meal for the money. "The Ag College cafeteria is a training ground for Home Economics students. The students work there for experience without any pay and the YMCA operates their cafeteria for profit," he reasoned. "Where does the money go?" Then he asked me to meet him again—downtown—when we would eat at the "Y" and compare.

When we visited the YMCA a few days later, it appeared that Harold was on to some-thing. The servings did appear larger, and were certainly as tasty as those from the college. Since we were both photographers, we decided to check the menu at both places so we could get

Sigma Delti Chi, professional journalism honorary for men, was founded in 1909 to help journalism students better equip themselves to become members of their profession. That's me on the left in the bottom row.

identical meals. One of us set up the camera on a tripod while the other picked up a meal in the cafeteria line. We then laid a 12-inch ruler across the plate to show size, put price labels on each serving and took our pictures.

Photo flash bulbs got attention. Someone at the YMCA came to our table and asked what we were doing. We said we were photojournalism students

120

practicing food photography. End of story with no further questions. A few days later, when we proceeded with Phase 2 of our project, the person in charge, who was on the University staff, did not like our explanation. She ordered us out and asked for our film. Fortunately, she was only the assistant manager and we convinced her that we had to complete our lab project on food photography.

Harold finished the story and we published it, with our photos, in the *Cornhusker Countryman*. I got a call to visit Raleigh Graham, the College ag editor, who was the magazine's faculty sponsor, and also a call from the Dean of Agriculture. I told the ag editor I didn't clear it with him because I was afraid he wouldn't let us run the story, even though it was true, and Harold had done so much work, he surely deserved to get the byline. He didn't really give me his blessing but said he appreciated my honesty. I felt he was not upset with the article itself, but with the fact that we hadn't cleared it with him. I was home free with him.

It was a few days before the dean could see me and I began to wonder if "truth" was really as good a defense for libel as we had been told in the "Legal Control of the Press" course required for journalism certificate candidates. He seemed interested and almost amused that we had noticed the apparent injustice and had the ingenuity and daring to do the story. He kept a good face by suggesting that in the future I should check with Mr. Graham before running a story that involved investigative journalism. There was never any public comment but, to our total surprise, the cafeteria manager quietly disappeared from the University's Home Economics staff and the Ag College cafeteria's food prices became more diner-friendly.

It Was Leo's Horse

When I returned to college after the war in 1946, I had enough money from playing bridge in the Navy to buy a car. With a $65 monthly check from the GI Bill, I generally had enough money to buy gasoline for it. But I still had to work if I wanted to buy food, shelter, clothing and recreation. Several of us who were in the same financial situation came back to Lincoln early to be in the front of the job line for the coming school year. Several of us were living at the fraternity house and the Nebraska State Fair horse racing season was under way. We each put 10 bucks in a pot to use for betting at the track. Our rules required a majority of the group at the track on any day to agree on the potential winner in every race, with a minimum of three "yes" votes before we could bet a penny of "pool" money.

One weekend day most of the house groupies had gone home so I went to the track alone. I decided that I would test my instincts by picking a horse in the first race but not buy a ticket. My horse was nearly last. On the second race I did it again and my pick got his legs mixed up on the home stretch and had to be hauled off on a trailer. It seemed that this might not be my day but I decided to go back to the barn area. Leo Cooksley, a fraternity brother who had graduated before the war (and before I enrolled at U of N), was a breeder of racing horses and Shorthorn cattle and had some of his horses at the track. I did not know him well but I had met him a couple of times at the house and I had visited him on one of my earlier trips to the track. I noticed in the racing program that he was listed as the owner of a horse entered to run in one of the later races. The odds were 30-to-1 but this might be a good time to go say hello to Leo again.

When I reached his shed row, Leo was brushing one of his horses. After a brief visit, he continued preparing his horse, and asked if I was going back to the grandstand. I assured him that I was, and he continued, "before the sixth race?" I told him that I wasn't having a good day but that I was indeed going back. Leo never wasted time with small talk. I didn't have a lot to say but tried to keep some conversation going, about horses, cattle, the fraternity, the Sandhills. He began to saddle his horse and looked at me again, "You are going back to the grandstand?" he asked again. Over the loudspeaker system I heard the call for the fifth race.

I told Leo I felt it was about time to go back. He reached into his hip pocket, took out his wallet and, under the secret pocket flap, there was a hundred-dollar bill. He squeezed the bill into a wad, put it in my hand and said, "put this on this filly's nose in the sixth race. And don't bet until just before they close the windows," he said. "I don't want it to change the odds too early." I gulped. I had never had a hundred-dollar bill in my hand before. I don't think I had seen a hundred-dollar bill since I was a kid of 12 and watched Zell Russell peel bills from a roll in his coat pocket to pay for a new tractor. I shoved it deep into my pocket, afraid someone would know I had it and whack me over the head on my way to the grandstand. Once there, I paced back and forth in front of the betting windows, waiting for the announcement that this was the last chance to place bets.

As I walked, I kept thinking about Leo and his bet. Leo had a reputation for being, if not stingy, at least very careful with a dollar. I decided to take advantage of his apparent knowledge. If he would bet a hundred on this filly—and put it all to win without a dime to place or show—even though I had never bet $5 on anything before, I could surely justify betting $5 this time. When they finally announced the last call, I walked to the window and plunked Leo's bill down for a win ticket. Then I reached in my pocket for a bill. I had a ten but no five. I laid the ten down and told the clerk I wanted a $5 ticket but he handed me a $10 win ticket and no change. I almost fainted. That was my meal money, but it was too late. I took my tickets and headed for the rail at the race track. I had my week's grocery money riding on this race and was determined to win—or lose—close to the action.

122

It was just another race until the horses came down the stretch toward the finish line. Leo's filly was in the pack but broke clear with about 100 yards to go and finished with a couple of lengths of daylight between her and the field. I began to breathe again. Then I looked at the pari-mutuel tote board to check the odds on our winner. She had been 30-to-1 when I first noticed that the horse was entered in a race, and then she was 20-to-1 when I bought the ticket. The board now showed 16-to-1. I went to collect my winnings and got back $168. I could hardly believe it. But I was too scared to cash Leo's ticket. His bet would pay $1,680. I didn't want to carry that much money without an armed guard so I went back to the barn and gave Leo his ticket. Somehow it seemed safer to carry the ticket than the money.

Leo thanked me for placing his bet. And I told him what I had done with his tip. Then he told me something that settled the case of nerves I had before making my bet, although this was well after the fact. His filly was a "barn" horse that week. The "in" crowd behind the track—the trainers and jockeys (and a few owners)—would pick a horse with pretty good ability but one that had been groomed for a special situation by managing to not get a recent win. The odds would build so having a winning ticket would have a good payoff. Then, the word was passed. This was the day . . . the horse . . . and the race.

Nobody bet early and nobody bet big. The "in" crowd did not tip off anybody not in on the deal until the last minute, if at all. The odds shrunk on the tote board, especially in the last minute before race time but it still made a nice bonus for a bunch of guys who worked hard for little pay in a business they loved. I do not know if it happens at other tracks or all tracks. I never told any of the guys at the house about my big win or how it came about but Leo (now gone to that track in the sky) and I always had something to talk about after that day at the track.

College Pranksters Import Own Fraternity

History has perhaps carelessly failed to record the time and the name of the person who showed up at one of the Burnett Hall journalism darkrooms with the rumor that there was a real college fraternity—honorary fraternity, that is—for photojournalism students. This was unique in that its grade score required that you were not on the probation list (especially good for camera buffs who sometimes struggled for good grades) and you must have completed or have been registered for at least one class in photojournalism. Oh, yes, it was coed.

This rumor probably brought different ideas to each of us who happened to hear the news. Our messenger heard it had started at the University of Missouri and that they were having a photojournalism day, photo display and membership event. We might even get a chapter for our own school if we applied. Our unofficial on-the-spot meeting authorized the bearer of such news to follow up. Sure enough, a few weeks later our delegation headed for Columbia. I (Phil Raynard) remember that Bill Poe, George Shaw, Bill Leroy and maybe Tom Reynolds (I am not sure about Tom) saddled up my Mercury convertible and headed south.

The trip was upbeat but not particularly memorable except for the fact that George Shaw needed something to drink and nothing was available. We were driving across Missouri and, by state law, all businesses dispensing alcoholic beverages were closed for election day in Missouri—or—that all booze would be locked up for the event. Have you ever crossed a state in the confines of a small automobile with an apprentice alcoholic? But even George survived.

The University of Missouri College of Journalism had impressive quarters and their chapter of Kappa Alpha Mu staged a photo show beyond our hopes or imagination. We returned with the charter for our Nebraska chapter and heady ideas for the first photo exhibition we would produce on our campus. Those of us who made the trip automatically became new members but we were eager to share the wealth by

Completing its first year on the Nebraska campus, Kappa Alpha Mu, photography honorary, encourages high standards in photography. Back row (l-r): Yost, Poe, Orr. 2nd Row: Hoaglan, Fine, Moorhouse, Munger, Hays, Albert. Front row: Reynolds, Farris, Sohl, Raynard, Morgan, LeRoy, Shaw.

inviting fellow photographers as new members—and we needed the money from their dues. To my surprise, I was elected president at our first meeting; payment, I felt, for having driven my car from Lincoln to Columbia.

As I look back while writing this in 2004, I believe this occurred in the spring of 1948. Curious readers could probably fix the date more surely, if needed, by checking to see if Missouri had an election at that time. I doubt that any Kappa Alpha Mu documents (we were never good at records) could confirm, in fact, is there still an active chapter at Nebraska?

New Friends and Jobs Away from Home

When I went to begin my college career in Lincoln I knew Don Cahill. He was two or three years older than I, but he had some major illness in the early grades and was kept out of school for a time to recuperate so he actually graduated from high school only a year ahead of me. It may have been his

124

age or the fact that he had more exposure to the world than I, but Don had acquired more maturity than simply a year of college. I didn't know him well because his family lived south of Stapleton and we lived west. His family went to the Catholic Church and I had been told by my dad to not associate with Catholics and I didn't know which they were. But Don and I had been on the same high school football team.

Don had roomed in a private home at 2991 Holdrege St. his first year in college but he had a new job that provided a one-bedroom apartment so I was happy to take over his old place. The rent was $6 or $8 per month including cooking "privileges" in the partially finished basement. Several of the homeowners along Holdrege Street and other nearby addresses had extra rooms and took in students. The University of Nebraska ag campus began at 33rd Street with the main entry to most classroom buildings in the area of 35th or 36th so it was a good morning walk, but who could argue? The room rates were in a scale based more or less on distance from school and mine, with one of the longest walks, was one of the cheapest. I shared a room, including the limited cooking facilities, with Don's brother, Jim.

Along the way to the campus, owners of several other large, older homes also took in students, many furnished both room and board. As we walked to classes and home again we got to know many students, some better than others. Dwight Johnson and Tom Mocroft were also in their first year of college. They lived at 3141 Holdrege so we became friends sharing the walk. There were several others but Tom and Dwight appealed to me as friends more than others, and apparently vice versa. I never saw them on weekends since I worked every minute possible to earn money to stay in school (the going wage for student work such as spading gardens, cleaning basements or attics, etc., was 25 cents per hour), but I learned that they both lived near Waverly, a town near Lincoln, and went home on weekends.

As we got into the second semester I began feeling a little more like I belonged in college and had that good job running the milk route every morning and working at the college creamery on weekends so I actually had some money to spend for the first time in my life. The other good part was that I was so busy working I had little time to spend any of my newfound wealth. I was surprised when Dwight and Tom invited me to a Monday evening dinner late in the second semester. I had seen that big house at 3605 Holdrege but thought it was a rooming house. I had little idea what a fraternity might be.

Well, that's where we went to dinner and I sat at a table with new initiates, Dwight and Tom, and had my first meeting with the housemother. Mother Wiebusch gave me a geography lesson, so to speak, by mentioning that she knew where my home town of Stapleton was located and that Dennis Clark, my Uncle Bill's best friend in high school, had been quite an AGR leader in Ag College until he died of pneumonia in his senior year. I didn't realize at the time that Alpha Gamma Rho was actually a fraternity or that I was being "rushed." A few weeks later I was invited back and asked to join. Looking back, I think that was the first time in my life that I was making a decision entirely on my own. Yes, I pledged, and with the war interrupting everybody's life plans, I was called to Navy flight training active duty before I was eligible to be initiated so I guess I was actually a fraternity "pledge" through the whole war, being finally initiated in the fall of 1946 when I got back in college.

After the war was over there was record enrollment of students on the campus and in all the facilities dealing with students. The new GI Bill paid $65 per month, plus books and tuition, to every single veteran (more to married students). That was enough to pay the monthly house bill so all I had to earn was "spending money" for such items as clothes and recreation,

Alpha Gamma Rho fraternity members at University of Nebraska, 1948. I'm in the 3rd row, far right.

including gasoline for my car, which I needed since I had classes on both the Ag and City campuses and bus service was not geared to classroom/course schedule timing. I would still be "working my way through college" but at a different level than the 25-cents-an-hour work available to students before the war who had to schedule almost every minute of their day and night. I also learned that sales jobs and piece-rate work let me earn more money per hour than "hourly" work, and that there were many opportunities in this field.

I registered for my first photography course and found the rate for photo work was much like a sales job. I liked getting paid for what I delivered instead of how long it took to do the job. I also found "student activities" that carried salaries in addition to the experience and satisfaction of being on the staff of campus publications. As I remember, the Ag Editor (sort of a new position created when I convinced the editorial board there was enough activity on the Ag campus to deserve a spot on the masthead) was the same

126

pay grade as Associate Editors, earning $15 per month. A year later when I became editor of the monthly Ag College publication, Cornhusker Countryman, I got $25 per month. As a photographer for the Cornhusker yearbook, I was paid for each photo they used, not how long it took to take the picture. My kind of job!

Sorority Rush Week "Queen Maker"

It was my second year of college after being in military service for a few years during World War II that I was asked by Thelma Baskin, one of the very interested parents in our town, for some advice or assistance. She wanted to be assured that her first daughter, Virginia, had at least an equal advantage in sorority rush week when she entered college in the fall. I guess I was the logical source since I had been at the University for some time (counting wartime absence), was a member of a fraternity and we had a bit of an acquaintance. The Baskins owned the Diamond Bar Ranch, one of the area's biggest acreages, which began at the railhead of the Union Pacific Railroad tracks and covered a lot of land to the north and west of Stapleton.

I had no track record in the Stapleton social world. My parents associated as little as possible with town people and discouraged their kids from contact with anyone who didn't belong to our church. This gave me a lot of catching up to do when I got home from the Navy. I would never be a member of the "in" crowd in Stapleton but Thelma was looking for every break for the first of her three daughters and the first to go to college. I was surprised when she asked me for advice but she wanted Virginia to get into a good sorority and I guess she felt that I was the nearest thing she had for a ticket to the never-never land of sorority life. That life would begin with rush week, when the eligible coeds participated in the "cattle call" before classes began that meant sorority membership for the chosen few and at least an imagined "in" during their entire college life.

She heard that I had developed a fairly active social life and participated in several college activities on my return to school. She was sure I could help and wanted me to list the "best" sororities for her daughter, the ones where I had the most dates and at which ones I had friends who could be helpful to her in college generally. How do you make that kind of a list? I nixed a couple as being "moneyed" or "haughty"—don't waste your time there (what I really meant was that I didn't have a single acquaintance there that would help), but I tried to tell her that two weeks after "rush week" both mother and daughter would be sure they had picked (or been picked by) the right house and would never look back, wondering about the choice.

I tried to be helpful and honest and, as it turned out, I had no idea how far-reaching my recommendations would be. Virginia went through rush week, got invited and pledged Alpha Xi Delta and I'm sure she was happy for life with her choice. As I remember, I told Thelma in my advance critique that this was a good house and I had several of their sisters in classes but somehow neither I nor my friends had more than occasional dates there. But the rest of the story comes much later.

Virginia did well in school, graduated and became a home economics teacher, yes, in Stapleton, our hometown. Meantime, both of her younger sisters, Marybelle and Lorajane, followed Virginia to U of N and, in turn, became "legacy" members of Alpha Xi Delta. And when my sister Barbara moved on from Stapleton High to the University, having been one of Virginia's students, guess what sorority she pledged. Bingo! And Lorajane, mentioned above, was Barbara's sorority pledge "mother." I'm sure all of the girls, and their sorority sisters, were happy with their choices. I never asked Thelma if she ever second-guessed me and my pre-rush week sorority ratings, nor have I ever brought up the subject for my sister to edit.

I've Got Keys that Jingle, Jangle, Jingle

Never the naturally studious, model student, I had always found studying to be less exciting and rewarding than many other activities, so I knew it would take serious effort on my part to re-acclimate and make the grade on my return to college after nearly four years' absence from the classroom. Navy flight school was demanding, but now I had to prove myself to myself, my family and friends all over again on my return to the college environment. I had always been able to apply myself—cram for a test, etc.—but it had been several years since I was a student with my own private personal future and goals other than those I had to share with the U.S. Navy. And I didn't even know where I wanted to go in this new adventure.

It was almost as if some great plan had returned thousands of veterans to the classrooms to be supporters and confidants for each other in this new post-war adventure. Most of us were decent and motivated students in that we were convinced that we'd have a better future if we went to college, so we had a reason to study and get on with our lives. Learning comes easier if you have some life experience to build on, which was a bonus for veterans. The new GI Bill paid our tuition plus $65 per month. What a bonanza! A great start for someone who previously had to earn every penny of his college expenses—quite an order when the going wage was 25 cents an hour. Living in an organized student house gave students an environment that eliminated many of the distractions for students on their own, as I was before the war. The Alpha Gamma Rho (AGR) fraternity house was especially good. The members were bright and motivated to be the best on campus.

While the "study hour" environment of an organized house helped most students hit the books, it seemed that veterans sometimes got "itchy" before study hour was over. Maybe we were not quite reacclimated to civilian life.

And college rules did give "adult" privileges to veterans, which helped. Add to this the fact that I had converted the income from a few years of playing bridge for money into a Mercury convertible. Either the Mercury or I found it difficult to honor study hour rules five evenings a week. When my "study bone" got itchy, I might walk down the hall jingling my car keys—or "willing passengers" might show up at my room if I was slow to get the urge, and remind me that this might not be a particularly good evening to study.

The outcome was usually the same. I almost always had three or four passengers by the time I got downstairs to face the scowl of Mother Wiebusch, our housemother. It was probably hard for her to admit that some of "her boys" answered my invitation and were on the way to some off-campus roadhouse for an hour or so. I had the feeling that I was her enigma. Other members told me she had mixed emotions, but she never refused when I picked her to be my bridge partner and hated to admit that she privately enjoyed it when I brought recognition to our house for some ex-tracurricular (not in the classroom) feat. She had to swallow hard when my actions embarrassed her finer self, or at least she never thanked me for "broadening" her life ex-perience in this manner. On second thought, maybe I didn't thank her very often either.

I've never known whether the collection of AGR brothers at the University of Nebraska made the best possible environment for unsophisti-

My study desk at AGR house; note press camera with flash on book shelf.

cated young college guys or not but I especially needed that kind of surroundings to feel comfortable while in the midst of, and slowly working out of, my growing pains. I was given a lot of direction when needed, with thoughtful room to develop as I was able. It turned out to be the kind of home I had never had before—most appropriate—and eventually appreciated. We can't go do it over. I have, over the years, learned that the invitation to join

AGR and my acceptance was the luckiest fate for me. I have no way to measure how much I returned to the fraternity and its members but I did recognize their gift and worked hard to repay them.

Among other things, I learned lessons from the least expected places and people. I imagine that brother Jim Monahan's family represented as much net worth as anyone in our fraternity. His family owned a lot of good ranch land in the Hyannis, Nebraska area. They had more land than cattle, so to speak. During the 1940s and '50s, their herd was not big enough to graze all their pastures so they bought several loads of their neighbors' weanling calves or yearlings in the fall to eat up the extra grass grown on Monahan pastures and market a year later after they had each gained a few hundred pounds at very low cost. This was during a time when yearling weights for many grass-fed cattle, thanks to small-sized cattle "show-ring" genetics at the time, were not enough to reach needed slaughter weights coming out of feedlots.

Monahan marketing in the late 1940s began, as it had in previous years, by shipping several railroad carloads of steers to the Omaha stockyards on fall weekends to be on the Monday morning market. Jim came to college with a new Ford club coupe which he used thoughtfully for his own use, or occasional other trips. Jim's dad, Earl, had a 1942 Lincoln Continental (the last pre-war model) which he drove from Hyannis to Lincoln, some 300 miles, on Sundays, then after spending the night at the fraternity house, the two drove Jim's coupe early Monday morning the nearly 60 miles to the Omaha stockyards (Earl didn't like exposing his Continental to Omaha traffic) to watch their cattle sell.

I learned that they had been selling several rail cars of steers every Monday, and one day I commented to Jim that they must have all the cattle out of the Sandhills by now. In his matter-of-fact way he answered, "Today we shipped the last of the 2-year-olds." That meant they would now start shipping the heaviest of their yearlings. They only sold the heaviest of their yearling crop, carrying the balance over to sell the next year as 2-year-olds. They had plenty of grassland and made plenty of hay . . . and what's another year to a steer? It could earn the seller a few dollars per steer by waiting.

In addition to what I find is an interesting and true story, the above serves as background information for another lesson learned at our fraternity house, at least by willing students, from an unexpected source. Our fraternity house was a near-century-old ranch house that must have dominated the landscape before they citified the area with streets and built homes for college professors after the area became the site of the University of Nebraska "ag campus." It was still a big old place that housed 30-plus college guys in reasonable comfort with a multi-bunk sleeping dorm and a lot of "study" rooms with three to six desks each, plus the housemother's apartment. It was surrounded by big old trees that had grown skyward, but some of the branches were competing with our roof for air space and making worrisome noises during windstorms.

One main branch seemed to be the major competitor for space up above the second story and the one making those wakeful noises during windstorms that sounded ready to rearrange the fraternity house shingles. That branch had to go. But when a tree trimmer bid $150 to remove the troublesome branch (remember this was in the 1940s; house bills were $75 per month for room, board and fraternity dues), Jim Monahan, aghast at the estimated cost, volunteered to rent a trailer and supervise branch removal, saving the house members what was a lot of money at the time . . . probably a fair piece of one of those yearling steers on the Omaha market. Jim knew the value of a dollar. So did I; in fact I was out trying to earn a few of them while Jim was saving some for the house by supervising a group of pledges learning the skill of branch removal. I guess we should appreciate all the free help we can get.

Those Mercury Memories

Little could I have imagined when I learned to play bridge, the impact of what could happen in future years as a result of that knowledge. Nor could I have imagined that more than 50 years later when I returned to a reunion of fraternity brothers, the first questions several would ask, after not seeing me for 50 years, would be about an automobile. Yes, they do have a connection. My first bridge lessons were in the Alpha Gamma Rho (AGR) fraternity house shortly after the Japanese dropped their bombs on Pearl Harbor. As an indirect result of the bombing, my bridge lessons continued during the next 17 months as a naval aviation cadet before I got my wings and an assignment to other than a training base.

I frequently played with one person as a partner in flight school. We played well together and, in a stroke of good luck, we were assigned to the same squadron in the Philippines. In my observation, most card games in the military are played for money. And it was our good fortune that the Navy had many bad bridge players. Our squadron seemed to move every month or two from one station to another as we wore out our welcome. We went from a shore base on Jinamoc Island in Leyte Gulf to a seaplane tender in Lingayen Gulf to a shore base at Sangley Point in Manila Bay to another tender and to another shore base at Puerta Princesa.

About the first day our squadron got settled at a new location, bridge junkies from the ship or station would saunter into our quarters, inquiring about possible bridge players in the new squadron. They could beat the few bridge players on their ship or station and were scouting for new talent. They were really looking for suckers. The other pilots in our squadron would tell them that Bidewell and Raynard played a little. Ben and I were far from world masters. We didn't want honors or credit; we played for cash. Our challengers seemed to be giving lessons to willing learners and, able to regularly beat their students, were looking for new challenges, especially somebody who would play for money.

I had decided before the war that I wanted a car when I returned to school, so I regularly converted my bridge winnings into postal money orders. When I got back to San Francisco after the war, I hit the car dealerships in and out of the Bay Area. I found a dealer that had a Mercury convertible in stock. He had ordered it for a local veteran but now it had arrived and the buyer didn't have enough money to buy it. I did.

It was Saturday afternoon in a small town. I had an envelope full of postal money orders. They had to be cashed at the post office. The dealer called the postmaster, who had gone home for the weekend. He came back and assured our car dealer that even though he didn't have that much weekend cash on hand, they could handle the transaction on Monday morning. I drove away with the car and in a few weeks I headed back to resume college.

That Mercury may not have been the sole developer of my personality but we earned a joint reputation. If you are in college and don't have your own car, you always want to be on good terms with several car owners who will double-date and share a car with you. And if that car happens to have a convertible top, so much the better. At the 50th anniversary reunion that I mentioned earlier several remembered incidents about my Mercury that I had forgotten. This included the seatbelt I had installed.

As a pilot, I always had a safety belt across my lap and when I hit the road without my belt, I felt as if I would fall off the seat. I found my security at an Army-Navy surplus store, where I bought an aircraft seat belt and had it installed. The convertible was cool. The seat belt was not. In fact, it was downright quirky in 1946. At least I didn't have belts for my passengers. It may have been the first seat belt ever installed on a civilian car.

One of my former double-date passengers recalled the Sunday afternoon drive in the country. You expect your hair to blow when you put the convertible top down but my back seat friends asked if the wind was blowing as hard in the front seat. My date happened to be double-jointed. She held her hand up above the windshield level and bent all her fingers back as if the wind had caused the gross malformation. Such a sight almost sickened the girl in the rear seat. Yes, I remembered that incident, but replaying the afternoon made it more vivid.

That rag top brought my first real thought of preserving assets. I knew I had better get some protection from the Nebraska weather. There was a 2-stall garage on the Cotner College property across the street from the fraternity house. A few phone calls produced the name and phone number of the college president, the only person with authority to lease the space. I went to his house to make the deal and leased a space for $8 per month until I finished school. I also got a date with his daughter, but we didn't hit it off as well as the garage and car did.

It was one of few convertibles on the entire University campus during the first year after the war. It was one way to "get girls" in a way I could not have imagined. I'll never know how Dr. Elliot knew, but one day, in an insurance course I was taking, he used my car to illustrate levels of risk. He proposed a situation where "Phil is a serious, law-abiding student. His insurance rating, hence the premium he must pay, is based on risk.

"On the way to and from class, that risk is low. But if students are standing at the corner bus stop and Phil offers them a ride, the risk goes up. When they all get out except one of the girls (he named a girl that was in our class), the risk goes up again. And when they decide to drive to Omaha—you get the idea." The girl whose name he mentioned did not know me and I did not know her. She asked Doc if he was talking about a real person so he introduced us and we even had a few dates. That was the most unusual way that my Mercury ever actually helped me to "get girls" and that might have been Doc Elliot's most memorable classroom example.

It Must Have Been the Feed

As I came through the door of the feed store, the bookkeeper greeted me with a cheery, "You'd better get out to Bennie Peters farm, their hogs are going crazy and they think it's the feed." Bennie Peters was a good customer. I was the sales/service man for a company that sold livestock feed, hybrid poultry and hogs, buildings, etc., to farmers in the Midwest. It was late afternoon in early fall.

As I got to the Peters farm and drove into the yard I noticed activity near the main hog barn. I drove right to the scene of the action. Bennie, his wife and junior high-age daughter were looking at a few pigs that were squealing, walking with a staggering, unsteady gait and falling down for no apparent reason. They were otherwise healthy looking, growing pigs near 130 to 150 pounds in weight. There were at least a hundred more pigs in the pen, apparently in good health. Why had these few been affected? That was my job to learn.

When did you buy your last feed supplement from our dealer? Did you mix it with the same home-grown grain that you've used with previous batches and in the same proportions? When did you first notice one of these pigs acting strange? How many are doing it now? Have they been in this same pen since you began feeding this latest feed mix? These were the first questions I asked the distraught farmer. The answers: Last week, yes, yesterday, five or six and yes.

I asked him to show me some of the mixed feed. It looked and smelled OK. I considered the possibility that some toxic weed could be growing in the pen and a few of the pigs had found . . . and sampled it. I told him I wanted to walk all over the pen looking for noxious weeds, inviting him to either come along or wait for me to end my walking tour. He chose to wait.

The pen was about 5 acres of alfalfa. Pigs graze on green, growing feed as readily as cows and sheep—and nutritionists recommended it. First, I walked along the fence since there is a strip near most fences that is difficult to plow and seed to new crop. This is the most likely place to find a toxic weed if one is growing somewhere. Along the way, I kept looking for spots of irregular crop growth but found none. I was most of the way around the fence when I noticed a "pig-sized" hole in the mesh fence that appeared to have had some recent traffic. I decided to see what was on the other side of the fence.

Across the fence was an old family orchard including dozens of apple trees. From the hole in the fence, a trail was developing to the heart of the orchard. Under the trees were bushels of windfall apples, lying in a pattern almost as if they had been raked into windrows, like hay. Then I noticed the next factor—bees—almost swarming over the windfall apples. I reached down and picked up one of the windfalls, cut a slice and tasted it. A little tangy, I thought. I tried another. The second apple was beginning to soften with age. A slice of this apple was aromatic as cider. When I touched it on my tongue—it tingled like carbonated cider—oops, hard cider, I believe.

Ready to face the owner with my case, I brought my apple exhibit, told him about the hole in the fence then cut a couple of apple slices for him to sample. It only took a minute for the message to become clear to the large, red-cheeked farmer. "Are you telling me that my pigs are drunk?" Bennie asked. I told him that I didn't know of a law against it but that I wouldn't tell anyone if he wouldn't. And I haven't . . . until now.

A Different Point of View

I was living in Denison, a county seat town in western Iowa. I traveled as a sales manager for Western Iowa. My younger brother, Rowdy, had just moved to town. He got tired of working his way through music school by giving guitar lessons, dropped out of college, took a job managing a local music store and giving lessons. I had become a homeowner when my company promoted my salesman for this area to a territory in Eastern Iowa and he had trouble selling his house. It was a plain two-bedroom home on a corner lot but a good bachelor pad.

Enrollment in the Denison Music Store lessons department exploded with the arrival of a college-age, guitar-playing bachelor. Girls wanted to take lessons from him, boys suddenly wanted to play guitar when they saw what a magnet it was for girls. Record sales soared and the music store became competition for the Candy Kitchen as a teen hang-out. So it was not a real surprise for me to see the sudden reaction at our bachelor quarters on a late summer afternoon.

Rowdy and I were sitting across the living room from each other, finishing cool summer drinks. From my position near the front door I could see Mary walking up the street. She was a high school senior that lived just around the corner from my house and frequently walked her dog. As she passed our driveway and was about to disappear from my view, Rowdy flew out of his seat and charged across the room and through the front door. I was shocked that he needed to talk to Mary so urgently. She wasn't walking fast enough to deserve such a speedy response. But what did I know?

He came back in the house a few minutes later. "Man, I really did it. Why didn't you tell me Mary was walking up the street?" he demanded. "What are you talking about?" I asked him, "I watched her walk the last half-block. I thought you were in an awfully big hurry to talk to her but I figured that was your business. What's the problem?"

"From where I was sitting," he said, "I saw her big boxer dog run across our lawn and raise his leg over that sickly evergreen shrub by our front entry. I had the perfect chance to slam the empty beer can into his ribs before he could soak it again. The first thing I heard was Mary screaming, 'What are you doing to my dog?'" Rowdy said, "I thought the boxer was roaming loose. I didn't know she was anywhere in the area." As for me, I didn't know that the picture window in my living room was big enough for two such different views of the same happening.

Crashing in a Foreign Land

I had worked into late Saturday afternoon in southeast Nebraska with one of the company's best salesmen. I was going north on Highway 34 at late dusk, almost dark, entering Plattsmouth, headed for Omaha and on home to Des Moines, Iowa. The terrain there is hilly—long slopes on big hills. As I crested one hill and my headlights came down to light the road, the first thing I saw was the rear of a large horse in my lane—and very near.

I hit the brakes and steered hard to the left. I had always known that the front seat of a car gets very crowded with a large draft horse as a passenger. Then I noticed that it was two horses, not one. And they were being led down the highway behind a car at an easy trot with the halter ropes through a window to a passenger in the back seat. The car had no lights.

Lucky for me—I missed the horse. But I lacked about 8 inches of missing the car too. I got enough of it to snap both halter ropes and give the car an excuse to park on the right shoulder while its driver and the horseman/leader scrambled to catch the horses, which were now totally loose on the highway after dark. My car came to rest on the left shoulder with the right front fender and wheel smashed.

I pulled out a couple of flares, lit them and planted them on the road bank and started walking back up the hill to a farmhouse with lights aglow to call for the sheriff and a tow truck. As I trotted up the hill, it occurred to me that I was driving a company car with an Iowa license. The accident was in Nebraska and it was Saturday night, just before Christmas. Could we even get a deputy to come to the scene of the accident? Then it hit me—I got out of college in Nebraska back in February but still had a Nebraska driver's license—but it was too late now to go get an Iowa license.

When I knocked at the farm house door and told the lady of the house that an accident had occurred, she said, "Dad, didn't I tell you I was afraid we would have an accident when I saw those guys, leading those horses behind that car with no lights?" To which I suggested, "Ma'am, will you please remember to tell the sheriff exactly what you just said?" Yes, she called the sheriff and I decided to ask him which tow truck to call after he arrived.

Then, as I walked back down the hill to the accident scene, doubt really set in. I just knew the horse-leading farmers were no doubt from an important local family—and me—with an improper driver's license and an out-of-state car. How long would it take to get the mess cleaned up and how would I get to Omaha to catch other transportation back to Des Moines?

Almost immediately a sheriff's car pulled to the road shoulder with its red warning lights blazing. The officer took new flares up the road, then came back and interviewed the farmers. They then left, walking and leading their horses along the road shoulder and the officer came to my car where I was waiting in the front seat. The temperature was falling. He invited me to the warm patrol car, began making an accident report and asked for my license.

"Are you related to Bill?" he asked me. Stunned, I asked, "Bill who?" Well, I see your name is the same as an old friend of mine from Stapleton. "No, he's my uncle," I said, still stunned. "Do you know Mike David?" he asked. "You mean the Mike David that owns the store in Tryon?" I asked. "He's my father-in-law," said the officer. "I'm Tom Solomon. I'm the sheriff and almost all the deputies are gone to Christmas parties so you got me," he told me.

Tom Solomon was a career sheriff in Sarpy County. The SAC air base was within the county and lying just south of Omaha, numerous events got in the news from this area and Tom was a frequent headliner. But on this Saturday night before Christmas he was the good boss who gave his employees the night off. He was at a crash scene on the roadside, and while we had never met before, he had found a friend he never knew. So, it seemed, had I.

He called the owner of the tow service—at a party—to arrange for the tow, and then asked me if I needed to get back to Des Moines—and drove

136

me to the bus depot in Omaha where an express was just minutes from leaving. And talk about a switch—the poor farmers leading the horses—they were from outside the county and Tom had never heard of them. He told them he didn't want to ever find that they had led horses on the highway in his county again—day or night. Happy Holiday!

Potato Salad

Living alone in a bachelor pad has advantages—and disadvantages. When summer rolls around and you want potato salad—and you don't want to gamble that the next deli will make better potato salad than the last few you tried, a bachelor will do a lot better if he learns to cook. I did, and after a few years, got to the point that things came out of the kitchen pretty well as intended. I even made a brief but reasonable collection of recipes.

The bachelor quarters I occupied at this time, became mine when my top salesman got promoted by the company. He had earlier purchased a finished basement with a walk-out entry on a large sloping lot. A family had finished the basement to have a place to live while they built a house upstairs. When they did not complete their building project, my salesman/friend purchased the basement and built a two-bedroom home on top of it. I was trying to help him sell his house so he could leave town to take his new job.

One day he said to me, "Do you know who should buy our house?"

"I don't have any idea," I said, "We've asked almost everybody we know." Then he threw the big pitch at me.

"You should buy it," he said. Then he added, "The basement is rented out for more than the house payments, I know you have enough money in the bank for the down payment so you can live there free." We checked and he was right. He agreed to leave their stove, buy a new refrigerator for me, and I became a homeowner.

It was early one summer evening and I decided to have some potato salad later in the week. It doesn't take much for one person. I boiled a potato, and then put on an egg to boil in the potato water. These bulk ingredients could cool in the refrigerator overnight and I could add the condiments and dressing later. A phone call brought an invitation for an evening out. I left almost immediately and returned a few hours later to find the front door open. I was living in the edge of a small town and I rarely locked the front door but at least I normally shut it. One step inside the door, my nose was hit with the most caustic of sulfurous odors. There seemed to be a bluish haze in the living room and I wondered if the renters had a fire in the basement.

I charged for the basement door in a panic and was met by the tenants who gave me the bad news. They heard a noise—an explosion combined with a clanging that sounded like the lid of a kitchen pan hitting the ceiling. And that's just what it was. I had gone out with that egg boiling on the stove.

In time, it boiled dry and finally exploded—all over the kitchen ceiling—and the lid flew across the room. But the stink was worse than the mess.

My tenants had heard the explosion and came upstairs, very carefully, to see what had made the noise. They had the good judgment to turn off the stove, open the front and back doors and windows to let the air circulate. And don't tell me "a watched pot never boils." I almost stood over the pot every minute until the replacement egg was safely cooked and cooled with the potato and other ingredients in the fridge.

Oh, What Fun it is to Ride . . .

I was hired out of college as the first "executive trainee" with a small, old company that was getting ready to charge into the 1950s with a new look, new products and a lot of new people. They wanted me to help create the Executive Training program, participate in it, then write the course of study for future trainees. They planned for one trainee (me) the first year, two the next year and then see whether to enlarge, modify or kill the program. I was the "guinea pig" who was hired to do it, and then write about it. A sort of study guide for future trainees.

The company was a manufacturer of livestock feed supplements but they also acquired a company that bred hybrid poultry. They also developed a breeding program for hybrid hogs. They had the belief that research and manufacturing were important but that the bottleneck in business was sales. Management felt that if sales were going good, their impact on the company was 90 percent. If they were going bad, the sales impact was 100 percent. Fortunately for me, I had "sold" and "written" or "edited" my way through college—ideal experience.

I began working with the nutrition staff, writing product information for both the user of the products as well as sales personnel. I also wrote the company publications for the sales department including testimonial stories from satisfied users of company products. We served much of the Midwest from the offices and factory in central Iowa at Des Moines. This required travel to take photos and collect stories from our customers.

The company president asked me to look for a well-trained, child-safe pony, on my travels, for his young daughter. One day, when a black and white pony "nosed" into the interview, the customer asked if I knew someone who needed the pony. It was kid-gentle to ride or drive on a cart, but his daughter was now in college and the pony needed a new rider. My boss made the deal and the pony lived up to every promise.

A few months later I spotted a sleigh or cutter (I never knew the difference, although I've been told that a cutter is for only one horse while a sleigh may have either shafts for a single horse or a tongue for two horses). This had shafts. Tied up high in a machinery storage barn, the upholstered seat was long gone to mice but the wood and metal were perfect. "How much for the cutter?" I asked. "If you have someone who will really use it, it's yours," he answered.

My boss and his wife were enthusiastic. We ordered a harness made to fit the pony and I set about to re-upholster the seat and repaint the body area. It was a pretty showy outfit in all. Black-and-white pony, black harness, black cutter with red upholstery, red and white trim paint. I harnessed and ground drove the pony but we had no cart for a test. Then we waited for the first snow to see if the pony was really as advertised. The first snow barely covered the ground, leaving a few spots of dirt or stubble, just right for a test drive. The pony was willing and apparently safe. But the sun came out. End of test drive, and it was early December.

Then I spotted a string of sleigh bells, in good condition, chrome plated and all. I bought them before the seller changed his mind—and before it occurred to me that our otherwise gentle pony might take exception to the jingle, jangle, jingle. I didn't want to be either a witness or a participant in a runaway over a string of sleigh bells. If you want your arrival to be a secret, don't wear sleigh bells! Those suckers don't have a "quiet" pedal.

After a dry winter, the last day of school before the beginning of Christmas vacation, the temperature dropped a few degrees below freezing and snow began to fall. By noon there was a few inches of accumulation and it was still snowing and I decided to go home (I was rooming in a loft on the property behind the home of the company president) and get ready for the first real outing with sleigh bells.

I made a few passes around the stubble field beside the pony barn with harness, bells and all. The pony seemed up to the occasion. The president's wife asked if we could go pick up their kids from the rural/suburban elementary school. Why not? We were about three or four blocks, by graveled road—and across a two-lane paved highway—from the school. Giant flakes of snow continued to fall.

We drove onto the school grounds about five minutes before the end of the school day beginning the Christmas vacation. The sight of 200 noses against the glass-windowed south side of the school made the whole project worthwhile. But trying to clear a path through the students a few minutes later to get out of the schoolyard and back on the road home was a test of wits, patience and horsemanship. That black and white pony made us all look good and gave us something to take home for the holidays—and to remember forever.

Water Witch

When I was hired to be the state sales manager for western Iowa, I visited several towns, deciding where to live, but the nod went to Denison. It was the hub of roads that led to the corners of the territory, a county seat and farming town with a population of about 5,000. I checked into a residency hotel and began to look for an apartment in my spare time.

One of the curios, for me, was a sign attached to an overhanging branch of a large tree on the road past the Crawford County fairgrounds: *Water Witching*. It had to mean something or it wouldn't be hanging there. I had heard the expression but had no idea what it meant. The owner of the hotel was a farm real estate broker and appraiser. He had lived in the town for years. I felt he should know what it meant—and that he wouldn't laugh at me for asking—so I asked him what the "Water Witching" sign meant.

He said that some underground formations held veins of water and other formations did not. That certain people allegedly had the power to hold a forked tree branch and walk over land where the owner wanted to drill a well. When he walked over a location with good underground water, the tree branch would bob or dip toward the ground. Now I wished I hadn't asked. Here was a man with a college degree in agriculture telling me a spook story. I kept a straight face—but couldn't wait to ask somebody else who would take me seriously and give a real answer.

I had spent most of my life in the Nebraska Sandhills, which I later learned was over the Ogallala aquifer, the America's largest underground lake. When we wanted a well, we drilled (actually we washed it) a well. And we hit water. If we wanted it 2 feet or 10 feet or a half-mile in any direction, we hit water. A water witch, if such a creature existed, would surely starve in the Sandhills. His services would have worked, but they were not in demand.

One of the customers for the products I sold was a farm with a landmark barn on a highway corner near Ida Grove. It was totally destroyed in a Saturday night fire one cold winter night. Monday morning my swine supervisor showed up to make a few farm calls with me—including the Schirmacher farm, where the fire had occurred. When we drove into the yard, here was big Wendell, the 20-year-old son who had been an All American high school football player but chose farming over all the college football scholarship offers.

He had a tractor-mounted post-hole auger sitting near several holes and this young giant was walking across the ashes with a wire in each hand. "Oh Phil, I'm glad you're here. See if you've got it," he begged me. "Got what?" I asked, and introduced the company man. Wendell needed to locate some water pipes that had been under the barn. He had heard that some people can walk across the ground with L-shaped wires in their hands, pointing forward, and when they cross a pipe the wires will swing toward each other and cross.

This reminded me of the hotel owner and the water witching story. I was not about to make a fool of myself in front of two grown men by walking around with two bent wires in my hands. But the hog specialist took the wires and began walking wherever Wendell wanted. As expected, the wires

140

didn't get the message and all that happened was Cliff got ashes on his winter overshoes.

Reluctantly, I took the wires. I took a few steps and like remote-controlled magnets, those wires moved together and crossed. As I continued walking, they went back to the "straight in front" position. Wendell screamed, "Hey, you got it!" I desperately hoped he was referring to sanity because I was having second thoughts about it and needed an endorsement.

"Try it again," he urged, and when the wires crossed again, I began soul-searching as Wendell began driving stakes in the ground. He quickly moved me over for more readings on a line perpendicular to the original track. Then he marked a spot where the two lines crossed, backed up the auger-equipped tractor and began drilling a hole, stopping only when we heard metal clicking. We were within inches of the T in the water pipe 5 feet below.

It took a secret discovery of numerous other buried water lines to convince me that it was not plain dumb luck, or even witchcraft. I have since met people who are real water witches (also called dowsers or diviners). While I apparently have the ability to locate pipes, I believe in, but do not have the ability to dowse for a well location. It is an eerie feeling to see those wires turn in your hands. It gives a little credibility to other supposed supernatural events.

How Do You Start a Rumor?

One of my jobs involved working with the nutrition and sales departments of a livestock feed manufacturer. After developing a new product at the research farm, we liked to conduct some feed trials with commercial feeders under on-the-farm conditions. "Farm conditions" can produce surprises . . . and our management always went crazy to avoid surprises, especially with new products.

We had combined several "far out" ideas to create a new grain supplement for fattening beef cattle. It worked so well in controlled tests that we hurried to get field test results to see if our test-farm trials would be repeated. I called our two salesmen with the best customer lists in heavy cattle feeding areas to suggest feeders with good reputations that we could use for our field trials. We began with two feeders in the Omaha trade area and two near Sioux City. Cattle were purchased at the stock yards and we used stock yards weights going in and out of the feedlot.

A few weeks after the tests began, I was visiting the Omaha market when a feeder I had just met told me he heard we were testing a new beef feed and that cattle were gaining so fast that the company was afraid nobody would believe it and were trying to deny the rumor. I asked him where he heard that, in the hope that (a) it was true and (b) I could track down the rumor.

He knew the names of both feeders in the Omaha area testing the new feed but said he couldn't remember who had told him. It was true that both had been doing well and one of the sets of cattle had been making fantastic gains but I felt some of the gain was because the cattle weights had been shrunk from travel and limited access or time to take a decent fill of available drinking water when purchase weight was taken. The rumor turned up many times and might have helped sales of the product as much as our advertising.

The new feed turned out to be revolutionary and the cattle on this test made daily gains almost beyond belief. The feeders who were conducting this test had no idea who started the rumor. But one unknowingly named the feed when he said his cattle gained like magic. We named it Beef Magic. Sales of this one new product grew to become half of our total sales volume in its first year and the factory had to add a shift just to make the new feed. The night crew named themselves the Beef Magic shift. We never did know or learn how the rumor started, but trust me—we did nothing to squelch it. After all, how do you start (or stop) a rumor?

Call Off Your Thunderstorm

If you were in the livestock feed business in the Midwest during the 1950s and selling to cattle feeders, you would likely visit the South Omaha stockyards fairly often for some reason. I was, and I did. One of these trips included a feeder doing a "field trial" with a new feed that we were about to put on the market, along with two of his cattle-feeding neighbors.

The first load of cattle in the first test pen was going to market. We were anxious to see how much the cattle weighed, how much they had gained and how the buyers liked them—and in a few days we would get the dressing percentage and carcass grade. We had all met at the test feeder's farm early in the morning and we headed for the Omaha yards on a cloudy spring morning that was threatening serious rain. We wanted to be at the stockyards when the bell rang and buyers began walking through the yards, looking at the cattle.

From Iowa, the most direct route to the Stockyards was over the Missouri River on the L Street Bridge, then straight to the main gate. Rain began to fall as we crossed the river, accentuated by lightning strikes and loud claps of thunder. We joked about the weather, the cattle, the new feed and would we get rained on or would the storm pass and give us blue skies. I was driving a nearly new 1955 Pontiac hard top. Lightning strikes came nearer and one of my passengers wondered if the car would protect us from getting struck. The area on the south side of L Street was mostly open land with a few big trees—the flood plain on the west side of the Missouri River. The road was two-lane with fairly wide shoulders, raised perhaps 8 or 10 feet above the land on either side. It was early morning and we almost had the road to ourselves.

Lightning strikes and loud thunder claps continued with heavy downpours, followed by lighter rain when, in my peripheral vision I saw a ball of fire in a giant cottonwood tree 100 yards to our left. The tree actually exploded, blowing giant limbs over a foot in diameter and several feet long flying high into the air. Instantly our car was far off the paving and onto the right shoulder as if we had been blown there—a full car width off the road—by the blast. My passengers saw and felt it too.

I may have overreacted in steering the car back on the paving and I pulled off the road at the next crossroad to stop and collect my wits. I asked if anybody was scared—besides me. The cattle feeder had commented that cattle on this feed had gained like magic. One of my passengers wisecracked that he had expected to see the magic in the feedlot, not alongside the highway. "You don't have to blow up any more trees for me," he told me, "I believe your stuff is magic. You can call off your thunderstorm."

Substitute Becomes All-Star

During the time that I was living in Denison, Iowa, and sharing my home with my brother, Rolland, he suggested that we should take two local friends to our ranch in Nebraska for a weekend of hunting ducks and pheasants. This was an easy sell and our invitation was instantly accepted by friends who had hunted together previously. We got along well so it looked like a nice outing.

Pheasant season opened at noon Saturday. The duck season had opened earlier and continued later. I had a busy schedule so we decided that brother Rowdy and one of our guests would go early and case the area for the best hunting. I would go Friday with the fourth hunter. Less than a week before D-Day for pheasants, one of our hunters had a family emergency and had to cancel. We needed a fourth, and we were not talking bridge.

Lee Bliesman, a Denison farm owner and realtor, was our anchor hunter. He asked if I knew Joe Vaage. "Yes," I said, "he's my banker, but he doesn't look to me like the outdoor type." Lee assured me that they had hunted together and he was sure we'd be satisfied if Joe would go so I went to the bank and told the teller I needed to talk to Mr. Vaage. He stepped out to the counter and I asked if he'd like to go hunting in Nebraska.

"Come in here," he almost ordered as he pushed me into his office. He went to a map and asked, "Where?" I pointed to Logan County. "Oh, boy, I never got that far out," he said. Then he asked what we were going to hunt. I told him we normally had good hunting for both ducks and pheasants. "Yeah, I'd love to go," he told me. Then I reminded him that I hadn't even told him what days we were going. "That doesn't matter," he said, "I always save some of my vacation for this time of year and this kind of deal. That way I'm always ready to go."

Rowdy and Lee left Wednesday and scouted all the regular places and asked about alternatives. They were comfortable with hunting ducks at the Milldale Ranch early Saturday morning, then driving about 15 miles to our home ranch to open the pheasant season at noon. Rowdy knew the owners. He got permission to hunt and the assurance that nobody else would be hunting there.

There were two nice lakes, each about 20 to 40 acres, and a quarter-mile apart. Then there was the South Loup River that connected to the lakes. They put decoys on the one lake. The other had about a half-acre of open water where the cows tramped down the cattails while drowning the flies. On the other (north) side of the fence was solid cattails. Ducks would crash trying to land there.

Early Saturday morning we drove to the lakes. The open area of the cattail lake was loaded with ducks that promptly flew away when we drove up. Lee and Joe gasped. They knew the hunting trip was over. But Rowdy and I had hunted there before. We flipped a coin, Joe and I won the cattails, Rowdy and Lee got the open water with the decoys and blind. Joe and I waded out along the fence to wait for game. We had a north wind and the open area was on the south.

After less than a half hour, we heard a single shot. Here came a nice flight of ducks, ready to land into the wind right in front of us. We each unloaded our three shots. The flight left and we retrieved our kill. Then we waited. Maybe they would come back. In minutes there was a shot at the other lake, and here came the flock again to land on our open water. Same story. One more repeat and we saw our last flight with the same results. We were within one bird of the daily limit for the four of us.

We decided on a head count and walked over to the blind on the other lake. Ducks had landed there but too far out for a kill so Rowdy and Lee shot once each time to spook them over to us. A short trip down the river flushed a teal so Lee filled our bag. Then it was home for the pheasant season. We limited out by the time we got through our second shelterbelt tree strip. Then comes the fun part of every hunting party—dressing the game.

Not only was my banker a dead shot but he had the fastest knife I ever saw. He dived into the cleaning job with gusto and before he had taught us his tips and shortcuts, the job was done. That slim-built, blond, anemic-looking banker was a tiger in disguise. He was an OK banker before we left Iowa. Now we were going back. I saw him in a new dimension and he had measured up well.

No True Believer Like a Convert

When I got into high school and got exposed to a bit of the world, as in high school ag class, I learned that other people were using fertilizer on some of their crops to increase yield. We spread barnyard manure on the sandiest knobs but we *knew* that our land couldn't handle fertilizer. It would burn up the crops. But I found it hard to accept that common knowledge as fact.

If fertilizer was potentially so damaging, why were the stalks of rye always bigger in diameter and standing inches taller, with bigger heads, producing bigger kernels where the seed had fallen and they grew up through a cow dropping than a few inches away with none of that potentially "damaging" fertilizer? I was sure that spot didn't get any more rain than the stalks a few inches away nor resist bugs any more. My dad could never give me a good enough answer to satisfy me. When I was in college after a hitch in the Navy, I decided to avail myself of the free soil tests being done by fertilizer dealers to determine how much of what fertilizer was needed. I couldn't wait to show my dad. "It's just to sell you something," he said. I took samples to college and got tests done. Similar results, both from the lab and from my dad.

We had just planted 60 acres of Intermediate Wheat Grass in rows, hoping to capitalize on the cash crop potential of selling seed with new recommendations for that crop. I dug out the soil test results from samples taken right under the middle of that planting. Still no sale. But when I came home from school months later, my dad had "invented" fertilizer.

He had used half the recommended levels on a 20-acre plot in the middle of the 60; a fourth of the recommend level along the highway (if it worked, he didn't want the neighbors to see failure) and none on the 20 farthest from the highway. At harvest time, the planting with no fertilizer had no seed. The plot near the highway had a crop worth harvesting, but on the 20 where he had used half the recommended level, he harvested nearly $200 worth of cleaned seed per acre.

It didn't end there; the popularity of Intermediate Wheat Grass went sky high the next year. He applied the recommended fertilizer—both the amount and formula—on the entire 60 acres and the seed price was out of sight. The net income from that one crop of seed was more than the value of the land. He couldn't wait to show me the stubble that the cattle grazed all fall.

And he had planted 40 acres of new alfalfa. We always had trouble getting a good stand of alfalfa. He used starter fertilizer, but not full recommendation, and had a record stand. Except that he had a thicker stand on the corners where he was afraid they had missed some ground on the turns so they went in and out on all the corners with the fertilizer spreader, but not with the seeder.

Then he said, "You need to see the pasture." Fertilizing native Sandhills pasture—you must be kidding! "When we got done with these fields, we had a few bags left," he said. "We just mixed them all up and spread them across the old prairie dog town and up the slopes on the edge of the dog town until we ran out of fertilizer." I asked him if it made the grass grow taller.

"We can't tell," he told me, excitedly. "The cows keep it grazed off so close to the ground—right to the inch where the spreader went—that it never gets 2 inches tall. They won't eat the unfertilized grass next to it as long as there's anything left to eat where we spread the fertilizer."

Small World—The Name's the Same

I met and worked with people over the entire Midwest in my job as trainee become sales promotion manager for a livestock feed manufacturer. They had varied backgrounds, financial accomplishments and attitudes but all were happy with my company and its products. The salesmen took me there to gather stories of success and accomplishment to use in advertising and promotion material. We did not collect failures and I was not a trouble shooter so I saw only happy folks.

I also supervised side-by-side or split-herd feed trials where a farmer would split a herd of similar livestock, feeding our product to half the herd while he fed a competitor's product to the other half. Rate of gain and cost of gain were recorded and our success spread by word of mouth in the local area and by company plan over a wider area. I took photos and wrote the history of the trials so I needed to have good interviews with the farmers.

Early in the sales history of a new feed supplement for fattening beef cattle, we conducted numerous side-by-side feed trials. Normally I went to the farm to interview the feeder and go over the feedlot, etc., with our local sales person before the test began or was authorized. This new product could beat any competitor and we were anxious to spread the news—fast—so several of our sales people were on their own to set up trials. When it was about to finish, I came to record results.

One such trial was at Wall Lake, Iowa. The feeder, Bill Raun, had split the herd but long before the test was over, it was obvious that we were leading and he had put a new lot of cattle on our feed. He continued the test and we needed the story and feedlot photos to make the test useful for us. When I was satisfied with the photos and story details I got off the track a bit and commented that his name was not common and that I had some friends in college named Raun.

"Ned and Rob?" he asked. When I agreed, he said, "They're my nephews. Are you from Nebraska?" I conceded I was and he asked where I was from.

"Up in the Sandhills," I told him.

"Where in the Sandhills?" he continued.

"Out near North Platte," I answered.

"Where near North Platte?" he came back.

"Did you ever hear of Stapleton?" I asked him.

"Do you know Bob Baskin?" he asked me and I said, "Sure, the train turns around in his pasture."

"Those are his steers in the feedlot. I've fed 'em for years."

Sometimes the best story is the story *after* the story. Best for me, that is, if not for the company.

Where's Lady?

Almost everybody who is not self-employed seems to be driven to climb that ladder to the supervisory or management level. And it's much later that most of the people who are successful at any or all these levels learn that the "good stuff" happens at the level where the company employee works with clients. When on my first livestock feed sales job, selling to farmers, I got to know Clint Whittlesea in Boone County, Iowa.

Clint was a good farmer and stockman but he excelled as a cow dog breeder and trainer. I never knew anybody with such a gold mine. He had a shepherd dog like I never saw before nor since. Lady was white with yellow-orange spots, long hair a lot like a border collie but her body was longer and slimmer and she was not that tall. The farm had cattle, sheep and hogs. Lady worked them all. And did it well.

Possibly the best thing about her was that she raised a litter of four or five pups every year. And she trained them herself. All Clint had to do was hang out with them enough that they could learn the hand signals, whistle and voice commands to go with Lady's actions. When the pups were 3 or 4 months of age, she would begin taking one pup at a time with her, leaving the others in the kennel area. By 8 to 10 months of age, they were trained.

Clint used a lot of my feed so I was at the farm often. But Lady and I had to be properly introduced every time. Until a member of the family told her it was all right, she was a fierce adversary. Even after being re-introduced, I have walked beside her, petting her on the back, and find her nipping me gently on the finger just to remind me that I was on her turf.

One day we were checking the condition of cattle in a lot. We opened the gate and Clint said, in a matter-of-fact tone, "Lady, watch the gate." She laid down in the open gate area and we walked through the cattle. Then we decided to look at the stock in the next lot, and the next and finally, about an hour later we were in the house drinking coffee.

Suddenly it hit Clint and he said, "Where's Lady?" Then he remembered we had left her guarding the first gate. We went back out to the lot and she was still faithfully challenging every steer that came near. No wonder Clint had deposits from buyers on every pup she would have for years.

You Know You Have a New Customer When . . .

During much of my life I have had more than one job at a time. Even when my job was a full-time position to do one specific job, management seemed to find a way to use part of me at something else. I was hired out of college as a so-called executive trainee. We built the training program as we went along and in some ways I was a high-class gofer, doing the odd jobs that nobody else was good at or they had enough status they could get out of.

Along with preparing product literature and publishing house organs and sales material, I wound up making tape-recorded on-the-farm interviews with satisfied customers for our radio commercials. I had completed most of the projects included in the training program and was going to transfer to a straight sales job. But there was no successor for the taped interviews so I agreed to continue that. It was a nice break from day-after-day farm calls.

My new sales territory was centered in Boone County, Iowa. It had been an abused territory in that the previous salesman developed a tendency to promise a customer whatever it took to get the order. Later, even though the product did all the customers really expected, it did not do what was promised, so they were mad—at him and the company. The company is always the last to learn of this behavior so we had some unhappy users and/or former users.

I spent my first several weeks visiting these people and got most of them to admit that the product did a good job—and that they really didn't believe what our salesman had told them. So after I got most of the former customers back in the fold, I began trying to sell to new customers. I enjoyed the challenge of driving into a farmer's yard, unannounced, and convincing him that he should use my product. Some bought readily, some bought later and some never bought at all.

One of the best farmer-feeders in Boone County was Ed Stumpenhorst. His account was one that I really wanted, but I was just not getting through to him. I did learn that he had moved to Iowa from Webster County, Nebraska during the drought and depression of the late 1930s but he never bought a pound of my feed. It just happened that one of my tours to make tape-recorded testimonials for our company advertising was going to be in his old home area.

I made interviews with three or four feeders in this area and after we were through with our tapes, I asked the farmers I was interviewing if they knew Ed when he lived there. When I asked the last feeder I interviewed in this area if he knew Ed, he said, "You bet. He was one of my best friends. Do you know him?" I explained that I was trying to get him for a customer and his long-time friend said, "Give me that microphone." He recorded a "Dear Ed—Hello" message for several minutes.

When I got back to Iowa that weekend I drove into the Stumpenhorst yard just about dusk on Sunday evening. Ed came to the door and I told him I had been to Nebraska and had a message from an old friend. His son's family was there but I told him that was OK and asked if I could come in. He wanted to know what the message was and I said I'd just play it, bringing in the recorder and plugging it into an outlet. It began to play the first interview. Ed said "I know him, does he use your feed?" Then the next interview began and they knew each other also.

Then the third began to run. These feeders were from different towns, but all in a 30 or 40 mile radius. The whole family sat listening almost in a trance. They acted like they just didn't believe it was happening. When the third interview was over and the personal message began, that big old farmer just cried, as did his wife, who was related to one of the people interviewed.

I was a little embarrassed but recovered when he asked if I would play it again. They served some dessert and coffee and I was invited back to talk about his feed program. It may have been a left-handed approach via Nebraska but I finally got this man's attention and he became a very loyal customer. Doing more than one job worked out OK for all of us this time.

The Flurry on the Fourth of July

Looking back on my days as a sales and service man, calling on farmers for a livestock feed manufacturer, it is easy to see why there are a lot of feed manufacturers. Many things can go wrong on the farm, mostly unrelated to the feed supplement, and few companies even try to follow up. It's cheaper to just let the user blame the feed company and change brands, assuming you will break even in the long run. You'll get as many as you lose.

My company grew by picking up the feeders that became disappointed with some other company's product—and by jealously guarding and giving service to the ones we had. And we had another reason in a few territories including the one that I worked. We had several flocks of parent stock hens that produced eggs for hatching commercial laying hens. We needed these flock owners to be good at managing because part of the company profit came from the sale of these eggs.

John Hasstedt, brother of the bookkeeper in our dealership, had one of these flocks. They had been raised from baby chicks on this farm, had been healthy for life and were just getting into full production when I got an urgent message from our bookkeeper. The flock of about 1,200 hens was getting up to about 1,000 eggs per day and in two days, dropped to about 30 eggs per day. What happened?

I went straight to the farm and talked to Mrs. Hasstedt, who took care of the flock except for heavy work like changing litter. Sudden drop in egg production is almost always the result of a shock. Many things can shock laying hens. I asked if they had ground new feed. No. Did you change floor litter in the house? No. Did a dog or other animal get loose in the house? No. It was early July and the house had automatic ventilating fans, had the power gone off to let the hens get overheated? No.

I then went to the house to begin snooping. I handled a few hens to see if they had lice or other parasites. No. The feeders were OK. The waterers were OK. I looked at all the windows and doors, the ceiling and floor. Nothing out of line. Desperate, I decided to walk around the outside of the house, probably as much to use time and let me collect my thoughts as to expect to find something. Then I saw a strange dent or break in two of the siding boards at the back of the hen house. Is this an old dent or a new one? She didn't know. Then the 19-year-old son, Roger, drove into the yard and came over to say hello. I asked him if he knew anything about the dent.

Sheepishly, he admitted that a few days earlier, on the 4th of July, he and some friends were firing homemade rockets. They found a tin can that fit nicely inside the pipe of a steel post driver. They put two giant-sized Fourth of July firecrackers in the post driver with a can full of mud for a bullet. This charge was apparently fired frequently during their holiday celebration.

They were afraid to be too close when the blast went off so they braced the post driver at a 60-degree angle with sticks. One of the blasts went off as the bracing gave away and the mud-filled can blasted into the back of the hen house. "Now that you mention it, I guess the hens did cackle and flew into a flurry but we didn't think much about it," he confessed. The hens molted (lost their feathers) but good nutrition brought them back into full "pre-fright" production in about six weeks. And Roger Hasstedt really worked at being my friend. I don't know how he smoothed over the loss of egg money with his mother.

Smile

When I started to college I wanted to become a high school ag teacher. No question about that. When I came back after nearly four years of flying for the Navy, I had no idea what career I wanted, much less what courses I wanted to register for at that moment. Finally, I asked Doc Downs, a dairy professor and our fraternity advisor for the University of Nebraska, what courses I should take to help my future career along.

Doc was a straightforward kind of guy. He asked, "What's easy for you?" I said, "No, Doc, you don't understand. I know what's easy. I want to know what I should take." First he wanted to know what was easy. I said "anything to do with the English language or livestock. Now, what should I take?"

"Have you thought of ag journalism?" he asked. I told him that I was doing just that, but just because I liked it and it was easy. He said, "Good. When you're in college, take what's easy for you. After graduation, do what you damn please." Now I was questioning him again: "what do you mean, do what you damn please?" But he pointed out that he, and several of the professors we both knew, had changed fields after graduation. I had a course—for now.

I always liked photography. It was magic. My first "big" purchase was a camera. So it was natural that I would register for a photo course my first year in serious journalism. And guess what? The teacher was a former dairy professor. Ray Morgan was a professional photographer outside the classroom. And as he began working on his master's degree, relating the physical measurements of the cow to her production, he used photography to provide proof.

He began using colored slides (rarely seen anywhere and never in the classroom) in teaching dairy science. Students registered for his classes not for the dairy, but because of the photos. The Chancellor heard about his work and called on him in the 1930s to set up a visual aids program for the U of N, a first in the history of college teaching. When he had the program going, Ray switched careers and transferred to photo journalism.

A few courses later when I registered for a photo "problems" course, to my surprise, Ray had learned that I, like he, was from ag college. My first "problem" assignment was to go to the University dairy and take a picture of three Holstein bull calves, with the same expression. That assignment, and others, taught me that I had as much patience as an animal—a crucial trait for a livestock photographer.

I almost followed Ray's lead. I had been registered in Ag College but as my interest in journalism continued, I transferred to Arts and Sciences and was a few courses in Spanish shy of graduation when I transferred back to get an Ag degree with a journalism certificate. My job began on Monday, graduation was on the following Friday. They kept my diploma in lieu of $25 for absentee graduation. I have never needed it so I guess they have it and I still have the $25.

I don't know if Ray was "playing God" in trying to build a career for me or vicariously re-visiting his old haunts, but most of my assignments in his photo class involved some scene in agriculture. When members of my family look back and wonder why I took so many photos of cows, horses and ranches—and so few of the family—they can blame it on Ray Morgan and Doc Downs, dairy professors who impacted my life.

And Your Assignment for Next Week . . .

Journalism, in my opinion as a former student and sometime practitioner, qualifies more as a trade school than being an orphan under the college of Arts and Sciences, which it was before it became a full "College of Journalism and Mass Communications" after my departure. We routinely got lab assignments—even regular course projects—almost as earthy as repairing dented fenders. I give our professors credit for exposing undergrads to the real world as we paired with *Lincoln Star* reporters on their beats.

Lincoln is a unique lab for journalism. It is one of few cities where you can report from the state capitol, county seat, city council and all the judicial branches plus the state university and several other colleges and the state prison, without ever leaving town. About the time you have to slap yourself to stay awake in county or city meetings you find yourself getting a new vocabulary of four-letter expletives in municipal court. And then came 1948.

The members of our advanced reporting class had a unique opportunity, or challenge. The three leading Republican presidential candidates were scheduled to appear on the campus within one week. Our assignment: Interview Harold Stassen, Robert Taft and Thomas Dewey next week. It seemed an easy job. Surely all candidates need press. We expected an interesting and memorable week.

Stassen was a former Minnesota governor and recently discharged Navy Captain. He held an informal coffee hour at one of the larger Student Union lounges on Tuesday. It was nearly a full house but he was open, smiling and cooperative. He made a brief statement of his goals and invited questions. He stayed and gave thoughtful answers as long as we had questions.

Taft was a U.S. Senator from Ohio. He was on the stage at the college theater the day after Stassen. I expected him to be aloof and dogmatic but not as open and cooperative as Stassen had been. He came across as a really warm, guy-next-door kind of person but he gave deeper answers that energized your thought processes and, for a dozen journalism-class reporters, stimulated follow-up questions. We were all amazed at his apparent understanding and his invitation for us to come on stage to ask questions when his general remarks were over.

Dewey was Governor and former Attorney General of New York. He was appearing at the auditorium on Saturday night. We could not learn his pre-speech schedule from anyone, including the local Republican Party officials. It looked as if most of our class would get two-thirds, but not all of our assignment. I was sure he would stay at the Cornhusker Hotel, the leading hotel in Lincoln. I called the hotel; they denied that he had reservations.

This was one time when, thanks to pure dumb luck, I knew the right person . . . one who knew more about the minute-to-minute schedule of my quarry than anyone else in the world. I had been on the high school football team with Don Cahill, the Stapleton grad that helped me get situated when I first came to Lincoln fresh out of high school. He was in management training at the Cornhusker and being bell captain was his assignment for a few weeks. I called him and found that the Dewey party had reservations.

We had the feeling that if they were so secretive about their plans, it might be tough to get access but I was determined to complete my

152

assignment. Don suggested that he make me a bellboy for a few hours and take a message to the room, if nothing else. Don learned that the schedule called for a mid-afternoon arrival at a little-used door, time to review his speech, dinner in the room and a limousine to the auditorium. He was not even meeting with local Republican dignitaries on the Lincoln stop. There were only two people with him.

Another college student worked part-time as a bellboy. Don decided that we should both take any calls to the Dewey suite, that two of us might be more able to distract an aide, if necessary, so I could get to Dewey for some kind of interview. He was right. Don deliberately misplaced a briefcase when the party arrived. About an hour later they called about it and were told that it was found and we delivered it to the room.

Dewey was sitting at a desk when we got to the room. We welcomed him to Lincoln and I told him I was sorry I had to work and would miss his address and asked if he could give a few answers for my assignment as a journalism student, working my way through college. His face became flushed and he accused me of being in his room under false pretenses.

It was much later when it occurred to me that I should have accused him of the same thing. What a contrast in attitude with candidates Stassen and Taft. While I did not have much of an interview to turn in as an assignment, I was the only member of the class who even saw all three, close up. And the professor made me Exhibit A for ingenuity for at least getting to see the candidate. It was enough to make you change majors—or vote for Harry Truman. Maybe writer Dorothy Thompson was right in saying that Thomas Dewey was "a person whom you must know intimately to detest adequately."

Maternity Ward Stand-In

As a sales/service representative for a livestock feed company, I found more real, salt-of-the-earth people than in any work I have ever done. One of my best potential customers was Jim Kelly. He was a solid livestock farmer who raised a good number of hogs, had about a thousand laying hens and fed several hundred steers every year. I got to know the Kellys after a neighbor recommended that I tell them about our hatching-egg poultry contract. They were allegedly good with livestock and had a really good hen house.

I stopped and explained the program and a few days later, after visiting with the referrer, they signed a contract. They raised the chickens and used our poultry feed, as per the contract, but did not buy a pound of feed for any other stock. One day I stopped for a routine check on the hen flock and Jim was in a bad mood, he was up all day and all night farrowing pigs. I told him I'd be glad to "midwife" his sows for the night—whatever night he chose.

I convinced him that I'd done it before. There was a cot and an alarm clock in the farrowing house, so I showed up in the evening after supper for my shift. He came out about 10 p.m. with hot coffee and found me attending a sow in labor as I took each newborn baby, put it under a heat lamp until she had finished, then put the litter back with the mother where they settled down. Jim saw I was on familiar ground so he left me and went to the house.

Next morning he came out to invite me in for breakfast. "What do I owe you?" he asked. "Nothing," I told him, "I like to keep sharp. But I'd appreciate it if you'd try our pig starter and let me visit about some other products." He was noncommittal but a few days later he left a message at our dealership that he wanted to see me. When I got to the farm, he wanted me to look at his steers. "They don't look thrifty," he told me, "and they look dirty around their eyes."

The local veterinarian had just told me it was a terrible year for lice. The steers were tame so I found one lying down, chewing his cud, and looked closely at the skin around his eye, then took a pinch with my fingernail. I got a couple of lice. We put him in a squeeze chute to find much of his skin caked with lice. Even though I told him it was a bad year for lice, the owner was aghast, like he had been accused of a felony. I convinced him that if we treated for lice and put the cattle on my feed they should really race to market. He agreed and we did . . . and they did.

As the months passed, I had a call almost every week from a feeder in the area that wanted me to explain my feed program, and became instant buyers. Rarely did one tell me that Jim Kelly had sent them, but the bookkeeper at our dealership commented one day that I sure had "a way with the Catholics. We've never done any business with them before," she said. I told her a good bedside manner in the maternity ward would work with any denomination.

Once a Horse Trader . . .

One of my first recollections regarding livestock judging was a photo of the classic style for a draft horse. That model was the Belgian stallion, Jay Farceur. Little did I know then that years later I would cross trails with the rest of the story when I was working as a sales/service representative in Boone County, Iowa. My acquaintances there included Lowell Good, son of Grant Good.

Grant had been a horseman, an exceptional judge of horse flesh and while he probably did not covet the title, I would have to call him a first-rate horse trader. He was a breeder of Belgian horses without equal. He had gone to France and found a young stallion with a great pedigree which he purchased and imported to Iowa. This colt was Jay Farceur. Good showed him to International Grand Championships and stood him at stud for many years at record prices.

Jay Farceur's greatest son, both for classic appearance and as a progenitor of great horses, turned out to be a colt sold to a horse breeder in a small town

154

in Southern Minnesota. Grant had gone to visit the young stallion several times and the owner felt Grant was effusive with his flattery. He never missed a chance to tell the owner that he would buy him back someday, but of course "someday" never seemed to come.

Then one day, without notice, Grant Good drove into the Minnesota farm, told the colt's owner he was there to buy him and asked the owner how much he wanted. The owner had a farm full of the colt's offspring and while he was not great at procuring mares, had enjoyed reasonable income from stud fees. He felt that his horse would never have much value while the sire lived, so he quoted a reasonable price. Grant wrote him a check for that amount, then he asked for permission to use the phone to call home.

Within an hour, a driver drove to the farm, loaded the young stallion onto a truck, and drove down the road. The next day, after the truck carrying his newly purchased stallion arrived back in Ogden, Iowa, Grant Good made another phone call—to announce to the world that Jay Farceur had died—on the day before he drove to Minnesota to buy back his No. 1 son.

Something New in the State of Maine

Bob Neumeyer and I had double-dated teachers in Denison, Iowa, and Bob married one. I had hired him to be a salesman for the livestock feed company I had worked for since college. He had done well and was promoted to the state sales manager's job in eastern Iowa. In 1959 we decided to take a vacation trip to the east coast together.

I had purchased a 1958 Oldsmobile, the dealer's demonstrator. It was big-bodied and road-hungry, the perfect vacation car. We went to Milwaukee and saw a baseball game, took the overnight ferry boat across Lake Michigan and drove to Canada and on to New York, where Bob's wife, Hollyce, had a stock broker cousin with extra room. It was a great base for a few days of exploring the area.

The stock broker cousins had tickets to the Yankees "old timers" game, and we made a tour of the New England states, including a visit with my brother Rowdy, who had been recalled to the Army and was putting in time at Ft. Devens, Massachusetts, and on to Maine. We found that at that time, most of New England felt it was a sin to eat out so, except for Howard Johnson, they hid all the restaurants from tourists.

But in Maine, we found a handsome, if weather-beaten, seafood house sitting high on a cliff above the pounding surf of the Atlantic Ocean at dinner time and decided to give it a try. We each ordered a different selection from the menu to exchange and sample a variety of their specialties. Then I threw their regimen into a tailspin.

I am not much of a seafood eater. The smell is at least mildly offensive to me but the taste of strong-smelling or strong-flavored fish really challenges my upchuck reflex. I have always hated the tartar sauce served with fish. It is almost more offensive to me than the fish smell itself. But shrimp or cocktail sauce, if generously used, helps me survive a seafood meal without gagging.

I ordered cocktail sauce with my order. The waiter stopped, got that funny look, like I had just insulted the founder, and asked exactly what I wanted. I said I just wanted "cocktail sauce, shrimp sauce, whatever you call it here. You know, what you serve with a shrimp cocktail." He still looked at me as if I were speaking in a foreign language, which turned out to be the case. He left with what I felt was an uncomfortable, quizzical look.

He returned to tell me that nobody in the kitchen knew what I had in mind. I asked him if they had ketchup. Yes they did. Horseradish? Yes they did. How about Tabasco sauce? Yes. But he didn't give me any satisfaction that he believed these should be in the same pot. I told him to get a bowl, use about 2 or 3 parts ketchup, 1 part horseradish and a couple of shots of Tabasco and stir in a little salt. No big deal.

It was a big deal. He returned with tray, bowl, ketchup, horseradish, Tabasco and a big spoon. Oh, yes, the entire kitchen staff tagged along with him. If they came to shame me into eating tartar sauce, they picked the wrong diner. I had never made the stuff before. Thankfully, I never had to. And I knew we had no manufacturer's sample to use for a comparison.

Bob gave me that look, like now you talked yourself into a fix. But I didn't disappoint them, or myself. I put the ingredients in the bowl in my suggested proportions, gave them a good stir and tasted it with a spoon. I was close enough for any seafood house. The staff watched, then they wanted a sample, although all looked as if they didn't really believe what they had seen. Some seemed to like it, others still didn't believe.

Soon our dinners were served. I don't remember the specific entrees or how we rated them on a score of 1-to-10, but thanks to the sauce, the ocean-view setting and the experience with the kitchen staff, we had a forever-memorable experience. When we finally rose to leave, our waiter and some of the staff came to present each of us with a menu—and generous applause. Some time I want to go back to Maine to see if that sauce ever caught on.

A Simple Mistake in Identity

I was sharing an apartment in Denison with a young attorney. We were overdue to host a party for our unofficial social group that included several people with better party facilities than our small digs. One of our friends was also a salesman of mine. He had purchased a finished basement and was in the process of building a house on it. We decided that the empty basement was the best party room around so we got permission to use it.

It was nearly Halloween and the Denison High School football team was to play a major game on Friday night. We imported a few bales of straw for

156

seats, a few pumpkins and cornstalks for decorations and the party was to begin after the ball game. We told the guests they were welcome to bring their own drinks if they liked, but that we would furnish hot, spiced cider.

We got several gallons of apple cider and borrowed a 3- or 4-gallon pot to heat the cider on the kitchen range in the basement apartment. We heated it to near boiling, then set the stove to keep it warm, while we went to the game. While most of our friends were not teetotalers, none were serious drinkers. A few complimented us on planning a "cider" party.

The friends collected at the party site after the game and dug right into the snacks and hot, spiced cider with the brisk evening temperature outside. Only a few minutes later I was surprised that the party had become so relaxed, almost raucous. I asked Bill, my co-host if somebody was spiking the punch or passing a bottle around. He had noticed the same attitude among the guests and claimed to be as surprised at their behavior as I was.

The next thing I noticed was one of the normally dignified schoolteachers in a bull-like charge with pieces of corn stalks for horns while her date, using another corn stalk as a sword, stabbed as if to make the living room a bull ring—as several guests applauded and screamed *Olé!* This party seemed to be getting out of hand and we had no idea as to why. We had not seen a bottle of liquid courage anywhere but we were sure somebody was spiking the cider.

Finally several of the guests had practically collapsed so Bill and I, who had been pretty dry in our hosting duties, began driving people home. We were still in a quandary about the mellow condition of most guests. We had not seen a bottle in the apartment and had not noticed people go outside and besides, they knew us well enough that they wouldn't have sneaked anything in, they would have been overt about it if they had done it. One guest later asked if we knew—did he switch from cider to booze?

There was a little cider in the bottom of the pot when we closed up shop so we dumped it down the drain. But the next morning we found a cider jug that was still about half full. Bill poured a little in a glass for a mid-morning refresher and got a funny look on his face. "Taste this," he said, almost threatening. It was real fuzzy tasting. We didn't notice; in fact, I don't think that either Bill or I even tasted it before the party. Try to explain to your guests that Mother Nature, with jugs not tightly sealed, had spiked the punch. With that spice and heat, nobody tasted the bite, but the spiced cider we served . . . was really . . . hard cider. *Olé!*

You Can be Great if Your Audience Doesn't Know

I took a sales job after about three years in the executive training program. I picked an abused territory and one that had been selected to supervise flocks of hens producing hatching eggs for the hybrid poultry division of the company. We delivered day-old chicks to farmers, who raised them and sold eggs to us for a premium price after the flock matured and began to lay eggs for the hatching season.

One of my jobs was checking to see that the birds were healthy and that the farmer followed prescribed vaccination and development schedules. I don't know whether confinement-raised poultry get sick or what sicknesses they get, but when they are raised on dirt that has ever had chickens nearby, they are likely to get an intestinal infection called coccidiosis. Flock supervisors expect it, see symptoms and prescribe treatment. No big deal— but I hadn't been there and done that . . . before.

As the first few thousand babies began to grow, I went to meetings and read textbooks about potential problems. And I clipped out a color description of what a chick with coccidiosis looked like—outside and inside—from Successful Farming magazine and from the Dr. Salisbury (pharmaceutical manufacturer) manual. They showed in detail how to do a post mortem exam and how to identify coccidiosis. I had a date with the hatchery serviceman to see what a sick chick looked like inside.

Then I made a farm call and noticed that some of the chicks did not look healthy. I inquired and found the farmer's wife had noticed it a day earlier but had not called. One chick that was a little over a month old and might have weighed half a pound had died. The wife asked if I could take it to the lab and get a post-mortem exam to see what had made it sick.

I told her I was not an expert but I would like to look inside right then, that I had surgical scissors in my pocket. When she agreed, I went into instant recall mode. I snipped the skin at the end of the breastbone, then a snip on each side and I was inside. Since chicks with coccidiosis go off feed, the intestine would be empty so I opened the large intestine to find large red blotches, just like the photo in the manual. The diagnosis was easy, I thought.

I retrieved the manual from my car and showed the lady with the chickens how closely our sample matched a "classic" case. I told her I'd bring medicine to treat the flock, took the chicken to town and conferred with the serviceman for the hatchery who said I had been lucky. Big relief. When I returned with medicine, the wife said she had never seen anyone do that kind of surgery and I looked so professional. She asked if I had ever thought of taking up medicine. I surely never told her that it was the first post mortem I had ever done or even seen.

I Don't Know Beans

The livestock feed company I worked for manufactured concentrated feed supplements. They were made of minerals, vitamins and high-quality protein ingredients and needed to be mixed with large amounts of grain and sometimes additional protein supplements like soybean meal. Our product

158

was far more concentrated than most of our competitors. It was sometimes a problem to get the product properly mixed with grain on the farm.

Some companies added the grain in their manufacturing plants but had to freight the grain back to the farm. There were some commercial mixers and we sold mixers but many farmers did not want an extra machine. In my trips around the Midwest, I found good feed mills every 25 to 50 miles. Almost all had extra capacity. This seemed a potential solution for both of us.

I had the idea of contracting with many of these mills to mix our product with local grains and become sub-manufacturers for us. When I presented the idea to a staff meeting, it seemed so obvious that some staff members felt there must be unseen problems. Management asked me to develop the program and set up test areas to see how it worked and how to solve problems that might arise.

The company gave me a desk and a secretary and asked me to check in with the production department as I developed the program and contracted with the first "guinea pig" sub-manufacturers. They estimated it would take at least two to three years with lots of meetings and trouble-shooting—maybe five years—to cover the company's trade area but it was such a natural, before a year was up, I had basically finished the job and was staying out of the office so they wouldn't know I wasn't working.

I returned from one trip through northwest Iowa and South Dakota when Bill, a staffer in the money department, asked me, "What's new out in the country?" He did this every week or two and I never knew exactly what he wanted to know. On this occasion I told him that I knew the country was going to have a record soybean crop. "How do you know that?" he asked.

I told him I had been in several areas where dealers told me they had sold thousands of bushels of soybean seed last spring to farmers who had never planted a bean before and the yields, in August, appeared to be very high. "Is that true?" he asked, probing deeper. "Who did you talk to?" he wanted to know. I named several of our people—salesmen and dealers—and he began to call them on the phone, immediately.

He probed them as he had asked me and finally he looked at me and said, "Phil, do you have any money you could afford to lose?" I didn't know what he meant but then he told me that the company always forward contracted feed ingredients at what they hoped would be low prices. This gave us a price advantage which could let us sell our product cheaper or make more profit.

"The Department of Agriculture will announce the next crop forecast in two days. If what you and these dealers tell me is true, soybean prices will drop through the floor. You can contract 100 tons of soybean meal for $250 (later was changed to $750) margin. It's no big deal for soybean meal to drop $5 to $10 or even $20 a ton in deals like this. If you own a hundred tons, that's $500 or $1,000 or $2,000. That's big money, with only $250 at risk!" he almost yelled at me trying to make sure I understood.

The next morning I told Bill I had $500 that I could spare and asked what to do. We went to the commodity broker and I contracted for my two units—200 tons—of soybean meal. I don't know how much Bill put up, but it made me look like a beginner, which I was. And he was right. The day after we made our contracts, the USDA announced an expected record soybean yield as usual.

Prices dropped exactly as predicted—over $10 a ton in a couple of days. I was up $2,000, less the $500 deposit, in a couple of days. I took $500 of my profits and contracted for 200 more tons and waited. In a few weeks I called the broker and asked about my account. He said I would make just over $6,000 if I sold. I gasped and told him to sell immediately. He suggested I could take some profit but stay in the market. "Sell," I told him. "I don't know beans about beans. Bill got me into this, now you get me out." I was uneasy until I got the check.

A few days later the northern Corn Belt had an early frost. Soybean prices shot up as fast as they had fallen a few weeks earlier. If I hadn't sold, most of my profit would have been wiped out. Bill came to me and asked, "What are you going to do about your soybeans?" "Oh, I sold out," I told him "I just felt uncomfortable. I just took my money and ran." He kept his position, hoping to wait for capital gains tax treatment (six months then). When he complained about the new, lower prices, I heard the adage for the first time in my young life oft repeated in later years, "Bulls make money and bears make money, but hogs get slaughtered."

Fair Weather Job Seeker

While it may be true that nobody can ever be totally objective about anything, I can guarantee that responding to job interviews in February makes objectivity next to impossible. After a dozen years with one firm, a company merger sent me to find a new job. The family ownership did not follow through on their promises so I went looking again. The interviews came down to American Breeders Service, with offices in Chicago and near Madison, Wisconsin, who had an opening as ad manager, and *Western Livestock Journal*, owned by Crow Publications in Los Angeles, who wanted to hire a new field editor. ABS was a leader in artificial breeding—biggest and oldest in their field with a good reputation among employees and a friend of mine was their account exec at the ad agency. The L.A. job also had good references and the industry leader. Both jobs seemed well within my interest and ability.

My ABS interview was in Chicago. The temperature was near zero degrees and there was enough blowing snow to make Lake Michigan a blurry mess. The people in Los Angeles met me at the airport the next week in short sleeves. What a difference, and what a chance if I really wanted to go back to the California that I liked when I was there in the Navy, even though our training was not always fun and games.

When I got back to the Midwest, I made a phone call to my ad agency friend to learn that they had decided to give me the ABS job. It was still an ugly, snowy winter. I called Los Angeles and told them I had decided to take their job—that I had never had a problem with rolling up my sleeves but having a job where I wore short sleeves was even better. And I called Chicago, asking them to remove my name from consideration as advertising manager. A fair weather employee if ever there was one. Incidentally, we have lived in California ever since.

A Good First Impression

Every freshman needs an advisor to get registered for the right courses, it seems. But I learned that you don't have to accept the schedule they arrange for you as final. I registered for Alexander's afternoon class in Animal Husbandry. Then a few weeks later I got a chance to work afternoons and since my mornings were open and a job meant the money I desperately needed, I got permission to change to Dr. Hanson's morning class.

My first day in class, I was given the last seat, alphabetically, after Warner and Wirth. Then we went to the barn for lab, where we practiced judging beef cattle, including a class of young Hereford bulls and a class of just-weaned Angus bulls. Before we handed in the cards with our placings, Dr. Hanson asked students to guess the average weight of the Angus bulls and put it on the bottom of our grading cards.

Several hands went up and he began asking class members for their weight guesses. I was not anxious to volunteer but these guys were saying numbers like 330 pounds, 350 pounds, 300 pounds, even as low as 250 pounds each. He began thumbing the cards and finally came up with mine and called my name. Apparently I had guessed the heaviest weight in class.

I had just come to college from the ranch where we had weighed dozens of calves. And I had heard that when it came to guessing weights, you added 10 percent if they were bulls and 10 percent if they were Angus. I felt they would weigh about 400 to 425 lbs. over our scales, and then added the 20 percent so I guessed 500 pounds each. I was surprised but the rest of the class just gasped when he announced that they had weighed an average of 530 pounds that morning.

This was not the first time I guessed cattle weights but this writing is not to show that I was either good or lucky on that day. The thing I want to point out is that I was wearing a bright red high school letter sweater. The "S" had been removed because I heard they would tear it off when you got to college. But when he called my name and I held up my hand, Doc pointed to me and said, "You in the red, what do you think they weigh?"

I got almost straight A's in Hanson's class, and in his nutrition class later. My work may have been good enough to get A's but I always felt part of it was due to the fact that I got lucky by having my good fortune in that first class, the late assignment of a seat out of alphabetical order—plus the identification that made me stand out—to be "memorable"—with that red sweater on my first day in class. Who says high school football doesn't help you in college?

No Wonder Bryan Lost

Pundits of the era might believe that James Lawrence's greatest claim to fame was that he was twice the manager of William Jennings Bryan's unsuccessful campaigns for President of the United States. Otherwise, Lawrence was editor of the *Lincoln Star*. The Journalism School at the University of Nebraska had a unique arrangement whereby students who were enrolled in an advanced reporting class spent a semester "riding shotgun" with regular *Star* reporters.

This was a rare experience at several levels. Lincoln is the Nebraska State Capitol so reporter beats covered the state, county and city government from the standpoint of legislative, executive and judicial departments, to say nothing of the state prison, the University of Nebraska and three church-sponsored colleges. But nature demands a balance. For the privilege of tagging along, learning from regular reporters, the Journalism department kept Lawrence on the staff as the lecturer and resident "editorial" authority.

There may have been a time in his earlier life when Jimmy Lawrence was an asset in more than name. That time had passed in the opinion of nearly 40 of us who were obliged to take his course. His night lecture was from 7 p.m. to 9 p.m. on Wednesday. There was a lab under another professor where we put together a newspaper twice a week; this made the course bearable. And fortunately, your grade was the average of your lab and lecture grades, according to Lawrence.

The first night we attended the lecture, Jimmy seated us alphabetically—an insult to juniors and seniors eligible for the course. Then, like a third grade teacher laying down the rules, he strode from one side of the room to the other, gripping his chin with each phrase as if "milking" out each word. "You will attend this lecture every Wednesday evening during the semester and one percentage point will be deducted from your final grade in this section for each unexcused absence. There are no excused absences. You will read five major newspapers, of your choice, daily, except that the *Lincoln Star* is a required newspaper, and you will keep a scrapbook of the four or five leading stories each day, for the semester, with your positive or negative comments regarding each story.

"One-third of your grade in this lecture section will come from your news notebook and one-third will come from each of two examinations, a mid-semester and a final exam. One-half of your final grade will come from this lecture and one-half will come from your laboratory. I have nothing to say about your grade in the laboratory section but I have everything to say about your grade in this lecture section."

This was the fall of 1948, the year of presidential elections, and Lawrence was in his glory. "You are so lucky to be in this profession and to be learning at this historic time," he lectured us. But that was only the beginning. I attended the first and second lectures and had clipped the lead stories from a few newspapers but then I heard that Lawrence rarely asked for the news notebooks at the end of the semester. Further, I heard that he almost never got his papers corrected nor turned in his grades on time so your lab grade became your course final grade.

Another *Daily Nebraskan* staff member, Cub Clem, was in the class. We agreed that since it was required for a Journalism certificate, we might have to re-take the class some day but for now we'd take a calculated risk. We would not keep a news notebook nor go to class until the mid-semester test, at least. If we got an incomplete, we could take the course again.

We went to see what the mid-semester exam looked like. It was right after the November elections. He listed about 20 states and asked for the approximate vote in each of these states for president, senator, governor, etc. "That is, if New York cast a million votes, I want you to say that 530,000 voted Democrat and 470,000 voted Republican for president, then give the approximate difference at the senatorial and gubernatorial levels—within 5,000 or so—and tell me why it came out the way it did." That was Question 1. The test continued.

We both left in about 30 minutes and never returned to the class. We heard that his final exam was just as bad—and that he did not even come to give the final exam, but sent his secretary, who did not ask for the news notebooks. I did well in the lab section and the professor recommended me for a job before the semester ended.

I got an "A" in his lab and when the final grades came out, that was my final grade in the course. The experience of traveling the beats with *Star* reporters was the best lab I had in any course but our experience in Wednesday night lecture would have neutralized that benefit if Cub Clem and I hadn't decided to take a chance on Bryan's losing campaign manager.

Sometimes it's Just Your Day

We wheeled off the Pennsylvania Turnpike for gas while on vacation in 1959, and the generator warning light on the dashboard came on. We were several miles from the town of Hershey, but there was a small town near the turnpike exit. It was after closing time for most businesses so we decided to get a motel room and rush to the garage in the morning—and pray a lot. After all, we were miles from the comfortable feeling of a hometown garage.

When we checked into the motel, I asked the owner if he knew a good auto repair shop. He said they had a good shop, he liked it so well that when he bought a new car, he bought it from that dealership, even though it meant changing from his previous brand of auto. "They are Oldsmobile dealers," he said, and because he knew the shop foreman he called him at home to make an appointment for us to go in the next morning. I was driving an Oldsmobile; maybe I was really in luck.

I pulled into the shop the next morning, fearing the worst since we were far from home. My car was logged in by the service writer and then it went straight to a service bay. The mechanic raised the hood and let out a whistle like a mating call. He yelled to all the mechanics, "Hey guys, come look at this one." It may have been a curio, at least in this part of Pennsylvania.

It was an Olds 98, a dealer demo, with all the gadgets. That included a six-barreled carburetor, air conditioning, air suspension and probably would have had more except there was absolutely no more room under the hood. Every time another mechanic came to look, I could see the price go up on the repair bill. But the mechanic didn't miss a lick. He did his diagnostic work and then told me our problem.

He told me that their dealership had only sold two cars in the past year with air conditioning so they carried almost no parts specifically needed for cars with air conditioners. The rotor on the generator was so worn that it was shorting out the brushes and I needed a new rotor. He said he would try a temporary repair by removing the rotor and cutting little grooves with a hacksaw blade so it would let me drive, hopefully continuing to charge, for a few thousand more miles.

I was "buying a pig in a poke" but I was a long way from home. He worked as fast as I could have hoped or imagined and in about three hours he told me that the car was ready to go and the office had my bill ready. I was anxious for the car but not the bill. Boy, were we in a small town! I don't remember the amount but I know it was less than I'd have paid at home. Sometimes it is just your day. And the repair lasted until we had it replaced when we got home.

The Graduates Wore White

I have always held stuffed shirts in contempt. I don't even care much for formal functions and prefer they just give the information over the phone or send it in the mail. This has had nothing to do with the fact that I only attended one of the several graduations that occurred where I have been involved, for one reason or another. I did show up when it really counted.

Our county had several one-room schools and a "promotion" ceremony was planned for all eighth graders, fairly advanced conduct for 1937. My horse never had a sick day in her life until the scheduled graduation day, when she had serious colic and I insisted on staying until the vet came and went. She recovered and I was in the ninth grade the next year, just like the kids who made it into town for the formal graduation ceremony that night.

High school graduation was scheduled to be a big deal. The school had even rented caps and gowns for the graduates—all 19 of us. But the weatherman had no control and a spring storm dropped a cloudburst on our area at the time most graduates were preparing to leave for the ceremony. The storm was so severe that the only graduates who attended were those who lived in the south end of town, near the school. And the two boys who lived in that end of town didn't want to be the only boys so they boycotted the event and only a few girls showed up that night to officially "graduate."

The next graduation that I had a chance to miss, thanks to having my college interrupted by World War II, was the day we got our commission as Navy Ensigns and wings as Naval Aviators. The Navy was impersonal, but insisted that you be present. If you had completed your requirements, you graduated. If it took another week to complete them, you graduated next week with another group of new Ensigns, but whenever it was . . . you had to be there.

The Navy had several "official" uniforms. They had several Naval districts, covering all bases within specific geographic areas. In the New York district, you wore Navy Blues every month of the year. Chicago wore Blues with a white hat cover, as did San Francisco. In Corpus Christi, Texas, where I took my advanced flight training and where I graduated, Navy Whites were the "uniform of the day" every day, summer and/or winter.

There were several hundred of us on the parade grounds on graduation day and it was an impressive sight. I'm sure Japan would have surrendered on the spot if a photo of our graduation class had been sent to Tokyo. The ceremony had no speeches; it was just long enough for remarks from the Admiral, a salute, and award of the Naval Aviator Certificates one at a time.

When I went back to college I even liked ritual and ceremony less than before. However even my dislike for wasting time on ritual had little to do with my next non-graduation. Mid-year graduation isn't a big deal compared with the tradition of June ceremonies. But college officials try to give importance to their institutions by insisting that you graduate on their terms—you attend graduation ceremonies.

I had a job that was to begin on the first of February. As I remember, that was on Monday or Tuesday. Graduation was scheduled for the following Friday. My new employer would probably have given me a few days to attend the ceremony but I didn't ask. The University of Nebraska wanted $25 for "absentee" graduation and I felt that was silly. I already had a job. I still have the $25 and they still have my diploma, which I have never needed.

My Chemistry Grade is in the Newspaper

Science was never my strong suit. I always had trouble concentrating on one topic. I did best when I waited until I had several jobs, and then did them all at once. My brain is happier riding off in many directions, exploring many options, than being stuck on one course. So it was no surprise that I'd have a problem trying to concentrate on topics as confining as science; any science.

Except that I needed the discipline of the required subjects demanded by an ag college, I'd have been happier taking liberal arts. When it came to math and science, instead of having to pin it down to a specific answer, I'd rather you tell me what you want it to be and let me write something to justify it. All the science courses require that you absolutely know the answer, their answer, not mine. You can't editorialize.

I was taking a basic chemistry course during my first semester in school after getting out of military service. I had also been named ag editor of the *Daily Nebraskan*. In the lecture, the chem teacher asked a question, and then picked the name of a student from his roster. Wrong answer. Then he asked another student. Another wrong answer.

This gave me plenty of time to thumb through my book and find the right answer, and by divine providence or other good luck, he said, "Well, let's see what our journalist friend has to say about this, Mr. Raynard, what is your answer?" I had written a story on the opening of the Ag Student Union for the paper that ran two columns wide down the middle of the front page that day, with my byline so it was easy for him to call me by name.

I gave the best answer of my college science career and good enough for Dr. Abbott. I don't think he ever asked me another question, but I didn't need it. My reputation was made in his course—far better than I deserved—and he gave me an 85 percent for a final course grade. But even more embarrassing than getting a grade I didn't deserve, every mention of a chemical function related to paper or ink, always brought his connecting that reaction to "our journalist friend." We had others in the class who were miles ahead of me in journalism and almost anyone else in the class knew more about even paper-making chemical reactions than I. But I continued to be his "journalistic" bookmark for that course. And it didn't end there. I think the chem professors compared notes.

I barely knew enough about organic chem to draw the benzene ring but I got a grade in the '80s, just for showing up. Thank you, Dr. Abbott, for paying attention to feature stories in the *Daily Nebraskan* and for giving me credit for stuff I didn't know. Another example of being able to editorialize the answers and get a grade I didn't deserve in, of all classes, chemistry.

My Dad, the Feed Salesman

Our ranch was just outside the perimeter of the geographical area that our company tried to cover when I was in the feed business. I made no effort to get my dad to use our products but one of my jobs was supervising side-by-side or split herd feed tests. The farmer used our feed for half the herd and a competitor's product for the other half and at market time we tallied up. We had a money-back guarantee that our feed would perform equal or better than any competitive product, and at lower cost, or your money back

My company manufactured a vitamin-mineral product which I named Pasture Plus, to identify it in company research trials, etc. It was designed to supplement pasture and enable cows to breed back more quickly after calving and promote herd health in general. I mentioned the idea of splitting our cow herd and testing the product—no guarantee, of course—but it would be a way for me to see how well the product worked outside our sales area.

We had enough fields to make the test easy but I was still surprised when my dad went for the idea. He was normally suspicious of anything new. *Why would he go for this deal?* I wondered. We put the cows in the test fields as soon as they calved so the cows would have a few weeks to rebuild nutritional deficiencies, if any, before breeding time. We had written a protocol to follow in the test but I left with little expectation that it would be carried out.

Several months later I was at home for a few days. First order of business was to see the cow/calf test. "Is it all right for the calves to eat that stuff?" was dad's first question. They were licking it up with their mothers from free-choice feed boxes. Since nobody kept records every day, we wouldn't know until next year at calving time which half of the herd had bred back best. But we got our first surprise when we began to weigh the calves. Supplemented calves were several pounds heavier than their non-supplemented mates.

At the next calving time, every cow in the supplemented herd was pregnant and they had bred on the first or second service. The calf crop was more uniform and since more were conceived on the first or second service, more were born earlier, hence heavier at market time. I tried to convince my dad to continue the test for another year but he said he was already smart enough, now he wanted to get a little richer, and supplement the entire herd.

Dad had a bad habit. He couldn't keep a secret. One day he called me at the office and asked if he could buy some extra feed for the neighbors. I assured him that it was OK—even encouraged—and signed him to a dealership contract so he could make a few bucks while he spread the good news. If anyone would have called him a salesman it would have scared him from ever mentioning the stuff again. This incident really gave me a great story to tell our salesmen and dealers at company meetings regarding the use of Pasture Plus. Yes, the name I stuck on the new product during development had stuck.

I never did know whether he sold it at full retail price and kept the mark-up or simply let the neighbors have it at his cost because he believed in the product and wanted to help. He never sold much of any other product we made but for several years he was our top Pasture Plus salesman, just because he couldn't keep from bragging to the neighbors about an unusual product that did the job. I occasionally wondered how well my earlier neophyte Hereford herd would have performed years earlier if Pasture Plus had been invented then.

Mischief in Vail

Most Americans have heard of the excitement generated at Vail—Vail, Colorado, that is. I have never stopped at that Vail. But there is a little town east of Denison, Iowa, on old Highway 30 that is called Vail. It also generated a little excitement. Like other small towns, Vail wanted a little notoriety, but more important, some income to support the expense of keeping a city hall.

They didn't have any good ideas for fame, but they decided that speed was their city meal ticket. They hired a town cop on a commission basis, reduced the speed limit on the highway to the lowest number allowed by law and waited for the money to roll in from speeding fines. It didn't take long. The cop had a hopped-up engine in his car that could catch any speeder, the mayor levied large fines and Highway 30 became a nurse cow for the town of Vail.

The town policeman parked nearly out of sight behind the large grain elevator at the edge of the road and waited, but not for long, day or night. Drivers just didn't slow to 25 miles per hour on Highway 30—until they had a flashing red light in their rear view mirror. The driver was taken straight to city hall to pay the fine and the cop went back to his stand by the elevator.

The situation continued for two or three years and might have lasted years longer except that the cop had the bad judgment to arrest several of the local people and the mayor had the bad judgment to levy the same fines on the Vail natives as on the out-of-town traveling—and speeding—public. It took months to learn who halted the arresting incidents—but stop they did.

One evening in early fall, as day and night shared about equal hours, the city's lawman had his high-performance patrol car parked in its usual space near the grain elevator waiting for east-bound traffic to produce his next prey. A serious speeder blew past, the cop car's engine roared, the flashing red light went on and the chase began—and ended!

Two young men, who lived in the area, had apparently been arrested at an earlier date. After they were fined, they decided to "get even." They found about 150 feet of steel cable and two large clamps. They attached one end of the cable to a utility pole at the edge of the highway. Then they let it lie in the weeds between the elevator and the highway for several days, waiting for ideal conditions to make their strike.

As dusk approached dark, they slipped in behind the patrol car when it returned from city hall, clamped the other end of the cable firmly to its rear axle and left, at least far enough to avoid getting hit by anything, but near enough to see it happen. When the accelerating car hit the end of the cable, the chase team flew into three parts. The rear axle stopped immediately, the bulk of the car continued a few feet down the road and the policeman was launched through the windshield.

Townspeople heard the noise and came to help clean up the mess. The policeman was injured but survived. The car did not. And it took several weeks to discover the guilty parties. I don't recall the punishment but I remember it as mild, compared with what might otherwise have been expected. I heard that the former speed cop later found employment in another city.

The Switch to Color

My company gave me a sideways "promotion" to a job as state sales manager for western Iowa in 1954. I had traveled most of the Midwest in my previous job but still I did an area search to decide where to live. Denison was slightly off-center in my territory but was the hub of roads leading in all directions so I settled there for five years until they asked me to return to the home office to become ad manager.

After a few months in a residence hotel while a local hardware store owner finished building an apartment complex, I became his first tenant. My old TV set was taking a while to warm up to a full picture. I visited with the local appliance storeowner about a new set but no deal. One spring evening I saw him walk past my apartment so I stopped him, invited him to come in to see that my set was actually operating so I could get a trade-in.

I went into the store a few days later to talk trade. He said he would bring a new set for me to try out, then we'd later make the deal. When he showed up to make the switch, he brought a color set. I told him to take it back—I couldn't afford a color set. He just wanted me to try it for a few weeks. We got no color shows most days, but a few on weekends. Then summer came. No color shows except one on Saturday night.

I told him to pick a good black and white set and tell me how much it would cost after my trade in. He wanted to leave the demo all summer; there would be a color show almost every day when the fall season began. He was right. The NBC station in Omaha kept one of the NBC color teams there a lot of the time, did the first "full color" day of telecasting in the United States. They broadcast a tendon transplant in a girl's leg—in bloody, living color.

An attorney moved into the apartment with me and together we hosted a lot of local people who came to see our color programs. I was told that only the banker and the appliance store owner had color TV. I was Number Three! Big deal. I still had to make a trade. Bob was going to want his demo set back. Maybe he would take a reasonable offer for the used set.

He priced it only about $100 above a similar black and white set so I said yes. But he didn't deliver the set I had used for months, he brought a new one, with "next generation" system inside. It moved with me to Des Moines a few years later, then it later took the trip to California in 1962 where it worked for years until sets with transistors replaced the old models using vacuum tubes. It was nice to have a set that wasn't always blowing tubes, but that "first color set" on the block was still one of the better buys of my life.

Hey Guy, You Have a Sister

My baby sister, Barbara, was born in the summer just before I started to high school. After four boys, she was more welcome in our family than spring rain during a drought. As brother Rolland later described the situation, the folks had quite a family—four hired men and a child. At any rate, I had finished high school and a year of college before she started to school.

The next year I went into the Navy for nearly four years. Then I went back to college and finally took a job—all without spending many days at home—and without getting to know my little sister. After several job assignments for the firm I began working for right out of college, I was living in Denison, Iowa, by 1955 when my sister began college.

Her college roommate was a girl's basketball star from Holstein, in the next county north of Denison. As they settled in and became comfortable in Lincoln, it occurred to them that I was less than three hours of driving time away and Lois had another half hour to be at her home. On one of these early trips, Barb asked if I had a good scissors, etc., because she needed some shaggy locks trimmed.

Whatever I did passed muster with her hairstyle critic and she made the trip regularly for her trim. Her hair at the time was sort of a casual bob and she seemed to like both the price and results well enough to come back on schedule for a combination visit and hair touch up. After this had been going on for a few years, she one day discovered a newly arrived purchase of mine, a picture cookbook published by *Life* magazine.

The book was coffee-table quality and besides, the recipes were good. In addition to the large format, *Life* magazine-quality illustrated pages, it had a book of perforated tear-out recipe cards and file box for storing them. I admit, it was a little gaudy for any bachelor pad, but I had actually cooked a few of them and they were good. It only took a few minutes until she said, "Thanks, I just found my graduation present." Another problem solved? Yes, and I quickly ordered a replacement cookbook which is still in use.

Just Being a Responsible Citizen, Sir

One winter evening when I was living in Denison, Iowa, and working as a State Sales Manager in the livestock feed business, I had been riding with Vince Book, one of my sales people, making farm calls. We had just left our dealer in Carroll and were en route to Vince's home in the small town of Gray, where I had left my car. It was full dusk and almost all the cars had their lights on.

Vince was driving south on Highway 71, in an area of long upgrades and downgrades. As we topped a hill, I saw what appeared to be headlights whirling in a circular pattern on the upslope of the next long hill probably a half-mile or more ahead of us. It was a pattern I had never seen and I told Vince to slow down, that there might be an accident ahead.

The paved road surface was mostly clear of snow or ice but the shoulder and all the fields had several inches of snow cover. As the evening darkened, the temperature dropped below freezing. When we approached the scene, there had indeed been an accident. A southbound tractor with trailer was starting up the long hill when the driver met a northbound sedan.

The truck was mostly in the left lane, southbound, with the tractor slightly on the left shoulder and the back end of the truck filling the left lane and extending a foot or two into the right lane. It had serious damage to the right front fender and the right half of the grill. The driver was just getting down from the cab as we arrived and stopped on the right shoulder. He was shaken but did not appear to have any serious injuries, if in fact he was injured at all.

The sedan was in the ditch on the right side of the highway, facing the road and at a 90-degree angle to the road. Its front end and windshield were smashed. I went to the driver's door and could see a man in the seat. He was cut and bleeding, moaning and seemed to be semi-conscious. He did not respond when I tried to talk to him. Vince had a blanket in the car, which I unfolded and covered the man in the wrecked car.

Soon another southbound car stopped behind our car. The driver asked if he could help, got out of his car, then he disappeared. When he showed up on the scene again, he was almost out of control. I asked him to drive to the farmhouse where we could see a light and call an ambulance, sheriff and wrecker. He collected his wits, got in his car and left. I was afraid we would have someone run into the truck.

I asked the truck driver for flares. He brought several out of the cab. I told him to get back in the cab or in Vince's car to keep warm. I lighted a flare on the bank behind Vince's car, then I headed up the hill, lighting one a few feet from the truck. I ran up the hill, lighting flares every 50 yards, then returned to the scene.

The injured driver was still sitting in the driver's seat and moaning. A few southbound cars had stopped on the right shoulder. I got a couple of big, strong young men to help tip the seat back to make the injured man more comfortable. In a few minutes, when the ambulance arrived, the emergency people moved the driver from his wrecked car into the ambulance. Meantime I had a chance to visit with the truck driver.

He had been driving south when the northbound car began inching across the center line and into his lane. He said he had flashed his lights to bright and then to dim, then started to pull onto the right shoulder but at the last minute he could see he would hit the car head-on so he swerved to the left. Most of the debris was at the edge of the right lane and on the road shoulder, confirming the truck driver's statement.

Several cars had arrived so I lit another flare and began directing the traffic, south, then northbound. Suddenly a northbound car came down the hill past the burning flares and toward the accident scene at a speed much too fast for road conditions, heading directly for the semi in the northbound lane. I waved the burning flare at him until he was a few car-lengths away.

When it became obvious that he was not going to get stopped, I turned and ran to the west ditch. The oncoming car crashed into the rear wheels of the semi and did a full 180-degree spin. The back end of the car apparently raised as it turned and the rear bumper ticked my right hip as it almost flew past me. I ran down into the wide, flat ditch and was so mad at the dumb driver who wouldn't stop that I was going to go back up and hit him. Then I felt that I had better cool out so I went back up the hill to replace the flares that were about to burn out.

When I got back from posting the flares, Vince had several people with flashlights looking for me. They had seen that car hit me after it hit the truck wheels but they didn't know where I went. They were looking under the car, in the ditch and even out in the field. Finally the deputy arrived. He had a good Speed Graphic but didn't act like he knew the first thing about how to operate it. I was experienced with that camera but it was his problem.

He got out flares for us but wanted photos before he took any statements. I showed him how to use the film pack in his camera and asked him if anyone had called a tow truck. He finally did take some names and phone numbers. After being on the scene for well over an hour, I found Vince and we headed to Gray and my car. I drove on to Denison and stopped at the restaurant where Ray Torczon, a friend and area Ford tractor rep was eating a late dinner.

I sat down in the booth with Ray and told him about the accident and ordered my dinner. Then it struck. My knees began to shake and suddenly I was not hungry. I ate a little of my dinner but when I went to get up from the

172

booth, I found my hip was hurting—my first effect from being hit by the car. In the next few days I learned to use my left foot on the brake since I could hardly raise my right one off the floor. That sucker had really hit me. It turns out he was drunk. The deputy arrested him at the scene.

We later heard that the sedan driver, who died at the hospital, had left an afternoon meeting feeling ill, and was returning to his home in Carroll. He had apparently made a miraculous recovery between the time he left the meeting and the trial, a few months later. I was called as a trial witness. The deputy's photos didn't come out so the trucker insurance company's attorney needed testimony to determine what happened. I felt sorry for the guy's family but in my mind, the truck driver's story seemed to be reinforced by the evidence.

The attorney for the family suing the trucker (and his insurance company) tried to make his case by getting me to contradict myself. He really annoyed me so I asked the judge if I could just tell the jury what happened instead of giving yes and no answers. Over the objections of the attorney, he said I could. After the trial, I got a check for three days' pay from the insurance company and a letter of commendation from the sheriff. Even with that, I do not recommend being at the scene of accidents unless you are a paramedic, a tow truck driver or an attorney.

Every Vote Counts

I met Bob Neumeyer shortly after I moved to Denison, Iowa, in 1954. I was a state sales manager for a livestock feed manufacturer and Bob was getting his start in farming after he was mustered out of the Air Force. We were among the eligible bachelors dating the area's schoolteachers. They probably never saw dates, before or after, who would be "talking about livestock feed" when they returned from the ladies' room.

Bob's dad was a substantial farmer feeder who fed several hundred steers and thousands of lambs yearly. And he raised most of the grain he fed. The farm had several hundred acres of hilly grassland that was well suited to a herd of purebred Angus cattle. My first encounter with Angus—a young mother with her first calf at side and a tin can on a toe—left me with much to be desired regarding the Angus temperament. But over time I learned to respect the genetic trait of the breed to develop flakes of internal fat within the primal cuts of meat rather than large strips or "seam fat" as more characteristic of some other breeds.

This flaking of internal fat contributes to a more flavorful, tender cut of meat. Bob and I frequently discussed this inherent benefit and the possibility of breeders ever being able to "take it to the bank" by selling Angus-sired calves for a higher price than calves of other breeds. Neither of us conceded that it couldn't be done but I maintained that it wouldn't.

173

Meat packers had never put their names on cuts of meat when they appeared in the supermarket meat case. This left only the Angus breeders—a nation-wide collection of people from 4-H kids to hobbyists to investors to serious, career cattlemen. And their only real connection was the American Angus Association, which recorded their cattle. The association is a group of staff people, hired and supervised by a board of directors, elected from the breeder-members.

Bob was elected secretary of the Denison Angus Association, a group of breeders in that area. When they decided to have a sale of breeder-consigned stock, the secretary drew the short straw when it came to managing the sale, making the catalog, spending the advertising budget, etc. Bob knew of my printing and advertising experience so he came running. I knew very little about purebred livestock sales but Bob showed me some catalogs from previous sales. We got the job done and the sale was a success. But we got no premium for meat quality.

Some years later I was working with *Western Livestock Journal* and Bob came to visit after attending a Jay Cees (Junior Chamber of Commerce) convention in Las Vegas. He rode with me for a couple of days and said that if the company had an opening for a field editor, he'd like to apply. Within a few months we did, he did, and he got the job. He was later offered a partnership by an Angus breeder in Idaho, which he also accepted. We continued to talk about Angus beef and our disgust that the breeders did not get paid for the quality they produced.

A few years later, the American Angus Association board of directors decided to fund a start-up program to market Certified Angus Beef. The program took money to administer and sales did not return enough profit to break even. Members were in love with the idea of a premium price for their product, but they did not love the idea of being banker for a financial loser.

As proof again that timing is everything, Bob was elected to the board of directors of the American Angus Association This position made him responsible to the Angus breeder-members from coast to coast for wasting their money on a pipe dream. As the program grew, so did the financial deficit and some of the board members began to wonder what kind of monster they had created and to waver in their determination to stick with the program. Bob and I continued to visit about the program. Bob could vote. I could only watch and/or encourage.

The last year of Bob's term on the board, they were again faced with voting to continue funding a program that had shown promise for years, but they couldn't take promises to the bank and the program was eating up all the funds they had available. There was dissention on the board and it appeared they might refuse to fund the "start-up" Certified Angus Beef program for another year. The board members' vote was evenly split with one member undecided. Bob convinced the undecided voter to join him in financing the program for one more year.

Funding was continued and the program broke even, financially, that year for the first time. Since then, many thousands of Angus-sired cattle have been bought, fed and marketed under the CAB program returning premium prices to cattlemen across the country. As a result, Angus bulls are in demand by cattlemen across the land, at premium prices. With this success, the American Hereford Association began a competitive "Certified Hereford Beef" marketing program. I wish them all well. Cattlemen need all the help they can get.

Journalism Lecture in a Snowstorm

When I was a state sales manager for Foxbilt Feeds, living in Denison, Iowa, I published a sales letter to the dozen salesmen and nearly a hundred feed dealers in my area. I wrote it on a typewriter but took it to the job printing folks at the *Denison Review* newspaper, who printed and folded it ready for mailing. I was the only state manager who did this but I felt it was one extra contact with all the people in my division and it saved phone calls and personal visits. This allowed me to spend more time hiring and training new people instead of maintenance.

It was my regular take-the-paper-to-the-printer day and it was snowing. As I met Dick Knowles, the publisher, in the office entry, he asked, "Hey, Phil, you took journalism, didn't you?" When I agreed, he said, "I really need you for a few minutes. The high school has been publishing its own paper but we made a deal to begin including it in the *Denison Review*. They have a new journalism teacher. I can tell them what we want for the newspaper but I'm the money man. I never studied journalism. Will you come along and handle that part?"

School was beginning the second semester. The old teacher was taking maternity leave and the new teacher was an English major who inherited the journalism class but had not taken any journalism courses. I organized my lesson plan while Dick drove a few blocks in the snow and to the classroom. It didn't take him long to tell them how many words made a column inch, how much space they had in each issue, etc., then it was my turn.

I decided to start them off with the five W's: who, what, when, where, and why, and let them ask questions. At the end of the period I was grateful for a room full of fairly bright kids with curious minds. We had to practically throw them out of the room. The teacher, Carrie Deuland, asked if I could come back again. She was attractive, single, new in town and I was the only single male who knew her. I said I'd be back, if it kept snowing. We both prayed for snow—for different reasons. She later married one of my friends but did not become a journalist.

Those Timely Postal Bonds

One of the best farmers I ever knew became one of my best salesmen when I was a state sales manager for Foxbilt Feeds. His name was Fred Grell. He was a satisfied user of our products that I happened to meet at one of our dealers and he immediately got my attention. He was towing a portable, hydraulic scaffold that he had invented and was trying to patent. But this wasn't his only good idea.

A few months later, when our company changed some territory boundaries, I got some new area and needed a new salesman. I called Fred to see if he would like the job. He liked the idea—as long as we didn't demand that he work full-time on feed sales. He was a farmer feeder first and feed salesman second. I felt he could sell more in a couple of days than most people could do in a week so I hired him on the spot.

I made a number of farm calls with him. I'd handle the conversation on one call to demonstrate how I sold and he would take the next call. I would later make suggestions for improving the presentation or endorse what he had done. It was an easy training session. He was already a customer and well satisfied, and knew why and how he used our products.

One day we visited a farmer. Fred knew the farmer's family but had not really talked to this person in recent years. The family had been good hog raisers and Fred heard that the farmer was involved in some hog breeding plan. He had heard about line breeding and had inbred his herd to close family members for several generations. He was sure he would soon breed the perfect pigs, even if he had been getting smaller litters and the pigs had very slow growth rates.

Fred acted briefly interested and asked him to keep reporting his progress and excused us. As we left the farm, Fred commented that he felt the farmer's father would be spinning in his grave if he knew what had happened to his great herd of hogs. And he commented, "When I find something as sick as his breeding program, I try to dispose of the carcass before it starts stinking, then start over."

But the best story that Fred ever told me was regarding the outstanding Ida County farm he owned. It was 480 highly improved acres of Class I soil. He began with 320 acres, then added the adjoining 160 when it became available. He had just married and began farming on a rented farm near his family home. The banker loaned him the money to buy the used machinery he needed. Then came the crash of 1929 and the depression that followed.

After the Roosevelt administration declared a bank holiday in 1933, they ordered the insurance companies to get rid of the farms they had repossessed during the preceding hard years. Fred felt he might find a good farm with a built-in loan to get started farming his own land. He found an excellent 320-

acre farm—a big strike for a young farmer to attempt and most of his friends would probably have passed it up—but Fred talked to the sales agent.

The insurance company wanted a down payment of $100,000, which they reduced to $50,000. Fred didn't even have $500. But his wife had made a comment about her father having some postal bonds being paid off and he didn't know what to do about reinvesting. The total of the bonds was $20,000. The time was near when the company had to transfer title to the farm. Fred went to the agent and asked if they would sell him the farm if he had $20,000 as a down payment. The agent reluctantly agreed that they would, but they only had a few days left.

That weekend Fred went to visit the father-in-law and asked to take him for a drive. They drove to the farm, then into the headquarters pointing out the great buildings and the fine farmhouse. Then he told his father-in-law he was trying to buy it but he was $20,000 short of being able to make on the down payment that the insurance company wanted to sell the farm. The $20,000 was immediately volunteered and the deal was made. Fred told me, "My father-in-law went to his grave without knowing that he made the entire down payment on our farm."

Family Football Feud

When I moved to my first assignment outside of the Foxbilt Feeds home office in Des Moines, the area I picked was in Boone County, for several reasons: We had a hatching flock breeding program in the area for our Ames In-Cross hybrid poultry company. The Ogden (Iowa) Hatchery was both a feed dealer and poultry service provider for the hatching flocks, the ex-salesman left a mess of customer relations that needed cleaning up. Good training for a new man. We had an experienced supervisor and it was near enough to Des Moines for me to continue working with our ad agency in making tape-recorded on-the-farm interviews for company advertising.

I found a "mother-in-law" apartment on the back of a house, across the street from a gas station where I was able to park my car inside, a bonus on cold Iowa winter nights. The apartment was owned by the couple who also owned the local clothes cleaning plant. Ogden had several kinds of Lutheran churches and my landlady knew all of the parishioners—told me which were friendly and which were feuding—so I wouldn't run afoul of the local religious politics.

I had an ownership map of the county farms and color-coded all the owners—Missouri Synod Lutherans got a red star, the Swedish Lutherans were blue, American Lutherans yellow, Catholics green, etc. I kept the book with me and checked it before I pulled into the driveway. Some farmers would not buy your feed if you named a member of the wrong church as a user, but just drop the names of several of his own church members and you likely had a new customer.

George Dunn was one of my early single male acquaintances when I moved to Ogden in the fall of 1951. His dad was one of the area's best cattle feeders. George was home from military service and trying to decide if he wanted to be a farmer. It was through George that I met the Doran family who owned and operated several good farms in the Beaver area near the west side of Boone County.

Jim Doran was an All Big 8 (All Big 6 at that time) football player for Iowa State College in Ames. He graduated in 1951 and was drafted by the Detroit Lions. At that time, rookies in the National Football League were paid $6,000 per year. He was voted the "Rookie of the Year" in the NFL and his brother Tom, who was acting as his agent, was trying to use this "Rookie" honor to get $12,000 for Jim's second year.

The fun part of this friendship was the evenings the four of us spent over a bowl of popcorn and a few beers at the Daniel Boone Hotel. Detroit had offered $8,000 and Jim wanted to sign. Tom tried to be firm. "They'll pay $12,000 or you'll farm," he'd tell Jim. "But Tom, I want to play," Jim would plead. It was a long winter and spring of negotiating. We never learned the exact figure but it was $10,000 or more that finally did the trick. Jim was a Lion again—and born 50 years too soon. Today they would have moved the decimal over a couple of zeros to re-hire the league's most valuable rookie.

Who Caught the Bouquet?

Early actor W.C. Fields is alleged to have said, "The only wedding I ever approved was that of my parents." I tend to agree, in many cases. In fact ceremonies, rituals and all kinds of formal functions have little appeal for me. If other people want to submit to ceremonies of any kind, they had better be adults, in my opinion, or shame on their parents. But even with this attitude, I got caught.

A friend in Denison, Fred Witt, pursued a schoolteacher all the way to the altar. We had frequently double-dated, in fact I had introduced them when Carrie showed up as the new journalism teacher and I assisted with her class the first couple of days, so I guess I wasn't surprised when they asked me to be in the wedding. It seemed an innocent request so I reluctantly agreed. After all, it was their wedding. It was to be held in the bride's home church in Huxley, a tiny town between Ames and Des Moines.

The upcoming event was routine until the day of the wedding rehearsal. It was about 90 miles from Denison to Ames and another 15 miles to Huxley. There were three or four carloads of participants or people invited to the dinner from Denison. Irv Keesling, and I went in my car but we goofed in timing the trip. We got to Ames early. Not enough time to do anything big, but too much time to have a cup of coffee or anything little. What to do?

At the highway crossroads in Ames was the Pontiac dealer who sold several cars to Foxbilt, the company that was working for. I said to Irv, "Let's go in and look at new cars. I haven't taken time to even look this year." He agreed and the owner saw me drive up and asked how many miles I had on the '55 hardtop. I told him and he said he just had to make a deal. He had a customer just waiting for that car. Sure!

That was the first year of the four-door hardtop. I had sworn at having to tip the front seat every time I had a rear seat passenger. "How much to trade for the front car in the show room?" I asked. He surprised me with the small difference. Maybe he really did have a customer for my car. "Is it ready to drive?" I had to know, because we were going to deal fast or never. It was, and we showed up for the rehearsal only minutes later with a new car.

After the rehearsal and dinner, we decided that Fred should have a stag party. He decided otherwise, took off at fairly high speed for downtown Huxley and we followed—with a new car odometer reading about 25 miles. He finally hit a dead end street after breaking in my new engine with a chase of several miles. If you always thought a new engine should be pampered, don't believe it. That was one of the best cars I ever owned.

The wedding was memorable for several reasons, not including the chase. As Carrie and her father began to walk down the aisle she whispered to him—almost complained—it was going so smoothly and she almost wished some memorable incident would happen. But it proceeded on schedule, right up to the "I do's." I had a funny feeling about Maxine George, the bridesmaid beside me. She had mentioned that she felt a little faint before the ceremony. I stole a glance and she seemed pale so I whispered, "Max, lick your lips."

A few seconds later she turned and bolted for the door to the pastor's study just a few feet from where we were standing at the altar. I followed, two steps behind. She collapsed just inside the study door and I could only catch a handful of dress between her shoulders to slightly ease her fall to the study floor. It takes quite an incident to shift attention from the newlyweds but Maxine did it. We missed the march out of the church that had been dutifully rehearsed. I guess the others improvised. They didn't say who caught the bouquet. I had my hands full trying to catch the fainting bridesmaid. Yes, it was a memorable wedding.

He Never Forgot

The first presidential election after I got out of college was in November, 1952, when Eisenhower defeated Stevenson. I was living in a loft apartment in the back of a property owned by my boss. The property had a painted brick colonial home framed by two giant elms with an appropriate set back from the county road. It had a large lawn and gardens plus the shrubs that separated the main residence from the second home, the apartment and the 12- to-15 acre field in the back.

Such a property required the services of at least a part-time gardener. This was no ordinary gardener. Tom Wilson was a hulk of a man at several inches above 6 feet and with a thick, muscular body that showed no hint of his age, approaching 70. He was a former coal miner but when the mines played out many years earlier, most of the miners found other work. Tom was president of the now nearly defunct local union.

His only union duties were dispersing some disability checks and keeping in touch with the few formerly active members still in the area. He had black lung disease so bad that it took enough digitalis to kill several heart patients just to keep him going. But Tom was not one to let black lung slow him down. He asked no favors. He had never learned to drive a car so he took a bus from his home in Colfax, some 20 miles to a junction near the property in the north-east edge of Des Moines, then made the return bus trip back to Colfax in late afternoon.

I had driven out of my driveway and up to the owner's garage. My boss and I frequently rode to the office together if we had no reason to take two cars to work as was the case this day. Tom arrived, sack lunch in hand, as I drove in. This aging near-giant was positively red-eyed as if he had been crying. It became quickly apparent that this was not just an election to Tom. He walked straight to my car and began to share his grief with me.

"It's them young working guys and the dumb housewives that did it," Tom almost screamed, "dumb sonsabitches, never hungry a day in their life, don't know what the world's all about, never had to beg at the back door of a grocery store or a cafe to get food for their kids. What are they thinking? Don't they know anything?" he asked, pleading to everybody, or anybody, or nobody, except I was the only one there. And he started crying again.

"Like a bunch of bees," he said—I'll never forget it, "They fan their wings on a piece of tin to make some noise, then they crawl in the hive and make honey for somebody else. I feel sorry for the good people that will be hurt by this," he continued. "There are thousands of people that will be hurt bad. I'll tell you, Phil, it's a hell of a thing when a man's belly tells him how to vote. Mine told me in 1932 and I never forgot how it felt. And I want to tell you how glad I am that it never felt that way again." For me, I think of Tom after every general election.

Magic in Her Hands

There are a lot of ingredients necessary to get good livestock photos. I found that I had one of them when I was in college. Ray Morgan, who was a former

180

dairy professor, was teaching photography when I knew him. When he learned that I was his only photography student from Ag College, he assigned me special projects that frequently included animal photography. It may not have been an easy job to take a photo of an architectural specimen. You had to get it properly framed and decide what time of day will create the best shadows, etc., but at least the church never moved. It was just you and the elements.

Livestock people want their photos to be just as elegant, as well-lighted and as perfectly posed as the church tower, except that bulls, pigs, horses or other livestock bring a built-in handicap. They are alive. And they don't respond, like people, when you say "smile." Few people have the patience to wait until all the elements are present. You must know how the animal should look and be in the right spot when that moment comes. Animals sense it. If you get nervous, they get nervous. I learned that I had patience with livestock, if not with people.

One of the first and hardest jobs in livestock photography can be getting rid of the owner. One day I was taking photos of yearlings for use in the Mid-Winter Quarter Horse Sale catalog. This owner had two well-bred colts to photograph. He was a school principal and knew his horses but they didn't seem to respect him. The first colt was super-alert and high-headed. I picked a spot that I felt would give us good background but the owner could not lead the colt with authority nor make him stop with his body, his feet, his ears and his attitude anywhere near the right spot at the same time.

Several neighbors came to witness the event but the colt wouldn't let anyone position his feet where I wanted them. One was a high-school girl that I felt might be able to handle the horse. The owner surely couldn't. I knew I would make an enemy if I "fired" the owner from his job so I suggested that he might move the feet, then asked, "Kathy, would you take the shank (halter rope)?" Instantly, this high-headed, unruly colt became a kitten. The owner positioned his feet and we got several good shots.

The next colt came out. He was a dead-head compared with the first one. What the first colt did wrong from nervousness, the second did from being sluggish and non-compliant. Again I asked the owner to position the feet and said, "Kathy, you were our good luck charm, why not try it again?" The minute she took the shank, the colt's head came up, his ears perked and his whole body became alert. The owner positioned his feet and our photos were in the box.

As I picked up my gear and headed out the driveway, Kathy, the girl wonder, was walking home. I picked her up, thanked her for helping and asked where she got the magic for handling horses. She didn't know. She just liked horses. She was 15, her family had moved from Washington and she brought her horse along—a 10-year-old stallion and potential racehorse that broke a vertebra when he reared over backward in a training starting gate.

181

She exercised horses for the owner and this unruly horse liked her so he gave her the stud. I used her for every horse photo job I had in the area until her mother got a job at John Deere and they moved away. She brought out the best in every horse she touched. Kathy had magic in her hands.

Photos of cattle, when halter-broke and fitted for a posed picture, can almost be shaped as if manufactured. Loose cattle are a different matter. Most livestock deserving of a photo have good physical conformation and are tame enough to let the photographer work at close range. But that's only the first part of the deal. It is still necessary to catch a "natural" pose that flatters the animal.

Some cattle have a good temperament and respond well with one or two handlers. If operating in a closed area, a photographer with one helper can do the job—the right helper. This must be someone who senses how much space the animal needs. I call this the "comfort zone." With some cattle it may only be a few inches or a few feet between the animal and the handler. For others, it may be 5, 10 or 20 feet. The handler must anticipate what the animal will sense and how it will respond to each move the handler makes. I have found few owners who are good in a small space with cattle. And ranch managers don't rate much better. Both are too busy. Most of the good handlers in my experience have been women or children. Like Kathy with the horses, she has the touch.

Bulls in a Blizzard

When Foxbilt Feeds promoted me to the job of state sales manager, I toured the western Iowa area that made up the territory I would supervise. I had been through this area several times in my previous work of collecting stories of feeders using our products and publishing company house organs but it was never with the idea of picking a place to live.

I remembered hearing an old territory manager saying you should not live in the center of your territory. That would mean staying overnight away from home in both ends of your territory but if your home was off center, you could drive home every night from working in the near end and be gone only when work took you to the long end. This meant Denison or Atlantic in western Iowa. Both were crossroads for several highways and both were county seat towns with enough population to provide needed services.

I had a college friend in each town, but Dale Landgren, the Hormel buying station manager in Denison, won by introducing me to several potentially helpful local people including his wife's schoolteacher cousin. I soon met some more teachers and young bachelors, including Gordon Halverson, the recently-hired Chamber of Commerce manager. I needed a Chamber membership like I needed the plague but Halverson invented a "traveling man's bureau" with a small membership fee and enlarged his membership by a bunch of fairly creative salesmen.

To encourage Chamber of Commerce membership, the manager had purchased a bunch of papier-mâché Hereford Bulls that had Chamber of Commerce membership medals hanging around their necks. When a merchant paid his dues, he was given the bull to put on display in the store window. Denison was in an area of many cattle feeders and later the founding city for Iowa Beef Packers (later becoming the nation's largest beef packer, then purchased by Tyson Foods) so the beef animal was an appropriate logo.

It was especially appropriate for me and for Bob Neumeyer, a local air force veteran whose father was a substantial farmer-feeder. Bob and I had dated schoolteachers and after a few months of "arguing feed" on double dates, Bob married Hollyce and I hired him to be a salesman for my Denison territory. We both joined the Chamber and were fairly successful in making our quota of new members.

Members in each bureau were responsible for recruiting within their bureau. Bob and I were on the membership drive and soon had every potential member for our bureau. At the end of the drive we suggested that if we sold a membership to a business that would be a member of another bureau, the recruiting team would get the otherwise unpaid dues to spend in their bureau projects. The board approved our idea.

A few days later a serious snowstorm closed country roads so Bob and I went to the Chamber office in a snowstorm and got the list of suggested members, old and new, who had not joined. I don't remember whether it was 12 or 16 names. We took enough bulls off the shelf for every name on the list, then we agreed when Halverson suggested we might leave one bull at the office in case we didn't sell everybody or possibly a merchant might not be tending his business on this snowy day. We may have resorted to "hard sell" once or twice but at day's end we had to go back to the office for that last bull. When the impressed Chamber manager told this story to the membership, we earned more respect from other members than we deserved.

That Good Bad Habit

In 1953 and '54 I was traveling through most of the Midwest in my job of contracting regional feed mills to be sub-manufacturers using our pre-mixes and formulas to make finished livestock feed supplements for sale to livestock feeders in each area at a freight price advantage to the feeder. It gave our salesmen a price advantage over the competitors and company sales were booming.

One of the mill owners I interviewed was in Ripon, Wisconsin. The mill was owned by a successful businessman named J. Stuart Nash. I had limited contact with him but his name, his contacts his personal habits and the man, were memorable. He took me to lunch in the Republican Club in Ripon, birthplace of the Republican Party, he informed me. After lunch we returned to his office where he took a one-hour nap. He had recently suffered a heart attack at age 52 and the nap was part of his recovery therapy. We later took a spin in his speedboat on Green Lake and a tour of the countryside in his Jaguar convertible. I was interested in his feed mill but the nap was more memorable for me.

The company promoted me to the new job as Division Manager sometime in late 1954 and I moved to Denison, Iowa. I inherited a handful of unhappy, disorganized salesmen who were starved for a little attention and supervision. It was easy to spend extra time with each man, building his morale and helping get new dealers and customers for the livestock feed that our company made. I tried to spend at least one day per week recruiting salesmen for my empty territories and one day or more in training new people.

George Lovitt was one of my new salesmen. He came from an old farming family in the Shenandoah area and was giving up driving a bread truck in the big city of Des Moines to enroll his kids in small-town school. He took to the new job in near-record time and I began spending my extra hours recruiting and training newly-hired men in other areas. Division 7 (my new territory) had been at the bottom of some 20 territories in the company when I arrived. Our sales were increasing and George was climbing within my territory. Then it struck.

I arrived at home one evening from a day of work in the territory (this was long before cell phones or answering machines). Mrs. Lovitt called to tell me that George was in the hospital. That morning he was ready to leave for a day of farm calls when he said, "I don't feel so good right now. I think I'll just sit in the rocking chair for a minute," and Melanie began making beds when she heard a strange noise and returned to the kitchen. George was on the floor, unconscious, having had an apparent seizure.

She called an ambulance and after an exam at the Shenandoah hospital, he was sent to Omaha for brain scans. When the medics determined his condition, he had surgery, tying off a blood vessel to his brain and was expected to be off the job for three to four weeks. I decided that I would try to keep his territory active by working two or three days a week making farm calls and put in the rest of the week in supervisory work.

Trying to make eight days of work fit into six days gets to be tiring after not too many weeks. I had just had lunch in Clarinda on a balmy spring day and was on my way to my first afternoon farm call. I was beginning to nod off when a giant elm tree appeared in a wide shoulder area on the right side of the road. The idea of a brief afternoon nap overpowered my urge to continue down the road so I parked and tipped the seat back. In an instant I was asleep.

184

I awoke as if shaken by a clap of thunder. How long had I been asleep? Only 15 minutes? I was amazingly refreshed. The afternoon was one of my most productive. That nap was great. I worked into the night. Then came tomorrow. My car had acquired a bad habit. Only minutes after lunch it homed in on another tree appearing along the highway. It shocked me, but I recalled J. Stuart Nash and his doctor's advice even though I hadn't had a heart attack. The idea of an after-lunch nap seemed wonderful but I wondered, *did I need this?*

I remembered how good I felt the day before—after the nap—so I did not fight the urge. Fifteen minutes later I awoke from sound sleep and marveled that only a few minutes' nap during the day refreshed me almost as much as a full night of sleep. For years I tried but never fully broke the habit. And for many years I was embarrassed to nod off after lunch but no more. I just lie down or lean back and whether I actually go to sleep or not, that next 10 to 15 minutes is magic. I even named the after-lunch siesta the Nash Nap and the urge to take the nap is my Nash Attack. Whatever you call it, I recommend it, even if J. Stuart Nash never did work for me.

The Corny Fisherman

My dad took me fishing a few times while I was in grade school. We went to the nearby Sandhill lakes to fish for pan fish: bluegill, crappie, bullhead—and he always felt he had to cast for bass. I was always ready to go someplace but by the second or third trip, I decided that fishing wasn't my idea of great fun. To me, fish are loaded with bones, they do not particularly taste good and they smell awful but the worst part is the protocol. Every real fisherman that I know insists that you must be quiet at all times if you are to be near him. It was never clear to me that fish even had ears. Why must we be so quiet? I can tell you that if a football fan had to swear to an oath of silence before attending a game, the stands would be empty.

Brother Jack liked to fish but he was a temperate fisherman. He could take it or leave it. Youngest brother Rolland (Rowdy) was the family's other fisherman and he was one of the intense, do-it-by-the-book type. When he lived with me in Denison, Iowa, and managed the music store, he couldn't wait to leave the shop in late afternoon and head for some kind of water somewhere, anywhere. He was slow to wake up in the morning—unless he was going fishing, when he was always awake before the alarm went off.

I would frequently get back into town from my traveling job in time to make dinner. I generally went to the music store first for his input on the grocery list and if he was gone, I'd stop at the grocery to pick up food, head home and start the meal, assuming that he would show up by dinner time. If he didn't show by our regular eating time, I would either eat alone or if it was a meal that would hold in place for a while, I'd leave for the gravel pit in the west edge of town to retrieve the fisherman or at least remind him that it was dinner time.

One afternoon I dropped by the store and he was gone so I went shopping at the grocery, then to the gravel pit. He was at it again and when I got near him and tried to talk he shushed me in his best fisherman style. He was about to catch a world record bass. Or I think that's what his signals meant. I walked up and down the shore and saw bluegills in the water so I put one of his rods together to have something to do while waiting. I noticed that the frozen corn in the grocery bag wasn't frozen any more so I baited a hook with a couple of kernels.

Those bluegills practically jumped out of the water to get that corn. There was a 3- or 4-gallon pail by his tackle box so I dipped some water out of the lake and put the newly caught fish in the pail of water. In time, he gave up on the lunker and came to where I was landing another fish. He couldn't believe it. Corn for bait! I thought we were headed for home but remember, he's a real fisherman. He just had to try using corn for bait on his granddaddy bass. He speared a few kernels and made a cast near the island where his trophy held court and zap! That fish almost jumped out of the water, grabbed the bait, straightened the hook and disappeared. Rowdy looked for a bigger hook but none seemed the right size so he dropped by the bait shop on his way home to get armed for tomorrow.

Tomorrow was Sunday morning and Rowdy slipped out early without even waking me. Just after sunrise he was back home with his trophy. Al, the music store owner was also a fisherman so he got the first phone call. After the preliminaries I was listening to one half of the phone conversation. "No, I don't know how big he is, Phil, can you measure that fish?"

We had no scales to weigh a fish so I got out a tape as the fish lay on our front porch. "22 inches long," I reported. "And he's really deep-bodied," I heard Rowdy add. Then after a minute Rowdy said, "Corn." After another pause I heard, "yes, I said corn—five kernels of frozen corn. You know Phil doesn't know anything about fishing and last night while he was waiting for me he put some kernels on a hook" . . . and he repeated the experience about the one that got away. Next stop for bass and Rowdy, straight to the store owner's home. Al and Nona even cooked that fish for Sunday dinner. I chose to eat elsewhere. I never did like fish.

He's Trying to Wreck the Company

I was hired out of college to be the first "executive trainee" with the unique dual purpose of helping write the training syllabus while participating in it. That was a consideration in picking me for their first candidate. Numerous college students worked in sales to earn the money to go to college but I was surely the only one they found with a combined livestock, sales and college

186

background with a journalism certificate. I admit, even now, that I was probably a logical choice for their "imagined" new job opening.

We developed the executive training program while I also worked as an assistant to the sales and advertising manager. They hired two trainees the next year but neither of them began their careers in the office as I had. They followed our syllabus recommendations by beginning as salesmen with additional training sessions. We tried to avoid "hand feeding" these trainees but instead made them compete in the business world for their living.

I spent some time every month during their first year with these two candidates in sessions set up specifically for our learning from each other. One of these trainees asked me if there was some way our company could become more "competitive" in the business. This floored me because I was supervising side-by-side feed tests where we agreed to split the herd and if our product didn't produce more return for less cost, we refunded the cost of our product. We never lost. What did this new guy mean more competitive?

Our products were great. The availability of equipment needed to use them properly was our shortcoming. Our concentrates were more concentrated than most competitors. The livestock feed business includes a variety of products. Some are concentrated protein, vitamin and mineral supplements to be mixed with farmer-raised or purchased grains. At the other extreme we found the companies that made complete feed products that included both the grain and supplements in the same mix, all shipped from a factory to dealerships in rural area towns.

Highly concentrated supplements have a marked price advantage because the farmer raises the grain part . . . most of the finished feed . . . purchasing only a small part that was shipped to him from a factory miles away. If the grain was included at the factory, a freight bill was a larger part of the cost of every pound of feed. We had most competitors whipped for nutrition per dollar. Our problem was availability of on-the-farm equipment to easily and accurately prepare and control the quality of our finished livestock feed. "How good is the best product on earth if it is difficult or impossible to use properly?" this trainee asked me.

I began to survey his area. There were two good stationary mills that had fairly sophisticated equipment but when farmers tried to get their feed mixed the mill operator tried to un-sell them on our feed and sell them his brand. When I talked to the mill owners I learned that their mills had plenty of capacity. They needed more business and didn't know how to get it. I felt we could make a win-win situation. If we came up with a program that gave these mill owners some new business and furnished an on-the-farm salesman for the mill owner, and at no cost to him, we could become industry leaders.

It would take some product re-formulation, leaving out some of the protein ingredients we had normally added at our factory but we could save freight if we could trust these local mills to use the same quality we had used.

We needed a new modified pricing and commission structure, contract enforcement and in-house education of our people, the mill operators and their employees. It was asking a lot but I felt we could do it.

I was sure this program would work but I kept fine-tuning my idea to get as many bugs out as possible before I told anyone else. Meantime I had been moved to a territory supervisor's job at Fort Dodge. I still kept checking with mill owners in my new territory. There must be something wrong with this idea, I reasoned, or somebody would already be doing it. Since nobody was doing it, maybe it wasn't such a hot idea after all, I almost admitted. Finally I was ready to spring my idea on our Sales Manager — win, lose or draw.

I had two things going for me and my program. From day one with the company, I had been a member of the "executive council" that the company chief operating officer named. It cut across all levels of supervision and job titles. This didn't make me always right but at least my idea could get a fair hearing. I wasn't too smart with the ways of the world or even our company at the time but I felt I could use a friend when I presented this new program to the full company management group. Our sales manager, Ken Lepley, was open-minded and a positive thinker. If my idea had any merit, Lep would recognize it, I was sure.

Lepley liked the concept and made few suggestions for my package. I was asked to show the idea to the office senior staff, then to a division manager's meeting. These guys all outranked me and included all my bosses. Several didn't buy the concept. I felt that underneath they resisted change and probably some of them felt insecure in their jobs and their ability to handle such a change. It was no "slam dunk." But management asked me to hire and train my replacement and begin to try the new "sub-manufacturer" program in areas with the approval of the state sales manager involved.

They gave me an office and a secretary and I was to make up the program as I went along—with supervision. I got no ringing endorsement. Nobody said it in so many words, but it became clear that I was going to be the one that had to make it work. One of the state managers accused me of trying to wreck—at least change—the company. And he didn't like it. It was my idea and it was going to be up to me to make it work. I started in two territories where the state managers endorsed the idea from the start.

Management said they believed in the idea enough that they were ready to go through "three to five years of hell" while we made the transition. I signed up the first four mills I contacted and all were the cream of the crop. The word spread and within a few months we had some of the best regional feed mill owners calling to see if they could get in on the program. And to our great surprise, we got unsolicited applications for sales and management jobs from top candidates . . . something we had never had in previous years, and this magnetism was just because of the new sub-manufacturer program.

Within a year and a half, I had the entire territory covered with sub-manufacturers and I was staying out of the office so they wouldn't know I wasn't working. It got boring so I asked for a new job. They gave me the western Iowa division. I was ready to move to a new job where I was selling a proven product—not a totally new concept. This territory happened to be dead last in sales among the company's 20 divisions. It couldn't get worse so it should be fairly easy for me to look good. But I was surprised that we got to be No. 1 in the company within five years.

That Genetics Puzzle

Working with livestock and livestock people on a first- or second-hand basis for most of my life, I have been exposed to a lot of genetics. My early world was full of horror stories about "inbreeding." I remember the theories of our neighbors when I was a kid. I didn't take genetics in college; it had tough prerequisites and a reputation as a tough course. I was an eager listener, though, when I began working with poultry geneticists at Ames In-Cross, the hybrid poultry firm that merged with Foxbilt Feeds, my employer when I got out of college.

One of the first lessons was a visit to the breeding houses. The best male was mated to his 12 best full sisters, then the best of that mating repeated. After 12 generations the hens were better producers and in better health than their original breeding stock. Most matings were not this successful but I quickly learned that most of the dire outcomes predicted by old friends were highly exaggerated or totally untrue.

We had dozens of highly inbred families that were outstanding performers. There are also some unspectacular results. Not all bloodlines respond well to inbreeding. Geneticists explain that whether breeding corn or hogs, inbreeding intensifies both good and bad traits in the bloodline. Real improvement comes from picking the best from one family, mated to the best of another family. Results will often be improved and will be more uniform if either or both families are line-bred.

Our company also operated a swine breeding program strongly reflecting the work done at the University of Minnesota by veteran swine geneticist, Dr. Winters. This was based on a rotational crossing program of three inbred lines. Inbreeding reduces the variance within each line, giving more consistent and predictable performance than with open-mated livestock.

I worked as a consultant for Wolfe Hereford Ranch for five years in the mid-1960s. On one of my first ranch tours, I was taking special notice of the livestock we had in line for our first production sale. A young bull really caught my eye. I asked Bill Wolfe about him. Bill tried to avoid my questions but I finally learned that the bull was "C35" in ranch numbers. He was the result of an accidental mating of the proven herd sire, HPM Lamplighter 20, to one of his own daughters.

At birth, C35 appeared to be one of the best calves on the ranch. He looked like a great prospect for the livestock shows but stock shows require a pedigree to prove the animal's age, name, parentage, etc. Bill felt this would show that he, the owner, was either a sloppy manager or crazy for mating a bull to his own daughter. Almost nobody in the business at that time would condone such a mating.

Since C35 was such an outstanding individual, Bill decided to breed him to unrelated females to give them a "double dose" of "20th" breeding. I had nothing to lose so I encouraged him. It worked. I also urged him to mate "20th" to more of his daughters. We produced many "double-bred" 20th sons and daughters. Then we mated C35 and other double-bred 20th sons to several "20th" daughters; triple-bred 20th, so to speak. This proved to be our best mating. We began breeding over 100 yearly.

In one sale, our third-highest seller was sired by HPM Lamplighter 20, his mother was sired by the 20th and his grandmother was sired by the 20th. We told buyers that if they liked the performance of a bull, buy him, because his calves have no choice but to look and perform like their sire, who was also the grandsire and great-grandsire. We never found a defect or even a slow-gaining animal in hundreds of these tightly line-bred matings.

Some livestock lines had problems with recessive genes that showed up when inbred. A few families in both Angus beef cattle and Holstein dairy cattle have a recessive gene that can produce syndactylism (mule-footed calves, also born dead). One of the most promising Holstein sires in the 1960s was Tidy Burke Elsie Leader. A sire of very feminine-appearing females with high production at an early age, he became a popular sire. He was sold to an artificial insemination firm for big money. Then the mule-foot trait showed up in his offspring.

Ed Cate, a Tulare, California, dairyman, had a son of "Elsie" that had dozens of great-appearing daughters coming into production. The AI stud service that had purchased—and destroyed—"Elsie" wanted to buy Ed's bull if he did not carry the mulefoot gene. To prove it, Ed bred his bull to a large number (I believe it was 25) of his daughters. They felt that if that many produced calves by this mating without a mulefoot, the bull would not be a carrier of the gene. I was at Ed's dairy when the 20th calved. Still a perfect record. But before all 25 calved, two calves were produced with the mulefoot trait. Sorry. No sale for the bull!

We didn't prove or disprove most of the old wives' tales with the livestock breeding I observed. But old friends Byron and Wanda Phillips became a working lab for one of the old truisms. If your parent was a twin, you won't have twins, but your kids will, or will it be your grandchildren? Don't you believe it. By was a twin. He married Wanda, whose mother was a twin. When they started their own family, we asked By to speculate if it would be twins.

He said they would have a litter and cited the genetics twin theory. They should have bridged the "skipped generation" idea, but all their kids were single births. If By and Wanda had been close relatives, would they have had twins? Minnesota's Dr. Winters said close relatives rarely marry, but not because of genetics. He claimed, "It's because they already know who their in-laws would be."

A Degree by Degree: Installment Plan Education

Brother Dick was almost an only child—or the second of three families—or a lostling that was overlooked, depending on which segment of time you consider at the moment. Being the firstborn in the family, I tailed my dad outside at an early age and brother Jack, born three years later, tailed me outside as soon as possible—and much earlier than I would have liked.

When Dick came along some two-and-a-half years later, there was no way he would have been welcome, nor able, to keep up with Jack and me. He would grow up being that "only child" until Rolland was born almost six years later. I never knew or cared much what Dick did for a good many years. I was growing up and he was a boring little kid who couldn't keep up and he soon learned that it wasn't productive to try. He did his thing, whatever it was; we did ours. Jack was three years my junior but since I skipped a grade, we were four years apart in school and were not in high school together. Dick was still going to our one-room country school when I went off to college and into Navy flight training so we really had a gap.

The next thing I knew he was at Kearney State Teachers College, now a University of Nebraska campus. With his first teaching job, he began looking ahead and was soon spending his summers in New York at Columbia University graduate school. He was switching careers, one course at a time, from teaching social studies to teaching art history and from teaching high school to teaching college. As he continued for several summers, one of our topics of conversation was what Dick was doing this summer—was he going back to Columbia? One year I took a vacation trip with friends that took us to the east coast and New York. Dick gave us a tour of Columbia and much of the city and then rode home with us.

Some years before, we had discovered a distant cousin who operated a greenhouse and nursery business in Delaware. One year when I asked Dick what he was going to do when his summer school was over, he reminded me of a pet saying that "one of the good things about friends vs. relatives was that you could choose your friends." He said he was going to accept an invitation to visit the Delaware cousin. "This time," he said, "I am going to choose my relatives."

A Cold Day in Iowa

Ames In-Cross was the name of a company that bred hybrid poultry for sale to egg producers across the country and to the hatchery men in various areas who in turn sold baby chicks to egg ranchers. This involved a longtime breeding program based on finding outstanding poultry families, then purifying the characteristics by testing, selection and line breeding. If a family became a reliable producer that combined well with other families, its value could be the difference between having a successful nationwide company or a failure.

Foxbilt, Inc., my employer at the time, merged with Ames In-Cross and I became advertising manager for the combined companies. I found it enjoyable and interesting to work with the geneticists to learn the traits of various families, then to develop marketing strategies for the commercial poultry. This was in the late 1950s when most of the country's egg production had not switched from the general farmer or small specialized egg producers to the giant egg ranches of today that are located within easy egg-hauling distance of most major cities.

Historically, the egg market cycle begins in September when school starts, family vacations are over and Americans return to a more stable living pattern than during the summer season. Birds, including poultry, naturally nest in spring. Hens begin laying eggs at 5 to 6 months of age and will live to be several years old, but their egg production is at its best during the first year. At the end of about a year's production, most hens molt their feathers and go out of egg production for a few weeks. Most poultry men market the year-old hens and replace them with newly raised pullets at this time.

These factors combine to make late winter and early spring the big months in the hatching business. Poultry breeders and hatching egg producers are going at full speed during the late winter and early spring to supply this market. To get more use from their incubators (high-cost, single-use machinery) they use their full capacity during the commercial hatching season, then use the incubators for hatching breeders and parent stock eggs during other months.

Poultry eggs hatch after 21 days' incubation. At Ames In-Cross, we tried to get two 21-day cycles of "breeders" through the incubators before they were filled with eggs for normal parent stock in February. This meant that from mid-December through January, our incubators were filled with eggs from hens that had been inbred for generations to identify family traits, intensify them and mate each family to various other families, looking for that "better" cross-bred bird. These eggs were valued at several dollars each, but they were, in essence, irreplaceable. The company's future was tied directly to the genes these eggs represented.

Iowa is well known for foul weather during the winter months, including frequent sleet and ice storms. Ames In-Cross headquarters were at Roland, a tiny town about 40 to 50 miles north of Des Moines. We constantly worried about loss of electric power and had tried to get the town to cooperate with us in buying a standby power unit. But incubators are well insulated and, if all power is cut off, will hold their heat within the "safe" range for incubating eggs for 48 hours as per manufacturer's guarantee. Neither weather nor power officials had a record of power outages for longer than two days in this area.

Then it happened. At the slack time during the Christmas and New Year holidays, a record sleet and freezing rainstorm hit central Iowa. Electric power lines snapped as tons of ice weighed heavily, far beyond the tensile strength of the normally stable cables. We were hours away from damage to the eggs but a nervous pall hung over AIC executives, still in contact with the office since several executives had left town for the holidays.

When the outage passed 24 hours we began to realize that we might be about 24 hours from seeing the company in ruin when the new crop of baby chicks that were to be our future breeding stock would become garbage. We had located a small generator that could furnish power for about half of the incubators but we were still looking for either a larger generator or a chinook wind that would thaw the ice and enable the Iowa Power and Light Co. people to restore our lines.

Then someone recalled an obscure new government plan to give some surplus military equipment to schools. This included Des Moines Tech High School, which had one or more giant generators made to power auxiliary military bases to help train future engineers. Wayne Fox, one of our founder's sons, knew a science teacher at Tech, made a call (some of the phone lines were also lying on the ground) and found that yes, they had a generator big enough to run not only our incubators, but the entire city of Roland. But we still had problems.

This generator was big. Really big. It had been brought to Des Moines on a railroad car and it took a special permit and one of Iowa's biggest lowboy trailers to get it to the school and it would surely take the same to move it to Roland. Since it was a school holiday, could we find anybody who would put his name on the line to let us "borrow" the generator from the school? And could we find any highway department official to permit us to haul this oversize load on the most treacherous roads we had seen in years?

Wayne Fox's contact at Tech High turned out to be our kind of guy. He was acting department head, still teaching by request, after being officially retired, to keep the department operating while the school board found a successor that they felt would carry on the envied tradition at the school. He had the resources we needed, the authority to make decisions, and he didn't give a second thought to "getting permission." He even lined up the same lowboy owner who had brought the generator to the school. And from the original permit, he tracked the official to his home to get another permit for the trip to Roland.

We still had about 12 hours to get our new power source online—if the incubators had lived up to their guarantee. Flashing lights on the highway patrol cars seemed to make the "oversize load following" escort vehicle redundant. As the "young, single guy" on the staff, I got to be the "gofer" in running errands and keeping the plan together, substituting as message carrier in lieu of the downed telephone lines. The trip was uneventful. We met little traffic and the generator, on its lowboy trailer, fitted nicely on a vacant lot where the Iowa Power main line entered our property.

There were few people present when the generator was connected. Our Tech High teacher had brought his favorite diesel-powered generator mechanic with a service truck full of tools to be sure our monster would make sparks. It was getting dark and cold. It looked like we might yet save the eggs as we still had about four hours left on the incubator guarantee. In the anticlimax of the winter, as electricians hurried, the automatic hatchery lights suddenly came on. These were the electric eye-controlled yard lights that normally lighted the hatchery area at night.

Iowa Power and Light Co. had given top priority to our investment and had miraculously restored power to our hatchery in the little town of Roland ahead of many big city areas. Yes, our volunteers started, then tested the generator, even though IPALCO had finished their job minutes earlier. We later made a deal with the City of Roland and Tech High (they actually had two of these generators, but had to own them for a year or longer before they could transfer ownership) to have a standby unit for both the city and the hatchery in the years to come. As far as I know, that "government surplus" generator may still be sitting by the hatchery, waiting for the next ice storm. But that was one freezing-cold Iowa day I'll long remember.

The Pots-and-Pans Guy

When I left home for college I had about $20 in the bank and another $20 in my pocket, a Regents' scholarship that gave me $50 for the first semester and $25 per semester for the next two semesters. I also had a little-known Montgomery Ward scholarship for about $500. I also had the promise from my parents that I should not expect any help from them. They kept their promise to the penny. One piece of good luck came along. My parents finally decided that they could afford to be gone from the ranch for two days and volunteered to drive me the 250 miles to Lincoln, where we happened to meet my cousins, Marian and Ed Taylor, at the State Fair.

When I got to Lincoln I found Don Cahill, who was a year ahead of me in high school and had both a car and a year of experience in the college world.

194

I found the student employment office and a cheap room that I shared with Don's brother, Jim. There were several candidates for every job, which meant the upperclassmen already had the jobs, except for filling silo at the Ag college dairy or spading gardens. That work paid 25 cents an hour and sometimes a glass of milk and some cookies—an occasional substitute for lunch or dinner.

I got through the first few months, then the Japanese bombed Pearl Harbor one Sunday and things changed. A lot of the older students became eligible for the military draft in an instant and many swapped college life for military life. Suddenly a job opened up for me at the college creamery. Then my 18th birthday came in February and I had to plan for a military career and put college on hold if I passed the physical exam. I was too close to the problem at that time to see the solution but after the war things appeared a lot different to me. I learned that I liked selling and that I liked freedom from being tied to an hourly job.

Toward the end of the spring semester in my first year back in college after the war, I got a job selling kitchen aluminum ware—pots and pans. I had bought a car when I got out of the service so I headed home to sell pots and pans to our old neighbors. The time was ripe. They were fairly flush with post-war income and, as a rule, had a bunch of ugly old pots and pans in the kitchen. I did not single-handedly convert the kitchenware in homes over a very wide piece of geography but I doubt that many college students made more money or learned more about selling that summer than I did.

My company had a sales manager who was a good motivator. The company sponsored a sales contest among all the salesmen. The top 40 salesmen in the company during the month-long contest earned an expense-paid week's vacation at Lake Taneycomo in the Ozarks. Our area manager put on his own contest within the company campaign. During the last week of the month, the sales leader in our area got a full set to sell—and keep all the money it brought. He had four men you might call "career" salesmen with several years' experience. It had been a contest to see who, if anyone from this group, could beat Jack Garska during any sales period. I was one of the new guys—the college student. Garska was regularly the sales leader.

I had already worked the area west of Stapleton where we lived. When the contest was announced, I concentrated on the townspeople. They lived closer together with less driving. I did well and almost every buyer referred me to one or more of the neighbors, but Stapleton is a small town. The last week I built a new list of prospects and headed south to the county line. My first call was Mrs. Newburn's, where my mother had roomed years earlier when she taught at the nearby one-room Banner school. She bought in an instant—didn't even let me take the pans out of the case—and sent me to a neighbor.

I was hot. I decided to push my luck. Charley Cooksley, an old bachelor, lived just a mile down the road. I had never sold to a bachelor. I noticed an open door on the granary so I walked in. Charley was nailing boards on a bin partition. A noisy fan was running so I had to yell to get his attention. He was so startled that he screamed and the hammer and nails went flying. He bought a set, a small set, but it was my first and only sale to a bachelor.

When I went to the Saturday meeting in Kearney, the veteran salesmen were already checking to see if they had topped Garska. None had. He had won again, until the sales manager asked for my sales book. I hadn't taken time to total my sales. When the checks were added, Garska went into shock. I had topped him but we both earned the trip to Taneycomo. It hadn't occurred to me that I could win, that I could top these veterans. I worked hard because I didn't want to look bad. I continued to earn my way through college selling kitchenware instead of taking hourly wage jobs. When the decision came for my first job out of college, my pan people made a good offer but I reasoned, why should I spend years studying agriculture to sell pots and pans? Instead, I became the first trainee in Foxbilt Feeds' new "executive training program."

You Have to be a Member

My first out-in-the-country sales job with Foxbilt Feeds was in Boone County, Iowa. I had been hired out of college as the company's first "executive trainee" to see if their idea for bringing up their own next crop of executives would work. My first training assignment was to understudy the sales manager, then I was to rewrite the company product literature, publish company house organs and be gofer-in-chief, working with all departments. It was interesting work and great training, but I finally decided that I had better take charge of my career . . . and the way to get ahead in this, or any company, was to make it in sales.

I picked an area that had been a good producer but the salesman had been fired for being casual with the truth. He over-promised. The district manager in this area was a solid, no-nonsense trainer and supervisor. I asked him if he would give me objective sales training if I signed on in his now "open" territory. I liked its location, being far enough from the home office to avoid constant scrutiny but near enough to get good service from the plant. The territory had one sometimes-fickle dealer and the previous salesman had been selected to place and supervise hatching flocks, producing eggs for Ames In-Cross, our hybrid poultry subsidiary. This meant I would get experience not possible in most territories.

When I began making calls on the list of alleged customers inherited with the territory, many were quick to condemn both the salesman and the company for promises with no follow-through. I learned to let them blow off steam on the first call, agree with them, then partially blame them for not telling the company when they were the only people who knew its salesman was behaving badly. In my first month on the job, I met a young, relatively new veterinarian in the area that was fast replacing the "old school" vet. In our first visit at an American Legion Club meeting, I learned that we were both looking for new customers. He was amazed that a feed salesman had actually studied nutrition in college and became a great recruiter for me. Needless to say, when a customer complained about his livestock health or vet, I mentioned "that new vet."

One of my first new customers was heading a membership recruiting drive for the Boone County Farm Bureau. I joined. Another customer, just over the county line in Greene County, was also recruiting. My explanation that I had joined in Boone County wasn't good enough. I joined again. A few weeks later I got a call from a farmer that I had called on earlier but seemed to be a confirmed Co-op feed customer. He was the program chairman for Beaver Township Farm Bureau and heard that I was an ag college graduate and that I would talk about nutrition if asked. He was asking, but had two conditions. No. 1, I could not mention the name of the company I worked for. No. 2, I had to join the Beaver Township Farm Bureau. The meeting was at George Grabau's house. He was one of my customers so I felt I would be on friendly turf, even if my invitation had conditions I never expected. I joined the Farm Bureau again.

Meeting time came and the program chairman introduced me without my company's name. I showed a university-produced movie on nutrition, made a short talk about some of the deficiency symptoms I'd noticed in the area, then said I'd answer questions. Several hands went in the air. I picked one farmer's hand and he asked if I worked for a feed company. I said I did. He asked which one. I looked to my program chairman, who seemed to be embarrassed. Before I could answer, George Grabau, our host, who was 6'4" or 6'5" with a voice to match—and General Patton's former aide—boomed out, "He's with Foxbilt Feeds. I use it." Word of our meeting got around and I was invited to talk nutrition at meetings in most of the county's townships. It helped my business grow even if I had to join the Farm Bureau three times that year. And I begged off when later asked, several times again, to join the Farm Bureau.

An Idea That Became No. 1

Blame it on the war, or maybe it was just meant to happen. Denison, Iowa, for many reasons, or perhaps for no particular reason, happened to be home to several single males who were all a few years past normal college age due to a few years of military service. I was one of that group, having moved to Denison to serve as a regional sales manager for Foxbilt Feeds for the Western Iowa territory. Gordon Halverson was hired as manager of the Denison Chamber of Commerce straight out of college. Bob Neumeyer was getting his start at farming, borrowing some of the machinery from his dad's operation a few miles out of town. We three were among the singles (all veterans) dating schoolteachers and looking for a little excitement.

Halverson saw the rest of us as potential members and as talent to make his outfit more lively. While neither Bob nor I really had a business, like most prospective Chamber members, Gordon talked Denison's single guys into joining for a minimum membership fee, and then they could work with whatever bureau suited them. Bob and I went into the "Ag-Industrial" bureau since it was expected that any industry in this Corn Belt town would be agriculture-based. Our members made a strange mix that included a cement contractor, a soft-drink bottler, a manufacturer of livestock watering devices, a dairy and milk processor, chick hatcheries, seed and feed dealers. Bob and I nearly qualified here, although we didn't stock or deliver our feedstuffs, we just sold it.

Most Chamber members wanted their businesses to grow, which, most felt, also meant that the town had to grow. The answer to their prayers would be a new business with many employees to bring new buyers for their goods. And many felt that the answer was already in town—a ghost of industry past, an abandoned Swift & Co. poultry processing plant on the highway on the edge of town. Some of our members were convinced that a new livestock packing plant bringing new money to the community could be packaged in that empty building. The chamber manager got the plan for forming an industry development corporation from the Iowa State Chamber and got good cooperation from most of the civic and business leaders. He also got the name of a highly qualified potential manager for a future packing plant, should we decide in favor of such an operation.

In a strange coincidence, election time for the chamber rolled around. There had been an unwritten succession order for becoming chairman of each bureau. Halverson, the chamber manager, felt the heir apparent in our bureau would not be a suitable chairman at this time, with the upcoming projects. He asked me if I would like to be bureau chairman. I told him that I was flattered to be asked but I had joined more to have fun than to build an empire and that I didn't want to be the new guy to run against any of the town's businessmen. "Would you serve if elected?" he asked. Feeling that nobody would vote for me, I agreed. He then got Bob to nominate me and I was shocked to win the election. This possibility hadn't occurred to me, but I kept my word. What do I do now, I wondered. I soon found out. All bureau chairmen automatically formed an advisory group working with the Industrial Development Corporation and our Ag-Industrial bureau was the lead group. I still didn't realize what was ahead.

Our "highly qualified" candidate showed up for an interview after we had studied his track record. We were sold, almost to a man, on Andy Anderson as the man who could ramrod our project. But one of the possible investors decided to do his own search. He had a relative in the executive placement business in Los Angeles, where Andy had recently worked for several years. He gave us a scare. He said his sister reported back. "This guy has too good a record," she reported, "nobody is that good." We continued to check, even with employers, employees and customers for several years back. It appeared that Anderson had spent a lifetime building a perfect track record, waiting for the right opportunity. This, he felt, was it. A few weeks later, we agreed. But then he shook many of the activists by telling them that there was no way that empty, abandoned building could fit into anybody's future. It was abandoned because it was outdated years ago and it would be more obsolete now than then.

Andy had grown up and was educated in Iowa. He decided early in life that there was opportunity for creative people in the meat-packing business and set out to get the best experience and ideas available. He finally found a banker to partner with him in building a packing plant in Boise, Idaho, with the most modern product flow and equipment. It was an industry leader. His partner was soon killed in a plane accident and, when Andy couldn't find another partner, they sold to Swift, the meat packing giant and he began looking for another opportunity. We were the best bet that had come along and he was ready to join up.

He sold the committee on finding a site with enough acreage for growth and parking. "Don't fence yourself in before you get started," he told us, "and we don't want to be too close to a town. Even the most modern packing plants create an odor. The city fathers will quickly forget about the new money you brought to town if they smell the place that brought it." We found the site and raised the money through the sale of stock in the new Crawford County Packing Co. to finance the construction and beginning of the proposed pork packing and processing plant.

How do you sell stock in a nonexistent corporation to naturally suspicious Iowa farmers and city fathers in a small county seat town? We used amateurs. It was mainly the members of the chamber of commerce, working in teams of two or three, making appointments and presenting the idea. Bob Neumeyer and I went together. Bob had grown up in the community and knew many of the farmers. My presence gave him moral support. We began making tentative appointments and followed up as soon as the managers had materials to show the financial projections. We couldn't wait to sell the first shares, or at least to see if we would get checks from these farmers for stock in a proposed but nonexistent corporation or if they would send us down the road. We must have been good salesmen or else this was a cause whose time had come because we were successful in selling the first stock in the new company. We even bought what we could afford.

By the time Andy had slogged through an Iowa winter with contractors and financiers, every person who worked with him was convinced he was as good as claimed. He was on the job early every morning for the better part of two years to get the place operating. The plant incorporated the most modern ideas and equipment. When he had hired and trained his crew, the operation was open for business and soon visitors from around the world came to see the country's most modern plant in operation. The city fathers basked in this attention, but were not enthusiastic about some of the packing house workers who came to town, even if most of the employees were local people looking for jobs. And when Andy told the city fathers that the plant must have a union contract to get meat unloaded, they were in for another jolt. He set up a local union, then had a union election where he got both the united packing-house workers and amalgamated meat-cutters on the ballot, and both decertified, almost before their national offices knew of the event. This gave the plant many months of union peace to start operations.

Before the pork plant was finished and operating, several of us visited with Andy on a fairly regular basis. He said that he was really happy with the way our area had responded and that he planned to run the pork plant for a couple of years to get it really humming then sell the operation. The stockholders would make a lot of money on their stock and would be willing to invest it—and more—to build a new beef packing plant. He said that was what he wanted from the start but knew we couldn't swing a deal of that size until there was a track record to show. An amazing amount of new machinery and systems were coming on the market but no new plants to integrate the new knowledge.

He felt a new-style beef plant could set the standard for operations and profits for years to come. He said he had some processors working on a plastic wrap for meat. He said the new plant would pack everything in primal cuts or possibly ready-to-cook portions in plastic wrap right at the packing plant. "There won't be any more "swinging carcasses" in the meat trucks of the future," he promised us—in the 1950s.

Andy's "dream" came true. They did sell the Crawford County Packing Co. to Farmland with a check of $350 for each $100 original investment after only a couple of years' operation. As soon as the deal with Farmland seemed sure, Andy came back to the Chamber and Industrial Development Corporation to see if they wanted to help kick off the new stock drive. This might be a tough sell. It would be several times as big as the pork plant. Yes, we joined the stock selling team again, going mainly to the people who had just made a nice profit on their last stock purchase. This was an easier sale. Would it be as good, we wondered.

The venture was called Iowa Beef Packers. And it did as Andy predicted. It brought new technology to beef packing and large profits for stockholders from the Denison plant. With the profits, they built new plants at South Sioux City, Nebraska, and across the country, becoming the largest beef packer in the United States. And did I make a lot of money from the stock I purchased?

You bet. When the price got up to $15 for every $1 invested, I sold before the price dropped, but a bit early. When investor Armand Hammer's Superior Oil Company purchased all the IBP stock a few years later, the value was over $100 to $1 for the common stock.

It may not have made millionaires on the scale of the Silicon Valley computer industry but a waitress in Sioux City had saved all her tips for years—$11,000 worth. When her boyfriend left Sioux City to join IBP's work force, she plunked it all on IBP stock which would have returned more than a million if she still had all the stock. Good for her. It was a once-in-a-lifetime experience for me. But think twice before becoming a candidate for a job you aren't sure you want. It may not turn out to be No. 1.

Temptations Resisted

When I was about a semester short of filling the University's graduation requirements, I had a call from Associated Press. I was to meet at their Omaha office for instructions about taking over their office in Lincoln. I had allegedly been recommended by the head of the School of Journalism and my hiring was a done deal. The pay offered was less than I was making for part-time work while working my way through college. I didn't make the meeting and I don't know whether the Lincoln office was closed or not due to my no-show. AP did not go out of business, at any rate.

A few years later, I was offered a possibly interesting job with an advertising agency in New Orleans. A college friend, Gould "Fig" Flagg, had become ad manager for Nebraska Consolidated Milling Co., manufacturer of Duncan Hines cake mixes, etc. The New Orleans agency was being considered to take over the Duncan Hines account but the mill also had a brand of livestock feed products. To get the cake mix account, the feed line was holding the agency hostage. The agency must hire an account exec, approved by Flagg, to take over the feed account. He called me and I was interested except for two things: I was already working for a feed manufacturer. I liked Duncan Hines mixes, but I did not respect their feed. I met Fig in Omaha on a hot summer day to discuss the deal. The news, as we met, featured the 100-plus temperatures in New Orleans. Crummy product and crummy weather and an "iffy" profession made me nix a job change, even with a big pay raise.

As the fallout from the merger between my employer, Foxbilt Feeds, and meat packer, Morrell & Co., caused the formation of a new feed company, I felt this was the time for a career change. I interviewed for several jobs. One was in Kansas City with the leading ad agency in the area. They offered the job of account exec with two product lines that I liked. They also wanted me to join their "creative" committee to replace a retiring longtime employee. The pay was good and I had pretty well decided to take the job until the next

Monday morning, when they called and said "We had another meeting and we're afraid you'll go somewhere else. We want to raise our offer." I guess I should have been thrilled but I began to wonder just how much more I should ask for. An offer came from a company more stable than an ad agency so I took it, probably tossing away my best chance to learn if I really had major league advertising ideas.

Much earlier, when I was a Navy pilot in the Philippines, I was tentatively offered the "career opportunity of a lifetime." World War II had just ended and I had survived long enough to get a promotion from ensign, the lowest ranking officer, to lieutenant junior grade. The Navy wanted to learn who would be in the service in the years ahead. Commanding officers could make "spot" promotions to the next higher rank to pilots requesting transfer from the Reserve to USN or permanent officers.

Our Commanding Officer was an Academy graduate with friends in high places. Admiral Byrd was in the process of assembling a new Antarctic team. Our CO said he could get me in as one of the seaplane pilots on the team. Such experience would "practically assure" that my spot promotion would be permanent and that I would have a "successful career" in the Navy. It would be a rare opportunity, I agreed, but I wanted to go back to college more than I wanted to go to Antarctica, career or not. As we flew over Alaska glaciers in a float plane while on vacation many years later I was still not sorry I hadn't signed on with Admiral Byrd.

Looking for a Summer Job

I had been back in school at the University of Nebraska for a year after getting out of the Navy in 1946 and decided I should try to get a summer job that had a future instead of taking the first week-to-week opportunity that came along. I had been selling kitchen aluminum pots and pans. I was pretty much my own boss, worked any time I needed money and was getting fairly good at the job but I didn't see it as leading to career employment. After all, I was in Ag College with Journalism as a double major. I kept an ear open for possible future career jobs and checked the want ads in the weekend *Lincoln Journal* and *Omaha World Herald*. One Sunday there it was: Opportunity for stable go-getter with long-established Midwestern company, livestock background helpful, write to Sales Manager, P. O. Box, Des Moines, Iowa.

I wrote my best letter and hoped for a few days, then came a phone call. My letter, it seems, was too good, and to the wrong people. They didn't have any "summer" jobs. They were looking for someone, well established in his home area, to be a salesman for a livestock feed manufacturer. But they were interested only in full-time, career people; a college degree was helpful but not required, the sales manager told me. But, he added, they were in the planning stages for an executive trainee program that they would like me to consider when I got out of college. They had a sales meeting scheduled for the next week for their Nebraska sales people in Lincoln and they wanted to visit with me at the end of the meeting. I agreed to meet and they brought the full load—the Nebraska Sales Manager—plus the Company Sales Manager and even the General Manager had all come for the Nebraska meeting.

They seemed like decent people but they didn't have an opening that fit me for the moment so I didn't include them in my plans. I think they were more alert to the opportunity than I was because every few months I got a letter from the sales manager to remind me that they were still working on the executive training program or some other bit of company news. Meantime I decided to spend the summer selling kitchenware unless an unexpected offer from some surprise source came along. But the next year the letters began coming again. I had the credits to graduate in February but considered taking some more courses, graduating in June.

The Foxbilt people were coming to Lincoln for another sales meeting in early January and would like to talk again. We met and they convinced me to become the first man hired in the Foxbilt Feeds "executive training

program." I helped plan the course, understudied the sales manager, wrote a "training syllabus" for new hires, rewrote the company product literature and outdated sales manual and helped hire and supervise the two trainees hired the next year. I actually became a jack-of-all-trades by my twelfth year in the company, beyond the originally planned program, and becoming a state sales manager and finally the company

Phil's successful, if brief, career as seed company ad manager.

advertising manager for the last few years before a company merger resulted in most executives forming a new company. I passed up a great offer from a Kansas City advertising agency, choosing instead to broaden my experience into a half-new field, consumer products, while enjoying the comfort of working for a firm that was also steeped in agriculture, as advertising manager for the Teweles (say "too-lees") Seed Co. in Milwaukee.

This was a family-owned company in its third generation and one of the industry leaders. They had long been big in farm seeds but also had a lawn seed and chemicals division that had become the second largest in that field. Each division had a sales manager but I was advertising manager for both divisions, giving me experience in consumer products, a new field for me, as well as the agricultural line where I had ample experience and a good track record. The current generation of owners felt pressured to out-perform their parents and grandparents and felt that a new program of bonuses for key employees would produce a record sales year. The company president met with the sales managers for farm seeds and for lawn products and me. He showed us the growth in sales for the past few years and projected the management's "hoped for" sales numbers for the upcoming year along with management's promised bonuses for the three of us at various sales totals. They made generous offers—if we could reach their sales goals.

We more than met their goals, but instead of giving us the bonuses we had earned, they decided to overhaul their entire plant. Ironically, the company only operated for one more year before selling out to a large livestock feed company. I'm sure we made the sellers a lot of money.

I did not wait for the verdict from another attorney, but went in search of another job, leaving Milwaukee in a snowstorm to interview for the position of field editor for the *Western Livestock Journal*. I also interviewed for the ad manager position with American Breeder Service, the country's largest artificial cattle breeding company, when a friend who was their ad agency account manager advised me of their opening. I interviewed at the ABS office on Wells Street in downtown Chicago on a blizzardy February day, then a couple of days later went to their farm and bull station near Madison, Wisconsin, where the climate was improved but still terrible. It was the kind of day to make a Midwesterner feel at home if uncomfortable.

A few days later I flew to Los Angeles to interview for a vacant Field Editor position at *Western Livestock Journal*. When the supervisor met me at the airport wearing a short-sleeved shirt on a balmy day, it was hard to be objective in deciding which job to take. When I had been in California in the Navy, I thought it would be a great place to live if I could find an honest job there. Ann had worked at UCLA before we were married and wanted to move back. This one would give Ann and me a chance to move to California for a job in an opening where I should immediately feel at home, even if not learning about a new industry. When I got back to Milwaukee I learned that I had been selected for the ABS job. I called Los Angeles to confirm their job offer, then called ABS, asking them to remove my name from their list. Coral's birth was due in a few days on about April first. With my Teweles job over in early April, things were working out just right. The one surprise was that Coral waited until April 15 to arrive. I made reservations for Ann to fly out with Coral (United Airlines required babies to be 10 days old to fly at that time). I hired a moving van and left for California where I leased a home, waited for Ann and Coral to arrive and began the new job in late April, 1962.

My Milk Route Had a Bonus

Someone told me there might be an opening for a student worker at the University of Nebraska college creamery. Don Cahill, a year ahead of me in high school, had a job there and had been helpful in getting me settled in to college life. I immediately applied and was told that Don had recommended me but they were not sure they could hire anyone less than 18 years of age. I was disappointed but a couple of days later there was a call at the rooming house asking me to come for an interview. I was hired on the spot, but just to fill in if other student workers were too busy with school activities to work regular hours. They suggested that I would probably be on a regular schedule soon if I was dependable in showing up for work.

A few weeks later—I had only worked a few days and it was early December—they asked, "Do you have a driver's license?" Yes. "Have you driven on Lincoln streets?" Not much, but I had only been in town a few weeks. (I didn't have a car and had to ride the city bus to go anywhere, like almost every other student in 1941.) Then the Japanese bombed Pearl Harbor and the person handling the dairy delivery route to the Student Union downtown, the women's residence halls and a couple of other stops, enlisted in the Navy. They needed a dependable early morning delivery person—starting now! A professor had made deliveries on the route a couple of times. It took him more than four hours but they felt that with a little experience I could trim the time so they would give me four hours' pay no matter how slow or fast I handled the deliveries. I had to walk (or run) the seven or eight blocks from my rented room to the campus dairy department building, where they kept the delivery truck in a heated garage, at 4 a.m. in the winter darkness, rain or snow.

The pay, like every other campus job at the time, was 25 cents per hour or $1 for every morning delivery trip. Not many students had it so good. I was already on the morning crew at the creamery getting an hour for helping set the cottage cheese milk in the vats before I went to school. After a couple of weeks I had learned how to load the morning delivery orders and had the trip down to two hours, later squeezed to one-and-a-half hours. That, plus the hour at the cheese vats gave me five hours' credit for two-and-a-half hours' work—double pay, so to speak. And there were other fringe benefits and/or surprises. The morning manager at the Student Union showed me how to make "breakfast sandwiches" with the egg salad or liverwurst or whatever I found in the cafeteria. They even had individual boxes of cereal for students who bought their breakfasts at the Student Union. And there was the surprise "skin show" on more than one morning when the delivery door at the women's residence halls was locked and I had to go in the front door and past bedrooms via halls filled with screaming coeds in various states of undress—on my way to the kitchen storage area to make my otherwise normal delivery of dairy products. All things considered, I probably had the best job on the campus . . . and I really needed it.

A couple more workers enlisted and I got on the weekend crew at the creamery with the opening to work eight hours every Saturday and, increasingly, some Sunday work. Our weekend crew members brought some of the groceries—bread, lettuce, salami, etc.—and we got free milk, cheese and ice cream—so our weekend meals were almost free too. With all that income and no time to spend any of it, I was actually saving money—putting money in the bank—while working my way through school—at the going labor rate of 25 cents per hour. For the moment, at least, I could say goodbye to spading garden plots or helping clean basements and/or attics for campus area homeowners for the standard wage—25 cents per hour.

I did have a new concern, however. My birthday was February 7, just two months to the day after the Japanese bombed Pearl Harbor (I heard the news when I got back to my room after the Sunday work was over), when I would be 18 years old and eligible, in fact, forced to register for the military draft, but that could wait. I was enjoying my time at school, the good fortune I had in getting the critically-needed income stream during my first trip away from home and the experience I got working at the college creamery.

"Write" of Passage into Management

Company personnel problems brought an unexpected move for me in the spring of 1953. A district manager had reached an impasse with one of the company's leading salesmen and our management voted with the salesman. This resulted in an area shake-up and an opportunity for a new district manager, who would inherit Bill Smith. Like many top salesmen, Bill was a chronic management problem for his previous company and for ours. And now he was about to become my problem.

I had known Bill for the three or four years that he had been with our company. I had done tape-recorded interviews with some of his customers for company radio advertising and some testimonial stories for company house organs but we had never had a "you vs me" encounter. When I moved into the territory as his new manager, all went smoothly to start, as I expected. I tried to motivate him to do his best. In addition to company sales contests, I got him to set a personal goal for the next 90 days, betting a 7-X felt hat that he had overestimated his ability. When he won, the hat cost me $50 but I earned $300 to $500 in extra commissions. But then the "old" Bill began to show up.

A salesman in an adjoining territory, and in another manager's area, found a feed buyer using our feed. He had been sold by Bill Smith, going outside his territory and his contract. I told that manager to have his salesman go sell a customer in Bill's territory but that didn't fly. I had to force Bill to give up the commission on the sale. He continued to test my management ability. I kept my cool and generally kept him at a fairly high level of production. I continued to find prizes he would work hard to win.

He was one of the best salesmen I ever saw, and his salesmanship was apparent early on. I once went with him to see a new customer, whose only previous contact was buying baby chicks in our hatching egg program, which required use of our feed. The chicks were a few weeks old and doing OK but we didn't have a long-term contract yet. We caught the farmer on his tractor in a blizzard. The farmer would not get in the car because he knew Bill would sell him something. Bill rolled his car window down about 6 inches and that farmer bought four different feed products for a total of more than $2,000. Bill had to roll the window down a few more inches for the buyer to write his check. That, to me, was salesmanship! But Bill continued to be a management problem. Since I was his manager, he was my problem!

One evening he called and wanted me to work with him the next day. I changed my schedule and met him at the car dealership. He had a Roadmaster Buick, called a "four-holer" because Buick had placed three chrome rings on the front fender of their regular cars, but four rings on their flagship, the Roadmaster. Its automatic transmission was called Dyna-Flow. On Bill's new Roadmaster, it flowed reluctantly. He had spent more than $500 at the dealership, had driven a replacement several times and had driven the new car less than 10,000 miles. Bill wanted to complain to me and have me furnish wheels for a day. The dealer had quit fighting the company to defend Bill's rights. That night I wrote a letter to the president of GM outlining the chronic problem.

It must have been a good letter. The day it hit Detroit, Bill got a phone call from Buick's area representative. He brought Bill a new car to drive for several days while they repaired his. In a few days his car was delivered back to him with a new transmission and a check to repay him for every penny spent to repair his car over the months. At our next sales meeting, Bill said he wanted to make an announcement to the assembled salesmen. This was spooky. Bill had been known to take over a meeting for any possible excuse and it could be difficult to get control of the meeting again. But what do you do when your best salesman wants to talk?

He embarrassed me into serious blushing when he told the men that if I ever asked them to do something, they should do it without asking why. He admitted that he had sometimes questioned me but that I had done something for him that nobody else in the world would—or could—have done. I got his car fixed—perfect—he said. I didn't need to. It wasn't my job. Nobody else would have done it—or could have done it—but I did. He wanted the group to know that anything they did for me in the future would come back with a bonus—and sat down. I recovered, in time, but I had never seen "that" Bill Smith before or since. He must have been sincere because he was never a problem for me again, but he still liked our "personal" contests.

Black Mountain Needs Big Spring

The California Department of Real Estate could probably test an applicant's ability to handle surprises but instead they let nature take its course and the agent either learns to respond to unusual situations or the applicant finds another occupation. In short, a lot of the contacts in this business will be surprises both good and bad, before and after your first meeting. I had a call from a potential seller with a "perfect" ranch for one of my buyers. This was an OK cow ranch but a better hunting ranch complete with water rights owned by the ranch, ponds, duck blinds, and fields planted to cover crops for pheasant, quail and upland game. The ranch house looked more like a gun club lodge than most buyers expect in a ranch house—and the price reflected the "double life" potential. But the visit wasn't a waste of time. The seller had "outgrown" his love for hunting, especially on a place more than a three-hour drive from his San Francisco Bay area home and business.

But it was his "business," not the ranch that became our common interest. He had been born into a family that owned the Black Mountain Spring Water company. Their business was outgrowing its present sources of spring water and the owner was sure that a "ranch broker" could locate the spring they needed. Its requirements were simple except that it had to be nearly pure H_2O with a minimum of impurities and the greater the flow and nearness to San Francisco the better. In the years that I had traveled ranches all over California, surely I would know where several such springs existed.

I had been on many ranches with springs in Northern California. I didn't know how many gallons per minute and I didn't know if they had impurities but this didn't sound like a tough assignment. Then I wondered, if it was so easy, why didn't he just put an ad in a good farm paper? Well, I could do that and make a nice commission on the sale of the ranch so I agreed to see what I could turn up in this new year. It shouldn't take long.

A couple of weeks later, in late January, I was at the Red Bluff Bull Sale. This sale has become the leading three-day social event for northern California livestock men, during which time a few hundred bulls, over a hundred working cow horses and a dozen or so well-trained cow dogs were to perform at their specialties and find new owners at substantial prices. If you go to the Red Bluff Bull Sale and don't see a specific neighbor or ranch owner from Northern California, you probably just missed him in the crowd.

208

I have attended all of them since 1963, except in 2005 when Ann was in the hospital at sale time.

I had just parked at the fairgrounds when I saw Fenton O'Connell near the first bull barn. He had probably owned or leased more total acres of cattle ranch land than anyone who headquartered within many miles of the San Francisco South Bay since the days of Miller and Lux, who a century earlier were "everywhere." I described my need to Fenton, knowing that he would be more likely than anyone to have owned or leased a ranch with "our" spring on it. He said, "Phil, have you been on my Hollister ranch where my son-in-law, John Bourdet, lives?" I knew that he owned a lot of land but I had not been invited to this one. Then I asked about the spring. He said it had never been officially tested or measured but it was "pretty big." He thought it would probably fill a 3- or 4-inch pipe. The spring was near the top of the highest hill on the ranch—an unexpected place for any spring, much less one with a big flow of water.

He said a geologist friend had tested a sample for purity years earlier in an attempt to learn the water's source. It had none of the contaminants expected from such a location and he felt the water had to be Sierra snow melt that mysteriously crossed the San Joaquin-Sacramento valley at some depth far below the known valley sources. He had no suggestion on how the water crossed the wide valley or how it came out only a few feet from the top of the highest hill within miles around. Fenton said he really didn't want to sell the ranch but he would like to have the spring captured and piped down the mountain with a couple of outlets for cattle water.

My buyer came to look and loved the spring, tested it and found that it was indeed, almost pure H_2O. He agreed that it would be cheap for him to pipe it down the mountain and put in a couple of cattle-watering outlets and with an existing paved road almost all the way from their plant, the ranch-plus-spring seemed perfect. What a deal. I was beginning to have visions of the commission I would earn from the sale. But the grandfather (who had founded the company) would not consider a lease. He would either own it or find another source so our deal died and I never found another spring with any decent level of purity at any price.

It's Company (Bank) Policy

In about 1965, I met Ezra Lundahl at the National Western Livestock Show in Denver. He was trying to sell his invention, a wagon to haul baled hay that had an undercarriage with wheels on an offset axle that "tumbled" to allow the wagon to cross irrigation ditches. The driver would raise and lower the bed just by pulling the wagon through a ditch.

His machine looked great but his descriptive literature, from the photos to layout—even the wording and grammar—left much room for improvement.

He saw some material I had done and asked if I could help him sharpen his image. A few weeks later I was in Logan, Utah, the site of his blacksmith shop, his ranch and his printer. We had nice weather for photos so I recorded his machine doing its thing, made notes about its capability and was about ready to leave town.

I had spent a few unplanned dollars so I felt I would be more comfortable if I had an extra hundred dollars in my pocket for the several travel days ahead. Instead of asking Ezra, I went into the First Security Bank branch across the street from the shop to cash a check. At the teller's window I was asked for identification and when I produced everything asked, the teller apologized because it was "bank policy" to not accept out-of-state checks.

She called the supervisor. He looked at the check, then went through all my identification, item by item, then apologized because it was "bank policy" to not accept any out-of-state checks. But he called the manager to come out of his office and up to the teller's window. He went through the same ritual but before telling me about "bank policy" he asked what I was doing in Logan.

When I told him I was doing some work for Ezra Lundahl, he couldn't dig into the cash drawer fast enough. He apparently did not consider that anybody, including me, could have come in and looked out the window and seen the name on the front of the shop across the street and conned them out of their life savings. The name on the shop, visible to us and everybody in Logan . . . Ezra Lundahl.

Cottonwood Ranch

The caller on the phone told me he had watched my ads for a long time and decided to call me when he decided to sell. He had a sizeable ranch in the Surprise Valley of California that he wanted to sell. He wanted me to tell him what I thought it would bring. I had to wonder why he had called me as there were good ranch brokers in that area, which was a long way from Auburn. Maybe he wanted my price to compare with theirs, maybe they knew him and didn't want to work for him. Word gets around in Modoc County.

Flattering comments are OK but I have always been suspicious of that kind of introduction. In this case, some of my mistrust was not justified. He was not an old-timer in the business and for some reason the ranch brokers in his home area just didn't advertise in the publications on his subscription list. In this case I almost wish they had, but I got irreplaceable experience.

It was a pretty good ranch. Overvalued, in the seller's mind, but we arrived at an asking price that let me maintain credibility. I listed it, prepared brochure material and began to advertise. After several weeks with no action, the seller, a Sacramento businessman absentee ranch owner, began to get

210

impatient even though I had warned him that it often takes several months or possibly more than a year to find a buyer for a ranch priced at $5 million.

He called to tell me that there was an international real estate exchangers meeting in Las Vegas in a couple of weeks and that he thought we should see if we could make a sale. We went and began circulating brochures. We got an offer to exchange for a gem—the world's sixth largest diamond.

I didn't know anything about gems but I had a couple of connections in Las Vegas. I called one who gave me the names and phone numbers of two certified gem appraisers/jewelers/exchangers. I learned that more jewelry is probably appraised in Las Vegas in any day, month or year than any other city in the world. Big players often get overextended and sell or hock gems to get out of town.

At any rate, this diamond was well known. It was big as a hen's egg but it was yellow and full of imperfections. It was big but extremely low quality as gems go. Every jeweler in town knew it, had appraised it and I was told it was in a safe in Phoenix. It was big, its value was fully established but not many people with funds to buy it had any interest in owning it. In short, it was a lot like Dudley's Cottonwood Ranch.

Their offer was on the table for a couple of days and I couldn't decide if my client was really serious about accepting it but it was his call. Finally he asked me if I thought he should make the deal. I told him that I believed in money a lot more than gems but it was his ranch. I wanted one thing to be absolutely clear, however. He had better find some money in the deal somewhere because I would not take a chip off that diamond for any part of my commission.

Inventing the Future
(The story of inventing the World's First Livestock Video Auction)

I have made enough sales on the telephone to have great respect for most of the people who call. There's an excitement in not knowing who will be talking to you every time the phone rings. This was true one day in early 1969. We had just moved to Auburn from Southern California a few months earlier. We didn't have much previous information about the town so we decided to lease a house while we got to know the area better before buying a home. We found a suitable house on our first trip to town and leased it for a year as the owner had just taken a job in another area. A few months later he fell out of love with the new job and was back in town, wanting his house back. We agreed to cooperate if he could help us find another suitable home. In a few weeks we found a new home and were just getting settled when the phone rang.

The caller was Ed Wright, an old friend that I met while working as a field editor for the *Western Livestock Journal*. I later arranged for an interview with management that resulted in hiring Ed in a territory next to mine. He later went to work with Harry and Skinner Hardy, father-and-son livestock auctioneers and livestock market owners. Ed was calling as an outgrowth of this job. He called to tell me that the Livestock Marketing Association was preparing for its annual Livestock Marketing Congress to be held in June at Monterey. They wanted someone from the state where the annual convention was being held to serve as chairman. Ed was it. He called to tell me they wanted to make this a meeting on livestock marketing from seed stock breeders to commercial cattlemen and finally to consumers.

They wanted to make the 3-day meeting to kick off with history of livestock marketing the first day, present marketing on the second day and project into the future of marketing on the third day. He wanted someone to locate and assemble this information and write the presentation. It didn't take long for me to tell him that I didn't know anybody who had the background to do the job, much less one with the time and ability to put it together.

Ed said, "We didn't call you for a referral. We want you to do it." I gasped and almost laughed. "I'm in Kansas City in the association office," he said. "I have them convinced that you can do it. They will pay all your travel and expenses but their budget doesn't have room for a very generous offer." He put Jim Fries, the public relations man, on the phone. I told him he had called the wrong guy. But I agreed to accept his invitation to go to Kansas City to discuss the project. They found a few more dollars to pay for the job and I finally agreed to do it.

I began putting the program together in the order they wanted to present it. And did I get a shock. There was no recorded history, anywhere that I could find, on livestock marketing. I went to visit the American National Cattlemen's Association, the National Livestock Feeders Association, National Pork Producers, Wool Growers, but none had even a hint of the documentation I needed. Libraries were little help. No government agency kept such records. The publicity man at the Kansas City Stockyards had acquired the diaries of one of the old commission house owners and gave me a few excerpts from his notes. Maybe I had enough history for Day 1.

When we got to present market conditions and our plan for Day 2, the staff at the association had the people and material that I needed. I visited every office employee and field man. I quizzed everybody about his job, what he did and how he felt it would contribute to marketing in the years ahead. I needed help and an inspiration from these people.

I was sitting in Dave Daniels' office engaging in "future" talk when I saw it unfold. I told him I could envision the livestock market of the future taking place in a new kind of building. It may be in a city, a farm town or at a rural crossroads. It would probably have offices for a branch bank (an ag lender), maybe a commodities and stock brokerage, a feed and general farm store, veterinarian office, possibly one or more machinery dealers and a livestock auction theater.

I suggested the sale ring or entry alley would be a scales so the stock in the ring would have their average and total weight flashed above the auction block and that we could have a giant screen where we could project live photos of stock, still at home on the ranch, that had been examined, weighed and graded by known, qualified livestock appraisers. We would be able to buy and sell stock, by the truck load or by the herd, with only the pictures in the ring. We would eliminate stress, shrink, handling, extra trucking, sickness and accident. We could sell or include insurance from portal to portal and with credit cards, special telephones and computers (remember this was 1969, before desk-top or notebook computers), eliminate drafts, pre-qualify every buyer and know the limit of his line of credit.

We could sell the cattle by video, put the buyer's debit card in a slot in the phone and it would take the amount of the purchase off his credit line and authorize writing a certified check, on the spot. At this point, Dave Daniels picked up his phone and asked the receptionist, "Where's Tad Sanders?" Sanders was head of the marketing association. We went to meet him in the coffee shop where Dave asked me to tell Tad (and a couple of other association men) my vision. I came as near as I could to repeating the conversation. When I finished, Sanders said, "We'll do it." It began to impress me that if Sanders would commit to this idea with only the first undeveloped idea of what it could turn out to be . . . maybe this was a serious idea. Until this moment, I was just running the procedure through my brain, as I explained my vision, to see how it sounded to me. But I felt that Sanders wouldn't have his job unless his opinions had substance.

When June arrived, so did the marketing congress. We had shocked a lot of people with our first-day presentation of the history of marketing. They heard information that few had ever heard before. But when we gave them a description of what I had envisioned on the third day, there was plenty of chatter as this nation-wide collection of disbelieving market men and other livestock people got their imaginations tweaked. Then the narrator said, "Now you are going to see what we have described, right here, right now."

These veteran market men stared in disbelief. We pulled the drape and had video screens, a telephone, and several seats for buyers and Ken Troutt, the 1968 World Champion Auctioneer. The cattle, to my surprise, were in Halferty Bros. feedlot in Plattsburg, Missouri, who I knew as Foxbilt Feeds customers a few years earlier when I was a feed man. The auction was in Monterey, California, the transaction went by phone to Kansas City then to a computer in New York and back to Kansas City . . . and confirmed back to Monterey to write that certified check instead of the less-than-certain bank draft that had been common in the industry to that time.

It did not revolutionize livestock marketing immediately but it got the attention of many marketing people that day. It took several years before another video auction was held but it became an important marketing medium within 25 years. It was an exciting day. I was glad to be the first to see it—both in my head before it happened and in the company of the country's leading livestock marketers when we finally did it in the flesh. I'm sure that video auctions would have happened somewhere if I hadn't done it then but I'm really glad that I "imagined" them first.

I Want to Talk About a Ranch

The phone rang in my office one day late in March, 1981. The caller wanted me to identify myself, which I did. He then identified himself and told me he was ready to leave Sacramento, wanted directions to my office and said he would see me shortly. His name was Barre (pronounced Barry) Stephens. All I knew about him was that his name was on several parcels of land southeast of Alturas, in the northeastern-most California county.

When Barre reached my office, we didn't waste much time on the weather. He showed me maps of two adjoining ranches. He wanted to sell the larger one, would not sell the smaller one unless someone wanted both, but he would price both in case that happened. He wanted to know if I was interested in listing it and when I could come to Alturas to see the property.

I was already scheduled to be there the following week so we set a date and I met him at the ranch. On the trip to Alturas I remembered another thing I knew about Barre Stephens. The leading ranch broker in Alturas was his best friend. It appeared that I was being set up to appraise the ranch so his friend could sell it and good old Phil would be sent packing. I have always been a slow learner so I went ahead and kept the date . . . and my word.

It was a little late to back out now. I showed up at the ranch on schedule and we toured the property. I asked him how much he felt the ranch should bring. He wanted $1.6 million. I felt it should bring $1.2 million but would be willing to list it a little higher. I told him my price and in a minute he said let's list it at $1.4 million. I kept waiting for him to thank me for showing up—and to tell me that his best friend was a ranch broker. But he said nothing.

At this point I decided it was my move so I took a listing agreement out of my brief and began to fill in the blanks. I kept asking for information and he kept giving it. Finally we got to the bottom line and the only thing left to do was to get the seller to sign the agreement. I pushed the listing agreement across the table, turning it so the space for the seller to sign was right in front of him. Now I knew his friendship would enter the picture.

Without hesitation, he picked up the pen and signed the listing agreement and handed it back to me. I tore the contract out of the pad, separated the

214

copy for the seller's file and handed it to him. I couldn't stand the silence. I said, "I have a question for you, Barre . . . aren't you and (I named the local broker) still friends?"

"Oh, yes, we're best of friends," he answered.

"If you are best friends, why am I sitting here?" I asked, "Why are you doing this with me?"

Then he told me something that really made an impression and something that I have quoted other potential sellers. He said, "Yes, we are good friends and he sells lots of ranches but it seems to me that he always tries to see how cheap he can sell them. From what I hear, you like to see how high you can sell them." No explanation or further comment was needed. Now, I had better live up to the reputation he had given me.

It took a few weeks with the stormy spring weather to take photos, get a brochure prepared and ready to begin advertising by early May. It almost seems anticlimactic but we got lucky and had an offer in June, got our counter-offers agreed and went to escrow on July 2. Modoc Title Co. was allegedly the slowest title company in California where no escrow ever closed within a month. But both the buyer and seller were friends of the title company owner, and both wanted a fast close so it closed escrow on July 31. Lucky again.

Invention: The Mother of Necessity

I published the *California Cattleman* under contract with the California Cattlemen's Association, which owned the magazine name and membership list. I was required to publish every month. They furnished the editorial material including industry news, the organization's goals, projects and accomplishments. I furnished the ads and occasional feature stories. If I sold enough ads to make a profit, I got to keep it. If I lost money, they were sorry.

Magazines thrive or fail on advertising. Many ads, big magazine; no ads, no magazine. Advertising from pharmaceutical, farm equipment, livestock feed and service firms kept the door open, so to speak. But livestock events and purebred breeder ads made the difference between publishing a skinny 24-page issue that didn't pay the rent and phone bill—and an 80- to 100-plus-page issue that made both me and the banker happy.

Every job has problems. But problems mean opportunities. One of the problems I had in publishing the *California Cattleman* was timing. Like shopping centers or restaurants, everyone wants to do the same thing at the same time so you are overworked and underappreciated. Then, when you need it most, nobody wants anything to do with your goods or services.

We had special issues that attracted advertising from different segments of the industry that were pretty well spaced throughout the year. We got permission to combine the July and August issues into a "Bull Buyer's

215

Guide" for breeders to advertise their bulls to commercial cattlemen buyers. This was our biggest issue of the year. Most California cattlemen buy new bulls in early fall, then turn them in with the cow herd in late November or early December so the calves began coming about September 1.

Nobody ever invented a saleable idea for the December issue. Cattlemen don't buy their cows a bull for Christmas. Breeders don't have "after Christmas" discount sales that need ads in the December issue. But one day an idea hit me that took our December issue from a skinny and pathetic dead loser to our second- or third-best issue of the year. The calendar!

Most people think that Pope Gregory or Julius Caesar invented the calendar. Not true. Oh, they may have devised a system that measures the passage of time. Big deal! I invented a calendar. One that I could sell. I had a full-page ad for every month. It was drill-punched so it hung on the wall with a full-color photo ad at the top and a memo calendar below it. I sold dates for sales, open houses, fairs, auctions, etc. in the memo calendar part. It was included in

Timing is everything. I shot this Ace Hereford Ranch bull in Gardnerville, Nevada, just before the other 40 bulls in the pen cleared the hilltop. This was the August photo in the 1973, first-ever *California Cattleman* magazine pull-out calendar, included in the December 1972 issue.

our December issue. It became the industry organizer for California cattlemen. And the next year you could find calendars in many of the country's livestock magazines. Copy cats!

We've been told that necessity is the mother of invention. I do not believe that for a moment. Nobody really needed a television set until someone invented it. Nobody needed a credit card or possibly—even the wheel—until somebody invented it. And absolutely nobody needed to buy a full-page, full-color ad in a calendar published by a cow outfit until I invented one. And it was the easiest ad space to sell in the entire magazine. We almost had fights to see who got to buy August or September or October. There seemed to be someone who had an event every month. And I even found someone who wanted a full-page ad in December.

216

CALIFORNIA CATTLEMAN
CCA

Published monthly, eleven issues per year,
July-August combined.

Vol. 55   No. 4
APRIL 1972

Office of Publication: WEBPCO, 246 North
Wenatchee Ave., Wenatchee, Wash. 98801.
Second Class Postage paid at Wenatchee,
Washington.

Business and Advertising Office:
P. O. Box 1618, Auburn, California

OFFICE (24 Hour) .... (916) 885-7378
PHIL RAYNARD (Home) ...... (916) 885-4978
GINGER WILTERMOOD .... Office Manager

Subscription price of $5.00 is included
in the amount of the membership dues.

Published for the
California Cattlemen's Association
Mezzanine, Senator Hotel   12th & L Streets
Sacramento, California 95814

Editor:
WM. B. STAIGER

INDEX
To Feature Articles

OUR COVER PHOTO

"We're searching for an animal that will bring more money," says Garrett Beckley, Linden. Some 11 breeds and extraordinary records kept by Garrett Beckley, Jr., have been used in this search. Our cover shows what the Beckleys have in mind with over 200 replacement females that survived this unusual performance test.

Beckleys want the maximum return per head and per acre from their 1,840-acre ranch. It has practically all been converted to irrigated pasture since purchased in 1946. Over 1200 cows were bred by AI last year (including 650 Simmental, 225 Limousin and 350 Red and Black Angus) and will breed 1400 this year. More of this operation is shown on page 14.

California Cattleman photo by Phil Raynard

TRAVELIN' AROUND

By Phil Raynard

AN OPEN LETTER TO RICHARD NIXON

Dear Sir:

I have been furious (as has almost everyone connected with livestock) since your vicious challenge to your latest economic advisory appointee to "Get out and do something about meat prices."

You claim to endorse free enterprise and those who live by it. Livestock Producers represent free enterprise as well as any segment of our population. But they have not prospered like industries with government contracts, quotas and subsidies.

Stockmen as a group have been among your best friends and strongest supporters. They have felt that you were their friend, even as late as the meeting a few days earlier with Agriculture Secretary Butz and leaders of the California Cattlemen's Assn.

The deepest cut of all — the one that added real insult to injury — is the hard fact that has headlined the livestock press of late, that *beef prices at the farm level* are finally *back up to 1952 levels.* How would you like to be pointed out as a villain to all your fellow countrymen by the man in the highest office in the land — just for getting back to where *you* were in 1952?

Also please consider that the average hourly earnings of most manufacturing laborers rose 230 percent during those 20 years (food marketing employees 250% — Government workers 330%) and corporate dividends 200 percent.

Yes, the cost of producing meat at the farm level about doubled during these 20 years. Thousands of dedicated, able, hard-working stockmen have lost their land, their businesses and way of life. Surely the survivors of this "death march" deserve better from you.

Why didn't you tell your new appointee to get out and do something about wages and dividends? This is inflation in the eyes of livestock producers. Why didn't you tell your new advisor — and the American consumers — that they paid 23 percent of their take-home pay for food in 1951 but now they spend less than 16 percent?

Why don't you use your office to help our people understand each other instead of trying to pit one segment against another? What happened to that candidate who pledged to "Bring us together?"

Can you name a single case in history when any group of Americans has been more unfairly accused by any president? We will be happy to make suitable space available for your reply if you choose to set the record straight. Our industry has been waiting more than a week for an explanation at the time of this writing.

Sincerely,

Philip N. Raynard, Gen. Mgr.
CALIFORNIA CATTLEMAN

7

Open letter to Richard Nixon (reprint of editorial from the April 1972 issue of the *California Cattleman* magazine) after Nixon "challenged" his new Economic Advisor appointee to "get out and do something about beef prices" which Nixon apparently felt were "too high." Cattlemen disagreed.

In Living Color

I don't know when the California Cattlemen's Association was founded but they began publishing a magazine in 1917. It was a not-too-glorified house organ of eight-to-16 pages for nearly 50 years until somebody decided to make a magazine to be a little proud of and at least one with enough advertising to pay for the printing. That's when they made a contract with Jack Parnell to sell the ads and publish it for the association.

Jack had no background and little interest in journalism but he could sell. He liked to make money, and wanted to become a livestock auctioneer so this was an ideal vehicle for him. I had a consulting business, handling advertising for leading purebred livestock breeders. I found that ads in *California Cattleman* really drew reader response so I was also hustling business for Jack . . . and my customers.

We moved north from the Los Angeles area in 1968 and Jack began getting a start in the auction business so I began selling ads for the magazine, and soon bought out half, then the full interest in the contract to publish the magazine. We had the best ads in the business, but no matter whether we used red or green or blue to accent the black and white cover, the ad was still basically black-and-white.

In the spring of 1970, we borrowed the full-color separations for a cover from the Shorthorn association. We had to borrow because it cost too much for us to handle the cost of color separations on our budget. Then we borrowed a cover from the Hereford people. We had many nice comments about the "brighter" magazine so I decided we had to find a way to have color covers. Would a purebred breeder pay our cost or more to have a photo of his cattle on our cover, I wondered. This idea was not covered in our contract with the association. I asked them if I could get paid for the cover—to sell it like an ad—and they agreed.

California-Nevada Hereford Association, February in the *California Cattleman* calendar, photo by Phil Raynard taken of bulls on stage at John Ascuaga's Nugget Casino.

218

Then I had to begin selling and scheduling breeders and organizations to appear on the covers months ahead so we could get good photos during good weather or when the breeder's stock was in good condition for a photo. This also brought another bonanza. Presses run eight or 16 pages in a normal "signature" which meant that if I had a color cover paid for, I also had the extra cost of a color run for eight or 16 pages paid for. This also meant that I could sell that many full-color ads and have the profit from almost all the extra color charges. Bonanza!

A more attractive magazine made it easier to sell advertising so the success fed on itself. A few years later I invented the pull-out advertising calendar that we included in our December issue for the upcoming year. The color photos from the recent covers were ideal, and already made, to use on the calendar ads for the advertisers. I have no idea how many color photos I took or how many ranches I visited during those years, but I did get well acquainted with a camera, a lot of California's purebred cattle breeders and many miles of California's ranch roads.

Don't Take it for Granted

Shortly after I left Crow Publications to do consulting and free-lance work, I heard that the Will Grant Agency, which handled American Cyanamid's west coast activities, wanted a photojournalist. I dropped by their office and found him out of town but his secretary affirmed what I had heard. She asked me to come by in a few days when Mr. Grant was back in the office and to bring some samples of my work, photos and articles that had been published.

I came at the appointed hour and found a dignified, rather commanding gray-haired ad agency owner with a desk about 7 feet wide. We visited a few minutes and I showed him some of the stories I had written, which he read, as I covered his desk with photos. He seemed to approve the stories and, looking at the photos, said, "Oh, these are fine. What camera did you use?"

In my first semester in photojournalism classes I saw pictures taken with a pinhole in a box. Since that experience, I have always resented the simplistic question from people who don't know what they are talking about and think that a good camera equals good photos. Mr. Grant's question triggered my resentment and I gave him a young upstart answer. "I don't believe anyone has ever realized the limits of the Brownie Box." Almost in horror, he said, "You didn't take these with a Brownie Box, did you?"

When I answered, "You mean you can't tell?" he conceded, "I guess you've got me there." I apologized for my brashness, pointing out that in my opinion, a camera gives control of light, time and area to expose but the photo was the result of being able to see what we want to record, then framing and shooting it. I quoted an unknown photographer who, when asked what he took his photos with (referring to what camera) said, "I take them with my heart." We went on to do numerous stories from Oxnard, California, to Lane County, Oregon.

A Lucky Click of War Chic

One of the better photos from the many years and thousands of animals that I ever photographed was one of a Quarter Horse stallion named War Chic. It was the day before deadline on the *Western Livestock Journal*'s monthly magazine when George Texiera called from San Diego County. He had just leased the horse and wanted to advertise in our next issue. But first, he needed a photo.

I told him to get the horse ready, that I was a little more than an hour away and would leave immediately to take the picture. In those days we got one-day photo processing at a Hollywood camera shop but we wouldn't have time to send the photos for him to OK. He could let me pick the photo—or else. He agreed, gave directions to the ranch, and I hit the road in late afternoon, we found a spot to pose the horse and began shooting.

I was using a Speed Graphic camera with 12 shots per film pack. I did a few broadside photos, then tried a few three-quarter front view shots. The horse was in a good mood and the photos were OK but I hadn't seen "that pose" until movement somewhere in the distance made the horse turn his head slightly and I fired. End of pack, end of photo shoot.

Early the next morning I ran the film to our photo shop, picked up the shots in the afternoon and called George. I told him I was sending him the proofs except for the one I had to send to the printer. He called me the next day and said the photos were good, but the horse just didn't look quite good enough and he wanted to cancel the ad. I agreed with the photos, but reminded him he had ordered the ad and we couldn't cancel, but I assured him he would like the photo we used.

About 10 days later the phone rang again. It was George Texiera. He had just picked up our magazine in the mail and that was "the best horse picture I ever saw" and wanted a "great big" enlargement to send to the stallion's owner. The next day the phone rang. It was Joe Hanson, calling from Idaho. He owned War Chic and had just received his copy of our magazine and "that is the best horse photo I have ever seen." He wanted 40 copies of an 8-by-10 enlargement. "What do you want to do with that many?" I asked him. Joe told me he hoped to book at least 40 mares to War Chic.

He said "I'm going to give one of these photos to every mare owner who books with me. They probably have other mares going to other studs. If they have an 8-by-10 photo of one of the stallions, are they going to tell other mare owners about some other stud or are they going to show them a photo of mine?" I'd have to agree that this Idaho farmer was thinking ahead of the

220

city slickers in this case. Incidentally, we filled both orders, and as long as War Chic lived, it was the only photo his owners ever used to advertise him.

Insuring a Rocket

Most fanciers of racing horses seem to have the conformation of a classic racehorse in a mental image. The same is true for the breeding stock expected to produce great runners. They want a long, sloping shoulder, short back, long hip, long forearm and short cannon bone. Rocket Bar, a stakes-winning Thoroughbred and leading sire of racing Quarter Horses during a period during the 1960s and '70s, almost exaggerated all of the above.

Rocket Bar was owned by George Kaufman, who had a horse ranch south of Modesto. Several times, when driving up or down the valley, I'd get the itch to see the horse again and marvel, not at his record on the racetrack or as a sire, but in just staring at him again. One day George mentioned livestock mortality insurance, knowing that I was an agent. He had just been offered a lot of money for the horse. He told me he had no insurance on him, but that after turning down over a third of a million, he would feel pretty dumb if the horse should die.

The premium on livestock insurance is not large and the commission was a small fraction of that; still, insurance on an animal with that much value would be welcome. Insurance companies will sell life insurance on a person for as much coverage as the insured is willing to buy. Trying to collect early on a life insurance policy is called murder. Trying to collect early on a horse is called fraud. While both have been known to happen, it's probably more common on a cow or a horse than on a human. And premature death seems to occur more frequently if the animal is "over-insured."

"How do you establish value on a horse?" George asked me. A real sale is always considered the best basis of value. An offer to buy is an indicator, but there are a lot of "would you take" kind of offers. Insurers call these fishing expeditions and not necessarily a good basis of value. My company gave its agents a pretty free hand to insure stallions for a value of twice its annual income from stud fees.

At that moment, George told me he had booked over 100 mares at $2,500 each but he was raising the stud fee to $3,500 and he felt he would not lose any mares. I was never good at math but that gave me over half a million in value to work with. When I told George, he asked me how much the premium would be. At that time and at Rocket Bar's age, it would be 4.5 percent per year, as I remember it. That meant a premium of over $20,000 per year.

George decided that he would feel well covered at $100,000. He said, "I'd be better off as a race horse owner if he was dead than if somebody else owned him." He had been the sire of as many as eight of 10 qualifiers for a single leading race. George felt he would get out of the business if anyone else owned Rocket Bar. We insured the horse, which gave me an excuse to visit and gaze in awe at his conformation.

About a year later, a syndicate from Oklahoma came to the ranch, bought Rocket Bar and moved him back east. And George kept his word, "I can't run against them," was his feeling. The minute their check cleared the bank, George scheduled a dispersal of all his horses and he bought the ranch in Idaho where he had worked as a boy and had always wanted to own.

That ranch stuck in George Kaufman's mind like this horse stuck in mine. I never took a photo of Rocket Bar. He always stood with his left front foot off the ground. That leg had been injured as a yearling. He ran, and won a stakes race, in effect, on three legs. But I somehow always looked past the crippled leg to see the otherwise incredible conformation and to respect the genes he passed on to his sons and daughters. Oh, how they could fly!

One Good Idea Can Be a Different Good Idea

I never believed in the trend to breed the "little" cattle that were popular in the 1950s and until the dwarf cattle begin to show up in the early '60s. It wasn't that I was smart enough to know, it's just that my dad always told me you sold cattle by the pound and it seemed counterproductive to intentionally breed cattle smaller than the land and the marketplace wanted.

In April, 1962, I began work as a field editor for Crow Publications, which published both the *Western Livestock Journal* and *Western Dairy Journal,* in the early 1960s. I was told that one of the best dairy herds was Sequoia Holsteins, owned by the father-son team of Mark and Bruce Borror. They also had an Angus herd of big, coarse cattle that were not much in demand. They were good prospects for advertising their Holsteins in the Dairy Journal but "just be nice to them about their Angus. They just aren't raising cattle that are in demand right now."

This was about the time that "performance testing" of beef cattle got its start and was criticized by beef breed representatives who had long used the show ring to establish a purebred animal's value, based exclusively on its conformation or body shape. The "performance" people felt that the real value was in an animal's rate of gain, feed efficiency, desirable carcass and reproductive efficiency.

The Sequoia Angus herd fit the performance category and as breeders went from the show-ring darlings with dwarf pedigrees that produced inefficient and even sickly cattle, they had to abandon the "popular" pedigrees and bring in blood of non-dwarf breeding. There were few Angus herds left in the country free of dwarf bloodlines. Sequoia and especially the Borror herd in northern California with similar breeding, owned by Mark's

222

brother, Dale Borror, and his son, Bill, were to become two of the new sources for Angus breeders nationwide.

My interest and belief in cattle that performed on the basis of producing meat, not blue ribbons, made me a natural enthusiast for breeders of "performance" cattle. I was the only "professional" that came to beef breeders' "weigh day" except for the breed association fieldman and county farm advisor. Most breeders still were critical of these "big, gawky cattle" but one by one they were forced to use the herd sires from the performance breeders to continue their herds.

After a couple of years with Crow Publications, I began a consulting service, handling advertising and marketing purebred cattle for some leading breeders. Then, after about a year, I got involved with publishing the *California Cattleman* magazine and selling advertising to breeders. This involved ranch visits with the owners and generally taking photos of sale animals to use in ads.

One breeder, Paul Pagliarulo, who owned Karolinda Angus near Delano, asked me if I could find a good set of heifers to use as breeding stock to augment his existing herd. I had just been at the Tehama Angus (owned by Bill Borror) weigh day and Bill had decided

Tehama Angus Ranch bulls. I took many photos like this for Tehama, a longtime consulting customer.

to sell his entire spring calving heifer crop of between 20 and 30 heifers. He wanted to concentrate on his fall-calving herd.

Tehama previously had destroyed registration papers on females and refused to sell them as breeding stock. They culled cows after they had produced a calf if they didn't fit in their future herd but put all heifers into the breeding herd or sold them without papers. This was a rare buying opportunity but there was no established price because the herd had not been in demand. I brought Paul to look and he bought the entire heifer crop. And shortly thereafter I began handling the advertising for Tehama Angus.

I told everybody how smart the Borror families had been to stay with their big-framed, unpopular Angus during the many years of being out of demand. And pointed out how many breeders had come to these two similar herds to make purchases of bulls with size and natural muscling to get their herds into demand on the new basis. Then, one day, Bruce told me the real reason they had such big-framed Angus. The reason pre-dated performance testing as we know it in light of its use and meaning today.

The Borrors had been partners in the Holstein breeding and dairy but both Mark and Dale had families and were running out of land so Dale decided to take his share and move north to Tehama County. Mark stayed at Springville. Most dairymen across southern and central California used Angus bulls to breed their heifers. Some bred their mature cows, using Angus bulls as "cow fresheners," selling all the calves and buying replacement dairy heifers.

Dairymen found that almost all beef cattle breeders produced bulls too small, physically, to breed a Holstein cow. They needed bigger Angus bulls to breed the taller dairy cows. Borrors sold their Angus bulls to dairymen. They had to keep raising the big Angus bulls. It may have been the dairy market as much as the "performance-breeding" beef market that made the Borrors so "smart" in breeding big Angus. But they were smart enough to take advantage of their position.

The Jug That Didn't Glug

You may have heard that everyone needs to own a boat and a swimming pool, at least once. There is also the saying that if you own a boat, you will always remember two dates—the day you bought it—and the day you got rid of it. I have never heard the same for pools. I have never owned a boat, but we did have a pool when we lived in La Mirada, at the south edge of Los Angeles County.

Swimming pools have two character-building options. You can hire a pool service to keep it clean and properly maintained for chemical balance, or you can do it yourself. The latter is much better from the standpoint of character building and giving the owners something to do in their spare time in addition to swimming or enjoy the pool-side goodies heralded by the likes of *Sunset* magazine.

For do-it-yourselfers, some pool chemicals come in gallon plastic jugs. You can have nerves of steel and still get splashes of high horsepower chemicals on your person. One day as I was doing my pool-side duty, it occurred to me that if that jug could breathe, it wouldn't glug, glug, glug and splash its contents on anyone in the area. Why hadn't someone invented one?

The solution was only a few minutes or problem-solving days away. A cork and a plastic tube gave unqualified proof that the idea worked. Now it was only a matter of finding what size the air intake needed to be—the fraction of the volume of air vs. the volume of content solution that was needed for free exchange of air for product. Anybody in the plastics business could mold the air intake into the neck of the jug.

My experience showed that the air bleed should be one-fourth the diameter of the bottle neck. But I had no experience with the U.S. Patent office, patent lawyers or marketing. I could see that if a patent earned even a fraction of a cent per jug, there were enough manufacturers shipping multiple carloads daily, just within sight of the Santa Ana Freeway to put an inventor on easy street for life.

I found patent attorneys in the yellow pages, picked one and made a call. He said it would be unlikely that such a simple invention hadn't been patented but he felt that if it had been, such an invention would surely be in use. The thing to do was to write my claims for what the patent would do, have them witnessed by competent people and initiate a search. He wanted $300 as a start. If we got a negative report with little effort, the balance would be returned, etc.

We were lucky and unlucky. It had been patented just over a year earlier by a man in Richmond, VA and his claims were almost word-for-word the same as the ones I had written. I called him and found that he was a chemical and bleach manufacturer serving a small east-coast regional market. He had made no effort yet to get anyone licensed to make or sell the idea. He wouldn't sign any kind of contract for me to market his rights so he—and I— could get a royalty from the patent. As far as I have been able to determine, he never did anything with his patent. The good luck part was that the search only took a few minutes and I got back half of the original deposit. And jugs still glug.

You Don't Drive a Bramer

Shortly after I began working with the *California Cattleman* magazine I was asked to take some photos of Brahman and Brahman-crossbred cattle to be used in a sale advertisement. A breeder was planning to disperse his herd and a sale date had been claimed. I met the owner at the ranch and was taking photos of both his Angus cattle and the crossbreds being used to produce Brangus which are five-eighths Brahman and three-eighths Angus.

The nearest I had ever been to a Brahman animal in my previous life was a day at the county fair when a bull had bucked his rider off, then jumped the arena fence, landed a few inches from the car fender where I was sitting, and ran off into a pasture. He didn't know I was there, but he surely got my attention and my admiration for his athletic ability, which I was later to learn, was consistent with the Bos Indicus or Brahman cattle.

I had my reflexes tested while taking a photo of a half-blood cow with her three-quarters Brahman calf. A few drops of Brahman blood generally makes a mother cow very maternal and protective. She took exception to my being inside her "comfort" zone and made several threatening steps toward me. Fortunately, she decided to give me another chance and did not make a full charge in my direction. There is no way to respond to the quickness and strength of an animal that weighs 1200 pounds or more for cows and up to 2,000 pounds for bulls.

We had taken some good photos and I noticed about a dozen young bulls from weanling to yearling age. They were standing in a row, almost as if lined up for a photo, except for the two at the end of the row. I took a photo of the group as they stood, then asked the owner if he could drive or push the last two up into the line. He said, "No, I don't think so." I was shocked.

Who says Brahman bulls are hard to ride? Photo taken at Ben Bartlett's ranch in California's San Joaquin Valley one day when I stopped to sell Ben an ad for an upcoming issue of the *California Cattleman* magazine (approximately 1984.)

Almost the entire herd had done everything I asked when I asked him to make it happen. My normal system didn't work for Brahmans. I had to learn a new way of thinking.

Then he asked me what I really wanted. I pointed out that the group was in a row, making a good photo, but it would be perfect if the two bulls on the far end would just step forward to be in an even line with the others. "Oh well, that's easy," he said, and began talking as he walked up to the group. He rubbed and scratched each one as he went down the line and when he got to the two at the far end of the row, scratched them, one at a time, under the chin and nudged them forward to exactly where I wanted them.

When they were in a perfect row, I quickly snapped a photo. Then I asked if they would stay in line if he walked out of my range. He walked away and they did as asked so I took a photo of just bulls without the owner so the sale manager had his choice of shots. Then the owner explained. "I didn't know what you wanted when you asked if I could drive those two bulls forward.

Bramers (most breeders don't call them Brahmans) don't like to be pushed but you can lead them anywhere. Bramers will run up to you when you're out in the pasture. Don't be scared. They won't hurt you, they're just curious. They're the most curious and friendly cattle you'll ever see." OK, but how do you know if they're just curious and friendly—not mad—until you're eye to eye? And one to one, a mere human being is badly

226

outnumbered with any animal as athletic as a Brahman, friendly or not. You can be "friendlied" to death and be just as dead as if you're killed to death.

Dog Trainer

In some 16 years of publishing the *California Cattleman* magazine, I took the photo that would grace its front cover almost every month during that time, and even more pictures to be used in ads promoting purebred bulls for sale to commercial cattlemen. And if I learned one irrevocable truth from this experience, it would be that dogs and cow photos don't mix.

Almost every cattle ranch has at least one dog. Ranch dogs may be Heelers, Border Collies, McNabbs, or even a Beagle/Dachshund cross that has conned his owner into thinking he has the heart of a cow dog, if not the talent, but they all belong. I also learned that you can criticize the owner, his wife and kids, his pickup or the breed of cattle he raises, but you had better love his dog.

When you really must have a good "cover quality" photo while keeping the peace regarding the owner's dog, you learn a new level of diplomacy. But the unhappy fact is that 99 of 100 possible cover photos will be ruined— totally died aborning—if a dog of any kind gets near the scene. Except for "art on the plains" paintings or photos of wild steers on cattle drives, cover photos require scenes to be calm and dogs do not make for calm cattle.

As early as I can remember, I had better results from handling livestock in a deliberate manner as by yelling, running and using dogs. This was mightily reinforced by a ranch hand we had when I was about 10 years old. He was magic with livestock. I learned to read the "comfort zone" for every animal and found this knowledge or understanding most important in taking livestock photos. Sometimes I had real problems getting ranch personnel to understand this and cooperate in taking photos.

Dick Moseman had years earlier purchased the Crowe Hereford Ranch east of Redding, including the reputation Hereford herd. He had agreed to put a photo of his herd on the front cover of the *California Cattleman* and I went to the ranch to take the photo. The photo was to feature cows with their fall calves at side. We were shooting in late winter or early spring. The weather was great when I arrived and we headed for the pasture.

When I got there, Floyd Santos, the ranch foreman, was rounding up the herd on horseback. He had four dogs with him. One was a mature female, the other three were nearly grown, green pups. I normally ordered all ranch dogs locked in a kennel, gooseneck trailer or some escape-proof enclosure before going near the cattle. Unruly dogs can ruin cattle photos. We had no such enclosure and both Floyd and his boss were long-known friends. I was stuck.

Floyd rode up and asked what arrangement I wanted for the photo. I pointed to the two large oaks on the horizon with Mt. Lassen in the background and suggested he might pick out the most attractive 20 to 30 cow/calf pairs, then bring them slowly—very slowly—toward me, between the trees. I had the camera loaded and would wait to see the cattle come over the hill, then start shooting as they came toward me.

There were about 100 pairs in the field that covered several hundred acres. Floyd rode off into the herd and as I watched in fear and disgust, a cow and calf ran to the west with one or more of the dogs in pursuit. Then I heard him whistle and soon a few more pairs broke away from the herd with his cow-dogs right behind. This continued for maybe a half hour or longer as he "culled" the herd down to the size and quality I ordered. I walked to the top of the hill, after a quiet period, and was surprised to find the remaining group about 100 yards from our target area and nicely under control.

Soon the lead cow's head appeared over the horizon, exactly between the two oak trees I had specified. Slowly the rest of the group inched over the crest of the hill behind her. As the balance of the group crested the hill, and as they saw me, they slowed to a stop and stared. I began shooting as he eased the cattle toward me, quickly changing film packs as they continued to perform as ordered.

It turned out to be one of the best "shoots" I ever had and we had a real job deciding which of several good photos to use. I thanked Floyd and told him he took my prize as a trainer of cow dogs. He said he could never have culled the herd and put the cattle where I wanted them without his dogs. At that moment I believed him, but I never told him it was the only time in my life it ever worked. He wins my prize as a dog trainer.

Real Advice to a Real Estate Beginner

My main job was publishing the *California Cattleman* magazine, which in our case, meant selling ads first, then putting the material into magazine form. I had recently received my real estate license and ran my first ads in the magazine. I stopped at Andy Joughin's (pronounced Jock-in) ranch near Solvang, on a crisp spring morning. Andy agreed to take an ad and we were walking toward a pen of Hereford bulls to get a picture of the bulls to put in the ad.

Andy was a pioneer Hereford breeder and one of the members of the old Tri-County Hereford Association that cooperated with Cal Poly in the first several bull sales that were jointly sponsored by Cal Poly and the Tri-County group. Andy wasn't a big talker but his mere participation in an event was as credible as a boost from most people when it came to giving credibility to the event. He was the quiet type but a heavy hitter. People respected Andy.

"I see you're in real estate," Andy volunteered, as we walked. This was a big surprise to me. Andy was a good walker, well over 6 feet tall with long, deliberate strides, but not a talker. In the years I had known him, he barely answered when spoken to, and I had never seen him start a conversation on a new subject. I answered that I had a license and felt there might be an opening for a ranch specialist.

"You'll do well," he assured me. "The magazine is a good place for people to get to know you. There aren't many people who specialize in ranches. You have a following already and one day you may have to decide whether you want to sell ads or ranches. But that decision can wait. It will take care of itself."

"I've owned several ranches." he continued. "People think I've made a lot of money running cattle. I don't know if cattle made me any money or not, but they gave me a good, honest front to own land. That's where I made money." I couldn't believe this. Normally an extra-quiet guy, Andy was "talking his head off." Then he went on, "You'll do well, especially if you can convince your buyers to always buy a good ranch. If you buy a good ranch, no matter how much you pay," he went on, "time will make you a smart man."

"And another thing—and don't forget this—every ranch I ever bought was w-a-a-a-ay too high at the time," he added with more emphasis than I ever heard from unemotional Andy, before or after. His message made sense to me at the time, but it seems better advice every time I recall it and with each ranch I sell. It's too bad that all of my prospective ranch buyers for all of these years didn't know Andy.

And You Think You've Been to an Auction

In the years I worked as a field editor for *Western Livestock Journal* and as the publisher of the *California Cattleman*, breeders and livestock sale managers bought ads and, as part of the package, I furnished ring service, spotting bids at the auction being advertised. In nearly 20 years, involving many auctioneers and other ring men, I saw or was a party to some strange quirks of human nature. But none match the story I was told about a dairy cow auction.

Harry Hays was a Canadian cattleman and dairyman who became a breeder of Holstein dairy cattle and sale manager of both commercial and purebred dairy cattle. He later became the Canadian Director of Agriculture and a Senator. We were talking about strange conditions that occur at auctions and he related one from his early days in dairy sale management.

He had scheduled an auction to disperse the herd of a good Canadian dairy farmer. The dairyman had a high-producing commercial Holstein herd of about 300 cows. He had reached retirement age. They scheduled the sale months ahead for an early fall date. Harry had advertised the sale widely and had received early requests for catalogs from many potential buyers. He felt lucky to have this herd for one of his fall sales.

Harry went to the farm, near Kenora, not far from Winnipeg and from the United States, a few days before the sale to get the cattle sorted and to get a sale lot number on each animal. He felt sure this should be one of the good sales in the area that fall. He had checked and re-checked everything he could imagine that could go wrong. Even the weather had been great. But he did not count on one item.

This was many years before weather satellites that let us know what kind of weather to expect. On the evening before the sale, a freak early fall blizzard blew into the area closing highways and cutting off all forms of communication. They couldn't even cancel the sale. On sale morning, two dairymen hired snow planes to bring them to the farm. Only two potential buyers for 300 cows. He and the owner saw certain disaster.

At sale time, the two "buyers" were sitting 10 feet apart in the otherwise bare bleachers. Harry said, "You have come a long way and I know that you both need cows. We won't disappoint you. We'll bring in a cow. You can bid until you stop, take as many as you want at that price. Then we'll do it again, until we're done." The bidding went fast and the price was soon up to the market price for good replacement cows when one buyer quit bidding. "You have the bid, sir, how many do you want at that price?" Harry asked the successful bidder, who answered, "I'll take 'em all."

"You Can Think of Something"

I began a consulting service for breeders of purebred seed stock when I left the *Livestock Journal* in 1964. One of the first clients to contract for my services was Bill Wolfe of Wolfe Hereford Ranch in Wallowa, Oregon, a leading breeder I definitely wanted. Bill wanted to change his marketing program to sell his year's produce at a yearly ranch production sale. In the past, he had to have someone able to deal with bull buyers on the ranch every day of the year in case a prospective buyer came along.

This was a wonderful idea on paper, in any other part of the country, but several purebred breeders in the northeast part of Oregon had tried to hold production sales and not one had been a success. Cattlemen in the area just refused to pay good prices at a public auction. I knew that Bill had the best herd in the area—probably the best in America—and a good reputation, but I knew we should move slowly. I felt we needed at least five years to make the change.

We decided to hold a production sale the first year to sell mostly females and a few herd sire prospects, appealing to other purebred breeders, and then include a few range bulls for local commercial cattlemen. My idea was to increase the number of bulls for commercial cattlemen in each year's sale, decreasing the emphasis on breeding stock for other purebred breeders. By the fifth year we would sell only bulls. This was Bill Wolfe's dream and my determined hope.

This was in the 1960s, when good range bulls brought about $600 per head. We hoped to make the sale average $1,000 per head on a minimum of 60 cattle in each sale. The first year we sold 40-plus females and 20-plus bulls, including several real herd sire prospects for sale to other purebred breeders. Our average price was a few dollars over our target of $1,000 per head and we were elated. But we did not sell a bull to a cattleman from either Wallowa or Union county.

We reduced the number of heifers in our second sale to about 35 head and increased the number of bulls, hoping to get a few local cattlemen to come bid at auction. I spent more of our advertising budget on local media, bragging about how many bulls sold for "under $600," determined to draw local buyers. When the sale was over, we had an average of just a few dollars per head more than the first sale. A few bulls went to our local counties but none with a Wallowa address.

I decided that our third sale was our make-or-break year. We had about 30 lots for purebred breeders and over 30 were range bulls for commercial cattlemen. I continued to advertise how many bulls we sold for "under $600." It really upset Fern (Mrs. Wolfe) to see us brag about selling "cheap" bulls but I insisted that our job was to get cattlemen to come, expecting a top-quality Wolfe bull at a reasonable price, then let "auction fever" take over when the sale began and pray that the auctioneer would earn his money.

Bill did not like to visit the ranches of people who had bought his cattle. He was afraid they would think he was trying to pressure them. They knew he had great cattle and bought them freely at the ranch by private treaty and paid good prices but refused to buy at an auction anywhere in the area. I got Bill to ride with me and call on almost everyone in the local area who had bought an animal from him in the past several years. Some were 4-H or FFA buyers, some were bull buyers, some female buyers. All were flattered that Bill Wolfe had come to visit and I took their photos and collected testimonials to use in local advertisements.

I bought an ad every week in the local weekly paper for several weeks before the sale, running photos and testimonials of local cattlemen in every ad—a different one every week. I bought the early morning market report on the local radio station. The rates were so low that I was tempted to overdo, but I kept the advertising just below the level that I felt the local people would feel we overdid it.

When sale day came, we still started the sale with a few high-dollar bulls. The first bull brought $5,250 for a half-interest. The second $5,000 for a half-interest and $4,500 for the third bull. I was at ringside and moved from one side of the ring to the other, passing Fern Wolfe (in a front row seat) on the way. She grabbed my shoulder as I went by, saying, "Oh, Phil, isn't this

231

just wonderful!" I answered, "Unless we sell some $600 bulls, what will I use in the ads to get people to come next year?" She said, "Oh, Phil, you have a whole year before the next sale. Surely you can think of something."

This turned out to be our best sale to date, but we did have some bulls that sold for $600 or less so I still had a "come on" to feature in our sale ads for the next two years of our five-year agreement. We had several Wallowa County commercial cattlemen buy bulls in this third sale. The next year the bulls sold well to local cowmen. In our fifth sale, the last year I worked for Bill, we sold only range bulls but we still averaged over $1,000 a head. They sold a few top bulls and females in consignment sales elsewhere at high prices. We had done what Bill wanted. We successfully changed his marketing program.

Protected to Death

How many times have you seen a situation where a strong-willed idealist has put his money where his mouth is—to learn that he was in love with an idea that turned out to not be the truth—but a smoke dream instead? If he had grown up with my early livestock mentor, Jake Sauer, he would have known better. Had he known of Allan Savory and Holistic Resource Management, he would have known better. I don't know where he got his idea nor do I know where Hollywood celebrities and other self-appointed advocates get their ideas. Most of these people, it turns out, act on bad advice. But most do not invest any money.

The specific case in point is a 3,700-acre ranch near Red Bluff, California. It was purchased by a man who could afford his foolishness, determined to return this "overgrazed and underappreciated" ranch to its healthy or fully productive state by building a terrific fence all the way around it, remove all livestock except the deer, rabbits and other native species and let nature heal itself.

This ranch had irrigation wells and several hundred acres of pasture that was irrigated with water from the wells. Combined with the other acreage of native pasture, this made an ideal cattle or sheep ranch where the stock could graze year around on the same ranch without being hauled from summer pasture to winter pasture and back again. The new owner capped the wells. Without irrigation water in summer, most grasses died and weeds took over.

The new owner built a good ranch headquarters with ranch house, horse stable and corral, machinery barn and a hay and feeding barn. He hired a ranch foreman who tended the ranch roads, the fence and the buildings. He watered the newly planted shade trees, including cork oaks. Otherwise he patrolled the ranch to be sure that no livestock grazed there. The ranch returned no income but had a sizeable expense for 25 years—long enough to

232

see how much a previously slightly overgrazed ranch would recover with complete rest.

The irony is that the more aggressive plants squeeze out the other plants. Good pastures rely upon a blend or balance of vegetation. Some species in nature will produce their best in wet years, some respond best to modest but regular rain. A different species or member of the pasture team will perform better each year. In nature, there would be grazing animals that tend to level the playing field for the various crops. But this owner, like self-appointed conservationists, did not see the big picture. Fortunately, it was his money.

In 25 years, the plant population on most of the ranch was nearly reduced to two undesirable plants, called weeds, because the other plants could not successfully compete on their own. And there were no grazing cows or sheep to control these aggressors and allow the desirable plants to compete. If you like yellow star thistle and medusa head, you would love this ranch. These are two of the most dreaded plants in California and in only 25 years without any grazing, these two weeds had displaced almost all of the desirable plants.

As Allan Savory observed when he was a game refuge manager in Africa, the feeding of the large grazing herds and the trampling action of their hooves as they grazed made a seedbed preparation hard to equal with any machine. And the stems that were not eaten were left to protect the seedlings when they sprouted the next season. In fact, Savory observed that the grass needs the animals as much as the animals need the grass.

We don't have any idea how bad this ranch would have become because the owner finally sold it. The new owner planted orchards on the formerly irrigated pasture acreage and began to pasture the balance of the ranch. We don't know how many years it might have taken to return the ranch to good plant diversity without holistic resource management. But 25 years of "rest" almost ruined the ranch.

Through the 1970s and '80s I frequently heard about the "Savory System" of pasture or ranch management. I did not know of any operations in California so I called his office in Albuquerque and asked for the names of Californians on the program so I could write a story for the *California Cattleman*. Savory invited me to attend one of his week-long classes (normal tuition $1,200) so I could understand what the ranchers would be telling me.

Savory was right. I would have missed the story completely had I written the story without attending his school. It is so simple when you see it in action alongside other ways of managing ranch land. But both this ranch and its owner would have profited immensely if that owner had been introduced to HRM before he purchased the ranch. What a waste of both money and good California ranch land that could have been saved.

Blame it on the Government?

When I worked for Crow Publications in the early 1960s, I worked on both *Western Livestock Journal* and *Western Dairy Journal*. One of my regular *Dairy* advertisers was Leonard Bartels, who developed and sold replacement heifers to dairymen in the Southern California milk shed. I sold him on the idea of using testimonial ads. The idea worked for him and it made work for me. But I got to meet a lot of good dairymen and travel a lot of back roads.

I was the guy who went to his customers, took their picture and wrote the ad copy about something unique to that dairy and an endorsement of the heifers they bought from Leonard. I felt there was an interesting story in every dairy or in its owner's history and that if I did my job well, I'd find the story, report it, and let our readers learn from our ads as well as our editorial.

I found a rags-to-riches story of a penniless 18-year-old immigrant who, in 30 years, had worked and managed his life and fortune to have enough equity to borrow several million dollars so he could develop a shopping center on his former dairy farm acreage. There was the owner of a top purebred herd that began with a heifer he took as part of his wages some 20 years earlier when he was an hourly wage milker in a dairy.

My advertiser was happy and I saw and learned many things from people I met along the way in doing this job. Dairies are busy places. Most dairy installations were able to handle several hundred cows and some milked several thousand at one location. This means meeting veterinarians, concrete-laying crews, feed truck drivers, salesmen for dairy equipment, hardware, vet supplies, machinery and feedstuffs. Boy, do dairies use feed!

One day I had an appointment to get a Bartels testimonial from a dairyman at San Ysidro. The dairy was only a few hundred yards from the Mexican border and on a nice hill overlooking Tijuana, the Mexican city at the U.S. border crossing check point at San Diego. We were near enough to see the city sprawl but just far enough away that we didn't hear the highway noise. As I began the interview, the dairyman's wife interrupted to tell him a long distance call was being returned so he excused himself for a moment.

As the dairyman left to take the phone call a hay salesman drove into the yard and introduced himself. We visited about various topics but he quickly hit on politics and his disapproval of almost everything at every level of government, to my surprise. I had always felt that political discussions were off-limits for any thoughtful salesman. Maybe he felt it didn't count since I was another salesman, not a customer. I encouraged him but kept my feelings to myself.

Suddenly the wind changed and the new southwest wind came wafting in to the dairy, which generated some odor, but there was no mistaking this "essence of Tijuana." Raw sewage, smog, every bad odor you could imagine. Immediately he switched topics. "Smell that! What's the difference between these two places, less than a mile apart, to make that much difference in the smell?" he asked. I began a quick cause-and-effect list in my head of the factors involved and I concluded aloud, "It can't be geography, it must be that dirty, rotten no-good government we've been griping about." The big-mouthed, I've-got-all-the-answers salesman got instant lockjaw.

Follow the Head Table

During most of my life I have avoided formal situations. I guess we all need a little boredom, just to build character, if nothing else, but being bored at formal functions really pushes me over the edge. I am willing to work on a board or committee if it is a worthy cause and have served as chairman when asked if I believe we can accomplish something.

But when it's over, I'd rather have one of the people whose situation was improved tell me how things are better now than to make a fuss over my being on the committee. There must be a lot of people who like that stuff. Otherwise why do we have such a long head table at every banquet? I agree that the message may get a better hearing if the teacher stands at the front of the class but if you don't have a message, I suggest you stay at home or at least sit down.

One of the built-in risks of representing a publication is the chance—in fact the certainty—that you will be invited to endless phony functions. You had better learn to say "thanks" gracefully and to determine in advance when you can say "no thanks" and get away with it. I think the outsiders really believe they gain publicity from including press representatives as guests when their group meets for almost any reason, and they may be right. This means a lot of free meals for a reporter but it also can mean sitting at the head table.

I rarely saw any real benefit from this attendance. The people in charge had it figured pretty well. They seated the press representatives at the end of the table, never near the podium and microphone at the center of the table. This told the assembled members that the press was important, but not that important. But I once got some mileage out of the alleged honor.

When I was editor of the *Western Dairy Journal* I got the usual press pass to one of the Los Angeles dairymen's association meetings. And I had the usual position at the head table—at the end of the table. Beef cattle banquets don't serve chicken. I remember a new manager of the California Cattlemen's Association who nearly got fired when he served a main course other than beef at a banquet. But dairymen had no such rules.

The main course was fried chicken. There must have been more than 200 people varying in table manners from total competence to the other extreme. But all seemed to have the idea that this was a banquet and you had better use a knife and fork, no matter how uncomfortable it made you feel. I glanced at the other people at the head table to see them uncomfortable, but apparently determined.

I wasn't the host but this seemed silly. And I have never liked eating fried chicken with knife and fork. Without another look to the right or left, I picked up a piece of chicken with my bare hands and took the first bite. The simultaneous sighs of the crowd almost bounced off the walls as everyone at the banquet followed suit. Seconds later, all the people at the head table abandoned their silverware. Several times in the months that followed, I later met a dairyman somewhere who reminded me—and thanked me—that I had the guts to enable those dairymen to eat chicken with their fingers.

Horseshoes and Lemonade

Rex Ellsworth is best known as a breeder of racehorses, including Swaps, winner of the 1955 Kentucky Derby. I first got to know him through an artist in the *Western Livestock Journal* art department. Grant said he was "related" to Rex. When I asked how they were related he said it was too far away to inherit anything but too close to marry his daughter. That's when he decided to quit as an exercise boy for his racehorses and take his art more seriously.

Rex probably owned more total numbers of Thoroughbred mares and more top-rated mares than any breeder in California if not the world. Other breeders prized their two or three stakes-winning mares and they were coddled and groomed to excess at most horse farms. Rex had dozens of stakes-winning and/or stakes producing mares running with foals in big pastures. None had been brushed nor had the knots pulled out of their manes and tails in months.

I later knew Rex better when I worked with racehorse breeders in sale management, mortality insurance and livestock photography. In addition to his horse breeding and training operations, Rex had a feedlot, some irrigated pasture and a sizeable ranch in New Mexico that I knew of. He used me to locate bulls when one of his livestock programs ran afoul.

I don't know that he ever operated a dairy but he raised hundreds of dairy heifers, bred them and sold them as replacement cows to dairy operators in the Los Angeles milk shed area. One year the market for Holstein heifers dropped so recalling the truism: if life hands you a lemon, make lemonade. He decided to at least delay his loss. He bred the heifers to Brahman bulls, shipped them to his New Mexico ranch to have crossbred calves. If the Holstein market recovered, he would wean the calves and feedlot them, breeding the cows back to Holstein bulls.

The cows began to get sore feet in the rocky New Mexico terrain. His local veterinarian suggested getting metal shoes for the cows so he mailed an order to the company where he regularly bought horseshoes. When they got the order for medium size cow shoes for 1,200 cows, they were sure the

236

order was in error for both the number ordered and the species. Rex had purchased many horseshoes but never shoes for cows. Nobody had ever ordered that many cow shoes. They wrote (they didn't call) asking Rex to re-check and confirm the order.

When the re-confirmed order got in the hands of the shoemaking firm, the heifers were limping in droves, some even had bleeding feet from walking on rock. The shoes were freighted directly to the New Mexico ranch where they had to put the entire herd through a squeeze chute to get them shod in what must have been the biggest shoe fitting in cow history. Rex saved the crossbred heifers, bred them to Angus bulls that I located for him. He found that the crossbred calves from dairy heifers he didn't get sold to dairymen worked well in the feedlot.

Always the trader, Rex sold Swaps after his Derby win. A few years later he had another colt, Candy Spots, that ran second in the Kentucky Derby, beaten by a horse named Chateaugay, sired by Swaps, the horse that Rex had bred, raced and sold. After the race, Rex was asked about the outcome and if he ever had second thoughts about selling Swaps. "Never," he said, "I needed 5 million dollars really bad at the time."

The Missing Briefcase

I worked with Caldwell-Heerman, a top racing horse sales firm, on a part-time basis in the mid-1960s to conduct horse auctions. The lead partner was Tom Caldwell who was one of the top horse auctioneers in the country. In this job, I worked with breeders who used the sales as a market place for their Quarter Horses and Thoroughbreds. We normally had two sales yearly. One was primarily a Quarter Horse sale at the Los Angeles County fairgrounds in Pomona and the other was a Thoroughbred sale held at Hollywood Park racetrack. That's the one you fly over if your flight lands or takes off from LAX airport. Tom also auctioneered at other sales.

My work involved processing entry forms, preparing the sale catalogs, including writing footnotes describing each horse, handling the sale advertising and occasionally taking on-the-ranch photos of horses consigned to the sale. On sale days, I was also one of the ring men or ring-side bid spotters who encouraged bidders and yelled their bids to the auctioneer.

It takes several people to see that the several hundred horses are properly stalled in the barns at the track, to get the sale facility ready, to conduct the sale, collect the money and get the horses shipped to their new owners. Most of these people spent several days before and during the sale, living out of a hotel near the Hollywood Park racetrack grounds.

The sale ran for three days with horses in three sections. The first day was for yearling racing prospects, the next was for breeding stock and the third was for horses in training or currently at the track. The event brought

237

together the widest range of humanity you can imagine. We had Arab sheiks, business magnates from several countries, captains of industry, Hollywood actors and studio people along with professional horse people and the full range of race track types, hoping for inside information to use in laying their next bet at the track.

Horsemen have some interesting quirks. While most businesses expect their transactions to be done by check, you had better be ready for bundles of hundred dollar bills at horse sales. In case the IRS happens to be looking in their checkbooks or over their shoulders, cash leaves no paper trail. That's the way many horsemen like it. So we had both race track security and privately-hired, off-duty, armed sheriff deputies near the table where the money is collected.

At the end of each day's sale, Tom Caldwell put the checks and cash in his briefcase and, accompanied by our guards, drove to the hotel where we had arranged to put it in the hotel safe immediately. I left the sale area with another ring man and drove directly to the hotel. Tom and the security men were only minutes behind. Some members of the sale crew who had left earlier were sitting in the coffee shop just off the hotel entrance. When I arrived, they yelled, asking me what one of the horses had brought. I went in and sat down with them at the large booth.

As we compared notes, Tom arrived in police escort, set his cash-filled briefcase on the counter at the registration desk for the hotel manager to deposit in the safe. But we saw Tom before the manager did. "Hey, Tom," someone yelled, "What did that last gray colt bring?" He turned and stepped into the coffee shop, sat down beside me and slipped the briefcase behind our legs in the booth.

We went over some prices and were congratulating ourselves about the sale when we noticed the hotel lobby full of policemen. What we didn't know was that would-be robbers had apparently been casing the sale operation, knew the route from the sale facility and knew that Tom took the money straight to the hotel safe. They arrived at the hotel just minutes behind him, charged in with drill team precision, guns drawn, and ordered the manager to open the safe.

The manager didn't argue, but he did set off a silent alarm as he began to open the safe. By the time it was opened and the crooks saw that it held no briefcase, the cops had arrived. We missed out on all the fun. We never learned what the cops were doing in the lobby until later when the manager told Tom about the close call. And to this day I've never deposited anything in a hotel safe.

A Bouquet for the Champion Bull

I began work as a field editor for *Western Livestock Journal* in 1962, a few days after our first daughter, Coral, was born. I got the Southern California territory that was shunned by other field editor types. I earned my paycheck by selling advertising, primarily to breeders of purebred livestock seed stock. Most of the income from their ventures came from the sale of bulls to commercial cattlemen in the area who raised cattle for the beef market. A few of the top herds also sold females to other breeders who wanted to upgrade their herds.

At that time, the main measurement of quality in beef breeding stock was the results from livestock shows. Breeders wanted to own a show champion, or the sons and daughters of show champions. Most of the beef cattle breeders in the Southern California area were doctors, lawyers or captains of industry who were in the cattle business to satisfy a boyhood dream or for income tax benefits, which were substantial at that time. Most were not long on livestock savvy but hired professional ranch managers or livestock showmen to do the dirty work while the owners stood in the Champion photo, holding the purple ribbon when their bulls or heifers won at the show.

Most of the purebred beef cattle in the 1960s were Herefords—red with white faces and feet. Some had horns, called Horned Herefords; some were naturally hornless, called Polled Herefords. In most of the country, Horned cattle breeders and Polled breeders feuded over the genetic quirk concerning horns but in Southern California they were above that or too naive to know they should.

They formed a Southern California Hereford Association to promote their cattle to the commercial cattlemen in the area but didn't know what to do about it. Most of the field men for livestock publications ignored area breeders. I was the first to take them seriously. I went to their meetings and convinced them to buy a full page ad for their group plus a one-column directory listing in every issue of our monthly magazine. Our commercial cattlemen readers responded by calling to buy bulls. This newly discovered fame whetted the breeders' appetites for more.

The American Hereford Association had long designated certain livestock shows to be called "Register of Merit" shows. Denver, Kansas City, Fort Worth and a few others were always ROM shows but other shows including state fairs in some states would get ROM designation for a year on a rotating basis. This designation gave elevated status to the show and it attracted herds from across the country.

Los Angeles had a show grounds called the Great Western where national show competitions were held for many agricultural commodities including dairy breeds. Any County Fair could have a show but everybody knew that no beef breed executive would let his breed take Los Angeles seriously enough to give status to a show held there. Not quite everybody. Some of these businessmen set out to get ROM status for the Great Western show, if only for a year.

I didn't want to miss a single detail of this campaign so I went to every meeting. Within a year they had won. Then the fun really began. They didn't know the first thing about putting on a cattle show but this group had leaders in their fields—the owner of a drugstore chain, a manufacturer of aircraft parts, an MGM studio vice president, a hospital owner, several physicians, CPA's, etc.

At a meeting someone mentioned that the Great Western show had always had the beef cattle show in a part of the large barn where the cattle were stabled while a regional flower show was held in an adjoining barn that would make a great show ring. What could we do with the flower show? In near desperation, I facetiously suggested that we might convince the flower people that instead of just having a flower show, the flower exhibits and landscape designs could find a new calling by enhancing the cattle show.

One of the members turned to me and said, "Don't dismiss that idea until you and I go and meet with their people. You may have invented a whole new kind of livestock show." We had the meeting and to our amazement, even though we did not have a nurseryman in the Hereford Association membership, the flower show people liked the idea and got approval of their members. When we brought the news to our cattle people, some derided the idea—what would the crusty, hard-drinking Scottish herdsmen say about such a sissified show?—but voted to go ahead.

"A Bouquet for the Champion Bull." Best 10 Head competitors in early 1960s Register of Merit Hereford show at Great Western show grounds in Los Angeles where the first "combination" livestock show and flower exhibition took place. Since that "pioneering" use of flowers at livestock events, purebred livestock shows and auctions across the country have used flowers and other plants to soften the scene.

When show time came, the flower people had made a waterfall at one end of the arena that served as a backdrop for photos of the show winners. Banks of flowers lined the walls on all sides. Pots of fuchsias and other plants hung from the overhead creating a ceiling of flowers above the show ring. The growers and decorators came to see how their flowers had enhanced a cattle show, or vice versa. The Great Western staff had outdone themselves. A bed of green-stained shavings carpeted the entire floor except for the white face of a Hereford bull sculpted in shavings in the center of the show ring.

I made a special trip to the barn with my camera the evening before the show opened to record the scene before the cattle trailed through it. And the Scotch herdsmen, whose attitude was the concern of the show planners? When they noticed that I was there with a camera, they asked me to take their

Angus "Best 10 Head" at Great Western Livestock Show in early 1960s shown by Twin Valley Ranch. Pictured l-r are Glen Bratcher, Secretary of American Angus Association; show judge Herman Purdy, actor and bulls' owner Fred MacMurray, his wife, actress June Haver, Wayne Pugh, ranch manager; Forrest Berry, Great Western board president and ranch herdsman Ralph Clark.

pictures in the ring. Walt McRobb spoke for all the showmen when he said, "I didn't think I'd live long enough to show cattle in a place like this. The other showmen are sure going to be jealous. You have started something. I hope it lasts a long time."

And that facetious remark of mine, enhanced by some business men who knew how to make things happen, did start something. From that day forward, almost every cattle show or sale, at least across the west where I have visited, has used flowers to "friendly up" the scene. Some may have only a few flower pots at ringside while others with bigger budgets make larger floral displays. I have never seen one that seemed quite as spectacular as the Great Western Hereford ROM show. But maybe, because it was the first, our memories of it get better with every passing year.

The Dirtiest Trick

We have all known someone whose personality invited the practical joke but I have never known anyone quite as open and ready as Tom Bolin. He was a news writer or associate editor for *Western Livestock Journal* when I was

241

hired to work for the same outfit. Tom could write a good story or rewrite a not-so-good story to improve it but he didn't "get" a joke, no matter how obvious, and anything subtle was miles beyond his grasp. Hollywood could not have cast anyone better to be the sucker for a practical joke. Tom's very presence made the jokester's juices begin to flow.

At the other end of the practical joke spectrum among my acquaintances is Bob Neumeyer, whose mind is always ready for a new trick. If you chance to meet Bob in the grocery store, don't be surprised at the bag of Brussels sprouts in your cart at the checkout counter. If you enjoy a good practical joke from either the giving or receiving end, having Bob around keeps your wits super sharp.

Bob and I had both left our jobs at the *Livestock Journal*. Bob was working for a competitor and I was doing consulting work with ranchers and purebred cattle breeders throughout the west. *WLJ* management had sent Tom to take over the northwest (Idaho, Washington and Oregon) territory that Bob had vacated. Tom had done a good job in the office, where he was given stories to edit. He worked through them and was ready for more, but field editors had to be organized. When Tom got up in the morning he didn't seem to know what he was going to do today—or tomorrow.

Bob picked Yakima as his home when he took the *Livestock Journal* job and continued to live there. Tom also moved to Yakima when they sent him to be the northwest field editor. I was in the area and was an overnight guest at the Neumeyer house when the conversation got around to how Tom was getting along after a few months on the new job, including a remark about his lifelong, near-paranoid fear of losing his job, no matter how unfounded.

It must have been Bob who made me do it, but I envisioned a phone call with Tom, making believe that I was a newly hired field editor being sent to work a week with Tom to familiarize myself with the area and the company. From my time in the *WLJ* office with Tom, I knew he was aware of the Bay brothers who were ag journalism graduates from Missouri and especially Ovid, the eldest.

Since Tom had no reason to suspect a joke, I felt I could convince him with some Missouri slow-talk conversation and, since Nelson Crow, our old publisher boss, was attending the National Cattlemen's Association convention in Portland, Tom couldn't check out my story and I could send him into orbit with worry. From Bob's phone I called and said, in my best Missouri slow talk, "This is Ovid Bay. I have been in Los Angeles and I rode to Portland with Mr. Nelson Crow. He suggested that I fly to Yakima on the morning flight and ride with you for the week to see how you do your job. What sort of a schedule do you have for this week?"

Tom immediately began to stammer. He said his schedule was tentative and he'd have to make some calls and the week's schedule would depend on what he learned from these calls. Tom was more than flustered; he was

242

becoming fully incoherent. Bob, listening on an extension phone, was barely able to contain his composure and thankful the phone had a "mute" button. Every time Tom tried to quiz me I answered that "Mr. Nelson Crow said I should ride with you this week," and his voice wavered again. He suggested that I call back later after he made his calls. I gave him my arrival time "in case we don't talk again tonight," assuring him that "Mr. Nelson Crow said you would meet my plane." Then I asked, sort of parenthetically as an interested bystander, "and what will you be doing in the future?" When he began to stammer again, I hung up the phone.

After we let him stew for a few minutes we decided to call back and tell him it was a joke. His line was busy. We tried every 10 or 15 minutes for over an hour but his line stayed busy. We finally caught him between calls and his "sigh of relief" could be heard for miles. He admitted that "you guys really had me convinced." And his phone calls . . . he knew that Nelson Crow really was at the Cattlemen's Convention in Portland but he tried to call everyone else in the company, one after another, to see if we were telling the truth but didn't catch anybody at home so we were home free, for the moment. I give him credit for maturity. He seemed to feel we were better friends after the trick than we were before.

The Bakersfield Ram Sale

A big, handsome guy, a few years younger than I, stopped to compliment me on the way I had handled things at a tour stop during one of the *Western Livestock Journal* ranch tours. He introduced himself and I wondered what I had that he wanted. He was almost effusive but I learned later that was just how Ed did things. A few months later, at another event, he showed up again and began visiting. He introduced himself again and said he was a salesman for a Los Angeles meat wholesaler, he grew up on his grandparents' ranch near Chico and he liked ranch people so he attended get-togethers.

The next time I saw Ed Wright was at another livestock event. We visited at length and he said he would like to apply for a job the next time a field editor slot was available. I passed the word to Nelson Crow and within a few months, Ed was working in a neighboring territory. We both worked areas that were served by the livestock auction at Bakersfield so it was logical that we would be the ring men for the annual Bakersfield Ram Sale.

It started off innocently enough. We had known sheep people. They struck me as no different from cattle people in that they were both independent types who lived off the land, appreciated their neighbors and were more than a little suspicious of anybody or anything to do with government. We had worked the ring, spotting bids, at bull sales. It didn't occur to us that selling rams to sheep men could be all that different from selling bulls to cow men.

The auction barn had a sale arena from wall to wall through the near center of the barn. On one side of the ring was an "in" gate to let the livestock in from the corrals out back, the auction block in the middle and an "out" gate on the other side. Stair-stepped bleacher seats for bidders filled the rest of the barn. They began at ringside ground-level, sloping up to the back row of seats some 16 to 20 feet above ring level. As ringmen, we stood facing the bidders with our backs to the ring, Ed on the right side of the auction block, me on the left.

After the introduction and terms of the sale, the first ram on the sale order entered the ring. A committee of stockmen had graded the entries. The champion sold first, followed in order of desirability, according to the judges, one at a time. As the bidding began, Ed and I took the bids, then yelled them in to the auctioneers. The champion went to a buyer in my section. I asked his name so I could relay it to the auctioneers and sale clerks to record.

When the buyer gave me his name, it sounded to me as if he had a speech defect and also a possible sneeze. As politely as possible, I asked him to repeat the name, which he did. It still did not sound like a real word to me so I asked him if he could spell it. He said, "Yes, he could, but it wouldn't help." This brought a laugh from several in the crowd. I had been to a lot of sales and asked many buyers to give me their names but this was a new one.

Poor Ed, he was at the other side of the sale crowd, wondering what had happened to me. I looked back at the auctioneers, Harry and Skinner Hardy, and they were practically falling off the auction block with laughter. Finally they told me they knew the buyer and would handle the name. The next ram sold to a buyer in Ed's area. Now it was his turn. These buyers looked like any other stockmen we had seen but their names were really different.

A lot of the sheep raisers throughout the country, and especially in this area, were of Basque ancestry. Basque people come from a unique piece of geography on the Spanish-French border where the language is unlike anything else in the world and their names, like Anchordoguy, Arciniega, Carricaburu, Duferrena, Elgoriaga, Etchegaray, Goicoechea, Marcuerquiaga, Ormechea, Ospital, Otegui, Pierresteguy and Urrutia are at best a challenge to non-Basque at the first reading or attempt at pronunciation.

Fortunately for Ed and me, they understood the shock these names can have on Anglophiles and they enjoy being unique. Several of the people from this sale crowd became my friends and we always had a memorable event in common. I learned to appreciate the Basque people and especially their unique and for me, selfishly rewarding cultural adjunct, the Basque restaurant. Take my advice and never pass one up at mealtime.

244

Dialing a Record

When we moved to Auburn in 1968, we rented a home to give us time to appraise the area and decide where we wanted to live on a long-term basis. We were assigned a new telephone number, which means you get the numbers left over after somebody picked the good ones. Auburn had only one prefix—885—so we got 885-4978. I soon began working with Jack Parnell, who had the contract to publish the *California Cattleman* magazine. His phone was 885-7378. Imagine that—both numbers ended in 78.

The magazine office was in Jack's carport (he had boxed in two cars' worth of his four-car port) and the magazine phone was an extension line of his home phone. Business grew and I soon got a real estate license. Conducting two alleged businesses and a home with a single phone line got confusing and became a traffic jam. We needed another phone and another number. Available numbers included 885-3978, a natural for us.

As our businesses grew, both Jack and I needed new file cabinets. There was not room for even one and since it was Jack's carport, I decided it was up to me to move. A builder had just begun the footings for a new office building on the way to our office so I stopped by, was sent to see the owner and had leased an office space before a brick was laid. It would take a few months to build; in the meantime, we got ready for the move. I felt that meant another phone line. Wouldn't it be good to have a number in series with 3978.

As it happened, Jack Owens, a local horse trainer and sometime cartoonist for our magazine, had the number we needed: 885-3979. I asked my secretary to call Jack and ask if he had any intentions of changing numbers. We had several months to plan and it would be a shame if he was changing and we didn't claim his old number when we needed it so much. She called but got a busy signal. The "calling Jack Owens" routine continued every few days for months. The line was always busy. We couldn't imagine what took so much phone time.

One day I remembered that we still hadn't talked to Jack and asked my secretary Ginger to try Jack Owens one more time. Imagine the shock when I heard someone ask why I needed Jack and looking up, he was just coming in the door. I told him I needed to talk to him about his phone. "What do you want to know?" he asked, "I just changed numbers yesterday. I had been on a two-party line with a neighbor for years but he sold to new buyers and they have teenagers. I can never get out and nobody can call us so I finally decided to get a private line."

He was reluctant to give it up because the phone company agreed to refer callers to his new number for 90 days. I told him we would forward his calls for years, so the phone company sent a form for him to release them and give us the number. Jack was also a Quarter Horse breeder and show judge. This meant a lot of phone traffic. We forwarded dozens of calls to his new number for months, even several calls years later but it's surprising when some people get the word. The latest was just a couple of years ago. Jack's card with his new phone number (now more than 30 years later) is still taped inside my top desk drawer—just in case.

Surprise . . . and a New Era

Dorsey McLaughlin owned Hot Springs Ranch with a good purebred Hereford herd at Healdsburg and a sheep ranch a few miles north of it at Cloverdale. I had met him on several occasions and my feelings about him were mixed. He was obviously a man of means from his contacts, friends, property and the brand of Scotch that he drank to at least mild excess.

His Healdsburg ranch became worth too much for vineyards to keep it in cow pasture. He had a great offer so he took that money and purchased a ranch at Salmon, Idaho. He had been a good advertiser for me in the *California Cattleman* but rather than letting him go quietly, I sold him on the idea of a goodbye/hello ad for the May 1972 issue, announcing that Hot Springs Herefords were moving to Idaho. We thanked California buyers for their patronage and promised to continue consigning Hot Springs bulls to California sales.

This was not the first "relocation" ad that had ever been run, either in the *Cattleman* or other publications. But I convinced him that he should run it in full color with a photo I would take on the scenic Cloverdale ranch where he ran some cattle in addition to his reputation sheep herd. It was our first full-color ad with an on-the-ranch photo. He lived in San Francisco and had managers on both his ranches and, while he may not have handled a pitchfork much, he was a "hands on" owner, tuned in to every purchase.

The photos turned out well—almost classic—and I met with Dorsey at the Healdsburg ranch house in the evening to get an OK on the ad layout and to get approval of the ad copy. Most breeder-advertisers can give you a few ideas for an ad but their expertise is in breeding cattle, not writing ads. Dorsey was a "hands-on" ad buyer too. His feel for word selection regarding buyer motivation was advanced, almost shocking. Had I underestimated his depth? Then he did it.

We were trying to make several points in one paragraph and I wanted to combine these several ideas while separating them from each other. I could run them in a series with dots, I reasoned to myself. Then he volunteered, "I don't know if you read Herb Caen (San Francisco Chronicle columnist) but he invented what I call three-dot journalism that might work here." That was exactly what I was thinking and I was wondering how to suggest it to him. Almost immediately the ad copy was done and I was on my way.

246

In the years that followed, our mutual respect and friendship grew. The photo of his Cloverdale ranch depicted the "ideal" California ranch scene. He later sold the ranch to the government to become a park. Since his cattle ranch was now in Idaho, I got his permission to use the photo in my ads for California ranch real estate. I had calls from potential buyers who wanted to buy the ranch in the photo. But I have used "three dot" journalism even more than the photo and I think of Dorsey and mentally thank him every time I do.

Nobody Here But Us Brokers

We get phone calls every week about ranches that we have advertised for sale. The caller typically asks questions about the ranch and asks us to send him our prepared brochure with ranch information. This is a routine event and we make a living by responding. Frequently we get a call a few days later from the prospective buyer, asking us to meet for a ranch tour.

Every year or so we have someone who seems a fairly typical buyer but on the way home asks, "Did I tell you I have a real estate license?" What he is really trying to do is get us to take half the commission off the sale price if he is the successful buyer. Real estate protocol demands that he must disclose that he is licensed—the first thing—on his original call. This rule applies whether the agent is representing a client or buying for his own account.

The story of an experience I had some years ago solved the problem of how to tell these "late confessors" our policy on commissions. When they bring up the "Did I tell you?" I tell them, "That's OK; here's how we handle that." Years ago I had a client looking for a ranch. I saw a property described in a newspaper ad that sounded right so I inquired. It was a great ranch in Garden Valley but not for this client so I kept the information on file.

A few weeks later I had a call from a former client who had looked at some ranches with me but didn't buy. This person was now ready to buy and when she described the property characteristics, I knew the Garden Valley ranch was just right, except that it was in a marginal location. This buyer had been divorced since our previous contacts. When she showed up to look at ranches, she introduced me to her new boyfriend who was an active real estate broker.

She assured me that her friend would not participate in the sale but before I convinced them to look at this "ideal" property that was badly located for them, my client and her friend were married. I finally convinced them to go look at the Garden Valley property, "just to get it out of your system." They loved it enough to overcome the location and made an offer immediately.

It happened that the sellers of the Garden Valley ranch, both the husband and wife—and both, coincidentally, named Marion Henness—were active real estate brokers and had the leading brokerage in the area. It is obvious how to handle the sale. The buyer is a broker. He gets half the commission—

Right? And the sellers are brokers so they get half of the real estate commission—right?

But wait! It seems that something is wrong with that reasoning. I am the person who represented the buyers who came to me for a ranch. And I am the person representing the sellers. They were conventional residential brokers with no ranch experience and they had never had any contact with the buyers until I introduced them. I was the only person acting as an agent.

Let me tell you how we handled that situation and how we have handled all similar situations since that time. The buyers and the sellers were unknown to each other. They came to me as clients. One wanted to sell. The other wanted to buy. I was the one who got them together and did all the work. I took the full commission and we all left happy and are all still friends. And there may even be a bonus. I convinced the buyer-wife to get a real estate license and she became a successful agent for several years until she moved to Oregon some years later for another business opportunity.

A Collapse of Memories

At 8 o'clock in the morning on Super Bowl Sunday, January 30, 2000, they imploded the Mapes Hotel in Reno. The collapse made the early morning network television news. It was 12 stories high and had opened in 1947 as the first high-rise hotel-casino in Nevada, if not in the world. The owner, Charlie Mapes, had a knack for keeping a hotel filled and the Sky Room was the showplace for the area featuring the leading entertainers of the day from Frank Sinatra down the list.

His long-standing friendship with two veteran breeders of Angus cattle, Wilbur May, and frequent hunting partner, Bill Volkmann, gave him easy access to the cattle community. Wilbur owned Double Diamond Ranch, located south of Reno, and Bill owned Hacienda de los Reyes at Selma, California, near Fresno. A good headquarters hotel made it easy to stage a livestock show or sale and attract a good crowd. Catering to the livestock crowd with special rates and performers that were popular with cow people helped make Reno a meeting place of choice for many livestock events.

As I saw the old friend collapse on television, I recalled a previous "blast" I had shared at the Mapes Hotel. I don't remember the event but it was an Angus cattle sale. Bob Neumeyer was managing Western States Angus Association and was sale manager. Since the Mapes Hotel was sale headquarters, Bob got the big corner room with the compliments of the hotel owner. Bob invited me to share the room which had an extra bed.

We were shaken out of our sleep by an early Sunday morning explosion. Instantly awake, if not fully oriented, we could see that our room seemed to be safely intact. We hurried to the big, curved corner window and saw a column of smoke across the street half a block away. We dressed quickly and went down to the ground floor to see what had happened and if the hotel was safe or whether we should run for cover elsewhere.

As we got to the lobby, Joe Monforton came in the front door, brushing glass shards off his hat and coat. Joe was a field editor for one of the livestock papers. He had been out for an early morning walk, passing the bank across the street from the hotel at the time of the blast. Glass windows came crashing down around him. Luckily for Joe, no large pane happened to fall where he was walking. As I remember, not a single pane of glass in the hotel was shattered, more than I can say for some people's nerves.

Fire trucks began arriving by the time we felt we were safely out of range of whatever was happening. As a crowd began to gather, we learned that the blast was in a paint shop across the street and the damage was limited to that building. It was exciting at the time, I can assure you, but it was a sad anticlimax or post-climax to see all the bricks collapse into the basement in a cloud of dust some 33 years later.

One-Hour Photos—Miracle of the 1960s

When longtime friend Bob Neumeyer became manager of the Western States Angus Association, he was determined to move the Angus breed out of the dark ages in the west. Herefords were the "cattlemen's breed" and Angus bulls were used mostly by commercial cattlemen as "heifer bulls" to breed first-calf heifers because baby Angus calves were generally smaller than Herefords. A few of the more thoughtful cattlemen used them to get the extra performance that heterosis from cross-breeding gives to the offspring.

The breed, including its major events, was controlled by a handful of eastern breeders. They were mostly "hobby" cattlemen. Their cattle operations were mainly income tax shelters and/or rich people's toys. Their interest in the broader cattle business was remote or non-existent. The major breed show, called the National Angus Futurity, was held in the east. Western breeders tried to compete with their Western National Angus Futurity but the "national" part was in title only. No eastern cattle ever came and the show winners got no recognition outside the western states.

Bob was determined to make a mark for western Angus breeders and the cattle they produced. The Western Futurity had been held in a county fairgrounds beef barn. He felt that the show had to get a new base to get nationwide attention, at least in the Angus breed. He hit on the idea of moving the show to Las Vegas. He found a willing co-conspirator in Dr. Bob Taylor, a Las Vegas physician and Angus cattle breeder. Doc Taylor knew "everybody" in Las Vegas. He had soon wrangled an invitation to use the Stardust Horsemen's Park for the cattle show.

News of the pending move to Las Vegas shocked breed officials and old-line breeders alike but they couldn't turn back the tide. Some eastern herd owners got the itch to go to Vegas, even if it meant having their cattle compared with those of western breeders. Prior to this, western herd owners had purchased cattle from eastern breeders but the unwritten rule seemed to be that cattle went west and money went east. Bob wanted to change this but he knew "those westerners" would have to do something special to get it done. He had to invent something that would make the eastern breeders recognize a western event.

Cattle show champion photos in the 1960s were in black and white and it took a week or two before the photographer got all the film processed and had time to print the photos. Doc Taylor tended to be an overachiever. Taking Bob through the Stardust facilities, Doc and the Stardust's promotion people even showed Bob their photo lab where they routinely processed color film in about an hour. Suddenly Bob got a vision of the impossible: could he flash color slides of the winners at the awards banquet on the evening of the show's second day, only hours (not several days) after the Supreme Champion was named?

Bob called me. He knew that I took livestock photos every day and that I had taken hundreds of livestock show photos. Would I do the photography, sort the slides and run the projector? The Stardust had already agreed to process the film. The winners would be announced—and color photo slides would be shown, for the first time ever, at the banquet in the evening after the show, beginning with the first class shown—the female junior heifer calf.

After the banquet dinner, the lights were dimmed and I flashed the first color slide on the screen. I can still hear the disbelief from the several hundred cattle people in the room. A few gasps, then one by one, people began doing double takes as they saw the images on the screen. It took several minutes and much whispering before everybody present realized that they were really looking at their show champions that were named winners only a few hours earlier. Until that minute, when their bull or heifer was flashed on the screen, they all knew there was no possible way to see photos of the winners on the same day as the show, much less at their banquet only a couple of hours after the last animal was shown. Credit Las Vegas with another miracle, but Bob earned nationwide recognition and respect for both the quality and number of the cattle exhibited, the Stardust and I shared credit for the magic of "instant photos."

The New Look in Livestock Photos

"What a great photo! You mean it was posed?" Yes, I'm afraid it was. The animal may have been trained, haltered and positioned, one foot at a time, or it may be that the photographer followed the animal until it naturally walked into the perfect pose, and camera ready, captured the animal on film in a split second. But it wasn't chance.

250

It probably doesn't occur to most people who look at livestock photos. What is the "proper" pose for a show animal and is it the same for animals in the show ring as in a pasture scene? I have no idea who started taking cow or horse photos in poses as they have been historically photographed. The pose is different for all classes of livestock, but each is designed to flatter each animal and to make each appear as near to the "ideal" animal as possible.

Dairy cattle tend to be taller at the rump than at the shoulders so the man with the camera must find, or make, a slight slope to elevate the front feet. The front feet are positioned straight under the shoulders and may be posed slightly wider or narrower than the animal stands naturally, depending upon the natural width of the front quarters.

The rear feet are positioned with the far leg straight under the animal as if a plumb bob were dropped from the pin bone at the tail head, down to the hock and dew claw on the far rear foot of a cow in production. The near leg has the foot positioned forward so the leg covers the near rear teat, leaving the front teat in view of the camera. The camera is positioned to be perpendicular to an imaginary line through the length of the cow and level with the middle of the cow. For an animal not in production, rear legs are reversed. Maybe it's not "natural" after all.

Thoroughbred horses are positioned much like dairy cattle except that they should be on level ground so the viewer can see whether the horse is high or low in front. The front feet are positioned much like a dairy cow except that the far front foot should be to the rear of the near one so there is daylight between the legs below the knees. The rear feet will show the horse in its most natural position if the rear feet are placed like a dairy animal not in production with the far leg forward and the leg near the camera placed so a line drops from the point of the buttock through the back of the hock straight down to the fetlock at the back of the foot.

The camera, for horse photography, is placed perpendicular to the center of the mass of the horse—approximately at the point of the cinch ring. If the horse's mane naturally falls to the right, you photograph the left side and vice versa. Thoroughbred (race) horses have been pictured this way for years, which gives a good historic comparison of horses over time.

Quarter Horse, Appaloosa and Paint breeders began posing their horses for photos like Thoroughbreds but these breeds didn't have years of tradition in their history and most of the breeders had little knowledge of history or respect for tradition. Photographers took photos from every angle. These breeds were pictured in some cases like the Thoroughbred but show photos were often taken as three-quarter front or three-quarter rear photos with all four legs squarely under the horse. Sometimes the head would be turned around to the side on three-quarter rear shots, sometimes straight ahead or as chosen by the photographer.

Beef cattle photos during the 1930s and '40s were mostly three-quarter front poses, and then the photographer retouched the entire animal except the head. It also was a growing trend to make beef cattle look short legged so the camera was above the level of the animals, which were bedded in deep straw to further give the look of short legged cattle. And cattle were always photographed wearing halters.

I felt that every animal worthy of a photo had a pose somewhere that made it look great, unretouched. I felt it was the duty of the photographer to find and record that pose. I began to vary from the previous norm when I took the catalog photos for the Santa Barbara Ranch sale, held at the Cow Palace in the 1960s. I posed the animals in halters, then had the herdsman remove the halters to take the photos, giving the appearance that it was their normal, unhaltered pose. Austin Moody, the sale manager, said it was the greatest set of sale photos he had ever seen or worked with.

Unfortunately, Moody was killed in a plane crash on his way to the Cow Palace—and the sale was a flop. But the age of "halter off" photography had its start. As the move to larger cattle returned to the beef business, buyers wanted to see what the cattle actually looked like, not the retouched photos of the past. I was taking a lot of photos on ranches and began looking for poses much like the broad-side photos of Thoroughbred horses. This was the position that showed the most honest pose of the animal and the most of its natural conformation.

I never liked to take show photos of beef cattle. There was always pressure to do it fast and they had always been done with all four feet squarely under the animal. It was like cutting out cookies. Most show animals were young

"Family Portrait" photo by Phil Raynard for Jess Hereford Ranch.

and the rear end of young beef cattle is always higher than the front so they appeared to be running down hill unless you elevated their front feet. I learned that if you gapped the rear legs like posing Thoroughbred horses—or beef cattle running loose in a field—it lowered the rump and made the animal look better balanced.

252

Mel Hansen is surely one of the best in the business of selecting, fitting and showing beef cattle. I believe the event was the Western National Angus Futurity after it was moved to Reno. I was the photographer. I had done the photography at a few lesser shows and decided to shoot this show using "gapped" poses instead of posing cattle with all four legs squarely under the animal as had been "traditional" for show photos.

Mel had probably shown and posed almost as many cattle as I had pictured. When he brought his animal to the winner's circle for a photo he posed it in the "four-square" position. I asked him to move the far rear leg forward and the near rear leg back. Mel is pretty blond and he is pretty big. He knew how to pose animals. Anyone in the livestock show business, including Mel, knew that. I knew it too, but I was on a mission, and persisted, quietly, to ask him to change the pose after he was satisfied that the pose was perfect.

His blond face began to redden as he glared at me. When he didn't budge, I took the needed photos then asked him to try it my way, just once. It took a few extra minutes but we pictured that animal in both poses. He later admitted that the animal looked better with the legs gapped. I don't think it took a year until show photos across the country were all taken in that pose. The old livestock show world was often considered to be phony . . . and got the photos it deserved. Today, nobody would consider returning to the retouched photo with the top line flattened and rear quarter rounded unlike any animal ever grew naturally.

Coyote Supply and Demand

People in agriculture have long been their own worst enemies in the world of marketing. Every farmer or rancher knows a little about supply and demand. They understand—sort of—that when they raise too much wheat or corn, prunes or almonds, cattle or sheep, etc., prices tumble. Everyone hopes his neighbors will plant few enough acres or breed few enough cows to keep bushels or other measures of production in line with reasonable price. But will any given farmer cut his own numbers back to boost prices? No chance. If prices happen to be good, he doesn't want to take a chance on missing out on the returns from a profitable year. That's probably the reason that government programs work as well as they do.

From disasters of drought, flood, disease, foreign imports and other unkind or severely damaging events to their incomes, their persons or their property, farmers have learned to never count their harvests until they're safely stored or sold. And most prefer a bumper crop with the accompanying low prices to the opposite with nothing to sell at high prices.

In the drought of the 1930s, the federal government began to subsidize the farm industry with the mixed goals of stabilizing farm income and insuring what bureaucrats called the "ever normal granary," making plenty of food available for the American people, come drought, plague, pestilence or plain old bad luck. This was the beginning of an uneasy partnership between the historically independent American farmer and his government.

Except for a few conservatives, most government officials welcome agreements of any kind that breed dependence on them or their programs. Good weather, new machinery, improved management, fertilizers, genetics and pesticides made bumper crops a regular occurrence. America's farmers were able to feed the world without trying but would not voluntarily limit production to the amount that could be marketed at a profit.

With the importance of agriculture to the country's economy, government officials felt it necessary to intervene, not only to guarantee a food supply, but to keep the farm economy healthy. Most farmers wanted no such partnership until government sweetened the pot to guarantee them a reasonable profit, year after year. As various programs continued, farmers became more comfortable but still suspicious. Finally, by the 1980s and '90s, many farmers admitted, and even sometimes bragged, that they were "farming the government."

It is relatively easy to contract the acres planted of various crops. Keeping the livestock population under control is a different challenge and one that has not yet been managed. As a result there are what economists call "cycles." It has historically taken 10 or 11 years for the "cattle cycle," with big inventory and low prices back to low inventory with high prices and on to big inventory and low prices. The sheep, hog or poultry cycles all have their unique numbers. And sometimes interesting factors play a part. There has been no "cattle cycle" in recent years.

It was early summer in the mid-1970s, and I was traveling much of the state of California to sell as much advertising as possible for the special Bull Buyer's Guide that ran in the July-August issue of *California Cattleman* magazine. Cattle prices were low as a result of too many cows in the country's collective cow herd while sheep breeders were enjoying high prices. It is not uncommon for two commodities to be at different phases of their price cycles.

I was calling on purebred cattle breeders in the area east of Stockton on a hot afternoon. Solari's is a country store near Linden. If you're in this area near lunchtime, this is the place to stop for a generous serving of minestrone with hard-crusted bread. It isn't a bad place for just a cool drink on a hot day, either. I stopped and found several stools occupied by local cattlemen. One man who had been sitting at the counter got up and paid his bill as I entered. This left me his seat between Ad Englehart, who was strictly a cowman, and Pete Ospital, who raised both cattle and sheep.

We began visiting about the heat and bad cattle prices. Pete broke the tone when he said that the number of sheep in the country was down and prices

254

were really great. "In fact," he said, "if I just had a few more sheep I would probably have enough money from sheep to make up for the losses on my cattle." This was the opening for the buckaroo at the end of the counter. He had it figured out. "We got too many cattle," he ventured. "Maybe we could get some profit back in the cattle business if somebody would teach more of them coyotes to kill calves."

Just a Little Practice

Livestock photography is a strange business. You may take show photos of a single animal in the morning and on-the-ranch action photos of a cutting horse or a cattle roundup in the afternoon. Southern California has so many horse owners it has been said there are more horses within 100 miles of downtown Los Angeles than any other place in the world. Having worked from Santa Barbara on the west, south to San Diego and well beyond San Bernardino to the east, I agree that Southern California is loaded with horses.

Almost every horse owner believes his is the absolutely greatest horse in the world and is eager to have a den or stable wall covered with photos of his pride and joy. Some even pay a photographer for his prize photo. I kept myself saddle-sore, helping trainers at stables and training ranches. It was common to arrive, after making a firm appointment to photograph a horse in training for an owner, only to have the trainer ask me to help him for a minute first.

You don't have to know anything to own a horse. And you don't have to be reasonable in your expectations. Several times I came to take posed still photos of a horse but the owner of a cutting horse in training arrived, unannounced, just ahead of me and wanted to see his horse work on cattle. The trainer would ask if I could "turn back" cattle for his work. I was often given a horse that had just arrived from the racetrack that hadn't cooled out yet from training and probably wasn't trained to neck rein besides.

One such date was to take photos of a horse being trained as a rope horse by one of the great performers and trainers, Norris Patton. He had just received a new set of roping steers and wanted to take a practice run to see whether a steer ran to the right, left, or straight ahead. And whether he ran straight out or if he might duck down to avoid the rope. He had a great old rope horse that had helped Norris earn a bunch in the rodeos and would give the calves a good run.

I decided that if he was going to practice, I might as well position myself in a good spot to learn where I should be for the steer Norris decided to use when we went for the trophy photo. I decided to shoot at 1/100th of a second, pretty slow for real action but I hoped that if I panned the camera to keep the image centered, I could freeze the image while blurring the background, giving the feeling of the speed involved in the action.

The first run was a flop, with the tricky steer ducking and turning away as the horse got near. The next steer stumbled and the horse was so near it was only luck that we didn't have a pile-up. The third steer ran straight away as we hoped and I clicked the shutter at what I hoped would be the right moment. Norris was satisfied with the steer so he brought out the colt he was training and we made a few runs, and I ended up getting one or more shots on each run.

When the negatives were hung to dry they all looked pretty good, but then the prints came up. We had done well with photos of the colt in training . . . but the "practice" shot of Norris and his old buckskin had miraculously recorded the last-second before the crash. I couldn't have planned it better. The loop was over the calf's head, lying against its neck, but the calf hadn't hit the end of the rope. Norris was just beginning to "throw off his slack" (tighten the loop), his right foot was just beginning to slip out of the stirrup, the old buckskin was beginning to set his feet for the stop but the dust hadn't yet begun to fly.

This photo was proof of the photographer's answer to the suggestion that "most of the great photos are mainly luck." I guess I would agree— with the note that it seems odd that most of that "luck" comes to people who have spent years to learn their craft, spent much time and money acquiring the equipment needed and the knowledge of how to use it and spent hours, days or a lifetime pursuing a given photo. Isn't it odd that most of the "luck" comes to those people?

I never did decide whether the photo should be called "Split Second Before the Crash," or a name to be selected by the viewer. You can be sure I didn't show it to the owner of the horse I was sent to photograph. The best photos of his horse's work would have paled by comparison. My practice shot was the best rodeo photo I had ever taken. I had no sale for it—it was just a "practice" shot—but it is still my "personal best" trophy.

Life Rediscovered From a *Wall Street Journal* Ad

I always read the "Ranches For Sale" ads in the Friday *Wall Street Journal* to see what other people are selling. I often advertised my listings that were more likely to be sold to an investor than a cattleman. In December, 1991, I saw an ad for someone looking to find a large orchard or a ranch with orchard-quality soil and, while it was barely coherent, I was interested. I didn't have a listing as large as the advertiser wanted but I had three adjoining properties that would come close.

I called immediately and the phone was answered by a person who needed help with both vocabulary and pronunciation. By proceeding slowly and getting him to repeat almost every word, I became convinced that this was a broker named Nabi Jon Kashifi and that his client was an Afghani national and would-be immigrant with enough money at hand for the down payment and enough in foreign banks to pay in full—when he could get it ashore. I drove to Nabi Jon's office in Walnut Creek with the map and information sheet combining three properties and had what I hoped was a presentable package. If I could talk to this broker in person, maybe I could understand him better.

My new friend and his client were Afghanistan natives. He was a captain in the army when word leaked that the Russians were coming. An outspoken anti-Russian, he knew his days would be numbered if captured by the Russian army. He left Afghanistan as quickly as possible. A family friend had taken his family to Los Angeles a few years earlier, so he quickly arranged for them to sponsor his departure. In only a few days, he was out of the country.

He was fairly well prepared to leave. He was college educated and spoke five languages. Unfortunately, none of them was English. When he arrived in Los Angeles he needed a job and he needed to learn the language that would open the job market to him. His sponsor helped him decide to become a real estate agent so he could help new families arriving in the United States. He kept his contacts in Asia and was doing well in real estate. Now he needed a special property for a special friend. I brought him the best I could find.

He didn't like it—too many houses and barns. Too much fence. He wanted bare land with a capability for orchards. Now he tells me. Reaching back in my rarely-used gray cells I recalled a ranch near Oakdale that George Rose had told me about months earlier. George was a land-owner and speculator. He had repossessed the ranch from a previous sale. I called George and scheduled a ranch showing. We met and drove over the land and Nabi Jon, the agent, liked it. We went back to George's office to get some supplemental material.

George went into his office, which was in the shopping center he owned in Oakdale. It was a mid-December afternoon. The shopping center was decorated for Christmas. In the middle of the parking lot was a freestanding building being used as a teen hangout, video rental, hamburger and malt shop. Nabi Jon suggested that we go to the building for a snack while we waited for George to check his messages and bring the ranch information.

We found seats at the counter, looked at the menu, and were ready to order when the server turned to face us. I couldn't have been prepared for what followed. Two grown men—the customer, who came with me, and the server—both began screaming, crying and mumbling strange words. Nabi Jon threw himself on the floor and began pounding it with his clenched fist. I didn't know how to ask what was happening so I just sat in amazement. Finally the crying stopped and, in broken English, I got an explanation that will satisfy me forever.

Our server in the malt shop—the owner of the business—was the son of Nabi Jon's U.S. sponsor who helped him flee Afghanistan for the United States. The two families had lost touch with each other with the passage of time and moving to new cities. What a shock to be present at this surprise reunion! The ranch sale was made, but the commission I earned was not the most memorable thing about this transaction.

A Kingdom for a Horse

Rodeo is big business. It's not General Motors or Amazon.com but in much of the West and Midwest, a decent promoter can fill the grandstand at almost any county fairgrounds and many larger venues with cash customers to watch the age-old contest between man and beast. Rodeo at its best is seen in the National Finals Rodeo. The event is staged at year-end and includes the top 15 contestants, based on money earned, in each rodeo event across the country. They compete on the best of the country's broncs and bulls for 10 "go-rounds" or rides to determine the world champion in each event.

The event has been staged in several cities since its inception but it has been in the Las Vegas convention center since about 1980. In the 1960s it was held in Los Angeles at the "old sports arena." In addition to the "rough stock" that tries the cowboys' skill, dozens of horses are used. Almost every calf roper, bull dogger, steer roper and barrel racer brings his or her own horse. Several competitors carry two or more horses as sort of spares in case the top horse goes lame or hits a bad streak. This is a business where time is everything. Success or failure, including world championships and thousands of dollars' difference in prize money, is measured in tenths of a second.

There is also great demand for horses that do not compete but are used for dignitaries to ride in the Grand Entry parade that opens each evening event. In a coliseum filled with thousands of cash-paying enthusiasts, with music and public address system blaring, many otherwise reliable mounts can more resemble the rodeo stock than the foolproof, unspookable, guaranteed-to-be-safe mount needed to carry a political dignitary or Miss America.

Enter Phil Livingston. He was an artist in the *Western Livestock Journal* advertising layout department. He had acreage at the north edge of the Los Angeles basin and performed a profitable niche service. He kept four horses in his intensive training barn. They were mostly consigned by professional rodeo cowboys. These were great young horses that Phil kept for a year, exercising and training each to participate as a roping or bull dogging mount.

In this training, Phil prepared these horses to keep their cool under every imaginable situation. He played loud music with intermittent gunshots and screaming, trailered the horses to rodeos and exposed them to every cause for a wreck. He looked for chances to use them in parades—indoor and outdoor. At the end of a year, all that got passing grades were ready for a professional

258

cowboy to carry as his second horse. Phil kept his name on the list as the supplier of absolutely foolproof, reliable mounts for any rider at any function needing a horse. It was a rare but important part of their training. One day, if they continued to respond to the training regimen Phil had for them, they would be performing in an arena full of noisy rodeo fans. If they were less than cast-iron solid in the noise and surprises of the rodeo environment, it would be better to learn it now than years later and miles down the road when it really counted.

In exchange for the use of these four reliable horses, for the many days' duration of the National Finals Rodeo, Phil got a whole handful of box seats to every event. That's when you find out who your friends are. I helped him with layouts for my special accounts and kept myself on that list. Those were the years before TV coverage of the event when you either showed up in person or read about it in the papers. The finals are now featured on cable and satellite TV networks so the tickets to the National Finals Rodeo aren't quite as exclusive as in the 1960s.

Flying Embryos

A full-color cover of the April, 1975, *California Cattleman* magazine showed a photo of two veterinary and reproductive doctors and a sedated embryo donor heifer, lying on her back in a surgical frame, all in surgical attire. This recorded the first transfer of embryos taken from donor cows in the U.C. Davis veterinary hospital and flown from the lab to the ranch, where the embryos were implanted in recipient cows with estrus periods drug-matched to the donors.

Transfer of embryos from a limited number of females with the most desirable breeding had been done for several years. The cost was substantial because of the special care and use of drugs to cause the development of several eggs instead of only one, as in normal ovulations. At first, the females were artificially inseminated with semen from a selected male, then a few days later, when the embryos had developed to the 8- or 16-cell size, they were taken in a surgical procedure and each healthy embryo was surgically implanted into a recipient female.

Most of the embryo collections resulted in anywhere from two or three up to 30 or 40 fertilized embryos in each collection, so it was necessary to have an unknown number of transfer-ready cows synchronized with the collection of embryos from a donor cow. The cost of getting a donor cow with her cargo of transferable embryos was so great that the cost per calf would be greatly reduced if the breeder could save most or all the embryos by having enough recipients ready.

Windswept Livestock Co. was owned by the Burroughs family. They had an excellent ranch on the west bank of the Sacramento River near Orland.

They had a dairy background, operating a dairy at Brentwood and had bought the Orland ranch to develop dairy heifers. They sold their dairy and began using beef-breed crosses on their dairy cows to produce beef animals. They used bulls of various breeds, then recorded the weights and the returns they got from the progeny of each breed cross.

Their records showed more profit with crosses using Simmental and Gelbvieh (European cattle breeds) bulls. They decided to become purebred breeders of these cattle. They advertised in the *California Cattleman* magazine, which I published. We became good friends and they invited me to record the procedures involved in the embryo transfers. Both of these breeds originated in Europe and importation to America began in the 1960s but Oscar Burroughs went to Europe and eventually got permits to import semen from a few special European sires he selected. This semen was used in the 1975 transfers.

It cost several hundred dollars per embryo to collect them and make these transfers in 1975. It was hoped that the breeder would be repaid by giving birth to high-value calves from embryos transferred to recipient cows. They got credit for the innovation, but it was hard to make it profitable. As usual, the pioneers took the arrows; somebody else made the money. Technology moved swiftly and both the removal of embryos from donors and implants into recipients were done non-surgically within a few years, at a fraction of the earlier cost.

By 2000, the cost per collection (which produces from five or six to a few dozen embryos), is about $300. A few dollars will freeze the embryos and a technician can implant an embryo in a recipient female whenever you like for a few more bucks. We are still not sure how much this technology has contributed to breed improvement. Ideally, we have reproduced the best breeding and used the poor-quality females as recipient mothers, but it is my opinion that the process improved the sale price of cattle produced by embryos more than it improved the overall quality of the cattle industry. In any case, it was satisfying to help record that speck of history.

What's Your Deadline?

I was hired by Crow Publications in April, 1962, to begin work as soon as our first baby, Coral, was born and old enough to travel to California. I would be a field editor for Southern California for *Western Livestock Journal*. I found early in my tour of the area that the dairy industry was being neglected by publications in the area, especially the breeders of purebred dairy cattle. When I suggested I might be able to bring in some new business, I also became a field editor for *Western Dairy Journal*, which we published.

This proved to be an industry in search of a publication, an interested reporter and an advertising medium. Within a few months we were sought out for many mutually useful contacts and events and I was named editor of the magazine. One day I had a call from a good source asking what I knew about the possible sale of the most prestigious purebred Holstein herd in the state. I had not heard about it but, if I wanted to look like a dairy editor, I decided I had better see if the rumor was true.

I left immediately for Hughson, a small town near Modesto and some 300 miles from Los Angeles. I drove straight to the dairy ranch office at the headquarters area. I had been there once before and had met the owner, Dr. Harold Schmidt, a few times on other occasions. He seemed to always need to be re-introduced. He was cool if not aloof. Maybe he was just shy. I was about to find out which, and hopefully a lot more.

As I got near the office I could see that the main activity was taking posed photos of numerous purebred cows. Harry Strohmeyer, the country's leading dairy photographer, had set his camera up with a great background and a large staff of people was grooming and leading cattle to the site to be photographed. I had never met Harry before and was thrilled to meet him and to see him practice his art. But I came to see the owner and, if my rumor was true, to get the story. I asked for Harold and was sent to the ranch office. He was eating lunch at a large desk. He invited me in and said, "I suppose you've heard about the sale." I asked if it were true but before he confirmed or denied, he began at the beginning. I listened.

"I was a poor kid on a small farm in the Midwest," he began. "I was 9 years old—you had to be 10 for 4-H but they let me in—and I had a little crossbred half-Jersey, half-Guernsey heifer. I led her into the show ring to be judged at the county fair and stood dead last. Heartbroken, I led her back to the stall and cried. I knew my heifer was the most loved, best cared-for heifer in the show. Why had they put all those other heifers above mine? I have spent the rest of my life getting the answers," he told me.

"In 1941, I got my veterinary degree and put my new wife and all our worldly goods in a Ford car and, with less than a hundred dollars in my pocket, we headed west. I felt that California was where the action would be in the dairy business." He told me that reproduction was the biggest dairy problem and he specialized in that field. Nutrition had not developed to meet the demand for high production in dairy herds, especially in California. He picked up a few well-bred purebred cows with breeding problems and established a herd that grew to become one of the largest and best purebred Holstein herds in the state.

He eventually added "Dusty Jo" to his herd. "Dusty Jo" was Rocky Hill Mont Burke Dusty Jo, the highest-producing and highest-classifying registered Holstein cow in the state and her presence gave a national reputation to his herd. As the story unfolded, I waited to ask the killer question: Did you sell the herd? But he kept on talking. This talker was the guy who had always seemed so shy or maybe so disinterested that I had always felt the need to re-introduce myself every time I met him.

Finally he paused and asked if I would like some lunch. I thanked him, but I had eaten on the way to the ranch. Then he said, "I appreciate the way you handled this. I was afraid I'd get a bunch of phone calls. It's hard to explain on the phone. So far I have had a call from the farm reporter for the *Modesto Bee*. I told him the idea of a sale was interesting and that I'd call him if such an event occurred. I was sure I'd get more calls. I don't like phone calls on sensitive issues. I like to look at the person I'm talking to if it's important.

"I suppose you have some questions," he continued. He was right. I asked first of all if a sale had occurred. He did not make any effort to swear me to secrecy. He told me that it was a done deal, with only a few details on time of delivery and payment dates to be concluded. I told him that I knew and deeply respected the buyers, the Sawyer family, that we were on good terms and I was pleased that he had found such a good home for the herd.

He told me that he had enjoyed building the herd but it had reached a point where continued improvement would be minimal and the sale of these several hundred cows would assure his financial future. Then he shocked me by asking, "What's your deadline?" I told him I was on deadline, and that the magazine would be in the mail the next Monday. Then he voluntarily told me that he would not give the story to anyone else until we were in the mail.

I told him that I was pleased and flattered by his offer, but a monthly magazine staff understands that we can't "scoop" traditional news media and that a monthly magazine editor doesn't worship deadlines and mailing dates as much as the publishers of daily papers. He said that he had no idea how we heard of the sale but that he appreciated the professional way we handled the event and that stalling a few publications on our behalf was the least he could do. Then I accepted the can of cola he offered for my trip home and thanked him. Yes, the sale was completed . . . and I never had to introduce myself to Doc Schmidt again.

Que es en Español?

Knowledge can be packaged and sold like any product. When someone is convinced, by whatever means, that you have expertise and experience important to him, you have the potential to sell that information. This is called consulting in the business world today, even in the world as it existed in the 1960s. I discovered this to be a marketable skill when Andy Anderson told me that he liked the ads I made and asked what I would charge him to handle all the advertising for his purebred Polled Hereford herd.

Andy was not the biggest or the best of purebred breeders but he was one of the most motivated. He wanted a great herd and he wanted the world to know it was great. I wondered how many other breeders were candidates for this service. While I considered what I should charge Andy, I made a mental list of others in the business who might be interested. Most of the prospective clients on my developing list were interested and several said, "How much?" I invented a charge that would be a monthly retainer for routine work plus a daily or hourly rate for special work. Most said, "Let's go." Suddenly I had a new business that would pay more than my regular job and I would have time for photojournalism projects and commercial livestock photography too. But there can be problems in every business.

Shortly after this transition, old friend Carl Safley became manager of the Carefree Ranch in Arizona. He wanted me to handle advertising for the ranch's registered Brangus cattle herd. We decided it would show a touch of class if we could furnish a "photo pedigree" of every animal offered for sale from the ranch. Most of the herd sires had already been photographed but our idea would require taking a photo of every producing female in the herd. A fair-sized job, but we felt it would be worth the effort and set a date to begin our photography.

Good livestock photos are not easy, especially when your cattle are not used to being handled and have never been haltered. They actually ran on thousands of acres of desert land north of Phoenix. We had a good set of corrals and most of the cowherd had been gentled to the point that they did not panic when a human was in the corral with them. Generally mild mannered, all cattle with Brahman blood hate to be alone. (Brangus are three-eighths Brahman and five-eighths Angus). Two or more may be gentle but a single animal will crash into any fence in an attempt to find a friend.

We decided to have a go at it. We got the first few to strike a reasonable pose and it seemed we might get several pictured that day but Carl's secretary drove out to the corrals a couple miles from the office to tell him to return an important phone call. Goodbye Carl; what about the photos? Carl spoke good ranch Spanish. All the employees were straight from Mexico and spoke not a word of English. I took two semesters of Spanish years earlier in college but I had not tried to use a single word of Spanish for years and had never learned the words to tell a vaquero (Mexican cowboy) how to pose a cow for a picture.

We wanted broadside photos of the animals with their feet neatly placed showing good balance. And we wanted the cow's head turned slightly toward the camera, enough to see her far ear and the brow of the eye that was away from the camera. Carl left me with two alleged helpers. Both were great with cattle but didn't understand a word of my instructions in English and had never seen anybody take a picture of a cow. How, I asked myself, do I tell them what I want?

I remembered that "ojo" was Spanish for eye. What was Spanish for ear? I pointed to my eye and said "*ojo*." Then I pointed to my ear and asked, "Que es en Español?" They quickly answered "oido" but I had not been listening to Spanish words for years so my listening, and pronunciation, were not too keen. Real down-on-the-ranch Spanish didn't sound quite like I remember my Spanish teacher many years earlier.

I asked them to repeat until I could say *oido* well enough to get by. Then I drew a picture in the sand, showing my helpers the position needed for the legs. I showed them which legs I wanted forward and which back, along with the angle of the animal's head. The cows in the corral with us became curious, even seemed to accept our presence and became more manageable and we got several useful photos—en Español—before Carl returned. And they, the unidentified masses and language critics who said I would never use my Spanish, what did they know?

Are We Still Under Budget?

I had known Dean Parker for several years. He was one of the West's top auctioneers and a leading horse sale manager. He had seen some of the ads I had made for my consulting customers and shortly after we moved to Auburn in 1968 he asked me how much I would charge to handle the advertising for his sale management business. We agreed on a price and on suggested agreements for advertising budgets with his future sale customers. I had been privately critical of the way most sale managers handled their advertising and welcomed the chance to show the horse-sale world that I could do better.

Within a few days, Dean had scheduled our first sale. This was in the days before the tax law of 1986 when a lot of high-income people were taking advantage of a loophole in a legitimate tax law that allowed depreciation and capital gains advantages for purebred livestock breeders. The owner that had contacted Dean was an investor whose taxman had suggested he buy a ranch and raise purebred livestock for tax reasons. He knew nothing about livestock but he didn't like cattle so he picked horses. He preferred Quarter Horses so he began buying at sales.

He learned that there were both racehorses and performance horses within the Quarter Horses breed. He bought some of both. Then he bred some of the racing mares to performance stallions and vice versa. After a few years of this mischief, his taxman advised him that he had to show a profit by the end of five years or the government would declare his ranching venture a hobby and he would lose all his tax advantages. The only way to create a positive cash flow from this mess was to sell out. He called Dean Parker. Dean appraised his herd and estimated a sale average of $600 per head. Dean had budgeted a reasonable amount for advertising.

I did not meet with the seller but Dean brought me a few photos of horses that were to be in the sale, show photos of a few horses being sold, and photos of a couple of sires represented in the breeding program but not in the sale. I could see that this was an uphill battle. We had very few strictly performance horses that had any merit and we had no racing-bred horses that had any record to point to. I felt we had to "blow a lot of smoke" without disclosing the fuel in our non-existent fire.

I listed all the appropriate publications with their advertising rates and decided which would get one page, which would get two. Then I had my chance to show how smart I was and why I was so critical of most sale advertising. Most sale managers would get the material from the owner, including a handful of old photos. He would call the publication or its field man, tell them the sale date and a little about the horses, send a couple of the photos and ask them to make an ad. Then he called the second publication with the same story, sent different photos and asked them to make an ad . . . and so it went.

The intent was for all to advertise the sale but the problem was that no two publications made ads resembling each other, so the readers got no hint that the ads in all the publications were for the same sale. A potential buyer could easily read one ad and give some thought to going to that sale. The next ad might cause the buyer to think this was a different sale on the same date. And when he had seen three or four ads with no apparent connection except the date, he couldn't decide which sale to attend so he didn't go to any of them.

I took our best photo, which was a stakes-winning Thoroughbred sire. He was not represented in the sale but his full brother, that didn't run a lick, was the sire of several horses in the sale and several mares were bred to him. I featured this photo, listed all the great Quarter Horse sires of the age that were represented in the sale, no matter how many generations ago, featured the number of horses selling, the date and location even though these horses had little to brag about. I went to my favorite print shop and had them set the type and make the ad exactly as I wanted it. Then I made a photocopy of the finished ad for every publication we were using so they couldn't change a letter. I wanted every reader and every possible buyer to see exactly the same ad and get exactly the same message, time after time.

About a month before the sale, Dean asked me if we were still under budget. I assured him that we were and still had a few hundred dollars for classified ads in local newspapers. Then I asked him why he asked. "This is really a bad set of horses," he told me. "They just don't have much to talk about. But we have had more requests for catalogs than any sale I ever conducted. I have talked to horsemen in several places who told me we sure must have a big advertising budget—they saw our ads everywhere." I told Dean that's exactly what we were trying to do. I told him that anybody else holding a sale, using the old scatter system of advertising, would have to spend a ton to match us with our approach.

Advertising and catalog requests don't pay bills. Income from sales does. What would happen on sale day? When the day came, this second-rate bunch of horses had attracted the biggest sale crowd of the season. But what about the payoff? Dean had suggested to the seller that he hoped they would average $600 per head or higher. When the sale was done, the average was over $1,000 per head. Did my advertising idea work? We'll never know, but Dean made sure we followed the pattern in all future sales. No other sale managers copied the idea. Maybe they never paid enough attention to learn what we had done.

Professor for a Day

It must have started in about 1974. I didn't imagine that it would be repeated so I paid no attention to the date or trying to remember it. I began work as a field editor for *Western Livestock Journal* in April, 1962, as soon as Coral was old enough to be allowed on a United Airlines plane. In October I made my first visit to the Cal Poly campus in San Luis Obispo where I was a ring man for one of the first Cal Poly "test bull" sales. A few years later I began doing advertising and marketing consultation work for ranch owners and purebred breeders, leaving WLJ employment, but I continued my contacts with the Cal Poly people.

After I bought ads in the *California Cattleman* magazine for my breeder customers and got great buyer response, it was easy for Jack Parnell to get me to sell ads in the magazine. It was after our move to Auburn when I began seriously working for the magazine and my name appeared for the first time on the masthead in the September 1969 issue. I soon became a part owner and publisher of *California Cattleman*. This brought a lot of public contact.

One of the people I met at Cal Poly was Frank Fox, a beef specialist. He was in charge of the bull test and sale, and taught a course in managing purebred beef cattle herds for college junior and senior students. He arranged for the class to tour several of the state's leading purebred herds. He also invited guest lecturers, including breed association field men and specialists in several associated fields, to appear when they were in the area.

Almost all breeders agree that advertising is necessary for the financial success of a purebred operation but few people feel confident about their ability to either prepare an ad or plan an advertising program. My experience in handling advertising for other livestock products gave me confidence enough to at least try. It may have been a false security but there is so little competition in the field that it is easy for a practitioner to look good.

I don't know if Frank Fox talked to some of my consulting clients or maybe he thought my specialty would be useful for his students or maybe he couldn't get anybody else to show up for a given date. Anyway he invited me to come and talk to the class about purebred cattle marketing and advertising in particular. Frank said I had a unique way of expressing myself. I think it was just that when I couldn't think of exactly the right word, I'd talk around the issue using other words until I made my point. Anyway he invited me back once a year for about 15 years until he retired in 1988.

The pay was enjoyable if not fancy. Frank took me to lunch and I got a tour and update of the campus, the college farm (Rancho Escuela) and the current test bull progress. I was always scheduled in the spring, generally a few weeks after the new bulls were brought in to go on test. I always hoped one of the students might become both a purebred ranch manager and a believer of my advertising recommendations but I am not selling ads any more so that doesn't matter.

I accidentally impressed a prospective ranch buyer when it happened that three ranches we looked at during one day had managers who remarked that they remembered my "lecture" to their class. I knew one of the managers had been there but I was as surprised as my clients when the other two brought up the event. I never became sought-after as a speaker but it forced me to organize my thoughts and sharpen my presentation at least once a year.

The Wagon Wheel Motel

I couldn't guess how many "Wagon Wheel" motels I have seen in my years of travel up and down the country's highways. I have spent the night at enough Wagon Wheels to make them a national chain, but I doubt that a single one was a member of a club, much less a regional or national chain. In many years of travel, I have learned that events make a place more memorable than it would be otherwise. Such was the case on a snowy night in Mackay, Idaho.

I was traveling with Bob Neumeyer, who was manager of the Western States Angus Association. Bob had helped some Angus breeders sell some bulls to commercial cattlemen in the Arco-Mackay area of east-central Idaho. The breeders had told the buyers that they would help sell the Angus-cross calves at market time, many months later. The bulls had sold well and this was payday—the time to keep the promises made nearly two years earlier. Bob had scheduled a special feeder calf sale at the fairgrounds. To assure a good market, Bob, as sale manager, had advertised the feeder sale and personally invited many known cattle buyers.

In a totally separate incident, a breeder in northern Nevada had called and wanted help in selling some Angus heifers. We went to see him on our way to Idaho. The road was long and narrow but, following directions, we finally came to a country tavern and restaurant with cabins for hunters and fishermen. It was nearly dark when we arrived. The front door entered into the bar. Bob asked the bartender if he could get directions to find the man who owned the heifers. "That's me," the bartender answered, "and I've decided to keep the heifers." Then he added, "Since you're here and it's about supper time and there isn't any place to eat for a few hours, go in the other room and pick up a menu." We took his good advice.

There had been about a dozen patrons in the bar. There must have been two dozen diners in the other room. There were a few fishermen, a few hunters, linemen for a utility company and nearby ranch families having dinner. The dining room furniture was sort of early Nevada goodwill store style, some made of wood, some with plastic tops and chrome legs like a 1940s Sears catalog come to life. One table was long, with about a dozen chairs that could have been in a Basque eatery if it had had a checkered tablecloth. The typewritten menu was inserted in a folded plastic jacket. Nothing stood out except the insert suggesting diners ask their server about the dinner special. We asked.

The waitress/cook told us it was a steak and, when I asked what kind, she said, "It's a Spencer steak, one you don't see often but it's a real good front quarter steak that we get from a real good supplier." She was right, I rarely see a Spencer on a menu, but it's probably my favorite. Bob and I both ordered it. In a minute we were served minestrone soup, then a salad that would have made the best restaurants in Reno or Las Vegas jealous. The steak also lived up to what we had come to expect at this no-name place in the middle of a long road. After dinner we headed for Idaho and a night's sleep. Great food is where you find it.

The next day we drove to the fairgrounds in Mackay. This was late fall and the weather was cloudy and threatening. Cattlemen had unloaded some of their calves before we arrived and they continued into the afternoon as the overcast sky began spilling rain, then snow, on the valley. We had reservations at the Wagon Wheel Motel. With the cattle fed and bedded down and darkness arriving early in the area, we headed for the motel. With as many Wagon Wheel motels as I have seen over the years, I had never seen this one before, and I have never experienced one quite like it since.

Several people were present to help with the sale. Ken Troutt was the auctioneer, Bob was the sale manager, and I was there to serve as one of the ring men, along with another of the publication field men. The motel had a large room with four beds, a picnic table and a fireplace. Outside, the covered walkway was wide enough to protect a long stack of firewood, as well as the guests, from the weather. There was even a stack of firewood and kindling beside the fireplace. We accepted the invitation and built a fire.

Returning to the motel after dinner, we swapped tales and played cards at the picnic table beside the fireplace as snowflakes floated down outside. The storm waned during the night but we awoke the next morning to a dreary gray day that settled into a freezing drizzle. But an active crowd assembled to make a strong and rewarding sale for the ranchers who had bought Angus bulls on faith many months earlier. Little did they know they could have had

268

an even more rewarding experience had they spent the night at the Wagon Wheel Motel.

The New Field Representative

Some people are walking victims for practical jokers. Among these, a few who are unable to defend themselves are not fair game for jokers' barbs. Conrad Burns was the perfect combination, being both the perfect target and at the same time, capable of either defending himself or turning the charge on the joker. In a time when most livestock breed associations were fairly flush with funds, Conrad was hired fresh out of college by the *Polled Hereford World* magazine as their field representative for the West Coast and Intermountain area.

I don't remember the exact year when he came on the scene but it was in the mid- to late-1960s. He appeared as "regular" as a guy can be who has slightly drooping eyelids, strawberry blond hair and a Missouri drawl. But Conrad didn't blend into the background. He could see humor in almost any situation, always had a wisecrack, was ready with self-deprecating humor and making himself the "goat" in a conversation. Love him or hate him, his personality stood out in any crowd and he was rarely short of words.

While we found each other at the same events over a lot of geography, it was at the PI (Pacific International Livestock Exhibition) in Portland that I recall two occasions when Burns was speechless. One evening, after the livestock events of the day, Bob Neumeyer and I walked into the lounge at the Imperial Hotel to see if there were friends to join for dinner. Dorsey and Barbara McLaughlin, California Hereford breeders, Tom McCord, the Hereford field man, and someone else, who I do not recall, were sitting at a table. It was one of several tables spaced along an upholstered seat. Bob and I sat at the next table, slightly separated from the group.

Soon after we came in, Conrad Burns and another livestock field man came in and sat at the next table beyond us. A few minutes later, two apparent "ladies of the evening" came in and invited themselves to sit at the table with Burns and friend. Almost before it became less than comfortable to be near them, Barbara said, "Bob, come here for a minute, I want to ask you a question." When Bob responded, it left a space between our group and those at the next table. Then she called for me to come help settle the argument. When I went to join Bob in the seat beyond their table, she told us her plan. She suggested that we go to dinner, leaving Conrad and Joe with the girls and see if they would excuse themselves and come with us or stay with their new guests. They stayed—and were still there when we came back from dinner.

On another evening, some seven or eight members of the livestock crowd went to dinner together. We began talking about some event that had occurred, favorable for Polled Hereford cattle, so Conrad volunteered to buy dinner for the table. What he had not realized when he picked up the check was that Bob Neumeyer, who was sitting by him, had picked up his wallet when it fell out of his coat pocket and quietly handed it to me. Most of the diners from our table had stepped outside before Burns reached for his wallet at the cashier's table. Bob and I kept an eye on the developments and, just before he had to begin washing dishes, I stepped in to ask if this would help, producing his wallet. But he laughed it off and, fortunately for me, never held a grudge, which was the thing to do since the grandson of the Parker Ranch owner, Hawaii's largest holding, had by now paid the check.

What, you may wonder, would a guy like this do as he matured? He took a job as a public relations man for a major livestock market in Montana, then began a market service for all the Montana markets over a chain of radio stations. Once again, Burns got involved, this time about the performance of a county supervisor and he was challenged to run against the offending politician. He did, and won. He was soon involved in a statewide issue and was next challenged to run for United States Senate. The opposing Democrats laughed at his entry at the time, but he won anyway and represented cattlemen as well as any joker ever elected to that august body but he got associated too deeply with the wrong lobbyist and lost, after three terms, in 2006.

Passport to Almost Everywhere

It didn't particularly spark my interest in chemistry, but from a very early age I was fascinated by the photo process and the camera, which was a magic box for me. A couple of my aunts frequently had brought a Kodak Brownie box camera when they visited and if they were kind enough to send a print or two at some later date, I was thrilled out of my wits, just by the magic of the process, which I surely didn't understand. The first "big money" purchase I ever made was for an Argus C3 camera, for something in the area of $10, from the Ward's catalog.

Our home ranch was almost directly beneath the airline route from Omaha to Denver so the first few photos I ever took turned out to be mostly sky with an airplane-shaped dot in the middle, since my camera did not have a telephoto lens. I recall a print of skinned coyote carcasses (we were fur hunters) and one of my favorite feed team hitched to the wagon. I'd really love to have that photo of the team now but both the print and negative disappeared long ago.

In those early years, it took months for me to get enough money to buy a roll of film and more months before I could afford to get it processed. It never occurred to me that one day I might have a darkroom or the savvy to make the magic of a photograph. I continued to be amazed by the ability to snatch a scene from the air and put it on paper. It would be years before I learned that there was another kind of magic in a camera. I still had that old Argus camera in the Philippines but film was hard to find and, if not shot and processed quickly, some kind of mold or fungus spotted your exposures. But just having it was enough for our squadron commander to make me photo officer. That led to the post-war assignment to get aerial photos of all the Philippine Islands, meeting a real photographer and getting a look inside a darkroom, plus some serious shooting and processing.

When I got back to college after military duty, I took a course in journalism and, the next semester, my first course in photography. The U of N Journalism school opened new quarters with six great new darkrooms and student privileges to develop and print your own work for experience—for free. Can you imagine the Military Ball, the most prestigious social event on campus right after WWII, with all coeds praying for a date with a veteran wearing his glamorous dress uniform loaded with medals and campaign bars? What an occasion for a photo. Bill Poe and I, both photo students, got the picture concession, a bonanza for two guys working their way through college. We both found dates who wanted to go badly enough to help recruit customers and keep records for us.

The old, bulky Speed Graphic or other press camera was the standard medium when I was in college. Fine grain film was not yet in use and the large negative and powerful flashgun made press cameras reliable for those who used them for both photos and as a passport to places not open to people without such impressive, if bulky "credentials." I was admitted to numerous meetings, court trials, city council meetings and legislative hearings that would have never been available to me without an admission ticket or at least a press pass, often not available.

The camera could also be an instrument for mischief in the hands of a creative competitor. I remember an evening when Bill Poe and I were taking photos of student-produced skits for the Cornhusker yearbook. Photographers for the *Daily Nebraskan* and other campus publications were also present. The show reserved several front-row seats for photographers. All the photographers were early to find their seats. Then all except Bill and I left their press cameras to claim their seats and went outside to visit or smoke.

I noticed that two of the Speed Graphics had focal plane shutters. I tripped the shutters, leaving the black curtain in front of the film pack. They wouldn't get any photos unless they noticed the "trip" and these photographers didn't know cameras that well. Two others had new film packs with the protector tab showing. I tore off the tab without pulling it through so they were left with a black curtain in front of the film. Result: We had the only photos and when they later had to borrow our prints for their publications, had to give us credit lines. College stuff, maybe, but great fun at the time.

Who knows how many opportunities have passed unnoticed? It happens that two of my acquired talents combined into an unusual niche, working my way through college. After the war, married veterans returned to college to find that the GI bill and a working wife let them keep most of the bills paid if the student also had a part- or full-time job. This left little money for a night on the town, especially when the price of a movie ticket and the babysitter both needed to be paid.

I happened to drop by the apartment of a fraternity brother to find the young parents trying to get baby photos. They had neither the patience nor the camera to get good results so I suggested that I would try to babysit for them at a future date, and take the whole evening, if needed, to get some photos—for a reasonable price. I was first-born in a family of five, which qualified me as a sitter. I had a first-rate press camera so we set a date and I got lucky with the baby photos. Thus was born my babysitting-and-photo business. The journalism school furnished the darkroom and supplies. All I was out was the film and a few hours. I was paid for both jobs and I studied after the kid(s) went to sleep.

A camera was important on my first job out of college. Company literature and house organs need photos. As finer grain film came along in the late 1940s and early '50s, the 35 mm camera began to replace larger format—and bulkier—cameras in most areas. The 24- and 36-exposure rolls eliminated a lot of reloading so I switched, except for photos where I felt we'd need a lot of enlargement. Then when I went to the Livestock Journal, I got introduced to the Hasselblad. It shot a 12-exposure roll but, with its lens quality and the occasional need for color cover photos, that camera, my job and I really fit hand-in-glove.

While few people had ever seen a Hasselblad and didn't know what it was, you were almost automatically invited to the head of the line if you carried one. It just looked important. I can't remember paying admission at fairs, race tracks, livestock shows and many other places if I had a Hasselblad hanging on my neck and its bulky case in my hand. But I remember one time when the camera almost kept me out. I had taken photos of Governor Ronald Reagan at an agriculture meeting and again in his office when he met with staff members of the Livestock Marketing Association to designate "Livestock Marketing Month" in California. No big deal. But the California Cattlemen's Association scheduled its annual convention in Reno during the time between the end of Reagan's term as governor and his election as president.

As publisher of the *California Cattleman* magazine, I had been convention photographer for years. Reagan was to be the banquet speaker. I don't know whether his security people were furnished by the government or the Reagan-for-President committee. In any case they took their jobs and my

272

camera seriously. They wouldn't let me in the banquet hall until they had taken my case apart, examined every lens and gotten the OK from the CCA.

That was an occasion when I saw the normally glib Reagan at a total loss for words. He was well-regarded for his policies by most members of the Cattlemen's Association and its president, Jack Owens, a plainspoken rancher from Red Bluff. I was seated at the first row of seats below the head table to make it easy to photograph the speakers. I was poised for the shot as Jack remarked in his introduction, "Governor, we cattlemen thought you were a pretty good governor and we admired your administration. But I have to tell you," speaking of Reagan's successor, Jerry Brown, who had few friends among the cattlemen, "it sure didn't take much to replace you." Reagan sputtered for a few seconds then he finally said, "Thank you, I think." I took my pictures and sat down, not knowing whether it was the Hasselblad, or whether the security goons would have felt so threatened by a less imposing camera but we really got noticed on that occasion.

Then there was the time when not "wearing" that camera was a gift from mother luck. It was the Cattlemen's convention in Oakland. I had been taking candid photos during committee meetings and, with the day's work over, most of the conventioneers headed toward their rooms to freshen up before dinner. I was walking down the hall, by chance with a group of cattlemen from Madera County.

Someone suggested that I come to the rooms with them to visit over some refreshment. I accepted their invitation but said that I wanted to take the camera and case down to lock them in the convention office and get rid of the load. "Madera County has a block of rooms down this hall, just knock on any door," said Mitch Lasgoity.

I left them, walked about 100 feet down the hall to the office, unloaded my camera gear and began to walk back to the Madera invitation but someone asked a question and I got into a discussion for a few minutes before leaving the office. As I turned down the hall toward the Madera County rooms, the conventioneers began coming out of the rooms into the hallway in total confusion and a bunch of policemen came rushing down the hall from the outside exit.

I turned to look in the other direction and saw more police coming from the main hallway. What had I missed in those few minutes, I wondered. It turned out that four street thugs had obtained entry, even though all outside doors needed a key to enter, and were waiting for the cattlemen to return. They robbed all the Madera County people of wallets, money and jewelry— at gunpoint—then had tied them up and fled. It was pure luck that I didn't show up with a big camera and without time to convince those armed robbers I had not done any shooting.

The Hasselblad generally got me by. And it took great pictures that could be enlarged to cover the side of a truck or a billboard. I haven't shot mine in years. It's too big for a charm bracelet and too expensive for a keepsake. I have made the change to digital. I don't carry a camera for admission any more, and it seems that images will be digital and online. I like some of my digital camera's features but I rather miss the go-to-the-front-of-the-line treatment I got with the Hasselblad.

I Just Stumbled Into It

After a few years as a field editor for *Western Livestock Journal* and doing consulting work for ranchers and purebred breeders, I began working with Jack Parnell, who had the contract to publish the *California Cattleman*, the house organ magazine for the California Cattlemen's Association. His livestock auction business was growing and he didn't need the magazine so he was glad to have me become a partner and later to sell me full ownership.

In selling advertising, taking photos and doing all the things necessary to publish a cowmen's magazine I met a rancher who one day asked me to help him solve a problem. His good hired man was going to retire, none of his kids wanted to ranch and he was past retirement age. "Who do you know who needs a good 500-cow ranch?" he asked me. A few days later I met another rancher who complained that the city was surrounding him and vandals were cutting his fence and shooting his cattle. "Where can I find a good 500-cow ranch?" he asked. Being the good, helpful publication field man, I got them together.

I had spent several years getting to know California's ranchers and driving California's back roads. I made several referrals and even had one buyer criticize me, saying that the ranch I told him about wasn't quite as good as he thought it to be when he bought it. I decided that I had let several thousand dollars of real estate commissions get away and if I was going to get blamed, I surely should get paid. I went to a real estate school, passed the test and got my license.

When I was notified that I had passed the license exam, I began looking for a broker where I could do an apprenticeship. I called several people who claimed to be "ranch" brokers but I wasn't convinced that they had either the background or current contacts to be called a "ranch" anything. They sold residential acreage properties and wouldn't know a real ranch on a bet. I had just spent several months working with Jack Linkletter. I knew that the Linkletters owned ranches and, even if they didn't have a broker they liked, they might know some that I should avoid. I called Jack and told him my situation. He said it was interesting that I had called. Yes, he had a broker that he liked and had used for several years. They would be on the phone in a few minutes to discuss a pending offer and, while he didn't know if Bob Koetitz wanted any new salesmen, they would visit and he promised me that Bob would return my call.

274

Bob called and after a few visits we made a deal. I ran a branch office for his Western Ranches firm for about three years. It was a good relationship and I could advertise my listings in my own ad in my own magazine, so to speak, since I published the California Cattlemen's Association magazine. My first listing was a ranch southeast of Sacramento but my first attempted sale involved a new listing from some people I had met at an Angus cattle event and the offer came from a man I met at a Polled Hereford sale. The buyer had sold his furniture store in Eureka. He wanted to move from the coast to a ranch in the North Central Valley. When I showed him the Barnes ranch it was love at first sight. He would be selling a highly improved 40 acres at Eureka and wanted to take that money to buy the Barnes ranch.

Before I got over to list the 40 acres, a neighbor who owned 200 acres of meadow at Fort Dick wanted to sell it and buy the 40. That meant that technically, I would sell the Barnes ranch to the man with the 200 acres and all the other transactions were "exchanges" for tax purposes. I was such a novice I didn't know it would be difficult at best and probably impossible to make the deal. I explained it to my broker and he said "Go for it," knowing, but not saying, it would be pure luck if it closed but—what the heck—he knew that I needed the experience.

In a little more than a month, the deals were all done and we closed escrow on the whole row of dominos. When I went to pick up my commission check at the Western Ranches office, my broker asked me if I knew what we had just done. Of course I didn't realize or understand everything that had happened but it was done and I was glad to get my check. It was then that Bob told me that when I told him what was involved, he didn't think we had a chance to close the complicated, three-ranch deal. Almost every time he had tried to make one of those double-jointed sales they had fallen apart, but he knew I'd get some valuable experience even though he knew I wouldn't get a paycheck. I was lucky. I got both the experience and the check. I did not realize at this time just how hard it was to make such exchanges, under normal conditions.

At Bob's urging, I prepared for, and passed the broker's test. I was later to learn that there was probably not another broker in California who knew both ranching and real estate as well, nor one more understanding and objective about my move to establish my own company. Recalling the complicated sale of the Barnes ranch to Guy Libera, I remember a similar situation some years later when Dave Van Cleve began working for me as a salesman. He needed a good ranch to sell and I had noticed a "for sale by owner" sign a few weeks earlier on a property in our home county. I didn't have time to follow up, but Dave did.

As it turned out, the ranch was approximately 5,000 acres, the remainder of the Whitney Ranch, and it was owned by a Beverly Hills attorney and two Litton Corp. executives. They had purchased it several years earlier and planned to hold and sell later at a big profit. The market had turned bad on them and now they seemed ready to cut their losses. In a short time Dave made the sale and went to escrow with a local rancher who had a reputation as a demanding landowner who would sue with the slightest excuse. I warned Dave that we had just walked into the lion's den, that he would get some experience but to double check every move and get everything in writing so we'd have perfect records if we got sued. I could not have imagined a worse buyer-seller combination but I felt we had to go on. After all, we were talking about the commission on more than a million dollars. At that time, there were not many million-dollar ranches.

I had indigestion almost every day that the ranch was in escrow, certain we'd get a ton of trouble, probably sued, and with no commission check to pay for it. I warned Dave it would never close but that since we were in the deal, we just had to watch every detail. I found an incorrect easement listed in the preliminary title report but pointed it out to the escrow officer before we took a copy to the buyer or seller. He was mightily relieved. This turned out to be an unexpected blessing. The City of Lincoln had condemned the right-of-way for a water line to cross the ranch to bring water from the Placer County Water Agency to the City of Lincoln's water department.

The buyer wanted a detailed map of the proposed water line location. This could have been a problem for engineers and difficult to produce but the title company was most cooperative in furnishing the map, in repayment, so to speak, for my saving them from earlier embarrassment. We had other minor glitches but all were quickly solved. Still I kept telling Dave that it would probably not close but, like the complicated Barnes Ranch sale, nothing could knock this escrow off course and it closed exactly on schedule—and without a lawsuit. I am still convinced that if an escrow is supposed to close, you can't stop it—and if for some reason it is destined to not close, nobody can bring it together. I won't mention the ones that "got away" and found some excuse to avoid closing when they appeared at the outset to be much better prospects with more important reasons to close.

Little did I imagine when I got a real estate license so I could get paid for "referring" ranches to potential buyers that I was really beginning a career change. I finally discovered that if I had intended to be twins, there would have been two of me. I was both magazine publisher and real estate agent from 1971, when I got my license until the end of 1985, when I made the switch out of the magazine and into real estate exclusively. All of my previous jobs prepared me to be a ranch broker. Even my ads in the *California Cattleman* magazine went to my primary clientele—without having to pay for them. Now I would have to pay for my advertising.

276

International Cattlemen's Expo

We had moved to Auburn in September 1968. I continued my consulting and livestock photography work and had begun to work with Jack Parnell who had the contract to publish the *California Cattleman* magazine. I was involved in writing some presentations for the Livestock Marketing Congress which was to be held in Monterey in May 1969. Little did I know that another project was to fall in my lap and the two turned out to be related.

I got a surprise phone call from John Chohlis. Any call I got from John would be a surprise unless he really needed my talents. He had been editor of the *Western Livestock Journal* when I worked there and we got to know each other as well as needed but we had both moved on. John had been hired by Jack Linkletter to help manage their family livestock interests, which turned out to be something neither of us had ever imagined. John was a city kid who had a graduate degree in Range Management and several years of selling ads to livestock breeders and writing stories about ranch operations but not a day of hands-on ranch management. I wasn't mad at John. I had just learned to protect my turf, that if we were working at the same place, he would claim credit for every good thing you did and blame you for all his goofs, when possible. The topic never came up but I'm sure that John knew that I knew. We could work together but I insisted that my area of responsibility be well defined and insulated from John's influence.

As it turned out, it didn't matter. Jack Linkletter was a fast learner. I once described him as someone who could hear you begin to describe an operation he'd never heard of but that he learned so fast he could finish your first paragraph. He heard somewhere that the livestock industry needed a new forum to establish the value of breeding animals by some criteria other than eyeball rating of their conformation compared to a so-called ideal animal.

The relatively new criteria of performance data, which recorded weights at various ages and rate of gain, hit a responsive note for some stockmen but it mainly confused what industry leaders thought they knew about livestock breeding. Linkletter wanted to combine the best existing criteria for evaluating cattle breeding stock and show it to stockmen, worldwide, if such a combined system could be simplified enough to be understood. Jack and John were sure it was needed. But the concept was too different from standard stock shows to give any other thinking person much confidence that it could be done.

As Jack imagined it, we would hold a "traditional" cattle show but it would be modified by something neither John nor I had imagined. Linkletter had an idea for a show based on genetic growth and carcass traits in addition to traditional eyeball appraisal. He also planned for a giant trade show where all types of new ranch machinery and technology would be on exhibit along with seminars and specialty clinics. He wanted to reproduce the video auction that I had invented for the Livestock Marketing Congress, which he had attended. When I told them I liked the whole idea, I was invited to Los Angeles to discuss the details. Did I think it was possible? Could we attract a large number of livestock and machinery exhibits and could we attract a large crowd? Was the idea realistic and possible?

If yes to all of the above, they wanted me to produce the show program including the sale of advertising to livestock breeders, machinery and equipment manufacturers nationwide. How much manpower would it take to handle the catalog? Jack asked me. I told him I felt that two experienced people working full-time from now until showtime could do it. He began to squirm. I added that I felt one good person could probably do it, and as he became less tense, I assured him in my most confident tone that I could work part-time for 40 percent commission and get the job done. "It takes as much time as you have," I explained. He had never mentioned my pay previously but he accepted my proposal on the spot, and I think that may actually have been the moment when Jack's idea became a viable project.

Within days, I got the go-ahead to begin contracting exhibitors and selling advertising. Jack had made tentative arrangements to hold the show in Las Vegas in early December, 1969. December is the time when casinos look for any kind of activity, even at reduced rates, because people stay away in droves. As we neared showtime and I had sold enough program ads to earn most of a year's income, Jack hired me to supervise the commercial exhibitors at the show to see that they all found the space that we had reserved for them and to help keep all of them happy.

This was all new for me but interesting. This was the first time the newly patented Melroe Bobcat, later to become a construction industry standard, had been seen outside North Dakota. The Melroe people made a hit with cattlemen by using the machine to clean the bedding and droppings from the stalls and alleys in the livestock area. Little did we foresee the number of these flexible, short-turning machines that would eventually be at work in nearly every feedlot or big livestock handling facility across the country and expand to every construction site. The equally new Gyrocopter flew exhibition flights daily but I never saw one in public again.

Kenny Vaughan, the Polled Hereford field man, was hired to supervise the livestock exhibits. The show drew a record number of commercial exhibitors and was one of the largest livestock shows in the country but it did not show the long-term growth possibilities that Jack Linkletter wanted so he turned the show over to Kenny, who held two more shows but, since it did not produce a wide industry consensus on changing methods of evaluating cattle, especially breeding stock, Kenny ended the show. It was interesting to be involved in this piece of livestock history, even though it was not to become a permanent fixture in that form.

278

RBSK

I know a lot of people who live at the end of dirt roads . . . and a lot more who live somewhere between the paved road and the house at the very end. When I was growing up in Logan County, Nebraska, there was not an inch of paved road in the county. We all lived along, or at the end of dirt roads. Our neighbors, the McPherrin family, stretched their fences and gates so tight that most potential trespassers found them intimidating without knowing that Old Mac had a reputation for being as unfriendly as a locked gate. I don't recall a single padlock on a gate. But I was growing up in the 1920s and '30s. I left home and started college in 1941. Things have changed in America since that time when most of the country's population was still rural. In Logan County it still is very rural.

California has a lot of terrain not well suited to building roads. When the early settlers found the best place for a team to pull a wagon from where they were to where they wanted to be, that became a road. There might be one family and one ranch that used the road or, in some cases, there might be a dozen ranches along that road as time passed and more settlers arrived. All the ranches along the road have easements allowing them to pass over the owner's property. When the people who lived along the road tired of trespassers, salesmen, poachers and other undesirables, they locked the gate.

I have seen many gates that had a chain and half a dozen locks (one for each property owner) affixed. An old friend, aircraft engineer Gage Irving, invented a lock for use on swinging metal gates that had flippers along a rod. Each flipper could be locked separately using different locks but when the padlock on any one flipper was unlocked, the locking bar could slide back far enough for the gate to clear the post. Copies of that system are now found on many of the gates mounted along hill and mountain ranch roads.

If we wanted to drive to a rancher's home when I was growing up, we just went there. But locks have made ranch brokers creative. We have to get a key to drive to a ranch headquarters today in many cases. When we get a listing to sell a ranch we are given a key to the lock on the entry gate. Needless to say, we protect the key and allow it to be used only for business. Loss or casual use of keys has helped the sale of combination locks. The owner can give the combination for his lock, instead of a key, to welcome guests. When the combination falls into any unwelcome possession, the owner simply changes the combination and begins giving the new combination to welcome guest, denying admittance to "spoilsports."

Every ranching community has a series of "dumb padlock" stories that are told at feed stores, sale barns or wherever ranch people gather, about losing a key, forgetting the combination or finding that the gate just didn't open that day. I remember one occasion when a padlock served as a "ranch country" IQ test. We had a ranch listed for sale in the Coast Range foothills. It was several thousand acres fenced into several fields. The ranch road went through all of the fields and all of the fences had gates that were closed during the grazing period. Some of the fields were leased to a sheep rancher who had a herder living in a camp wagon. The herder had been told that we would be crossing the ranch and what kind of car we drove. I once stopped to visit with the herder but his English was no better than my Spanish. But somehow I felt that beyond the language problem, the herder was really not too bright and mentioned it to the owner. He agreed. He said that his herder had trouble in remembering how to open the combination locks . . . all set to open on four zeros.

No matter how well keys or combinations are protected, there can be times when I need to be on a ranch and somehow my combination numbers or padlock key does not open the lock. In case such an event occurs, I always carry an "open sesame" RBSK (ranch broker's skeleton key), which looks a lot like a pair of long-handled bolt cutters. Early in my career as ranch broker I learned an important lesson about the use of an RBSK from a veteran.

Harley May was a ranch broker in Oakdale. He was a former rodeo bulldogging champ, about 6-foot-4 and on the impatient side. He was preparing to show one of his listings to me and was surprised to find that the owner had put a new padlock on the entry gate. Harley had purchased a new set of bolt cutters for just such an occasion. He swore as he placed the jaws on the padlock and reached out to the end of the 3-foot-long handles. As he squeezed, a jaw from the new cutter snapped and zinged into the air. In that one lesson, I learned that, when necessary to cut, make it the chain instead of the tempered steel lock.

Don't Ask a Cow

Everybody who works with livestock and especially people who keep up with "impartial research" can assure you that genes breed true and that if it works in Bakersfield it will work in Arroyo Grande. If you have worked with livestock very long you know that a cow is not capable of being psyched out. She is not going to respond better to a placebo than the real drug. So be it. I happened to witness a situation that proves that the things we have always known to be true may not be true at all. This series of events came in the late 1970s and early '80s when Tejon Ranch management decided to terminate the purebred Hereford herd. The livestock manager, Harold Thurber, had built a great cowherd. It was one of the pioneer performance-tested herds in California. I had been present at several "weigh days" and had taken numerous photos at Tejon as a witness to their performance testing program.

Huasna Ranch owners had purchased several bulls from Tejon, liked their performance and had expressed an interest in starting their own purebred herd. When Tejon made the decision, the herd was sold as a unit to Huasna.

280

Each animal in this performance program was weighed every year and each calf was weighed at 205 days of age and again at 365 days. Mothers of good performers are kept in the herd and those with lesser performance are culled. After a few years of this kind of testing, certain cows and cow families become obvious foundation cows, the kind to build a herd on. Tejon and Huasna agreed to have Harold continue as a consultant to help the new owners produce good bulls, some of which Tejon wanted to buy back for their commercial cowherd. He asked me to witness his consulting work and follow the progress and outcome of the herd in its new quarters.

Unknown to me at the time, Richard and Bert Snedden, at Rancho Santiago, had used Tejon bulls for years and were delighted that the herd was being held as a unit so they would continue to have a good bull source from a fairly small piece of California so the bulls would be acclimated to their range conditions. They just kept buying these bloodlines from Huasna. Tejon Ranch was at the top of the "Grapevine," the curvy stretch of the Tehachapi Mountains that lay between Bakersfield and the Los Angeles

Photo of Tejon Ranch registered Hereford cowherd on ranch pasture near the top of Tejon Pass on I-5 north of Los Angeles. Tejon was the largest privately owned property in California (283,000 +/- acres in 1964).

basin. At a quarter of a million acres, Tejon was the largest contiguous privately owned ranch in California. It is about 100 miles, as the crow flies, from the Tejon headquarters to the Huasna Ranch. Snedden's ranch is almost in the middle between the other two but just north of a straight line. There are similar range conditions at the three locations except that much of Tejon is from 3,000 to over 4,000 feet elevation. Huasna is in the mountain foothills at about 1,000 feet elevation with some coastal influence weather, including frequent morning fog. The Snedden ranch lay between the two ranches. All are in the low-rainfall area near Bakersfield.

After a few years, a partnership break-up ended the Huasna operation and the herd was sold at auction. As Richard Snedden told me, they decided to buy some of the best performing cows from both the years at Tejon and Huasna and start their own purebred herd so they could keep using bulls from these bloodlines that were acclimated to the area. Performance records were public information so it would be easy to see which of the cows they wanted to start the Snedden herd. They were surprised to find that a dozen or so of the best performers at Tejon were in the mediocre group at Huasna and some of the so-so cows at Tejon became performance leaders at Huasna.

"How were we to decide which cows to buy?" Richard asked me. They bought most of the top performers from both locations on sale day. They also bought some of the "middle of the herd" cows. Surprisingly, most of the top performers for Sneddens had not been "best" at either previous ranch. Since the bottom cows were sold as culls from both Tejon and Huasna, we never learned how they would do at Santiago. Maybe science teaches us a lot of things that we have long known to be true but that are not really true when the rubber meets the road. These old Hereford cows showed us that we don't have to modify test conditions very much to play havoc with the results. Is this also true in testing other things we've "always known to be true"?

The Blue Ribbon Idea

When I arrived in Los Angeles to begin work as a field editor for the *Western Livestock Journal* in 1962, the field services director took me to visit a few of the larger customers, purebred livestock breeders who bought ads in our publication on a more-or-less regular basis. He gave me a brief history of the ranches, the herds and the owners as we made our calls. Then he sent me out with a list of breeders in the area that might buy advertising to promote the sale of their breeding stock. One of the first solo calls I made was at Blue Ribbon Ranch.

I have no idea why I picked this name from the list of prospective ad buyers but it was high on the alphabetical list, and by pure chance, a good choice. I met Walt McRobb, one of the best known of the veteran Scottish-bred herdsmen in the business. He was slim and 50-ish with a craggy face but he had a gentle voice and manner. He had an eye for cattle and could pick a prospect in the pasture and make it into a show champion. And unlike numerous herdsmen or ranch managers, Walt was willing to defer most management decisions to the owner. This was a good decision in the case of Blue Ribbon Ranch because the owner was A.D. "Andy" Anderson, a take-charge kind of guy who began making decisions early in life as a half-orphan kid selling newspapers on the steps of the Brown Palace Hotel in Denver.

Andy craved attention from anybody who could make Southern California breeders feel they belonged. For the moment, I filled this need. Andy had a booming business in aircraft parts and owned a couple of blocks of real estate along Century Boulevard that led to the main entrance to Los Angeles International Airport, but his ranch, with its herd of cattle, was his primary recreation and ego object. Finding someone to put his name in print, even if he had to pay for it, was the answer to his prayer. He subscribed to

282

the breed Association magazine but had rarely seen its representative. When I arrived to sell him an ad it was as if he had found a friend for life.

When his ad appeared in the *Western Livestock Journal*, my publication, he called to ask permission to run our ad in the *Polled Hereford World*, his breed's national publication. This was a big surprise for me so I asked my boss, who gave me the OK. I didn't know it yet, but this was the preview to a new career for me. I suggested a couple of changes to make the ad better for a national audience and Andy was in business. A few weeks later he asked me how much I would charge to set up a year-long advertising program, make his ads, etc. I asked my boss if I could do this in my spare time and got his blessing. Then I had to decide how much to charge.

Andy couldn't keep a secret if his ego was involved and in a few weeks other breeders began asking if I would do their ads. In fact, he became an unofficial recruiter for my new cause. With this kind of start and in an industry that had no "ad agencies" to design ads or project a year's ad program including the budget, it was easy to compete with the other area publications. My competitors—ad salesmen with other papers—recommended me. I was doing their work for them. I pushed my publication first but I got paid for doing all their ads.

Western Livestock Journal, my employer, published a weekly livestock newspaper, which was pretty much straight livestock production and marketing news and a monthly magazine, which was more dedicated to feature stories. The magazine had a horse section with lots of stallion ads in advance of the breeding season and continuing well into the spring. The horse-racing industry uses January 1 as the birthday for foals, even if they come in June or December. This gives an advantage at the race track to early foals, and as a result we sold a lot of ads in the fall and winter months to help mare owners decide early which sire to select for each mare.

It's difficult to have a good livestock ad without good photos. The Livestock Journal had a 4-by-5-inch Speed Graphic camera in their storage room that none of the employees knew how to operate. I had cut my teeth on one in my first college photojournalism course so it was mine to use and I used it frequently, especially for posed horse photos and later for magazine cover photos. They also outfitted each of the field editors with a Hasselblad camera. I had to get checked out on it but the Hasselblad could produce work unmatched for quality. I began doing freelance photography for both horse and beef cattle breeders. My employer encouraged this, feeling that if I took the picture, I had the first and best chance to sell an ad. After a few months I began to sense some beef cattle breeders were beginning to put more emphasis on rate of gain, cost of gain and other performance traits than on show ring success which had long been the major factor in determining the value of purebred livestock.

This was the first time I had really seen show ring success as "opinion of a judge on a given day" contrasted with rate of gain and carcass value. And while it was possible to have cattle that were successful performers in both the show ring and as physical and/or genetic performers, they were surely more than twice as difficult to breed. It seemed to me that all the beef breeds were at crossroads. Were they going to rely on show ring results to decide the conformation of cattle or would they increase the attention to the market evaluation of the beef carcass as the guide to the future? I felt that every breeder should have a goal and make his own decisions but I didn't need to know which was most important. I could write good ads for both.

I decided that I could have more fun and income from a number of regular customers paying me a monthly retainer fee (plus overtime charges) doing advertising work than having a job with a monthly paycheck. And I'd have time for free-lance photography and livestock mortality insurance on the side. I made a list of leading breeders in the west. I picked a handful—the best of both cattle and horse breeders—and began my contacts. I was surprised how easy it was to sell the idea when I showed them ads I had created for other breeders and explained the concept. It had not occurred to most breeders that they could or should have thoughtful, long-range programs to promote the sale of the breeding stock they produced. Had I invented a new business or a new industry?

Breeders who built their herds mostly on the basis of the show ring results of their herds and were generally more likely to be serious advertisers. Pictures of champions make potential buyers aware of your herd and to accept the show ring results as measures of value. But serious competition was building from breeders who felt their customers would profit more from the economic factors such as fertility, rate of gain and carcass value than from winning blue ribbons. There were not many "performance" minded customers in my Livestock Journal territory. The owners rarely looked deeper than the blue ribbons; not into the actual profit a rancher made if the stock he raised produced a better carcass in less time and/or on less feed. I felt this "carcass judging" and ranching for profit would one day rule the industry so I began seeking out breeders who paid more attention to the scales and rate of gain than on the blue ribbon lovers.

One of the happy accidents from my early work with the *Western Livestock Journal* had been my acquaintance with the Borror families. Brothers Mark and Dale Borror were breeders of Holstein dairy cattle but their respective sons, Bruce and Bill, were more interested in their Angus beef herd. Dale and his son, Bill, chose to move from the south-central Tulare County area of Springville, to the northern California area of Tehama County, where they would specialize in Angus. Mark and son Bruce stayed on the home ranch with their breed-leading Holstein herd but Bruce also continued the Angus. Management people at the *Livestock Journal* told me

284

that I should work with Borrors' outstanding herd of Holsteins with ads for the *Western Dairy Journal* but their big, plain Angus weren't much in current breed circles. Be nice to them, I was told, but their kind of Angus beef cattle aren't very popular today.

I got the list of "performance" breeders for all the beef breeds when I started my new ad agency work and began making ranch visits, especially on "weigh day" so I would know which herds had proof of performance. In herd after herd, for year after year, I was the only "industry" person present for "weigh day" at performance-minded breeders except the County farm advisor and generally (but not always) the field man for that breed. I made these visits solely for my own information but they convinced most of the performance-minded breeders that I was "ahead of the curve" in being interested in their welfare. The statistics convinced me that Tehama Angus, as the Borrors named their herd, was the Angus breed leader in California, if not the country.

At one "weigh day," Bill showed me a set of weanling heifers from their spring-calving herd. He told me he had decided to discontinue spring calving and would sell these, the last of their "spring calvers." He gave me permission to sell them, about 25 or 26 head. The price would be top of the market in those days, suggesting $325 per head, plus commission, but the buyer would have to take at least 20 to get that price. A few days later I made a routine ranch call on a breeder, Paul Pagliarulo, who I had never met before. He asked me where he could get a top set of heifers to build a herd on. What a coincidence. I told him about the heifers, he came to look at the heifers and their weights and decided to buy them—all similarly bred and made a great foundation herd. I got a nice commission on the sale and the sale assured Bill Borror that I would be a valuable team player so he hired me as his advertising and marketing consultant. But it took five years for me to convince Bill that he could hold a successful one-breeder annual bull sale.

Bill had long wanted to hold his own Annual Angus Bull Sale but he felt that if the commercial cattlemen did not attend in good numbers and pay good prices for the bulls, the herd's reputation and marketing future would surely suffer. Up to that time there had never been an Angus breeder bull sale attempted in California. I was convinced that these cattle were good and that Angus were being accepted well enough that we could hold a successful bull sale. After five years of advertising, using Borror genetics and my photos and wile, we held the first one-breeder, on-the-ranch Angus bull sale in California on September 28, 1978, heralded with the line, "35 Years of Performance." It was a success by all standards. Our relationship continued for five more years until the Tehama Angus Bull Sale was firmly established as the industry leader and I told Bill he didn't need me any longer. I began spending that time on real estate and Borrors have never had a bad sale in the 30-plus years of bull sales since.

285

It was fun, but challenging, to sell a service that did not, and never had existed. One of the first on my list was Bill Wolfe, the Wallowa, Oregon breeder of Polled Herefords with probably the best and one of the nation's largest herds of that breed. He wanted to have a ranch bull sale to sell most of the year's produce in one day instead of having to keep someone on the ranch every day of the year in case a bull buyer happened to come along. I convinced Bill that it would probably take five years to make a full change. He became my first client from outside California and/or my *Western Livestock Journal* sales area to pay me a monthly retainer.

Another early Angus herd among my consulting customers was Double Diamond Ranch at Reno, owned by Wilbur May of the May Company department store family. He knew merchandising better than he did cattle breeding but he knew a good bit about marketing and he had a manager and a herdsman who knew the cattle side of the business. When I told him about my service he didn't argue for a minute about the price for my services. He simply said, "It's about time" and asked me to tell him how much each of the top five Angus herds in the west spent for ads. I itemized the top spenders by scanning livestock publications, measuring the ads and multiplying by the cost per column inch and reported back. He told me to prepare a budget to spend more than any of the others and to work with his ranch managers to decide what we wanted to say and where to say it." They weren't all that easy . . . nor that marketing savvy.

The list of livestock-oriented operations that used my advertising services grew and came to include a couple of Quarter Horse breeders and some livestock marketing and auction firms. I was determined to only work with cream-of-the-crop people and it seemed that I would find a saturation point fairly soon, considering that there is a limited difference between herds as developed by different breeders. It seemed it would soon become difficult to find credible reasons for a buyer to consider one herd over another. I was surprised—and pleased—to learn that my accepting a herd gave it credibility among buyers. And I learned it the hard way. I helped a herdsman for one of the "leading breeders" sort their bull crop into three pens (good, better, best) based on my appraisal of each animal's value. When I brought a potential bull buyer to the ranch a few days later I was shocked to find several bulls had been moved to higher priced pens than I had graded them. That was the first customer that I ever "fired."

Another surprise was the change in places to advertise. The *California Cattleman* was a monthly newsletter published by the Cattlemen's Association for its members with a few pages of "institutional" or "good will" ads but not a lively read. Jack Parnell, an old friend, saw promise and got a contract to publish it, sell ads and bring in some lively editorial. I soon saw it as a "comer" and began placing ads in it for my customers and got instant results. Almost as soon as this happened, Jack needed an ad salesman to help compensate for the time he was spending to promote his growing livestock auction business. We had just moved to Auburn and I had been impressed with the results of my ads in the *California Cattleman* so I was glad to join up.

Both our businesses grew and I took over his publisher contract. I kept all the phases of the business going for a while. Finally the Cattlemen's Association got a new publisher for the magazine after 16 years and I produced my last edition of the magazine in December, 1985. I continued to create ads for a few loyal consulting customers.

I got one of my best customers by suggesting that he buy an ad congratulating his competitor whose bull had just been made Champion over my future client's bull. The Pedretti Hereford Ranch had shown both the champion single bull and the champion pen-of-three bulls for several consecutive years at the Red Bluff Bull Sale, one of the west's criterion bull sales. In January 1982, it looked as if Pedretti would have the champion again but the judges made a competitor champion instead. Pedretti's bull was the reserve, or second-place, bull. I suggested to owner Gino Pedretti that he buy an ad with a picture of both bulls, congratulating the first bull to top them in many years, with photos of Pedretti's champions for the past several years. He liked the idea, ran the ad and got many favorable comments from other breeders, customers and potential customers.

When I approached him about becoming a regular client he said OK and some 25 years later I still did his ads, along with the other top Hereford breeder, Bruce Orvis of the Orvis Cattle Co., the oldest registered Hereford herd in California, which dated back to 1918. He heard about the Red Bluff "congratulations" ad shortly after it was printed and, with an oral "non-competitive" OK from both herd owners, hired me to do his work too. As of this writing in 2006, I still handle their ads. Over the years, as my real estate business grew, I discontinued working with all the other breeders except for taking occasional photos of somebody's horses or cattle. Whoever said there aren't a lot of ways to make a living? I'd never have learned this in college!

The Troubled Years

We were on a roll, so to speak. Both our daughters were getting good grades in school, the *California Cattleman* magazine was doing well, my relatively new ranch real estate business was being accepted and I was getting a share of cattle ranch sales and we had moved to a new home that we had both planned and built. Moving to Auburn had been a good decision, it appeared. I considered hiring a field man to help me sell magazine advertising, to help with livestock sales work and begin real estate school. I had been working hard and needed a spare tire to both let me concentrate on new business and have a little time off. I interviewed recent Cal Poly grads. Nobody with the proper credentials seemed to be interested in doing my job until I asked a few friends and discovered that one had changed his company's sales structure that left no position for a long-time employee that seemed to have the experience I wanted. He needed a job and I had found my man.

He learned our business and made friends quickly. I had time to follow up ranch sale leads that I would have previously had to forget because of an over-promised schedule of my time. Business continued strong, my new hire became an accomplished advertising salesman and we kept the *California Cattleman* magazine as a leader in the field. Then with no warning I found that we were short of money in the office bank account. Some of our regular advertisers had not paid their bills. When I began checking each one I learned that they were paying my salesman, who had been spending our advertising dollars—getting some of the customers to loan him money to finance nights of partying when he was allegedly on business, spending days and nights away from home—to be repaid when we ran their next ad—and we were now closing in on pay day. I faced him over it and he confessed that he had "borrowed" money from customers but said he could not repay them or me and he was too embarrassed to go to our customers and explain the situation or even to stay with me if I gave the explanation to our customers.

He resigned and went to Mexico. A few months later he suffered a fatal heart attack. I was stuck with paying the printer and keeping my business afloat. I had to make ends meet somehow, and I didn't know for the moment how it would work out. I fell behind on house payments, office rent and our magazine printing bill. All of our creditors were understanding and stayed the course. I never knew whether they were "good guys" or simply figured it was their best and/or only chance to get paid, but we had a few tough years. I didn't think I had been a spendthrift but maybe life had been too good. I could see no choice but to keep on keeping on and we were finally able to close a few good-sized ranch sales and with the commissions earned I was able to pay off the creditors and customers who had loaned money or extended needed credit to me during those dark and troubled years.

The Cattle Show with a "Classic" Moment

Si Williams, one of the leading livestock auctioneers in the Northwest, undertook the management of the first "Western Charolais Classic" show and sale to be held in Caldwell, Idaho, in March, 1967. Charolais is the name of a breed of beef cattle imported from Europe, primarily France, and many of the first American breeders were located in the Pacific northwestern states, along with a good number from Utah. I had done a little work in the northwestern area with a few consulting customers, including livestock photography and livestock insurance sales, but was not widely known in the area and we were still living in a Los Angeles suburb. I had met Si at a few of the livestock sales but we did not have a long association so I was surprised to be asked to be the official photographer for the show and sale. Or maybe everyone else said NO.

Si had covered most of the bases—too many, it turned out—in helping me do my job. He had contacted a professional photo studio in Caldwell and arranged to process my day's work during the night after the daily events so we would have samples to show the subjects and potential photo buyers when they came to the event the next morning. That was the good part. The bad part was that they were closing their darkroom for a few days as they moved to a new location as per an earlier agreement. I could take the photos during a day of showing cattle, then rush to the darkroom that evening and by midnight we had "proof" sheets (and some finished prints) the next morning to show the participants and cattle owners. The problem came at the end of the show when their darkroom was closed and I had to get all the prints made at my regular Los Angeles photo lab a few days later, and mail to the cattlemen after the show.

I give the breeders credit; for a breed of cattle new to the area with not many breeders, they brought out a respectable number of cattle with acceptable quality and most of the owners or showmen were reasonably competent in preparing and showing their stock. But overall, this event had many moments when it resembled a rodeo more than your traditional livestock show. A lot of the show entries were barely broke to lead and many of the cattle that were brought in only for the sale were barely under control when haltered and taken out of the stall. (Some were entered in the sale but some were only there to compete in the show.)

The first night in the darkroom, after a day of showing cattle, we processed the film and printed proof sheets to show the owners of the animals in the show and/or sale. I also printed a few 5-by-7 and 8-by-10 photos so I had some samples for a display to show the owners how the finished photos would look. In addition to photos of the cattle in the show, I went through the yard area to see if I could find candid photos to display. In one pen I found two good cows, each with an attractive calf at side. Some cattle, like people, really show off for the camera. These two pairs did a great job at posing and I took several photos to be sure I had a good one to print. The next morning I set up a display board with sample photos in various sizes that I had taken the day before during the show. I also had a couple of candid photos of people, a few of good show animals and the best shot of the two mother cows with calves at side.

Several of the owners came to look at the proofs of their cattle and ordered the prints they wanted and paid for the prints to be delivered later. As time passed that morning before the scheduled activities, I was kept busy showing photos and taking orders. One exhibitor informed me that I had taken a photo of his pair of cows with calves. I congratulated him on having great photo models as he told me his experience in being one of the first Charolais breeders in the area and seemed reluctant to let me talk to other exhibitors who wanted to order photos—in fact, he became a real time robber and pest. He didn't suggest that he wanted to order photos and I had nothing else to tell him.

He continued to interrupt when I tried to take orders from other exhibitors. Finally he asked me for the photo I was displaying of his cows and calves. I told him the price (as I remember we got $7 for 8-by-10 and $5 for 5-by-7 prints) but he said he would give me a dollar for the photo. I said, "No deal!" Then he said, "Well what will you do with it? It's not worth anything to anybody else." By this time—losing my patience—I said, practically yelling, "I'll show you what I'll do with it" and reached up and pulled the photo off the display board, tore it to shreds and threw the scraps in a wastebasket. Then it hit me—I had become so upset with this breeder that I had raised my voice and created a real scene. I had just insulted an important senior citizen. He was plainly out of line but he was a board member of the group that had hired me. When you deal with the public it is a good idea to stay under control no matter what. But before I could weigh what had happened, or even collect my wits or apologize, the 30 or 40 people sitting and standing in the room broke into applause.

I was aghast! I had no idea why these people, his cohorts and fellow breeders, would applaud when I had just lost control and blown up at what should have been my customer. My nonbuyer turned and left. I had a big audience made up of his fellow breeders and I felt I'd be fired on the spot. But one of the other breeders in the room came up to me and said that everybody in the room had wanted somebody to put the guy in his place for years. He was one of the early Charolais breeders; they gave him credit for that. But he was someone who always had ego trouble, as a big-time church official—almost all these Utah neighbors were members of the Mormon Church—or simply in daily affairs in the community. He was a self-important, arrogant bore who always wanted more than others got. This, it turned out, was the moment they had been hoping for. It finally arrived and they were thrilled to see the guy get what he had apparently earned, again and again. I'm sure I wouldn't be so lucky if I tried for a repeat performance, but I'll long remember the applause I got from his fellow breeders.

Being unable to deliver our photos promptly because of the long-planned move of the local photo studio as the cattle show and sale was closing was an unfortunate glitch in timing. These were good people and I was breaking new ground. I had to wait a few days to deliver the prints but the show repeated (and I was the repeat photographer) for several years of what was considered a successful run by buyers, sellers and the little old photographer who lost his cool for a moment and won the hearts and applause of the show participants who had never before found the courage or occasion to give a troublesome neighbor a dose of needed medicine. But nobody got a photo of that.

Buy It Before the Price Goes Up

I got my real estate license in 1971 after I learned of several ranch sales that had been made because I had told a prospective buyer about a ranch I knew to be for sale, or prospective sellers of someone ready to buy. . . several times, and decided I should be getting paid for what I knew. I also hoped the business might be even better if my job was selling ranches instead of just telling potential buyers about ranches, or potential sellers about buyers. It did not turn out to be a "get rich quick" idea but it was a pretty good long-term choice for me, as I write this in 2008, some 37 years later. If I have learned anything in this time, it is that we have poor memories—and also that we are not able to see very far ahead.

I didn't get a real estate license that limited me to selling ranches only in Placer County, where our home and office are located. Placer is pretty much a "cull" county when it comes to serious, productive agriculture. There just isn't a lot of soil that produces enough of our typical agricultural produce to justify owning it. Oh, yes, there was an early development of rolling foothills soil for fruit orchards, being augmented and/or replaced by wine grape vineyards and boutique wineries but there are not many acres of land with high quality soils and gentle terrain that encourages what we think of as "typical" agriculture—large-scale row-crop or forage or orchards. But land has other uses. There is a great demand for smaller, personal or residential ranch properties, with emphasis on "residential."

One time I took inventory and discovered that I had sold more than 20 ranches within Placer County over the years—several of them twice—and a few I had sold three times. And it wasn't a matter of selling the right ranch to the wrong buyer, or vice versa. There is just a fairly high turnover of ranch properties when the owner's occupancy and ownership is based on a non-agriculture job as compared with counties where most of the income for owners comes from the land and what it will produce in strictly agricultural use. And every time the property sold, the price went up. No two situations are identical but a typical sale from the basis of advancing price over time can be represented by a "nearly typical" property. This was strictly an agricultural ranch since it was not in the sought-after "foothill beauty" category, but it was bought every time on the financial basis of its agricultural production.

I was running an ad in the Sunday *Sacramento Bee* for a ranch I had listed for sale. In checking my ad copy, I noticed another broker advertising a ranch property that interested me. "260 acres, irrigated cropland, more than 100 ac. rice quota, $260,000." It was a county away but it looked like a real buy for several potential buyers. It was listed by a broker acquaintance so I called him immediately (Sunday) to ask what was wrong with the property. It just looked too cheap. He assured me that he just had it "listed well" and it was a good buy. I asked him to send me information and he assured me that a farm manager was available to show me the ranch. Then he added, "What about that ranch you have advertised in the same paper? I haven't been to Auburn for a while, why don't I just run up for lunch and we can exchange ranch information tomorrow."

We had lunch and I couldn't get back to the office fast enough. This ranch looked like it could work for any of several potential buyers. I went there the next morning, did a ranch tour, added a little information to his brochure and made copies that I sent to three or four potential buyers. The next morning I had a phone call from one of them, Ron Matulich. He asked me, "What's wrong with that ranch?" I told him what the listing broker had told me, that it was just "listed well."

"Can you meet me at the Oroville airport in two hours?" the client asked. I met him. After a ranch tour he asked me to check on the 60 acres that jogged into it. I called the absentee owner, who agreed to sell and we went to escrow the next day on the whole 320 acres. Sale price: $330,000. That was in December 1989. About four years later the buyer needed some money to buy a property just listed for sale near his home ranch two counties away, so he called me and asked how much the 320 acres would bring.

We listed it for $500,000 and sold it a few weeks later for $490,000. He ran a bunch of cows for four years and made $160,000. It sold to Frank Hurling, a retired Chevrolet dealer, who needed a place for his growing purebred Polled Hereford herd in 1993. Frank improved the place a little (he replaced some fence and added a covered area onto the end of a barn to allow his crew to work cattle in all weather conditions). In the summer of 1997, Frank decided that he had raised enough champions and called me to sell the ranch again. We closed escrow in October, 1997, for $800,000, with the Belden family, and it became a Brangus ranch. As much as I'd like to have a good ranch to sell, those Beldens and their Brangus haven't felt the urge to let me sell it a fourth time. I like satisfied customers but Beldens, aren't you satisfied yet?

The Calculator that Measures Time—by its Size

We moved our office from Parnells' enclosed crowded carport to the new building at Highway 49 and Palm Avenue in Auburn in early January, 1974. We had been scheduled to move by New Year's Day but the contractor hit a few snags and we moved on January 10. And the check has continued to be due on the tenth of the month ever since. So what's the big deal over a moving day? There was a boxy old "compact" calculator, introduced at the

292

same approximate time, that moved with us. The new machines got smaller and smaller but the prices didn't follow. It's hard at this time to believe, with small, hand-held calculators selling for less than $5, that it would have cost more than $100 for a model that could either plug into 110-volt current or operate with a couple of small batteries.

It seemed to me that prices should be falling and I decided that I would buy one when the price fell below $100. They did and I did and that new Kings Point Micro Memory machine moved with us. I paid $99 and change for it. It is 3 inches by 6 inches and a full inch thick. I don't know when the last batteries ran dry but that machine has been sitting on my desk since we moved in January 1974, plugged into the wall outlet. It still works. I have another calculator on my desk, or sometimes in my briefcase, that is about the size of two soda crackers. You can't plug it into anything and I'm not sure you can change its batteries but it didn't cost more than $3.95 and it might have been a free promotional item. Who said "they don't make 'em like they used to?"

We may have another way to measure time—the size of the appliance for sale. It may not get down to the minute or even the year that a particular unit was made but we have fallen in love with miniaturization. I learned professional photography using a big old Speed Graphic press camera in the 1940s. There are still some Speed Graphics in use but when I got my first real job that used some of the journalism training I got in college, it was in the 1960s and my employer furnished a newer and smaller, if not much lighter weight, Hasselblad camera. It was so capable of quality work that I really resisted the move to the digital camera. I couldn't believe that a camera could take pictures without film . . . but it did . . . and for much less money. The digital was so capable I found a buyer for all the darkroom equipment in our office. Now I wonder where I can get my money back for a perfectly good Hasselblad or find another job for it to do—like that old brick-shaped appliance on my desk that marked a certain date in the progress of miniature calculators.

Does the Post Office go with the Ranch?

Ranch real estate brokers get some amazing requests for items not normally included in the sale of land. I remember one potential ranch buyer who liked the ranch but "fell in love" with the cattle brand. "If the brand goes with the ranch, we have a deal," he nearly dared me. I promised him we'd make the deal as I wrote up the contract, and then convinced my seller to make me an honest man. But what do you say if the buyer asks, "Does the Post Office go with the ranch?" What Post Office?

I hadn't seen Rancho Lilac for nearly 50 years. I happened onto the property in 1962 during the first few days of my job as a field editor for

Western Livestock Journal. It was listed among other prospective advertisers for our publication. The ranch and its herd were owned by Col. Irving Salomon, a retired Army officer who hobnobbed with the rich and famous and was instrumental in the United Nations formation at the end of World War II. While a promoter of Henry Cabot Lodge as a potential Republican presidential candidate in the 1964 election, he was also welcomed by Harry Truman, Eleanor Roosevelt and politicians from around the world.

The "Lilac" part of the name came from the early identification of the settlement in the application for a post office in the growing community called Bear Valley in 1874. The "Bear Valley" name came from a legend that a man had killed an enormous 2,200-pound grizzly bear on the property shortly after the Civil War. The "Bear" name was dropped and changed to Valley Center after they learned there was a "Bear Valley" in Colorado. The post office was located at the Rancho Lilac site, named for the California Lilac Ceanothus bush growing wild in the area, approximately 40 miles north of the greater San Diego area. Neither the ranch nor the post office was for sale, only the cattle raised there.

I don't think the Colonel spent much time at the ranch—I met him there once—but he was well represented where cattle were involved by Willis Goode, long-time ranch manager, Texas expatriate and good judge of breeding stock. Willis was an authority on Hereford cattle pedigrees . . . and especially on the offspring of Anxiety 4th, a foundation sire of the Hereford breed. He ran a good outfit and liked my ranch visits, hoping that I would help sell some of the bulls he raised every year. My job was selling advertising, but it endeared the ad salesman to the ranch owner and manager to recommend the bulls raised on the ranch and their blood line.

A lot of cattlemen did buy Hereford bulls from the ranch, but even more people were interested in the curio firmly planted in the front yard at Ranch Headquarters. "Rancho Lilac," according to the *2002-2003 Orange Book,* "was the site of the smallest post office in the United States. The post office, which still exists, was not much bigger than a phone booth. It functioned from 1881 until about 1912." I was not on the scene until some 50 years later but the post office I saw still stood just off the main ranch entry, proud and well cared for on a 3-foot-long piece of plank attached to a sturdy post with neatly shingled roof over the top of the four or five boxes. It still served as a country mail outpost for a few nearby ranch families, with daily mail deliveries from San Diego and Escondido. The "real" post office, dating to a time before the turn of the twentieth century, escaped my view or even my knowledge of its existence until the U.S. Navy very indirectly helped me revive the story.

In May, 2008, I was attending a reunion in San Diego of fellow Naval Airmen who had flown seaplanes during World War II. (Martin PBM's and P5M's, also called "flying boats," land and take off from water.) Rancho

Lilac was located toward the north part of San Diego County, but I went to this reunion with a special mission. Would the old Rancho Lilac, as I knew it, still be around or would it have been subdivided into so many acres of residential housing tracts, city streets, schools, shopping centers and the like? After all, this was May, 2008. I hadn't been in north San Diego County since the early 1960s. I met the son of a deceased airman from our group who lived nearby, had his car at the reunion and had enough curiosity to drive me—or let me ride with him—as we went in search of the old Rancho Lilac.

We were referred to the nearby library and museum. I was shocked to find that the original post office (that I had never seen), all 3-by-4 feet of it, held a position of honor as sort of a welcoming committee just outside the museum front door. When we went inside, the ranch, the post office and the reason for its location became apparent. The "heirs of Rancho Lilac" had given $250,000 to help build the museum, along with a lot of memorabilia. The museum docent lived near the ranch and gave us the directions we needed.

I noticed "deferred maintenance" to the white board fence that lined the driveway. The row of 16-inch-diameter eucalyptus trees were now 2 feet in diameter. The guest house where Eleanor Roosevelt and other dignitaries had occasionally spent the night needed paint and new windows, but the front pasture field—the biggest piece of flat land within miles—was still large and flat and growing a nice crop of cattle feed. My memory of the ranch nearly 50 years earlier came rushing back. But the man driving the pickup truck coming down the ranch entry road was not Willis Goode. The aging driver, who had been a neighbor years earlier, when both Willis and the Colonel were alive, now leased the land from the Salomon heirs.

I'm looking at the Rancho Lilac Post Office in its new, permanent home guarding the entry to the Valley Center, California museum. From 1898 to 1912, 50 homesteaders along Lilac Road had mail delivered by stagecoach to this post office. In 1912, the Valley Center Post Office took over deliveries in the area. The building measures 5-by-8 feet. It stood for 106 years in its previous location (Photo by Jim Stephens).

Instead of chasing us off the ranch, he was thrilled that we had found the place and stopped to visit.

And I had another "flashback" to my days as a field editor. Subscribers rarely drop in at the office to view the products advertised but I remembered the day when one with two sons in their later teen-age years dropped in at our office looking for guidance in stocking their newly-purchased Oregon ranch. I remember his name was D.D. Williams. He lived in the Los Angeles area and, while his ranching background was limited, he had been a *Western Livestock Journal* subscriber for some time. They had a group of yearling heifers and wanted two young Hereford bulls to mate with them. I had been at Rancho Lilac a few days earlier and had photos lying on my desk that I had taken of their yearling bulls. One of the Williams family noticed the pictures, and asked if these bulls were for sale. I picked up my phone, caught Willis Goode in his office, and made an appointment for the buyers. I did not deserve all the credit Willis gave me for "selling" his bulls but that sale made him a ready buyer for an ad in any future issue of the magazine. And the buyer did not get, nor want, a post office with his bulls.

Space—It's a Matter of Perspective

My cousin Mike was born and grew up in Honolulu, on the island of Oahu. We were living in the Los Angeles area when Mike took his first trip to the mainland. I had not seen him since he was just a preschooler when I was in Hawaii as a Navy pilot late in World War II, visiting his family during my frequent weekends ashore, so his arrival was a welcome visit. He worked through his high school years assembling Honda motorcycles and was going to Chaffee Junior College for their aviation mechanics course.

He flew to Los Angeles a couple of weeks before school started and planned to stay with us until he got settled at college. He freighted two motorcycles over by ship, strapped to a pallet. They arrived about a week after Mike flew over and he was beginning to feel pretty cooped up by the time his wheels arrived. We drove down to the port where he unstrapped the first bike for the ride home, followed by another trip to retrieve bike No. 2. We got home in the late afternoon with the last bike and Mike said he needed to take a little ride before dinner. He had driven my car around our neighborhood so I didn't worry that he had no road map in his pocket. He knew the way home.

Time passed. It got to be dinnertime but Mike hadn't made it back. After a reasonable wait, we decided that he must have ridden beyond our neighborhood, but that he was a big boy and we didn't have a definite dinner date so we sat down to eat without him. In the middle of dinner, the phone rang. The first thing that Mike said was, "Hey, Phil, where's Hemet?" Mike had never ridden on a highway other than on his home island. Oahu is only about 50 miles across from end to end. He had traveled nearly that far when he got to Riverside but he got confused in the maze that connected several

296

highways and instead of returning home, he was headed south on the "inland" route to San Diego. When he finally decided that the road home had given him the slip, he escaped from the freeway and began looking for a landmark, or at least a telephone.

The directions I gave him for getting home seemed to work. He showed up a little more than an hour later—more than ready for a late dinner—and relieved that he had been able to call home for directions. He said he just didn't realize how much space there really is out there. "I never realized how far you could ride," he said. But when I showed him a California road map so he could see where he had gone, he just shook his head. Maybe he had never seen a map of the area before. Mike rode with me for a few days, making ranch calls in my work as a field editor for *Western Livestock Journal*. He commented often that he just couldn't believe we could drive so far and not see the ocean, yet we were probably never 100 miles from it. What a contrast to the place where I grew up in Nebraska where few people had ever—or would ever—see the ocean. Somehow I don't think they teach a very good geography course in Hawaiian schools. But maybe this is something you don't find in a classroom. Maybe you have to see space yourself for it to have real meaning.

Phil's Daughter

There are 10 counties in Nebraska that have a population of fewer than 1,000 residents (2000 census). Logan County, where I grew up, was seventh-lowest, with 878. The two counties to our west are lowest in the state, at 546 and 462. There are two towns in the county: Stapleton, the county seat, got to a high of over 400 in 1940 but has shrunk to fewer than 300. Gandy has about 25, with only a few occupied houses. The rest of the county's citizens live on ranches.

There is now a paved road (U.S. 83) through the county going north-south from Mexico to Canada and another (State Highway 92) going east-west, crossing at the county seat town. There was not a foot of paved road in the county when I was in high school. As ranchers buy the ranch next door, another family leaves and the population shrinks. Locals laugh that the paved roads help the departing families get out of town.

These counties have limited need for political offices as known in most of the country. They elect a board of supervisors for each county. Some elect county treasurers, clerks, etc., but supervisors hire a county executive in most of these low-population counties. Some are full-time, some are part-time employees. Most of these counties have a secretary who keeps the court house open for business and logs the daily activities for all departments.

Our daughter Coral graduated from high school in 1980, and took a trip that summer to visit her grandmothers living in Nebraska and Iowa. She flew into Denver, but the last leg of her trip was by Greyhound bus as planes don't fly into Stapleton. She tried to call en route to update her arrival time but Grandma had left early so nobody answered the phone. Coral tried to call information to double-check the number, but when she gave the operator the town name, nobody could find a directory for the town, leaving Coral wondering whether she was even heading in the right direction. When she finally got off the bus in North Platte, she found that the Stapleton phone directory was a couple of pages stapled together.

Grandma couldn't let Coral be in Nebraska without reading at least one book by the state's leading author, Willa Cather. They went to the county library to check out the book and found a high school classmate of mine was keeping the county records, including checking books out of the library. My mother had been library treasurer for 30 or 40 years, but Mildred felt she should have some other identification for the record. My daughter could hardly wait to get back home and tell me she had a new way to tell when you are in a small town. In the library log, identifying the book and the borrower, Mildred had written, "Phil's daughter."

The Crib

Can there be long-term happiness for a couple who went to the same hangout but for different reasons and at different times? I don't know when the Cornhusker Hotel was built in Lincoln, Nebraska, but it was the capital city's leading hotel for many years. Important guests for almost any occasion in those years were sure to be booked at the Cornhusker. I don't remember how many floors it had or how many rooms. I do know that it had a ballroom and a Grand Ballroom and several other places to accommodate groups of varying sizes. But for Ann and for me, and probably most other people who knew the Cornhusker during their college or early post-college years, the most memorable place was what might be called the coffee shop in other hotels. In the Cornhusker, it was called The Crib.

Coming from Nebraska's Sandhills area, we made our own corned beef for main courses and sandwiches and we raised our own cabbage. So we were well acquainted with the alleged favorite dinner of our imagined-if-never-proven Irish forebears, but nobody in my immediate family had exposed me to the memorable Reuben sandwich. Since I don't remember who it was that ordered one for me, I give full credit to the Crib in the Cornhusker for my introduction. And I never forgot it.

Meantime—actually it was a few years later—Ann finished college and took a job in the personnel department at the University of Nebraska. She also found her way to the Crib. She may also have eaten a Reuben sandwich but she happened to order a piece of the famous Cornhusker Cheesecake. That, to her, earned the "memorable" stamp. In time we met, but not in

Lincoln and not at the Cornhusker. We met in her hometown of Denison, Iowa, where I saw her having dinner with her mother and a friend, and I asked the restaurant owner for an introduction. While we did enjoy our individual featured items from the menu, I don't believe that we ever stayed at the hotel overnight.

One day just a few years ago, we happened to be watching some "news of the world" program on television when we saw the implosion of the Cornhusker. It had apparently lived a long and prosperous life and was ready to be replaced. New owners rebuilt on the same site and called the new hotel the Cornhusker, although it is under different ownership and management. Over the years Ann made cheesecake from every recipe she found that she felt could be the Cornhusker recipe. Needless to say, none was. Had she just forgotten how it tasted? Would it still taste as good as it did when she first discovered it? Then I happened to sit at a banquet table with some old college friends at an animal husbandry department event when I commented about the Cornhusker cheesecake recipe search. My friend's wife told me her friend had all the recipes from the old hotel management and yes, she would gladly send the cheesecake recipe—and she did! What a way to end a "lifetime" search.

That Dark-Haired Girl

In 1959, I was working for Foxbilt Feeds, and was soon transferred to Denison, Iowa. A college friend living in Denison helped introduce me to my new sales territory. I checked in to a residence hotel and was on the list at a new apartment house under construction. Since the hotel had one of the town's best restaurants, I didn't even have to go outside in the winter weather to eat dinner. In a few weeks I had met a few single men and most of the female schoolteachers. Within a few months I had moved into a new apartment and was feeling comfortable in the new territory.

Many months later I happened to go back to the hotel restaurant for dinner. Most of the customers were locals or traveling men but this evening I noticed a couple of older ladies with a very attractive dark-haired girl. The restaurant manager

Ann at college-era evening on the town (early 1950s).

299

knew "everyone in town" so, after they left, I asked her who the dinner guests were. She knew. In almost minutes I had a call at home with the pedigree and possible way to arrange a meeting. After their warnings that I had to be an honorable suitor if not a saint, I got a date . . . and, as it turned out, a date for almost every evening while she was in town. I would never have had the first date without the "club women" and their influence, though.

Her name was Ann. She was on her way to a new job in Los Angeles at the UCLA job placement center. She wrote as promised. I accepted her invitation to visit when summer vacation time arrived. A few weeks after she left Denison for Los Angeles, I visited the Oldsmobile dealer on the day the new 1960 models arrived. My banker was also in the show room and volunteered that if I wanted to buy one, "I'll cover your check." I did and he did. The salesman and I picked it up in Omaha on Halloween evening, the last car delivered before the GM strike in late 1959. It would be my passport to Los Angeles next summer. I hadn't been in California since I bought that Mercury convertible to take back to college with me when I got out of the Navy at the end of World War II. I would see if Ann seemed as wonderful as she had in Denison.

In California we "did the town" for several days: Disneyland, a helicopter ride, San Diego where my brother Jack took us deep-sea fishing in his boat. And I asked Ann to marry me. She stalled for an answer while she explained that women outlive their men by several years and I already had nearly a 10-year head start. I never knew whether she just wanted me to sweat or if it was a big issue. In any case, she said "yes." We agreed to be married before Christmas. By pure coincidence we had met on October 13 and were engaged on July 13 (we were surprised when we looked back), so we decided to be married on December 13, 1960. She wanted a "private" wedding so we were married in the living room of my longtime boss in Des Moines. I hired a photographer friend, who printed a quick wedding photo that we could use in our surprise Christmas card—a surprise, because most of our friends didn't know that we had ever met, much less married. We planned to have more photos printed after Christmas, but a fire burned Adolph's studio, along with several businesses in that block, and the negatives of our wedding photos.

Christmas for an Almost-5-Year-Old

No, I don't remember what I got for Christmas when I was 4 years old. I have a decent memory for some things but that event totally escapes me. But one of the most rewarding Christmas memories was our daughter, Holly's, fourth Christmas. She was born in early January. That has a built-in unfairness. It's hard to build another head of steam less than two weeks after Christmas for a birthday party worthy of the occasion to last all year.

300

We hadn't had much experience at managing this problem in our Christmas/Birthday celebrations in previous years. There had only been three and what does a kid remember? But this year she was older. She was going to be just a few days short of 5 years old at Christmas. She was beginning to have a feeling for elapsed time.

We had kept our Christmas plans and her presents under control enough that the birthday celebration a few days later would not be a total anticlimax. She had visited school with her sister and wanted to start attending herself. We found and renovated a kindergarten-sized school desk with attached chair. Except for the desk, we got little things, saving a few "big" presents for her birthday.

Christmas morning began with stocking stuffers, then moved to the tree and finally to the desk. Here her flashback to the morals from all the Christmas songs struck her and we knew we had handled this Christmas about right when Holly, tearing the ribbon from a present, enthused, "Boy, I sure been good!"

Wounded and Alone in a Foreign Land

Nebraskans don't have a lot to be proud of in comparison with some other places. We don't have any ocean beaches. We don't have any mountains—unless you count the Badlands and they aren't that bad. We don't have weather that makes a vacation-bound family drool. We don't even have a major league ball team, unless you count University of Nebraska football.

Nebraska had a good team when I was in college there in the 1940's. We couldn't beat Oklahoma with any regularity, but we had a good chance against almost anybody else. And they have been at or near the top of the heap in national rankings most of the years since that time. And unless you are being recruited to play football, does a school's football success have that much bearing on where your child should go to college?

When Holly, our younger daughter, graduated high school and was accepted to attend UCLA in 1987, it didn't occur to me that the family would be forever shamed if she didn't wear red during football season. We were glad she would be going to a good school and one with no out-of-state tuition. And how would we know that her roommate, as a Sports Medicine intern, would be a water girl for the football team and have access to tickets. Little did I know, or could anyone imagine, that such a blessing would turn out to be a mixed one.

It also didn't occur to me that Nebraska was on the UCLA football schedule or that it would matter. Holly got tickets and invited me to attend the game in the Rose Bowl, UCLA's home stadium. Needless to say, I went. Our tickets were in the middle of the UCLA student section, the east side of the Rose Bowl. And for an afternoon game, you really need sunglasses with a

301

dark tint. As it turned out, I would need sunglasses to hide behind—to heck with the glare.

Facing into the west and the California sun was more than I bargained for. But maybe the view of the field contributed more to my misery than the sun. That afternoon I saw why UCLA senior quarterback Troy Aikman would soon be the overall No. 1 pick in the NFL draft. Aikman threw a pass well past everybody on the team—the Nebraska team, that is. The UCLA receiver was right there and the misery began. Nebraska got the ball but did nothing with it. UCLA got it back, and Aikman struck again. This continued and finally, when I looked at the scoreboard it was UCLA 28, Nebraska 0. And the first quarter wasn't over.

Nebraska finally got its act together and played a respectable game but they never did find a play that would take 28 points off the opponent's score so they lost. So did I, from almost any angle, and in addition to the humiliation of the lop-sided score, the ribs on my left side were badly bruised from Holly's elbow jabbing into me every time UCLA made a good play. It was an ordeal but it's nice to have your daughter convinced she has chosen the right college for all the right reasons. What father would do any less?

Holly's interest in college sports waned considerably after two seasons of UCLA football. As a sophomore she reluctantly agreed to attend home games only when enticed with offers of free tickets and other goodies by her Sports Med roommate who preferred to hitch a ride back to campus with Holly rather than wait for the team bus. By grad school she hardly remembered the school colors and was completely unaware of any season aside from spring, summer, winter and fall. But things do change. Only minutes after the football team from the University of Florida (where Holly teaches) had beaten Ohio State in the 2006 final Bowl Game in January, 2007, Holly called to say, "Hey Dad, did you know this is the first time in history that any university has been national champion in both basketball and football at the same time?" "Yes, Holly, I read the possibility in the sports pages before it happened and I watched the game on TV but I'm glad you called me to confirm it."

Major Advice

Holly graduated among the top few in her high school class and applied to UCLA as a Sociology major, having liked whatever preview of the field she was afforded by her high school psychology teacher. But before she could take a college sociology class, she had changed her mind several times and was puzzled as to what she should major in. I suggested foreign language as she seemed to like Spanish and Russian and always got good grades in them. She dismissed my idea: "languages are just easy for me." I said math courses are easy for some people who have to study hard in foreign language classes.

They all count, don't they? I told her what my college advisor had told me, "In college, take what's easy for you; when you get out, do what you damn please." I'll probably never know if my counsel was either heard or heeded, but she went on to study several foreign languages and now teaches Czech at the University of Florida.

Reader's Digest to the Rescue

Indigestion and acid stomach are not the normal topics for a stimulating conversation. Stomach ulcers are members of the same family. And like "family jokes," they are better kept within private conversation groups. I know, because I lived with all of the above for too many years. A trip through the super market was a test of ulcer vulnerability. Stomach muscles contract when you walk along the wrong aisles. Orange juice was a no-no and an apple really turned you inside out, so to speak. Canned pears were always friendly and fresh pears were normally OK, but many fresh fruits and melons depended upon your sensitivity on that day.

My doctor prescribed Tagamet for years and I was constantly warned to get my sleep and avoid stress. I had to be hospitalized for a bleeding ulcer in 1980 and again in 1983. I was frequently reminded that ulcers are not caused by what you eat—but by what's eating on you. I did not agree with any of the above advice but I had no evidence that it was wrong.

One day I read a story in *Reader's Digest* about a new discovery of bacteria called *H. pylori*, which hid in the stomach and caused ulcers. The article claimed that a new treatment could rid a person of these bacteria in two weeks and for very little cost. I called my family doctor and told him I wanted to try the new *H. pylori* ulcer treatment. He was aware of it, had prescribed it once, but didn't seem to be as excited about its prospects as I was. But he wrote the prescription.

The treatment involved two antibiotics and Pepto Bismol tablets. It only cost about $25. I took one antibiotic twice a day, the other antibiotic three times a day and the pink stuff four times a day. It sounds more like a math story problem than a medical treatment but I did my best to follow the instructions. On the second day I began having stomach cramps. It seems those bugs didn't like being hustled out of their comfortable bed. They settled down, but only to interrupt my comfort zone again about a week later with phase 2 of the eviction ritual, then I ran at a quiet idle for the balance of the two-week treatment.

And did I get instant relief from the dreaded ulcer and the food problems? My stomach was ready for most foods in a few days but I had to get my brain healed up before I was ready for a fresh apple, orange juice or a raw tomato. It apparently takes a while for your brain to disconnect from your stomach. It has been years since I felt my stomach muscles cramp up at the sight of forbidden foods, or since I took a Tagamet pill. . . and years since anybody has lectured me about ulcers being caused by "what's eating on you." Thank you, *Reader's Digest*.

A Little Shaky

I had survived blizzards and tornados well-known to Nebraska and other inhospitable areas. I even flew through the eye of a hurricane when on Navy duty in Florida and took a direct hit with another Florida hurricane and a Philippine Typhoon, the hurricane's far-east counterpart. My "nerves of steel" had been well tested but suddenly and quietly one evening after dinner they got another trial.

We were living in La Mirada in about 1964. I had just finished eating and I slid my chair a few inches back from the table when I felt I was going to fall off the chair. I didn't know why nor which direction I was going to fall. Then I noticed the hanging light over the dinette table dancing a jig. As I began to comment about this funny feeling, my peripheral vision, looking through the window pane in the dinette back door, picked up the sight of an apparent water gusher spouting in the air outside near the pool.

My wife was more quick-witted than I. She asked, "Are we having an earthquake?" and grabbed our 2-year-old and bolted out of the house to the deck of the pool outside. Then it became obvious that she was right. The quake was one of the few that don't quake, but instead creating a rolling effect. The water rushed to one end of the pool, then to the other. Each time the wave hit the end of the pool, it shot a spout of water some 12 to 15 feet in the air, then repeated the spout at the other end of the pool.

After a few minutes, our stomachs settled down and while the pool water was still sloshing, the spouts were not overflowing quite so wildly. We went around to the front of the house, only to see neighbors, up and down the street, also coming out to their front yards. About half the homes on both sides of the street—all those with pools—had water running down the driveways. A real estate agent could know in a few minutes' drive down our street, which homes had pools.

About 10 years later I was sitting in my office in Auburn, talking to a client in Davis on the phone. My chair began to squirm and I could feel the entire office do a gentle dance. I interrupted our line of thought, saying, "I think we're having an earthquake." He responded, "I wonder where it is."

"It's somewhere nearer to Auburn than Davis," I commented. Then he said, "Hey, I feel it now." In a few minutes we heard on the radio that a quake had hit Oroville, which is probably 60 to 65 air miles from my office. The quake's epicenter was believed to be under the dam or the deep end of the lake, backed up behind the dam.

Exactly a week later I was meeting clients in Oroville. Four of us were seated in the Prospector Inn restaurant for lunch. I asked our waitress what she did and where she was when the earthquake hit. She said she was waiting on the very table where we were sitting. And she pointed to an emergency door a few feet away, saying, "I went straight out that door. I was the first one out."

She brought our water and we began to order lunch when I noticed water in our glasses was trembling. Our waitress was next to notice—and she retraced her steps from a week earlier—straight for the door. She was the first person out the emergency door again when the "aftershock" to the original Oroville quake a week earlier, struck as we sat in the restaurant.

Early one morning when Holly, our younger daughter, was attending UCLA, the phone rang and almost got us out of bed. Her apartment was shaking in the tremble from the nearby Sylmar earthquake. We reassured her that most earthquakes are not severe and that the quaking would be over any minute. Before our reassurance had any quieting action, she said, "my closet door just came open—and my ironing board just fell out." How much reassurance can you honestly give a scared girl when this is happening? I have been through the eye of a hurricane, near the center of a tornado and the middle of blizzards but never ground zero of an earthquake. Maybe I'm naive but I still prefer the quake.

We Have Some News

During the 16 years that I published the *California Cattleman* magazine and the preceding years as a field editor for the *Western Livestock Journal*, I sold a lot of sale advertising to attract buyers to attend livestock sales. And part of the service that went with the buyers' purchase of advertising was serving as a ring man or bid spotter at the livestock auctions that we advertised.

In the 1970s and '80s there was a regular sale circuit in the fall where the auctioneers and livestock publications field men sometimes had a series of sales in various locations at least three or four days per week. Sometimes we seemed to measure time by where we were on a given day. "We're at Kundes' sale so it must be Wednesday; we're at Gardnerville so it must be Friday, etc." I tried to keep up with ads and stories from hotel rooms and I called home every night.

One night I called home from San Luis Obispo, home of Cal Poly University, on the night after the bull sale. It was the first Tuesday in October and it was probably after 9 p.m. I was surprised that Holly (our 9-year-old) answered the phone. "Holly, what are you doing up at this hour?" I asked.

"We have some news," she answered, "and I wanted to tell you."

Just then her sister, Coral, picked up the other phone and without any introduction of the topic, said, "Hey dad, I won the Toyota."

"Sure you did. What are you talking about?" I asked, forgetting that our local grocery store had, for several years, held a "customer appreciation" night on the first Tuesday in October. For several weeks in advance of the date, every customer got a ticket to complete with name and address and deposit in a barrel for a drawing. They gave away bags of groceries and weekend trips. These were awarded whether the winner was present for the drawing or not.

The grand prize was a new car, which was exhibited near the front door of the supermarket for several weeks in advance of the drawing. The winner of the car had to be present or they would draw names until someone came forward to claim the car. We decided to put Coral's name on all our tickets, as did several friends. There were thousands of customers and we knew our chances were slim but at least we were competing only with our neighbors.

Coral's name was the first to be drawn for the car, a new Toyota. My phone call was only a couple of hours after the drawing. Yes, she was excited, but almost as excited was a secretary in a neighboring office. A few days later she asked me in the office hallway if that was my daughter who won the drawing. When I told her this was true, the secretary asked, "Did she need it?"

I answered, "She's 17 and didn't have a car."

"WOW!" was her loud and enthusiastic response. Yes, it was a WOW! People really do win those drawings.

It Ain't Easy Bein' Grandma

Bringing up a family in the drought and depression of the late 1920s and almost all of the 1930s was more than my young parents knowingly bargained for when they set out in life. Their parents had traveled to get from where they were born to the promised land they were looking for to be their new homes. My grandparents all moved to Nebraska from somewhere else. The Brothers family arrived from Iowa and the Raynards came from Canada to Nebraska, then to Idaho and back to their new Nebraska home, which turned out to be permanent.

My parents were both the first generation of their families to grow up and reach voting age, then settle in the home communities where they were born and/or spent their early lives. Their parents had prospered to some extent and built new homes and farmsteads on their homesteaded claims but one generation hardly makes a tradition. They were also the first generation to go to school past the early grades and to be influenced by "higher education."

Aunt Lyndall, my dad's oldest sister, completed registered nurse training before she married. Hazel, the next sister, married young, perhaps more in line with previous generations. Marjorie and Lillian, the younger sisters, both went to college, one at a time, each helping the other with expenses, then

306

Marge went through nurse's training. My mother was fourth in her family's birth order and the first to go to college, called "normal school" for a year of teacher training.

My mother was born in February, 1899, and my dad a year and a month later in March 1900. They married late by standards of the day, a month after my mother was 24 and a few days before my dad was 23. I was born a year later, in 1924. They had moved to a new farm, built a home, barn and other outbuildings. They had bought a new Model A Ford and had two more sons, Jack and Dick, before the crash of 1929 and the Depression that followed.

It is not for me to comment on the cause or impact it might have had on each member of my family but my parents were each the most obviously religious in their families. My mother was determined to raise religious children and felt that some over-exposure would assure the outcome. My dad never openly agreed but always cooperated with her. They didn't want their kids to associate with any that weren't their religious equal, which reduced the pool to near zero. We were not allowed to fraternize outside our group and there were no eligibles in the group.

That solved the problem for a few years but not forever. Being the oldest, I was the trailblazer, but hardly an aggressive one. In time, I went off to college, then into the Navy. Jack also enlisted in the Navy in WWII, and Dick went to college. My mother was always one to avoid a frontal attack, favoring the glancing blow when possible. One day when all the family was at home, apparently expressing her feeling that some of her big boys were old enough to be married—even though she had done her best to keep any of us from ever having a date—she commented that she was afraid she was never going to be a grandmother. I responded, "Don't give up hope. You'll probably make it before Barb (our baby sister) is out of high school." That was probably not the answer she wanted but it reminded her that she might need a new perspective and it ended her not-too-subtle hints.

Time passed and her first grandchild, our daughter Coral, was born. Then Barb's first born, Sabrina, came along. And was Grandma in seventh heaven? It might seem so, but she lived in a very traditional neighborhood. Now she had two granddaughters to brag about, but named Coral and Sabrina? I am not sure she ever accepted the fact that Coral could be a person's name. I think she told her neighbors it was really Carol. And who but a belly dancer would have a name like Sabrina? She finally had two granddaughters, but was too embarrassed by their names to tell anybody in our home town she was a grandmother. As it turned out, it ain't easy being grandma in our family.

A Change of Pace

During the summer of 2000, Ann and I took a trip to Europe with her sister Nancy and brother-in-law Dick. We visited the home of William Brewster, Ann and Nancy's "Mayflower" ancestor at Scrubbe, England, and researched their father's roots in Sweden. While Dick and Nancy left us to visit friends in Finland, we added Denmark and Ireland to our own schedule.

We took the high-speed train from Stockholm to Copenhagen, where we stayed a couple of nights and learned that the pork barbecue at the internationally famous Tivoli Gardens amusement park (Denmark's version of Disneyland, sort of) lived up to its reputation. They serve a roll of paper towels with your order. Yes, you need the paper towels.

I had long wanted to visit the racehorse breeding area in eastern Ireland and to see the Irish National Stud where several of the best racing sires in Ireland were kept, so we made that part of our itinerary. I had done little research except for visits with a former client, an Irish-born engineer who I happened to meet because he wanted me to sell a ranch not far from Auburn, and a real estate agent working in the next county who was not only Irish born but claimed to be a schoolmate of the veterinarian at the stud. They both gave me general directions to the Curragh in County Kildare southwest of Dublin. This area, I was told, had miles of grassland similar to the bluegrass area of Kentucky where many famous American stud farms are located.

I never owned a racehorse but I have ridden many miles far from any racetrack, having learned to ride a ranch horse at an early age. I had taken a lot of horse photos and worked at length with horse pedigrees and auctions and have long felt a little magic when I look at a great horse. I felt that if we were spending most of a month in Europe, we could give a couple of days to my fascination for good horseflesh.

I didn't have specific directions to the horse area but I felt that if I looked for signs to "Kildare" or "The Curragh" that I could get off the main highway and ask directions. I was far from comfortable driving on the left side of the road as we drove southwest from Dublin when I was shocked to see an office building with the name Irish Thoroughbred Breeders Association in large gold letters. I made the next exit and backtracked to the office.

I didn't even know that there was an Irish Thoroughbred Breeders Association. I had known and worked with the California Thoroughbred Association so I felt this was a place where I might get some of the answers regarding the location of horse farms. Little did I know. They gave me a map of all the racetracks in Ireland, good directions to the National Stud, to the Curragh racetrack and a bed and breakfast where we could spend the night near the track. Then I got the real surprise.

I told Paula O'Neill at the Breeders office that I'd like to visit a few stud farms if possible. She made a phone call but got an answering machine and

308

asked if I would call her after her office opened the next morning. She wanted to make an appointment for us to visit Kildangan Stud just a few miles away. It was the farm owned by Sheikh Mohammed and she told us that once you have visited the National Stud and Kildangan, a tour of any other farm is anticlimactic.

The next morning we went across the road from our B & B to Curragh race track to watch dozens of horses in training get their morning exercise then called Paula, who had made an appointment for us to see the Kildangan operation that afternoon. Such a deal. I had known of the Sheikh as a buyer of top racehorses and heard he had purchased a farm in Kentucky but did not know he had one in Ireland. This was his main operation, nearly 1800 contiguous acres divided into eight units with large, newly-built brick horse facilities at each unit plus its own community for farm personnel. Now we would get to tour it and see its famous horses.

My lack of familiarity with the area roads and bad time management got us on the road to Kildangan nearly an hour before our appointment. Just as I began to consider what to do with our spare time, a large sign on my left brought our next surprise: "Ireland Department of Agriculture—Official Bull Test." Yes, I like horses but I have been closer to far more cattle than horses and I have worked with many cattle breeders involved with performance-tested herds.

It had never occurred to me that Ireland had a department of agriculture, much less that it would test bulls. But here I was, with time to kill. We turned

Ann, Phil and Holly Raynard in the Czech metro. Built during the Russian occupation, the underground railways are described by Czechs as the "only thing the Russians did right."

into the entry road and, in minutes, I was on a private tour of their impressive three-barn facility. For me, at least, it was one of the highlights of our trip.

We were really enchanted by Ireland and its people. They all seemed anxious to visit, answer questions, give directions and be helpful if possible. And it seemed that every Irishman we met loved horses.

Ann spotted a stuffed pony in a shop in Kildare that she just had to buy for 2-

year-old grandson Ryan, and she carried it all the way home when it was too big to fit in our luggage.

The next year, my sister Barbara and her husband Garvin called and mentioned that their bank was arranging a trip to Alaska for their group and had space for two more people. We had enjoyed our trip the previous year, so we signed up. We had nothing to do with the timing but we were lucky enough to tour almost-always-cloud-covered Mt. Denali (McKinley) on all sides for three days without a storm or serious clouds. . . a "miracle!" And what a contrast between the Alaska frontier and the European lifestyle we had enjoyed a year earlier. Our tour bus frequently had to stop to observe the 100 percent wildlife right-of-way of a grizzly mama and babies crossing the road. While leaning out the window to take a picture from our tour bus, I had to wait for another monster bear to take a few steps so it would all fit inside the camera viewfinder.

We also got to share an evening with the "Alaska branch" of our family. Some years ago, my brother Rolland had joined a western band, and he played lead guitar for an eight-hour shift in a 24-hour club in Fairbanks. After his death, we had nearly lost touch with his family, who had stayed on in Alaska, but they held a "reunion dinner" for us. Rolland and Barbara were the "young ones" in the Raynard family, and were a few years behind myself, Jack, and Dick. This was the largest family reunion in some years.

We were back in Europe in 2003, after daughter Holly, who was studying in Prague, had called to invite us to visit. Czech archives and libraries routinely close for a while each summer, so she would have some of time to show us around.

I get to examine this Lipizzaner broodmare up close in Slovenia pasture. Foals are dark when born but become white as they reach maturity.

We rented a car, a Skoda, the most popular brand in the Czech Republic and apparently the only one manufactured there, and drove with her through central Europe down to Slovenia. We thought Holly's knowledge of languages would be an advantage, but everywhere we went many of the servers and busboys spoke fluent English.

Another surprise was the European building style. It seemed that the buildings in London were all in solid rows of houses six to eight stories high and all painted gray or brown. In Prague and eastern European cities they were still six to eight stories, but instead of gray and brown, they were painted red, green, blue, orange, white, various pastel shades, or even black.

And many of the buildings, much higher than they were wide, were thoughtfully named with bakeries, pharmacies, laundries, and other stores on the first floors with stairways to the upper levels and rents scaled in reverse proportion to the height of the floor.

Holly had asked if we had any special places to put on the "must-see" list. I wanted to see the white Lipizzaner horses perform. I thought they were based in Vienna, not too far from Prague. Holly learned that they performed in Vienna in spring and early summer, but they would be gone by the time we arrived in July. She reported that the Lipizzaner horses come from Lipica, Slovenia, a little country I had

Ann and I in Piran. The "gray" buildings in the background would be seen as surprising shades of pink, green and orange in a color photo.

never known, joining the northeastern points of Italy. The Lipica stud farm was built there in the 1500s, but the horses were moved and split up over the centuries--not unlike European territory. The breeding farm would be open in the summer and housed many of the Viennese performers. What a surprise! We got to stay a few nights at the Lipica Hotel, visit the mare barn, the stallion barn, take a lecture tour and see the developing "almost ready for prime time" team of reserve horses perform. We stopped on the road beside the breeding ranch with several hundred tree-studded acres of pasture where the mares and foals seemed to enjoy the visiting tourists as their ancestors had done for centuries. From there, we explored some of Slovenia's other

311

attractions: Piran's scenic coast, an Alpine crater lake, and Postojna's extensive network of caves which houses a lesser-known performer, a blind flesh-colored amphibian known as the "human fish."

I was impressed to find, if not the place where beer was invented, the highpoint of land use, crop planning and field selection: acres of barley joining fields of hops vines climbing on trellises. We never saw a brewery, but one must have been nearby.

We returned home enlightened, refreshed and a bit in awe of East European style and people. Adding to our excitement, a few weeks after we got home, daughter Coral presented us with granddaughter Mackenna.

All In Good Time

Ann was pregnant when we moved to Milwaukee. The management and most of the employees at my old company decided to start anew, leaving the old name and factory in the hands of John Morrell & Co. Things had been downhill since merging the companies and the old gang decided there had to be a better way. I had been with the company for over 12 years, since college. I decided that, while I might not be the perfect ad manager, I had done well enough to try something new. I was hired as ad manager for a seed company in Milwaukee.

We were lucky to find a nice rental home fronting on the Milwaukee River and a new doctor who endorsed natural childbirth and settled down to start our family with the birth anticipated on about April 1. Both the job and pregnancy seemed on schedule. Then things crashed at work. The sales managers for farm seeds and lawn products, along with myself, were the three executives on a bonus plan. I handled ads for both divisions. We agreed to sales quotas reflecting reasonable increases over the previous year with bonuses for exceeding quota that could have paid as much—or more—as our base salaries.

Farm seed is sold during the winter. You plan and work all year, then seed dealers fill their warehouses. The spring planting season lasts a few weeks and most of a year's work gets rung up on the cash register in that time. We had an incredible year. The sales managers had been at the company a year before I was hired but company sales in their first year barely made quota so they got no bonus.

This year our sales topped the highest anticipated level and the three of us who had planned and worked overtime began to anticipate our payoff. Then the boss called a meeting and said that the company had earned so much money that they had enough to improve the seed plant and the bonus would have to wait. We had no written contract so we were out in the cold, and in Milwaukee, it can be really cold.

312

I took advantage of the bad news. Both Ann and I wanted to go to California if we could find decent work and this seemed the time to look. An old friend told me that *Western Livestock Journal* was looking for a field editor. I applied and got the job. I had the Southern California territory. The job was to begin about April 1, or as soon as the baby could travel so we settled in to wait. The pediatrician told us on a visit in late March that we were on schedule and that our next meeting would be in the delivery room—or come back in a week, which we did, and he prescribed pills to hurry things. Our next meeting would be in the delivery room—or come back in another week, which we did.

We barely left the house for two weeks because we knew that at any minute we would get the signals but the signals didn't arrive. Finally on April 14, one of our neighbors invited us to play cards at their house next door. We had just dealt the first hand when Ann asked, "Beulah, do you have a towel?" Her water had broken. We went home, called the doctor, picked up the long-packed bag of maternity items and drove to the hospital. A few hours later—and two full weeks late—Coral arrived. Ann recalled that she also came two weeks late.

Such was not the case some six years later when Holly, our second, was born. We had again moved during pregnancy, this time to Auburn. Holly was

due about the first week of February so we weren't much prepared for a delivery through the Christmas and New Year's holidays. We did have a baby sitter that lived a short block away and we had mentioned that we might need her services on short notice in a month or so. Not

Family photo taken on the back deck of our Auburn, California, home (2005). l-r, Phil, Ann, our daughter Holly, grandson Ryan Flood, daughter Coral Flood, son-in-law Harold Flood, granddaughter Mackenna Flood.

to worry. If the daughter was not available the mother promised to come. But late in the afternoon of January 4, a month early, Ann suddenly needed a towel again. I called the doctor, then the baby sitter. She was not at home but her mother promised to walk down the drive to our house to stay with Coral.

Auburn doesn't have fog, but the dense low-flying clouds that afternoon resembled fog. We hustled to the car, met the sitter in the driveway, and we headed toward the hospital just over a mile away. We barely got to the emergency entrance, where the nurse and I delivered Holly on the gurney. From the emergency unit they called the doctor, who was making afternoon rounds in the hospital, knowing that he'd have plenty of time to finish his afternoon schedule and get to maternity for the delivery. As it turned out he wasn't needed in maternity; he got to emergency in time to help clean up.

Years later, with Coral's pregnancy, she was due in mid-January. As delivery time approached, the doctor knew whether it was a boy or a girl, but Coral and Harold didn't want to know; they bought baby clothes in green and yellow and waited to be surprised. The expectant parents' family and friends began to speculate about both the delivery date and sex. I am not much into dreams and rarely remember a thing about my dreams but one night in early January, I had a dream about the pending arrival.

I related the experience, telling everyone that the baby would be a boy and that it would be born, very late, on February 2, my mother's birthday. In my dream I had seen the baby at a few months of age, trying to imitate the "pop" noise I made by pursing my lips. My dream got the sex right but even dreams can't be right about everything, Ryan was born minutes after midnight on the early morning of February 1, two weeks late compared with the doctor's schedule—or a day early for great grandmother's birthday anniversary of my dream.

The Trailer in the Oaks

My business had grown nicely in Northern California, mostly cattle people, while my clients in the Los Angeles area had a lot of horse people in the mix.

Cattlemen paid their bills more promptly so they figured strongly in our family plans. I followed the quick money. We checked the papers in several areas for "Homes for Sale" and "Homes for Rent" since we knew nothing of the residential real estate market when we decided to move from the Los Angeles area to Northern California.

Wildlife in our back yard includes our "regular" doe (with rare triplet fawns) in photo taken from our back porch, curious as wild turkey hen tries to guard the turf for her out-of-camera-sight hatchlings.

Sacramento was so big we concentrated on Auburn where we had friends and were impressed by the Sierra Foothills.

314

We did not find many homes on the market either for sale or rent and since we didn't get a firm feeling about which neighborhood we might like best, we decided to rent until we knew the area a little better. Good choice! One homeowner had taken a new job out of town so he was anxious to get his nearly new home occupied. A few months later our landlord found he didn't like his new job that much and wanted to move back home. He had wanted a written lease so he was glad to help us find another suitable home to rent. We found another good home in the same school district whose owner had also just taken a new job out of town. Before that

Ask why I left Nebraska after you see the "two-tree orange grove" in our garden. The mandarin tree on the left (fruit ripens about Thanksgiving) and the navel tree at right (ripening early in the new year unless serious freeze strikes.)

year was out, they, too, wanted their home back so we found another rental and began looking for a new home and/or building site in earnest and started developing plans for our new "dream home."

Building sites were not that plentiful. Most of Auburn's vacant lots were the generic type that had been passed up in favor of the "preferred" lot next door. We also felt that we would be more comfortable building on acreage rather than a standard residential lot, if the prices weren't too far apart. We did not find much selection in either so we finally bought the home we were renting and kept watching. One day I saw what looked like a mobile home almost hidden from roadway view by large oak trees. I drove up the entry road to find the owners living in the mobile while their new home was being built. They didn't know if any of the surrounding lots were for sale so I went to the county recorder's office and got the name of an alleged owner of two lots joining the home under construction. His name was in the phone book so I called him.

"Do you work at the newspaper?" the surprised landowner asked as soon as I told him the reason for my call. Moments earlier had placed an ad for tomorrow's paper to sell "buyer's choice" of his two lots that joined the lot with the home under construction. He couldn't believe that he was getting a call from his ad before the newspaper was even printed. Ann and I spent much of the weekend walking the two lots and deciding. He wanted $15,500 for our choice, which was $500 more than the asking price for the best building lot we had previously found in Auburn. Fortunately, I had just sold a ranch and had a commission check in the bank so even though he wanted so much, we were prepared to pay cash. Now it was time for us to get started on house plans.

We had been collecting house plan magazines and ideas from all the homes we had lived in. We began to put them on paper and when we were satisfied with our plan and its pet features, we went to an architect and told him to package it. The spring of 1978 came late, following one of the record wettest winters. I hired a local builder/developer, who I got to know when he bought a ranch from me some months earlier, to build our home. We were ready to start on the first of April, but spring rains stalled us for two weeks. The dozer knocked down a few oaks and flattened a building pad. We waited for two more weeks but had several springs and seepages break out in what would have been the center of the home so we were stalled. They put a French tile (a 4-inch perforated plastic tube) just uphill from the building site and the "springs" under the future home dried up in a few days.

By April 15 it was still too muddy to get a lumber truck on the site so a contractor dumped a load of "DG and cobbles" (decomposed granite, resembling coarse sand, and cobblestones 4 to 8 inches in diameter) on the muddy entry drive. The driver then drove over them with a large four-wheel vehicle, smashing the cobbles deep into the muddy mess to establish a base and leaving a smooth, firm surface as the DG formed a crust all over the area. A truck drove in the next morning on the new driveway with our first load of lumber and workmen began to frame the foundation.

We wouldn't move in for months, the first week of October, but we were finally building our new home. We planted a "one-of-each" family orchard and built a deer fence around it. It was great to be living in the "dream home" we had planned. Imagine a native Nebraskan, married to an Iowan, with both a mandarin and a navel orange tree at 1,400 ft. elevation and producing real crops. And we have daily visits from deer mamas with babies, our "resident doe" with yearly twin fawns (she even raised triplets a few years ago).

A Letter to Ryan

As you celebrate your second birthday, I hope and expect that you will have a long life filled with good days. To me, good days are the ones when you awake with a clear head and the ambition to get going and make something happen with no need for several cups of coffee to wake up and an hour to harness and direct your thoughts and strength into productive channels. I have personally had very few bad days. For all my life, except for a few days when bad planning or unfortunate scheduling of events outside my control denied me at least a few hours to sleep, I have awakened with the motivation

316

to begin the new day with a head thinking clearly enough to let me answer the phone or make daily plans.

When I was in approximately the 20- to 40-year-old age bracket I was a "night person," generally doing my best thinking at night. This was in contrast with my long-time friend, Carl Safley, who told me he would only make serious decisions between 7 and 11 a.m. He felt that he was at his mental peak in the morning. I don't know which hours find me at my mental peak or whether they have changed through the years. I remember one occasion when I had been busy during the daytime for several weeks but I was also trying to piece together a new manufacturing program that I had imagined for my employer and the new marketing plan it necessitated. This was before hand-held dictating machines, so I drove with a pad on a clipboard lying in the front seat beside me. As new ideas for developing the program crossed my mind, I would take a pencil from my pocket—while keeping my eyes on the road—and write a few words on the pad to help me recall the thought at some later date.

One late afternoon when I was driving home from supervising salesmen in my territory, the notes on my clipboard representing this blur of different ideas began to merge into a coherent plan. I parked in the driveway, went straight to my desk and began typing. I was not conscious of the process but my mental juices flowed through my fingers and onto the typing paper like cider squeezed from the press in Grandpa's apple orchard many Septembers ago. Finally I felt hungry, thirsty and out of energy. It was nearly 3 a.m. and I had not eaten dinner nor thought about it. But I had typed many pages— almost the entire program I had been nursing for weeks, consciously and subconsciously. With few changes, the company adopted my deranged night of work and weeks of semi-conscious visions to become its new manufacturing plan with the marketing program to execute it. That project also gave me the new job of putting the program into action and supervising it for a few years. I was a "night person," on that occasion, at least.

That said, I am sure you can be successful whether you turn out to be a night or day person. How you wake up in the morning may be more important but that can be managed. Your mother awakened able to discuss any topic or to continue the conversation where it was when she went to bed. Your Aunt Holly would only groan and order us out of her room, even when we tried to obey her late-night order to "wake me early tomorrow." In time, both were equally civil. And both could handle any challenge. It didn't make either of them a better or worse person. They just had different sleeping, waking and working patterns.

I doubt that you can choose whether you are a "night" or a "day" person, and I doubt that you can voluntarily make the change. It's hardly "as simple as night and day" to make the change, in fact I have changed from being a night to a day person but it was not deliberate; it just happened over time. I

317

was always able to be awake as soon as the alarm went off and I was never thick-headed for half the morning like some "night" people. I have generally found myself waking up just before the alarm went off if it had been set at the same time for a few days. I can still work into the night if necessary to get a job done but I like my regular bedtime more than I did at an earlier age.

Outside influences can wreck, as the saying goes, "the best-laid plans of mice and men." I am referring to the years when my younger brother, Rolland or Rowdy, as he became known, was living with me in Denison, Iowa. He was the guitar player and music student in the family. He worshipped the great "pickers" (guitar players) of the day such as Merle Travis, Les Paul, George Van Eps and the man at the top of his heap, Chet Atkins. When any of these guitar players performed within several hours by highway from where we were, he began a campaign to convince me that I just had to hear their performance.

I resisted many of his urgent needs but we did go to Kansas City to hear Merle Travis and St. Louis to hear Chet Atkins. And do you believe he talked his (our) way to talk to both of them in the dressing room or green room after the performance! Rowdy had done all he could do, near our home, in the isolation of the North Platte, Nebraska, music market, where his band played western music on the local radio station while he was still in high school. He thought he had figured how the idea of "self accompaniment" on the guitar was possible and he couldn't wait to talk to these players to see if he had it right. As it turned out, he did. And Atkins even put his famous Gretsch guitar in Rowdy's hands to demonstrate if he was doing it right. He was.

It was good that I was "night people" at that time and age as we turned around after the performance near midnight and headed home, some 300 or 400 miles away. But just because your grandpa did stupid things at an early age does not necessarily give you license to repeat the stupidity. Some things are important to prove. This was more important to Rowdy than to me and he was no doubt more satisfied for having done it but years later I can't argue with any serious conviction that we shouldn't have done it.

This is probably one of the last "Letters to Ryan" that I will be writing for you in these Bio Bits. The project started a long time ago as an idea, years before you were born or imagined when your mother urged me to put some of my memories on paper so members of the family could know something of life as I saw and lived it at an earlier time. Neither my father nor grandfather had done that so in that sense, we never knew what they did and in the same thinking, who they really were.

While the idea was frightening, I decided that I would try to write about a few of my most memorable childhood events. I listed some possible topics as they popped into my mind, let them incubate until one jelled to a point that one day I felt ready to write about it. The first words hit paper in 1992 when "The Day I Killed the Boar" began to flow out of my fingers at the keyboard

318

and onto paper, with surprising ease after the first few lines were written. Yes, it took some editing.

I could never have written a chronological autobiography but little bits of my life story seemed manageable and somehow the handle, "Bio Bits," hit me. That title covered the topic for me and reduced the pressure that would have been involved in writing about the events of my life, and all in the order they occurred. The Bio Bits idea of which story to write next was like watching popcorn and guessing which kernel would be the next to pop, bouncing from high school events to incidents from any of my several "careers," and back to another memory from my early life . . . just as I happened to recall each story. The exception is my Navy career.

The first part of my Navy stories follows the Navy pilot training sequence my life took from the Japanese attack on Pearl Harbor through my enlistment and training, up to getting my wings. The second part follows the "popcorn" system again. It may not be logical but what in life is really logical? I'm sure that most lives, like mine, and in spite of trying to manage your time and activities, has quite a bit of "popcorn" mixed in with the plans we worked so hard to perfect. I wish you happy reading and pleasant memories—as I remembered and recorded them—for you, for other family members or for anyone else who happens to read them.

P. S.—Mackenna

Almost every railroad train had a caboose until 1984, when rail moguls sent these relics to parking lots, and with each one, a brakeman and a lot of nostalgia. We had grown up expecting that quaint car at the end of every train. We didn't know the trains could run without this ever-present curio. To us it seemed as inevitable, if not as important, as the locomotive. The railroads saved the cost of building and pulling the cars, and also the paychecks for the employees who rode for so many miles in the hundreds of cabooses on trains across the nation. I'm sure the stockholders were happy that the company didn't have to maintain that picturesque relic at the end of every train, but railroaders and observers alike were stunned with the absence of that brakeman and his caboose, like a writer choosing to not use a period at the end of a sentence.

At a later date and without public exposure, our family was seemingly complete with the arrival of Ryan Flood, our first grandchild, in February, 2000. But welcome as our first grandchild would be, Ryan was not destined to be an only child. A little more than three years later, baby sister Mackenna arrived in late July, 2003. How lucky can you get! I always thought it would be great to have a big sister to break the ice for me with my parents and the world but that was not to happen. I did finally get a sister but not until I had graduated from the eighth grade, much too late to give me the "big sister" guidance I had hoped for.

Looking back at the birth order, my mother's family had a son, then four daughters; my father's family was two girls, then a boy, then two girls, then a boy. My family had four boys, then a girl, or as our youngest brother Rolland used to say (growing up on the ranch with more work to do than could ever be done), four hired men and a child. Ann had a younger sister but her father had two younger sisters, her mother had two sisters and a brother. We had two girls, as did my sister, but my only brother who had children had two sons (the last chance to keep the family surname alive) and a daughter.

As much as we might like to control birth order, for the moment we had better prepare to deal with what we get and take advantage of whatever benefit we find from what we have. One thing is certain—like a lot of things in life, we can't change it. Another thing that happens on its terms but not necessarily on those of the parents and/or grandparents is the date and time of an expected birth. Our first grandchild was due in mid-January, according to the pediatrician. I don't dream often but when I do, watch out.

One night, weeks before the arrival, I dreamed that the pending grandchild would be a boy, born on Feb. 2, my mother's birthday. I have never been much of a dreamer, either in number or assigned importance but this was one of my most vivid dreams. I was so convinced that I announced the future arrival date and sex. It was as plain to me as anything I've experienced in a dream. I just knew it would happen that way. Well, my dream got the sex right but missed the delivery by a full day. Not bad for an amateur dreamer some months in advance. I had no dreams or visions of the anticipated delivery date or sex for Mackenna and it turned out just fine. So, back to the advice department.

As I write this, both of you are young. Ryan just past 7 and Mackenna within a few days of 4, I couldn't be more pleased with the way you both have developed to date and the way your parents have brought you along. I hope you'll remember and appreciate some of the times when they have given you positive direction and be motivated to thank them for it someday in the future. I'll long remember the welcome you have given your grandmother and me and the times, too many to count, as each of you reached that age, grabbed the pen and pencil from my shirt pocket as special toys to revere, to make an old man feel important to his grandchildren for a moment then be returned to the pocket a few minutes later, in safekeeping for a reprise performance at some later date. Yes, grandchildren are important.

Happy Holly

Our second daughter was due in early February but the first of her "precocious" acts was arriving a month early, late in the afternoon, during a winter fog. Natives of Auburn, California, swear that Auburn, at 1,200 to 1,400 feet elevation, is above the fog; ("it's just a low-flying cloud; they have fog down in the valley") but if you need to drive somewhere during that kind of weather, it's hard to tell the difference. Our teenage babysitter lived a short block up the street and we had arranged with her mother that one or the other would come to take care of 6-year-old Coral if we had a maternity call. Coral had been a late arrival but we had the maternity bag packed weeks ahead of Holly's due date. This was more than six years later. We hadn't

Six-year-old Coral holding 1-week-old Holly (January 1969).

even re-read the baby name list before the afternoon when Ann suddenly said, "oops, Phil, please get a towel, quick." That was the same warning we got while visiting at our next-door neighbors' house the eve of Coral's arrival. But Coral was two weeks late; this was a month earlier than the due date. I grabbed a towel for Ann and called our neighbor, Monica, to see if she or her daughter could come babysit—in a hurry.

I hustled Ann out to the car in front of the house as Monica came hurrying up the driveway in the dense fog. Her daughter was not home from school yet. I quickly let her in the door to meet Coral and called to alert our family doctor. I learned he had the day off but a partner was making his rounds at the hospital. "Go ahead to the hospital; the doctor will meet you in the maternity ward." As we neared the hospital, which was barely a mile from our house, Ann broke the silence, "Phil, hurry or we'll have the baby in the car." How much do you hurry in a fog? I did the best I could, driving straight to the emergency door and rushing in to get a nurse. Holly was born on the gurney in the space between the car and the emergency room. The nurse and I were in attendance but Holly was in a hurry. They paged the on-call doctor, who got to the emergency room in time to help clean up. I called home to see how Monica was getting along with Coral. It all happened so fast they barely had time to get acquainted.

Holly was a tiny baby, but apparently healthy and, at barely more than 5 pounds, large enough that they didn't put her in the preemie nursery. As soon as the hospital staff got Ann and Holly bedded down and stable, I went home to get supper for Coral and myself and tell her she had a new baby sister but the new sister had no name yet. Coral was curious about her little sister. "Can I play with baby?" she asked, and "How big is baby's head?" I told her the baby was very small and wouldn't be able to play for a while. The hospital did not allow young family members in the maternity area at that time but we noticed an outside window in Ann's room and we went around to look in. We couldn't see the baby very well but the attempt was apparently satisfying and Coral began planning how she would play with "baby."

Holly quickly took her place in the family. Her first unusual trait seemed to be that she was always happy. She could worry the family with a fall down a flight of stairs and most kids her age would be screaming from either pain or fright but Holly would get up, possibly bruised, but always laughing.

But a few years later, it was not so funny when she plopped on her backside, going out the front door and onto the ice-covered north entry to our Auburn home. Auburn weather tends to be mild compared with the area where Holly's parents spent their early lives. Snow is rare and it is not necessary to drain your garden hose to protect it from freezing. But in a freak weather pattern that hit Northern California in December 1972, several inches of snow accumulated over the entire Northern California area and slight daily thawing left morning ice on all the protected areas. Eighty-year-old trees in the Berkeley arboretum were killed from freezing. I was in Monterey for the California Cattlemen's' Convention. Their local newspaper had a photo of homes along the famous ocean-front 17-Mile Drive (where it never snows) that had snow on their roofs for several days. Cars parked at the hotel had engine heat melt the falling snow and night-time temperatures froze the puddles. Apparently the weather was the same at our house and Holly seemed to never learn that that normally dry and friendly north entry would make her feet fly out from under her every time she went out the front door. Holly survived and the ice melted, eventually.

I think kids always want to go when and where the family car goes. I can remember wanting to go but, if my memory is accurate, there were not so many trips in the family car as today. With gasoline costing from 17 to 20 cents per gallon it could cost $2 to $3 to fill a 12- to 15-gallon gas tank and you always reconsidered the expense of an unnecessary trip. When I was a child, that meant we rarely went anywhere but church. And as time passed we saw many changes in our way of life from those days in the 1920s and '30s. Instead of being farm-bound in your thinking and your life, consider working for wages and monthly income compared with doing jobs that didn't exist in the drought and depression days.

In my job, during the 16 years as publisher of the *California Cattleman* magazine in the 1970s and '80s, I sold ads, wrote articles and performed many jobs that the casual reader would never imagine were in the realm of magazine publishing. But I made few business trips that would have been much fun for a daughter to tag along. It happened that on one particular autumn Saturday I needed a photo of some young bulls at Windswept Livestock Company and I also had the obligation to be a ringman (bid spotter) at the Guertin Brangus Ranch fall auction sale. Fortunately they were located only about 20 miles apart and neither was more than 100 miles from our home.

Holly must have been 7 or 8 years old at the time . . . old enough that she wanted to go wherever I was going, but young enough to need a little direction, especially in risky situations, such as sitting or lying on the grass in the middle of a pasture full of curious year-old bulls. That was the reason I wanted her with me on this trip. I needed photos of a group of year-old bulls for the next ad I planned to run for Windswept. I had personally been involved in such photo-taking adventures many times and knew what yearling bulls would do in this situation and I had never known any that were not highly curious but always fully dependable. They might lick you . . . maybe cattle have a flavor test . . . but they mean you no harm. I knew, though, that when a year-old animal weighs a thousand pounds, watch out. It could hurt just as much being a victim of curiosity as a victim of anger.

We parked at the gate entering the bull pasture. I loaded my camera and entered the field, inviting Holly to come along. She had never been near enough to touch a bull, much less find herself in a pen full of them, even young ones, and these cattle are fast growing, weighing about a thousand pounds each. Young bulls are difficult to photograph. Their curiosity makes them want to touch or lick anybody or thing within reach. It was almost impossible to get them far away enough to get more than three or four in a photo. I wanted a photo of 40 to 50 bulls, not just a piece of the two or three nearest to the camera. I had to get them away from me and Holly was to be my bait. I let the bulls form a half-circle while I backed out of the action. They got near enough to lick Holly but I got her to make them back up with body movements, making the bulls form a half-circle facing me and the camera so I could take my photos. While never completely comfortable, she finally got the hang of it and I got my photos. I'm sure Holly was fascinated by both the photography and the response of these young bulls, as well as the livestock auction that we attended later in the day. She never did show an interest in either as a career.

She did, however, show talent that was useful in livestock publications. Holly was handy with anything artistic. One year I had an idea for the Central California Bull Sale ad artwork. This was a bull sale held in Stockton and managed by my former partner, Jack Parnell. Area breeders of all beef breeds were invited to consign some of the bulls they had produced where bull buyers could come and buy on sale day. I felt we needed photos—head shots, preferably—of bulls of all the breeds represented in the area, for use in sale advertising. But it's difficult to get photos of bulls representing the many breeds, especially with a similar size, shape and background. It occurred to me that artwork might be our best answer.

I knew of Holly's artistic talent but I had never tried to see if she could do pencil or charcoal drawings. I collected photos of the many breeds; some were headshots, some full bulls, etc., but I felt we had models enough to "copy" in drawings. I didn't want to waste good paper until I learned how well Holly could draw, so I just got a large sheet of typing paper. I asked if she could do a charcoal drawing of a bull head in similar size for each breed in the sale. It was just after noon that I gave her the assignment.

I went back to see how she was getting along after an hour or so, thinking that if her first couple of bulls were OK, I would have her do all of them. It would be quite a project but I planned to ask her to do one bull's head for each of the breeds. What did I know? In that brief time she had finished all the bulls—a bull for each of a dozen breeds—and they were so good we kept the ones she had done on typing paper without asking her to do them all over again on art paper as I had originally planned. The sale management continued to use those for at least the next 20 years of bull sales—and for good reason. Only a few bull buyers ever knew who did the bull heads art work—when they chanced to ask me where we got such good artwork, I simply said it was Home Grown!

I was a Guinea Pig for Six Years
(Or, *I was in a Ginkgo Evaluation of Memory Study*)

I got a letter from my doctor. I dutifully read most of the mail addressed to me, even some that appears to be form letters. I know that this is often a waste of time but at least I learn if there are pending items that might concern the way I live my life and/or want to forget what someone would like to make my obligation. I received such a letter several years ago from my eye doctor, notifying all patients that he would no longer do certain surgeries for members of a medical group insurance plan that was reducing their payments to surgeons for some procedures. I was beginning to have some impaired vision in one eye and cornea surgery seemed to be in my future. Dr. Hardy had been my eye doctor for several years and we were both parents of UCLA students. I wanted to stick with him for the surgery.

Having no desire to pay cash for this procedure when I had been paying into a group insurance plan for years, I inquired about alternative insurance groups and found that I could transfer my coverage to the medical group affiliated with U.C. Davis and that they would accept me. This insurance plan paid cooperating surgeons enough to make Dr. Hardy satisfied if not happy. I couldn't transfer Ann's coverage since she had an existing condition that they frowned on so she stayed in our current group but I switched and got on Dr. Hardy's favored insurance payment list. A few months later he

324

performed the surgery and at the end of the insurance year I transferred back to our old group. End of story? Of course not.

Health care providers, like the rumor about elephants, do not forget. That little foray into the medical never-never land for Dr. Hardy's good graces left my name on the U.C. Davis books. My health care inventory matched the requirements for an upcoming project so (aren't computers wonderful?) when they became one of a half dozen University Medical Schools that planned to participate in a nationwide test of gingko biloba and its possible effects on memory, I would be among a few thousand people more than 75 years of age, in a five-year-long, double-blind, nation-wide trial. I was invited to join these "guinea pigs" in this study. We would neither pay, nor get paid, for participating and all we had to do was report as scheduled two times per year for a health exam and an accompanying series of memory tests during the upcoming five years. As the test continued, funding became available to allow the test to continue for an additional sixth year of study. Participating institutions included the medical schools at Johns Hopkins University, Wake Forest University, University of Pittsburgh and the University of California Davis, which is located in Sacramento.

The evaluation was a "double blind" survey with neither the participants nor the administrators knowing who got pills with the real drug and who got placebos. The pills were sealed in a card—a week per card—one pill for morning and one for evening, every day until the next evaluation time. Every pill looked just like every other pill—about the size and brownish color of Advil. If we forgot to take a pill at any time on our schedule we left it sealed in its card so they knew every week and month if we took all of our pills or how many we forgot. They also wanted participants to bring all medications being taken for any other purpose to every evaluation meeting so they could possibly learn if there was any action of outside drugs on the test results and if there were relationships with any of the other drugs used.

My final evaluation was October 17, 2007, but it took 13 months to evaluate all the participants since some had enrolled in the study group several weeks or months later than I, and reported for their final evaluations in the following weeks or months, so the concluding test results were tabulated after the last participant had finished the entire regimen. We have now learned which patients were taking the real material and which got the placebo—and if there was a difference. Did the stuff work? We got final results in November 2008. There were 3,069 participants nationwide. More than 100 participants died from unrelated causes during the six years of testing (we had to be past our 75th birthdays to enroll). We, the participants, were first to get the final test results. And would you believe? *The stuff didn't work!* Ginkgo *did not reduce* the onset of *Alzheimer's disease* or *heart attacks*. Officials continue to examine differences, if any, in cancer or depression. We took over 33,000 test visits, more than 3 million ginkgo and

3 million placebo tablets but more than 500 people developed Alzheimer's disease. I apparently didn't . . . and *I was in the placebo group!*

Never that Far from Home

When Columbus sailed his three ships to what turned out to be America, there is no record that he met somebody he had known from a previous occasion, or somebody who knew him from . . . well, you get the idea. It's a small world, however, and my limited experience proves it to be getting smaller. Like most of my family and/or acquaintances, we have not been world travelers of note. But we have been urged out of our home towns on a few occasions. I think that every journey turned out to be fun and surprising in many ways. On one trip, Ann and I had been invited to share a visit to England, Norway and Sweden with her sister and brother-in-law. Ann's sister, Nancy, put the itinerary together with her wits, her travel expertise and her computer and she masterfully scheduled the trip to include a visit to the home of their "Mayflower ancestor" William Brewster in Scrubbe, England, and locate the Swedish side of their family.

She asked if there was anything I would like to see during our time in Europe. My only request was to see if there was race scheduled at Epsom Downs, the horseracing track in southwest London, during our time in the area. I felt that would probably be the most likely place I could name with a personal connection for me. I had worked with the sales of the Thoroughbred breed of racehorses, their buyers and sellers, and felt this could be the nearest to an "international" connection I'd ever be able to make to any of my jobs. Nancy found one. Brother-in-law Dick and I went to the track while the sisters signed on for a tour of downtown London. The track was so long that on a simple 1-mile race the horses started not in front of the grandstand— where in the states horses would finish a mile race after running a lap—but far across the infield. I would guess they were at least several hundred yards of distance and a mile of track away. The race did at least finish on level ground in front of the grandstands.

Ann's request showed more class than my racetrack. She had always had a fascination for the Sami people in extreme northern Sweden, reindeer herders who earned their living in an unforgiving climate. We flew to Lulea on Sweden's east coast by SAS, then boarded a bus to Jokkmokk, well above the Arctic Circle. Our bus was invented for this particular situation. It had a handful of seats behind the driver and about an equal number up on the second level for other passengers—more than was needed to haul the 10 or a dozen people on this particular trip. The rest of the space—the rear two-thirds of the bus—was for freight. And the freight part seemed more nearly filled to capacity than the seating area. I had never seen such an invention so

I scooted up the stair to the upper level, in hope that I'd have a better view of the scenery.

By pure chance, another passenger on the upper level of this bus was a man who was a great visitor. He was a native of the area, went on to earn graduate college degrees and had retired from a position in California's Silicon Valley as an inventor and corporate executive. He came back to his homeland to visit family and got the job as headmaster of the government public school system that taught ABCs to the Sami people in the area. Most people would find this area a wasteland full of scrub pine trees. I began visiting with my fellow passenger on the bus trip and he told me that the acreage of pines was the "money in the bank" and/or "retirement plan" for people in the area. He explained that there was such a small number of daylight hours during most of the year in the area that the pines only grew a few inches per year. But they had value. Someday they would grow big enough to harvest and whoever owned them at that time would have some income. Meantime, people invested their money in the land covered with young and growing trees. Every time a tree grew a few inches, the investor earned a little potential return—either to sell as most industrial country investors would sell stocks or other property—or to hold because most of the trees would not be harvested during the life of the person who bought the acreage of young trees. "You can always take your title to the bank and get some money," he explained. There must be an appropriate expression for dull activities that covers the effect of saying "exciting as watching pine trees grow above the Arctic Circle."

Getting from England to Sweden took a little imagination and dumb luck. Shipping over to Norway for a tour of the glaciers along the inland waterways, even in late spring, was quite a show. Then we began using our railroad passes, an ingenious system of buying a pass that gave permission to ride any train anywhere in Europe for a period of time. You travel unscheduled from wherever you are to where you want to be. At a time like this it's helpful to know at least where you are and/or where you want to go. We got off a train at an uninhabited crossing and took the wrong train. Late at night we pulled into a station where we could get back on track and on schedule but it was near midnight and the station was unoccupied. We hadn't eaten for several hours and prospects were not good until I went out the backside of the station, saw a light and heard unintelligible conversation in the nearby darkness. An "interesting" restaurant, of sorts, was just closing. I walked in, asked if they could serve us and found they had about four possible meals. We were in Sweden, had only Norwegian money and the chefs were Turkish immigrants cooking pasties or kabobs like you never saw. They made the exchange; we ate, then went to the railroad depot to "rest" or try to sleep until morning on the hard wood benches. We got a lesson in "international" travel that is fun now; an "experience" then.

After making all of our scheduled events, we were back in Stockholm where Dick and Nancy were going to Finland to visit a former exchange student who had lived with them a few years earlier. Ann and I saved a few days at the end of our trip to fly to Dublin, on Ireland's east coast, then we would be on our own without connections except for our reservations to fly home a few days later from Shannon Airport near Ireland's west coast. We had long wanted to visit Ireland, the supposed home of my Raynard ancestors (although the family had no history, names nor addresses for these unnamed relatives) but a land with hospitable people, a heritage of horse racing as well as the probable origin of the "curry" comb, which I had often used in my early life to groom the hair on our family's livestock. That grooming device was allegedly invented by people at an earlier time in this part of Ireland called "The Curragh." This is an area with hundreds—perhaps thousands—of acres of rolling grasslands; great horse pasture, the Irish counterpart to the bluegrass area of Kentucky.

It was also the site of The Curragh race track and horse facilities, along with a couple of hotels, some restaurants and at least one very good bed-and-breakfast facility just across the street from the five-eighths mile pole on the Curragh track. The secretary at the Irish Thoroughbred Breeders Association office knew the owner of the B and B and made reservations for us, noting that their roomer for the night had an interest in racehorses. When we checked in, we were invited to rise early the next morning to see the owners exercise their horses in training in a large grassy area of rolling terrain just beyond the Curragh racetrack. I took her good advice to find the hills alive with horses and riders and a large parking lot filled with horse vans. I had noticed earlier in our visit to Epsom Downs that there were not the shed rows of horse stables on the grounds as at American tracks. Not far from the Curragh was the Irish National Stud where mare owners brought their best mares to Ireland's top Thoroughbred sires . . . and nearby was the classic Japanese Flower Gardens—acres of a different kind of beauty.

Owners brought their horses to the track, whether for training or for races, in vans on the morning of the event. They train in early morning but race in the afternoon so the same parking area works for both. On this morning there was a sea of vans parked while the hills were covered with dozens of riders. Some horses were apparently just getting exercise while others were practicing the procedure of getting into and out of the practice starting gates and others were wet with sweat from strenuous workouts. But it seemed that there were a lot of interested people standing around the parking area, watching their horses work or just visiting. I guess I didn't have the appearance of a native so one of the trainers introduced himself and asked where I was from. He pointed out some of his charges that were galloping over the hills and asked if I would be long at the track. He wanted me to meet his father, who owned a number of horses and would be arriving soon.

328

In minutes we had the meeting. The father called himself a dairyman who just couldn't get horses off his mind, and finally bought his first horse, then another, etc. He said he was dumb enough to go to America to meet an auctioneer and agent who helped him buy the first of his "imported" horses. That "horse auctioneer" turned out to be Tom Caldwell, the man I had worked with for several years at horse sales in California. I still have the Irish horseman's business card. He identified himself as J. C. Hayden, Racehorse Trainer. He made me the hero (or curiosity) of the moment as he introduced me to every horseman nearby as "Auctioneer Caldwell's friend from California." I hope I made his day; he surely made mine.

We enjoyed almost every minute we spent in Ireland, including the "mountains" in the south-central part of the country but they wouldn't have looked large, even compared with the gentle terrain of the Nebraska Sandhills. I felt more comfortable when I finally got over the urge to get far to the right shoulder (while all cars are supposed to drive on the left) when meeting a car on the narrow Irish roads, which are often restricted by hedges on both sides. We had a period of concern the day before we left. The big news of the moment was the trucker strike scheduled for the day we were to leave for home. We got a motel as near the airport as possible since the local radio reported that all roads leading to the airport would be blocked by striking truck drivers. I asked the cabby who took us from the rental car check-in to the motel what to expect. "Don't worry," he assured us. "I'll pick you up in the morning and I know the back ways to get to the airport." The driver kept his word, driving around the main arterials which were, in fact, blocked with parked trucks. Instead he took us down residential streets and almost back alleys but he got us to the check-in on time, as promised, and we boarded the plane, taking wonderful memories with us as we left Ireland.

The Reunion of 9/14/01

Ann's high school graduating class in Denison, Iowa, had scheduled its 50th reunion for the weekend of September 15, 2001. As a totally unrelated event, the University of Nebraska College of Journalism had planned to hold the dedication of Andersen Hall, its new home, for the same weekend. And to make a full calendar, the *Daily Nebraskan* college newspaper picked this weekend as a reunion time for former staff members, making a double celebration for J-School grads and guests.

Despite personal restrictions, the travel schedule was a neat fit. Ann had an agreement with a Denison classmate living in Marysville, only 40 miles from our home, who didn't like to fly. They would meet in Sacramento for a train ride to Omaha. I would fly to Omaha, rent a car, pick up the girls when their train got to town and make the 75-mile trip from Omaha to Denison. I would then have a day or two to visit old Denison friends before driving down to Lincoln for my Journalism events. This would be the kick-off event for a Raynard (Ann and Phil) vacation to visit relatives while Ann's friend Donna Gibson Peterson had her own schedule.

Our plan was doing fine with no glitches: Donna arrived in Sacramento from Marysville and we drove the 30-odd miles from Auburn in plenty of time to meet her at the railroad station. They claimed their sleeper-car reservations a bit before noontime on Monday, September 10, boarded the train and headed for Omaha. When I saw the train get under way with the girls safely on board I returned to Auburn. My air reservation to Omaha was the following morning. I would spend the night in Omaha, then meet the girls at the Union Pacific depot about 7 a.m. Wednesday for the trip to Denison, then wend my way back to Omaha and Lincoln for my events that would occur on the weekend.

When I turned on the television Tuesday morning to get the overnight news I was in shock if not disbelief. The TV screen showed a burning World Trade Center in New York from a plane crash—then another plane crashing into the second tower. You didn't really need a journalism background to know there would be a major glitch in air travel on this day. I tried to call Southwest Airlines to confirm my scheduled flight but got busy signals for hours. Then the government announced that all U.S. flights were cancelled until further notice. I gave up calling Southwest, knowing there would be no Omaha flight today. But what about the girls? *What would this do to railroad travel?* I wondered.

Meantime, word of the plane crashes reached the Amtrak train as it arrived in desert country near the Nevada/Utah border early Tuesday morning. Poor Ann and Donna, what did they know of what was going on? News on the train was spotty at best. Then the train was stopped; all luggage was taken off and all passengers had to identify and stand near their bags until everything was matched and identified. After all the matches were made, they got back on the train. But they were now in "never-never land" and hours behind schedule. The train had to stop at each of the several tunnels along the route through the Rocky Mountains while train personnel walked the tracks inside the tunnels from end to end for possible dangers. Needless to say, the train passengers had now been out of touch with the world for hours.

I couldn't reach anybody by phone that might have solutions to my travel problems but I remembered that Donna had mentioned that she had a Budget rental car reservation in Omaha, "just in case." A call to that office confirmed her car reservation; they were glad for a contact call, even if we were both far out of touch. They promised to attach a note to Donna's reservation so we might get in contact again when they arrived in Omaha. Southwest Airlines finally called me on Thursday to confirm that we would be allowed to fly on Friday and I would be welcome on a flight to Omaha, if I still wanted to go.

330

The U of N Journalism folks were sympathetic, but since about half of their expected guests were already in Lincoln—early—for the Friday night event, they decided to go ahead with the dedication and repeat the event a year later for those who got cheated out of this one.

Meantime, when the girls finally arrived in Omaha many hours later, they got my message from the car rental people. They called and Ann agreed to ride to Denison with Donna and use the room we had reserved.

With schedules now scrambled, I arrived in Omaha at about 10:30 Friday night, much too late to drive to Lincoln for the Journalism building dedication, which had occurred some hours earlier. Instead, I spent the night in Omaha, updated Ann with the new schedule, then drove to Lincoln to fulfill some prior commitments before going back to Denison on Sunday— and the vacation was back on schedule, sort of, for the rest of what we had planned. Damned Arabs! At least they didn't fly our Southwest airliner into the Denison, Iowa, high school.

Early the next week we flew to Detroit to visit Dick and Nancy Christiansen, Ann's sister and brother-in-law. After a few days there, we got in line to leave the Detroit airport, and our luggage was run through a newly introduced "radar" scanner (they called it), but they didn't scan us before letting the luggage and us board the plane to Indianapolis. And we had the story of the "latest in air travel" to tell my sister Barbara and brother-in-law Garvin as they picked us up for a visit to their farm on the Illinois side of the Wabash River. I don't remember the procedure on leaving Indianapolis airport a few days later, so their security process must not have been as intrusive as the creative Detroit scan (which we never saw again) in those first days of post 9/11 air travel, as I write this several years and many air trips later.

The First Granddaughter

My mother (under conditions beyond her control) had four sons, then finally a daughter. As the boys grew older and none married, she often commented that she was afraid she was never going to be a grandmother. I once answered that she shouldn't be in such a hurry; she would probably make it before Barbara (our baby sister) got out of high school. That may not have been the answer she wanted from her firstborn son, but the other boys felt the comment was fitting and agreed that she had earned the answer. In time, however, she did get that first grandchild in the form of our daughter, Coral. She was also the first grandchild for Ann's mother, who had kept her cool very well while waiting for the arrival.

Coral was the near-perfect child for inexperienced parents. I was not fully inexperienced since I was the oldest of five and had plenty of "glancing blow" experience that comes from just being the first and watching what happens naturally to the next four siblings. But even the "model child" can surprise doting parents. She had worn glasses from about her second birthday and one day, for no apparent reason, when we were all at poolside, she walked out on the diving board and announced, "I have to break my glasses." She took them off, snapped the nose-piece in two and dropped both halves in the pool. We still have not had a good explanation but you can be sure we asked. She liked stuffed animal toys to be "poofy" (with long fur). She must have been about 3 when she got a flowery new summer dress to wear to my cousin Mike's wedding. We never did learn where she got the idea that she would be the star of the show but she was a little taken aback when we arrived to find several grown-up girls, also wearing fancy new dresses. If the "wedding" occasion was not oversold, it had apparently been "overbought."

Coral was a good student from day one, but she had really bad luck with picking "best" friends. It began when we moved from La Mirada on the Orange/Los Angeles county border at the end of her kindergarten year to Auburn, where we have made our home for 40 years, and counting. We were at fault for the first loss by moving and leaving Paula from kindergarten but the next two or three friends just happened to be in families that left town after a year or two for some unpredictable reason while we didn't go anywhere. She wanted to be in Campfire and the club needed a leader so Ann volunteered for several years.

Shortly after getting her driver's license she was stopped for speeding on the highway with a load of her friends in Ann's car. She was embarrassed; we were surprised and I don't think she ever had another violation. The next year she won a new Toyota when our neighbors (the ones without kids of driving age) joined us in putting Coral's name on the tickets they put in the barrel for the annual "customer appreciation" prize drawing and party by our local, privately owned grocery. When the secretary/office manager for my *California Cattleman* magazine and real estate business resigned to take a job in Sacramento, Coral, who had done some work in the office, agreed to fill the vacancy, at least on a temporary basis. This was a tricky job. In addition to traditional office work, we had a photo darkroom and processed our own film and printed photos for use in the magazine and real estate brochures.

At the same time, Coral was in college, trying to decide on a career. After changing majors frequently during her first two years of college, Coral finally decided to major in journalism. She had always been good with words and I was pleased that she had followed my track from many years before when Doc Downs advised me to "take what's easy for you; when you get out of school, do what you please," and I chose journalism for "easy." Coral married her longtime boyfriend, Harold Flood, while still in college, and both juggled jobs and classes while finishing their degrees. As Coral's studies progressed, she was a top student and was selected to make the commencement speech for her department. She was hired by her favorite professor's wife as editor of a legislative newsletter monitoring bills affecting children. After a few years she was hired by a leading lobbying firm as a legislative analyst, and was promoted to manager when the position opened a few years later. Her employers let her reduce her hours and do part of her job at home after the kids were born, but the schedule and the commute became more difficult as Ryan and Mackenna got older. She stopped working outside the home when Mackenna was about a year old, and has a busier schedule now than when she was working.

Proof of the Pudding

My mother was a pretty good cook, especially when you consider that she had come up the hard way—before refrigeration was common on the farm. I was the first born and since we generally had a hired farm hand to help dad with outside work, I was available to be nursemaid for the younger siblings until I matured to the point that I could handle a team of horses and do serious outside work. This included an introduction to cooking for the family.

Mom had a book of recipes for desserts or other things she didn't cook for the family on a regular basis. I don't know where it went but I'd like to have her recipe for maple nut cake. I never had much of a sweet tooth and never cared for fluffy cakes (she was proud of her 12-egg-white angel food cake) but I always asked for her maple nut cake for my birthday.

Great recipes must be scarce. My wife and daughters have dozens of recipe books and there are endless magazines with new recipes for every occasion but we have found that humanity would be well served if 90 percent of them were used in the old Copper Clad range to make heat for the few really good recipes that exist. In my bachelor days I had a few standard mixes but often went begging when the occasion demanded something better.

I remember when Bill Norelius shared an apartment with me. We decided to roast our own bird for Thanksgiving guests. I didn't trust Sunday newspaper recipes and we didn't have a cookbook so I called Hollyce. She was married to my good friend and top salesman, Bob Neumeyer. "Hollyce," I explained, "Bill and I want to roast our own Thanksgiving turkey. Do you have a tasty, fool-proof, old family recipe for turkey stuffing?"

She called back in a few minutes with the magic potion. Our guests raved. I still have that hand-written recipe card. In the 50 years since that event, the recipe has been often used and given to several people who liked the results. When I later asked Hollyce about the recipe she told me she couldn't find her recipe at the moment and since they were ready to leave town when I called, she just gave me the first thing she found in a current magazine.

I had never tasted lasagna until after I was married and was uneasy when my wife, Ann, suggested it for dinner but she made it anyway. It was great. We had it often and for several years I ordered it away from home but no more. Hers was the best. Where did she get the recipe? It was not a family recipe from her Mayflower or Swedish ancestors. She got it from a lasagna noodle package.

How Much is That in Cereal Years?

It is the first few days of the year 2000. I am walking down the cereal aisle in the grocery store and notice that Wheat Chex cereal is on sale for $3.79 per box (as big as the corn flakes box), a serious discount from the $4.99 "regular" price. I had a flashback to an earlier time. It wasn't many light years but it has been 26 years since we moved into our current office on January 10, 1974. Ours was the first office completed in the new building at 161 Palm Avenue in Auburn. The owner had his carpenters finish the offices as the tenants' occupancy dates arrived.

Sue Reeves was our office manager and secretary shortly after we moved in. One day we happened to be discussing cereal. The topic of the moment was the sugar-coated cereals that were coming onto the market. How do you resist the pressure to buy sugar-coated cereals for your kids? Sue might have flunked all the psychological experts' kid-raising recommendations but she said she had a rule: We don't buy cereal that costs more than a dollar per box. And that eliminated all the sugar-coated ones. I didn't remember that any box of cereal ever cost less than a dollar. The wheat farmer got 7 cents a box then—5 cents now.

But on the same time/price comparison, I remember when I would come home and announce that I had just listed a big ranch for sale. The asking price was almost a million dollars. Both the seller and I agreed that the price was high but "things were going up." Now we sell less than half of that same ranch for more than the then-magic sale price of a million dollars.

I don't remember what year it was but I will always remember the shock during Jimmy Carter's administration when I filled my car's gas tank with gasoline near Alturas, California, and the attendant had to call his company's credit card office for an OK on my card because the tank full cost more than $15. Boy, has that ever changed!

334

The price I paid for the Mercury convertible I bought when I got out of the Navy in 1946 eludes me but I remember that I paid $2,300 for a new 1953 Pontiac two-door sedan when I moved to Ft. Dodge. I forget what the 1955 Pontiac hard-top cost but when I got the 1960 Olds four-door hardtop as the last car delivered before the GM strike, it cost almost exactly $4,000. We picked it up in Omaha on Halloween evening, 1959.

I paid $12,500 when I bought Bob Neumeyer's house in Denison and $13,900 in 1960 for the house in Des Moines. The best lot in town was priced at $14,000 in 1977 when we paid $15,500 for our acreage in the Auburn, California, suburbs. In 2000, an adjoining lot was worth over $200,000. Old friend Andy Joughin was right when he advised me early in my real estate career to "convince your client that no matter what he pays, if he buys a good ranch, time will make him a smart man." I agree about ranch values, but what can Sue Reeves tell her kids about sugar-coated cereal?

Super Scab

Some years ago I had cut the end of my thumb, near the nail, and it seemed to never heal. I had tried Band-Aids, adhesive tape and ointments, in a series and sometimes in combination. As the saying goes, it was far from my heart, but it continued to nag for days until one day I was using some Super Glue and spilled some on the old cut.

I tried to remove it with a Kleenex but it stuck. I pulled most of the tissue off but I was literally stuck with the remainder. I worried about the glue causing infection. Not this time. In a couple of days the remaining tissue fibers came off and the cut seemed to be forming a scab for the first time in days. It continued to be sore so I deliberately put a couple of drops of the glue on what had been a persistent cut. By the time this layer had worn off, the cut was healed.

I nearly forgot about the incident until some months later when by chance I heard a medical brief about a former successful prizefight cut man who had his "secret" cut medicine. He was world famous for putting his magic potion on even the most severely bleeding cut fighter between rounds and rarely having the cut get reopened during the remainder of the fight.

The medical report told us that the magic potion used by the cut man was simple old Super Glue. Augmenting that information from my "medical research" the medical people had found that the glue, in addition to sealing up the cut, was an excellent medication and sterilizer. This makes me wonder how the prizefight cut man knew what to use—or did he just stumble onto it like I did? At any rate, I have used it on myself and others ever since, with great success.

It's Not Home Any More

I drove west from Stapleton. The road was paved with asphalt. Where was the good old dirt road that Bud Danker had graded regularly with his trusty four-horse team and the manually-adjusted road grader they had pulled for years? I had to watch carefully to orientate myself to be sure I knew where to leave the highway to get on the old road that led to our ranch and the home I knew. I had returned to Stapleton for the 50th reunion of my high school class, which graduated in 1941. I hadn't been there in several years and expected some changes, but it hadn't occurred to me that the new owners of the ranch were magicians who could make the old cement-block ranch house totally disappear.

My parents retired from ranching in 1965, built a new brick house in Stapleton and sold the ranch to the McPherrin family, our long-time neighbors. I returned to attend my dad's funeral several years later and drove to the old farmstead. It was relatively unchanged from the home I remembered. It was bought and paid for, so the McPherrins had no obligation to get my permission to do anything to what had been my family home for so many years.

Grandpa Raynard had used native Sandhills sand itself to make the blocks. Then he had built the square block house with four rooms and a large pantry downstairs, and two bedrooms and a big storage closet upstairs. I don't know the year it was built, but I believe it was about 1908. He added Phase II a few years later when he built a large kitchen with basement. It was in the basement where he installed a new Delco 32-volt electricity generator with storage batteries. Electricity was installed in every room of the home and added to the barns and other outbuildings. And the basement had a bathtub. No indoor toilet replaced the outhouse while I lived there, but my parents remodeled the house after I was out of high school, turning the old giant pantry, strategically located near the center of the house, into a full-blown bathroom.

Grandma Brothers' farm on the north had been sold and re-sold since I lived there. The old Barner place on our west side was now operated by Glenn Dee, the Barners' second son. McPherrins owned their old home ranch to the east, where I often rode a horse to carry phone messages or summon one of their family members if the call was too personal for our ears. The Means place on our north was purchases by McPherrins many years earlier. Ralph Reynolds had moved to the old school section south of our place after my dad gave up the lease but both Ralph and Mrs. Reynolds had died and I didn't think to ask who operated it or if anyone still lived on the place.

Our barn was south and slightly east of the ranch house, standing tall and proud. The windbreak made of vertical 1-by-12 boards, a full 6 feet tall, still stretched to the east from the northeast corner of the horse barn to the cattle shed, forming a stud paddock and sometime corral for riding young horses or branding and vaccinating cattle between the two buildings. The barn was painted white. I had almost forgotten that it was white. I remembered it as a red barn with vertical white bats. It was after I was out of college that Dad had painted all the barns with white paint. This was a jolt at the time but after a few looks, I decided they looked better with a shiny new coat of white than the badly-weathered coat of red they had worn when I first knew them. They may have looked better but I was still uncomfortable with the change.

Nesbit School, the one-room country school that every member of my generation of the family had attended, was closed and the site abandoned. It sat on a lot that Grandpa gave the school district years earlier by easement. The lot had been cleared and even the fence was removed. The schoolhouse was sold and moved to a farm just west of Stapleton. I don't know what happened to the barn at the school where I had tied Jada or Midget every day for the eight years I went to Nesbit School when we lived on the school section. The barn should have been big enough to have some value. I doubt that the coal shed or either the boys or girls outhouse was worth saving. The road that ran through the ranch from east to west past the school had also been closed and the land returned to the adjoining pasture.

The "Mailboxes on the Wheel" were gone. This was the landmark at a T in the road a mile from our home where someone, years ago, had buried one end of a machine axle in the ground. The big iron wheel, rotating on the axle, made a base for numerous mailboxes. The mail carrier could stop and, by rotating the wheel, fill all the boxes without moving his vehicle. There was a community story about a tourist viewing the landmark: "47 Brothers and 45 Moore." Two of the families getting mail there were Chauncey Moore, Box 45, and M.D. Brothers, my grandparents, Box 47. I remember about 10 mailboxes when I ran to and from the wheel, which served as a school bus stop when I was in high school. The population had declined in 50 years. Now three boxes, side by side on a new post, were all that was needed.

The ranch entry road from the old highway, running a quarter mile south to the ranch headquarters, still had alfalfa fields on both the east and west sides. The grove of cottonwoods was depleted to a few trees. They may have outlived their genetic lifespan. Grandpa had planted them when he homesteaded the land in 1908. The apple orchard south of the cottonwoods had also lived well beyond their expected life span and had grown out of control with no pruning.

We had planted a Chinese Elm hedge in the 1940s along the east side of the entry road through the farmstead. Jack and I had pruned every branch that grew into the driveway while the rest of the family went to Canada on vacation. The elms had claimed nearly half of the road. Dad almost collapsed when he saw the new "haircut" we had given them but joined in the praise when a neighbor told him how much better it looked. The hedge needed another pruning.

But the new owners almost snatched away my birthright when they took a bulldozer to the landmark cement block home. They basically pushed it into the basement when the old electrical wiring threatened to burn the place down. The house was impossible to update to meet current building code. Plumbing, wiring, insulation and the limiting floor plan were all against it. Except for the memories, the new double-wide modular home was a screaming improvement.

Raynard family in our La Mirada, California, backyard in 1962. Pictured, l-r: Richard, Barbara, Rolland, Eunice, Jack, Harvey, Phil.

The cement block house earned and deserved its memories. The new one likely never will. I didn't realize until later that they had bulldozed the hackberry tree near the yard gate on the way to the barn—probably to bring in the new house. Thankfully, the owners did not disturb the matched pair of box elder trees east of the house, supporting many summers' worth of hammocks that generations of kids had lazed and swung in. Take photos of your keepsake memories. You can see them whenever you get the itch. But seeing the "improved" version of the old place can help you decide it might have been better to not return.

Those Were Dates to Remember

My parents were lifelong Republicans. I don't think they ever saw a good Democrat or a bad Republican. I never knew whether she really believed it or if she just said it to make my dad uncomfortable, but my Grandma Brothers, to her dying day, was an avowed Democrat. She never said why she was a Democrat; she just was. With this heritage, my parents convinced me that Franklin D. Roosevelt was scum and everything he did or said was suspect. I didn't have any serious political convictions so I generally accepted my parents' opinion on politics when I went into the Navy. I got accustomed to having Roosevelt as president during a year and a half of flight training, but it wasn't an endearing relationship. He was my commander-in-chief but the association wasn't personal as far as I was concerned.

We were at Corpus Christi going through our second tour of Operational Training, preparing for combat duty. We returned to the base from a training flight to see the flags flying at half staff. What had happened? The date was April 12, 1945. When we got to the BOQ (bachelor officers' quarters) somebody had a radio turned on and we heard for the first time that Roosevelt was dead. He was never my hero. I had never seen him. I was a Navy pilot, barely 21 years old, and had been through a rigorous training program. I should have been fairly mature and able to accept the news of any public official dying but I really felt empty inside. NAS Corpus Christi was a sober place that day. I think everyone on the base was shaken.

I remember one of my roommates, Bob Nichols, from Southwest City, Missouri. He may have spoken for most of us except that some of it was personal with him. He said that he should believe in Harry Truman, a fellow Missourian, but "Truman is a small-town politician who was our senator with no experience at being president." We had no choice. We were in the middle of a war and we suddenly had a new boss.

I had no knowledge and no expectations for the new president. We soon went to San Diego in final preparation for overseas duty. At San Diego we were in training, officially, but we carried live ammo and bombs. In a few weeks we got orders to join a patrol bomber squadron in the Philippines where we inherited an aging plane that had been flown by the original squadron commander's crew. In the Pacific area we heard (unofficially) from every source that we would soon begin the campaign on the Japanese homeland. Everyone knew that the Japanese would not give up easily and that the future would be bloody.

We soon got orders to return to San Diego to pick up a new plane, fresh from the factory, to replace our old one. This was in early August, 1945. We had been to Saipan where the skies were filled with B-29 bombers from nearby Tinian, the newest Air Corps super bombers that would help take Japan. When we got to San Diego our plane wasn't ready so we were sent to Camp Elliot north of San Diego to wait for the plane's delivery. A couple of days later we got an early Christmas present from our new president and a hearty endorsement of his policies. On August 6, 1945, Col. Paul Tibbets, flying the Enola Gay, a B-29 bomber, dropped "Little Boy," the first atomic bomb known to the world, on Hiroshima.

We didn't know that there was such thing as an atomic bomb, but it was welcome. Almost before we had time to react to the first bomb, a second bomb was dropped two days later on Nagasaki. We could smell victory. And the new guy we got for a president instantly became the hero for everyone in uniform. Our new quarterback had just thrown two touchdown passes. In dropping those two bombs, Harry Truman saved thousands of American lives. He authorized the killing of a lot of Japanese—although probably far fewer than would have died in an invasion of the homeland—but remember,

339

this was a war. And they started it. Like Roosevelt's death, these were days to remember.

When the Japanese government asked for peace on August 10, and on the official VJ day on August 15, our crew was still sitting at Camp Elliot waiting for our new plane so we didn't get to see how the news was received in our squadron in the Philippines. We heard about it a few days later when we got there and we were overjoyed with the news at San Diego. We even wondered if they would send us back to the Philippines. That was optimistic dreaming and of course we would have missed out on some great experience. A few days later we were sent back to the squadron but August 10th and 15th were big dates. When peace terms were signed on the battleship Missouri on September 15, it was probably important but to me, totally anticlimactic compared with those August events.

In another date to remember, the Great Western Livestock show in Los Angeles was always held around Thanksgiving time. I especially remember this show a year after I helped introduce the first combined livestock and flower show in the same arena. I had been running errands just before the Hereford judging and drove back onto the show grounds where I met Ed Wright, another publication field editor and good friend. Ed had just parked and was walking to the show barn where I was temporarily parked and was as wide-eyed as I had ever seen him. "Did you hear the news?" he asked. Before I could even ask what news, he blurted, "Kennedy has been shot."

"Are you sure?" I asked, in total shock and disbelief, then turned on my car radio for further confirmation of this unnerving and "impossible" news.

We rushed inside the barn to the show ring where the Hereford cattle show was in progress. Bob Jones, president of the Southern California Hereford Association and a CPA with a national accounting firm, was at ringside. We gave him the news and as soon as he was sure we weren't kidding, he picked up the microphone and announced the news to the unknowing—and unbelieving—crowd. This 100 percent activist Republican was as shaken as the rest of us on November 22, 1963, another day I will always remember.

The Good Stuff

Don't expect this to be a road map to ambrosia. The writer admittedly has warped taste about a few things. It started when I was young. I may have seen somebody cut the frosting off a slice of cake and set it aside for later. I did part of that. I cut the frosting off and ate the cake but then left the frosting on the plate. I never had a sweet tooth. Sweet things made me gag, even as a child. They still do, to a point. With this qualifying introduction, welcome to some of the good stuff I have discovered in years of travel.

My first real job after college was still a part of a training program but I was out of the office in a sales job. I had rented a mother-in-law apartment with limited cooking privileges so I ate out a lot. If you lived in Ogden, Iowa, in the early 1950s, that meant eating a lot at Rudy Pestotnik's Lincoln Cafe. It sat in the middle of Ogden on the south side of Highway 30. Ogden was lucky to have Rudy. Day in and day out, few towns had a better menu or better prepared food, but especially in the morning. I don't know when Rudy got up but he made a giant tray of cinnamon rolls and another of sticky buns loaded with pecans. That was the motivator to get up early. I remember the tray of cinnamon rolls always lasted until late morning but not the pecan sticky buns. Nine a.m., tops. A testing machine might have proven that they were as sweet as the frosting I cut off a cake but they didn't taste that way to me. No, I don't have the recipe.

My uncle Hank owned a 40-acre field on the south side of the highway that jogged into our property. It cornered a 40 on the north side of the road that we leased from Joe McGue for years. When Joe died, the heirs offered to sell us the 40. Dad bought it and traded it to my Uncle Hank. This squared up both properties—or so it appeared on paper—unless you liked crab apple jelly. A giant tree on the line between Hank's property and the McGue place raised a crop of crab apples every year. I tasted the jelly at Grandma's house and knew we had to have some so we picked apples every fall until Hank retired and sold the property. Years later I returned for a visit to the old homestead. The buyers had removed the boundary fence that separated Hank's place from the McGue 40 and with it that big old crab apple tree. Oh well, maybe that jelly wasn't really as good as I remembered it.

I was spending the day with a salesman in Page County, Iowa. He was a feed salesman and I was his supervisor. We were calling on livestock feeders in the Clarinda area. This was a county seat town and the place where 4-H clubs were invented and '40s band leader Glenn Miller was born. George suggested that we visit a client near the Missouri border and go to Blanchard for lunch. Blanchard for lunch? Blanchard was not a town. It was barely a crossroads with a mom-and-pop grocery, a school and a lumber yard/hardware store that was our dealer.

Where do you eat lunch in Blanchard? I wondered, unless he had relatives there. Over the basement entry at the side of the hardware store was a small "café" sign but the good stuff was inside. Two local women had served "home-cooked" meals there for years and people came from miles around. How about roast beef sandwiches on fresh homemade bread or a roast beef dinner and "picked fresh this morning" berries for a strawberry shortcake? The menu was limited in the number of entrees but not the quality or flavor.

During the years that I published the *California Cattleman* I was present at a lot of livestock affairs, including dozens of bull sales where purebred livestock breeders sell their year's produce. This event generally begins with a free lunch provided by the breeder. The publication field men that served as bid spotters, attended many sales and we knew the quality of the cattle produced by each breeder but we never talked about it openly. We drove from one sale to the next, day after day, during the busy fall sale season and buyers, sellers and bulls blended together. The season could get boring but each place had memorable events.

We began rating the breeder sales by the quality of the lunch they served. Tehama Angus always treated the sale crowd well at lunchtime, as did Nugget hotel and casino owner John Ascuaga at his Hereford sale. But the runaway winner was the sale of Polled Herefords at San Jose, owned by HP computer inventors Bill Hewlett and Dave Packard. It was the first time I ever saw an electric-powered contraption with a series of vertical spits, rotating choice tri-tip roasts surrounding an expanded metal core of charcoal embers. They were barbecued to a perfect medium rare by lunchtime as the Basque bakery bread arrived, along with other lunch goodies and tubs of fruit salad loaded with fresh strawberries and melon balls. What thinking field man wouldn't recommend those cattle to anyone with a cowherd?

The drought and depression of the 1930s also brought poverty. We learned, as a family, to survive. We had livestock. Prices were so low it hardly paid to sell our produce and livestock. We couldn't get enough money from our produce to buy food so we ate what we grew. We cured our own hams, bacon, corned beef and dried beef, soaking them in brine using a mix from Morton Salt Co. It involved marinade in a crock and injecting the meat with salt brine, followed by drip-dry hanging in a cool, dry place such as our basement. The pork was good but the dried beef was more akin to big chunks of jerky than the stuff you buy in stores today or got served in a military mess hall. If you shaved it thin, cross-grain, and used real butter in the cream sauce, it made great chipped beef on toast.

Today's ham is not as different from our basement cure as was the dried beef. Some kind of ham is needed for another of my "good stuff" memories, three-day navy bean soup. It takes a cup of dry beans, 6 cups of water, a couple of dozen black peppercorns and a few bay leaves. Soak in water overnight, bring to a boil and simmer for an hour then refrigerate. Add a pound or more of ham, cubed, bring to a boil and simmer for an hour the next day, then refrigerate. On the day you want to eat the soup, add water up to the original level, a garlic clove, medium onion, quartered, and simmer for about an hour until the beans begin to lose shape, then serve. Eat the peppercorns if you like but discard the bay leaves. You also discard the bay leaves if you make my pot roast. I once used arm roast but packers don't make them any more so I like a tri-tip or other rump cut. Add potatoes, carrots, an onion and your favorite meat spices. But please, no french fries with pot roast as a grossly misguided Fresno restaurant operator once did when Bank of America had the annual California Livestock Symposium get-togethers in that city.

When it was chokecherry time, our family drove 30 miles to pick wild chokecherries and currants from the banks of the Dismal River. This operation had two separate and unequal parts. Picking is awful. It takes a jillion cherries to make a gallon. Each berry is a medium-sized pit, surrounded by flavored skin and almost no meat. Then when you begin to make jelly, they are mostly pits. This means an awful lot of picking, which is bad enough by itself but I always had to be partially responsible for keeping little brothers Jack and Dick out of trouble if not helping to pick berries.

Fortunately we had time to forget these troubles by the time we ate the jelly. The only fruit to match those two for flavor, in my opinion, is the Damson plum in our Auburn garden. The preserves are so good we haven't gone to the trouble to make jelly. There was another plum that made me aware of how good plums could be. Jack and I discovered a secret open area playground in the middle of thicket while picking wild plums for plum butter. That was a double winner. We got away from the "grown-up" world and wild plum butter was out of this world.

One yearly event on our ranch, though different, was nearly as painful as picking chokecherries and was guaranteed tearful. In the end it was possibly as rewarding as chokecherry jelly. This was the ritual of digging, cleaning and grinding horseradish. We always had three perennial plants in our garden: asparagus, rhubarb (my Grandma Brothers called it pie plant) and horseradish. Asparagus and rhubarb were simple to prepare, especially if you didn't use too much sugar on the rhubarb. Horseradish gave off an aura that made a sissy out of the rankest onion. It was easy to dig and brush clean in water but it had to be ground to be used on meat and if you were the one who ground the horseradish root, you cried. It was guaranteed to clear your sinuses and tear ducts.

A few years after he picked up the homestead on the land west of Stapleton, Grandpa Raynard planted a large orchard, just south of the protection of the cottonwood grove planted earlier. These trees must have been nearly 30 years old when I lived with my grandparents, doing chores for my room and board, so I could ride the school bus to high school. Apples get ripe at different times of year with some mature in midsummer and other varieties coming on line every week or so until late fall. Frost comes fairly early in Nebraska. I remember my dad as once saying the average "killing" frost in our county was September 27. I don't know if that meant only the tenderest plants got killed or how many survived after that date. We did get the apples picked and stored in the cellar shortly after school started.

I did not know much about apples. We did not have any soil good enough for an orchard on the school section where we lived. I was surprised that some were ripe and gone while others were still hard as stones. The fruit from one tree amazed me and gave me one of my earliest claims to fame. I later was told that it was a variety called "Greening" that produced large—giant is more accurate—fruit that had to be picked before it was ripe, then it ripened in the storage cave or cellar some weeks later and could be kept for months without spoilage. They were not only green; they were the original green giants.

The orchard was never given fertilizer or hormones but the smallest of these Greening apples were the size of softballs; large ones like the biggest cantaloupe. One of these, plus a sandwich, made lunch for any school kid. We ate our bag lunches in the high school gym and everybody saw what everybody else had for lunch. "Everybody" is a vague term but we had nearly 100 kids in high school and about a third lived in Stapleton so we probably had about 50 to 60 eating lunch in the gym. We had a barrel-full of Greening apples. I had one every day for months and almost every day I had an audience to see the size of the apple in my lunch.

I went home for Christmas when I was in college but I had Christmas and birthdays in some strange places while I was in the Navy. That was when the world discovered that popcorn was the parcel protector that you could eat. What I wanted as a birthday cake was what my mother called a "maple nut cake." It had no maple and was really a spice cake with nuts baked in a loaf pan, but it was the walnuts that made it great. I got one sent to me at Navy air bases all over the country and in the Philippines. The only food as welcome, but impossibly hard to ship, even with popcorn, might have been gooseberry, blueberry or rhubarb pie. Good stuff.

Typing 1, Etc.

My computer began acting strangely last week, as if it didn't have a brain in its Apple head. It wasn't getting the message to the printer that I wanted it to write a letter and instead began sending information to me about things I didn't know existed. Why, after nearly eight generally trouble-free years, would it become my enemy? Not that we had ever been great friends, but we had sort of a gentleman's agreement to coexist and not cause each other too much grief. Even a call to Harold, my son-in-law, who generally has some kind of road map to get me out of minor computer glitches, didn't cure its insubordination. Then I saw the time indicator at the top of the screen. It was yesterday. Suddenly I recalled a similar incident about four years earlier when I noticed a slow response to some of my ideas and learned that the battery had run down in four years. Well, it was four years later and I got another new battery. My computer acts like it just had a brain transplant. It lets me sound relatively coherent again.

This prompted me to recall my eagerness to take Typing 1 in high school and the thrill of learning a new method of communication. Once I learned to type I never again felt the urge to write anything longhand. It has been long enough since that happened that I can compare it with my reluctance to accept the tractor as the new power source when it arrived in our community. I was ready to learn typing and accepted it eagerly but the tractor did not excite me at all.

When it came on the scene, I wondered what an electric typewriter might offer over my old mechanical model. I took a test drive and found that the words practically jumped off my fingers and onto the page. I had to have one. Several typewriters later my machine was getting casual about delivering some services and I was not assured by my repairman that it would be "cost effective" to repair the old friend. I was not ready for all the functions that computers could perform nor did I feel I needed many of them but I had seen how easy it was to read proof and correct errors when using the word processor function. While I was a fairly accurate typist, the idea of ending erasures and correction fluid had great appeal. This was in 1993 and I was assured that the industry had peaked out on innovation and that what I could buy then would be near "state of the art" for years to come.

I did not know the difference between a PC and a Mac except that they used different systems that were not compatible. I asked both my daughters, who were literate in both systems, which I should get and without hesitation, both said "get a Mac." When I asked why, both said I would get impatient and stick my fist through the screen if I got a PC.

Now, in 2001, I find that my 8-year-old unit is too slow to get any satisfaction from "getting online." I am not interested in looking at a screen all day but there are some services online that could be helpful and possibly almost necessary in the near future. To change systems now, with the new PC operating systems, including the mouse, wouldn't be such a challenge to my patience. There is more software available and at lower cost for PC units than for a new Mac. Decisions, decisions. (Incidentally, my Mac crashed; it was replaced with a PC in 2004.)

My Almost Big Brother

"What is that set of photos?" I asked myself as I began to uncover one of the accumulations that occur in my office from time to time. They were photos taken a couple of years earlier when I visited my late uncle Bill's ranch in Montana. I was never on the ranch while Bill was alive. I had been "too busy" to keep in close touch with him. With Bill, you had to be the one who kept in touch by either visiting him on his turf or being where he happened to go. He did not write and I don't know that he ever made a long-distance call but he was a good person. He lived his life, with you or without you. He accepted all people for what they were and made no demands. I hadn't seen him since we both returned separately to Stapleton 10 years earlier, for my

345

class reunion, shared with several other classes. I did not miss him when we didn't see each other but he was easy to like. Finding those photos made me recall our lives together . . . and apart.

Six years can get you included, or excluded. I was in the awkward position of being six years younger than my Uncle Bill, my dad's baby (and only) brother. I was too young, in the early years, to be included with Bill in anything other than a family activity. My first recollection of Bill was not of him but of Trixie, his white-and-black-and-brown rat terrier. She was special, which made Bill special. I had never seen a dog so tiny and she had a fancy collar with metal studs all the way around and Grandma let her in the house. With all that, she had to be special. We had greyhounds and they were not "house" dogs. I don't recall an event that ever included Bill and Trixie and me, nor how long she lived, but she is firmly in my mind, connected to Bill.

We both went to the Nesbit one-room school but Bill was one of the "big boys" six years ahead of me so we had little in common except for our last name. He was not remembered as a student. I remember when I started to high school and told him that Louise Plageman was my English teacher. When she took roll the first day she asked if I was "Billy's brother." I didn't understand the implication when I told her I was his nephew but Bill was quick to tell me that it wouldn't do me any favors to claim him as a relative in any class, especially English.

Bill was proud of the school's football team. He was a three-year letterman at tackle and I later heard that he had told someone he would have quit high school in a minute but for football and his coach, Willard Waldo, who was also the ag teacher. I told Willard about this many years later and he said that Bill and the town were all proud of that team. It was the first time the school had a "break even" season with as many wins as losses in the few years since they began playing football. Bill's class graduated in 1935.

Bill was a member, if not the ringleader of a gang-of-four in his class that included Dennis Clark, George Wallace and Byron Kesslar. There were not many possibilities to get into trouble in Stapleton in 1935 but the evening of a graduation practice, in a few idle moments, the four wandered through the empty school and found a typewriter in the principal's unlocked office. They had seen, but they had never used a typewriter. They couldn't resist the temptation to see their names in print. All, that is, except Bill, and he was probably the most likely of the four to be involved in mischief.

When the authorities discovered the dirty deed the next day, the guilty ones had to get their parents to sign a paper of permission to graduate. Dennis and Byron confessed to their parents, who signed. George Wallace felt he couldn't handle the problem with his parents so he conned his mother into demonstrating her signature on a piece of paper and he later filled in the permission part. But the mystery was why those three would be involved

346

without Bill. He explained his innocence by saying he didn't plan to take up typing and didn't see that he had anything to gain by typing his name.

After graduation, Bill worked at home on the farm, then after Grandpa died, my dad partnered with Grandma, and we moved to their farm. Bill lived in the tenant house with Grandma, working for my dad. He also bought and trained saddle horses, including a brown gelding in 1939 or '40 called Seabiscuit after the famed racehorse of the day, and hunted coyotes with hounds. Coyote hides were worth $10 to $15 dollars apiece. Farm laborers earned $30 to $50 per month so a few coyote pelts really changed your standard of living.

I remember one day when I was riding with Bill. We jumped five coyotes in a five- to 10-acre weed patch, probably a litter of young ones. Fortunately for us, all the hounds chased the same coyote. In a short burst, the pack of hounds made the catch. We tied the coyote on a saddle and rode back through the weed patch to see if any had returned. One had, and we soon had a second coyote on the saddle, and we continued riding through those weeds until we got all five. And even though Bill was normally a good sport, he never gave me a dime from those five pelts.

When Nebraska farm labor jobs became scarce, Bill went to Idaho with a neighbor boy, where they heard that jobs were available in the sugar beet and potato harvest. He worked there until December 7, 1941, the bombing of Pearl Harbor. The next day he and nephew Ray Barner enlisted in the Navy. The war followed and he made the Navy a career, retiring as a Chief Gunner's Mate in 1963 after more than 20 years' service. He returned to the Montana ranch he had purchased a few years earlier. As a new landowner and outdoor lover, he was anxious to build a home.

Much of the ranch was forested so Bill began falling trees to build his residence, a cabin about 16 feet by 24 feet. The Navy did not train gunner's mates to build log cabins but he cut the trees and built one, alone. He finished it just as winter set in so he retired to the city for the winter without cutting holes for the door or windows and later imagined aloud the frustration of a hunter lost in a storm who sees a sheltering cabin, only to find it had no windows or doors. He continued cutting and built a storage shed, an outhouse and a stable with two large stalls plus a storage area. He used large (very heavy) poles for the stable but built it and the other buildings alone, erecting the poles with the help of a pinto mare and the leverage of an A-frame hoist.

Numerous family members stopped by. My brother Jack and his wife, Mary, parked their motor home at the edge of the clearing near Bill's cabin to spend time for more than a dozen summers. I was often invited to visit but never "found time" while he was alive. After Bill's death in the spring of 1999, none of the bachelor's relatives wanted, or could afford the ranch. Incidentally, it sold for $1.2 million with no power, water or phone.

Character 101

I don't remember the 1929 crash on Wall Street but I well remember the Depression that followed. It hurt everyone in the country. There hadn't been many rich farmers before the crash but there were fewer after it. Rich and poor got hurt by the hard times. Market prices for farm products fell along with other commodities and wages. We couldn't get enough money for our produce to make a living but the salvation for people living on farms was the fact that we could "live off the land," so to speak. We raised our own livestock and the hay and grain to feed our stock. Many of the wage earners and their families in the city were out of jobs and had no recourse. For many, it was either the government bread lines or hunger.

The Nebraska Sandhills were too far from a city for us to ever see a bread line but we heard about them and saw photos so we were convinced the story was true. Farm families were grateful that they had home-raised grain, meat and eggs, even if we barely got enough for our produce to pay for hauling it to market. I vividly recall a meeting years later, in the 1950s, with a grain elevator owner who showed me two telegrams in a picture frame on his wall. His grandfather had been a Western Iowa lamb feeder. During the worst of the depression, he had shipped several train carloads of fat lambs to the Chicago Stock Yards livestock market. One telegram informed him that the sale price of the sheep lacked $5.60 of paying the freight bill due for hauling the sheep. "Please pay this difference," he was told. His seven-word reply telegram read, "Have no money. Will send more sheep."

While farm families suffered the low prices, they at least had food for the table. 1932 had below-normal rainfall and crop yields suffered, so we had even less produce to sell at those record low prices. The drought continued in 1933 with an even shorter crop yield and 1934 was a total disaster. Pastures barely grew any green grass. Corn in our community never got big enough to have any value, even as green feed for cattle. Wheat, rye and oats would normally make enough growth from winter moisture alone to be a crop worth harvesting. The winter wheat and rye never matured enough to head out so we pastured what little green growth we had. Spring-planted crops barely sprouted. Some weeds did grow and we cut and stacked them, mostly Russian thistles, for livestock feed. We learned why they were called "weeds" when the cattle got so little nutrition that many of our cows lost their calves from nutritional abortion. Now, with the drought, farm families had no money and were challenged for home-grown food.

We had some spring rain in 1935 and grew a partial crop but the drought was not over. Our first return to near normal crops came in 1939 and '40. The national economy also recovered slowly. There were no spare dollars anywhere when I graduated from high school and enrolled for my first year of college in 1941. I was 17 years old and had hardly spent a night away from home. We ended our Sunday afternoon game of playing catch with a football in the church parking lot across the street from my cheap student room. I turned on my roommate's radio to hear that Pearl Harbor had been bombed. I had no training or experience that could have given me any real understanding of what that news meant—but I knew. I didn't know everything but I knew enough. That was the most sobering event in my life at the time. It was sobering for America too.

My first thoughts were of aunts Marjorie and Lillian, my dad's younger sisters, who had moved to Hawaii. I knew they lived in Honolulu and I knew that Pearl Harbor was in or near Honolulu. I had never been there nor seen a map of the city so I didn't know if they were near or far from the action. The first follow-up broadcasts would report that damage was strictly limited to the Pearl Harbor Navy base and immediate surrounds so I had less concern for their safety and more for my long-term and immediate career implications as well as fear for the country. I was to learn later that my aunts had an apartment in the Punch Bowl area a few blocks north of Beretania, a main east-west thoroughfare that paralleled the beach a few miles east of Pearl. They could hear the planes and explosions but could only see planes before and after their dive attacks on the naval base. We had no TV and news traveled slowly in those days. When I visited there three and a half years later courtesy of the United States Navy, I took photos from a spot near my aunts' apartment, of ships leaving Pearl Harbor on their way to sea.

We were a broke country, inching our way out of a financial disaster with a "Depression" military made up mostly of young men who joined up to get a bed, a square meal and a regular, if small, paycheck. It had been more than 20 years since the end of World War I and, although the European countries were still up to their old antics of swapping soldiers' lives for real estate, it hardly occurred to enlistees in any of the U.S. military branches that they might be involved in a war. A military person was not held in much esteem and the uniform of any service branch was neither stylish nor prestigious. I was trying to get established in school and to find enough work that I could pay my $6 per month rent and have something left to buy groceries. Jim Cahill, my roommate at the time, was good at macaroni and cheese. When I was lucky enough to get a job at the University creamery we had free or very cheap cheese and milk, which helped.

I didn't know it at the time but I grew up that Sunday. And so did everyone in the country. America was just coming out of a deep financial depression and so was almost every one of its citizens. But we both, the country and the people, had resources that we began to draw on immediately. It is widely recorded in the history books so I don't need to say more about it. During the 1980s and '90s I was frequently concerned about both our country and our people.

We had it so good for so long that I really wondered what would happen if we ever had to face another "Pearl Harbor." I was concerned that most of our younger generations had lived in such unchallenging times that I feared they might be flabby in both mind and body, an easy mark for enemies, home-grown dissidents—including those running for office—or foreigners. I had commented to acquaintances about my concern on several occasions.

Within days of my last criticism of our soft young Americans came the suicide attacks on New York and Washington, our "Pearl Harbor for the 21st Century"—our 911 call on 9-11-01. Now I wonder if the 70-year-old veterans had been as concerned about our country and the character of our people in the late 1930s and early 1940s as I had been some 60 years later. I see the December 7, 1941, enemy attacks on Pearl Harbor and September 11, 2001, on the World Trade Center/Pentagon as similar but different.

Both were surprise attacks on U.S. soil that I believe could and should have been known and prevented if our FBI and CIA spy organizations had done the job they were created and paid to do. They differed in that the Pearl Harbor attack was the Japanese nation attacking our military. The Trade Center attack was organized and carried out by a splinter political group of no particular country and the attack was on civilians, not our military people. We suddenly had to fight an enemy with little apparent public base or organization in a 21st Century cave-to-cave type of warfare.

We had incredibly different preparation for our separate crises. I was too self-involved at the time of Pearl Harbor to be objective, but looking back and comparing the response of our people some 60 years apart, it seems to me that our current generation is made of pretty good stuff after all. We came upon our character by different routes. We in the World War II generation knew that the privation and "fulfillment denied" of the depression-age 1930s and '40s had honed us to be both mentally fit and determined. How do we explain the character and resourcefulness of our 21st century's overindulged generation? The important thing, to me, is that even though it might appear that both generations were badly but differently prepared and certainly not alert to a crisis pending in the immediate future, we both had the character and visceral resources when it counted.

Hyphenated Mischief

It would be interesting, if not outright fun, to be a "Hyphenated American." But it's hard. It seems you have to be a real opportunist to be a "hyphenated" anything. What kind of an American is a Canadian-American? Does that qualify? Or is a Canadian already an American? If my Canadian ancestry qualifies me, wonderful. It is not many generations since my grandfather was an immigrant from Canada, as was my dad's oldest sister. Dad was just born too late to qualify. How stupid or "non-opportunistic" of him! There are thousands or millions whose immigrant ancestors are more generations removed than mine who insist on being "hyphenated." But they don't think it's fair for me to use the hyphen.

Isn't that unfair? How can I get anybody to lobby for my interests as a Canadian-American as they do for every other kind of hybrid or "hyphenated American?" Immigrants to the United States from the first country to our south are gladly "hyphenated;" why not those from the north? Native-Americans, African-Americans, Asian-Americans have parades, lobbyists, get government programs, school preferences, tax benefits, special privileges, business and personal loan benefits—even their own holidays, and a long shopping list of special treatments because of that hyphen. They can and do but I think I'll decline.

It is my observation that the smart ones get rid of the hyphen as soon as possible. The early Irish immigrants, the Irish-Americans, began getting jobs as policemen and laborers, endured "Irish Cop" jokes for a generation but they soon got smart and became absorbed into the society and the economy, trading their hyphenated ethnicity for broad acceptance and opportunity. I am positive that African-Americans and Mexican-Americans will be considered second-class citizens by much of our society, and especially by themselves, until they shed their hyphenated status. And with the departure of the hyphen will go the parasites who have leeched profitable careers as self-appointed champions, both in the press and in the political circles, of these formerly second-class, "hyphenated" Americans.

If you want to be an American, stand alone as an American. The sooner you walk without the crutch of hyphenation, the better for you and the better for the rest of us. It may once have helped you up but now it holds you down. It may have helped you walk but it will never let you run. Get rid of that hyphen and you will singularly become an American. Then you will neither need nor accept the crutch given you by well-wishers and alleged benefactors whose campaign for your benefits is really a campaign for themselves in the form of praise, money, endorsements or votes, to the detriment of the people they claim to help. Remember that "second-class" is hyphenated. American is not. Take away my soap box but don't try to hold me down with a hyphen that means, for the entire world, **second-class** citizen.

Memories from the "Old Days"

Aunt Hazel and Uncle "Let" lived in Stapleton in the early 1930s. Hazel was my dad's older sister, who married Lester Barner. Uncle Let owned a truck and partnered with Shorty Upton in hauling grain, hogs, family possessions, etc. as Stapleton's only movers of whatever needed moving. I enjoyed our trips to town to play with the Barner kids. They had Harold, Evelyn, Thelma, Raymond (a year older than me) and Melvin before a recess, then Bob, Russ,

Keith, Jim and Myrtle. I think they moved to the farm somewhere during the last five.

I remember playing on old truck tires, swinging from a questionable tree branch and exploring. The block across the street was mostly a vacant lot but on the far side of the block was the Moran residence and mill. "Shag" Moran ran the mill and would grind everything from baking flour to livestock feed. If you needed cracked wheat for cereal, brown or white bread, or even rye flour, Shag could do it and if you just wanted a small bag of cracked wheat, he would do it "on shares," keeping part of your grain for his pay. This was a great incentive as most people in the 1930s had a little grain but less money so we could get our flour virtually free.

My mother didn't like to do business at the Moran mill. She thought he was dirty and he looked the part but it was "clean" dirt. "Shag," probably got his name from his appearance. He wore old clothes, his hair nearly reached his collar, topped with a tattered bill cap made out of cloth, I think. He was so covered with flour dust we could hardly tell where his white eyebrows, hair, cap, or shirt ended and Shag began. Even his shoes were white. He was one of the town characters from his appearance alone. Probably in his 40s or 50s, he was stoop-shouldered and walked with a bit of a shuffle in his gait. Except for the mill dust in the air, he was a good neighbor. We kids liked to watch the mill operation but he always made us keep a safe distance from the action. *What was dangerous about the mill?* we wondered. I never knew whether Harold Tatman got his flour from Moran's mill but I remember my Aunt Hazel bought bread from Tat's Bakery. She got two loaves of day-old or maybe two-day-old bread for a quarter. With five big kids—and five little ones—to feed, two for a quarter was a real bread deal.

A few years later I noted another memorable "twofer" when I got to Lincoln to begin college. I didn't use them, but Cheaper Drug on O Street sold two packs of name-brand cigarettes for a quarter. But just a couple of blocks west on the north side of O was Brick's Diner with 25-cent cheeseburgers and 15-cent malts. This was in the fall of 1941. I later worked a few hours a week as an usher at the Capitol Theater, which showed mostly second-run movies. I don't remember the price of the evening ticket but it was a quarter for an adult and 10 cents for kids in the afternoons. One of the curiosities from the theater was the lost-and-found depository for items picked up by the cleaners in their daily sweep-down. There was the expected collection of combs, earrings, candy bars, shoes and other apparel items that had been dropped or removed and forgotten by the owner. I still wonder how one person managed to leave without a hint that something was missing when he left an artificial leg, shoe and all.

Many years later, during the mid- to late-1950s, I was asked, as a trusted friend, to participate in a serious financial decision. Fay Leemkuil owned the gas station where I traded in Denison, Iowa. He had a Phillips 66 franchise but that was not the source of his financial dilemma. Soft drink machines of that era did not take paper money and make change as they sent your drink down one slot and your change down another. This was an insulated box measuring about 2 by 3 feet with a hinged lid on top. The drinks all came in glass bottles and hung by their necks in metal slots. To buy a drink, you raised the lid, slid the drink of your choice down a maze of slots to the take-out and inserted your nickel. The coin tripped the gate and you lifted your drink from the cooler.

One day when I filled my car with gas, Fay approached me very seriously and asked what the customers would think if he raised the price of drinks from a nickel to a dime. He explained that prices had gone up so much that he was paying almost 5 cents for every bottle and suppliers had told him another raise was coming. He could get the machine changed to take dimes but not pennies. He would have to double the price he had been charging. "I don't care if they buy fewer drinks," he told me. "I have drinks as a service and I don't want a price increase to make my customers mad so they quit coming to my station." I reassured him that I wouldn't leave. He changed to a dime. I stayed with him and I think everybody else did too, but it was a hard 5-cent decision for him at the time.

An incident from my military life in the Philippines involving price or fairness did not concern me except as an observer. Military life is rarely on an even keel. It mixes days of boredom with moments of extreme pressure. The dull days give an excuse to pump imagined life into otherwise non-events. A soldier from somewhere in the Pacific wrote to *Yank*, the military publication, that he and a friend had gone to the PX and purchased Hershey bars. His friend got five almonds in his bar while the writer got six almonds in his. How, he asked, could this have occurred and was it fair? This started a letter-writing campaign that ran for weeks with various imagined explanations offered for the unfairness. Then one day someone volunteered the solution. He wrote that the incident was obviously a grave error and assured the victims that all the guilty parties would be brought to face military justice for the wrongs. Meantime, he explained the error by saying that the soldier who got the bar with six almonds had somehow gotten an officer's candy bar by mistake. End of letter campaign.

Four Men and a Jeep

I have a vague memory of an automobile in the era of my childhood called the Willys-Knight (later Willys-Overland). I didn't know anybody who owned one and my memory of it is more the fact that it existed than what it looked like or how it performed. It was one of several brand names vying for sales as new ideas competed for the easy money of the period called the "Roaring Twenties" and the vanishing dollars that followed during the financial crash and depression of the 1930s. Most of these companies failed to survive and most experts would probably not have picked the Willys name to be one of the survivors. But the experts wouldn't have known a war was coming and that someone at Willys would have an idea that would thrive on war. That idea was the Jeep.

I was never in Europe during World War II so I don't know if there are miles of jungles with no roads where we needed to be to fight a war. But I was in the Pacific, from where there were fellow veterans who swore that we beat the Japanese on the ground because we had the Jeep and the Japanese did not. There was a saying that four men and a Jeep could go anywhere. If it couldn't carry the four men where they needed to go, the four men could push, pull or carry the Jeep. It was the original "four-wheeler." It and other "look-alikes" have all but replaced the horse for covering a lot of area for checking cattle, riding fence, etc.

In one of its configurations, the Jeep also became the ideal vehicle for ranch real estate brokers. I got our first Jeep in the form of a Grand Wagoneer, a mid-1970s model, when we sold the Glide Hill Ranch in the low foothills of the California Coast Range. We were taking a ranch tour with Mrs. Glide only a few days before escrow was schedule to close. I admired her Wagoneer and asked her what she would do with it after the ranch was gone. "I'll take it back to the dealer and ask him what he'll give me for it," she answered, "I won't need it in my condo." I volunteered that I'd give her a hundred dollars more. "Oh no, you won't," she barked at me. "He never did me any favors. If you want it, you'll get it at his price." And she kept her word.

This was the buy of the season. It was 2 years old with less than 10,000 miles and she had it serviced, cleaned and polished regularly. The front tires showed irregular wear from improper alignment. That wouldn't do for Mrs. Glide. She had the alignment checked and delivered it with all new tires. We drove it to nearly 300,000 miles with a minimum of service, then we purchased a second in a chain of used Wagoneers.

The Glide Jeep was a bronze-colored 1975 or '76 model. Its eventual replacement was a gray 1980 model, which was replaced by a red 1986 model and then by a white 1990 version, the last year the Grand Wagoneer was made. I'm not sure a better ranch vehicle was ever made. It had good clearance, short turning radius and good power. It can take a client to almost any point on any property. If it just got decent mileage it would be ideal but nothing is perfect. One of these years I'll have to change ranch cars or occupations. I don't remember how, but I got along before I got the first Jeep. It was more luck than thoughtful research that we got it but it served so well for so long. Maybe I'll discover that there is another model as good when I'm forced to do it.

College, Pearl Harbor and Phil Joins the Navy

By the time I graduated from high school, I had a Union Pacific Carl Gray scholarship for $100 and a Montgomery Ward scholarship for about $500, and my high school teachers told me I was capable of college work. What else do you need to go to college? First, you need to get to the town where the college is located and I didn't have a ticket. Hey, when you grew up in the isolation of rural Nebraska—and I mean very rural—you start with the elementary stuff.

I had a few lucky breaks. Don Cahill was two years ahead of me in high school. He was established and had a room at the University. I got his address and the phone number of the house where he was rooming. My parents drove me to Lincoln, and while we were there, decided to go to the Nebraska State Fair. We sat at a picnic table to eat lunch and were shocked to find that my cousins, Ed and Marian Taylor, had also picked that day, time and table for lunch.

Don sort of adopted me when I got to Lincoln, arranged for me to room with him, took me to register for work at the college employment office and introduced me to the manager of the college creamery, where he worked. Oh yes, Don had a car, which was rare for students in September 1941. Almost everybody took the city bus everywhere they went. It was even routine to take dates to and from events on the bus at that time. It beat walking.

I had less than $20 in my pocket when I got to Lincoln and about the same in my meager bank account. I needed work, constantly. Odd jobs, like spading gardens, cleaning attics and garages, even helping chop silage at the Ag College Dairy, paid 25 cents per hour. And when a kindly lady offered a bonus of an extra quarter or a glass of milk and some cookies when you finished spading her garden, it really was a bonus. During some bad weeks, it was also supper.

Room rent was $8 per month, which was hard to raise. That meant 32 hours of spading gardens or cleaning attics. By late fall the college dairy hired me for part-time work. I was put on the weekend shift, working eight to 10 hours almost every Saturday and/or Sunday. Not only did I earn $4 to $5 almost every weekend, but our student crew could use milk and cheese, free, for lunch while at work. We alternated bringing lettuce, sliced meat and bread. The University of Nebraska even furnished ice cream for dessert. With all this good fortune, it began to appear that college and I were going to make it, together.

We got our work done by early afternoon on the first Sunday of December so I had a few rare afternoon hours to myself. Roland Essman and Bob Gingery roomed across the street. Roland was in my class; Bob, who was a cousin to movie actor Robert Taylor, was a junior. They were passing a football in the vacant church parking lot so I changed out of my creamery clothes and joined them on the warm (for December) afternoon.

When our game broke up and I went to my room, Jim Cahill (Don's brother who became my roommate when Don got a job with room furnished elsewhere) was at his desk. I turned on Jim's radio to learn that Pearl Harbor was being bombed. I had barely been outside our rural Nebraska county, would not be 18 until the following February and I didn't know what "deep thinking" meant, but this event got my attention. I may have felt the impact more than some other students. I had two aunts in Honolulu. Marge and Lil, my dad's younger sisters, had lived there for a few years.

Every male college student began to see military implications. Surely this attack meant war. I had temporarily ended my military "career" a few weeks earlier. I had a knee injured in high school football and it still nagged me when I thought about it, especially when marching as one part of the dull, required ROTC class. I complained to the officer and, after a few referrals, I wrote to Dr. Carr, the Stapleton physician who had treated my knee injury.

Dr. Carr wrote back saying that he had attended the injury and felt the marching could be bad for my knee so I was excused from ROTC. And almost the best part, I got back the $10 deposit when I returned the uniform and $2 for the "credit hour" of tuition. I later learned that this was a temporary reprieve that did not end my military career.

America was indeed at war. The Selective Service System began drafting men by the hundreds locally and by thousands nationwide. ROTC seniors were pulled out of college and sent to officer training schools, then on to active duty. Others in our classes were drafted. It was difficult to concentrate on school when we didn't know who would be missing from the next day's class as they were drafted or enlisted.

When I turned 18 in February I had to register for the draft and began to give serious thought to the military career that seemed to be inevitable in the near future. We all wanted to see how good we were. This was a chance to find out. The consensus among the college men was that the Navy Air Corps had the toughest requirements. We agreed we'd first try to enlist in that but if we couldn't make it, we'd next try the Army Air Corps.

If we failed with both aviation branches, we'd try to get into one of the programs that kept us in college or enlist in the regular Navy. If we couldn't make any of these, let them draft us. It didn't occur to most of us that the two preferred programs involved learning to fly an airplane. Their attraction was that they were just so difficult to get into—the macho thing, I guess.

Several of us began visiting recruiting offices to see what military programs were available. In Lincoln and some other Nebraska cities, the Navy was taking enlistments in what was to be called the Cornhusker Squadron. They seemed to be in a hurry to recruit at least the list of possible candidates, but it took weeks after the first tentative sign-up to schedule our first written test of intelligence, aptitude or whatever. Then several weeks passed before our first physical exam.

Finally, the nucleus of the first group that began enlisting passed all our preliminary tests and were assembled in Kansas City for our final physical exams. For those of us who passed, there was a swearing-in ceremony for the "Cornhusker Squadron" enlistees on December 2, 1942, almost a year after the Pearl Harbor attack. And we got a lecture on our conduct including the note that nobody could be in more than one branch of the armed forces at any one time.

This turned out to be extremely good news for me a few days later when I received a letter from the University Registrar to report to the head of the ROTC. The good Colonel informed me that I had not registered for ROTC and that there was a law requiring all male students of state universities to be enrolled in ROTC. I told him that I had been given a medical reprieve from ROTC a year earlier because of a knee injury.

That explanation pacified him for the moment but the eager colonel followed through and dug that old reprieve out of the files and I got another letter. He was irate, informing me that I only had a one-semester reprieve. Where was I last semester? And this semester? I didn't really like the Army ROTC program and wasn't going to be badgered into some cull outfit. Then I asked him about the "not being in two branches of the armed forces at once" idea, telling him that I had just enlisted in the Navy Air Corp which made me ineligible for ROTC.

That really blew his mind. *How can you pass the toughest test of physical ability in all the military while you aren't able to march in ROTC?* he wanted to know. I told him I had improved in the past year. But he agreed that I could not, in fact, serve in two branches and said, "Young man, you have just enlisted yourself out of this man's university. I cannot let you attend the University of Nebraska, where I am professor of military skills and tactics, and let you out of ROTC."

That simplified my problem. I didn't know how long it would take for the Navy to call me to active duty but I felt it would be hard to concentrate on college anyway, so I told the registrar that I had enlisted. The University gave half credit for any course if you had a passing grade. I sold my books, got a tuition refund on the extra hours and went home to wait. As it turned out, I also broke horses and hauled hay to feed cattle until I was ordered to report for active duty to flight prep school in April, 1943.

About a month after I went home, I received a letter notifying me that Congress had passed a law allowing enlistees to also be in ROTC while in college, awaiting call to active duty. I had my mind made up, I had won my battle with the military and was not about to take advantage of their "generous offer" to return to college for a few weeks. Ironically, when I returned to college after more than three years of active Navy duty, I was given enough University credit hours, in lieu of ROTC, to qualify as a lieutenant in the army, which I declined.

To Fly or Not To Fly

Our news these days is full of situations where unfairness is exposed and class-action law suits litter our courts. Maybe what we need is a good war. In the military, when we fell the apparent victim of an unfair ruling, we had no legal option. When I enlisted, the agreement was that if a cadet "washed out" or was disqualified from flight training, he was released from the Navy to civilian life with no strings attached except for the jurisdiction of his local draft board.

Some of my fellow cadets washed out but went home and enlisted in the Army Air Corps. They had already had good ground school and in some cases, some flight training. Either the Army Air Corps was an easier program or the Navy training gave them a boost, because most of them completed Air Corps training and got their wings.

Just after I got to Tucson and had begun flight training, the Navy decided to change policy. We had to sign a new agreement. We had our choice to resign from flight school and go home right now, or agree that if we stayed in training and washed out, we would be automatically enlisted as apprentice seamen or possibly become eligible for other unnamed Navy programs.

If the powers wanted to find how a person performed under pressure, this was the perfect test. I had taken four or five training flights of about 25 to 30 minutes each at the time. My instructor said he felt I was probably going to learn what was needed to solo, but it was just too early to make any guarantees. We had to sign the agreement in the next couple of days—too soon to know if I would ever solo.

By now I was fairly determined to fly but I didn't want to throw away all my other options and be one of thousands of "enlistees" in the shipboard Navy in the event I got a tough, unfair check pilot or any of a dozen other unknowns and wind up washing out of the flight program. I didn't want to go home a "quitter" but it was hard to sign up to give away a lot of your life potential in the event of some bad break.

We were flying out of Gilpin Field, at that time a dirt runway a few miles northwest of downtown Tucson. We flew in the morning when the desert air was cool and reasonably stable and we went to class in the afternoons when the turbulence of the hot summer afternoon air made it difficult to know whether the pilot or the weather was in control of the plane. We were expected to solo in less than eight hours of dual flight time.

At Tucson, we flew Waco UPF-7 open-cockpit bi-planes—almost twins to the Stearman "Yellow Peril" planes we'd fly later in Primary Training. Ground school and air regulations were the same at all bases. This plane was more difficult to handle than the single-wing light planes used at all other bases but we got no credit for that. We had to solo or else. We never took more than one flight per day and our deadline to sign the option drew near.

Most of us signed the last day. None of us had soloed. A few were afraid they wouldn't make it, right or wrong, and signed to go home. A few days later the first cadet in our platoon soloed. As the days passed, we tried to reassure each other, while knowing that pep talks didn't make us any more capable of flying that plane off the ground, taking it around the pattern and landing again. Maybe we were just nervous.

I felt I was getting the hang of it. I didn't feel my instructor's hand on the stick, but he never gave me the feeling that he thought I would make it. Then one day—I had about seven hours of airtime—we were making touch-and-go landings and he took over when we landed. He put on the brakes, pulled off the runway and said "Try it a few times without me. But look at me when you go by. I'll wave you on or wave you to stop and pick me up. And remember, it will be lighter without me." Man did that front seat look empty after he got out.

I turned the plane around and taxied back to the end of the runway. The plane just jumped into the air without the instructor. I know I looked for other planes more than ever before. I looked constantly for a place to land in case the plane's engine died. A railroad track ran along one side of the airport. We took off over a cemetery located just upwind from the airstrip. A fresh grave had been opened in the cemetery below for a funeral and nearby a flock of buzzards circled beyond the downwind turn to return to the airport. Just the omens you need.

I brought the plane in for the first touch-and-go landing. The instructor was right. It was lighter and I was a little higher than ideal but I looked over at him and he motioned me on. I opened the throttle and took off again. I was numb, but functioning. I came around for the next landing and got the plane down at about where it should have been, and got another "go" signal. With the next landing, my instructor "thumbed" a ride like he was hitchhiking. I braked to a stop, wheeled around and picked him up. I had soloed!

I have lost contact with all the others who were cadets, flying from Gilpin Field in Tucson, and since my pilot's flight log book (which would have a record of every flight) turned up missing in action after the disposal of all my stored Navy uniforms and memorabilia following the estate auction when my mother moved from her residence to a senior care facility, I have no official record of the date of my first solo flight, along with a lot of other career details. I estimate that I soloed sometime in September or October of 1943.

I agree with many seniors who are surprised at "recalled incidents" or attempts to recall events from earlier times in their lives and find it difficult or impossible to retrace their tracks. In the years that I did consulting work on a ranch not that far from Tucson, I mentioned in casual conversation that I had been among the first Navy cadets—or anybody—to live in the newly-completed women's dormitory, Yavapai Hall, on the U of A campus, when stationed there as an aviation cadet. We flew in early morning when the desert air was fairly stable. If you flew in the afternoons, thermal currents bounced light aircraft almost out of a pilot's control so the Navy thoughtfully scheduled our flights in early morning and our ground school for afternoons when air-conditioned classrooms were immune from desert thermals. I remembered the events but felt no compulsion to go re-locate or visit the Gilpin Field facility. That was in the 1960s.

When the Mariner-Marlin Association of veterans who had flown in our Martin-manufactured seaplanes held their annual reunion in Tucson in April, 2009, I had the urge to go visit the Gilpin Field where I had flown my first flight, or at least see if anybody still lived there. Was it still in existence or was it just so many residential subdivisions? When I could not find anything familiar on the best AAA road map I called the Arizona Historical Association and a docent sent a lot of Gilpin Field history back to me. I wasn't driving the bus that transported we cadets to and from the airfield but the graveled road from downtown Tucson to the airfield was 90 degrees off from my remembered direction. I had long remembered that we took off in a southeasterly direction and made our first left turn over the largest cemetery I had ever seen. The cemetery is still on the map. But there was no Gilpin Field. Driving to the area, we found a large building that could have been a hangar, but now with a stone façade. We drove down a nearby street to get to the back of the hangar where the original "Gilpin Air Lines" sign was barely visible through the weathered paint. In about the right location and the right angle was a city street now named "Runway Drive," in memory, I suspect, of the dirt airstrip where I first flew an airplane solo. . . and none of the other 200 or so airmen knew nor cared that there had once been an airstrip there.

"I'm Frank Albert"

The Navy learned that we could fly. We had 40 to 50 hours of flight time at WTS. Some had signed out and some had washed out, but most of our platoon soloed and the survivors headed to Pre-Flight School. Now the Navy would learn how we responded to a heavy curriculum of college-level math, navigation, aerology (weather plus), Navy law and protocol and a demanding athletic regimen.

My Pre-Flight base was at St. Mary's College, Moraga, California, just east of the San Francisco Bay Area and almost in the shadow of Mt. Diablo. The campus was augmented with several large "temporary" buildings for dormitories, classrooms and athletic venues. With the emphasis on physical training at this stage of training, many of our officers were college and professional athletes who had gone through a 90-day officer candidate school and served as coaches and battalion officers. They were referred to, very unofficially, as "jock-strap admirals."

When we first assembled at St. Mary's they called our names and we fell into platoons, alphabetically. Most of the platoon officers were Ensigns (the lowest commissioned rank in the Navy). An officer reported to each platoon and marched the cadets off to an open space where we were given the "at rest" command and the officer gave a brief lecture about what we should expect at Pre-Flight school. Most of these officers were big and muscular athletic types.

The officer that came to our platoon told us about the other platoon officers. He named the All-American basketball, football, gymnastics, swimming and track performers. It was credible. We even recognized a few. But our officer was not an ensign. He was a lieutenant junior grade, the next higher rank, and he didn't look big enough or muscular enough to be an All-American anything. How, we wondered, did he get here?

He told us our regular platoon officer was Ensign DuBose, a former All-West Coast guard from San Jose State and was away today, playing for the St. Mary's Pre-Flight football team. We wondered what our guy did, if he was an athlete. Maybe he was a swimmer or a diver—they don't need to be big. Maybe he was just a regular Navy officer and not an athlete at all. Finally, before he marched us back to the barracks, he said, "I'll be your battalion commander. I'm Frank Albert." The All-American quarterback and Heisman Trophy winner from Stanford University who defeated Nebraska in the 1941 Rose Bowl, later with the San Francisco 49ers pro football team.

It's All in Knowing How

The alphabet was a great friend for me in Pre-Flight School. The Navy was not too creative in assigning people to their living quarters. Everything was done by the alphabet. If there were six platoons in a battalion, Platoon A would include cadets whose last names began with A, B, C and D. Platoon B would include E, F, G, and H, etc. Little wonder that Charlie Rea and I got to know each other pretty well. I don't know what Charlie learned from me but he taught me pragmatism.

I never knew whether he was "saving it" for a really stressful situation or if he was just lazy. He made every move count and resented anyone who wasted his time or energy on something he deemed unimportant. Charlie was from Indiana but a cadet named Peer, from Missouri, just couldn't get the message. Charlie was on his bed, as usual, and Peer kept asking questions. Charlie asked him to go away and bother somebody else, to no avail.

Charlie was a wiry, 5-foot-9-inch, 160-pounder. Peer was a couple of inches taller and probably 180 pounds. Charlie rolled off his bunk, picked Peer up with one arm under his knees and the other behind his shoulders, folded him like a book, took him out the back door and dropped him in the rain barrel. "Dammit, Peer, leave me alone," was his only comment. Everyone in our corner of the barracks broke into applause when a soaking-wet Peer returned.

Pre-Flight School was the station where they tested our athletic ability, our survival instincts and determination to continue in the flight program. We spent time in most contact sports including boxing and wrestling, we ran and ran and ran and swam and swam. But the "eliminator" was the obstacle course. Every cadet had to complete the course in less than 10 minutes or get "washed out" of flight school.

The course included climbing walls, crawling through barrels and tubes, hand-over-hand up ropes, jumping across water hazards, etc. We took a practice run the first week in Pre-Flight. They told each of us how many minutes we took so we knew how much we had to improve. We could make a timed run any time a supervisor was present and if we beat the 10-minute limit, we never had to run it again. We would have free time while others had to keep running.

Charlie suggested that we should go over in our very limited free time and "psyche out" the course, practice a little and work on the hazards where we felt we could gain the most and try a timed run. After a couple of practice runs and cramming on a couple of the time-consuming obstacles we asked for a timing and we both passed.

I think the obstacle course was the only athletic event that could cause a cadet to wash out. Passing meant that we could skip that part of physical training and use that time on the classroom where a failing grade or a low average would send you packing. I don't know how many other cadets figured it out but it surely made life easier for us. The Navy didn't give prizes for top performance in any one event. We only had to be good enough at everything to stay in the program . . . not that this was easy.

I just said that the Navy didn't give points for good performance—they only took off for failure. In fact, that is only partly true. When our battalion was about a month from finishing Pre-Flight, I was one of 20 cadets called to a special meeting. They wanted some more lighter-than-air (blimp) pilots so they picked the 50 cadets in our battalion with the highest grades in ground school, then they took the 20 cadets from that group with the highest grades in navigation.

They told us that we faced about eight more months of hard work and training to get our wings if we stayed in the conventional flight program—and that a fairly high (probably 20 to 25) percentage would wash out. If we agreed to transfer to lighter-than-air training, we would have our wings in 12 to 16 weeks and unless we committed a felony there was hardly any chance that we could wash out.

What a proposition! Back in Tucson a few months ago, I had to decide whether to quit or sign to stay in the Navy, even if I washed out of flight school. I signed to stay in and take my chances to solo or wash out. I soloed so I was still in the program. One of the reasons that I decided to gamble and stay in the program was that I wanted to fly. Now I had flown. At this point I had done everything the Navy asked. But I had to make another decision.

I really thought it would be fun to fly a blimp and the idea of cutting out months of flight school was appealing. Flight school was not easy by any standards. But I knew they didn't send many blimps overseas. Flying a plane for the Navy almost guaranteed travel. I think 16 or 18 of the "blimp class," plus the next two to four reserves, took their offer.

I decided to stay in the regular flight program, whatever came. More than once I thought about this decision and wondered if I had made the right choice. I'd still like to fly a blimp (Goodyear, are you listening?) but I think it was more fun to take off and land on water or on a carrier than it would be to fly a blimp. You can't do everything in one lifetime, I guess.

Iron Mary Alert: There's A War Out There

We had been through a few months at Flight Prep School (in my case, at Cornell College in Mt. Vernon, Iowa) where we did a semester of college science and athletics in 90 days. This was followed by about the same time at WTS School (I went to Tucson, Arizona) where we continued ground school and learned to fly, and soloed, logging about 50 hours of flying time.

As cadets, we had been under a good bit of physical and mental pressure but never really got the feeling that our lives were at risk. Sure, trainer planes don't fly themselves and novice pilots can do stupid and possibly dangerous things, but we didn't get the idea, in general, that we were facing death. Nobody felt pressed to "get his life and estate in order."

A few more months in Pre Flight School at St. Mary's College, California, put heavier pressure on us. Ground school training was accelerated as they gave us more concentrated and advanced schooling in navigation, meteorology, plane and ship identification, survival training, and the most intense athletic discipline we had ever seen—allegedly similar to the training for military Frogmen, SEALS and Green Berets.

Apparently the Navy brass wanted to sort out everybody who was not first rate at handling both physical and emotional pressure. As it turned out, the plan was well founded. When we went on to Primary Flight Training (NAS Livermore, California, for me) we were immersed into a flying schedule that now reminds me of rush hour on the freeway. And we didn't have cell phones or even radios.

We went to the flight line the first day on base to get introduced to the open-cockpit bi-plane, Stearman N2S or its identical twin, the Navy-built N3N, widely known as the "yellow peril." This was quite a move for most cadets who had learned to fly in a tamer model, enclosed cabin, side-by-side seating Piper Cubs, Taylorcraft or other light civilian planes.

Those of us who had taken WTS at Tucson had to scramble at the time, but now we were well ahead because we flew the Waco UPF 7. They

Aviation cadets "learn the ropes" in these basic, almost "foolproof" training planes, instructor pilot in the front seat and cadet in rear. I soloed in a Waco UPF-7 but in primary flight squadron we flew the almost indistinguishable Navy N3N's or Stearman N2S open-cockpit trainers, pictured here.

were built on almost exactly the same frames as the planes we would fly at Primary, except that the Waco was harder to get the tail down properly for a three-point landing (tail wheel plus both wheels of the main landing gear).

We continued ground school and athletics but not quite at the frantic pace we had at Pre- Flight school. After all, we were on the flight line almost half the day. The Navy schedule kept us busy and we were ready for bed every night when we had lights out when they blew Taps. Everybody, that is, except the cadets practicing night flying. Every barracks had loud speakers to make announcements but they were always quiet after bed time. Not quite!

A few days after we got to Livermore, we were nicely bedded down for the night and "Iron Mary," the speaker system, blared out: "Close friends of Cadet Petrocelli, please report to sick bay immediately." And just as immediately, there was chatter throughout the barracks as we speculated as to the outcome and the cause. We had heard a few minutes earlier that there had been a night-flying crash. Next day we learned that we were right. Our bellies tightened up a bit before taking off the next day. We now really had to face the fact that we were in a war. We were far from the front and the Japs didn't kill Cadet Petrocelli, but this really was war.

364

Flying In Formation—From the Front Seat

Open-cockpit planes meant several things that were fairly obvious if you were doing it, but not so obvious to others. The seats were front and rear, not side-by-side. The instructor sat in the front seat and talked to the student pilot through a Gosport tube. We all wore helmets and goggles. The Gosport was plugged into the cadet's helmet ear holes and the instructor had a funnel-shaped mouthpiece, a bit like the hearing aid in pre-electricity days.

The student had no way to talk back, which I guess was the way they Navy wanted it. We nodded for *yes* and shook our heads for *no*. The instructor had a rear-view mirror to see you. The student rode in the back seat for both dual and solo flights. The plane always felt the same from the back seat and we had to learn a lot of new things before learning how the plane felt from the front seat.

When we had learned to take off and land, leave the area of the airport and return, perform the required aerobatic maneuvers and become good enough at night flying to get back to the airport and land without accident, we were ready to check out in the front seat. We had a few take-offs and landings in the front seat to get the feel of the change in weight distribution in the plane and the difference in perspective from the front seat.

We got a feeling of confidence when we moved to the front seat. I never knew anybody to wash out from the front seat. And formation flying, the only discipline left on our Primary flight training agenda, was a sign that we were becoming military pilots. Formation flying without radio contact, teaches you to respect your fellow pilots and to respond to hand signals. A three-plane formation with an instructor in only one of the planes gave us enough understanding to fly in formation.

Our first exposure to instrument flying at Corpus Christi, Texas, was in a closed-cockpit plane like this.

We continued to practice our formation flying this way until we completed our duty at Primary and were transferred to Corpus Christi, Texas, for advanced training. But one of my last flights was a surprise.

Many famous athletes and Hollywood celebrities served in the military and mostly without undue attention. Like several other actors and people with a public image, Robert Taylor, a leading movie actor of the era, had been a private pilot and, after an indoctrination program, became a Navy pilot and got an assignment as an instructor at NAS Livermore. He showed up at the flight line like any other instructor and a friend of mine became his first student.

It was still a little exciting when he was assigned as our instructor for the formation flight. The next evening I had been invited to dinner with a college fraternity brother who went through a Navy officer program and was stationed at nearby Pleasanton waiting for overseas duty. His wife had come to visit until he went overseas and they were living in an apartment there.

When I got to their apartment they had that "cat that swallowed the canary" look and told me they had invited the couple in the next apartment (without identifying them) for dinner. My friends were aghast when the neighbors, Taylor and actress wife, Barbara Stanwyck, showed up and he said something like, "Imagine seeing you again so soon." A memorable way to leave Primary training at NAS Livermore.

The Long Texas Summer

If you are going to be in Iowa, I guess spring and early summer are about as good as it gets. That is the way my Navy experience—I am reluctant to call it a career—began. Heavy athletics in the Iowa summer sun was not my choice but moving to Tucson, Arizona in August would not be most people's idea of relief. In the Navy, you go where you are sent.

Winter rain and fog is the worst time to be at St. Mary's College, a few miles east of San Francisco, but at least we had weather to our benefit for the most rigorous athletic training period of flight school. Late winter and early spring is the best time to be at Livermore, a few miles east of St. Mary's, and be flying. But it is not anybody's sane choice to go to Advanced Training at Corpus Christi, Texas in April to endure the hot, humid, coastal summer. But endure we did.

The first adventure at Advanced Squadron was learning instrument flying. Several satellite fields were located inland from Corpus Christi, where we spent a few weeks in each new stage. The idea of flying, not by looking outside, but by your interpreting what you see and hear on instruments, was a little scary. We first had to check out in advanced trainer planes, with enclosed cockpits and retractable landing gear.

The instructor still sat in front with the student in the back seat, but these planes were enclosed and we used radios to talk to each other and to the tower. It was spooky when we began to fly "under the hood" with a 360-degree canvas curtain keeping you from seeing anything outside the plane's cabin. The instructor in the front seat had full view of the world so we were safe, but inhibited. We had to learn how to fly by radio range signals and orientate ourselves. We collapsed the hood for landing.

One night we had to circle while they removed a no-wheels landing. Training planes had a horn that sounded an alarm if you reduced power at low elevation without having your wheels down. A cadet was in the landing pattern on his final approach—with wheels up. They noticed his error from

366

the tower and tried to tell him, by radio, to put his wheels down or to go around again before landing. Later, when they held the inquiry about the accident, he said he couldn't hear the voice on the radio because the "wheels up" warning horn was making so much noise.

Goodbye Carriers, Hello Flying Boats

During this period, we had a chance to request the type of plane we would fly in advanced training. I had no preference to fly carrier-based planes versus multi-engine planes. We heard a rumor that if you got assigned to seaplanes for training, you might get Naval Air Transport Service (NATS), the Navy's "airline" and sought-after duty. I thought it might be fun to take off and land on water—I had flown from land—so I requested seaplanes.

I don't know if it was somebody reading my mail, divine intervention or chance, but I got assigned to seaplanes. I had many years earlier been aboard an old Ford Tri-Motor passenger plane, sitting on the ground, when it landed at the North Platte airport, but I had never been in a plane with the wingspan (115 feet), length and interior space of a PBY Catalina seaplane.

That first flight was an adventure. We boarded the plane on land. Then we rode down a ramp into the water with a cable to a tractor onshore easing us forward until we cleared the ramp when swimmers detached the wheels, called beaching gear, and the cable connected to the tractor. We turned up the

Our first multi-engine and first seaplane experience came in a Consolidated PBY-3 in advanced squadron training at Corpus Christi Naval Air Station.

engines and began to water taxi—like a large boat with two 1,000-horse-power engines doing the work. This was almost as big an event as my first flight in a plane, which was also my first training flight, or even my solo flight, both in Tucson.

Flying gives you contrasts with riding a horse or driving a car. You always watch for a place for an emergency landing, for example. Flying seaplanes gives you new perspectives compared with flying landplanes. Seaplanes are designed to fly over water, take off from water and land on water. Landplane pilots can be uncomfortable flying over large stretches of water and the converse is true with a flying boat over wide stretches of land.

In either case, with two engines, you don't expect to make a full-blown emergency landing. Seaplanes will suffer some damage from landing on land, but landplanes don't float if you ever have to land on water.

We had a fairly complete instrument panel on the planes we used as instrument trainers but the PBY had two engines. This meant a duplication of all the instruments to indicate the performance of each engine. And the training plane had a radio so we learned how to operate that along with airway protocol. But now we had radio with several channels plus radar, bomb sights, machine guns and we were flying planes with the capability and equipment used in combat. Fairly heavy stuff for a country boy less than 20 years old.

But the biggest shock for me to digest was flying over water—far enough from shore that no land was visible. We had instruments that showed what direction we were flying, our altitude and airspeed. We had a radio compass that could tell us the direction back to Corpus Christi or Houston or New Orleans, but there was no mountain range, no river, no railroad track, highway or power lines to lead you back to the airport.

I can assure you that the word, Navigation, has a different meaning when you can't visually determine your location on the globe, than it has as a noun or a category of training to describe the activity of locating a geographic position. And I was not the first to notice this. The plane designers placed a navigation table just off the flight deck where you could keep a running record of your position and what to do next to follow your flight plan.

Navigation was a pain but now I was thankful that I had been selected for training as a seaplane pilot. We had a sextant for star shots, a lot of the world had Loran stations that sent out radio waves and all that good stuff. Compare our facilities with the single-engine pilots and the tiny navigation board clipped to a knee, hoping their dead reckoning calculations would get them back to the carrier, day or night.

Another up side of flying seaplanes was the feel of the plane on water. There is no sensation like the plane, ready to break water on takeoff or when you feel the first tickle of water on the bottom of the hull in landing, then the feeling, like a big sigh, when landing speed slows enough that the plane sinks into the water from its position up on the step at first touchdown. There is almost a career involved in the water work necessary in handling a seaplane from the moment you untie the plane from a buoy in the seaplane harbor until you take off. And another from the time you touch down in landing until you have tied up to the buoy again or are back up on land after a flight.

No doubt a railroad engineer or cross-country truck driver gets acclimated to the noises of the engine that pulls them. I had to learn the new noises of two engines, each larger than I'd ever turned up or heard before. The strangest for me was learning how engines purr when "in sync" at exactly the same speed. Once you hear the "out-of-sync" noise your skin will always crawl when you ride with the pilot of a multi-engine plane who is casual about synchronizing engine speed.

There are advantages in having a galley and bunk room on board. There is also the other side, such as having flights long enough to make either of the above appropriate. When you and your crew are on a flight of eight, 10, 12 hours or longer, it can get a little lonesome out there. But is it worse to have a long flight with a crew of eight or 12 than to have a flight, not quite so long, but you are out there all alone?

The "Volunteer" Air Force

Where do Marine pilots come from? It never crossed my mind until one day in what would ordinarily have been an hour of physical training. Our battalion was instructed to report to a meeting room, not in athletic gear, but in the uniform of the day. One of our battalion officers informed us that we were at the stage when we made our preference to either stay in the Navy after graduation or request transfer to the Marine Corps.

I never knew whether it was a recruiting idea or if there was a regulation that required us to specifically request it if we were to be in the Marine Corps. At any rate, they had a Navy pilot and a Marine pilot who were going to tell us—a mini-testimonial as it were—why we should choose to stay in the Navy, or transfer to the Marines, also technically a branch of the Navy.

The Marine was present—a Major with rows of battle ribbons—and an uncomfortable aura or military protocol, was introduced. He was hardly up to full speed by the time his half-hour was over and was interrupted with a messenger who asked him to go on since the wind had come up, making a water landing and beaching a single-engine scout plane time consuming, so the Navy pilot scheduled to talk, would have to appear at a later date.

Taking advantage of the opening, the Major practically fought a war for us, had to throw everything overboard to keep his torpedo bomber airborne then, when later accosted, shot down a whole bunch of Japanese Zero fighters (with guns they had thrown overboard) and limped back to the ship. We had enough cool to keep from laughing, but none of us wanted the embarrassment of being in his branch of the military.

Next day we skipped another hour of athletics to listen to the Navy pilot. He came in from the flight line with hair mussed and without a necktie. He sat on the edge of the desk, told us to interrupt him whenever we had a question and did the best PR job imaginable. He came across as the guy you'd most like to have in your outfit. We never knew how much planning had gone into picking people for various jobs in the military. Sometimes it seemed as if we won the war because of the good placement of people, at other times we won in spite of it.

When our battalion officer finally had to call time and end the session, he told us the instructor pilot had been shot down, had a Navy Cross, some Distinguished Flying Crosses and Air Medals and a Purple Heart. He had been transferred to our training base as part of his recuperation. At the end of each session, there was a sort of "altar call" offering application forms for anybody who wanted to "volunteer" for the Marine Corps.

The next week, we were invited back to hear another Marine talk about his adventures as a Marine Pilot. This was not our first choice for humor but it beat going to athletics. We got word that the Marines really needed a bunch of pilots but we had a standoff. They kept inviting us but nobody signed up. Only one Marine graduated the week I did. He was a King Ranch heir who applied to flight school from Marine Corps enlisted duty so he was not new. But he was a good guy who took several of us to the ranch at Kingsville one weekend when we were stationed at Cabaniss Field nearby.

Wings at Last

Instructor pilots and the aviation cadets they teach are a pretty capable lot by almost any measurements. But the people who really know their business are the yeomen who keep all the records of requirements met, and get everything in order for weekly graduation ceremonies. They are the miracle men and women. I suppose after having one every week, we'd begin to see the pattern. Every cadet has a check sheet with a space for every required item.

All cadets have to check out in basic training planes, complete instrument

My flight school graduation and award of Navy "Wings" at Corpus Christi, Texas, September 20, 1944, one of approximately 140 graduates that week. I'm in the front row, on the left.

flying, pass every ground school class and meet every athletic requirement. Each type of advanced training has different required flights. Cadets training in seaplanes with me from the first day we were assigned to advanced squadron may graduate weeks earlier or later. A few days of bad flying

370

weather or the inability to make any one of several required flights might delay graduation by several days or weeks.

Our graduation planners have only a few days to make a schedule. Good weather in the morning with windy afternoons—an airplane that misfires as you prepare to take off and has to return to repair—your check pilot turns up sick on the day of your check flight—a week of stormy weather delays your long-distance navigation flight. These are but a few of the reasons you graduate earlier or later than your otherwise classmates.

When a cadet gets pretty well along in advanced squadron, his confidence is finally at a level that justifies going to buy the new uniforms with Ensign stripes to replace the Aviation Cadet insignia, from top to bottom. But you may get less than a week notice from flying your last required flight until the day you gather on the parade grounds with maybe 100 or so others for graduation, to get your wings and shake hands with the Admiral.

Enlisted personnel know of the tradition that a new officer gives a dollar bill to the first person who salutes him after graduation. They swarm at graduation like vultures over a carcass. I later wondered if this was a ruse to have a big crowd present for the ceremony. My first salute came from Chet Weichman, a cadet from Wiota, Iowa. We had been friends since reporting to our original battalion at our very first Navy assignment at Mt. Vernon, Iowa.

We had been training in different squadrons. He was flying single-engine planes and we hadn't seen each other for several weeks. He had just washed out a few days before my graduation. I got my wings and a 14-day leave, plus travel, on my way to my next base. He was going on to begin life as a seaman. It was an interestingly bitter-sweet occasion. Nobody ever said war was fair.

Hail the Conquering Hero

My mother was always a thrifty person, even compared with our neighbors and other people who lived under depression and drought conditions. It might be fair to call her stingy. This applies to expenditures of money for food, shelter and clothing as well as expenditure of emotions. A polite "thank you" was the best you got from her, no matter what you did. Celebrations were for others.

She always wondered aloud if I couldn't have earned an A+ instead of an A or an A- in a course, but I was never once praised for getting straight A's. My parents never came to attend a single football game when I was on the team. They complained about every "away" game when I wasn't at home to do evening chores on schedule.

They had reluctantly signed the permission form for me to enlist in flight training when I asked them. I got tired of trying to justify their signatures and finally asked them if they'd rather just wait until the government drafted me to be a foot soldier. They suggested that I might get an agricultural deferment but when I said "No thanks," they finally signed. When I had to decide whether to resign or agree to be a Navy enlisted man if I washed out, they simply said they would be disappointed if I quit—hardly an endorsement, but the best I would get.

They never said they were proud when I got my wings, but when I came home on leave, on my way to operational training at Banana River, Florida, I was shocked when they had a "reception" at the house one evening with coffee and goodies, including my favorite cake, inviting some high school classmates still in the area and a few other friends. I don't remember all who attended but there was one surprise.

In my Navy officer dress uniform, September, 1944.

Harry Frey was one of the smooth city guys. He was a year ahead of me in high school, the football fullback and no peer for a little old country boy freshman. As time passed this neutralized a bit. Harry was old enough to enlist in Naval aviation before I did and was called to duty in the battalion ahead of me. When the Navy made us "re-enlist," Harry had soloed and almost finished WTS training but signed out and got an agricultural deferment from the draft.

He lingered at the end of the evening reception, wanting to visit a little more with me after the other guests departed. He asked a lot of questions about going through flight training after he got out and finally asked me if I would sign his "short snorter," the pilot's "rite of passage," which was exchanging signatures on a designated dollar bill. He said, "This is a real occasion. I got this when I soloed but I never got the signature of a real Navy Ensign. And getting one that I really know makes it special." I nearly choked. Those wings, on this occasion, were almost magical enough to let you fly without a plane.

Having wings didn't make you omniscient or foolproof. The high school principal invited me to be featured at a school convocation. Apparently I was the first Stapleton graduate to become a military pilot and the first Navy officer, maybe the first officer in any of the military. They had even acquired a movie about naval aviation showing fighter plane take-offs from carrier decks and flying boats from water. I told the students a little about flight training and told them how fast things change—that the planes in the latest movie were now "mostly obsolcte." That "obsolete" comment was the only quote in the school paper about my appearance.

Where Do I Go From Here?

The first time the Navy gave me individual travel orders was for my leave and railroad ticket to my next duty base. Maybe they felt that if I got through flight school I could find my way to the next station on my own. Actually, this was the most difficult one for me to find. Each training base got feedback from the cadets at the next base so we speculated about which Pre-Flight station or which Primary Flight station we might attend. And we knew where they were located.

Upon graduation, I got orders to report to NAS Banana River, Florida. Where is Banana River? My ticket didn't even tell me where to get off the train. But again, luck was with me. I happened to be at the hometown implement store when owner, Bill Baskin, asked where I was going next. I told him the base name and, having been a Navy man in WWI, he said, "you'll like it there. It's at Cocoa-Rockledge, a double-name town on the east coast of Florida."

I got my wings on September 20, 1944. I was scheduled to arrive in Florida about mid-October. Naval Air Station (NAS) Banana River was an Operational Training

Beach crew washing a PBM Mariner seaplane at Banana River Naval Air Station in Florida. I went through operational training here in 1944, finishing just in time for Christmas leave.

Station where we would check out in PBM Mariner planes. They were flying boats, similar to the PBY's we had flown in Advanced Squadron. They were

373

larger, had two engines but they were more powerful than the PBY's. This was the plane we would fly in combat when we finished Operational training.

The crew on PBM's included three pilots, two in the cockpit rotating with one at the navigation table, and nine enlisted crewmen, including three each aviation machinists, radiomen and ordinance men. We had turrets in the bow (nose), dorsal (top) and tail (rear) of the plane with twin 50-caliber machine guns. We also had a single gun for each of the waist hatches (side doors). The radiomen and machinists not manning their stations doubled as gunners.

We had barely begun to fly PBM's when a hurricane came to town. The Navy did not schedule hurricanes. We did, however, respond to them. When the hurricane approached (this was before they got names), experienced crews flew planes to Pensacola and Jacksonville. Since we had more crews than planes, new crews were assigned to quarters or allowed to go ashore (Navy jargon for off the ship or base). Basically the base shut down. This was a mild hurricane but heavy rain with winds approaching 100 miles per hour can make a real mess, even if you don't get hit by a falling palm frond. It was my first of many negative experiences with the American Red Cross. One of the crewmen's wives had an acute appendicitis attack and the civilian hospital refused to admit a Navy dependent.

We called for a Red Cross ambulance to take her to the base hospital. They said she had picked a bad time to be sick. They would not put their vehicle and driver "at risk in this weather." Dick Combs, a pilot friend, had a car in Florida so we loaded the crewman and his ailing wife in the car and drove to the base hospital, barely getting past the security people on the causeway and Navy base entry gate because roads were closed except for "emergency" traffic. She recovered but my opinion of the American Red Cross did not.

Later training flights included bombing and gunnery practice. We carried practice "dummy" bombs under the wings which were released with remote switches in the cockpit. But gunnery practice used live ammo. We also flew through the eye of later hurricanes while conducting hurricane patrols as part of our training. It is really memorable to break through the rain and wind to see a circle of dead calm 10 to 15 miles across in the ocean below while flying inside the eye of the storm.

We continued to practice night flying and instrument flying. One day I was having a particularly good flight and the instructor let me make an instrument landing (with vision outside my side of the cockpit blocked by a canvas curtain). Then taxi back to the end of the take-off area where I made an instrument take-off. Those are experiences that tax your nerves and make the juices flow at the time, but great memories.

One of our last flights before graduating from Operational Training was to complete an overnight navigation flight. We flew to San Juan, Puerto Rico, for an overnight just a few days before Christmas. The decorated store windows in downtown San Juan, even in wartime, gave me my first chance to experience Feliz Navidad, Christmas in another language.

In wartime, the main military fringe benefits were the mail and the movies. When we prepared to leave San Juan, after a day lay-over for routine service on the plane, we were loaded with mail and movies to drop at an Island that I had surely never heard of, even though it was not far off the Florida coast. There is a band of islands, called Cays. We were to land at one called Great Exuma.

I was at the controls when we came in to land. The map showed a beautiful bay with a harbor several miles long. An Army station was located almost on the beach. This was mainly a weather and security station, but they had a right to get mail and movies. I called the radio tower and was given clearance to land. It was a nice day and a beautiful bay with Caribbean island scenery on three sides.

As we approached to land, I could see big rocky outcrops in the bottom of the bay that were obviously only inches below the surface of the water. The map showed a large bay with nothing less than 100 feet from the surface but such did not seem the case. I decided that I did not want to rip the hull out of my plane on a rock so I applied power and went into a climb.

The concerned tower radio operator called me to ask what had happened, why I had chosen not to land after such a perfect approach. I said I was afraid of the rocks, even though the map assured their depth. I had turned chicken. I was reassured that such had happened before but that the water was so clear it was deceiving. He said we could not even swim deep enough to touch the top of the rocks. Big deal. He wasn't flying the plane.

We landed on the next pass. There were no buoys to tie up so we dropped anchor and a boat came out to take us ashore. When we deposited the mail and exchanged movies, we got back to the plane. We took the dare. Not one of us could swim far enough down to even make the rocks appear closer than they did from the surface. That water was so clear we could see fish far away—until one of the fish turned out to be a large barracuda. End of swim. Prepare to take off for NAS Banana River.

Home for the Holidays

The Navy had trouble "getting it right" with our operational training. They sent PBM crews overseas with a senior pilot, called a Plane Commander, and two co-pilots. The problem: we went through Operational Training with three fresh new pilots in a crew. This meant that we had to exchange one of our pilots for our new Plane Commander, then let him work with our crew to become a team. They discovered their error and changed the arrangement in the class behind us at Banana River.

We got orders back to Corpus Christi where Bert McDonal, from our Banana River crew, was assigned to another crew and we picked up Bill Kress who had flown a tour of duty as a co-pilot in a PBY squadron in the Aleutian Islands to be our new Plane Commander. But en route Corpus Christi, we got a 10-day leave plus travel over the Christmas holidays. They might serve you roast turkey for Christmas dinner but the military made little fuss otherwise about holidays. The Navy Brass felt there was a war and they had to act responsibly.

When my little group was transferred from Flight Prep school in Iowa to our WTS base at Tucson, Arizona, there was such demand for railroad passenger cars that we had to travel in compartmented cars with roomettes for each two of us. The military always gave railroad tickets. If you had other transportation for any trip, you could cash your ticket and hitchhike, ride with your family or even take Greyhound. They just wanted you to be there on time.

Living on a military base means living in or near cities that make a big part of their economy from the military personnel. They were patriotic, in a subjective, money-grabbing way. Cities varied, seemingly in proportion to the years they had been a military base. Traveling to places that did not make a living off the military bases showed a different America. I guess it's easier to look good when your life and livelihood aren't at stake.

I had a ticket on the Florida East Coast Railroad to Chicago. A morning arrival gave me several hours layover until my train headed west at around 6 p.m. Chicago, despite the war, was dressed for Christmas. I went into a downtown restaurant for lunch but it was packed. As I stood near the door, a stranger got up from his table, walked up to me and invited me to have lunch with him.

I was suspicious but he reassured me by saying that no serviceman could buy a meal in Chicago for the duration of the war. I had never heard news of such a rule but it seemed a good idea for the moment. He asked where I was from, where I was going, what kind of plane I flew. I thought he must be a spy but he was just an interested citizen. When we had finished lunch, he insisted on paying, and we went our separate ways.

I headed toward the railroad station. I had a ticket from Chicago to North Platte and I wanted on one of the "Cities" trains. The Union Pacific had the City of Denver, City of Los Angeles and City of San Francisco. They left about a half hour apart and all went through North Platte so the earlier the better for me. The first to leave was all reserved but I got on standby and took the first vacant seat when one of the scheduled passengers didn't show.

My seat was at the end of a car with two double seats facing each other. The other seats were reserved by a "black shoe" regular Navy Ensign (pilots could wear brown shoes with their winter "aviation green" and "summer tan" uniforms not issued to officers limited to shipboard duty) and two girls from

Clarke College in Dubuque. One was going to spend the holidays at the other's home in Colorado. After we were out of the Chicago area, we went to the club car and a few minutes later a railroad porter asked me and the other officer if these girls were our companions. I said I guessed they were.

Good choice. We were about to leave Illinois and the club car had to close as we entered Iowa, a "dry" state. The porter shuffled us into a diner with nearly a car full of military men and their dates who were chosen to be guests of a Council Bluffs produce man. According to the story, his son was killed early in the war and every time he returned home from Chicago, he entertained all the military men on the train that trip.

Such treatment. He had a corsage for each of the girls. He had full steak dinners for the group, wine (Iowa let you drink it, you just couldn't buy it) and dessert. In fact, we ate our way all across Iowa. And when we got to the station at Council Bluffs, our host got off the train to more applause than I had heard in my whole life. What a day! Being in uniform, far from a military base, was surely the way to be appreciated. Getting home, even for Christmas with the family, would almost be a letdown.

When I got to North Platte, I learned that it had become famous countrywide for the canteen that operated in the Union Pacific station. Women's clubs in every town for miles around took turns as hosts. There was always free coffee and donuts, cake for service men with birthdays, help to call home, etc. It was even featured in *Reader's Digest* and at least one book, I was to learn later. For the moment, people amazed me with their response to anyone in uniform.

Being home was almost an anticlimax. Gasoline was rationed so you were inhibited as far as making trips was concerned. I later learned that I could have gone to the ration board and received a few gas stamps. Later, that is. Most of the high school classmates were gone or self-conscious about having an agricultural deferral from the military. It was still good to be home, but I had orders to get back to Corpus Christi, Texas, again.

The Navigation Teacher

Most pilots find that Operational Training is good preparation for going to overseas duty. That was the idea. But the Navy didn't figure everything out until our crew was in training. We went through training in Florida with three newly commissioned ensigns in a crew. At Corpus Christi, we replaced one of our original pilots with a more experienced pilot as Plane Commander.

He had a lot of flight time, but in a different plane than we were flying now so everything we did was old hat to all of us except the new guy. We almost had to slap ourselves to keep our attention sharp much of the time. And the base instructor personnel expected "learner" levels of performance.

We were one of only about a dozen crews with an experience level that didn't need teaching and explanations except for our new plane commander.

One day we returned from a flight and were taxiing to tie up to a buoy. The wind was blowing so we headed directly into the sea wall to make the buoy that was bouncing in the high surf. When our ordinance man in the bow of the plane had the buoy in sight, ready to tie up, the water bounced it away or to the other side of the plane. Tower operators were responsible for successful beaching and tying to the buoy—and responsible if a plane missed the buoy and crashed into the sea wall. When at the buoy, they brought out beaching gear, attached it and pulled the plane on shore.

An experienced pilot could blip the engines by turning off the ignition in brief spurts to cut the power and let the wind blow the plane backward, then we made another pass at the buoy. This happened three times one day. I just ignored the tower operator and continued to approach the buoy until we tied up. Then I called and congratulated the operator on her understanding that we were an experienced crew and totally safe and not candidates to crash into the sea wall only a few feet away. She did not endorse my macho appraisal of the situation.

We had flown navigation flights, including Puerto Rico, from Banana River but our Plane Commander hadn't done it so we were scheduled to fly to Panama. A major weather front was in the area so our flight was postponed for a couple of days, then finally rescheduled late one afternoon. Not far out of Corpus Christi, the threatening weather worsened.

The non-pilot navigation teacher told us he was considering calling in and canceling the flight. But by the time he made a decision, we were far enough into the storm that the odds of finding good weather seemed better ahead than behind our present position. We flew on into the night. It was stormy and turbulent. We tipped the radar receiver up but it showed the turbulence was too high for us to fly over. We dropped down to 200 feet to find some reasonably stable air. We were in heavy rain, but we could fly.

We had a drift sight that attached in the rear belly hatch of the plane. If we dropped a flare in the ocean, we could read the drift and estimate our dead reckoning track. The problem was that we were flying so low that the flare was out of range for the drift sight. I went back to the rear gun turret and "guessed at" the drift from the angle of the guns. Flares showed me approximately how frothy the waves were so I could estimate the speed and direction of the wind.

Navigation training flights are designed to test the competence of the crew in its use of navigation aids. These included the above-mentioned but included star shots with a sextant, Loran lines, radio compass, when appropriate, but this weather had eliminated all traditional navigation aids. We tuned the radio compass to a New Orleans radio station and got one

378

reading but we were otherwise flying by dead reckoning—almost by the seats of our pants.

We had extreme turbulence. Half the crew was sick, as was the navigation teacher. Between dry heaves, he paced through the plane chanting, "We'll all be killed. Even if we get through I'll give you a "down" because you aren't using any navigation aids." I asked our plane commander to throttle the teacher, that he was upsetting the crew, but Bill was too nice—or gutless. The useless tutor raved on.

Finally I intervened and told him "You outrank me and you're the teacher but you're upsetting my crew. Go to the bunk room and shut up. If we find you anyplace else we'll know you have gone crazy—and we couldn't keep you from jumping overboard. I want you to know that this crew is going to get through. It's up to you whether you do or not. The idea of navigation is to get there. And if we get through, we're going to get an 'up,' understand?" He went to the bunk room, and eventually to sleep despite the plane tossing in the turbulent weather.

We had a full dinner and breakfast aboard but Hewitt, our ordinance man-cook, couldn't keep pans on the galley stove. I finally got hungry enough to peel a grapefruit and eat it. I had never been airsick, even in aerobatics, but that grapefruit hung in my belly for a long time. It was years before I enjoyed grapefruit again. A few hours later we cleared the storm. Radar picked up the Yucatan peninsula just as my dead reckoning navigation predicted . . . and hoped . . . straight ahead and within minutes of our ETA. You can't navigate better—or be luckier—than that.

I went up to the dome and took a few star shots and had them plotted on the navigation chart before the sun—and the navigation teacher—showed up. He went to the navigation table and saw the course plotted. I told him breakfast was ready and he decided we had done a pretty good job. We altered direction for Honduras and later for Panama. But the fun wasn't over.

That storm sat in the Gulf of Mexico for days and the authorities wouldn't clear us out of Panama to fly home. Fortunately, Norrie Nedela, my co-pilot, and I had the presence of mind to bring our pay records with us. We went to the Navy station and drew some cash. We had nothing to do so we got aboard a ship at Cristobal, the north (Atlantic) end of the canal for a trip through the canal to Panama City, then we rode a commuter train back. I do not know where the navigator went but he showed up for the daytime trip back to Corpus Christi a couple of days later. Neither of us mentioned that stormy night. And we got an "up" on the flight.

We joked during the many months of training that we were in Naval aviation to dodge the draft. Now it was really beginning to seem so. For example, my college roommate after the war had been in the Army Air Corps on B-17's and flew two tours of duty as a plane commander from England over Germany but I had more hours of flight time when I left the states as a co-pilot than he had in his entire career, training and combat combined.

It was finally spring in Corpus Christi and almost a year since I had reported there as a cadet going to advanced squadron. We weren't anxious to get overseas to combat but we were bored to death, waiting for our new Plane Commander to get comfortable with our planes and his new job. He began looking for some way to avoid another tour of duty—we felt. He would find it a few weeks later in San Diego.

Overqualified

In September 1944, I graduated from flight school at NAS Corpus Christi, Texas, with a commission as an Ensign in the Naval Reserve and certification to wear the gold wings of a Naval Aviator and qualified in PBY Catalina flying boat. Then I went to Operational training at Banana River, Florida, where I checked out in the PBM Mariner, also a twin-engine flying boat, patrol bomber. After this I went back to Corpus Christi with my crew to pick up and train a new Plane Commander en route to being assigned to overseas duty.

We hit a series of winter storms in the early months of 1945, limiting the training flights, giving the dozens of pilots, as well as our crewmen, hours and days of idle time. I had earlier decided that I would like to get a private (civilian) pilot license. Since I had plenty of flight time, all I needed was to brush up on the difference between military and civilian aviation rules and pass the CAA (Civil Aeronautics Administration) exam to get the license.

I convinced a few other pilots to join me. We went to town to get the CAA rules and material to study for the test. We got the book and had plenty of spare time to study so we shortly took, and passed, the exam. We were going to get our Private Pilot licenses. That is the permit which lets you to fly a plane for personal use but not for pay.

When the administrator checked our log books, he found we had enough flight time to qualify, not only for a Private license, but for a Commercial pilot's license which allowed us to fly for pay, including carrying passengers. And that is the license we were issued. The real surprise, however, which we didn't consider, is that we had qualified for single and multi-engine, land and seaplane rating. This was one of the last things I got before leaving Corpus Christi. Thank you, Uncle Sam, for making the flight time possible and the time off to take the test.

Ready to Go Overseas, Almost

Our crew completed the schedule for our second Operational Training to break in a new Plane Commander. We got orders to NAS San Diego where we joined the active fleet. It seemed like a new phase of training but we carried live depth charges for regular anti-submarine patrols. There was at least one patrol bomber in the air at all times from San Diego, NAS Alameda (San Francisco Bay) or Whidbey Island (Seattle) flying coastal patrol.

In addition, we were training, at least to the extent that every hour flown or every landing, take-off or every minute of water work tended to improve the ability of a crew to function. The Navy constantly rotated crews through this regimen to provide coastal security while "warehousing" crews ready for combat assignment to the Pacific theater. We knew it was a matter of weeks, or maybe just days, until we would "TransPac" fly our plane across the Pacific to our next assignment.

Our crew and plane were also available for utility flights. The most memorable such assignment came when we were used to check out another pilot. He had flown several types of Navy planes and had several flights in PBM's but needed more experience in landings and take-offs so we were "it." In addition to our regular crew, we had the PPC candidate pilot and a check pilot. They were making touch-and-go landings in San Diego Bay.

This is the dullest kind of flying. In essence, we were all just passengers except for the duty aviation machinist who kept the engines doing their thing. I was in the forward bunk room, my co-pilot was at the navigation table just off the flight deck. Part of the crew had a card game in the after station. Our new Plane Commander had been excused from the flight since he surely wasn't needed.

After several touch-and-go landings, the plane landed again, slowing down as if it were a final landing. Then they taxied back near the Ferry slip to begin a full take-off. As they neared take-off speed the plane tipped to the left, then the pilot corrected, tipping back toward the right, but he over-corrected and the right wingtip float hit the water. Then he over-corrected to the left, the left float hit the water hard and the plane did a 180-degree turn at about 60 to 70 knots.

Bill Brady, our 2nd radioman, came running through the front bunk room where I was lounging, screaming "get to the rear, she's going down." I was instantly in a mixture of sea water and gasoline from the ruptured gas tanks in the hull underneath me. As the water gushed around me, I had to dive and swim down through the hatch (door) to the after bunk room, then dive again through that hatch to the after-station and I was instantly swimming in San Diego Bay. The front and rear parts of the plane had torn completely apart near the middle of the fuselage.

The crewmen who had been playing cards were also swimming. My co-pilot, the student and check pilots, along with Jack Barrath, our plane captain, and Frank Mennuti, our first radioman, all went forward from their stations and climbed out through the top of the pilot cockpit. The front part of the plane, wings, engines, etc., were either afloat or sitting on the bottom, and were high and dry.

I began counting heads. Was everyone accounted for? Erv Conley, our 3rd ordinance man had blood running all over his head from cuts he received as the tail section tore off. We found everybody else except Colbeck, our 2nd aviation machinist mate. I yelled to the pilots and crewmen still high and dry on top of the plane's floating cockpit, wings, engines and forward section. They were well above the water, maybe they could see something we couldn't see from our spot in the water, at sea level. No Colbeck. Everybody else was visible.

Then, like a drowning rat, glug, glug, plump, here came Colbeck, popping up out of the water, only a few feet from me. He had been watching the take-off and landing exercise from the clear plastic dorsal gun turret on top of the after station. He had gone down with the plane but the turret held air for him to breathe until he was able to open the escape hatch and pop out.

The crew from the rescue boat helped us all out of the water and took us to sick bay where I held Conley's hand while they shaved his head and stitched his jagged metal cuts—over 100 stitches. Except for wet clothes, I was the only other casualty. I had a badly sprained elbow, which was put in a binding and sling. I always had fair ambidexterity but the plane wreck is when I really learned to eat left-handed.

The accident happened in late morning, probably 10:30 to 11 a.m. but it was after noon by the time we all got to the hospital, put on hospital gowns while they dried our clothes and double-checked every crewman to see that we still had two arms and legs with fingers and toes, then change back. They hustled us into the hospital dining hall but most of us had left our appetites somewhere out in San Diego Bay. You think you have good nerves but a test like this makes you re-evaluate. We were shaken for the moment, but all came back to fly again.

A Crew Without a Commander

We never knew exactly what happened to our new Plane Commander. He may have found an angel with a different plan for his future but he never showed up again to fly with our crew after the crash. We flew a couple of times with other pilots, and then we got orders to join VPB-28, a patrol bomber squadron, in the Philippines. Most crews flew out in their own planes. We got to miss that boring ordeal. You may well wonder what VPB-28 means, and for good reason. The Navy does things its way and, in general, it has worked fairly well for 100 or so years. "V" means heavier than air (the Navy also had blimp—lighter than air—squadrons.) "PB" means patrol bomber, and "28" means there were 27 squadrons commissioned somewhere before ours. It isn't sexy, but it's the Navy's way, and we're stuck with it.

382

Now that there are no more seaplane squadrons in existence, this doesn't seem a fitting place to change the history of naval aviation.

We got orders, in early summer of 1945, to fly Naval Air Transport Service (NATS) to Hawaii, then to Manila. A new commanding officer had been assigned to the squadron and we went out to be his crew. We took over the plane flown by the previous squadron commander before he and his crew were rotated back to stateside duty.

Our new skipper was Lieutenant Commander William Clark, a 1940 naval academy graduate who had done previous duty as a shipboard Navy officer, then applied to flight school. After he got his wings, he was assigned to Alameda for extended training and checked out as a Plane Commander. The squadron had just moved to NAS Sangley Point near Cavite City, across the bay from Manila, when we got there to meet our new Plane Commander and begin a duty tour of several months, covering several islands and bases.

We barely learned how to get in and out from our base on the southwest edge of Manila bay when our squadron was moved to a tiny island in Leyte Gulf called Jinamoc. It was shaped like a wedge or teardrop, a little over a mile long from north to south and less than a mile wide. There was a narrow band of water on the west between Jinamoc and Leyte and another on the east between us and the island of Samar. The seaplane harbor was on the south end with ramps down into Leyte Gulf. The base was a Quonset hut complex except for a small native village at the north end of the island.

Being the skipper's (squadron commander) crew had to be the best duty and worst duty available. He gave us our full share of good duty and good flights. We also got more than our share of the bad. Our crew flew on almost every holiday. We got the night patrols that nobody wanted. I guess I was a freak but I liked night patrols. I felt our radar was as good as theirs and we were always watching for ships. They might not always be watching for us.

Soon we settled in to making routine patrols, but the skipper was working overtime so much on official squadron and Navy work that he needed to skip several flights. I had more hours of flight time than he and far more in PBM's so I was sent to take a few "qualifying" flights and became a Plane Commander. From that point on, it was really my crew and the "Skipper" flew with us when he had the time. Then we added a new pilot so we had two pilots in the cockpit rotating with one at the navigation table whether the skipper was with us or not.

Navy Pilots "Overtrained?"

There were times when cadets in training felt that new information and deadlines came as fast as we could manage to digest but in contrast, we often felt we were being "overtrained" and a lot of us had to keep slapping ourselves to maintain focus on information being parceled out too slowly to keep us sharp and interested. As an example, they spent many hours and dollars training every cadet in the swimming pool. Their response was that they were spending more than a million dollars on training every pilot and they didn't want to lose a single one because his plane got shot down and the pilot couldn't swim.

While life as an aviation cadet was not a hard one as military life was concerned, a lot of us got impatient. For example, it may have been fun but how many times did we need to repeat any given aerobatic maneuver once reasonably competent. Some of us joked that Naval Aviation training was a good and honorable way to avoid the draft. As an example of comparative training and pilot readiness, my college roommate after the war, Dale Nahrstedt, flew two tours of duty (30 combat flights per tour) as a plane commander pilot in Army Air Corps B-17's over Europe. But I had more hours of total flight time when I left for overseas duty as a co-pilot in the Navy than he had flown in his entire career, training plus combat, in the Army Air Corps.

Jinamoc Under Attack

It took a few days to settle in to flying from Jinamoc, making mostly anti-ship and anti-sub patrols in the Southern Philippines, from our location in Leyte Gulf. Our base was pretty bare bones with minimal services. We had a mess hall (the Navy fed its airmen well) and laundry, a Quonset for an enlisted men's club land a similar officers' club facility and a sick bay with the standard pharmacist mate.

If we got hurt or real sick, we went to larger facilities a few miles by boat to the west at Tacloban on the Island of Leyte. The same was true if you needed any personal items more than toothpaste and shaving cream. The base actually had a skeleton crew as a naval air base that included beaching crews to get our planes into and out of the water, maintenance people, fuel and ammo storage and a post office. There was a small outdoor theater and a few movies, including State Fair, which played every few days.

We had a large island on our east and another on the west. They seemed to give us pretty good security from the enemy. And our Quonsets sat near the edge of a cliff about 30 feet straight down to the beach. Good security. But one morning just before sunrise, the attack began with a blast. It awakened any late sleepers. Then the fallout began banging on our tin roof. Corrugated steel Quonset huts give protection from the weather but not much from bombs. And they make a great echo chamber for all kinds of noise.

Eight pilots lived in our Quonset. We all hit the deck under our beds, mostly grabbing our side-arm pistols on the way. Then it was quiet. Really quiet. I looked around and saw Glen Armstrong cocking his .45 revolver. I had already cocked mine. I slipped on my pants and shoes. It was still quiet.

384

Deathly quiet. Two other pilots began to follow us. Two of us went to the screen door in the south end of the Quonset toward the cliff and beach, and two went to the north door.

We looked out cautiously. Nothing. I pushed the door open a few inches with my gun barrel. Nothing. Glen and I inched out the door, one going to the right, the other to the left. The pilots at the other end of the Quonset did the same. Nothing. When I got to the edge of the Quonset the only thing in sight was the pilot coming around the corner at the other end. We stood still, looking everywhere to the right and left. Still nothing.

Tom Grote noticed a sizeable dent in the Quonset about 5 to 6 feet above the ground and almost directly over my bunk. None of us knew whether that dent had been there before or not. Then somebody noticed a chunk of coral about the size of your head, between our hut and the next one. Then a couple of pilots came out of that Quonset. They didn't remember that rock, or the several other large rocks lying nearby.

The second blast came almost in our faces, dead ahead. Like the Old Faithful geyser, a spout of water blew into the air, but it was spiked with a few pieces of rock. We raced back inside the Quonset. At least the tin roof would keep the rocks from hitting us. In the quiet that followed the second blast, we began to hear the chug-chugging of a bulldozer. It didn't sound very Japanese to any of us.

The Seabees had been working on a project, blasting a hole in the rock on the beach below—and they thoughtfully did it early in the morning before anybody was out of bed so nobody would get hurt if a little rock happened to go astray. Friendly fire or enemy fire—neither is a suitable war zone alarm clock, no matter how far you are from a real point of combat.

We Have a New Plane for You at the Factory

We were barely settled down in our squadron in the Philippines when word is received that VPB-28 is to be the beneficiary of a new plane to replace one from our war-weary fleet. One catch—you have to send a crew here to pick it up direct from the factory at NAS North Island in San Diego. This is another example of the mixed curse/blessing from being "the Skipper's crew."

My full crew had orders to take "the next available transportation" to San Diego. One of our planes flew us to Sangley Point in Manila Bay where we went by Naval Air Transport Service (NATS) to Pearl Harbor in Honolulu. A couple of days later we caught another NATS flight to San Diego. I marched up to the office with my orders and requisition for the new plane but either I had the wrong paper or we were at the wrong place or we were there at the wrong time. No plane.

The Navy didn't know exactly what to do with us so they sent us to a base out north of San Diego called Camp Elliot. I never learned what the real mission of the base might be. It seemed to be a sort of warehouse for Naval and Marine personnel being reassigned. My instructions from the Naval Air Station brass were to check in by phone every morning from Camp Elliot at 0800 until our plane arrived.

Fortunately for our sanity, we were told early in our Navy careers, always take your pay record with you. You may need a pay day. Day after day we checked in at 0800 in the morning, then we had to find our own mischief for the rest of the day. Just outside the Camp Elliot main gate was an arcade to cure boredom for several hundred Navy men killing time until reassignment.

After nearly two weeks, they finally said they had no confirmation of a plane for us to fly back. We were to take "the next available" transportation back to our duty base. NATS had no openings so we got passage on the Takanis Bay, an auxiliary or "jeep" carrier—slightly smaller than the full-sized aircraft carrier—but a big ship. It would leave in a couple of days. We were ready to leave the boredom of Camp Elliot. But we didn't count on the next move.

They dropped the atomic bombs while we were twiddling thumbs, shooting out targets and taking one-day liberty tours from Camp Elliot. I had heard that a girl from Stapleton (my home town in Nebraska) was living in San Diego so I called her. George Campau, an old friend from Stapleton and college, had Navy duty aboard a destroyer. He had just called her to say his ship was in port. A few days later we got the news that Japan had asked for peace and the war was over. I called her again and George had just arrived. I was invited to help stage a "victory party." In retrospect, I don't remember asking my crew if they had partied or not—assuming that they, and everyone else in the military, celebrated in one way or another.

With the "peace" announcement, a lot of things changed in our day-to-day lives. Ending the war meant we would be riding a ship, going to Hawaii, under supposed peace time conditions without fear of a submarine attack. But even though we knew the war was over, we constantly had that nagging thought—what if some Japanese sub commander hadn't read his mail? Even with this overtone, our trip on the Takanis Bay was one to remember.

It had a full ship's crew but no squadron full of pilots and air crewmen. The flight deck was bare but the hangar deck below was loaded with fighter planes, in transit for somewhere in the Pacific. It was carrying a few passengers including a few shipboard officers and enlisted men in transit, heading for new assignments, in addition to our crew. We only used a small fraction of the space provided for dozens of flight squadron personnel.

I was just an ensign, the lowest commissioned rank in the Navy, but as a plane commander, I was assigned to a stateroom designated for "senior air officer" and was invited to eat with the ship's captain. The skipper introduced himself as Commander Willet. My memory wheels began to turn and my response was to ask if he had a daughter who was a member of the

386

"Navy Juniors" who attended the "junior officer" tea dances at the Hotel Del Coronado. He assured me that such was the case—and he seemed surprised that I would have remembered.

The next day we found a fourth for bridge and sat near the aft end of the flight deck playing cards. The weather was perfect. The ship's speed and direction canceled the wind so we could deal cards for hours without ever having one turn over in the breeze. I was sitting just inches from the rear of the flight deck looking toward the bow with my partner looking down almost into the screws churning the water as we headed southwest.

A ship nearly 700 feet long, in calm ocean, is about as stable as the seagoing Navy gets. Walking along the deck, you would never notice that it was less stable than the sidewalk in your home town, but it was definitely in motion. The bow and the front of the flight deck rises high in the air, then nearly dive (in slow motion, of course), making the horizon well above the deck. At the same time, it rolled from side to side. There is no motion in my experience that is comparable. You can survive it; I did, rather easily, in fact.

My stomach was immune to air or seasickness. But the peripheral view, looking toward the bow of the ship while playing cards for hours, began to upset my normally stable insides. We changed position after I noticed it and looking down into the boiling water from the ship's screws quickly settled my ailment. We watched the flying fish and porpoises fly formation near the bow of the ship on our vacation trip to Hawaii where we caught NATS back to the squadron.

Jinamoc, Aircraft Livery Stable for the Philippines

Our island wasn't that big. It isn't on any of the standard maps available in libraries for civilians today; in fact it was barely on the detailed maps we carried in our planes. Jinamoc was at the north edge of Leyte Gulf, a little speck in the strip of ocean that lay between two major islands—Leyte and Samar. We were near the center of the Philippines, I guess, had a decent seaplane harbor and a fair-sized parking lot near the ramp area where we brought planes ashore for parking and service and the base had personnel for getting us back into the water.

For no particular reason that I ever knew, we had a Grumman Goose amphibian plane that probably had an owner somewhere—we just didn't know who nor where. It had the factory manual with it but it didn't seem to be assigned to any squadron or other Navy unit. It was a nice, if small, two-engine amphibian. It could land and take off from water, but it also had retractable wheels that let you land on regular air strips. Or you could land on water, pop out your wheels, and run it right up the ramp out of the water and onto the parking area.

Ed Luck, an LSU grad, was a lieutenant junior grade and Don Teeters was an ensign in our squadron. Ed was a plane commander and Don graduated later than I had and was just recently assigned to our squadron. We were the pilots most interested in flying the Goose, except for my crew chief, Jack Barrath, who was an excellent Aviation Machinist Mate. He was our mechanical expert and consultant. He had some maintenance experience on a Goose at a previous assignment.

No pilot in our squadron had ever flown one but our squadron commander gave us his permission to study the manual and turn up the engines to see if it seemed to be in operational condition. We did and it was. Next, he gave us the Navy's permission to water taxi and even take it off if it seemed to perform OK. It seemed to be reliable so we began making mail runs to nearby islands. The Skipper was glad to have us fly it, just to have it and to have trained pilots available for flights, if it happened to be the most suitable plane for the situation.

Teeters had attended and possibly graduated from the Minnesota School of Mines and had studied to become a certified gemologist when he went into flight school. He knew a good bit about rocks, pearls, mother-of-pearl, etc. We heard that there were lots of pearls in Iloilo and Cebu City. One day we "borrowed" the Goose, loaded up with about 20 cartons of cigarettes, some material from the parachute loft and a few nylon knit tow targets with occasional bullet holes—all items in great demand for barter in the Philippine civilian market place.

We landed in the harbor at Cebu City and tied to a buoy. Natives came out in boats to meet us and bring us ashore (I don't think they had much excitement on normal days but we were new if not exciting). With rare goodies to barter, we met such a welcoming committee our feet hardly touched the ground until we got to the city square. Don got pouches of pearls and mother-of-pearl along with other gems that I had never heard of. I didn't even know what was available for barter with any value. It was a fun trip for me, a profitable one for Don Teeters.

This was the first of several "peace time" or non-military flights made by our squadron and our crew in both the Grumman Goose, our squadron PBM's and other planes. Some were "humanitarian" and some, as our flight to Cebu City, for experience, selfish satisfaction, and plunder. Remember, we had a lot of time on our otherwise idle hands.

The Best (If Risky) Air Taxi Service in the Navy

Toward the end of the war, a shell-shocked sailor went berserk with "combat fatigue" or some other psycho problem. He had taken a "Tommy gun" (Thompson .45 caliber semi- automatic machine gun) and shot up a local platoon or company of the Philippine Army in an imagined enemy raid. He

388

had been captured, disarmed and returned to the United States for confinement, treatment or whatever seemed the appropriate outcome.

The Navy was conducting a court-martial hearing (in his absence) to determine what damages he had done and possibly award payment to the injured, families of the dead, etc. We got a call to pick up some witnesses and fly them to the base on the island of Samar, not far from our base. A Navy chaplain and two Shore Patrols (SPs)—the Navy's police department—came to Jinamoc by boat from nearby Tacloban on the island of Leyte, to be our diplomatic escorts.

We were to land at Catbalogan bay on Samar, meet natives in a dug-out canoe, who would take the chaplain and SPs ashore and return with the witnesses. Then we would fly them about 70 miles to the Guiuan Navy base on the south end of Samar so they could testify at the court martial. Most of the PBMs were flying or getting routine service so the squadron commander suggested we fly the PBY Catalina, a flying boat normally used for patrol bombing, air-sea rescue, etc., except for our squadron post-war use.

The PBY was another story. It had been left in the parking area on Jinamoc Island. It was assigned to a Combat Aircraft Service Unit but the Navy discovered that the unit's commander had been "supervising" family hard wood forests in the Philippines. He was sent home and the plane was parked. It was the "modified" luxury model. Gun turrets had been removed and plush seats had been installed in the bunk room and rear area of the plane. And it was a "Land Cat," an amphibian with retractable wheels that could land on a hard-surfaced airstrip, or it could land on water, then the pilot could extend the wheels and taxi it up a ramp out of the water and onto a land parking area.

Ed Luck, Don Teeters and I were the pilots that had been flying the Grumman Goose that was a sort of "orphan" plane left at Jinamoc. But it was mainly Sam Worthington, Glenn Armstrong and I who flew the PBY on the rare trips when it was used. I always included Jack Barrath, my PBM crew chief, as the aviation machinist and crew chief when I flew either plane and I liked to have Glen Eidemiller, my first ordinance man, to handle beaching.

Armstrong had another assignment so I asked Teeters to fly in the other seat with me. We taxied the plane down the ramp from the parking area into the ocean, retracted our wheels, checked our ignition and took off. Our landing would technically be "open sea" except that Catbalogan Bay, a short half-hour flight away, was well protected for a routine landing.

We dropped anchor since there were no buoys to tie to. Almost immediately a native dugout canoe with outrigger approached the plane. We opened a waist-hatch door, hung a pad over the side and warned the boaters to approach us carefully. The chaplain and SPs got in the boat and the natives rowed it ashore as we waited, a couple of crewmen went swimming, and I took a couple of photos while we waited for the boats to return with the natives. In about 30 or 40 minutes we had two boats returning with our native witness passengers.

We had a crew of six including two pilots, a machinist, a radioman and two ordinance men. The chaplain and SPs made nine and we had five natives for a total load of 14. That is more than the normal crew on a PBY Catalina but we had a light load of gasoline and no bombs so our takeoff should be easy, fortunately. We had an east wind and the bay was on the west shore of the island so I had to taxi well away from the island since we would be taking off into the east wind directly over the island.

It was the wind direction that set me up for one of the stupidest things I ever did in an airplane. We took off into a nice breeze that left slight ripples on the water and the plane practically popped out of the water and into the air. We climbed out of the bay and headed south to Guiuan at the south end of the island of Samar. The base was near the end of a miniature Florida-shaped peninsula but less than 2 miles across.

The Guiuan area of the island had a ship harbor on the west side with some iron buoys for boats to tie to, and a few rubber buoys to accommodate seaplanes. It was only 50 or 60 miles from our base and while we flew over it regularly, I had never landed there. As we approached the Navy base, I called the control tower to get landing instructions. I knew the wind was east since we had just taken off a few minutes earlier into an east wind from the bay 70 to 75 miles away on the west side of the same island.

A new paved airstrip had just been completed across the south end of the island at Guiuan. It ran almost from shore to shore, beginning a few hundred feet from the ocean for the rise from sea level up to the airstrip probably 20 to 30 feet elevation. I asked to land in the seaplane harbor but with an east or west wind, the landing and takeoff pattern was the same for land or water landings. You just flew a longer, or shorter downwind leg. As they gave me clearance to land, they asked if my plane was an amphibian. I answered in the affirmative. (Of course, a PBY-5A is an amphibian. That's what the "A" is for.) I didn't think of the landing and takeoff consequences.

The tower operator then said, "You are cleared to the strip." Somehow that seemed reasonable and my crew chief, who had listened to the radio, told me that the wheels were down and locked and I began to throttle back as we approached land. The plane was in a nice glide and I cranked on more elevator tab and eased off the throttles. As I approached the end of the landing strip I saw the top of a palm tree outside the window in my peripheral vision. I looked at my instrument panel. The airspeed indicator showed 50 knots. This plane can't fly at that speed, can I be on the ground, I wondered. I eased the yoke slightly forward and the nose wheel touched down. We were on the ground all right. I couldn't believe it. I was so preoccupied with the landing I didn't even feel the wheels touch.

390

The tower operator called to welcome us and I looked up the strip to see the "follow me" jeep coming to lead us to a parking area. We taxied to a spot near the tower, a crewman came out and put chocks at the wheels and I called the tower to report that we were at the chocks. I killed the engines, hung the radio headset on the yoke and looked over to my co-pilot, Don Teeters, and said, "Would you believe that was the first time I ever landed one of these suckers on land?" He said "if that's true, you don't need any lessons," but I know he didn't believe me.

Then the awful truth hit me. I had risked the lives of the innocent natives, the chaplain and SP's as well as the crew and myself. Why? I really don't know except that the wind was east and we flew the same pattern to land on the strip as for the harbor and the tower operator had given me permission. Then came the second truth: I had landed it. Now I had to take it off. I had never done that either. Fortunately the Navy wanted us to pick up some mail and movies so we had time to get a cup of coffee to settle my nerves.

Leyte Gulf is probably 70 or 80 miles across—from the tip of Samar on the east to Tacloban harbor and city on the island of Leyte on the west. Our home island of Jinamoc lay in the north end of the gulf. The battle for Leyte Gulf has been called the greatest naval battle in history. It was allegedly the turning point of World War II with the Japanese. You can look down into the water but you can't see the sunken ships. According to historians, the ships are there—enough to start your own Navy if you could float them all again.

This was not my problem. The war had ended but the people at Tacloban would be thrilled with the mail and movies we were bringing. Tacloban had a seaplane harbor where I had previously landed, but it also had an airstrip. When I got the PBY in the air, taking off from Samar, why not land on the strip when we got to Tacloban? No boat would be needed to get ashore. It was a short hop, the tower gave me landing clearance and we approached the runway. Just as I was touching down I heard the most sickening, grinding metal noise imaginable. Then it hit me, I hadn't put my wheels down to land and I was grinding off the bottom of my hull—the boat part of our flying boat—on the runway.

I pushed the throttles to the limit and we were airborne again. I didn't know how we would land with a hole in the bottom of our seaplane. Maybe we could land near the shore in shallow water, I thought. Then the tower operator called. "Navy 665, do you have a problem?" I told him I heard an awful noise, would he look to see if our landing gear was down. He asked if I had ever landed on a metal air strip. Landed on one—I had never seen or even heard of one.

The tower operator assured me that our gear was down and we were clear to circle and land, then he told me about metal airstrips. When the landing crews took Tacloban Harbor from the Japanese they brought Navy Seabees ashore with bulldozers. They hit the beach like ants, leveling the site and interlocking strips of perforated steel were connected to make a firm—if noisy—airstrip. Transport planes landed with supplies only a few hours after a beach landing.

I can recall several landmark days and decisions in my life. The decision to ask my grandmother to let me stay with her so I could go to high school was probably the first. The decisions to go to college, to enlist in the Navy Air Corps, to sign the new agreement to "fly or else" when I hadn't yet soloed in flight school—these were times when I had made decisions that would affect, if not seriously change my life.

But the events of this day and the decision to land on the airstrip instead of the harbor at Samar and the shock of that clattering noise of the Tacloban metal airstrip made this the most memorable day of my life up to this time. You can be sure I did not tell our squadron commander that I had never landed a PBY on land before nor that the clanging iron strip at Tacloban had tested my nerves to the limit. Sometimes, and especially this time, I did things as if my gray cells knew it was under control all along. Luckily, for the innocents who trusted their lives to luck and my normally reasonable judgment, I was in control—barely.

West of Tokyo

The war was barely over but we shortly began to see what would happen in converting to a peace time operation, even though we were far from full-fledged peace, even in the Philippines. Our squadron had operated at several locations. We had flown from Lingayen Gulf on the Luzon coast north-west from Manila where we were based on the seaplane tender, USS Pocomoke. We had been shore-based from Jinamaoc Island at the north edge of Leyte Gulf and from NAS Sangley Point, at the southwest edge of Manila Bay. Our squadron had also been tender based at Zamboanga at the southwest end of the Island of Mindanao and just south of that from the island of Jolo and even further south at Tawi Tawi.

We were ordered to the naval base at Puerta Princesa on the east side of the island of Palawan, the southwestern-most island in the Philippines. I enjoyed our Philippine duty more at Puerta Princesa than any base, not only because the war was over, but because I had enough experience by this time to be more comfortable in the jungle climate. Also, we had gone to the Philippines as the crew for the new squadron commander, William Clark, a 1940 graduate of the Naval Academy who had gone to flight school after some sea duty tours in the shipborne Navy, then was sent through flight school. He was replacing the squadron's original skipper who had taken VPB 28 to the islands months earlier and was now being rotated to stateside duty.

I had been flying PBMs for a year and had a good many hours—more than our commander—and since he had time-consuming obligations as the squadron commander, I flew as the plane commander much of the time with the skipper making a couple of flights per month. Finally he sent me to check out and earn "plane commander" status so we would be "legal" under Navy rules. The base on Palawan was located with a different relationship to other activities on the island than any other place where we operated. It had a large, nearly level area near the base where there was a small, scattered native village and several military installations with varying duties. Just off the edge of our area of operations in and near the bay, the Army Air Corps had a long air strip with squadron area, they had a P-51 fighter squadron, a P-38 photo-reconnaissance squadron, the Navy had a combat aircraft service unit (CASU) with bomb depot, aircraft parts storage, etc. and a limited base operations contingent.

On one of our first days, we went to the Navy officers' club where my geography knowledge got a jolt with the "West of Tokyo Officers Club" sign over the entry. Is that possible? I wondered. Maybe Palawan is really far

VPB-28 Officers aboard USS Pocomoke in Lingayen Gulf (1945). Front row (l-r): Short, Raynard, Reech, Dalton, Worthington, Teeters, Howard, Fog. 2nd Row: Dooney, Mix, Simdars, Martin, Clark (c.o.), Quillen, Grote, Callier, Summercorn. 3rd Row: Dunton, Rasmussen, Levi, Hefele, Watson, Folz, Wilkinson, Gay, Strand. Back Row: Stall, Harman, Livingston, Bartlett, Bidewell, Grosskreutz, Stare, Neihaus, Brown.

enough west at the end of the Philippines to actually be west of Tokyo. Next morning we dug out the maps. We normally flew with detailed charts that did not include a large area and the Pacific Ocean is big enough to fill a lot of small area maps. The Philippine Islands are so far south of Japan that it's not easy to tell which is west of what, especially on maps of small areas. The big area map made it easy. Every speck of the Philippines was west of even the westernmost dot of Japan. The O-Club sign was right by plenty.

The Navy officers club was only a few hundred yards south of the landing strip that the Air Corps used. We were enjoying a cool drink and watching as the P-51 pilots were shooting touch-and-go landings. The P-51 was a fast and lethal fighter but all planes have their idiosyncrasies. Flying over water, many planes were stable enough that if the plane lost its power, the pilot would fare well by making a full-stall landing on water. The plane would float long enough for the pilot to climb out and into the water, or a life raft if one was aboard. Rumor was that if a P-51 lost its power, the pilot had to parachute out. It had a big belly air scoop that would allegedly scoop up water on contact and instantly flop tail over head and sink with no chance for the pilot to get out.

Even parked, the P-51 was a thing of beauty, but in the air, the P-51 was a joy to watch. Suddenly I saw a plane coming in without his landing gear down. I yelled, "Look, Ma, no wheels," in time for a few of the other pilots to look, but the plane went beyond our line of sight and we forgot about it. Forgot, until the next day when the news on our flight line was that a P-51 had indeed, come in without wheels, just enough to hit the tips of the propeller on the airstrip but the pilot put on power, regained flying speed and went around for another landing with only a few bent propeller blades to show for it.

The first real sign of the oncoming adjustment to peace was the departure of the Air Corps photo squadron. They took the P-38s but left everything else where it sat. We inherited their dark room, cameras, chemicals, etc. I had recently been designated as our squadron photo officer—I guess because I was about the only pilot who had a camera or took pictures. I had never been in a real dark room nor loaded any camera beyond an Argus C-3 until we got orders to photograph all the islands in the Philippines along with some aerial cameras, but one of the Army sergeants had been in sick bay when his outfit left. He stayed a few days to check us out a little. There was an 8-by-10 view camera and he showed me how to take the big rolls of Kodachrome film and cut out sheets of film and put them in the film holders for the big view camera. You should have seen the beach scenes, the PBM's landing, dried fish hanging on racks outside a native village, banana and papaya trees, etc. But that's another story.

The skipper decided that the photo officer might just as well also be the gunnery officer since the war was over and most of our shooting would be with a camera. It didn't seem like much of a deal until the Admiral pulled out the CASU unit personnel and our squadron inherited its entire armament inventory. Little did I know this would be a mixed blessing. I didn't look forward to being responsible for the maintenance of the machine guns and the ammo depot that had tons of bombs and who knows how many rounds of machine gun ammo.

But Warrant Gunner Hassett (a warrant officer is the top enlisted rank) came with the deal. Nobody in the Navy knew more about this job. I showed up every couple of days for a cup of coffee and let Hasset run the bomb depot. The other bonus was the new jeep for the CASU "commanding officer." Under the rules in place, ridiculous as it sounds, I was him. The jeep had less than 3,000 miles on it and the new paint showed that whoever drove this must be important. It was so shiny I'm sure our skipper was jealous but he never suggested a trade.

In just a few weeks, all the army units were withdrawn from Palawan and our squadron with a limited Navy base contingent shared the area with only the natives, who kept a low profile. We spent free hours in the countryside learning how to harvest ripe papayas and bananas, keeping reasonably close to civilization and open space. We were forbidden to travel far beyond the base for several weeks waiting for a good old Army infantry unit to clear the remaining Japanese from a few more miles of the island's roads. The war was over except for a few possible renegades.

Beer King of the Philippines

Our squadron was ordered to Puerta Princesa, on the east side of the island of Palawan, at the end of the war. While I never did a census of the area, there was a spread-out native village, a good runway with an Air Corps establishment alongside, a small, deserted army area and a harbor installation where we were based. Native homes were long on bamboo and palm fronds. The military units operated from Quonset huts—dozens of them—of varying sizes. A rock-surfaced road connected these units and continued for most of the length of the island, we were told. But it was barricaded and we were not allowed to go beyond 10 kilometers to either the north or south because the Japanese had not been officially cleared from these outlying areas.

The seaport of Puerta Princesa had a small but substantial dock and was apparently able to handle fair-sized military and/or cargo ships, either before or during the war. It also had several metal barges or floating piers tied to the dock. The seaplane takeoff and landing area was several miles across and we had a beaching area to bring the patrol bombers ashore for major maintenance. We tied the seaplanes to buoys anchored near the beaching ramp. Crews swam out with beaching gear—large wheels with air tanks for flotation that attached to the sides and rear of the plane. A tail line was then attached and a tractor pulled the plane up the ramp and onto the parking/service area.

A few weeks after arriving at Puerta Princesa, a seaplane tender (I believe it was the Casco) that had been our base a few weeks earlier in Lingayen Gulf, pulled into port. The air officer that we worked with when on his ship, was also the recreation officer. He was one person that we had played bridge with, so he knew me, but they wouldn't play for money so we were still friends. He came to see me when he came ashore and told me that his ship had received orders to sail west, going home to the U.S. East Coast. He had charted the ports they would make and the number of days of liberty and found that he had nearly 200 cases of beer more than they needed. Any kind of beer would be not only welcome, but priceless barter in the Philippines— and this was bottled Budweiser, not Fort Pitt or Iron City or other frequent wartime brands.

There was a lot of stuff to drink in the Philippines but except for an occasional shore liberty or the goodness of some ship's recreation officer, we hadn't seen a bottle or can of decent beer in months. He was just *giving* us 200 cases. He might have intended it for the squadron but we didn't take any chances. Jack Barrath, my plane captain, shared housing with the two other chief petty officers from our squadron in a Quonset hut that had been "decorated" by Seabees and inherited by our chiefs when abandoned by the Seabees shipped out to other duty.

It was divided into private rooms. Beds were not GI cots but handmade with woven strips of rubber for springs. It had a kitchen with a toaster and coffee maker and a native Filipino house boy. It also had part of a Quonset attached that had an ice-making machine and insulated ice storage area. It was also next door to a Quonset for storage with solid ends and a padlock. That is the place we selected for our hoard of Budweiser. As they set the cases off the ship on the dock, our crew hauled 6-by-6 loads to the storage hut about 25 to 30 cases at a time, until the job was done, except for a few cases which were put in the cooler.

The next day we had a day off so we set out to see what kind of barter we could arrange. With my crew chief, Jack Barrath, we put a cold case (the short-necked bottles made a nice flat pack) in the back of the jeep, covered it with a camouflage rain parka and put another case on top of it covered by another parka. The Navy normally fed its air crews pretty well but the distance from home and the limitations of refrigeration sometimes made for monotonous menus. We headed to the commissary at the local Air Corps base to see if we could swap for something to give variety to our table fare.

We drove to the mess kitchen. The only person in sight was someone sitting on a box, sharpening a knife on a steel. Jack stopped about eight or 10 feet from him and turned the engine off. Dressed in a T-shirt and khaki pants covered by a white apron, he noticed our arrival—barely. I broke the silence, asking, "Sarge, what would you give for a case of cold Budweiser?" Without looking up or missing a lick at his knife sharpening he said, "Ain't no beer on this island." I reached for the parka, pulling it off the beer case so he could see it. That's all it took.

"Cover that son-of-a-bitch up," he ordered as he looked up, and threw his knife, sticking the tip of the blade several inches into the sand. "Come here," he motioned, as he opened the heavy door of a walk-in freezer. He took two large canned hams off the shelf, giving them to Jack. We hadn't had ham for weeks. As I contemplated our hoard of beer I hesitated, with some thought of giving him both cases. He felt I was backing out so he quickly reached for two similar-sized cans of turkey. I then told him we had two cases. He went to a different shelf and came out with a full loin of filet mignon steaks. We gave him both cases and were asked to come back any time. Our squadron had three Chief Petty Officers who shared the "Chiefs' hut" where the beer was stored. They knew about the beer. My crew of nine enlisted men, including Jack Barrath, had moved the beer so they knew. The beer was our secret and we shared whatever we could barter for. We quickly learned that we could trade a case of 24 bottles of beer for a case of 12 fifths of the best scotch or bourbon. We didn't use much of that but it was nice to know.

Then we discovered that the Army had a Coca-Cola warehouse or bottler on Guam. The Air Corps had brought in a squadron of twin-engine night fighters called "Black Widows." They made frequent flights to Guam and brought back four cases at a time in the empty second seat. This was the first Coke to hit Palawan in ages but we learned that their pilots were just as starved for beer. Maybe more starved. A case of our beer was worth two cases of their Coke.

We got the real lesson in beer power a few weeks later. Our squadron had a dozen crews and a dozen planes. It had been organized in the states and they flew the planes out to the Philippines. I never knew when they shipped out but it had been many months, mostly flying night patrols at low altitude with radar on. A ship made a bigger blip on radar than a plane so we had the advantage in the plane vs. ship duel. Most patrols were six to 10 hours so it didn't take many months to get a lot of hours on our engines. We had all PBM-5's with Pratt-Whitney R-2800 radial engines. This may have been the best gasoline airplane engine ever made but they only last so long. We needed some new engines.

Our skipper (squadron commander) was a great guy but a Naval Academy graduate and he did everything "by the book." We used to kid him by saying that while we were brought up on Mother Goose, his mother read Naval Regulations to him. It seemed that if he needed the Navy's answer to a problem, the book of Navy regs (Navy vernacular for the official book of regulations) just fell open to the passage he needed. This was wonderful for his "fitness report" that the admirals used to determine which officers got promotions but since most of the supply clerks were "reserves" and not "regular Navy" people, we sometimes got results quicker with non-military schemes and scrambling than his doing it by-the-book.

The best information indicated that there were eight new Pratt & Whitney R2800 engines at the depot in Manila. That's only enough for four planes and there were two other squadrons operating in the Philippines. The skipper was writing wonderful letters to the Admiral's office but we got no engines. Our plane needed new engines worse than any other plane in VPB-28. I don't know about other squadrons. We made a run to Manila one day and I went to the supply office where we met the enlisted man in charge, a Chief Aviation Machinist Mate, the same rate as Jack, my plane captain. We began visiting about shortages and quickly learned that Manila, like the rest of the Philippines, had no beer.

I told him that we didn't have a lot of beer but enough to bring him eight cases for a pair of R-2800 engines. We had put eight cases on board before we left Palawan, just in case. He said that he could let us have them for eight cases per engine. They were shipped the next day. We delivered our eight cases on the spot and the balance a few days later. We arranged for two more engines in the next two weeks. Our skipper was pleased when the engines came, knowing that his "Navy way" using official channels had done the job—until a few days later when he got a note from the Admiral saying that other squadrons had planes needier than ours. When he asked me point blank, I had to tell him that our beer and "reservist" wile had made the deal.

The harbor officer for the Navy base was Chief Warrant Officer Hutto. We weren't close friends but we had visited a few times and he remembered that I had told him I went to an Ag college. Within a month or two of inheriting the hoard of beer from the departing seaplane tender, Hutto drove his jeep out to the ramp where my crew was servicing our plane. He asked, "Aren't you some kind of an agriculture guy? What do you know about weevils? Don't weevils eat grain?"

"I don't know much about 'em," I told him, "Whatever made you ask?"

"I've got a ship in port with a few hundred cases of beer that is packed in barley so the bottles won't break. They were going to unload it but they found some weevils in the barley and seaport regulations won't allow it ashore. This is stateside-bottled Budweiser and my conscience won't let me send them out to dump it over the side at sea. What can we do with weevils?" I told him that I didn't know much about weevils but I knew they weren't swimmers. "Just set it off on those metal barges tied to the pier with metal cables. We'll take the bottles out, dump the barley in the water, put the bottles back and bring them ashore. You can sign that the contaminated material was buried at sea." He agreed.

I collected my crew and we began dumping weevil-infested barley into the bay, putting the bottles back in the cases and loading them on the squadron 6-by-6 truck for the trip to our beer storage bunker. If this had been our first new cases of beer—before we got the cases from the Casco—removing the bottles, dumping barley and replacing the bottles would have been too monotonous to endure for 200 cases. Knowing that we already had more beer in storage than we could ever imagine using made the job even more boring. After about a dozen cases—and we didn't see even one

398

weevil—we cut the barley-dumping part out of our beer disposal project. The beer went to our storage Quonset, weevils (if there really were any) and all.

Our squadron was transferred to Sangley Point for temporary duty a few weeks later. We had a squadron beer party but we left the rest of the beer locked in a Quonset hut on Palawan. I got enough "points" for rotation back to Hawaii, leaving the squadron behind. Since I have never heard of a weevil infestation in the Philippines, it just might be that a Quonset hut at Puerta Princessa still holds 300-plus cases of beer, well "aged" since 1946.

Our War Was Mostly Boring

Ernie Pyle and Bill Mauldin never visited our outfit. They went where the action was. The very name of our type of plane and duty, patrol bombers, tell you that we are more prepared to cruise than fight. Fighter planes had a different shape, a different power plant and were made to do a different job. Why would anybody want to be a patrol bomber pilot? The duty wasn't all bad. And when you consider the options, being bored in wartime may beat the alternatives. We had a lot of room to move around, we had a bunk room and a kitchen aboard and we were always based on calm water. But it really comes down to the fact that you go where the Navy sends you.

When we put in our requests for type of duty while we were in flight school (several of us actually got what we asked for) we had been told to put in for seaplanes. "Seaplane pilots get Naval Air Transport Service (NATS) duty," they said. That was the Navy's airlines. If true at the time, things changed by the time I got my wings. I asked for seaplanes, I got assigned to seaplanes . . . and I flew seaplanes. Some months later I did take a couple of flights on NATS.

As a patrol bomber squadron, we were based in a calm-water bay or gulf that had either a seaplane harbor with launching ramp to get the flying boats out of the water for service and storage or we operated from a seaplane tender located in a body of water that had a decent harbor to land and take off plus a number of rubber buoys anchored to the bottom of the bay. We tied our planes to the buoys when we were not flying, getting back to quarters aboard ship by boat.

Our squadron, VPB-28, flew mostly night patrols. We flew (as best I remember) at 200 to 500 feet above the ocean with our radar watching for Japanese ships. At this altitude we were high enough to clear the masts of the ships, should we chance to find one, but low enough that the ship's radar would probably not be able separate our blip from the ocean's image. We had the advantage because almost any ship would show up on our radar screen. We could pick up and identify ships as friend or foe at a distance of about 50 to 60 miles. This gave us some distance to prepare for an attack and climb to a higher elevation to begin a bombing run. Our squadron, VPB-28, was awarded a Presidential Unit Citation for sinking the most enemy shipping of any Pacific squadron but I was still in training—too young to be a hero in this war—but I filled a slot.

Our other duty was search and rescue. And you may be surprised to learn what much of our search activity was about. I'm sure most people never knew that the Army operated a lot of ships during WWII. In our experience, most were small, inter-island freighters with a crew made up of a commissioned officer in command and one or more enlisted or non-commissioned persons, who could allegedly send and receive Morse code, plus a native crew. We didn't get too many calls to search for "overdue" ships during the war but they got more casual with their schedules and locations after the war. We frequently would find a ship, after flight crews had searched an area for several days, anchored in some cozy bay, with women's laundry hanging on clothes lines strung from mast to mast.

When we finally got radio or blinker contact, they reported that they were making their own repairs and expected to be under way in a few days. We later learned that some member of their native crew would tell the crew and its officers how many beautiful girls lived in the village on the bay that happened to be near their route. Since the urgency of the war was over, why not investigate? In other words, a vacation stop. In time, we learned to fly the coast near the last reported position of the ship and we would almost surely find the lostling.

Clark Field was the big Air Corps base northwest of Manila. It seemed to be the Officers Club of choice for Army Air Corps pilots so we got called every time one of their planes was "overdue." Actually they had already landed at Clark but didn't file an "in" report. We did a search, with binoculars, of the aircraft parking area at Clark Field before we flew over an inch of Pacific Ocean looking for the overdue plane. I don't remember a single search over water for an "overdue" ship after we learned this shortcut.

We occasionally had a legitimate search. Sam Worthington's crew, from our squadron, dropped the first life rafts to the survivors of the Indianapolis. And one day we had a daytime search to the Indo-China coast, several hours away. We could receive and send radio messages for several hundred miles by using a "trailing wire" antenna. We had several hundred feet of woven metal cable with a lead weight to make it follow in a line when we unreeled it from inside the plane through a port in the rear of the plane, a bit like a giant fishing line. The radioman "tuned" the reception by cranking the wire in and out to get the best signal. It was especially important to crank in all the cable, and the weight, before landing on water.

A radio message cancelled the search that was the reason for our flight just after we got to the Asian coast. This was some geography that we had never seen so we decided to explore for a few minutes. The housing there at the time was mostly thatched roof construction, probably bamboo

400

framework. We saw several homes with a fairly large central room and passageways out to small rooms in several directions. I later heard that the parents lived in the big central room and the children, single and married, live in the annexes.

We didn't take our flying boat very far inland from the ocean (seaplanes are not good at landing on dirt—even in rice paddies) but we did fly low over some of the buildings to see what the homes and countryside looked like, close up. We soon ended our joy ride, then turned and headed for home when it appeared that the whole area was rice paddies. Imagine our surprise when we began to crank in our trailing wire antenna and there was no resistance to the cranking because the weight was gone from the end of the wire. We'll never know whose thatched roof we decorated but I'm sure the owner was just as surprised to find a lead weight from our antenna in his roof as we were to find it missing.

Spoolix

I don't know whether the date has been changed by act of Congress or by a presidential order. Both of these entities seem to feel free to change the date for us to celebrate various holidays. But in 1945, Navy Day was in October. And that was one "Navy Day" that I'll never forget. As the newly appointed squadron gunnery officer, I was thumbing through old squadron files and got the shock of my life. I gasped, almost screamed, when I found a letter to the parents from the squadron's previous commanding officer. He was the man who had been relieved by my plane commander, our squadron's new commanding officer.

Our skipper heard me and asked what happened. I told him, "This just has to be the guy."

"What guy?" he asked.

"This file shows that Charles N. Boyle, an air ordinance man, was killed by enemy gunfire during a bombing run on a ship as a member of a VPB-28 air crew." The incident was only a few months before we arrived as new members of VPB-28. We had heard that a plane had taken a hit in the bow turret—an explosive anti-aircraft shell—but the plane had sunk the ship and returned with several bullet holes. The bow gunner was killed but no other crewmember was injured. I had never heard a name before. Then our commander officer asked why it was such a big deal to me—"like it was personal." I asked and he agreed that he had time for a little story—a really personal story.

I was a freshman at the University of Nebraska. It was an English class the first period after lunch. A dull teacher and a 1 o'clock class don't make for a good combination. I always tried to be prompt to give myself a chance to stay awake and get a decent grade. There was one student who seemed to have a real problem with getting to this class on time and almost every time he was late the teacher would comment, "Mr. Boyle, is it impossible for you to get to class on time?" He never responded and while I did not really know him, I always recognized him if we happened to meet on campus.

As time passed and Pearl Harbor was bombed and we became involved in World War II, most men of college age became eligible for the military draft. I don't know why he decided to join the Navy Air Corps; I did it mainly because it seemed the hardest branch of service to get into. It had the toughest physical and mental requirements. In conversations with my friends, we would ask each other, what's the hardest branch of the service to get into? We generally decided we'd try Naval aviation. If we couldn't qualify for the Navy, we'd try for the Army Air Corps. If we couldn't make that, we'd enlist in the Navy or try for some program that let us continue in college. If none of those worked, let them draft us. The word "macho" hadn't been invented at that time, but it was a real accomplishment to be a member of the exclusive Navy Air Corps.

We gathered in Lincoln to take our first written and physical exams, I saw several fellow students that I recognized, and Boyle, from my English class, was one of us. Later, when those of us who had survived "Round 1" went to Kansas City for final physical and written exams—and swearing in for the winners, Boyle was one included in our group from Nebraska in what the Navy called the "Cornhusker Squadron." We reported for our flight prep training at Cornell College, Mt. Vernon, Iowa. Del Reeder was one of my roommates (the Navy did things alphabetically) and one of Boyle's closest friends from the University. I got to know Boyle from his frequent visits to our room. I never learned why he was called Spoolix.

We got split up after we graduated from flight prep and went on to our first flying base. I went to Tucson. Del Reeder and Spoolix both went to another base. I later heard from "Reed" that Spoolix had a brother, an Army Air Corps pilot, who got shot down over Europe. Spoolix resigned from flight training to attend aircraft gunnery school with the comment that it took so long to get wings in the Navy the war would be over before he could get into combat and have a chance to avenge his brother's death. Later, when I was in operational training, I heard that Spoolix had been killed. Little could I have imagined that it would have happened in what was to become my squadron, and only a few months before I got there.

The squadron record showed that he had been buried in the military section of Santo Tomás, the historic cemetery near Lingayen Gulf. The squadron had been flying from the same ship that was anchored in the same bay that was our home at that time. Our squadron commander, Lt. Cdr. William Clark, never missed a chance to promote the Navy's cause. This discovery was in early October, 1945, a couple of weeks before Navy Day, the day we jokingly called our skipper's second birthday. He said that he and the parents would appreciate it if I would go to Santo Tomás cemetery, take a picture of the grave, write a letter of our relationship as a Navy Day present to Spoolix's parents, who were still living in Omaha. What an awful assignment. It sounded to me like a job for the chaplain but when your commanding officer has an idea you respond. He sent Bruce, the squadron yeoman, with me.

Yes, the parents were appreciative but apparently I did not do a good job. I was disappointed to hear some years later that they had brought his body back to Omaha for burial in a family plot beside his brother, who they brought back from Europe. Even my photo showing them the peaceful place where he was buried and my letter to them did not convince them that Santo Tomás was an appropriate resting place. I still remember Navy Day—but especially that Navy Day—and I remember Spoolix.

Christmas Salad

Our crew was in a unique position. When we joined Squadron VPB-28, we were the crew for the new squadron commanding officer, William Clark. He was a Naval Academy graduate who operated "by the book" in Navy terms. He went to flight school after tours of sea duty as a regular line officer. His flying experience was adequate but limited, compared with officers of the same rank who began and continued as pilots. What he may have lacked in flying experience, was balanced by our crew. We had been through an extra tour in operational training due to a plane commander who got re-assigned before we went overseas.

It seemed to us that the Skipper wanted to be sure he wouldn't be accused of giving his crew favors by giving us the jobs nobody wanted, like Christmas Day patrol, long night patrols, etc. Then he would seem to have a conscience attack in which he gave us a fun job. This could be anything to break the monotony of the routine post-war training flights that we flew regularly when there was no ship lost or plane overdue. One such flight came in December, 1945. Christmas mail was piling up in the Philippines. If we could get the bundles to the Mariana Islands, there was plenty of transportation from there to the States.

We got the job. We flew to Sangley Point NAS in Manila Bay where we were loaded with bundles of mail for a trip to Tanapag Harbor, Saipan, the primary seaplane harbor in the Marianas. This favor was repaid when we flew the "Christmas Day Patrol" and the Skipper, proving that he was willing to share our suffering, flew with us. We frequently flew without him when his squadron duties needed his time. In fact, he later requisitioned another pilot for our crew so we could have two pilots in the cockpit at all times plus having one pilot at the navigation table keeping our position up to date as the other crews did.

The Navy had a reputation for taking good care of its air crews. If there was good food available anywhere, we got it. But the choices were limited some of the time and we were in a time of repeat menus with little fresh food. But when Hewitt, our 2nd ordinance man and 1st cook called up from the galley to alert us of our Christmas dinner, he jokingly said, "Skipper, sorry we don't have turkey, but how do you want your Christmas steak?"

Going along with the joke, Captain Clark answered that he'd like it medium rare. "And what kind of dressing would you like on your salad?" he asked. Continuing with the joke and knowing that there was no salad material in the Philippines, the skipper said "Roquefort, please." Hewitt was a former cab driver from Norfolk, Virginia, a constant joker and never short of conversation. He was also a good cook.

In minutes, here came the tray of food for the Skipper's Christmas Dinner and it was indeed steak—medium rare—with french fries and fresh green salad with real lettuce—with Roquefort dressing. We had eaten french fries instead of dehydrated potatoes when we were in Sangley Point a few weeks earlier but we hadn't seen lettuce for months. One look at that tray and the Captain called the galley. "Hewitt," he asked, "where did you get that steak and the fresh lettuce? Even french-fried onion rings!"

"Skipper," Hewitt responded without a second's hesitation, "I'm good, but I can't make french fries out of dehydrated potatoes. Sometimes we just have to shop around. Do you like this better than the goodies we get from Navy Supply?" Captain Clark, waiting to swallow before answering, repeated, "I know you're good, but where did you find food like this?" Hewitt almost interrupted him with "don't ask foolish questions, Skipper, and send us back to Saipan before this gets stale."

What Hewitt didn't say was that we had heard from Air Corps pilots flying Coca-Cola back from Guam and swapping for our beer that Saipan was beer-starved, so we stowed four cases aboard the plane from our warehouse before we left on our Christmas mail run, just in case. We'll never know how much Christmas mail didn't get home because we were trying to relieve the beer shortage on Saipan, but first things first. We were beaching our plane immediately after landing to conduct a post-flight inspection when we noticed a fleet of trucks hauling crates of produce from a newly docked freighter in the port.

Hewitt and Jack Barrath, our plane captain, intercepted the truck driver and worked out an "exchange." They got a crate each of lettuce, onions and carrots plus two crates of potatoes for our four cases of beer. The minute we got back to Palawan, they all went into the cooler at the Chiefs' Quonset hut for future use—such as our patrol a few days after arriving home—and "sharing" with other crews. And it was still crispy fresh for our Christmas Day patrol with the skipper several days later.

In Living Color

I never knew when Kodachrome film was invented. I think I once heard of medical photographs in color in the 1930s but the product selection was limited in the war years. And we only had film that made transparencies—Kodachrome. It would be years before we would get Kodacolor film that made color negatives. I had shot a roll or two of Kodachrome in my 35 mm camera when I was one of the Navy Aviation cadets in training at Tucson in the late summer and fall of 1943. But the Navy was over-protective of its interests and did everything possible to discourage any private photography on or about Navy facilities. We were not allowed to have a civilian camera on the flight line, officially, at training stations.

At the end of the war, our squadron got orders to photograph all but a few of the major islands in the Philippines from the north, south, east, west and overhead. If it matters, there are about 3300 islands in the Philippines, as I remember. We did this with special aerial cameras and Kodachrome film. I didn't know a lot about photography but the skipper had named me the squadron photo officer so it fell on me to check out cameras and film to other crews for part of the "shoot" but a lot of the work fell on my crew.

In a totally different assignment, our squadron "inherited" the equipment from an Air Corps photo squadron when they were ordered to take their P-38's and leave the area, leaving a bunch of aerial cameras, cases of black and white and color film, photo paper, chemicals and a full dark room for processing both black and white and color film. A special extra and something that seemed to me to be very un-military, was an 8-by-10 view camera with a dozen film holders and a sturdy tripod. I don't know how it ever got assigned to an aerial photo unit, but we had it. There was no cut film to use in the film holders so we cut 10-inch sections from a long roll of Kodachrome film that was 8 inches wide to fit in the film holders and headed for the countryside.

I photographed the native villagers, their huts, the fish drying in the sun, banana and papaya trees and farmers plowing with their water buffalo. Other days I took photos of palm trees along the sand beaches and many shots of our planes taking off and landing in the seaplane harbor at Puerta Princesa. These were all Kodachrome transparencies, but not 35 mm slides. They were all 8-by-10 inch transparencies like you would expect to find only in a display at a photo shop. In fact, there was no place else in the world where photos anything like these could have been found in 1945. I packed them in a box—a pile about an inch thick including pieces of paper between each of the photos in the stack.

When I got back to Honolulu after heading home from the squadron, I went to Kodak of Hawaii to see if I could get a back-lighted frame to display the transparencies. I almost attracted Kodak security. "Where did you get

405

these?" the man at the store asked me, in a tone that sounded like he thought I had stolen them. But he finally settled down and called some of the other employees to see the photos. They had no suggestions about displaying them so I packed up and went back to Aunt Marjorie's apartment, my home off the base when I was in Hawaii.

I spent several enjoyable months working at the ComAirPac office on Ford Island in Pearl Harbor, Hawaii during the spring and summer of 1946 before returning home to Nebraska and college. I had flown on a Naval Air Transport plane from the Philippines to Hawaii but it was a different deal when I got orders home from Hawaii. I got a ride on a Navy troop transport from Pearl Harbor to San Francisco.

When I got off the ship at San Francisco, one of my bags was missing. It was the bag that had all my wartime overseas souvenirs, including my old Argus C3 camera, all of my black-and-white photos with their negatives, the 35 mm slides I had taken during those months, and that incredible stack of Kodachrome 8-by-10 inch transparencies. I still miss them. I don't even have one photo of my plane or my crew. Some may have had real value but that's not the important part. I feel so empty not having any tangible evidence of those memories. For all these years I have seen them only in my mind.

PBM Purple Heart

Almost all of our night patrol flights began alike. We took off at dusk and flew a pre-determined heading and distance, then turned to fly in a direction that was approximately a right angle to our original course. When we had flown on this leg about the distance of two radar sweeps, we then returned toward our base. We were looking for Japanese ships, mostly lone freighters. We flew at low level, high enough to clear the tallest masts but low enough that our image blended into the water on the radar of any Japanese ship.

We normally flew three to four hours out, a few minutes (less than an hour) across the end segment, then three to four hours home. It is being generous to call this boring work. Thank goodness for mechanical autopilots. But we had to be alert at all times because in a moment of inattention we might miss the blip of a ship on the radar and either fail to find and destroy our enemy's life blood, or even be detected by the enemy's radar and shot out of the air with no warning as we passed over an enemy ship. All friendly planes and ships were equipped with IFF (identify, friend or foe) equipment that, when challenged, sent out a radio signal. This was designed to keep us from shooting our buddies down and was effective unless some Dilbert had forgotten to turn his machine on or tuned it to the wrong frequency. We always checked our IFF and machine guns after takeoff.

We often flew three or four plane patrols, each plane flying a modified pie-shaped, so-called "sector search" with the three or four-plane contingent combined to "clear" a large section of ocean of shipping for several days. When you look at the size of the Pacific Ocean or even a segment between the Philippines and the Asian shore, you realize that your chance of making contact or clearing any serious part of the area of enemy shipping is slim. But we kept on flying. We felt that we had at least thinned the population of enemy ships or satisfied ourselves and the Navy brass that there were darned few ships in the area after these patrol sweeps. And we conducted them with fairly consistent regularity. A ship would take several days to cross the area that our flights could clear in one night.

After you have flown several of these all-night patrols it gets easy to become casual about the urgency of the flight. Two things contributed heavily toward our keeping awake, if not alert. If our skipper ever got the feeling that a crew was less than totally diligent, that crew would be in deep trouble. And there was always the possibility that you would be dozing when you happened to fly into the range of the enemy, either on sea or in the air, and get rudely awakened. It was like the proverbial needle in the haystack that we would either find, or be found, but we did pay attention and always had someone watching the radar PPI scope.

One night we were patrolling an area that had been swept clean only about a week earlier. We were about three hours out when it appeared that there was a blip on the radar. When you have been watching that screen so attentively for so many hours, it's hard to believe that you really have a target. The blip was about 40 miles away, nearly straight ahead, and it appeared to be a fairly large ship. While we hadn't seen them, we were told that large Japanese ships generally sailed in a convoy with some military escort but the small ships went to sea alone in the apparent belief that we'd never find enough of their lone, small ships to have a big effect on the war, no matter how many we found and sunk.

Our pilots and our most experienced radar men studied the blip on the radar scope for a few minutes. Flying just above 2 miles per minute is slow by today's standards but you close on a ship pretty fast. We challenged its IFF and it did not respond. If it was one of ours, it would have returned its identification when challenged or risk being sunk. We decided that we had a target and as we closed on the ship, the crew prepared for a bombing run. That meant climbing and preparing to circle the ship, dropping a parachute flare on the moon side of the ship, then continuing the circle until the ship was silhouetted against the light of the flare and moon. There was no light and no sign of activity on the ship.

When we were fully down shadow from the ship, we had manned all our guns, armed the bomb releases and began a dive on the ship, losing altitude and picking up speed. There was still no light showing and no apparent activity on the ship. We dropped our first two bombs just as we passed over the ship. We had caught the ship personnel sleeping or at least not paying attention. Lucky for us!

One of the bombs exploded against the side of the ship, tearing a large hole in the side at about the water line and blowing away part of the deck, according to crewmen watching from the rear of our plane. As soon as we dropped the bombs, we pulled up and began to gain altitude, circling to make a second run to drop our remaining two bombs. As we circled, we could see a fire breaking out on the ship. We began the dive for our second run but just before we got to the ship we had to pull up to stay above the flames, to drop our bombs. Then we saw the first crewmen emerging on deck from ship's quarters below. Eidemiller, our bow turret gunner, fired what looked like a fiery rope of 50 mm ammo on this opening near the ship's bridge, making the deck hatch opening a forbidden area. A second bomb appeared to either hit near the original hole or else the fire exploded, according to our tail gunner our only crewman with a view.

As we began to climb after dropping our last bombs, somebody in the ship's crew apparently got to an anti-aircraft gun on the damaged ship and began shooting at us. We were nearly out of range for such armament. I don't know whether the Japanese used a tracer for every 10 or 20 rounds but there was lead in the air judging by the tracers we saw as we sped away from the damaged, and possibly, sinking ship. We immediately returned to our cruising altitude, exhilarated but shaken. With jangled nerves, we set course for home, thankful that we had done our job without getting hit.

Dawn was beginning to temper the night's darkness when we arrived back at our base. We could see well enough to land under normal flight conditions. We circled the bay, settled down for a routine water landing and began to taxi to the buoy at the ramp where we would tie up. The beaching gear would then be floated out and attached so our plane could be pulled up on the beach for a routine post-flight inspection. Another plane was tied to the buoy so we taxied in the bay, waiting to get instructions to either wait our turn for the beaching buoy or to tie to one of the buoys anchored elsewhere in the bay and come ashore later.

PBM patrol bomber planes are flying boats. They land on the hull and from that point the plane responds much like a motorboat except that a PBM has a 118-foot wingspan and has permanent floats mounted below both wingtips. The floats are positioned so they do not both touch the water at the same time. The plane tips slightly to one side, supported by the float on that side, but turning will make the center of gravity shift and the float under the other wing will then support the plane, keeping it nearly level. The plane could fall sideways into the water, except for the support of the wing floats.

As we continued to taxi, the plane was tipping too far to the left and the left wing float was sitting too low in the water. I had no idea what was wrong but called the after-station and asked a crewman to climb up through the top deck hatch and walk out on the right wing. The plane did not respond so I asked for another crewman on the right wing. The left wing float was still half under water and the plane was still tipping left. "Let's have another crewman out on that right wing," I called. That did it. The plane shifted and tipped toward the right. Then it became apparent why we had been tipping left. Water began spewing out of the left wing float. That gunner hadn't hit us where it hurt, but a bullet had apparently gone through our left wing float. Later, when they repaired the hole in the wing float, a repair crewman painted a Purple Heart over the patch—but not for long. Our commanding officer was a Naval Academy graduate and didn't take kindly to anything "out of uniform," so when he saw it, the purple was quickly painted over with a good shade of black to match the rest of the plane. Our souvenir had disappeared. No sense of humor . . . and no photo souvenir of our encounter.

I don't know if you believed this entire story or not. Actually, the first few paragraphs and the last paragraph are just as it happened. We don't really know where we got the hole in the wing float that took on water but when we discovered it and the creativity of the repair crew with the purple heart paint and Hewitt, our equally creative ordinance man, crew cook and good humor man, when he saw what the repair crew had done, suggested the skeleton of this sea story very much as I wrote it, just because it seemed a plausible basis for an imaginary encounter for a crew that was lucky enough to never see any enemy action. I have no idea where to find Hewitt today (he had been a taxi driver in Norfolk, Virginia when he enlisted) but I hope he—and all our readers—approve of the way I described his little trick. There really was a hole in the wing float.

Junior, Sir

Nobody has ever documented one of the most obscure statistics in Naval Aviation, to my knowledge, so I don't know the age of the youngest pilot who ever earned his wings. I know that our 41st president, George H. W. Bush, was among the youngest. He was born a few months after I was so he was a year behind me in school but he was ready to enlist the minute the Navy removed the "two years of college" requirement for aviation cadet enlistments. George enlisted. I was in college when the Japanese bombed Pearl Harbor and I became eligible for the military draft as soon as I reached my 18th birthday but I wasn't in a big hurry. I was never going to run for president. I began inquiring about my options but my draft board hadn't classified me yet. I decided that the Navy Air Corps was the hardest to get into so why not try? It hadn't really occurred to me that I'd ever have to learn to fly an airplane. That would come later.

When enlistment time came, I was healthy and fell between the physical size limits of 5'4" and 6'4" and passed the mental and psychological tests so the Navy took me, for better or worse. By the time I got through the enlistment regimen, the Navy flight training program had added a couple of new phases so Mr. Bush spent fewer months between enlistment and graduation than I did. As a result, he had gone to sea and had been shot down by the time I got my wings. I still was one of the youngest pilots. Besides calendar age, I had a youthful appearance, a fair complexion and was never over 5'6" tall, so someone along the way called me "Junior." The name stuck with me during the years I spent in the Navy.

Military protocol is based on respect for rank and seniority. But in most cases it didn't hurt if you looked—or at least acted—the part. I probably wasn't so good at that either. I rarely if ever "ordered" my crew, or any member of the crew, to do anything. If the crew had a job to do, even though the Navy gave me the right and authority to order the job done, I always made it a team effort. When our crew had a plane to clean, we cleaned it. If I had arranged liberty or had a cache of beer, we enjoyed it. We were a team— and it worked.

But my enlisted crewmen, and there were nine of them—almost all older than I—often called me "Junior," especially if no "senior" officer was present. In what could have been an embarrassing moment, Jimmy Hewitt, our 2nd gunner's mate, a former Norfolk, Virginia cab driver and the least "orthodox" military in our crew, called me Junior, just as our squadron Executive Officer happened to walk upon the scene. Jimmy quickly added, "Junior, Sir." That "sir" became a permanent addition to my name within my crew and others in the squadron.

That executive officer was not only second in command in our squadron but he was also a Texas Aggie where military bearing was worshipped. After the war was over we had a more relaxed attitude but few promotions. I jokingly became the "Bull Ensign" of the Philippines, waiting to become a lieutenant junior grade. I quit wearing ensign bars on my shirt about the time a squadron efficiency survey was published. An astonished Martin (the exec) had called me "chief," suggesting I was an enlisted petty officer without collar insignia, not a commissioned officer. He asked me, "Raynard, you are the youngest pilot in the squadron, you have the oldest plane, your crew has the worst military discipline, they even call you Junior, but your plane has been ready to fly more days and has flown more hours than any plane in the squadron. How do you do it?" I told him it wouldn't serve any purpose to tell him, a Texas Aggie just couldn't understand.

A Change of Islands

By the spring of 1946, the infantry units on the Island of Palawan had made raids through the country side and jungle near the main thoroughfares on the island. We were allowed to drive our jeeps almost from end to end—the full length of the long, narrow piece of real estate—without real danger of being fired upon by lone Japanese soldiers who didn't know the war was over. There was not much reason to drive the length of the island except that the jeep trail we called a road was there and we were there and we didn't have much else to do. We saw a little of "normal activity" in the native Filipino villages. Our flights were not as urgent as they had been a few months earlier. We flew a few "training" trips to keep the planes and crewmen well tuned and combat-ready but we knew it didn't matter all that much if we got a bit flabby, both in body and mental attitude.

I had tasted papaya fruit at the Navy BOQ (bachelor officers' quarters) mess at NAS Kaneohe but I didn't know whether it grew on a tree or a vine. I didn't know there were several kinds of bananas and that some varieties are fried, much like potatoes. Papayas, as it turns out, grow at the top of tall, slim trees. They do not have branches on their skinny trunks but have a cluster of large leaves at the top and the fruit, called melons, grow just under the leaves, around the trunk, up high in the air. We could see that the melons were not all getting ripe at once and while one or two might have a bright orange color, others were solid green or had yellow-orange highlights as they began to ripen.

The fruit might be 30 feet in the air, or higher. *How do you pick them?* we wondered. We began by shaking the tree, hoping the ripe fruit might fall. It did. Splat on the ground. Then one of us figured that if we had people standing by as "catchers" when one shook the tree, a good catch would return some delicious fruit. It worked. We began our "papaya shake-down" and brought the fruit back to chill in the walk-in reefer attached to the chief's Quonset. Banana harvest was quite a contrast. A banana stalk seems to be an annual, like corn. A banana stalk, several inches in diameter, yields in a few hacks with a bolo knife and you simply pick the bunch of bananas off the floor of the jungle or planted area. Near the native homes were structures like old-fashioned clothes lines except that they were used to hang fish to dry in the sun for eating at a later date.

We began to get regular groups of replacement pilots and crewmen and our old crews began to get replaced, one or two people at a time. New crewmen arrived to take the place of veterans as their names worked to the top of the list for rotation to stateside duty and probable discharge of reservists. Our skipper gave me every chance and every incentive to make the Navy a career. I had just been promoted from ensign to lieutenant junior grade. He said he would take advantage of a Navy regulation that allowed commanding officers to make "spot" promotions to officers who applied for duty in the permanent Navy, advancing my rank. He also felt he could get me assigned to be one of the seaplane pilots in the contingent for Admiral Byrd's upcoming Antarctica expedition. He said that being a member of such an adventure would practically assure me a good Navy career.

I didn't take the bait for any of the Navy jobs. I told him I had decided to go back to college but that I had an aunt living in Honolulu so I'd like a few months of duty in Pearl Harbor if he could arrange it. He said he had an old Navy friend who was a personnel officer who might be able to help me, wrote a letter on my behalf, put it in a sealed envelope and put me on the next Naval Air Transport Service plane to Hawaii.

I checked in with the skipper's old friend in the personnel office a few days later, giving him my letter of introduction. He turned out to be the personnel officer for ComPac, the office of the Commander of the Pacific fleet. "You're one of Bill Clark's boys," he commented quietly as he read my letter from the skipper. I never saw the contents of the letter but I think my old boss had given me a pretty good recommendation. "There's a job over in ComAirPac," he mentioned as he seemed to stare into space, hoping that a listing of job openings would suddenly appear. "I thought I'd better send a lieutenant or lieutenant commander over but Bill Clark thinks you can do it," he said, nodding approval of his decision. "We'll cut you some orders; you can pick them up tomorrow."

I came back to the Commander's office the next morning to pick up orders to my new active duty. He had assigned me to sort of an accounting job. We had five other officers and a few yeomen to write letters or recommendations when we needed secretarial service. The other officers were all assigned on "temporary" duty. I was assigned to "permanent" duty. I wasn't sure of the difference until I discovered that I was the department chief, even though two of the officers in my unit had higher rank than I did. But the big difference was that there were seven Jeeps assigned to "Junior Officers" attached to ComAirPac permanent company.

We were on Ford Island in the middle of Pearl Harbor. The place was crawling with admirals, captains and commanders. I think they outnumbered the "junior" officers on the base. But many of the high-ranking officers and most of the junior officers were on temporary duty. In fact, there were only five junior officers attached to "permanent" company for those seven jeeps. Such duty! My own jeep to take into Honolulu every afternoon after work.

And the "work" was interesting, even if it resembled accounting. Our group had the job of going over the battle reports for the Navy's entire Pacific air war. There was a report every time a plane took off and one for every time it landed. What was the purpose of the flight, what was done or not done, what ordinance was used and what damage was done to both enemy and allied forces. Then if reports had not been filed, we made recommendations to the "awards" section for their decision to award medals, battle ribbons, etc. It was really exciting to review some cases but mostly as boring as an all-night patrol flight over miles of Pacific Ocean for much of the air war. Reports on every plane from VPB 28, my old squadron, which sunk more tons of enemy cargo than any other squadron, got my full

412

attention until I learned that the statistics were generally just as boring as most of the flights.

I hadn't taken a single course in journalism at the time but I noticed that there was a glaring difference in the reports filed by air combat intelligence (ACI) officers regarding pilots in one squadron compared with those of another group in the same battle. One might report in detail using compelling words that made every move of every pilot in a dogfight come to life while another did his duty with all the emotion of counting sheep. We could see that some pilots would probably be awarded distinguished flying crosses and air medals for the same things that got little mention from the ACI officer as a result of the same battle but in a different squadron. Sometimes I took it on myself to re-submit a report of some particular action. I never saw results from my efforts except in one surprising case where I decided that a pilot surely deserved a better report than the one submitted. I said to one of my crew, "This guy should get a medal."

I was never stationed in Pearl Harbor during the war but I'm sure it was a "tight ship," for years after the attack, surely more alert than the relaxed attitude in early 1946. While it was the Navy's Pacific headquarters, it was operating at a peace time pace. One morning I was picking up an information package from an office some distance away and happened to meet Eddie Liebendorfer. He had been in our original Cornhusker Squadron as a cadet but I hadn't seen him since advanced training squadron. He was flying a JM-1, the Navy version of the Air Corps' B-26 except that ours had a few feet more wingspan and a single vertical rudder. He asked if I'd like to take a ride. I had never really flown from the cockpit of a land plane since training squadron and I had never been on a JM-1 so I was eager. Little did I know.

I learned why the B-26 was called the "flying prostitute," with "no visible means of support." It had the slim Davis wing and had very little lift at slow speed. I don't know the length of the paved airstrip on Ford Island but Eddie taxied it all the way to the last foot of cement, locked the brakes, turned up the power to check the ignition, applied full power then released the brakes. About half way down the runway we began to feel a little lift so he put the wheels in retract position and we finally cleared the deck as we looked up at the upstairs windows of the BOQ in time for a slight turn as we cleared the runway and found ourselves over water. I was never so glad to get airborne. Towing a target on a half-mile cable for battleship gunnery practice was tame after this, my last flight in a Navy land-based plane.

A few days later I was surprised to find another pilot who I had known a little when we both flew PBY seaplanes in advanced training in Corpus Christi but never since that we could recall. He was 3rd pilot on the Mariana Mars, the large Martin-manufactured, four-engine seaplane. He said they had done a 120-hour engine check and were going to make a test flight. Did I want to go for a ride? What a chance meeting. I could hardly wait! I cannot remember either the measurements of this giant or the horsepower of its engines but it had a spiral staircase up to the flight deck and I think you could play basketball in the main hull or freight-and-people-hauling part of the plane. I had seen a B-29 close-up and it was slim as a pencil by comparison. This plane was massive. I could hardly visualize getting something this size in the air.

It really fooled me. Of course we were empty. We had a small load of fuel and no cargo. It got up on the step almost as soon as the pilot applied full throttle and it popped off the water after a shorter run than a routine take-off in the PBMs I had been flying. I sat in the co-pilot seat and had the controls for probably half of the hour flight. Once back on water, the pilot let me practice my water taxi technique during a delay that kept us from the beaching ramp. I couldn't believe it. This plane had reversible pitch props on the outboard engines. You killed both inboard engines when you were sitting on the water and you could make the plane spin in one spot by having one prop running forward and the other in reverse. It was push on one side and pull on the other. We had to blip one engine on the PBMs and our smaller plane took much more space to maneuver. We finally got clearance to the ramp and my last flight at the controls of a Navy plane was over, even if I didn't realize it at the time.

This Guy Should Get a Medal

There have been several times in my life when I have had difficulty in accepting the score as the outcome of the game. This feeling is frequently hard to justify and acting on it has sometimes brought me trouble. I hate to see someone get a reward for something he didn't do and I am just as determined to see right prevail for someone who has earned a reward. I saw many examples of both in those months when we were examining the battle reports from World War II. We were advised to generally accept what had been reported at the time of the incident but when I saw a glaring example of bad reporting or failure to give credit when credit is earned, I regularly took some time and effort, as per the advice from our commanding officer, to edit or completely rewrite the original report. One case really got my attention.

Philip T. McDonald didn't win the war all by himself but he happened to be in a unique place at a unique time and, like all the people we call heroes, he met and surpassed the most laudable performance we could have expected, if not imagined. McDonald was a Navy F6F fighter pilot in the second battle of the Philippine Sea, which I believe was also known as the "Philippine Turkey Shoot." There were rumors that the Japanese air force was getting depleted of first-line pilots by this time. If not true at the beginning of this battle, it was true by the time it was over. It was also a

414

battle that made "aces" of several Navy pilots and sent the remains of the Japanese navy air force on its way home, a defeated outfit.

I don't remember the squadron number or the ship where they were based but several of the pilots had multiple "kills." This would have been remarkable if it had occurred during daylight but this was a night battle. All the pilot had to use in locating the enemy was radar and, at close range, fire from the exhaust. With such a handicap, the battle lasted less than an hour and McDonald had six kills verified and two or three additional "probable" kills. Five kills earned a pilot an "ace" rating and a certain Distinguished Flying Cross recommendation. But that was only the beginning of the McDonald story. When he returned to the ship, he called the tower and said he would make a pass at landing but asked them to look, because his plane took a few hits and it didn't sound right when he put the landing gear down.

When he got over the carrier, the spotlight confirmed that the plane was damaged and his landing gear was shot away but that he still had a tail hook. The landing signal officer told him they would prepare for a crash landing. McDonald radioed back that if he made a crash landing it could jeopardize all the planes still in the air that needed to land as all were getting low on fuel. "I'll pancake it in the water beside the ship and you can send a boat out to get me," he said, "I could kill a lot of people if I don't make a perfect crash landing. I'll circle until you can get a boat in the water or until I run out of gas." They put a boat with a floodlight over the side, he landed in the ocean beside the boat, got out without a scratch and was back aboard the carrier within a few minutes, wet, but alive and safe. End of report. . .almost.

I had seen reports of the activities of several pilots that I felt had been badly under-reported. I didn't want to cheapen the requirements to earn any military medal but this McDonald story really upset me. His ACI officer had barely made a report and had not apparently made any recommendation for any major medal. We had pretty good records available and I got several of the staff to dig out everything we had on Phil McDonald. He was from Horton, Kansas, and had two confirmed kills to his credit before this event. His ACI officer had made only a routine report of his earlier flights. There are a few medals that can be awarded for cumulative efforts but the big awards are most often made for action in a single event.

I felt we had the event and I went for broke. I wrote a new report to the Awards section to recommend a Congressional Medal of Honor. My report used the action in shooting down a good piece of the Japanese air force as the background, but his real heroism was in choosing to make a water landing, at night, so his fellow fighter pilots could land safely on the carrier, free from possible damage that might be caused by crash-landing his disabled fighter. I had never heard of the guy and I would never see him, but we were both Navy pilots. If the situation had been reversed, I would hope he'd do the same for me. I gave it my best shot and felt better as we continued to count planes, bombs, ammunition and damage. I almost forgot the few special letters I had written.

A few weeks later my job was done, I got orders to go back to San Francisco to be relieved of active duty. I was out of the Navy, for all practical purposes. When I got back to Lincoln to register for the fall semester in 1946, I first checked in at the fraternity house. It was great to see the people I had left behind nearly four years earlier. There were new members who had joined when they returned for the spring semester last year. A few weeks later the house was abuzz with a call from a new member I hadn't met. "Phil McDonald is coming back next semester." He had attended for a semester, joined our fraternity, then transferred to Kansas State University to get a course he really wanted under a "reputation" professor. Now he was going to come back to get his degree at Nebraska. I hadn't made any connection between events of today and those of some months earlier.

When Phil arrived at the fraternity house, I learned that he had been a Navy pilot. Yes, a little visiting about our careers in the Navy confirmed that this was that same Phil McDonald. But I didn't know what my friends in the Awards Section had done with my hard work, so I kept my little secret. I was not going to mention how or why I knew anything of his past. So much for my inspired work, but obviously nothing had happened as a result of my report. Nothing, that is, until one spring day when University officials scheduled a convocation. High-ranking Navy officers came to award a medal to Philip T. McDonald. No, my persuasive report of his accomplishments did not reward him with the Congressional Medal of Honor, as I had recommended. Officials had, however, taken my report seriously. They had awarded the Navy Cross, the second-highest honor in America's list of military awards, to the little red-headed fighter pilot from Horton, Kansas, who had thoughtlessly been passed over for the reward that I felt he had earned. Ironically, he majored in entomology and worked for a pest eradication firm after college until he was killed in a flour mill accident a few years after graduation.

The Mustang at the Gate

The timing was good. The Navy put me on inactive duty in early August of 1946 in San Francisco. This gave me a little over a month to get some civilian clothes, an automobile and register for college. The first person I called was George Campau. He had been a year behind me in high school at Stapleton and a Navy veteran who had arrived home from destroyer duty some few months earlier. His family had moved to Oakland, across the Bay from San Francisco, shortly after George enlisted in the Navy. We had kept in touch during our Navy years. He was running a mom-and-pop grocery and invited me to come spend a few days before I headed back to Nebraska to enroll in college.

George had a car and knew the territory and was glad to have a guest from the old days in Nebraska. What a break for me. He showed me the sights, day and night, and I even found and bought a Mercury convertible, just the car for my upcoming college years. After a few days I headed north to visit my Aunt Edna, my mother's younger sister, and her family in Portland, and my brother, Jack, on Navy duty at Astoria, a few miles away. Cousin Stan Carl was just home from Air Corps duty so we visited Portland's highlights for a few days, then I went to see Jack. He was assigned to a unit that was decommissioning ships at Astoria Naval Station. Jack's job was delivering bags of mail to the various units on the base.

I went on the base and talked to Jack's unit commanding officer, who said that their business was not critical and he would sign leave papers for Jack in a minute but it wouldn't do any good because there was a lieutenant junior grade "mustang" on the base who guarded the entry to the base commander's office. For months, this guy had refused to let anybody with leave papers in to see the commanding officer. A "mustang" is an officer who had been an enlisted man that had later been given a commission. I had served with some who were the best in the service but a few mustangs seemed to feel their power was long overdue and they went out of their way to overplay their authority. He was apparently one of these who really relished the authority to guard the gate for his commanding officer.

Jack had never had a day of leave since the one everybody got after finishing boot camp. I asked Jack's unit commander if he would prepare leave papers and I would at least try to get in to get the CO's signature. I was wearing my Navy Pilot wings, which often threw the people from the shipboard Navy for a loop. I would be unknown to the offensive Mustang. I decided that I would not tell him that I had leave papers for his boss to approve. I told him that I had just left duty in the Philippines and that I was bringing greetings from my commanding officer there to his boss, the base commander. I don't think my story really needed to be that good. I was sent in immediately and when I produced the leave papers, he signed them. Then I noticed that nobody had filled in the blank designating the number of days Jack could be gone. When I went back to Jack's unit, his unit commander was amazed and gave Jack 21 days. He asked me how I got past the mustang. I told him I flew past; I guess the wings did it.

Jack was dismissed from duty to go on leave immediately. He went back to the barracks, packed his bags and we headed to Aunt Edna's home near Portland to tell her goodbye before leaving for Nebraska. She decided to accept our invitation to ride with us and the next morning the three of us headed east. It did not occur to any of us to call or write to our Nebraska family to tell them that I was out of the Navy and that we were heading their way. The trip was uneventful until we got to a desolate stretch of Highway 30 in Wyoming where a thunderstorm hit. It was raining hard when the hail began. We had seen plenty of hailstorms but none of us had ever been in a hailstorm in a car with a canvas top over our heads. As the size of the hailstones increased, I spotted a deserted gas station ahead. We pulled under one lane of the roof overhang as a west-bound car pulled into the other side where we waited for the storm to pass. Some of the hailstones were nearly the size of golf balls but thanks to the protection of the old gas station, I never learned whether my canvas top was hail-proof.

When we got home to the ranch in Nebraska, the house was empty. A hired man showed up and said that my mother had gone to Grandma Brothers' house to help put up wallpaper. We headed down the lane to Grandma's house a mile away. It had been Aunt Edna's home as a girl before she finished college and took a job in Oregon many years before. My little brother, Rolland, welcomed us and ran inside the house to announce our arrival to the unbelieving wallpaper crew, including Grandma. I had begun my return to civilian life.

Ahead of My Time

Spending more than three years on active duty in the Navy during World War II gave ample opportunity to play cards. I served with several of the same people through 17 months in a handful of training stations as aviation cadets. As cadets, Ben and I played bridge together, and fairly well. Somehow I completed the required flights a week before Ben so I got my wings a week before he did. I got orders to Banana River, Florida, and we said goodbye. Next week, here came Ben and we were back together again, but in different training classes. We were all flying PBM Mariner patrol bomber flying boats. There was a difference, however. My class took operational training with three newly graduated pilots in a crew; Ben's class was assigned two new pilots with a veteran pilot as plane commander so they trained as a crew, ready to join an overseas squadron when they completed their PBM operational training. This meant we would say goodbye again. My crew went to Corpus Christi, Texas, where we exchanged one of our three new pilots for a veteran who became our Plane Commander. Then we went through operational training again.

When Ben's group completed training they went straight to the Philippines. A few months later, my crew, with our new Plane Commander, was sent to the Philippines. We were both in VPB-28. Hello again. Patrol bombers flew long flights—mostly six to eight hours or longer. We often flew at night, looking for Japanese ships on our radar. We flew low enough to hopefully avoid their radar. But ships made a bigger blip than a plane so we had a definite radar advantage over the Japanese navy or merchant ship.

418

Each crew serviced its own plane the day after a flight, then we generally had a day off so there was plenty of time and opportunity to play cards.

Ben and I were not great bridge players. But the Navy had many bad bridge players, mostly people who didn't know how bad they were, so we had an advantage from the start. And our squadron moved constantly—every few weeks—from shore station to shipboard duty aboard seaplane tenders, from island to island. We generally won all the money that the alleged players on one ship or station were willing to lose by the time we got moved to other quarters and some new, innocent players. I don't know what Ben did with his winnings but I bought postal money orders (an easy way to convert money overseas to take home). I rarely drew any pay during my time overseas, using my bridge winnings for all personal expenses.

When I got to California and was separated from active duty, I wanted a car to take back to college. I found a dealer who had a Mercury convertible that had been ordered by a veteran while he was overseas. The car was here but the would-be buyer had called the dealer to say he didn't have the money to buy it. I did. I cashed some of those postal money orders. I had no guilt feelings. I felt no need to find all the lousy bridge players who had paid for my car and give them a ride. There was one problem, however:

For several years I had worn a seat belt during every minute that I was in the seat, whether I was the one in control or not. Driving without a seat belt made me uncomfortable—like I was going to fall off the seat—so I went to an Army-Navy store (the only place you could find a seat belt in 1946), bought an aircraft seat belt and attached it to a reinforced floorboard. I got funny looks from friends when I went back to college in the fall of 1946. The convertible was cool. The seat belt was not. But I was comfortably belted, if 20 or 30 years ahead of my time.

Martin PBM 5 similar to the planes we flew in our squadron, VPB 28.

419

CPSIA information can be obtained at www.ICGtesting.com
Printed in the USA
BVOW010400031011

272577BV00006B/5/P

9 781589 097292